UNMAKING IMPERIAL RUSSIA

MYKHAILO HRUSHEVSKY AND
THE WRITING OF UKRAINIAN HISTORY

Unmaking Imperial Russia

Mykhailo Hrushevsky and the
Writing of Ukrainian History

Serhii Plokhy

UNIVERSITY OF TORONTO PRESS
Toronto Buffalo London

© University of Toronto Press Incorporated 2005
Toronto Buffalo London
Printed in Canada

ISBN 0-8020-3937-5

Printed on acid-free paper

Library and Archives Canada Cataloguing in Publication

Plokhy, Serhii, 1957–

Unmaking imperial Russia : Mykhailo Hrushevsky and the
writing of Ukrainian history / Serhii Plokhy.

ISBN 0-8020-3937-5

1. Hrushevskyi, Mykhailo, 1866–1934. 2. Ukraine – History,
Revolution, 1917–1921 – Registers of dead. 3. Historians – Ukraine –
Biography. 4. Statesmen – Ukraine – Biography. I. Title.

DK508.47.H78P56 2005 947.7'0072'02 C2004-904281-5

This book has been published with the help of a subvention from the
Ukrainian Studies Fund Inc., New York.

University of Toronto Press acknowledges the financial assistance
to its publishing program of the Canada Council for the Arts and the
Ontario Arts Council.

This book has been published with the help of a grant from the Canadian
Federation for the Humanities and Social Sciences, through the Aid to
Scholarly Publications Programme, using funds provided by the Social
Sciences and Humanities Research Council of Canada.

University of Toronto Press acknowledges the financial support for
its publishing activities of the Government of Canada through the
Book Publishing Industry Development Program (BPIDP).

To the memory of historians
who fell victim to the Stalinist terror

Contents

Preface

As I tried to answer the question of when this book originated and who helped me most in my work on it, my thoughts kept returning to a day in the early 1980s. I was in graduate school at the University of Dnipropetrovsk, and my undergraduate adviser, Iurii Mytsyk, showed up on my doorstep with two books in his bag. One of them was a pre-1917 edition of Mykhailo Hrushevsky's *Illustrated History of Ukraine*, and the other was Mykola Zerov's *Lectures on the History of Ukrainian Literature*, published in 1977 by the Canadian Institute of Ukrainian Studies. My guest had reason to believe that he was under investigation by the authorities for anti-Stalinist remarks that he had made at a private meeting. He was expecting a search of his apartment and wanted to get rid of the compromising publications in his home library. I agreed to take both books for safekeeping. I had read Hrushevsky before in the special collections of the Moscow, Kyiv, and Lviv libraries, but this was my first opportunity not merely to gulp down excerpts in the course of short research trips, but to read a whole book carefully at home, thinking about what I was reading. Hrushevsky's book struck me as a revelation about the Ukrainian past – a truth hidden from us by official Soviet historiography and the regime that it supported. It was my first encounter with an alternative account of East Slavic history, one that went far beyond the class-struggle-driven and Russocentric narrative of Soviet historiography. Its scholarly appeal and the fact that it was prohibited in the USSR made it especially attractive in my eyes. From that point on, I knew what the history of Ukraine was and how the Soviet version had to be reconstructed to meet the demands of historical scholarship.

In the early 1990s, when the Canadian Institute of Ukrainian Studies, the publisher of the second 'prohibited' book brought to me by my former professor, invited me to participate in the Hrushevsky Translation Project undertaken by its Peter Jacyk Centre, I was given the opportunity to become much more intimately acquainted with Hrushevsky and his work and to fully appreciate his talent as a historian. My work on the project – an English translation of Hrushevsky's ten-volume *History of Ukraine-Rus'* – also gave me ample opportunity to put the historical narrative that had so impressed me in the early 1980s into a much broader context, comparing it not only with the anemic Soviet narrative of the USSR's last decade of existence but also with a number of other narratives with which it had interacted and competed. In the process, I lost my earlier belief that I knew what the history of Ukraine was supposed to be, but maintained my admiration for Hrushevsky and the historiographic revolution or paradigm shift that he accomplished through his writings. The actual text of this book grew out of my work on the Hrushevsky Translation Project.

Thus, my thanks go to Professor Mytsyk in the first instance for entrusting me with one of his prohibited bibliographic treasures. I am also grateful to those with whom I have been working at the Peter Jacyk Centre. In my work on this project, I have benefited greatly from their support and expertise. I particularly appreciate the advice offered me by the director of the Centre, Frank Sysyn, and the cooperation of the managing editor of the Hrushevsky Translation Project, Uliana Pasicznyk. My special thanks go to the senior editor of the project, Myroslav Yurkevich, who edited the original text of my book and helped me handle numerous editorial and bibliographic problems. Without his help, support, and encouragement, this book probably would still be in the making. In the course of my work on the manuscript, I benefited greatly from discussions with my colleagues at the Canadian Institute of Ukrainian Studies and the Department of History and Classics at the University of Alberta. Zenon Kohut read the text and strongly supported the project from the very beginning. John-Paul Himka offered advice on improving the manuscript, while Bohdan Klid and Andriy Zayarnyuk shared their insights into East European social and intellectual history. I would also like to thank Peter Matilainen, who, as always, was very helpful in dealing with computer glitches, viruses, and the author's inability to grasp some basic principles of the cybernetic work ethic.

My stay at the Ukrainian Research Institute of Harvard University in the spring semester of 2002 as Petro Jacyk Distinguished Fellow allowed me not only to complete the first draft of the manuscript but also to benefit from the expertise and advice of Roman Szporluk, Lubomyr Hajda, and the Eugene and Daymel Shklar fellows at the Institute, Volodymyr Kulyk and Olia Hnatiuk. During my tenure as visiting professor at the Department of History of Harvard University in the spring of 2003, I had very helpful discussions on the content of my book with Terry Martin, David Brandenberger, Eric Lohr, and Kathleen McDermott. I am also thankful for the support and encouragement given to me by Dr Roman Procyk. Hiroaki Kuromiya read the manuscript and offered useful advice on improving it. Special thanks are due to Lubomyr Wynar for his help in acquiring unpublished materials, as well as to colleagues in Ukraine who shared their knowledge of Ukrainian and Russian history and historiography. I would like to thank Oleksii Tolochko, Natalia Iakovenko, and Vladyslav Verstiuk for their advice. I learned much from my discussions with Ukraine's leading experts on Hrushevsky – Ruslan Pyrih, Iurii Shapoval, Vasyl Ulianovsky, and Ihor Hyrych – as well as with the intellectual leaders and organizers of impressive conferences on Hrushevsky and his historiographic legacy, Iaroslav Dashkevych and Iaroslav Hrytsak. My special thanks go to Hennadii Boriak, Liudmyla Demchenko, and Halyna Svarnyk for their help in gaining access to archival materials in Kyiv and Lviv.

A grant from the Peter Jacyk Centre helped cover expenses related to bibliographic research and editing of the volume, while the Jaroslawa Demianchuk-Paclavsky Exchange Fellowship awarded to me by the Ukrainian Research Institute at Harvard University, as well as a grant from the Kennan Institute at the Woodrow Wilson International Center for Scholars, were instrumental in helping me finish the project. I am also grateful to the Social Sciences and Humanities Research Council of Canada for a publication grant and for financial support for the publication of this book from the Ukrainian Studies Fund Inc. (New York). At the University of Toronto Press, my thanks go to Suzanne Rancourt, Barbara Porter, and Miriam Skey for their advice and assistance. Last but not least, I would like to thank my wife, Olena, who not only encouraged me to undertake the writing of the book and put up with my research trips to Ukraine and long stays at Harvard, taking care of our two teenage children, but also brought order to my chaotic filing system – not the least important prerequisite for writing a scholarly work.

My research and writing of this book led me to contemplate not only the historical analyses produced by the scholars I discuss but also the terrible price that many of them were forced to pay for their loyalty to their political beliefs and the conscientious practice of their profession. The book's protagonist, Mykhailo Hrushevsky, who was arrested in 1931 and exiled from Ukraine, died under suspicious circumstances in 1934. His daughter, Kateryna Hrushevska, a historical anthropologist, was arrested in 1938 and perished in the GULAG during the Second World War. Hrushevsky's younger brother, the historian Oleksander Hrushevsky, was arrested in 1938 and died in the spring of 1943 while in exile in Kazakhstan. His nephew Serhii Shamrai, also a historian, was arrested twice, in 1933 and 1937, and died in the GULAG in 1939. Their fate was shared by many other historians in the USSR – people of various nationalities – who had their lives and careers destroyed by Stalin's terror machine. I dedicate this book to their memory.

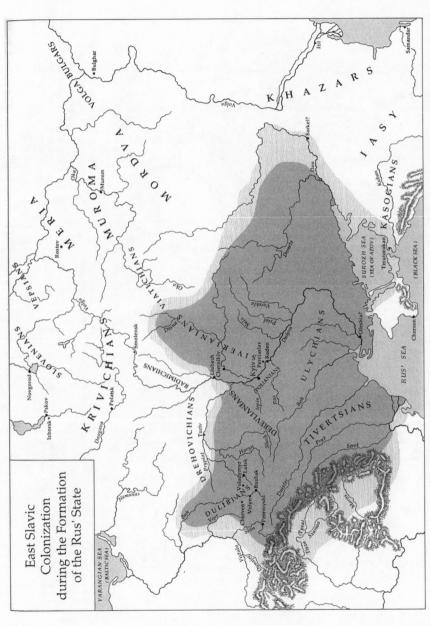

East Slavic
Colonization
during the Formation
of the Rus' State

Reproduced from Mykhailo Hrushevsky, *History of Ukraine-Rus'*, vol. 1 (Edmonton and Toronto, 1997), by permission.

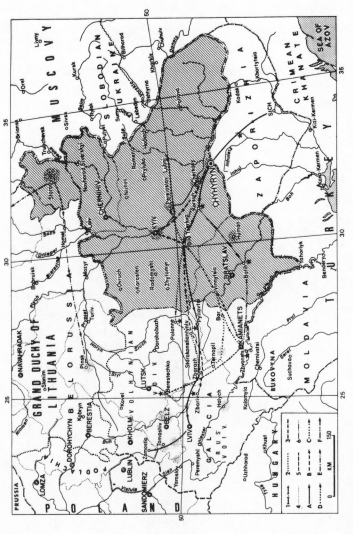

1. Border of the Kingdom of Poland in 1648
2. Boundary between the Polish Commonwealth and the Grand Duchy of Lithuania
3. Westernmost limit of Ukrainian ethnic territory
4. Voivodeship (palatinate) boundaries
5. Northernmost limit of the lands of the Zaporozhian Cossacks
6. Border of the Hetman state according to the 1649 Treaty of Zboriv

A. Khmelnytsky's first campaign (1648)
B. Second campaign (1649)
C. M. Kryvonis's campaign (1648)
D. Khmelnytsky's third campaign (1650)
E. I. Zolotarenko's campaign (1654)
F. Cossack campaign of 1652

The stars mark main battles of the Cossack-Polish War, and the speckled areas mark local rebellions.

Reproduced from Volodymyr Kubijovyč, *Encyclopedia of Ukraine*, vol. 2 (Toronto, 1988), p. 471.

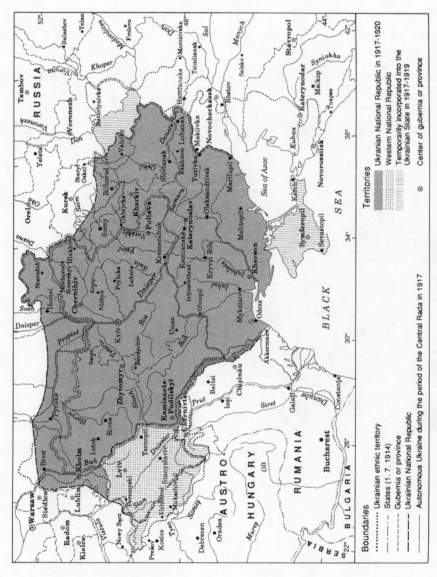

Reproduced from Danylo Husar Struk, ed., *Encyclopedia of Ukraine*, vol. 5 (Toronto, 1993), p. 409.

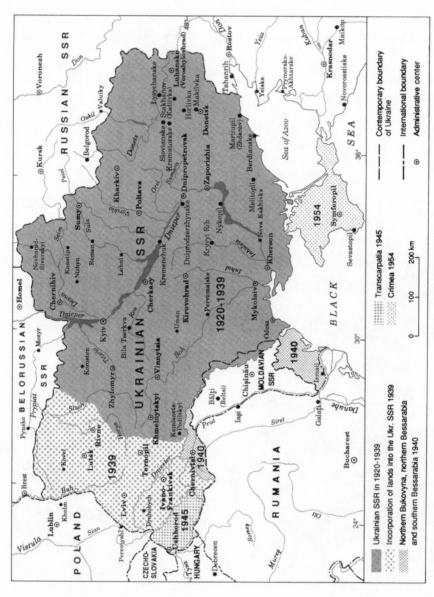

Reproduced from Danylo Husar Struk, ed., *Encyclopedia of Ukraine*, vol. 5 (Toronto, 1993), p. 441.

UNMAKING IMPERIAL RUSSIA

Introduction

The eleventh edition of the *Encyclopaedia Britannica*, which appeared in print in 1911 and presented the pre–First World War compendium of Western knowledge about the world, introduced Kyiv (Kiev) to its readers as a 'city of Russia.'[1] Some eighty years later, following the dissolution of the USSR, the fifteenth edition of the *Britannica* (as revised in 1993) referred to Kyiv not as a Russian city but as the capital of Ukraine.[2] The history of Kyiv was also treated quite differently in these two editions of the *Britannica*. If the authors of the eleventh edition claimed that 'the history of Kiev cannot be satisfactorily separated from that of Russia' and presented it as the seat of the first Christian church, school, and library in Russia, the authors of the fifteenth edition treated it as the capital of Kyivan Rus', which was defined as the first East Slavic state.[3] Behind the terminological change adopted by the editors of the *Britannica*, who replaced the words 'Russia' and 'Russian' with 'Rus',' 'East Slavic,' and 'Ukrainian,' lies the major geopolitical and cultural shift that took place in Eastern Europe in the course of the so-called short twentieth century (1914–91).[4] The editorial changes also reflected a major paradigm shift in the sphere of East European historiography – a change closely associated with the geopolitical shift in that part of the world. The present work is primarily concerned with this historiographic transformation.

The specific paradigm of Russian history that was profoundly restructured in the course of the 'short twentieth century' was a product of imperial Russian historiography. Imperial Russia, as distinct from Muscovite Russia before it and Soviet Russia after it, had an established view of itself as a tripartite nation. For a long time the Russian imperial elites officially maintained that the Russian nation consisted of three branches: Great Russian, Little Russian (Ukrainian), and White Russian (Belarusian). That view, which came into existence in the aftermath of the Muscovite government's occupation of the eastern Ukrainian and eastern Belarusian territories in the second half of the seventeenth century, expired (on the official level, at least) with the collapse of the Romanov regime in the flames of the 1917 revolution. The rise of independent states on the territory of Russia, Ukraine, and Belarus spelled the end of imperial Russia and undermined its concept of a tripartite Russian nation.

The dismantling of the institutional, intellectual, and spiritual heritage of the empire did not begin or end with the Bolshevik victory of 1917. Its demise resulted from the failure of the pan-Russian project of the nineteenth and early twentieth centuries, which sought to establish a modern Russian nation on the basis of the Russian, Ukrainian, and Belarusian ethnic groups (nationalities). The failure of the imperial Russian state to assimilate the Ukrainian peasantry to the Russian nationality was closely related to the development of the Ukrainian nationalizing project, which succeeded in turning most Little Russian peasants into Ukrainians in the course of the revolution and immediately after it. The Belarusians followed suit, reducing the builders of the modern Russian nation to little more than their Great Russian core. The imperial Russian authorities, who realized relatively early the danger of a split in the 'Russian nationality,' strove to prevent the development of the Ukrainian movement. Twice in the second half of the nineteenth century they attempted to stop the spread of 'subversive' ideas in Little/Southern/Southwestern Russia, as the Ukrainian provinces of the empire were known at the time, by prohibiting Ukrainian-language publications. These measures proved futile. Efforts to accomplish the linguistic Russification of the Ukrainian peasantry through the educational system were quite weak, lacking both resources and consistency on the part of the government; moreover, the official campaign against the much more obvious danger, that of Polish influence in central and western Ukraine, required the assistance of the Ukrainophile intelligentsia and thus had the ultimate effect of strengthening the Ukrainian movement in those regions.[5]

When pressure on Ukrainian activists in Russian-ruled Ukraine became too strong to withstand, they crossed the border into neighbouring Austria-Hungary, where the Habsburg regime was much more tolerant of the nation-building efforts of the local Ruthenians, as the ethnic Ukrainian population of the region was known at the time. In the late nineteenth century, the Ruthenian intellectuals of Galicia and many of their compatriots in Bukovyna, not unlike their counterparts in Dnipro Ukraine, were torn between two competing nationalizing projects, Russian and Ukrainian. Ironically, the prohibitions imposed on Ukrainian-language publications in the Russian Empire resulted in the transfer of Ukrainophile nation-building initiatives to Galicia, which helped local Ukrainophiles defeat the Russophile (Muscophile) nationalizing project in the Habsburg realm. Galicia became a veritable Piedmont of Ukrainianism, preparing the ground for the rapid expansion of the Ukrainian project in the Russian Empire during and after the Revolution of 1905. The Russian imperial government's exclusive reliance on repressive methods clearly backfired.[6]

The failure of the pan-Russian enterprise, like the collapse of any other imperial project, was closely associated with the dismantling or deconstruction of its historical narrative. Neither process took place overnight. In the case of the Russian imperial narrative, its disintegration began with the penetration of romanticism and populist ideology into the realm of historiography and acquired a new dynamic in the 1890s, given the growing dissatisfaction with the legacy of the 'statist' school in Russian historiography and its subsequent revision. This process reached its nadir at the turn of the 1930s, before the Stalin-era attempts to reassemble the Russian historical narrative under the rubric 'History of the Peoples of the USSR.' The forty-year period from the early 1890s to the mid-1930s also proved crucial for the fate of the Ukrainian national narrative. The formulation of the new historical paradigm, which brought about the 'nationalization' of the Ukrainian past and established Ukrainian history as a separate field of study, provided the young nation with a birth certificate and curriculum vitae sufficiently respectable to support an application for membership in the exclusive club of modern European nations. Not surprisingly, the delimitation of the past between Russia and Ukraine turned into a process involving numerous encounters, conflicts, and negotiations between individual historians and entire historiographic schools throughout the nineteenth and twentieth centuries.[7]

No historian was more intimately involved in that process or played a more prominent role in the demise of the old imperial Russian narrative and the forging of the new Ukrainian paradigm than Mykhailo Hrushevsky (1866–1934). Hrushevsky was one of the most eminent figures of the Ukrainian national movement of the late nineteenth and early twentieth centuries. He took an active part in the work of Ukrainian scholarly, cultural, and political organizations, becoming the first head of the independent Ukrainian state in 1918. Hrushevsky received his graduate degree in history from Kyiv University. His professor there was Volodymyr Antonovych, a well-known historian and founder of the Ukrainian 'documentary school,' and his field of specialization was Ukrainian history of the medieval and early modern periods. Upon graduation, Hrushevsky accepted a position at Lviv University, where he taught Ukrainian history from 1894 until the outbreak of the First World War. He served as president of the Shevchenko Scientific Society in Lviv, headed the Ukrainian Scientific Society in Kyiv, presided over the Historical 'Institutions' of the Ukrainian Academy of Sciences, and held its Chair of Modern Ukrainian History. Hrushevsky was persecuted both by the tsarist regime and by the Soviet authorities. In the early 1930s Hrushevsky was arrested by the Soviet secret police and released, only to die under suspicious circumstances in 1934, effectively becoming a martyr for the Ukrainian cause.[8]

If one were to apply Miroslav Hroch's periodization of national movements to Ukraine, it would become apparent that Hrushevsky was a leading figure of the Ukrainian movement in all three stages of its development.[9] As the greatest Ukrainian national historian and a prominent political activist, he played a leading role in stages A (scholarly interest), B (patriotic agitation), and C (the rise of a mass movement), partly because those stages overlapped and varied in different parts of Ukraine. In a fascinating way, Hrushevsky's life brought together a number of very different periods and trends of the Ukrainian national revival. It encompassed the cultural and political struggles of late nineteenth- and early twentieth-century Lviv and those of pre-revolutionary and revolutionary Kyiv, the life of émigré circles of the 1920s, and cultural and political developments in Kyiv and Kharkiv during the first decades of Soviet rule. Hrushevsky was a major figure on the Ukrainian cultural and political scene in all those centres throughout the period, and one could hardly overestimate his role in shaping the modern Ukrainian nation and its view of itself, of its past and future. Hrushevsky's major scholarly work, which preoccupied him throughout his life, was the *History of Ukraine-Rus'*, his ten-volume magnum opus published in Lviv and Kyiv between 1898 and 1936.[10] It covers its subject from ancient times to the mid-seventeenth century and is widely regarded as the major achievement of modern Ukrainian historiography. The *History* was impressive proof of the maturity of Ukrainian scholarship; it was also a major cultural and political statement strengthening Ukraine's claim to national distinctiveness and ultimately supporting the cause of its political independence.[11]

This book examines the dismantling or deconstruction of the Russian imperial narrative, and construction of the Ukrainian one, as fundamental elements in the unmaking of Russian imperial identity and the creation of Ukrainian national consciousness. Approaching these problems through the life and writings of Mykhailo Hrushevsky, I do not limit myself to analysing the role of the historian as nation-builder by tracing his involvement in the political transformations of the period, but go on to examine how particular historiographic concepts suggested and promoted by Hrushevsky were related to the formation of the new national identity.[12] It would be difficult, if not impossible, to overestimate the role of history in the formation, maintenance, and subsequent disintegration of national identity. Every nation has its 'story,' and agreeing on that story is essential to becoming and remaining a nation. The modern era became a golden age of history by dramatically increasing the demand for 'stories,' which were sought after not only by monarchs, their courtiers, and diplomats of premodern times, but also by incomparably larger numbers of nation-builders, state elites, and citizens. History, dressed in national costume and divided as a scholarly discipline along national lines, not only provided nations with their own exclusive 'stories' but also gave much-needed legitimacy to their existence.[13]

In dealing with the widely discussed and highly challenging topic of the construction of national identities, my study takes as its point of departure Benedict Anderson's maxim that modern nations are in fact imagined communities.[14] I treat the deconstruction of imperial identities and their replacement with new national ones in the context of the paradigm of the 'making, unmaking and remaking' of nations, originally suggested by Roman Szporluk as an approach to the interpretation of Ukrainian history.[15] I extend his maxim that 'one nation's fall is another nation's rise' to the realm of imperial and national identities and historical narratives. As the foregoing discussion indicates, my approach to the interrelation of history and nation-building is based on the assumption, broadly accepted in contemporary scholarship, that the development of national identity requires the construction of a coherent historical narrative. My other key assumption is that the 'othering' of ethnic groups (often dominant ones), in opposition to which the new identity is constructed or reconstructed, plays a major role in the formation of national grand narratives.[16]

For the purposes of this study, I treat the historical narrative as an intellectual framework that serves, according to Alun Munslow's definition, as 'the primary vehicle for the transmission, and arguably the constitution, of historical understanding.'[17] In this book I discuss a number of historical narratives that belong to two major categories, imperial and national. The Soviet historical narrative is in a class by itself, for at different stages of its development it included numerous elements of both the above-mentioned narratives in varying proportions. For present purposes, I regard every historical narrative as a product of a number of different discourses, which I treat in the broadest terms – again, in accordance with one of Munslow's definitions – as a 'shared language terrain.'[18] The interrelations between the dominant and oppressed/alternative discourses in the Russian Empire and later in the Soviet Union are treated here as a process of negotiation through which the creation, maintenance, and deconstruction of different historical narratives took place.[19]

In my analysis of the decline of the Russian imperial narrative and the emergence of the Ukrainian one, I distinguish Russo-Ukrainian relations in the sphere of culture and identity from Russia's relations with the non-Slavic nations of the empire in those same spheres. It is the first set of relations that I discuss in this book, and my treatment of the crisis of Russian imperial narrative is related first and foremost to the failed imperial project of creating one modern nation on the basis of the three East Slavic peoples of the empire. I treat Russia's relations with the non-Slavic nations of the former empire only in the course of discussing the Soviet historical narrative, which sought to establish a common historical identity for both the Slavic and the non-Slavic peoples of the former Romanov realm – a project all but ignored by Russian imperial historiography. Thus, when I write about Russian imperial historiography and the Russian imperial narrative, what I mean is the dominant historical narrative of the Russian Empire, not a narrative centred on Russia's relations with the subject peoples of the empire. The latter simply did not exist, for Russian historiography of the time all but ignored the historical experience of the non-Russians, treating the whole empire as a Russian nation-state. As Andreas Kappeler has correctly noted, 'the Great Russian historians of the nineteenth century, Karamzin, Soloviev, Kliuchevsky and Platonov, wrote national history, like the majority of historians in other countries.'[20]

My interpretation of the Russo-Ukrainian historiographic encounter of the nineteenth and twentieth centuries in terms of the interrelation between different historical narratives builds on research undertaken in the last decade by Stephen Velychenko, Zenon Kohut, David Brandenberger, and Serhy Yekelchyk.[21] A distinguishing feature of my approach is that I begin the ascent to the heights of the historical grand narrative from the level of the individual author, examining in depth how those narratives interacted in the writings of Mykhailo Hrushevsky, by far the most important actor in the whole process. In taking a close look at Hrushevsky and his role in the restructuring of East European historiography, I have been helped enormously by the recent boom in research on Hrushevsky and his legacy. The boom began in the 1960s in North America, where *Ukraïns'kyi istoryk* (The Ukrainian Historian, published in Munich and New York), the official organ of the Ukrainian Historical Association, emerged as one of the main vehicles for the popularization of Hrushevsky and his ideas. Its editor, Lubomyr Wynar (Liubomyr Vynar), became a leading specialist on Hrushevsky, producing dozens of studies on the life and legacy of the great master and promoting research on Hrushevsky as a distinct field of historical study. The late 1980s saw the publication of the first English-language scholarly biography of Hrushevsky by Thomas Prymak.[22] The English translation of Hrushevsky's ten-volume *History of Ukraine-Rus'* was a project that the Ukrainian community in North America conceived in the 1960s and began to realize in the 1990s with the publication of its first volumes by the Peter Jacyk Centre for Ukrainian Historical Research at the Canadian Institute of Ukrainian Studies, University of Alberta.[23]

The disintegration of the Soviet Union in 1991 and the proclamation of Ukrainian independence in August of that year made Hrushevsky one of the major heroes of the new Ukrainian state. A great historian, a socialist politician, and head of the first Ukrainian parliament who was also rightly perceived as a victim of Stalinism, Hrushevsky was an ideal father figure for the builders of the new Ukraine. Although his legacy was interpreted in different ways, it was embraced by all Ukraine's major political forces, from the nationalists and national democrats on the right to the slightly reformed communists on the left. The ruling elite contributed to the veneration of Hrushevsky by treating him as the first president of Ukraine, although in reality he was president of the Central Rada.[24] Monuments to Hrushevsky were erected in the major cities of Ukraine. Academic institutes vied with one another for the right to bear his name, and streets were renamed in his honour: thus, both the parliament and the government of Ukraine are currently located on Hrushevsky Street in downtown Kyiv.[25]

Hrushevsky's transformation from prohibited author to national hero generated enormous interest in the man and his work in Ukraine's post-Soviet academic community. The ten-volume *History of Ukraine-Rus'* was reissued in Kyiv, with the print runs of some volumes reaching 100,000 copies.[26] The publication of Hrushevsky's collected works in fifty volumes has recently begun in Ukraine,[27] while Hrushevsky's previously inaccessible diaries and memoirs have been published by Serhii Bilokin, Leonid Zashkilniak, and Ihor Hyrych.[28] A number of monographs and hundreds of articles dealing with Hrushevsky and his writings have been published in Ukraine in recent years.[29] Special library collections in which Hrushevsky's works were concealed during the Soviet regime are now open to the public. The same is true of formerly closed archival collections containing numerous sources on Hrushevsky's life and career, especially in Soviet Ukraine during the 1920s. A number of books based on previously inaccessible archival materials were published in Ukraine in the 1990s. Among the most important is a book by Ruslan Pyrih that draws mainly on Communist Party archives.[30] Pavlo Sokhan, Vasyl Ulianovsky, and Serhii Kirzhaev, and recently Oksana Iurkova have researched Hrushevsky's work in the Ukrainian Academy of Sciences, mainly on the basis of that institution's archival collections.[31] Thanks to the efforts of Iurii Shapoval and Volodymyr Prystaiko, partial access was obtained to the former KGB archives, with the subsequent publication of archival materials pertaining to the secret police surveillance and persecution of Hrushevsky. Today Hrushevsky is probably the only person investigated by the Soviet secret police whose GPU/NKVD special file (*delo-formuliar*) has been studied by historians and partly published.[32] In the last several years a number of interpretative studies of Hrushevsky's historical views have been added to the already impressive body of Ukrainian Hrushevskiana. These include the historiographic studies of Vitalii Telvak and Vitalii Masnenko,[33] as well as an in-depth analysis of Hrushevsky's writings based on the application of postmodern approaches by Volodymyr Vashchenko.[34]

The opening of the archives in the early 1990s and the research conducted by Ukrainian scholars over the past decade has contributed immensely to our understanding of Hrushevsky himself and the multiple contexts in which he acted during the last decade of his life. In researching the development of relations between the Russian and Ukrainian historical narratives, I often had to cross the boundaries that divide the contemporary historiographic map of Eastern Europe, where the old-fashioned approach based on empires and states still holds its ground against the aggressive advance of the national paradigm. I studied subjects and topics defined by that map as belonging to the realm of Russian imperial history, the chronicles of the Habsburg Monarchy, the annals of the Russian Revolution and, finally, the records of the Soviet Union. In a number of ways, this book deals with all the above subdivisions of East European and Eurasian history, while also touching on a variety of topics in Russian, Ukrainian, Belarusian, Polish, and Austrian history. Studying the career and activities of Mykhailo Hrushevsky helped me bring together all these realms and periods, which are now compartmentalized by modern historical scholarship.

This study of Hrushevsky's intellectual biography and scholarly activities thus affords unique insight into the encounter between Russian and Ukrainian historiography and identity at a crucial juncture in their development. It also touches upon a number of other historiographically important topics, and I hope it contributes to the better understanding of historiographic problems related to those topics. The major themes discussed in this book include the disintegration of the Russian and Austro-Hungarian empires – a process to which Hrushevsky contributed immensely through his scholarly and political work. Another subject of my study is the history of the Russian and Ukrainian revolutions, in which Hrushevsky played a major role as head of the first autonomous and then independent Ukrainian state in 1917–18. The cultural revolution in the USSR and the role of academics and academies of sciences in that process is another important subject treated in this study. No less important as a field of research has been the history of the USSR as a multinational state and the role of the Soviet policy of *korenizatsiia* (and, in the case of Ukraine, of linguistic and cultural Ukrainization) in the shaping of Soviet-era institutions and identities. All these major topics of East European history of the late nineteenth and early twentieth centuries figure in one way or another in the present work.

In my research on Hrushevsky's role in the construction of Ukrainian historical identity, I was often haunted by the 'accursed' question of modern historiography: to what degree was my protagonist biased in his interpretation of history, and what was the relationship between evidence and paradigm in his historiographic construction? Ever since the early twentieth-century rejection of the Rankean view of historical writing as a discipline that could describe the past as it actually happened, debates between proponents of history as a science and their 'relativist' opponents have shaken the historical profession.[35] That debate was given new impetus by the advent of postmodernism, which prompted traditionalist historians to try to prevent history from being 'killed' by the new methods.[36] In the present work, which is influenced to some degree by postmodern approaches (as the description of my research methods makes apparent), I often interrogate my sources by posing the 'accursed' question, seeking to determine to what degree Hrushevsky's interpretation of history was driven by his nation-building agenda as opposed to a 'scientific' study of sources. My answers, which vary from one case to another, are presented in the text, but my work on this project has strengthened my original belief that, although influenced and often driven by a very specific nation-building agenda, Hrushevsky made an enormous contribution to the expansion and deepening of our knowledge about the history of Eastern Europe.

'Getting history wrong is an essential factor in the formation of a nation,' wrote Ernest Renan,[37] basing this observation on his analysis of the nation-building experience in nineteenth-century Europe. Contrary to Renan's statement, the national historians of the nineteenth and twentieth centuries generally believed that they were finally putting things right and returning the histories of their peoples, usurped by oppressive states and dominant nations, to their rightful owners – nations awakened from long intellectual slumber. The national historians of the nineteenth and early twentieth centuries, unlike their postmodern successors, were convinced of their ability to uncover the truth about the past.[38] As Anthony Smith has argued, national historians were generally faced with a twofold task: to endow their emerging nations with ancient and glorious histories, thereby justifying claims to autonomous or independent political existence; and to present those histories in a scholarly manner so that they might be properly recognized by neighbouring nations.[39] In pursuing the latter task, these historians contributed tremendously to the development of historiography as a scholarly discipline. As Hrushevsky's example attests, the deconstruction of imperial narratives and the promotion of national ones in the course of the nineteenth and early twentieth centuries not only extended our knowledge of subjects traditionally at the centre of attention of imperial historiographies but also helped change the field in qualitative terms. The advent of national historiographies dominated (as in Eastern Europe) by imperial paradigms helped shift the attention of historians and societies alike from political to social history; from dynasties and states to peoples; from elites to masses; from ruling nations to submerged ones, thereby contributing to the development of the type of historical vision that we share today.

In conclusion, a few words about the chronological framework and structure of this book. It covers the period from 1890, when Hrushevsky published his first scholarly work, to 1934, the year of his death. This period coincides with an all-important stage in the development of Russo-Ukrainian relations in general and their historiographic dialogue in particular. The 1890s saw the rise of the concept of Ukrainian political independence. That was also the period in which Russian imperial historiography faced an ever more insistent challenge from representatives of national and Marxist historiographies. The year 1934 was in many respects a turning point in Soviet history. In the political sphere, it marked the end of a period of relative pluralism in the Soviet political system and inaugurated the era of Stalin's despotic rule, as the assassination of Sergei Kirov in December of that year opened the door to a campaign of mass terror. The same year witnessed a major turn in the development of Soviet historiography, which was supposed to follow the new guidelines set forth by the supreme party leadership represented by Joseph Stalin, Andrei Zhdanov, and the soon to be assassinated Kirov.[40] The period of autonomous (if not completely independent) development of national historiographies was effectively over, and their amalgamation into the Russocentric 'history of the USSR' was about to begin.

The book consists of two parts, each divided into three chapters. Part 1 discusses the interrelations between the imperial Russian historical narrative and the newly emerging Ukrainian national paradigm. The first chapter deals with Hrushevsky's biography and the development of his political and cultural views from his student years at the Tbilisi gymnasium until his brief tenure as leader of an independent Ukrainian state. The next two chapters discuss the interrelated process of the deconstruction of the Russian imperial narrative and the construction of the Ukrainian national one. Chapter 2 analyses the reclamation of the Ukrainian past in Hrushevsky's historical writings. The third chapter focuses on the main principles and methods employed by Hrushevsky in constructing his national narrative of Ukrainian history. Part 2 comprises three chapters that focus on the encounter, conflict, and negotiation between the national and class-based paradigms of Russian and Ukrainian history under Bolshevik rule. Chapter 4 discusses the evolution of Hrushevsky's political and cultural views in the 1920s and early 1930s. Chapter 5 deals with his reevaluation of the major problems of

Ukrainian history as exemplified by his treatment of the Khmelnytsky Uprising – a topic that Hrushevsky studied throughout his scholarly career, which spanned more than thirty years. Chapter 6 looks into the relations between the Russian Marxist, Ukrainian Marxist, and Ukrainian national historical narratives during the first decade of the existence of the USSR. It analyses the processes that led to the official suppression of the Ukrainian national narrative, making it exceedingly dangerous for professional historians to imagine Ukraine outside the prescribed Russia-based historiographic scheme.

In the text of this book, the simplified Library of Congress system is used to transliterate Ukrainian, Belarusian, and Russian personal names and toponyms. This system omits the prime (') used to transliterate the Cyrillic soft sign (ь) and, in masculine personal surnames, the final 'й' (thus Hrushevsky, not Hrushevs'kyi). The same system is applied in non-bibliographic references to persons and places in the endnotes. This simplified transliteration has the virtue of presenting East Slavic names to the reader in a form well adapted to standard English orthography.

 In the bibliography and bibliographic references in the endnotes, where the reader must be able to reconstruct Cyrillic spelling precisely from its Latin-alphabet transliteration, the full Library of Congress system (ligatures omitted) is used, and the titles of publications are given in modernized orthography. Variant spellings of authors' names are noted in the bibliography. In endnote bibliographic references, the author's name appears in the language of the given publication. Thus, in references to Hrushevsky's Ukrainian-language publications, his surname appears as 'Hrushevs'kyi,' while the Russian form, 'Grushevskii,' is used with his Russian-language publications. Similarly, the historian Viacheslav Lypynsky figures as 'Lypyns'kyi' in endnote bibliographic references to his Ukrainian-language publications and as 'Lipiński' in references to his Polish-language publications.

 Unless otherwise noted, all translations of quoted material are mine. As mentioned in the preface, Mykhailo Hrushevsky's magnum opus, the *History of Ukraine-Rus'*, is currently being translated into English by the Hrushevsky Translation Project of the Peter Jacyk Centre for Ukrainian Historical Research at the Canadian Institute of Ukrainian Studies, University of Alberta. Volumes 1, 7, and 8 have been published to date, and quotations from them appear frequently in my book. In bibliographic references to the *History,* the author's name appears in its simplified English form, 'Hrushevsky,' which is used in the series.

Toponyms are transliterated from the language of the country in which they are now located. Thus, Ukrainian forms are used for geographic names in Ukraine: Kyiv, not Kiev; Kharkiv, not Kharkov; Lviv, not Lwów or Lemberg; Odesa, not Odessa; the Dnipro (not Dnieper) River, and so on.

Because Ukraine did not become a united country until the twentieth century, I have capitalized the names of the various Ukrainian lands (Eastern Ukraine, Western Ukraine, and so on). The same principle applies to the capitalization of Western, Southwestern, and Northern Rus', which were not regions of a centralized polity but developed into the three East Slavic states of Belarus, Ukraine, and Russia.

The Julian calendar used by the Eastern Slavs until 1918 lagged behind the Gregorian calendar used in the Polish-Lithuanian Commonwealth and Western Europe (by ten days in the sixteenth and seventeenth centuries, eleven days in the eighteenth century, twelve days in the nineteenth, and thirteen days in the twentieth). Pre-1918 dates in this book are generally given in both styles, with the Gregorian-calendar date in parentheses, for example, 7 (17) April.

Part 1

Nation and Empire

When Muscovite Russia was turned into a modern state through the efforts of Peter I, his associates and successors, it took on the name of the Russian Empire. Thus the modernization of Russia took place under an imperial banner, and that coexistence of two contradictory projects under the auspices of a single state could not but affect another modernizing project of the day – the creation of the modern Russian nation. Peter's appropriation of the name 'emperor' for himself and 'empire' for his country in 1721 brought a new name but not a new self-image to the Muscovite elites, who prided themselves on their Byzantine heritage and ruled over the vast territories and numerous peoples of the former Mongol Empire. Indeed, Peter's imperial acquisitions appeared small and inconsequential in comparison with the territorial gains of his famous ancestors Ivan III, Ivan IV (the Terrible), and even his own father, Aleksei Mikhailovich. What was definitely new in Peter's imperial ideology, however, was the definition of the empire in national – Russian – terms. The concept of the nation that defined European politics of the early eighteenth century and was brought to Russia by Peter as part of a Western 'package deal' was indeed novel to the Russian elite. It was to serve Russia well in its competition with the West, as it helped define and legitimize Russia as a distinct nation and mobilize its resources for confrontation with the Western powers. Yet the new self-proclaimed nation was in fact an empire – a multiethnic conglomerate of numerous races, cultures, and peoples gathered together by the power of the Muscovite tsars, who had now become Russian emperors. Thus the Western concept of the nation was imposed on an empire non-Western in origins and development. The paradox was to haunt East and West alike for generations to come.[1]

Among the Russian imperial elites, one group was better prepared than the rest to apply the concept of the nation to Peter's realm. That group comprised the learned Kyivan monks whose services Peter retained to help him formulate and disseminate the new Western ideology and silence its main opponents, the Russian Orthodox Church and the growing number of Old Believers. The Kyivans, represented by the tsar's chief ideologue, Teofan Prokopovych, and the de facto head of the Russian church, Stefan Iavorsky, came from Eastern Ukraine. Until 1654 that territory had been under Polish rule, and it was there that the modern concept of national identity began to develop in the last decades of the sixteenth century. It was also there that the term 'Russian' (derived from *rossiiskii*, the Hellenized adjectival form of Rus') was routinely applied to the local Ukrainian population and the idea of the nation as distinct from the state (the ruling elite of the latter being Catholic by religion and Polish or Lithuanian by nationality) was first elaborated in the East Slavic world. It was in his addresses to Ukrainians whose loyalty Peter was trying to gain after the revolt of Hetman Ivan Mazepa that he used the word 'fatherland,' probably for the first time in his official pronouncements. Eager to gain the emperor's favour after the Battle of Poltava (1709), which had turned out so disastrously for Mazepa and his ally, Charles XII of Sweden, the Kyivan monks were prepared to move their 'Russia' from the banks of the Dnipro to those of the Neva and help endow the empire with its new identity. It is hardly surprising that the sons of Little Russia (as Eastern Ukraine came to be known in the Russian Empire) were among the most active 'nation-builders' of eighteenth-century Russia. The identity to whose development they contributed naturally included them and their homeland, turning eighteenth-century Russian national consciousness into a complex tangle not only of national and imperial loyalties, but also of Great Russian and Little Russian (Ukrainian) ones.[2]

By the end of the eighteenth century, most of the Ukrainian lands were under the control of the Russian emperors. Only Galicia, Bukovyna, and Transcarpathia remained in the realm of the Habsburgs, while the other Ukrainian territories, from Lutsk and Kamianets-Podilskyi in the west to Kharkiv in the east, were part of the Russian Empire. In terms of nation-building, those territories can be divided into four major sections that differed from one another in historical development, political tradition, and social structure despite their common ethno-cultural characteristics. The first region, Left-Bank Ukraine, was controlled until the 1780s by an autonomous Cossack polity known as the Hetmanate. It was the only region of Ukraine that met Andreas Kappeler's definition of an 'ancient' nation – a distinct ethnic group with its own history of statehood, distinct political and cultural tradition, and native ruling class.[3] All other parts of Ukraine lacked some or all of those characteristics. In Right-Bank Ukraine, the peasantry was dominated in political, economic, and cultural terms by the Polish nobility. The far eastern Sloboda Ukraine, centred on the city of Kharkiv, was rooted in the Cossack past but had no history of political autonomy. Its ruling class consisted of Great Russians and numerous Ukrainian noble families that ruled over the ethnically Ukrainian peasantry. Southern Ukraine, which developed around Katerynoslav and Odesa, featured an ethnically mixed population. Although Ukrainian peasants constituted an absolute majority, the region as a whole was dominated in political, economic, and cultural terms by Russian nobles, officials, and entrepreneurs.

In the nineteenth century Kappeler's 'ancient' nations had a clear head start in the formation of modern national identity, and it is not surprising that the former Hetmanate led the other Ukrainian ethnic territories in their national 'revival.' Its leading role in Ukrainian nation-building was fully apparent in the fact that two toponyms applied in the early nineteenth century exclusively to this region, 'Little Russia' and 'Ukraine,' came to encompass all of Ukrainian ethnic territory.[4] Although the nobility and clergy of the Hetmanate also staffed the ranks of the nineteenth-century Ukrainophile movement,[5] the Ukrainian national revival began in the early decades of the nineteenth century in Sloboda Ukraine, where the University of Kharkiv was founded in 1805 and the romantic school of Ukrainian poets and writers was formed. The revival then came to encompass Kyiv, whose university was established in 1834, with Mykhailo Maksymovych, a founder of modern Ukrainian historiography, serving as its first rector. By 1846 the Brotherhood of SS. Cyril and Methodius, the first Ukrainophile political organization, was formed in Kyiv under the leadership of another Ukrainian historian, Mykola Kostomarov. The brotherhood was uncovered by the secret police and its members arrested, but Kyiv, the ancient capital of Rus', situated on the boundary of the former Hetmanate and serving as the administrative centre for the Russian provinces of Right-Bank Ukraine, firmly assumed the role of capital of the Ukrainian national movement.[6]

The ideas of the SS. Cyril and Methodius Brotherhood, which envisioned Ukraine as part of a broader Slavic confederation on a par with Russia, were developed by the Ukrainophile *hromady* (communities), most of whose members subscribed to the populist ideology, with a strong emphasis on the cultural needs of the Ukrainian people. The leaders of the *hromada* movement, which eventually spread to other major cities of Ukraine, including Odesa, featured such luminaries of the national revival as the publicist and political thinker Mykhailo Drahomanov and the historian Volodymyr Antonovych, founder of the Kyiv 'documentary' school. The shift of the centre of Ukrainian activism from Kharkiv to Kyiv during the 1830s and 1840s coincided with the transition of the national movement from its first stage, defined by Miroslav Hroch in relation to the small nations of Europe as the heritage-gathering phase, to the second, characterized by growing political activism. The politicization of the Ukrainian movement was nevertheless hindered by government initiatives ranging from prohibitions on Ukrainian-language publishing enacted in 1863 and 1876 to the arrest and exile of Ukrainian activists: in that regard, the actions taken against the Brotherhood of SS. Cyril and Methodius were just the beginning.[7]

The struggle of Ukrainian activists for the enhancement of their national identity was fought on two fronts. The first was represented by Russian society and the imperial government, which embarked on the project of creating a modern Russian nation after the Polish Uprising of 1830. The second front extended through Ukrainian society itself, which was dominated by proponents of all-Russian unity. In the projected formulation of Ukrainian national identity, elements of imperial discourse interacted closely with those of national discourse, not only in the sense that national discourse opposed imperial discourse and vice versa, but also that two distinct national discourses and nation-building projects were in competition with each other. One, pursued by officials of the Russian government and some of the leaders of Ukrainian society, was the project of creating a larger Russian nation by taking over the construct of eighteenth-century Russian imperialism and turning it into a modern national identity on the basis of the Great Russian cultural and political tradition. The other was the project pursued by the Ukrainophiles, who had to deconstruct the all-Russian imperial tradition developed in the course of the eighteenth century, reappropriate the contribution made to it by their Little Russian ancestors, and build a distinct Ukrainian history and identity on that foundation.[8]

In the Ukrainian case, the problems normally associated with the emancipation of nations from imperial political and cultural dominance were complicated by the close entanglement of Russian and Ukrainian identities. Characteristic of the problems encountered by the

Ukrainian national movement in the Russian Empire was the fact that some of the most oppressive government measures, such as the Ems Ukase of 1876, which banned Ukrainian publications, were adopted on the initiative of those circles in Ukraine that regarded themselves and Little Russia in general as part of the Russian nation.[9] Except for the legacy of the Cossack Hetmanate, Ukrainian activists had very little in the way of a usable political, cultural, and historical tradition on which to develop their nation-building project. While the traditions of the former Hetmanate were indispensable to the Ukrainian movement, the Hetmanate itself presented the authors of the Ukrainian project with an innate difficulty. As noted above, it was the clergy and elites of the Hetmanate who acted as leading architects in the construction of Russian imperial identity. The political tradition of the Hetmanate embodied in the anonymous *History of the Rus'*, which circulated in manuscript during the early nineteenth century, stressed the glorious Cossack past and the particular rights and privileges of the Left-Bank nobility. It did not, however, argue for a separate Ukrainian identity, but demanded a place of honour for Ukrainians in the political and social structure of the Russian nation.[10]

The Ukrainian movement faced a highly uncertain future unless it could resolve the problem of multiple identity represented by the political tradition of the Hetmanate. The Little Russian legacy had to be adapted in such a way as to promote the creation of an exclusively Ukrainian identity. That task was all but impossible without the construction of a distinct Ukrainian historical narrative.

Chapter 1

The Historian as Nation-Builder

Hans Kohn, a Western pioneer in the study of East European nation-building, maintained that East European nationalisms differed profoundly from their West European counterparts because of their orientation toward the past. 'Nationalism in the West,' wrote Kohn, 'arose in an effort to build a nation in the political reality and the struggles of the present without too much sentimental regard for the past; nationalists in Central and Eastern Europe created often, out of the myths of the past and the dreams of the future, an ideal fatherland, closely linked with the past, devoid of any immediate connection with the present, and expected to become sometime a political reality.'[1] Kohn's differentiation of East and West European nationalisms was viewed with scepticism by many students of the region. One of the most prominent, Hugh Seton-Watson, flatly refused to accept the notion 'that nationalism in eastern Europe is something different from nationalism in western Europe, that it is something essentially reactionary and harmful without the positive features that made west European nationalism, in earlier centuries, a force for progress.'[2]

Further research on European national movements has indeed shown that the adaptation of historical myths and the construction of glorious pasts were essential elements of nation-building projects in both parts of Europe.[3] Still, what continues to give pause to students of nationalism in Europe is the role played by historians in shaping nationalist ideologies and nations themselves in the eastern part of the continent. There, unlike in Western Europe, historians not only endowed their nations with imposing traditions but also crossed the line between the writing and making of history, taking a direct hand in the construction of their nations and securing independent statehood for them. The symbol of the Polish uprising of 1830 and leader of the great Polish emigration in Western Europe, Joachim Lelewel, was one of the East European historians who successfully combined historical scholarship with political activism in service of a national cause.[4] Two prominent Romanians, Mihail Kogălniceanu, an eminent historian and Romanian foreign minister in the 1870s, and Nicolae Iorga, another great historian and president of the Romanian Council of Ministers in the 1930s, come to mind as political activists and authors of East European national histories.[5] Also no stranger to historical scholarship was a professor of philosophy at Charles University in Prague and the first holder of the chair of Slavic Studies at the University of London, and subsequently the first president of Czechoslovakia, Thomas Masaryk.[6] The prominence of historians in the struggle of East European nations for their independence indicates among other things the importance of the historical element in the broader undertaking of destroying empires and constructing nations in modern-day Eastern Europe. In this sense, national projects in that part of Europe were indeed different from those in the West. So was the social role of historians.

In many ways, Mykhailo Hrushevsky ideally fit the profile of an East European historian-awakener of his suppressed nation. In Ukraine he merely continued the tradition of political activism established by his predecessors in the field of Ukrainian history. Mykola Kostomarov, the author of the first scholarly monograph on Ukrainian history, also wrote the first political program of the Ukrainian movement, and, as noted above, headed the clandestine Brotherhood of SS. Cyril and Methodius.[7] Hrushevsky's own professor at Kyiv University, Volodymyr Antonovych, was a leader of the Kyiv Hromada.[8] No less active in politics were some of Hrushevsky's younger colleagues, such as Dmytro Doroshenko, the author of the first survey of Ukrainian historiography (1923) and of popular histories of Ukraine published in the 1920s and 1930s, who was also a minister in the government of Hetman Pavlo Skoropadsky (1918).[9] Hrushevsky's main ideological rival of the 1920s, Viacheslav Lypynsky, the founder of the 'statist school' in Ukrainian historiography, served as the Skoropadsky government's ambassador to Austria.[10] Hrushevsky was only one of many Ukrainian historians who took part in the Ukrainian national movement, but he was by far the most prominent in political importance and scholarly achievement.

Hrushevsky's life and activities well exemplify the interconnections between nation-building and historical writing in Eastern Europe in the late nineteenth and early twentieth centuries and are thus of particular interest to students of the demise of empires and the rise of nation-states in that part of the world. This chapter examines Hrushevsky's life and political activities up to the Revolution of 1917, focusing mainly on the development of his political ideas, and more specifically on the evolution of his views about the Russian-Ukrainian entanglement. The chapter follows Hrushevsky from his years at the Tbilisi gymnasium and Kyiv University through his professorship at Lviv University and involvement in the Ukrainian movement in the Habsburg and Russian empires, culminating with his role in the Revolution of 1917 and the emergence of independent Ukraine. The elements of Hrushevsky's intellectual biography presented here provide a background for understanding the development of his historical views, which are discussed in subsequent chapters.

The Shaping of a Populist

In the course of his long academic and political career, Mykhailo Hrushevsky never forgot the place where he was born – the town of Kholm (Chełm) on the Polish-Ukrainian ethnic border, a battleground of several nationalizing projects throughout the nineteenth and a good part of the twentieth century. Hrushevsky often addressed the problem of the Kholm region in his numerous articles and historical studies, claiming Ukrainian rights to that territory.

Hrushevsky was born in Kholm on 17 (29) September 1866. The time and place of his birth are highly symbolic for the history of the Ukrainian national movement. Hrushevsky's father, Serhii, like many of his compatriots, came to the former Congress Kingdom of Poland as part of the government-sponsored program to Russify the area after the Polish insurrection of 1863–4. Unexpectedly for the government, the de-Polonization of Ukrainian ethnic territory helped keep the Ukrainian movement alive in the empire. Quite a few government recruits sent to the Congress Kingdom in the 1860s shared Ukrainophile sympathies. This was especially true of those who, like Serhii Hrushevsky, came to the Kholm region as teachers at the invitation of the head of the local school administration, Feofan Lebedyntsev (1828–1907), the subsequent publisher of the Ukrainophile journal *Kievskaia starina* (Kyivan Antiquity).[11] Among the cadres recruited by Lebedyntsev to the Kholm region was one of Hrushevsky's future literary mentors, the famous Ukrainian writer Ivan Nechui-Levytsky.[12]

Serhii Hrushevsky was a descendant of an Orthodox priestly family in the Chyhyryn region on the Right Bank of the Dnipro. Thanks to multiple reprints of his textbook of Church Slavonic, he became widely known and even well-to-do. Even though he spent most of his career in the North Caucasus (the family moved there from Kholm in 1869), he was deeply attached to his Ukrainian roots and passed on his love of Ukraine and its culture to his children.[13] 'The vital attachment to the Ukrainian element that I can recall within me from a very early age must, of course, be credited entirely to my father's legacy,' wrote Hrushevsky in his memoirs.[14] Hrushevsky's mother, Hlafira Opokova (Opotskevych), came from a family with a strong Polish cultural bent. She was educated in Polish and Russian, although she knew and spoke Ukrainian. She was also the one who started Mykhailo's education at home, using a Russian grammar as a textbook.[15] Although the family's link with Ukraine and its culture remained unbroken, the young Hrushevsky was growing up in a Russian linguistic and cultural environment.

In 1880 Mykhailo's parents sent him to Tbilisi (the family was then living in Vladikavkaz) to attend a classical Russian gymnasium. There he became an avid reader of Russian and Western literature. Among other authors, he read Vasilii Zhukovsky, Mikhail Lermontov, and Ivan Turgenev – his favourite Russian author at the time – as well as Byron, Emile Zola, Alphonse Daudet, and Leopold von Sacher-Masoch.[16] Paradoxically at first glance, the years that Hrushevsky spent at the Tbilisi gymnasium made him more attached to his distant homeland than ever before. It was in those years that his interest in Ukraine and its history and culture took concrete form under the influence of books and articles on Ukrainian and Russian history and literature.[17] The gymnasium library had no books on Ukrainian literature or history (the only exceptions were collections of popular Ukrainian songs, which Mykhailo read with deep interest), and Hrushevsky used his trips to Ukraine, which the whole family occasionally visited during summer vacations, to acquire books on Ukrainian topics; he also ordered them by mail. In his autobiography Hrushevsky specifically mentioned works of Mykola Kostomarov, Panteleimon Kulish, Apollon Skalkovsky, and Aleksandr Pypin among the books that most influenced him, as well as collections of Ukrainian folk songs published by Mykhailo Maksymovych and Amvrosii Metlynsky.[18]

It appears that the young student was particularly impressed by the journal *Kievskaia starina*, published by the members of the Kyiv Ukrainophile circle known as the Hromada. Serhii Hrushevsky subscribed to the journal, which began publication in 1882 under the aegis of his former director in Kholm, Feofan Lebedyntsev. Mykhailo noted in his memoirs that by acquiring the issues of the journal published in 1882 and subscribing to it in the following year, his father gave him 'tremendous pleasure and, perhaps without anticipating it, indicated the path of my further activity.'[19] What was the political and cultural orientation of *Kievskaia starina*, and what impact could it have had on the upbringing of a young student? In its first years, the journal published numerous articles on Ukrainian history, literature, and folklore, thereby promoting local Ukrainian patriotism and culture. Conversely, the journal was a product of the political circumstances of the 1880s, which were unfavourable to the Ukrainophile movement. As a result of restrictions imposed on Ukrainian publications by the Valuev circular of 1863 and the Ems Ukase of 1876, the journal was published in Russian. Its content also reflected a major shift in Ukrainophile activity of that period from the political sphere, as was the case in the 1870s, to the cultural one. Under pressure from the authorities, a leader of the Ukrainophile movement, Volodymyr Antonovych, professor of Russian history at Kyiv University and one of the most influential contributors to *Kievskaia starina*, tried to stay as far away from politically sensitive topics as possible. Lebedyntsev, the journal's publisher, was largely responsible for its Orthodox and anti-Polish stand, as he tried to acquire a subsidy for its publication from the Holy Synod.[20]

Despite the anti-Polish overtones of many contributions to *Kievskaia starina*, the orientation of the Kyivan Ukrainian movement of the 1880s toward apolitical cultural work largely paralleled the dominant trend among Polish national activists of the day.[21] After the defeat of the uprising of 1863, they declared their loyalty to the foreign states controlling Polish territory and focused on 'organic work' – the development of Polish culture and society in apolitical forms.[22] It was only in the 1890s that the clear politicization of both the Polish and the Ukrainian national movements began, and the leaders of both camps strongly rejected the limitation of national activity to the cultural sphere. It was from this new perspective that Hrushevsky later gave an unflattering assessment of Ukrainophile activity in the 1880s. 'Cultural work,' he wrote in 1906, 'developed in two directions. One, represented in part by the *Kievskaia starina* circle, had – I shall permit myself to express it this way – a more all-Russian character. It relegated political and social work, in a more liberal or conservative direction ... to the all-empire elements, so to speak. It was the Ukrainians' place to build a super-

structure over that activity in the form of studying Ukraine and preserving the tradition of the Ukrainian language and literature at least in
the most modest scope – "for home use," as the expression went – that
would not arouse charges of separatism.'[23] In his memoirs, written in
1918, Hrushevsky somewhat softened his assessment of the journal,
noting that 'it could be said of *Kievskaia starina* in its first years that "the
glass from which it drank was small, but its own," and that glass was
fairly clean.'[24] For all the reservations that Hrushevsky expressed in the
revolutionary year 1906 about the activities and ideology of *Kievskaia
starina*, it was the journal that turned him into a Ukrainian patriot.[25]

In 1883 Hrushevsky, then a seventeen-year-old student of the sixth
grade at the Tbilisi gymnasium, began to keep a private diary that
provides unique insight into the formation of his world view.[26] As it
appears from his diary, Hrushevsky's adoption of Ukrainian identity
was a conscious choice. Like other leaders of the Ukrainian movement
at the time, Hrushevsky had to master a language and culture that were
foreign to his milieu. Hrushevsky began his diary in Russian, but in
time included more and more excerpts in Ukrainian as he tried to
improve his written command of what he considered his native language. Following a long diary entry written in Ukrainian in September
1883, Hrushevsky noted in Russian: 'Yesterday I read what I had written: my command of the language is poor. There are many words I do
not know; thoughts that I cannot express with the vocabulary that I
have. But what am I to do: I must practise the language as much as
possible. I have already suffered great harm from the circumstance of
having spent my childhood in the Caucasus, far from my homeland,
among foreigners. Nevertheless, I am bound to know the Little Russian
language, and, given the impossibility of studying it in practice, I must
be satisfied with the few methods available to me: reading Little Russian books, synopses in the Little Russian language, and so on.'[27]

Hrushevsky's reading of Leopold von Sacher-Masoch's novel *Die
Ideale unserer Zeit* in Russian translation also led him to comment on the
problem of choosing a language in which to write. He believed that
Masoch, the son of the Lviv police chief, was a Ukrainian by birth, and
regretted that he had forgotten his native language and become a German author at a time when Ukrainians needed good writers of their
own. Hrushevsky commented as follows on Masoch's 'choice' to become a German writer: 'It is clear that he has a fine knowledge of his
native Galicia and could probably converse in his native language.
Perhaps it was also not to his liking that his writing would not have

gained such a reputation if it had been written in Ruthenian, but it would have been all the more valuable to Ukraine, and from Ukraine it would slowly have spread across the whole world.'[28] Hrushevsky also regretted Nikolai Gogol's choice of language.[29] These comments in the diary reflected Hrushevsky's own dilemma at the time.

Far from his family, which was then living in Vladikavkaz, and even farther from the ancestral land that he glorified in his poems and diary entries, Hrushevsky developed a very strong attachment to Ukraine, which he viewed as his homeland.[30] In the romantic dreams that he recorded in his diary, the young Hrushevsky aspired to devote his life to Ukraine and gain a place in history by serving his homeland. He wanted to be 'the leader of a Ukrainian circle; to become, as they say, the leading fighter of all the boys who love their Ukraine.' 'Well,' wrote the young Hrushevsky in his diary, 'perhaps God will help me become leader: I shall work as much as I can to that end. And I want it very much, for these leaders will shine in history above all others.'[31]

From the very beginning, Hrushevsky's romantic nationalism had strong populist overtones. He was concerned first and foremost with the plight of the people, and while he was not prepared to idealize the peasantry, he was extremely unforgiving in his assessment of its 'exploiters,' whether Ukrainians or foreigners. Recording his impressions of Ukraine in his diary, Hrushevsky wrote that idyllic scenes of Ukrainian life did not blind him to its negative characteristics. 'Through the rainbow prism of my love for Ukraine,' wrote the young student, 'I discerned much that is unenviable – poverty, drunkenness, bowing low to the strong, strivings to abandon one's milieu, and so on. Of course, it would be as unjust to blame the people for all that as to hold up the peasant as some kind of ideal of honesty and nobility. The general exploitation of peasant labour had a particularly unpleasant effect on me. Although the Poles, Jews, and Germans are generally foremost in that regard ... the Russian [East Slavic] "bourgeoisie" also gives the peasants no respite.'[32] Hrushevsky's thinking about the role of the native elite in the exploitation of the peasantry was clearly influenced by his reading of Ukrainian history. In his diary, Hrushevsky compared the situation of the peasantry in his own day to that under Polish rule, commenting ironically on the role played in the exploitation of the peasantry by the Cossack officer stratum. According to Hrushevsky, that stratum, 'overflowing with patriotic feeling and cursing the Poles, tore the skin off the very same "common people" (not all did so, of course) whom it had resolved to defend, all the while considering itself the veritable bastion of the Ruthenian nationality.'[33] This critical approach to the history of the Ukrainian elite, fully developed in the writings of many regular contributors to *Kievskaia starina* and picked up by the young Hrushevsky during his gymnasium years, would long dominate his historical writings.

Especially important for Hrushevsky's intellectual development were the writings of Mykola Kostomarov. Kostomarov's idea of the betrayal of the popular masses by the elites, who first sided with the Poles, then with the Muscovites, and eventually returned to their own people under the banner of the Ukrainophile movement, would later become an important element of Hrushevsky's own interpretation of the history of Ukraine. Following Kostomarov, Hrushevsky noted in his diary that the Ukrainian movement was not the result of an anti-Russian intrigue but evolved naturally out of elite interest in the popular language and culture.[34] Hrushevsky fully accepted Kostomarov's argument that the Ukrainian people spoke their own language, not a corrupt version of Russian. Commenting on Kostomarov's thoughts about Ukrainian literature, Hrushevsky noted in his diary: 'As for those who say that there can be no literature in Ukrainian, that is a lie: if a man wants to express his thoughts in his native language, he has the right to do so; hence a native literature can exist and has the right to do so. Here, it seems, one may adduce the principle that anything can exist and has the right to exist when it is needed; when it is prompted by a need.'[35]

Notwithstanding all the influence that Kostomarov and his ideas exerted on the young Hrushevsky, he was quite critical of Kostomarov's federalism – an attitude that was to become more moderate with the passage of time. Upon learning of the death of Volodymyr Barvinsky, a leader of the Ukrainian movement in Galicia, Hrushevsky recounted in his diary Barvinsky's views on the Ukrainian issue and objected to his idea of a Slavic federation. 'But I am thinking,' wrote the young critic of federalism, 'how to avoid any harm to us from this "federative" model: we have already had a scent of this federation and are well aware of what it implies; we have already been with Lithuania and then with the Poles "as equal with equal and free man with free man," and we have already seen more than enough of it. No, first we have to regain our freedom, win it back, then bring our land properly back to rights, repairing all that is amiss, and only then make all sorts of unions and "federations."'[36]

There is little doubt that the young Hrushevsky's suspicion of federalism was rooted in his distrust of the prospective future members of such a federation – Poland and Russia. In complete accord with the general line taken by the editors and authors of *Kievskaia starina*, Hrushevsky considered the period of Polish rule in Ukraine to have been the worst for the Ukrainian peasantry. Surprisingly, his attitude toward the Russians was no more favourable, and he often used derogatory terms – *moskali* and *katsapy* – when referring to them in his diary. This negative attitude toward the Russian role in Ukrainian history could not have originated with Hrushevsky's reading of *Kievskaia starina*, but can easily be traced back to Taras Shevchenko and some of the writings of Mykola Kostomarov that did not appear in *Kievskaia starina*. Although, as Hrushevsky wrote, he was not a 'fanatical worshipper' of Taras Shevchenko, he admired the verses of the 'great Taras,' as he called him, and defended him against accusations that his works were lacking in social content.[37] To Hrushevsky's mind, the Russians were directly responsible for the persecution of Ukrainian culture and attempts to deny the existence of a distinct Ukrainian people with its own language and literature. Commenting on Mykola Petrov's article on the history of Ukrainian literature serialized in the *Istoricheskii vestnik* (Historical Herald),[38] Hrushevsky wrote in his diary: 'Let them now assert – these *katsapy*, who have become so overbearing, and have forgotten how the Tatars and the Poles once gave it to them hot and heavy, and have become so eager to breathe down the necks of others – let them assert, I say, that there can be no Ukrainian or, better, Ruthenian people with a life of its own; that it cannot have its own literature. It is no great thing to stick a gag into a man's mouth and say, "Look, he cannot speak: he is struggling and trying to get something out, muttering something under his breath, and that is all." Let them just give Ukraine its freedom, and then they will see with what fine flowers Ukrainian literature will pride itself among the others.'[39]

During his gymnasium years Hrushevsky came under the strong influence of Russian radicalism. The reading of back issues of the journal *Russkoe slovo* (Russian Word), the organ of Russian radical thought, to which he gained access during one of his trips to Sestrynivka, a family estate in Ukraine, introduced him to nihilism.[40] Entries in Hrushevsky's diaries reflect the influence of the ideas of Dmitrii Pisarev, which were then extremely popular among Russian gymnasium youth. Hrushevsky's favourite author at the time was Ivan Turgenev, and his favourite literary character was Bazarov in Turgenev's *Fathers and Sons* – a 'nihilist' of the sort admired and popularized by Pisarev. Also close to Hrushevsky's heart were Pisarev's ideas about forging a new man – one prepared to sacrifice himself for the common good.[41] Hrushevsky's attitudes to society at large were also shaped by the ideas of Petr Lavrov, whose thinking influenced generations of young intellectuals in the Russian Empire. Lavrov promoted the ideal of the 'critically thinking individual' (a formula employed in Hrushevsky's diaries) and saw the intelligentsia as playing a crucial role in Russian society by educating and awakening the people. Like Lavrov, Hrushevsky believed in the special role of the intelligentsia in society and refused to idealize the popular masses.[42]

The young Hrushevsky graduated from the Tbilisi gymnasium an ardent supporter of the Ukrainian cause; a believer in the existence of a distinct Ukrainian people with its own language and literature and in the natural right of Ukrainian culture to develop freely. Hrushevsky saw the source of that right in the common people. Living in a society in which young people embraced populist ideas en masse, reading the nihilist *Russkoe slovo* as well as the loyalist and conservative but Ukrainophile *Kievskaia starina*, Hrushevsky had evolved into a particular type of populist. In the tradition of Ukrainian populism, he hated both foreign and native exploiters of the people. He dreamed of bringing freedom to his native Ukraine and the unification of its ethnic territory, rejecting the idea of a future federation with Russia and Poland. In his memoirs, Hrushevsky retrospectively assessed his views as follows: 'My world view took shape in a moderate liberal direction with populist deviations and a cultural and national coloration.'[43] Hrushevsky's diaries attest that his actual views during his last years at the Tbilisi gymnasium were more radical than he was later prepared to admit.

In 1886 Hrushevsky came to Kyiv and enrolled at the St Volodymyr (Vladimir) University, then a hotbed of Ukrainophilism. In Kyiv Hrushevsky met many of the authors whose works he had read in *Kievskaia starina* and other scholarly and literary journals. Back in 1885 he had unsuccessfully attempted to make contact with the leaders of the Ukrainian cultural community in Kyiv through his acquaintances in the North Caucasus. Now he could meet many of them in person. Hrushevsky's university diary, which, like his previous diary of the Tbilisi years, was written with unusual openness and sincerity,[44] gives us a unique insight into his spiritual life, although it has much less open discussion of issues pertaining to his interest in Ukrainian affairs. In the late 1880s and early 1890s Hrushevsky maintained close contacts with the leading members of the 'Old' Ukrainophile Hromada in Kyiv and supervised the activities of the Ukrainian circle at the Orthodox seminary, but his diary is silent about these matters.

Mykhailo's father agreed to finance his son's education in Kyiv on condition that he not join any student circles and stay away from politics. The young Hrushevsky honoured that condition for quite a long time, concentrating first and foremost on his studies. Ukrainophilism was a punishable offence, as Hrushevsky knew even during his years in Tbilisi. His grandfather Zakharii became quite upset when he saw Ukrainian books in Hrushevsky's possession, and both Mykhailo and Serhii Hrushevsky were worried about possible consequences when they decided to order Ukrainian books by mail from the Ukrainian bookstore in Kyiv in 1882.[45] Hrushevsky became even more aware of the dangers associated with the Ukrainophile movement during his years at Kyiv University. Not only his father, but also his uncle, who resided in Kyiv, warned Hrushevsky against taking part in student meetings.[46] Some of his close friends at the university had problems with the police because of their Ukrainophile activities. There can be little doubt that Hrushevsky was cautious about what he wrote in his diary because he did not want to give the police the evidence they were seeking against the members of the Ukrainian movement.

There was another reason why Hrushevsky's university diaries differed from those of his gymnasium years. Clearly, the Hrushevsky who entered Kyiv University was a very different person from the one revealed in his Tbilisi diaries. During his last months at the gymnasium, he suffered a major psychological breakdown that took more than three years to overcome. The crisis was caused by the denial of a medal that Hrushevsky deserved and badly wanted to receive because fellow students had stolen questions for the matriculation exam – a traditional student prank at that time.[47] Hrushevsky's mental breakdown turned him into a very religious individual who often attended church services and was known among other students as an extremely pious Christian. Hrushevsky later referred to this stage in his life as a period of deep religiosity and explained it by psychological traits inherited from his mother, who was also extremely rigid in carrying out her religious obligations. In his memoirs Hrushevsky wrote openly about 'a certain lack of psychic balance in my character' and stated in that regard: 'At every moment, at every stage of my life I must have a certain goal before me to which I must devote myself completely and without reserve, straining my energies to the utmost, to self-oblivion, and I feel normal only when I can devote myself to the attainment of that goal with no obstacle.'[48] Eventually, Hrushevsky managed to turn this trait of his character into one of the sources of his success.

Hrushevsky's psychological crisis coincided with and probably was exacerbated by the need to make some difficult choices. One of the most fundamental was whether he should devote his life to serving God or the people, as he had dreamt of doing in his gymnasium years. It appears that by 1889 Hrushevsky had overcome his psychological problems and resolved to serve his people. The first step in that direction was to join the Ukrainophile student movement. The promise Hrushevsky gave his father not to join the student movement was effective only up to a point. With the growth of Hrushevsky's reputation at Kyiv University as an outstanding student and potential professor, he came under increasing pressure to join clandestine Ukrainian student organizations. In the end Hrushevsky's religious piety was put to good use by his Ukrainophile advisers, as he agreed to lead the Ukrainophile student circle at the Kyiv Theological Seminary.[49] Once Hrushevsky decided to devote his life to serving his people, he had no doubt that his research would be devoted to Ukraine. That conviction made it relatively easy for him to decline recruitment efforts on the part of professors who specialized outside Ukrainian history. In December 1888, when Iulian Kulakovsky, a professor of ancient and Byzantine history, approached Hrushevsky with an offer to specialize in ancient philosophy, praising his knowledge of Greek and hinting at the possibility of a postgraduate degree, Hrushevsky responded that he was not interested. He noted in his diary: 'I thought myself a hero, declining advantage for the sake of Ukrainianism.'[50]

In Kyiv, as in Tbilisi, Hrushevsky maintained a mostly negative view of the roles played by Russia and Poland in Ukrainian history. In 1888, while at Kyiv University, he published two reviews of works devoted to Slavic studies in the Lviv periodical *Pravda* (Truth), criticizing pan-Slavic tendencies coming first from Poland and then from Russia.[51] Judging by another of Hrushevsky's reviews, published in *Pravda* in 1892 (this time of a study of the Ukrainian nobility by Aleksandra Efimenko [Oleksandra Iefymenko]), Hrushevsky had quite a negative attitude toward historical Russia/Muscovy, which exploited conflicts between the Ukrainian masses and elites to enhance the centralization of the Russian state and curtail Ukrainian autonomy.[52] When one of Hrushevsky's acquaintances, the Russian scholar Fedor Uspensky, suggested that he was choosing his research topics out of patriotic motives, Hrushevsky recorded the comment in his diary with no indication of disagreement.[53] Nevertheless, the compatibility of his patriotism with scholarly objectivity was a question that bothered Hrushevsky. He discussed it with Nikolai Ogloblin, a Moscow historian and native of Kyiv whom Hrushevsky met repeatedly in Moscow during his visit there in February and March 1892, and noted in his diary: 'But I am still uncertain before my conscience: am I tendentious?'[54]

By the time of his graduation from Kyiv University, Hrushevsky was well read in the Russian, Ukrainian, and Polish historical literature, had a good knowledge of European historiography, including writings on British, French, and German history, and possessed sufficient knowledge of ancient and modern European languages to embark on a successful scholarly career.[55] Among Ukrainian historians, apart from his supervisor, Volodymyr Antonovych, Hrushevsky was especially well read in the works of Mykola Kostomarov, whose book on Bohdan Khmelnytsky, the first scholarly monograph on Ukrainian history, had impressed him the most. 'Yesterday I spent the whole day reading *Bohdan Kh[melnytsky]*. It makes too strong an impression on me: sometimes I cannot read it; it is so difficult,' noted Hrushevsky in his diary.[56] Among Polish historians, Hrushevsky was clearly influenced by the works of Michał Bobrzyński, a representative of the Cracow historiographic school. He paid special attention to Bobrzyński's statements on the historian's need for a broad education and on the importance of objectivity in historical research. The latter question particularly interested Hrushevsky with reference to his own Ukrainophilism. Another important question for the young student, especially given his populist upbringing and the strong populist influences among professors and students at Kyiv University, was the role of the individual in history. He read Nikolai Kareev's study of the philosophy of history and discussed the role of the individual with his acquaintances in the Ukrainian community.[57] He also read Thomas Carlyle's famous study on the hero in history, concluding that the book had more to do with poetry than with philosophy or historical research.[58]

As for Hrushevsky's views on the philosophy of history, they underwent a profound evolution from the rejection of philosophical positivism to its complete acceptance. In July 1889, reacting to a letter from a friend, he recorded in his diary his thoughts about Western education and Western influences: 'I received a letter from S. – very sad. He writes that without European education we shall perish. I am always somewhat displeased when people go overboard in making obeisance to European education; I am afraid, as it were, that instead of what is truly good in that education, people will substitute the false worship of false and fickle intellect, such as positivism, etc. For there is certainly good where there appeared true humanism, freedom, the rights of the individual, and concern for the infirm, not to speak of scholarly attainments.'[59] Thus, Hrushevsky accepted Western humanism and scholarship but rejected some of the more recent trends in European thought that he termed 'positivism.' He was to change his views on that point in very short order. As Hrushevsky's diary attests, in his last years at Kyiv University he became well acquainted with the works of some representatives of positivist scholarship and sociology, including Henry Buckle and Thomas Malthus. He familiarized himself with European philosophy, read Hegel, knew the works of Charles Darwin, and was especially well read in European political economy, including works by Adam Smith, David Ricardo, and Karl Marx.[60]

As Omeljan Pritsak has noted in his study of Hrushevsky's 'historiosophy,' his writings on Ukrainian history were profoundly shaped by positivist terminology and ideas, which found expression, inter alia, in his belief in progress and evolution.[61] In that respect Hrushevsky followed his professor, Volodymyr Antonovych, who was influenced by the positivist ideas popular among Polish intellectuals of the late nineteenth century.[62] Hrushevsky's acquaintance with leading proponents of positivism among the historians of the Russian Empire – his professor at Kyiv University, Ivan Luchytsky,[63] and his Moscow acquaintance Nikolai Kareev[64] – attracted him to that school of thought. Later he cooperated in scholarly and political affairs with Maksym Kovalevsky, an ethnic Ukrainian and one of the most original positivist thinkers in the realm of sociology.[65] It was Kovalevsky who invited Hrushevsky to teach a course on Ukrainian history at the Advanced School of Social Sciences in Paris in 1903. All the above-mentioned scholars worked in historical sociology, and Hrushevsky often considered himself a historian-sociologist, as he was influenced by the ideas of the Paris sociological school, especially the writings of Emile Durkheim and Lucien Lévy-Bruhl.[66]

During his years at Kyiv University, Hrushevsky developed into a scholar in his own right. He began his scholarly career under the supervision of Volodymyr Antonovych, whose article on the history of Kyiv in the first issue of *Kievskaia starina* had impressed him so much, and whom he already considered his teacher when he was enrolled in the gymnasium.[67] It was under Antonovych's supervision that Hrushevsky published his first scholarly works, an essay on Ukrainian castles of the sixteenth century and a history of the Kyivan Land up to the end of the fourteenth century.[68] The publication of his master's thesis on the history of the Bar starosta district in 1894 was followed by a two-volume collection, *Documents of the Bar Starosta District*.[69] Hrushevsky's first major study, his graduate thesis on the history of the Kyivan Land, acquainted him with the Rus' chronicles and the rich literature on the history of Kyivan Rus'. His master's thesis made him an expert on Rus', Lithuanian, and Polish archival materials and introduced him to the study of major topics in Ukrainian, Lithuanian, Polish, Crimean, and Ottoman history of the early modern era.

The book on the history of the Kyivan Land made Hrushevsky's name known to broad circles of historians specializing not only in Ukrainian but also in Russian history. It was positively reviewed by Ivan Filevich[70] and somewhat critically by Pavel Miliukov, who criticized Hrushevsky for an alleged lack of source analysis in his narrative and noted that he was a moderate supporter of the 'Ukrainophile theory' on the continuity of settlement in the Kyivan Land from the days of Kyivan Rus' to the Lithuanian period.[71] The book had a strong Ukrainian undertone indeed, as it attacked Mikhail Pogodin's theory of the Great Russian origins of the Kyivan population during the princely era and developed the views of Mykhailo Maksymovych, Volodymyr Antonovych, and other Ukrainian scholars on the continuity of Ukrainian presence in the region.[72] The study, written on a topic suggested by Antonovych, was a continuation of the work done by Antonovych's students on the history of the particular 'lands' of Ukraine. Hrushevsky's study was clearly superior in scholarly quality to the master's theses written by Antonovych's previous students, including Petro Holubovsky,[73] Nykandr Molchanovsky,[74] and Dmytro Bahalii.[75] Hrushevsky's work was awarded a gold medal by Kyiv University, brought him the recognition he was seeking in the scholarly community, and helped him apply successfully for postgraduate studies at the university. It also eventually contributed to his appointment to a teaching position at Lviv University.

In the Habsburg Monarchy

Despite Hrushevsky's desperate attempts during his first years at Kyiv University to stay away from Ukrainophile organizations, he eventually became very closely associated with the leaders of the Old Hromada in Kyiv. Apart from Volodymyr Antonovych, these included such individuals as Oleksander Konysky, the editor of the Galician newspaper *Pravda*, who lived in Kyiv and was one of the young Hrushevsky's closest advisers, and Vasyl Vovk-Karachevsky, whose daughter, Mariia, he wanted to marry.[76] All these authoritative leaders of the Ukrainian movement predicted a great future for the young scholar, and at receptions at Vovk-Karachevsky's house, Hrushevsky was often seated next to the most respected guests, such as Konysky and the leading Ukrainian composer Mykola Lysenko, who was also a member of the Old Hromada.[77] Antonovych not only encouraged Hrushevsky's research and growth as a scholar but also recommended him to others as his best student and thought that one day Hrushevsky would become as respected a scholar as he was.[78] Antonovych's support and recommendation were crucial to Hrushevsky's appointment to the chair of history at Lviv University, which was originally offered to Antonovych himself. The appointment represented a major success for the young scholar, fresh from the master's program, who was immediately given the rank of full professor. In the Russian universities he would have qualified at best for the *dotsentura* (associate professorship), obtaining tenure and promotion to full professorship only after the defence of his doctoral dissertation, as was the case with another of Antonovych's students, Dmytro Bahalii, at Kharkiv University. Hrushevsky's supporters in Kyiv were jubilant about the appointment. Konysky, for example, wrote to one of his correspondents on hearing the news: 'For me personally this is an ineffably great joy! This is the moment with which the history of our national education and culture will begin.'[79] Konysky's words were prophetic indeed.

In his autobiography Hrushevsky presented the background and significance of his appointment to the position at Lviv University as follows: 'In the Ukrainian circles of Kyiv in which I moved, great importance was attached to the reform of the Shevchenko Scientific Society. Following the so-called "agreement" of the Ukrainian populists of Galicia with the government, support was expected from the Polish side for the Ukrainian cultural and educational movement. At the beginning of 1891, Professor Antonovych, having returned from a trip to Galicia, told me of the plan for a chair of Ukrainian history at Lviv University; the chair had been offered to Professor Antonovych, but he did not want to take that burden on his old shoulders and recommended me. I accepted the plan with enthusiasm, given the importance then attributed to the Galician movement in Ukrainian circles: in Galicia they hoped to create an all-Ukrainian cultural, literary, and scholarly centre and, through the work of literati and scholars of all Ukraine and through its achievements, to break the system of proscription of the Ukrainian word and nationality in Russia, revive the national movement there, and so on.'[80]

The chair of Ukrainian history at Lviv University with Ukrainian as the language of instruction was the fifth Ukrainian chair at that institution (the others were in Ukrainian language and literature, civil law, criminal law, and theology),[81] which had ceased to be a German-language school in 1871 and was supposed to offer instruction in the languages of the local population. Under the circumstances, that meant Ukrainian and Polish. In a few years, however, Polish academics took complete control of the university, creating a situation in which any new chair with Ukrainian as the language of instruction could be established only as a result of strong political pressure. Ukrainian populist politicians, led by Oleksander Barvinsky,[82] demanded a chair of the history of the Ruthenian people (*ruthenischen Volkes*) but had to settle for a chair of world history with special emphasis on the history of Eastern Europe. A report of the imperial minister for religious affairs and education, Paul von Gautsch, found that 'under prevailing conditions, there are no grounds for the exclusion of the Ruthenian population of Poland from the history of Poland, which might give rise to a conflict between the Polish and Ukrainian populations that would be harmful to the country and the monarchy.'[83] In hindsight, it is quite clear that Hrushevsky's appointment to the chair of 'world history with special emphasis on the history of Eastern Europe' helped make that 'exclusion' not only possible but obligatory, from the political viewpoint as well as the scholarly one.

How did a young graduate of Kyiv University, as Hrushevsky was at the time of his appointment to the chair, manage to acquire such an important post? As Barvinsky stated in a letter to one of the Polish proponents of the 'new era,' Prince Adam Sapieha, both sides needed not just a professor but an experienced 'statesman' who could reconcile Poles and Ruthenians and serve as a contact in dealings with Ukraine. He and his colleagues saw Volodymyr Antonovych as just such a person, but the viceroy of Galicia, Count Kazimierz Badeni, and the Austrian authorities had reservations about him, treating him as a politically dangerous pan-Slav.[84] Nor was Antonovych interested in the position, for which he recommended his best student, Hrushevsky. As his graduation from the master's program became imminent and Antonovych's Galician friends realized that they would not be able to get the master himself, they decided to settle for his student. Hrushevsky accepted the idea with enthusiasm and began to prepare himself for the appointment.[85] He gave his formal agreement on three conditions: he would accept the appointment only at the level of full professor; he would not move to Lviv until he had defended his master's thesis and published the documents related to it; and he would not change his religion.[86] These conditions were accepted and in April 1894, even before Hrushevsky's defence of his master's thesis, he was appointed full professor of world history at Lviv University, effective 1 October 1894, by order of the emperor himself.[87]

Hrushevsky was viewed as an acceptable candidate, if not an ideal one, by all the parties involved. The Polish professors of the faculty of arts at Lviv University, where the new chair was located, were in favour of the appointment, although they expressed regret that this young and talented scholar did not know any languages other than Slavic ones. This inaccurate assessment probably reflected the fact that prior to his appointment in Lviv, Hrushevsky had published his works exclusively in Russian and Ukrainian. Count Badeni obtained information on the candidate's political background, which was corroborated by the Ministry of Foreign Affairs. In these reports Hrushevsky was characterized as an individual who devoted all his time to scholarship and was neither a pan-Slavist nor a radical nationalist, but gave his political allegiance to the Young Ruthenian/Ukrainian orientation.[88] In other words, Hrushevsky was characterized as an adherent of the Ukrainian populists, a party that supported the 'new era' and thus fit the requirements. The authorities were apparently trying to avoid the appointment of a Russophile or a pan-Slav supporter of the Russophile movement – an orientation of which they suspected Antonovych. The Austrian bureaucrats assured the emperor that, once appointed, Hrushevsky would renounce his Russian citizenship.[89] He never did so. But even more than the emperor, Hrushevsky was to disappoint the Polish professors at Lviv University and his own supporters among the Ukrainian populists. He came to Lviv above all as a representative of the Kyiv Ukrainophiles and embarked on his own agenda, which was not easily reconciled with the plans of the Austrian government, the Polish ruling elite, or even the leadership of the Ukrainian populists.

For some of Hrushevsky's Ukrainian backers, the surprises began with the young professor's inaugural lecture, delivered at Lviv University on 30 September (12 October) 1894.[90] He presented a view according to which the history of the popular masses served as the principal theme of Ukrainian historical development. As Hrushevsky saw it, the economic, cultural, and spiritual life of the people was the principal subject of historical research, with the history of the state and elites removed to the periphery of the historian's attention.[91] The lecture, crafted in the best traditions of Ukrainian populism, presented the history of Rus'/Ukraine as a history of the popular masses. Its principal thesis was based on the inaugural lectures of Mykola Kostomarov at St Petersburg University in 1859[92] and Volodymyr Antonovych at Kyiv University in 1870.[93] While it probably would not have caused any controversy among the Ukrainian public in Russian-ruled Ukraine, that was not the case in Galicia. It appears that many conservative members of the Ukrainian community were shocked by Hrushevsky's presentation of Rus' history as a struggle of the popular masses against their rulers, while the younger generation was eager to embrace that thesis.[94] But even the students were shocked by Hrushevsky's desire to treat them as equals and by his addressing them as 'comrades,' seemingly an accepted practice in Kyiv, but one that was viewed with suspicion by the politically more conservative Galicians.[95]

Hrushevsky came to Lviv and began to work in Ukrainian scholarly and cultural circles under the auspices of individuals like Barvinsky, who spared no effort to develop and strengthen the Ukrainian project in Galicia. This allowed Hrushevsky to get an early start in Lviv, but it took him a while to reformulate the Ukrainian project in Galicia according to his own views, and not those of his allies. An early beneficiary of the policy of political compromise with the Polish elite for the benefit of Ukrainian culture, Hrushevsky soon became disappointed with it and distanced himself from his former benefactors, such as Barvinsky, who remained loyal to the 'new era.' When young and still very religious, Hrushevsky met Barvinsky for the first time in Kyiv in October 1890 and was very gratified to find that Barvinsky was 'for religion.'[96] But that was also the time when Hrushevsky rejected the socialist ideals of the Protestant sects on the grounds that they undermined the Gospel. Lviv saw a very different Hrushevsky. Much later, Hrushevsky would write that intellectually and politically he had been brought up in the 'strict tradition of radical Ukrainian populism.'[97] In Galicia, that tradition fully manifested itself in Hrushevsky's political, scholarly, and cultural activities.

During his first years in Galicia, Hrushevsky sought to take a position 'above the battle' and avoid excessive involvement in party politics so as to draw support for his scholarly and cultural projects from all quarters of Ukrainian society. The years 1898–9 were a major turning point with regard to Hrushevsky's involvement in Galician politics. The 'bloody' Galician elections of 1897, in which the Polish administration put pressure on populist candidates who did not support the 'new era,' led him to break with proponents of the Polish-Ukrainian compromise. After some hesitation Hrushevsky also turned against the 'new era,' citing his disappointment with the behaviour of the Polish politicians, who had not kept their part of the bargain.[98] He wrote in his autobiography: 'It was still more disagreeable to learn that the hopes of favourable circumstances for Ukrainian cultural and special scholarly development, of a favourable attitude toward the Ukrainian national idea on the part of the government and the Poles with which I went to Galicia, relying on the assurances of Kyivans of the older generation who were better acquainted with Galician conditions, were based on false assurances from the Poles, who, by means of the "agreement" and at the price of certain concessions in the sphere of national culture, sought to crush any oppositional, freedom-loving movement among the Galician Ruthenians.'[99] In 1898 Hrushevsky explained his opposition to the 'new era' in a letter to the newspaper *Dilo* (The Deed).[100] Later he commented on it in an essay of 1910, where he explained his critique of the policy as follows: 'It was entirely clear to anyone of sober disposition that only actual strength could give the Ukrainian movement serious achievements in the cultural sphere, as in every other aspect of Polish dominance in Galicia.'[101]

Hrushevsky strongly believed that the only way to acquire cultural and national rights for the Ukrainian population in Galicia was through uncompromising struggle with the Polish ruling elite. Hrushevsky's stand on Polish-Ukrainian relations was closely linked to his populist ideas, for he saw the struggle against Polish oppression of the Ukrainian nation as a struggle against the social oppression of the Ukrainian popular masses by the Polish elite. That elite possessed the fullness of administrative and economic power in Galicia and, in Hrushevsky's opinion, consciously strove to deprive Ukrainians of a high culture, hindering their transformation from an ethnic mass into a nation (or 'nationality,' as Hrushevsky called it).[102] Indeed, the leaders of the Polish national movement in Galicia, especially with the rise to prominence in the 1890s of the National Democratic Party led by Roman Dmowski, aggressively pursued the Polonization of the Ukrainian peasantry, claiming that if the Ukrainians wanted to build their own nation, they would have to prove their right to do so in open confrontation with Polish society.[103]

Very soon after his arrival in Galicia, Hrushevsky became interested in the activities of the Ukrainian Radical Party – a political grouping with strong socialist leanings. He was also looking for ways to bring the radicals and moderate populists together in one political party. Hrushevsky not only began to cooperate closely with the famous Ukrainian writer and poet Ivan Franko, a political radical, but also met with other leaders of the Radical Party to discuss the possibility of joining radical and populist forces.[104] The time for action came in 1899, when most of the populists, dissatisfied with the 'new era' policy, decided to create a new party by allying themselves with a group of radicals. This resulted in the formation of the National Democratic Party, led by the populist Iuliian Romanchuk. Both Hrushevsky and Franko were elected to the party presidium – Hrushevsky, in fact, became its deputy leader. He apparently came to the conclusion that he could no longer limit his activities to scholarship and should go into politics. For both the Ukrainian and the Polish national movements, the 1890s were marked by a revolt against the earlier paradigm of 'organic' work (or 'cultural' work, as the Ukrainians called it) and the establishment of political parties with clear goals on their agendas. Thus, during the last years of the nineteenth century, Hrushevsky was also leaving behind the era of *kul'turnytstvo* – the exclusive concentration of Ukrainian intellectuals on cultural and apolitical activity – and making the scholarly and cultural achievements of previous generations accessible to the general public. In Miroslav Hroch's terms, Hrushevsky was successfully crossing the boundary between the 'scholarly interest' and 'patriotic agitation' stages of the Ukrainian national project in Dnipro Ukraine and going on to the 'mass movement' stage in Austrian Ukraine.[105]

The program of the new party, drafted by Franko, possibly with some help from Hrushevsky, included a number of politically bold statements. In the social sphere, as noted above, it called for a Ukraine 'without serf or landlord.' It advocated national autonomy for the Ukrainian lands within the Habsburg Monarchy and expressed support for the Ukrainian movement in the Romanovs' realm. As the party's ultimate goal, the program proclaimed the achievement of the cultural, economic, and political independence of the united 'Ukrainian-Ruthenian' people. It was the first time that a major political force, not a marginal leftist group, had put these slogans on its banner, and Hrushevsky had much to celebrate upon the creation of the new party, which subscribed to the all-Ukrainian agenda so dear to his heart. But the honeymoon did not last very long, as real power in the new party remained in the hands of the former populists, who often paid only lip service to the national and social principles that Hrushevsky viewed as a sine qua non. He soon became disenchanted with the new party and suspended his participation in politics for a time.[106]

Hrushevsky had come to Lviv with a twofold task. On the one hand, there was a need to strengthen Galicia's links with Eastern Ukraine and support the Ukrainian project in Galicia, which was not only under attack by Polish officialdom but also had to compete with the Russophile project of turning the Ruthenian peasants not into Poles, as the authorities wanted, nor into Ukrainians, as the populists were endeavoring to do, but into Russians. Hrushevsky's scholarly and cultural activities in Galicia, supported by financial and intellectual assistance from Russian-ruled Ukraine, would help the Ukrainian project prevail. The other element of Hrushevsky's mandate was to attain in Galicia the goals that the Kyivan Ukrainophiles could not achieve in Russian-ruled Ukraine. Hrushevsky's teaching at Lviv University was a major accomplishment in its own right. The position of the Austrian authorities, who believed that Ukrainian history did not constitute a scholarly subject or that it was politically inexpedient to separate it from Polish history, did not prevent Hrushevsky from teaching courses in Ukrainian history or postulating its existence as a distinct scholarly discipline. The Russian authorities did not give similar scope to Antonovych in Kyiv or Bahalii in Kharkiv. Teaching in Ukrainian at the university level was also forbidden in the Russian Empire. Thus, in Lviv Hrushevsky gained opportunities that could not even be dreamt of in the Russian Empire, and he was eager to use them to their full capacity. His courses in Ukrainian history gathered huge audiences, as most Ukrainian students at Lviv University attended them. Hrushevsky made good use of his seminars to prepare talented young students for scholarly work in Ukrainian history.

His major achievement was the publication of the first volumes of his multivolume *History of Ukraine-Rus'*. Initially Hrushevsky intended to write a three-volume popular history of Ukraine but then came to the conclusion that a solid, thoroughly researched account of the Ukrainian past was required. He began work on the project early in 1897, and the first volume appeared in print at the end of the following year. When Hrushevsky abandoned the idea of a popular history of Ukraine, he expected that his scholarly history would require five or six volumes, then extended it to seven, eight, and nine, and eventually stopped planning how many volumes it would include.[107] The first six volumes

covered the initial periods of Ukrainian history, those of Kyivan Rus'
and of Lithuanian and Polish rule, and included chapters on Ukrainian
economic, political, religious, and cultural life in the second half of the
sixteenth century. With volume seven, Hrushevsky entered the third
(Cossack) period of Ukrainian history. The seventh and all subsequent
volumes of the *History*, which constituted a separate series titled The
History of the Ukrainian Cossacks, were published between 1909 and
1936.

Needless to say, Hrushevsky's aggressive development of Ukrainian
studies gained him no support among the Polish academics, who initially looked down on their young colleague and later, disturbed by his
actions, tried to use political pressure to curtail his activities. They were
too late. Hrushevsky held the position of full professor, behaved independently, and followed his own course despite the admonitions of
the university authorities.[108] Hrushevsky's plans, in fact, reached far
beyond the walls of Lviv University. Among his many nation-building
projects, two deserve special attention. The first was the nationalization
of scholarship, entailing the formation of a Ukrainian scholarly elite
and the establishment of a prototype of a national academy of sciences.
The other was the nationalization of higher education and the founding
of a Ukrainian university. The two projects were interrelated, and the
progress of the first created important preconditions for the achievement of the second. Both were crucial to the success of Ukrainian
nation-building.

Hrushevsky's ruling passion, especially during his first years in
Galicia, was the Shevchenko Society, which his Kyivan mentors Konysky
and Antonovych wanted to turn into a thriving academic institution.
Later, Hrushevsky viewed the Shevchenko Society and its counterpart
in Eastern Ukraine, the Ukrainian Scientific Society, which he headed
from its foundation in 1907, as forerunners of the Ukrainian Academy
of Sciences.[109] The society was founded in Lviv in 1873 as a literary
association, at the initiative and with the financial support of Ukrainians in the Russian Empire, in order to help Ukrainian authors circumvent the restrictions imposed on Ukrainian publications by the Valuev
circular of 1863. In 1892, at the behest of Konysky, who had been a
founder of the society in 1873, and Oleksander Barvinsky, who was its
head at the time, the society was transformed into a scholarly institution and began the publication of its journal, *Zapysky Naukovoho tovarystva
im. Shevchenka* (Memoirs of the Shevchenko Scientific Society).[110] Its
first issue began with an article by Mykhailo Hrushevsky, then still a

student at Kyiv University,[111] and during its early years the journal relied heavily on materials and scholarly advice from Russian-ruled Ukraine.

Hrushevsky devoted enormous energy and all his organizational and scholarly talent to turning the Shevchenko Society into a premier academic institution. After his arrival in Lviv, Hrushevsky assumed responsibility for the scholarly aspect of the society's activities and was formally elected its head in 1897. The way in which he organized its work shows that he viewed it as part of a larger nation-building initiative. The main emphasis was on the humanities – history, language, and literature – the areas of scholarship immediately related to the construction and preservation of national identity. Hrushevsky aspired to transform the society from a Ukrainian literary and cultural club, which it was during the first years of its existence, into a scholarly institution whose work, publications, and opinions would be treated with respect not only by Ukrainians themselves but also outside the Ukrainian community, in both Austria-Hungary and the Russian Empire. The first obstacle on the way to achieving that goal was the existing leadership of the society, headed by Hrushevsky's benefactor Oleksander Barvinsky. The latter, like many of his supporters in the society, was a political and cultural activist who wanted to use the society as an instrument of party politics. The old guard objected to the admission and then to the promotion within the society of scholars who did not support its political views. Hrushevsky was able to overcome this opposition thanks to his impeccable scholarly credentials and skilful manoeuvring between the different factions of the Ukrainian community. His election as head of the society led to a change of its statute that ensured the prevalence of scholars over community activists in its ruling bodies.[112]

Turning the Shevchenko Society into an institution respected in the scholarly world required years of hard work. When Hrushevsky arrived in Galicia, he was assured by his Kyiv mentors that literary authors and scholars from Eastern Ukraine, who were not permitted to publish their works in the Russian Empire, would flood the Shevchenko society's *Memoirs* with their articles. The prediction proved wrong, and Hrushevsky had to rely almost exclusively on his own contributions and those of his students at Lviv University.[113] Eventually, his efforts at reforming the society paid off. By 1914, when Hrushevsky ceased to head it, the society had published more than ninety volumes of *Memoirs*, more than sixty volumes of its literary and socio-political journal,

Literaturno-naukovyi visnyk (Literary and Scholarly Herald), and eleven volumes of historical sources in the series *Zherela do istoriï Ukraïny-Rusy* (Sources on the History of Ukraine-Rus'). Even more important, owing to many years of work in the Shevchenko Society, Hrushevsky was able to educate a new generation of scholars specializing in various aspects of Ukrainian history. They included such historians as Myron Korduba, Stepan Tomashivsky, and Ivan Krypiakevych, who were to gain future renown.[114]

Hrushevsky's other major nation-building project, as noted above, was the establishment of a Ukrainian university. Unlike the reformation of the Shevchenko Scientific Society, which Hrushevsky managed to accomplish in a relatively short time, the university project proved impossible to achieve, as its realization depended not only on the support of the Ukrainian community but also on the attitude of the authorities, especially the Polish ruling elite of Galicia, which continued to subsidize the Shevchenko Society but drew the line at approving a university. It was in 1897 that Hrushevsky voiced the idea of establishing a separate Ukrainian university. He also came up with a plan of establishing parallel Ukrainian chairs at Lviv University that would eventually be separated from the institution. In the following year the issue was raised by a Ukrainian deputy on the floor of the Austro-Hungarian parliament in Vienna, while the Shevchenko Society sent the government a memorandum on the matter.[115] The Ukrainian demand for a separate university clearly antagonized Polish academic circles. The year 1901 became one of open confrontation between the Polish university administration and the Ukrainian students. That year saw the administration forbid Ukrainian theological students to fill out their registration forms in Ukrainian, followed by a conflict between Hrushevsky and the dean over the use of Ukrainian at faculty meetings. When a student meeting adopted a resolution demanding the establishment of a separate Ukrainian university, the administration refused to cooperate and expelled some of the participants in the student meeting, although the students, in Hrushevsky's opinion, were prepared to settle for the introduction of courses with Ukrainian as the language of instruction in the faculties of arts, medicine, and law. In protest against the actions of the administration, a number of Ukrainian students withdrew and transferred to other universities of the empire. Although Hrushevsky opposed the withdrawal, he was accused by Polish academics of having provoked student unrest.[116]

The conflict obliged all Ukrainian political forces and the leader of the Ukrainian Greek Catholics, Metropolitan Andrei Sheptytsky, to come out in defence of the students. Ukrainian politicians presented the government with a special memorandum on the establishment of a Ukrainian university drafted by none other than Hrushevsky.[117] He also elaborated on the issue in a number of essays, countering arguments raised against a Ukrainian university by Polish academic and community leaders. Hrushevsky based his argument on the principle of 'national justice,' which was often invoked by Polish leaders to advance their agenda in the Habsburg Monarchy. He maintained that Ukrainians constituted the majority of the population of eastern Galicia; like the Poles, who had obtained a university of their own in Cracow (the principal city of western Galicia), they had the right to establish a university in the eastern part of the province. Countering Polish arguments that there were not enough students for the prospective university, Hrushevsky cited enrollment statistics to the effect that there had been close to 800 Ukrainian students at Lviv University in the winter semester of 1905. He compared that figure to the total enrollment at Chernivtsi University, which had only 400 students registered, and remarked that no one questioned the existence of that university. Hrushevsky also rejected the Polish claim that there were not enough Ukrainian professors to staff such a university, as there was little if any interest in scholarship on the part of Ukrainians. Hrushevsky ridiculed that argument, noting that one could speak with no less accuracy of a lack of interest in scholarship among the Poles of the Russian Empire, where the number of Polish professors at Warsaw University was steadily declining because of government policy. Hrushevsky went on to claim that the Ukrainians could staff their university with professors within a three-year period, just as the Poles had done at Lviv University in the early 1870s. He believed that the Shevchenko Scientific Society had a role to play in that undertaking.[118]

The 'Liberation of Russia'

Hrushevsky had been sent to Lviv by the leaders of the Kyivan Old Hromada with an all-Ukrainian mandate – one that he never forgot during his residence of more than twenty years in Galicia. The essence of that mandate was to help turn Galicia into a 'Ukrainian Piedmont' where Ukrainian national culture, scholarship, and ideology could be developed free of the restrictions imposed on the Ukrainian movement by the Russian authorities. This idea mirrored the concept of a 'Polish

Piedmont' developed by the Polish leaders in Galicia, who considered Austrian rule more favourable to Polish national development than German or Russian rule. Activists of the Polish movement saw Galicia as a proving ground where Polish society could develop political, cultural, and social practices forbidden elsewhere on Polish territory.[119]

As Hrushevsky learned when he decided to leave the scholarly ghetto and present his nationalizing project to a wider world, there were serious obstacles on the way to realizing the Kyivan Ukrainians' dream of turning Galicia into a Ukrainian Piedmont. Even with the victory of the Ukrainian project in Galicia, the imperial border between the two parts of Ukraine made it extremely difficult to import Galician achievements into the Russian Empire. This became apparent after the publication of the first volume of Hrushevsky's *History of Ukraine-Rus'* in 1898, when he began thinking of ways to make the *History* and his other works accessible to readers in Eastern Ukraine. The ban on importing Ukrainian-language books into the Russian Empire was an almost insuperable obstacle. The Kyiv intelligentsia's circumvention of the Ems Ukase of 1876 by moving Ukrainian publishing activities to Galicia clearly allowed the Ukrainian printed word to survive one of the most difficult eras in its history and conquer Galicia, but that did not solve the problem of disseminating it in the Russian Empire. Unless the empire lifted its ban on Ukrainian publications, the whole idea of the Galician Piedmont and the raison d'être of Hrushevsky's work there was in serious trouble.

Hrushevsky had to act, and in 1899 he waged the first battle of his campaign to abolish the ban on Ukrainian publications. That year, when the Eleventh Russian Archaeological Congress was scheduled to be held in Kyiv, Hrushevsky and his students and associates at the Shevchenko Scientific Society submitted their proposals for participation in Ukrainian. On the one hand, this was a natural way of proceeding, given that Lviv historians published their research exclusively in Ukrainian. On the other hand, Hrushevsky was fully conscious of the political, cultural, and scholarly implications of his initiative in the imperial Russian context. Later he wrote in his autobiography: 'I raised and squarely posed the issue of allowing papers to be read in Ukrainian.'[120] Hrushevsky's demarche caused confusion in Russian government and academic circles. The organizing committee of the congress did not reject the Ukrainian-language papers, as it accepted papers written in other Slavic languages, but refused to publish them in Ukrainian in the proceedings of the congress. That compromise, suggested by liberal-minded members of the committee, was superseded by a ban imposed by the Ministry of Internal Affairs on the presentation of scholarly papers in Ukrainian. At this point the imperial Ministry of Education entered the scene and proposed a new compromise, according to which the presentation of Ukrainian-language papers would be allowed not at plenary sessions open to the general public but only at panels with no more than twenty-five people present. This proposal was rejected both by the congress organizers and by Hrushevsky and his associates. The papers that were to have been presented at the congress were published in two volumes of the *Memoirs of the Shevchenko Scientific Society*. As Hrushevsky noted in his autobiography, 'it was also necessary to document that these claims for the recognition of Ukrainian as a scholarly language were backed by genuine scholarly work.'[121]

The negative ruling of the Ministry of Internal Affairs was provoked by public statements made by proponents of the all-Russian idea, who protested against giving the Ukrainian language the same status as Russian at the congress. The attack on the liberals in the organizing committee was led by Hrushevsky's former dean at Kyiv University, Timofei Florinsky – the same individual who, following Hrushevsky's defence of his master's thesis in 1894, had sarcastically invited the young scholar to defend his doctoral dissertation at Kyiv University in the Ukrainian language.[122] In the eyes of Florinsky and other Russian nationalists, Hrushevsky emerged after the Eleventh Archaeological Congress as the leader of Ukrainian separatism. Once it became known in Russia that Hrushevsky had signed the declaration of the Ukrainian National Democratic Party calling for a united and independent Ukraine, he was accused not only of undermining Russian cultural unity but also of challenging the political unity of the empire.[123] Another even more important consequence of the language scandal was that it made the general public aware of the existence of Ukrainian scholarship and put the issue of lifting the ban on Ukrainian-language publications on the political agenda. As Hrushevsky's student Ivan Krypiakevych later wrote, Hrushevsky's stand on the issue 'made a great impression in academic circles in Russia. Everyone began talking about Ukrainian scholarship; they also began talking about unjust restrictions on the Ukrainian language.'[124]

In terms of the future of the Ukrainian language at scholarly conferences held in Russia, the scandal of 1899 also had a significant impact. In the short run, it was more negative than positive. To avoid further problems, the organizers of Russian archaeological (in fact, historical) congresses, which were held every three years, decided not to invite Galician scholars. That was the case at the twelfth congress, held in Kharkiv in 1902, where papers were read only in Russian. The tactic was only partly successful, as keeping Galicians away from the congresses was not enough to keep the Ukrainian language out of the congress proceedings. The following, thirteenth, congress, which took place in Katerynoslav at the time of the 1905 revolution, was addressed in Ukrainian by its honorary chairman, Mykola Sumtsov of Kharkiv University.[125] In fact, the ban on scholarly publications in Ukrainian was broken by Hrushevsky even earlier, in 1903, in connection with preparations for the Congress of Slavists that was to be held in St Petersburg. After lengthy debate, the Ukrainian language was allowed at the congress, but the congress itself never took place.[126] The papers submitted to the organizing committee were published nevertheless, and some of Hrushevsky's Ukrainian-language articles, including his most famous essay on the traditional scheme of Russian history, which deconstructed the all-Russian historical narrative and cleared the way for the introduction of a Ukrainian one, were published in a collection issued by the Russian Academy of Sciences.[127] The irony of the situation lay in the fact that although the Slavic congress never took place and the Ukrainian language was never heard from its podium, its organizers went further than the liberal organizers of the Kyiv archaeological congress had been prepared to go: they published the papers in Ukrainian.

In the autumn of 1904 Hrushevsky became involved in polemics with one of the foremost Russian 'Ukrainophiles,' Aleksandr Pypin. He tried to persuade Pypin to publish a Ukrainian-language article in *Izvestiia*, the journal of the Department of Russian Language and Literature of the Imperial Academy of Sciences (*IzORIaS*). Sometime in the summer of that year, Hrushevsky wrote to Pypin, offering for publication one of his Ukrainian-language articles and citing as a precedent the earlier publication in *Izvestiia* of a Czech-language article by Jiří Polivka.[128] Pypin responded in September 1904, refusing the article. He stated that although the department was not indifferent to the fate of the 'Little Russian literary language,' it preferred not to take a position in the conflict between local dialects. Pypin argued that *Izvestiia* was a Russian publication, not a pan-Slavic one; that the article in Czech was published as an exception, as it was bibliographic in nature and its author did not know Russian, while Hrushevsky knew the language.[129]

Hrushevsky shot back that his own article was no less specialized than Polivka's and that Pypin's claim about *Izvestiia*'s being a Russian publication left no place for the Ukrainian language in Russian or Slavic studies. Not without irony, Hrushevsky wrote: 'Here again we have the same vicious circle in which the Ukrainian question keeps turning in Russia. The Ukrainian language, literature, and the like are excluded from the Slavic dialects as an integral part of the "Russian" disciplines but are not included in the corpus of the latter. In consequence, there is no place for them either in Slavic courses, publications, and the like or in "Russian" ones, and ultimately they are excluded from scholarly practice. Regarding the Ukrainian language from its own viewpoint as an integral part of the Russian language (see, for example, the draft of its Slavic studies bibliography), the department could, with perfect consistency, make room on the pages of its organ for the (Little) Russian language alongside the (Great) Russian one.'[130]

Nevertheless, Hrushevsky's main argument was based not on the assumption that the Ukrainian language was entitled to a 'Russian' status but on the assertion of its complete independence. Hrushevsky found it strange that a knowledge of Russian should prevent anyone from writing in his native language. He and his countrymen were writing in Ukrainian not out of ignorance or inability to learn Russian or any other foreign language, but because their own language was capable of serving as a medium of intellectual communication. The capacity of the Ukrainian language to perform scholarly tasks had long been established, claimed Hrushevsky. The purpose of his article was to inform the scholarly community in Russia about the work of Galician scholars, while its socio-political task was to make a 'breach in Russian censorship policy, which excludes the Ukrainian language from use in scholarly writing.' Hrushevsky called on the department to treat the Ukrainian question not as a political football but 'from a principled viewpoint, i.e., from the viewpoint of free self-determination.' We do not know whether Pypin ever responded to this letter from Hrushevsky (he died on 26 November [9 December] 1904),[131] but Hrushevsky's call for members of the academy to support the 'self-determination' of the Ukrainian language did not fall on deaf ears. In the final analysis, it was the attitude of the Russian philologists at the academy that helped lift the ban on Ukrainian publications.

The year 1904 marked an important step in Hrushevsky's campaign to introduce the Ukrainian language into Russian imperial scholarly and cultural discourse. By the end of that year, permission had been granted to import his *History of Ukraine-Rus'* into the Russian Empire. That breakthrough, which was directly related to the coming revolution in Russia, resulted from a letter that Hrushevsky wrote to Prince Petr Sviatopolk-Mirsky, the new Russian minister of the interior. Judging by the draft preserved in Hrushevsky's personal archive, his appeal to Sviatopolk-Mirsky was a continuation of his earlier attempts to convince Russian officialdom to lift the ban on importing the *History* into the Russian Empire. Hrushevsky petitioned the heads of the Imperial Directorate in charge of publications in 1902 and 1903 but received either empty promises or no answer at all. Finally he decided to write to Sviatopolk-Mirsky, taking him at his word, as the minister had made an official pledge to 'alleviate the situation of the printed word in Russia and introduce freedom and justice into national relations.'[132] Citing the Ems Ukase of 1876, Hrushevsky complained to the minister that even the few copies of his *History* sent to individual scholars and educational institutions had for the most part been confiscated by the Russian authorities. Hrushevsky was determined to use every argument he could muster, appealing even to East Slavic solidarity: as a Russian subject, he wrote, he was ashamed and indignant that a Polish-language book on fifteenth-century Polish and Lithuanian history written by a former schoolfellow of his was allowed into Russia, while the fourth volume of Hrushevsky's own *History*, which covered the same chronological period, was not.[133] Whether the motive was the prince's anti-Polish animus or, more probably (as Hrushevsky wrote in his autobiography), his desire to calm Russian public opinion in the wake of defeat in the war with Japan and growing popular discontent, permission was granted to import the *History of Ukraine-Rus'* into the Russian Empire.[134]

In 1904 Hrushevsky also managed to publish in St Petersburg his survey of Ukrainian history – the first to appear in the Russian Empire since the 1840s. The project was the result of an invitation from Maksym Kovalevsky, a prominent Russian sociologist of Ukrainian descent, to deliver a course on Ukrainian history at the Advanced School of Social Sciences in Paris. Hrushevsky gave the course in April and May 1903, reworking it into a book in the summer of that year. Hrushevsky's *Survey History of the Ukrainian People* was written in Russian and crowned his long campaign to circumvent the ban on his works in Russia by publishing in languages other than Ukrainian. In 1900 Hrushevsky approached a number of German publishers to issue a German translation of his *History of Ukraine-Rus'* but, as he wrote in his autobiography, 'the unusual nature of the subject (compare Gautsch's argument) and the great dimensions of the work were an obstacle: publishers responded negatively.'[135] Not until 1903 did Hrushevsky find a publisher for the first volume of his 'big' *History* in German (at his own expense) and a brief history of Ukraine in French. The next step was to find a Russian publisher, which proved difficult. After prolonged negotiations, Hrushevsky decided to publish the book at his own expense.[136] It was a success and was reissued twice before being replaced by Hrushevsky's Ukrainian-language *Illustrated History of Ukraine* in 1912.[137]

During the Revolution of 1905 in the Russian Empire, Hrushevsky's activities began to shift more and more toward Kyiv. By intellectual upbringing and psychological make-up, Hrushevsky was definitely a product of the Kyiv cultural and scholarly atmosphere and did not feel completely at home in Lviv. Apart from that he saw new prospects for his political, cultural, and scholarly work opening up in Dnipro Ukraine and was eager to take advantage of those opportunities. Until 1905 Hrushevsky had been forced to suspend his trips to Kyiv and other centres of Ukrainian political and cultural life in the Russian Empire. He remained a Russian citizen, and his friends in Russian official circles warned him about the danger of such trips to Eastern Ukraine. Given his active participation in Ukrainian cultural and political life in Lviv, Hrushevsky's well-wishers apparently did not exclude the possibility of his arrest in the Russian Empire. The 1905 revolution changed the situation radically. Not only could the *History*, previously banned in the Russian Empire, now be sold there, but Hrushevsky himself was able to travel to the empire and was allowed to publish his political writings in Ukrainian and Russian periodicals.[138] Hrushevsky's professorial status made it easier for him than for other Ukrainian activists to publish pro-Ukrainian writings, and his readers encouraged him to do even more in that vein.[139]

A number of important battles were won; the door to the Russian Empire was now open; but the campaign to lift the ban on Ukrainian publications still lay ahead. The publication of Hrushevsky's *Survey History of the Ukrainian People* in Russia was met with open hostility by proponents of all-Russian unity.[140] The *Survey* was used by those forces as an example of what could be expected of the Ukrainian movement once the ban on Ukrainian publications was lifted. That was the leitmotif of an anonymous article published under the pseudonym 'Kyivan' (*Kievlianin*) in the newspaper *Grazhdanin* (Citizen). Its editors treated the article as an expression of the opinion of the Kyiv 'Russian Assembly' – a club of Russian nationalists – on the issue. The anonymous author claimed that lifting the ban on Ukrainian publications would amount to a revision of the treaty of 1654 between Tsar Aleksei Mikhailovich and Hetman Bohdan Khmelnytsky, that the publication of scripture in Ukrainian would help spread Protestantism (*shtunda*) in Little Russia, and that freedom of association would help establish militant organizations among the peasantry along the lines of the Galician Sich societies. Hrushevsky responded to these accusations with an article titled 'Phrases and Facts' published in the newspaper *Syn otechestva* (Son of the Fatherland) in April 1905. There he claimed that his opponent had a poor knowledge of history, as the treaty of 1654, which in fact gave Ukraine the right of self-government, had already been revised by the Muscovite bureaucracy, which took away Ukrainian freedoms. He further asserted that the restrictions on Ukrainian publications should be abolished without delay and that the Russian Empire was badly in need of restructuring (*perestroika*).[141]

Hrushevsky's debate with the 'Kyivan' took place at a time when the government, under pressure from the Ukrainian community, was looking into the possibility of lifting the ban on Ukrainian publications. In December 1904, the imperial cabinet decided to examine the issue, stating that the restrictions had initially been imposed to curb the Ukrainian movement, which in fact constituted no threat to the government, while the ban on Ukrainian publications was hindering the education of the peasantry. The cabinet asked for advice from the Russian Academy of Sciences, Kyiv and Kharkiv universities, and the office of the governor-general of Kyiv. All these institutions recommended the lifting of the ban.[142] The following year, 1905, saw the publication of memoranda prepared by the Russian Academy of Sciences and Kharkiv University in support of abolishing the ban. For Hrushevsky this was a dream come true. The text of the academy's memorandum, which was immediately translated into Ukrainian and published in *Literaturno-naukovyi visnyk*, appeared later as a separate brochure. In his introduction to the Ukrainian publication of the memorandum, Hrushevsky stressed the section in which its authors claimed that the ban on Ukrainian-language publications in Russia helped promote such publications in Galicia, where they took on an anti-Russian character.[143] Thus the achievements of the Ukrainian project in Galicia were not only recognized by Russian scholars but also used as an argument in the high-level debate on the future of the Ukrainian language in the Russian Empire.

In the spring of 1906 the Russian government issued new regulations on publishing activities that silently dropped the restrictions imposed on Ukrainian publications by the ukase of 1876.[144] The obstacles that had hindered the development of Ukrainian cultural and political life for decades were removed, and the Galician Piedmont could now start sending its books and journals to Dnipro Ukraine. Hrushevsky had every reason to be satisfied.[145] In an article titled 'The Ukrainian Piedmont' (1906), addressed to a Russian readership, Hrushevsky wrote: 'In the last decade of the nineteenth century, Galicia, despite the highly difficult conditions of its own national and economic existence, has become the centre of the Ukrainian movement, and in relation to the Ukrainian lands of Russia it is now playing the role of a cultural arsenal in which resources for the national, cultural, and socio-political revival of the Ukrainian people have been created and perfected.'[146]

The spring of 1906 brought the election to the First Russian Duma of a number of Ukrainian activists, as well as many deputies who, though not active in the Ukrainian movement, considered themselves to be of Ukrainian origin and were sympathetic to the Ukrainian cause. These deputies formed a Ukrainian caucus in the Duma that published a Russian-language newspaper, *Ukrainskii vestnik* (Ukrainian Herald), between May and August 1906. Hrushevsky went to St Petersburg as soon as the deputies began to assemble for the opening of the first Russian parliament and was immediately accepted by them as the unchallenged leader of the Ukrainian movement. It was Hrushevsky who, more often than not, defined the political course of *Ukrainskii vestnik*, to which he contributed numerous articles.[147] Hrushevsky was eager to share his experience with the political leaders of the Ukrainian movement in Russia. In the above-mentioned article, 'The Ukrainian Piedmont,' which appeared in the second issue of *Ukrainskii vestnik*, Hrushevsky acquainted the Ukrainian public in the Russian Empire with the Galician experience, not only with regard to the development of Ukrainian culture, but also in the organization of Ukrainian communal and political life, spheres of activity unfamiliar to the leaders and rank-and-file members of the Ukrainian movement in the empire prior to the 1905 revolution.[148] In his first speech to the Ukrainian deputies of the Duma, Hrushevsky 'acquainted those present with the results of forty years of constitutionalism in Austrian Ukraine and indicated the obstacles with which its social and cultural movement had had to contend and that must be borne in mind so as to avoid them in the construction of political and social relations in Russia.'[149]

One of Hrushevsky's most important contributions to Ukrainian political discourse in 1905–7 was his introduction of the 'Ukrainian question' to broad circles of Russian imperial society. Hrushevsky's articles also reached out to those of Ukrainian origin who did not read Ukrainian and were not involved in any type of Ukrainian cultural activity. These two audiences were the main target of the numerous pamphlets and essays that Hrushevsky published in the Russian Empire, in both Ukrainian and Russian, throughout the 1905 revolution. In a number of articles, he presented a survey of Ukrainian history designed to help the reader understand the origins of the problem. He also explained the development of Ukrainian political thought up to the Revolution of 1905.[150] Hrushevsky did not discuss the 'Ukrainian question' in isolation but treated it as part of a much broader political problem. In 1907 he published many of his political writings of that period under the title *The Liberation of Russia and the Ukrainian Question*.[151] The title of the collection embodied the main idea of Hrushevsky's writings of the day: the solution to the 'Ukrainian question,' which Hrushevsky saw in the granting of national-territorial autonomy, was presented as a necessary condition for the 'liberation of Russia.' That term was used in the Russian Empire to define a broad movement of the imperial intelligentsia and a public-opinion campaign designed to force the authorities to adopt a constitution. In Hrushevsky's view, the 'liberation' agenda had to include not only the adoption of a constitution and the granting of political freedoms to the population at large but also the reorganization of the Russian Empire on a federal basis. 'Russia is an "empire of peoples," among which the ruling nationality constitutes a minority. It cannot develop freely and successfully as long as that restructuring does not provide for the free and genuine existence and development of its component parts – its peoples,' wrote Hrushevsky in his introduction to *The Liberation of Russia*.[152]

Hrushevsky defined the 'Ukrainian question' as part of the national question in general – in his opinion, one of the most important questions that the Russian Empire had to confront on its way to the 'liberation' of its society. An important element in Hrushevsky's reformulation of the 'Ukrainian problem' was his refusal to treat it as an issue of restoring the historical rights granted to Bohdan Khmelnytsky by the Russian tsars and then taken away by the imperial government. Hrushevsky occasionally used that argument, but only in a supporting role. For a historian to marginalize a historical argument was surely no easy matter, especially as his more radical rivals within the Ukrainian ranks, such as the early proponent of Ukrainian sovereignty, Mykola Mikhnovsky, used this argument to legitimize their claim to independence.[153] By moving the historical argument to the periphery of his political discourse, Hrushevsky was in fact parting ways with the age-old tradition of Little Russian autonomism, whose leaders had continuously referred to the return of the rights guaranteed to Ukraine in Khmelnytsky's day as their political goal.

Hrushevsky also removed the 'Ukrainian question' from the framework defined by the concepts of 'all-Russian' culture and nationality. He considered the existence of a distinct Ukrainian nationality with its own history, language, literature, and culture to be an issue resolved once and for all. The official stand of the Russian Academy of Sciences, whose memorandum of 1905 suggested that the all-Russian language was in fact the Great Russian one, while the Ukrainians required education in their own language, significantly reinforced Hrushevsky's argument. The 'Ukrainian question' according to Hrushevsky, was not part of the 'Russian question,' but had much more to do with the 'questions' of the 'non-Russian nationalities' – the Poles, Finns, Georgians, and so on. The Ukrainian question could be solved, in Hrushevsky's opinion, only as part of the solution of Russia's national problem in general, which entailed a reorganization of the Russian Empire along national lines, with national-territorial autonomy for the non-Russian peoples. None of those peoples was to be treated preferentially by the authorities or to be discriminated against on the grounds of its alleged 'immaturity.'

Even though the goals of Ukrainian autonomy and the federal restructuring of Russia were among the traditional slogans of the Ukrainian movement, Hrushevsky's reformulation of these demands within the context of the right to national self-determination and constitutionalism put the Ukrainian movement on an entirely different basis. The change in status of the Ukrainian movement – from one struggling for a more prominent place within the all-Russian ethnic hierarchy to one that rejected that hierarchy altogether and adopted the goal of creating its new national identity outside the all-Russian ethnic construct – was vehemently rejected by the proponents of all-Russian unity. Still, the position taken by the leaders of the Ukrainian movement during the 1905 revolution and the reality of political struggle and dissension in the empire influenced even them. In 1910 Prime Minister Petr Stolypin, an outspoken supporter of Russian nationalist organizations, issued a circular in which he included the Ukrainians among the non-Russian nationalities of the empire. The 'error' was soon corrected by the tsarist authorities, but this had little impact on the way in which the members of the Ukrainian movement now saw themselves and their people.[154]

It made considerable sense for Hrushevsky to present the Ukrainian agenda as part of the solution to Russia's nationality problem in general and to seek support not only from the Russian liberals but also from the non-Russian national movements. The major stumbling block on that road appeared to be the 'Polish question.' An alliance between the Polish national movement, represented by Hrushevsky's adversaries in Galicia – the Polish National Democrats, led by Roman Dmowski – and the Russian liberals, led by Pavel Miliukov's Constitutional Democrats, was in the air from the first days of the revolution.[155] From Hrushevsky's viewpoint, that was a dangerous alliance, as it could lead to the solution of Russo-Polish problems at the expense of Ukraine. Exasperated with Polish rule over the Ukrainian part of Galicia, Hrushevsky feared a similar situation in the Russian Empire if the Vistula Land – the former Congress Kingdom of Poland – were to obtain autonomy. That could legitimize the continuation of Polish rule over the Ukrainian population of the Kholm region, replicating the situation in Austrian Galicia. Another concern of Hrushevsky's was that the achievement of national-territorial autonomy by the Poles within the Russian Empire would curb Polish opposition to the regime and weaken the forces of the non-Russian peoples striving for their national rights. Without the Poles, neither the Ukrainians nor the other non-Russian peoples would be strong enough to achieve national-territorial autonomy on their own. All these considerations influenced Hrushevsky's stand on the issue of national autonomy in the Russian Empire and account for his repeated appeals to all the non-Russian nationalities to maintain a common front against the regime, as well as his demands to the authorities not to discriminate among the nationalities and treat all of them as equally entitled to national-territorial autonomy within the empire.

Apart from the 'Polish question,' another important ethnic and religious issue that attracted Hrushevsky's attention during the 1905–7 revolution was the 'Jewish question.' Hrushevsky, who considered the Jews of Ukraine no less victimized by foreign dominance than the Ukrainians themselves, enthusiastically welcomed the submission to the Duma of a bill to abolish the pale of settlement. In an article titled 'The End of the Ghetto,' Hrushevsky wrote: 'The draft law on civil equality submitted to the Duma should remove from the Ukrainian lands of Russia one of the most shameful relics of the Middle Ages that continues to hang over them, through no fault or volition of their own, that is, the pale of Jewish settlement.'[156] Hrushevsky did not consider either Jews or Ukrainians responsible for their mutual animosity but

blamed the Polish and then the Russian government for creating the
'Jewish question.' He also attacked the foreign rulers of Ukraine for
causing the Jewish pogroms, stating that 'centralist socio-economic and
nationality policy, which condemned the Ukrainian masses of the region to irredeemable ignorance, to cultural and economic poverty, depriving them of all opportunity for self-determination and development,
created the other pole of that terrible question, which does not cease to
stun us with the most terrible conflicts that have often reduced social
thought to a despairing standstill.'[157] Hrushevsky despised the restrictions and persecutions inflicted on the Jewish population by the tsarist
authorities. He saw the Jews as possible allies in the cause of Ukraine's
liberation and hoped for future cooperation between Ukrainians and
Jews. Hrushevsky believed that all 'conscious' members of Ukrainian
society were bound to welcome the abolition of the pale of settlement,
which would turn the artificially divided segments of the Ukrainian
population into compatriots, working together for the benefit of their
homeland.

Hrushevsky's political pamphlets of 1905–7 show him operating
within the context of a number of discourses, notably populist (drawing
up the agenda for the Ukrainian cultural elites) and nationalist (employing the paradigm of the national revival). Within the parameters of
the populist discourse, the people were important to Hrushevsky as the
source of legitimacy for the program of Ukrainian nation-building. It
was the need ascribed to the Ukrainian people for free cultural, national, and economic development that Hrushevsky strove to satisfy
through the proposed autonomization of the Russian Empire. It was
also in the name of the people that he called upon the Ukrainian
intelligentsia to join the Ukrainian movement. At the same time, in
Hrushevsky's national discourse, the 'people' were not to be used as an
instrument to divide Ukrainian society into opposing groups of 'haves'
and 'have-nots' but rather to unite the prospective nation in the struggle
for its rights. Social issues, even such important ones as the agrarian
question, were now viewed by Hrushevsky through the prism of the
national paradigm. He believed, for example, that the distribution of
land to the peasantry would benefit the Ukrainian nation, predominantly made up of peasants, while hurting the Poles in Ukraine – a
nation of landlords.[158] Hrushevsky also skilfully navigated within the
dominant political discourses of the time. He often attacked the Polish
elites within the framework of the 'national justice' discourse they had

constructed, while presenting the Ukrainian agenda to the Russian liberals as part of the program for the 'liberation of Russia.'

During the first decades of the twentieth century, the Ukrainian movement found itself in very different situations in the Russian Empire and the Habsburg Monarchy, with well-developed national institutions in the latter and only the first signs of their emergence in the former. The immediate goals of the movement were also different in the two empires. Hrushevsky's populism, with its strong socialist overtones, which was a stimulus to the democratization of the well-developed Ukrainian movement in Galicia, could have created insuperable divisions in the young Ukrainian political movement of Eastern Ukraine and was therefore modified by Hrushevsky in favour of a more inclusive policy and discourse. The strategies that Hrushevsky employed in his writings published in the Russian Empire differed from the ones that dominated his Galician writings. Instead of challenging and attacking the leaders of the Ukrainian community, as he had done in Galicia, in Dnipro Ukraine Hrushevsky was more concerned with uniting the scattered forces of the delayed Ukrainian revival. These two strategies were related to very different images of the national 'other.' If in the first case the enemy was the Polish elite, and often Polish society at large (to the degree that it supported the policies of the elite), in the second it was the right-wing proponents of all-Russian unity, the Russian bureaucracy, the imperial regime, and so on, but never Russian society as a whole.

The differentiation between regime and society that was so striking in Hrushevsky's writings for the Russian public and so seldom apparent in his works written for Galician consumption is to be explained first and foremost by the political conditions of the time. The Ukrainian movement in Russian-ruled Ukraine was much more dependent on the support and cooperation of Russian political parties than it was in Austria, where it could not rely on the good will of the Polish parties and could easily survive without their support. There was also another factor, perhaps of even greater importance: in Ukrainian consciousness at the turn of the twentieth century, the image of Russia and the Russians had not acquired the characteristics of an ethnic 'other' to the degree that Poland and the Poles had done. In Eastern Ukraine Hrushevsky had to wage a long and difficult campaign to convince not only the authorities but the Ukrainian intelligentsia itself that Ukrainians indeed constituted a separate nation and that the intelligentsia's first duty was to serve that nation, not some general 'all-Russian' cause.

Between Two Revolutions

From 1905 on Hrushevsky's political and cultural work in Dnipro Ukraine took more and more of his time and energy, but that did not lead him to abandon his involvement in Galician political and cultural life. Hrushevsky became more active in Galician politics after 1907, with the passing of a new electoral law in the Habsburg Monarchy that introduced universal male suffrage, thereby changing the political scene in Galicia.

Hrushevsky's interest in party politics in Galicia reflected his general position on the issue of Ukrainian nation-building. He favoured all political alliances that could promote the independence of the Ukrainian political process, rejecting and condemning those that might compromise its independence and hinder the national self-determination of the Ukrainians of eastern Galicia. For example, Hrushevsky welcomed the alliance of the Ukrainian National Democrats and the Jewish Zionists in the elections of 1907 but vehemently opposed the creation of a Ruthenian parliamentary club uniting Ukrainian and Russophile deputies. The declaration of two of the five Russophile deputies that they considered themselves Russians gave Hrushevsky additional ammunition in his struggle against Russophilism and the Russian nationalization project in Galicia. So did the political alliance between the Polish National Democrats and the Russophiles. Hrushevsky condemned the Polish National Democrats' revival of pan-Slavic ideology, which was intended to improve relations between the Polish elite and the Russian imperial government on the basis of common anti-German sentiment. As these forces were opposed to the Ukrainian cause, Hrushevsky appealed for an end to the pan-Slavic tradition of the Ukrainian movement and stressed the importance of Germanic influences on Ukrainian culture and history. He also encouraged his readers to seek allies among the Belarusians and Lithuanians.[159]

Hrushevsky avoided membership in political parties but clearly favoured the National Democrats, whose meetings he again began to attend. Despite his interest in their activities, Hrushevsky had never been reluctant to criticize the policies of the party leadership. In 1911 he collected some of his earlier articles on political topics and published them as a brochure titled *Nasha polityka* (Our Politics). In these articles, Hrushevsky sought to mobilize Ukrainian society to struggle for its economic, cultural, and national rights. Hrushevsky, who had consistently followed Antonovych in stressing the importance of scholarly and cultural work for the Ukrainian cause, was now placing special emphasis on the need for political action. The main targets of his critique were the National Democratic leaders and representatives in the Vienna parliament and the Galician diet. Hrushevsky criticized their activities from the viewpoint of the 'people,' claiming that the people's representatives had an obligation to recognize their needs and lead them toward national and social liberation. The main deficiency of the National Democratic Party, in Hrushevsky's opinion, was its lack of principle, which meant readiness to compromise with the Polish authorities and settle for small concessions instead of fighting for the long-term goals of the Ukrainian movement. For most of his years in Lviv, Hrushevsky remained a staunch opponent of compromise with the Polish authorities and their rule in Galicia. He strongly believed that Ukrainian national and social liberation depended on a resolute struggle for the attainment of the rights offered to the Ukrainians by the Habsburg political system but illegally denied them by the Polish elite.

The publication of *Our Politics* caused an uproar in Ukrainian society and a great deal of trouble for its author. It spurred the leadership of the National Democratic Party, as well as Hrushevsky's old and new enemies in the Ukrainian scholarly community, to stage a revolt against him in the Shevchenko Scientific Society, forcing him to resign from its leadership. A new statute was adopted that gave voting rights to non-scholarly members and took them away from corresponding members in Eastern Ukraine – a constituency traditionally loyal to Hrushevsky. In the opinion of one of Hrushevsky's most talented students, Ivan Krypiakevych, who stood by his teacher during the conflict, the situation was not eased by defects in Hrushevsky's character – his authoritarianism and intolerance of opposition.[160] Eventually, he had to resign.[161] Although this was a major blow to Ukrainian scholarship in Galicia, even these drastic changes to the society's statute did not affect its scholarly character, which Hrushevsky had firmly established. Throughout the First World War and the interwar period, the society continued to function as an unofficial Ukrainian academy of sciences in Polish-dominated Lviv, where Ukrainian scholars had no other forum to present, disseminate, and popularize their scholarly findings.

Among the reasons that may account for Hrushevsky's unwillingness to make any compromises in Galicia, which eventually cost him the leadership of the Shevchenko Scientific Society, was his ever deeper involvement in the politics of Dnipro Ukraine. One of the consequences of the 1905 revolution that was not reversed after its end was the lifting of prohibitions on Ukrainian-language publications in the Russian Empire, which allowed Hrushevsky to move his scholarly and cultural activities to Dnipro Ukraine. The publication of his *History of Ukraine-Rus'*, which was transferred to Kyiv beginning with volume six, was only one of the signs of this major shift. While remaining active in Galician politics, Hrushevsky became heavily involved in Kyiv politics as well. He worked diligently there, trying to persuade the Russian government to establish chairs of Ukrainian studies in the universities of Ukraine. He also played an important role in the publication of the Kyiv newspaper *Rada* (Council), which he agreed to edit, inviting Symon Petliura, the future leader of the Ukrainian government of 1918–21, to serve as managing editor of the publication.[162]

From 1906 on Hrushevsky had definite plans to move to Kyiv himself; his family (wife and daughter) lived there most of the time. In 1908, during his brief visits to Kyiv, he was often busy supervising the building of the family home, which was finished by the autumn of 1909.[163] In 1908 Hrushevsky applied for the position in Russian history at Kyiv University. His competitor was a professor of the Nizhyn Historical and Philological Institute, Volodymyr Savva, a specialist in early modern Russian history.[164] Among those supporting Hrushevsky's application for the position were the philologist Volodymyr Peretts and the historian Mytrofan Dovnar-Zapolsky, both of whom held chairs at Kyiv University. The legal historian Mykola Vasylenko published an article in the local newspaper *Kievskii golos* (Kyivan Voice)[165] supporting Hrushevsky's application, but the university chose Savva for the position.

Hrushevsky's plans to base his activities in Kyiv encountered resistance not only from proponents of 'all-Russian' unity but also from certain leaders of the Ukrainian movement there. The expansion of Hrushevsky's activities in Dnipro Ukraine met with suspicion and resistance on the part of other leaders of Ukrainian circles in Kyiv. Among those who voiced their concerns were the writer Borys Hrinchenko and the literary scholar Serhii Iefremov, who apparently feared that the leadership of the Ukrainian movement in the Russian Empire might pass from them to the strong-willed Hrushevsky.[166] Probably the greatest surprise for Hrushevsky was that his return to Dnipro Ukraine met with resistance from his former literary mentor, the renowned Ukrainian writer Ivan Nechui-Levytsky. Unlike Hrinchenko, Nechui-Levytsky was concerned less with the possibility of Hrushevsky's taking control of the Ukrainian movement in Kyiv than with his alleged attempts to 'Galicianize' the Ukrainian language and Ukrainian cultural life in

Dnipro Ukraine. In 1907 Nechui-Levytsky wrote a brochure against Hrushevsky and his alleged linguistic 'Galicianization' that served as a basis for subsequent attacks on Hrushevsky from all sides of the political spectrum.[167]

Despite all the difficulties that he encountered in Kyiv, Hrushevsky went on with his projects. In December 1906 the editorial office of *Literaturno-naukovyi visnyk* was moved from Lviv to Kyiv with the help of one of the leaders of the Ukrainian movement in Eastern Ukraine, Ievhen Chykalenko, who was also the movement's devoted financial sponsor. The transfer of the editorial office of *Literaturno-naukovyi visnyk* ultimately played an important role in Hrushevsky's efforts to bridge the gap between Ukrainian cultural life in the Russian and Austro-Hungarian empires. Hrushevsky's other major preoccupation in Kyiv was the Ukrainian Scientific Society, which he headed. That new institution was supposed to play in the Russian Empire the same role that the Shevchenko Scientific Society had played in Galicia. Hrushevsky was elected president of the society's executive board and thus gained control of the activities of the two major Ukrainian scholarly organizations. In Lviv Hrushevsky continued to edit the Shevchenko Society's principal journal, the *Memoirs of the Shevchenko Scientific Society*; in Kyiv he assumed the editorship of the major periodical of the Ukrainian Scientific Society, *Zapysky Ukraïns'koho Naukovoho Tovarystva* (*ZUNT*, Memoirs of the Ukrainian Scientific Society). Hrushevsky's organizational energy and talent were enormous. The fact that he headed the Ukrainian scholarly societies in Lviv and Kyiv and edited their periodicals, as well as *Literaturno-naukovyi visnyk* and a number of other Ukrainian journals, led not only to numerous complaints on the part of Hrushevsky's rivals in Ukrainian cultural circles but also to some confusion among opponents of the movement. The Kyiv-based Russian nationalist Anatolii Savenko erroneously assumed that *Literaturno-naukovyi visnyk* served as the periodical of the Ukrainian Scientific Society in Kyiv and that the Kyiv Society was named after Shevchenko and had been transferred by Hrushevsky from Lviv to Kyiv.[168]

With the end of the revolution and the reimposition of restrictions on all forms of political activity in the Russian Empire, Hrushevsky was forced to change the focus of his activities from political propaganda to cultural and scholarly work. But even then he never completely abandoned political activity, insofar as it could be conducted in the post-1907 Russian Empire. In the era of government repression of political opposition in general and the Ukrainian movement in particular that followed the Revolution of 1905, Hrushevsky remained faithful to the program that he had formulated for the Ukrainian movement during the revolutionary period. In Dnipro Ukraine he cooperated with the Society of Ukrainian Progressives, whose political goal was the achievement of Ukrainian autonomy. Hrushevsky was a staunch supporter of that postulate of the Ukrainian movement and led the Ukrainian progressives in their attempt to convince the Russian Constitutional Democrats, especially their leader, Pavel Miliukov, to support Ukrainian demands for autonomy in 1914. The Constitutional Democrats, for their part, were prepared to push for the introduction of the Ukrainian language into the school system but considered federalization dangerous to the Russian state. Hrushevsky was eager to cooperate with the Russian liberals and peasant representatives in the Fourth Russian Duma on other issues close to his heart, including the establishment of chairs of Ukrainian studies in Ukrainian universities and the introduction of Ukrainian as the language of instruction in elementary schools, but refused to give up his demand for Ukrainian autonomy.[169]

The 'Polish question,' especially the issue of the Kholm region, remained at the centre of Hrushevsky's attention between the two revolutions, and in 1913 he did not hesitate to render public support to a government plan, promoted by the Russian nationalists, to establish a separate Kholm gubernia, thereby removing it from the prospective Polish autonomous region. He explained his position (and that of Ukrainian activists in general) on that issue in a letter read to the deputies of the Third Duma by a member of the Constitutional Democratic Party.[170] The Jewish question also continued to concern Hrushevsky. In 1913 he commented with disgust on the trial of Mendel Beilis in Kyiv, condemning manifestations of anti-Semitism in Ukraine and holding the imperial government responsible for them because it was preventing the development of culture and education among the Ukrainian population. He knew that the Beilis case would tarnish the image of his homeland but was proud that the jury, which consisted of simple Ukrainian peasants, pronounced Beilis innocent.[171]

One of the main goals of Hrushevsky's activity in Dnipro Ukraine between the 1905 revolution and the outbreak of the First World War was to preserve and secure the concessions that the Ukrainian movement had obtained from the government during the revolution. He was eager to use those concessions in order to move the Ukrainian idea from the narrow circle of the urban intelligentsia to the countryside and develop national consciousness among the vast masses of the Ukrainian peasantry. It was in this period that Hrushevsky became engaged in the publication of Ukrainian-language newspapers for the peasantry, *Selo* (Village, 1909–11) and *Zasiv* (Sowing, 1911–12). He was also active in publishing and reissuing his own popular writings on Ukrainian history. In 1907 he published a popular history of Ukraine, *Pro stari chasy na Ukraïni* (About Old Times in Ukraine), and in 1909, a popular biography of Bohdan Khmelnytsky, *Pro bat'ka kozats'koho Bohdana Khmel'nyts'koho* (On the Cossack Father Bohdan Khmelnytsky), both intended for a peasant readership. Hrushevsky's Ukrainian-language *Illustrated History of Ukraine,* which replaced his Russian-language *Survey History of the Ukrainian People* and was addressed primarily to the Ukrainian intelligentsia, was issued four times before 1917.[172]

Hrushevsky was actively inculcating national consciousness into the Ukrainian masses, and it would appear that his efforts were yielding the expected results. Readers in the Russian Empire were now gaining access to his publications and writing to him in Lviv to express their opinions, request advice, and the like. A court clerk from Berdychiv, Petro Saviovsky, wrote to Hrushevsky in his capacity as editor of *Literaturno-naukovyi visnyk,* complaining about the distrust of Ukrainians in the Russian Empire and asking whether there were any translations of Gogol into Ukrainian. 'It is most unfortunate,' wrote Saviovsky, echoing some of Hrushevsky's own concerns of his gymnasium years, 'that Gogol was a great literary capacity but wrote such a marvellous poem as *Taras Bulba* in a language other than Ukrainian.'[173] Hrushevsky was receiving correspondence not only from the Eastern Ukrainian intelligentsia but also from workers and peasants.[174] A peasant from the homestead of Poluianiv, F. Shelest, wrote to Hrushevsky in Lviv that he and three other peasants had subscribed to *Selo* and were glad to have read its articles about Taras Shevchenko. Shelest welcomed the 'progressive' orientation of the newspaper and the Ukrainian language in which it was written: 'Your bulletin is to our liking not only because it is freedom-loving and progressive, but also because it is written in our native Ukrainian language.'[175]

The outbreak of the First World War caught Hrushevsky vacationing at his summer house in Kryvorivnia in the Carpathian Mountains. Because of wartime conditions he was unable to return to Lviv, but the Austrian military authorities would not allow him to stay in Kryvorivnia. Faced with the advancing Russian troops, Hrushevsky embarked on a long and challenging odyssey. He left first for Budapest and Vienna and then for Italy, finally arriving in Kyiv in November 1914. There

Hrushevsky was arrested by the Russian authorities, who exiled him to Simbirsk.[176] On the eve of the First World War, Hrushevsky was perceived both in the Russian Empire and in the Habsburg Monarchy as the leader of the Ukrainian movement. His treatment by the authorities of those warring states during his three-year odyssey may therefore be viewed as a good indication of the way in which the Russians and Austrians approached the Ukrainian problem.

It is not surprising that the attitude of the Austrian government to the Ukrainians and their leader at the beginning of the First World War continued to depend mostly on the position of the Polish ruling elites in Galicia. The Polish National Democrats exploited the outbreak of hostilities to direct the state apparatus against their enemies in the Ukrainian camp, whom they accused of Russophilism – a treasonable offence, given the state of the war between Austria and the Russian Empire. Throughout his years at Lviv University Hrushevsky had remained a Russian subject, which made him an easy target for accusations of Russophile sympathies. He was also well known for his lack of deference to the Dual Monarchy. In the first weeks of the war an issue of *Literaturno-naukovyi visnyk* containing an article of Hrushevsky's with an unflattering characterization of the recently assassinated Archduke Franz Ferdinand had been confiscated by the Austrian police. Recognizing the danger to Hrushevsky, leaders of the Union for the Liberation of Ukraine, an organization of young Ukrainian activists established in Vienna in close cooperation with the Austrian authorities, helped the historian leave his summer house in the Carpathians first for Budapest and then for Vienna.[177] Despite the intervention of the well-connected members of the Union, the Austrian police kept Hrushevsky under surveillance while he was in Vienna and issued an arrest warrant charging him with Russophilism after he left the city.[178]

Even less tolerant of Hrushevsky as leader of the Ukrainian movement were the Russian authorities. In late August 1914, long before Hrushevsky crossed the borders of the Russian Empire, a warrant was issued for his arrest. It was executed on 28 November, a few days after Hrushevsky's arrival in Kyiv. He was imprisoned and, following numerous interrogations and a search of his houses in Kyiv and Lviv (now occupied by Russian troops), sent to Simbirsk.[179] Only a media campaign in his defence, featuring such prominent Russian academic and political figures as Aleksei Shakhmatov and Petr Struve, saved him from being sent to an even more remote Siberian location. Some of Hrushevsky's colleagues at the Russian Academy of Sciences, such as

Shakhmatov, stood by him and worked hard to make possible his transfer from Simbirsk to Kazan, and finally to Moscow. Others, like Sergei Platonov, took a more ambivalent approach, advising the Academy of Sciences to exercise caution in advocating Hrushevsky's transfer from Simbirsk. Hrushevsky's situation improved only as the revolution drew near and he was allowed to move first to Kazan and then to Moscow, where he was able to return to work on his multivolume *History of Ukraine-Rus'*.[180]

Why did the Russian authorities consider it important to arrest and exile Hrushevsky despite the protests of some of the most prominent Russian intellectuals? An answer to this question may be found in a book published by S.N. Shchegolev, an imperial Russian censor and 'Little Russian' by background, prior to the First World War. Entitled *The Ukrainian National Movement as a Contemporary Stage of South Russian Separatism*, the book not only presented a detailed history of the Ukrainian movement in the Russian Empire but also made a strong case against Hrushevsky and other leaders of the Ukrainian movement in Galicia.[181] Many of the ideas advocated by Schegolev made their way into a report filed in January 1915 by the head of the Russian police directorate in occupied Galicia, Colonel Mezentsov. Hrushevsky was presented there as the leading Russian 'Mazepist' in Galicia. In the official Russian lexicon, the term 'Mazepist' was a synonym for traitor and separatist: given wartime conditions, Hrushevsky and other leaders of the Ukrainian movement were considered potential traitors.[182] In his report Mezentsov portrayed the whole Ukrainian movement in Galicia as Mazepist, with its leaders aspiring to carve a Ukrainian kingdom under Austrian protection out of the Ukrainian ethnic territories of the Russian Empire. Mezentsov claimed that Hrushevsky, as leader of the Mazepist movement, had been summoned to Kyiv by his accomplices in the Union for the Liberation of Ukraine to conduct Mazepist propaganda among the population and Russian troops stationed in Dnipro Ukraine.[183]

The aggressive Russian stand against the 'Mazepists' resulted in a thoroughgoing campaign against the Ukrainian movement in the Russian Empire. The authorities shut down almost all the Ukrainian institutions and their media. In that context Hrushevsky's arrest was little more than a logical outcome of government policy toward the Ukrainian movement. With the outbreak of war, the defenders of all-Russian unity and old enemies of Hrushevsky, such as his former dean, Florinsky, were given unlimited opportunities to go after their main ideological foe. Russian newspapers were eager to give space to authors who accused Hrushevsky of every conceivable transgression against the Russian Empire. If in Austria Hrushevsky was accused of being pro-Russian, in Russia he was accused of being pro-Austrian. This was the leitmotif of an article published in the newspaper *Kievlianin* (The Kyivan) by Hrushevsky's former professor, Iuliian Kulakovsky.[184] The article provoked Hrushevsky's response in *Rech'* (Speech) that in turn triggered the investigation into Hrushevsky's anti-Austrian activities in Lviv. Hrushevsky ridiculed Kulakovsky's assertion that he was responsible for the formation of Sich Riflemen detachments in Galicia merely because his former students had joined them. He could no more be responsible for the actions of his students, stated Hrushevsky, than Professor Kulakovsky could be responsible for the actions of Hrushevsky himself.[185] Kulakovsky's unbridled accusations reflected the new atmosphere that took hold of Russian society during the war, making it difficult for Hrushevsky's friends to defend him against government sanctions.

In his letters to the exiled Hrushevsky, Shakhmatov tried to cheer up his colleague, expressing relief that Hrushevsky had been sent only to Simbirsk and not to Tomsk gubernia, as the military had advocated. He attempted to persuade Hrushevsky to suspend his political activities, saying that it was necessary to call a halt to the internal struggle in order to ensure the success of the external one – a clear reference to the course of the First World War.[186] Hrushevsky, for his part, adopted a stand best reflected in the words of another Ukrainian exile, Taras Shevchenko: 'I am tormented, I suffer, but I do not repent.' His spirits were clearly low, but he refused to give up political activity even in exile. In the summer of 1915 he wrote from Simbirsk to his supporters that the war was dragging on and it was impossible to postpone all activity until its end. Hrushevsky advised them to take advantage of the change of ministers in the imperial cabinet to lobby for lifting the ban on Ukrainian activities imposed at the beginning of the war. He suggested a program for the Ukrainian movement geared toward the responsibilities of individual ministers. From the minister of internal affairs, the Ukrainians were to demand an end to the prohibition on Ukrainian publications, liberalization of censorship, and improvement of conditions for Galician internees. The minister of education was to be lobbied for recognition of Ukrainian-language education as a private matter, as well as for the introduction of Ukrainian subjects in the curricula of teachers' colleges and secondary schools. From the Procurator of the Orthodox Synod,

activists were to demand the introduction of Ukrainian-language ser-
mons in churches and an end to the Russification of the clergy.[187]
Hrushevsky remained involved in Ukrainian political life after his transfer to Kazan and then to Moscow.[188] Even in exile, he flatly refused to give
up his role as leader of the Ukrainian movement in the Russian Empire.

   Hrushevsky's opponents in the Habsburg Monarchy and the Russian
Empire accused him of acting on behalf of each other's governments,
although it is patently obvious that both accusations could not be true.
But was at least one of the warring sides right? There is no evidence to
suggest that Hrushevsky's activities aimed directly at the disintegration
of either Austria-Hungary or the Russian Empire. Hrushevsky appears
to have been quite candid when he stated in his response to Kulakovsky
that his goal was the regeneration of Russia on the basis of the free
development of its nationalities. Hrushevsky certainly was not an Austrian patriot, and the pro-Austrian stand taken by the leaders of the
Ukrainian community in Galicia at the beginning of the war, as well as
the activities of members of the Union for the Liberation of Ukraine,
held little appeal for him. On the contrary, a meeting of the Society of
Ukrainian Progressives held in Kyiv at Hrushevsky's initiative before
his arrest in November 1914 urged the Union to refrain from speaking
on behalf of all Ukraine.[189]

   As Hrushevsky's own recollections suggest, from the very beginning
of the war he wanted to go to Kyiv.[190] The desire to secure his property
in the Russian Empire because of new regulations issued by the Russian
government upon the outbreak of the war – the reason for leaving Lviv
University cited by Hrushevsky's colleague Kyrylo Studynsky[191] – cannot, of course, be taken at face value. The version of events presented by
Hrushevsky himself seems much more credible. In his autobiography
Hrushevsky claims that he returned to Kyiv at the urging of his friends.[192]
Depending on the course of the war, new opportunities could arise for
the development of the Ukrainian movement, including the achievement of Hrushevsky's main political goal at the time – Ukrainian autonomy.[193] Hrushevsky wanted to be at the centre of the coming events,
and that centre was clearly Kyiv. By leaving Austria-Hungary, did
Hrushevsky miss his opportunity to become the 'Ukrainian Masaryk,'
as some of his later critics have suggested?[194] Apparently not. By 1914
Hrushevsky had little if any influence on Ukrainian politics in Galicia,
and his only future as a political and cultural leader lay in the Russian
Empire. By going there in November 1914, he clearly lost in the short
run. Given the dismissal of the Austrian court case against him and the

inconclusive results of the Lviv University investigation, it is unlikely that Hrushevsky would have encountered in Lviv the fate that awaited him in Russia. There can be little doubt, however, that by going to Kyiv Hrushevsky won in the long run. The fall of the Russian autocracy found him in the role of national martyr and recognized leader of the all-Ukrainian movement, not somewhere abroad, but within striking distance of Kyiv. It was in Kyiv that the future of Ukraine and the Ukrainian cause was decided, with Hrushevsky's active participation, in the course of 1917 – one of the longest years in Ukrainian history.

The Birth of Ukraine

In March 1917 Hrushevsky finally returned to Kyiv from his long exile to be elected chairman of the Central Rada – the institution that he turned into Ukraine's first parliament in the course of the year. He led the Rada and all Ukraine to an assertion of Ukrainian statehood and independence. It was a stormy process punctuated by four proclamations ('universals') of the Rada. The first proclamation, issued in June 1917, declared Ukraine's intention to begin the process of acquiring national autonomy. The second, published in July, informed the population that the Central Rada had decided to postpone its declaration of autonomy in exchange for recognition by the Provisional Government in St Petersburg as the regional government of Ukraine. The third proclamation, issued in November in the wake of the Bolshevik coup in St Petersburg, declared the formation of an autonomous state, the Ukrainian People's Republic. By the end of the year, that republic had acquired de facto independence, which was officially proclaimed in the Fourth Universal of January 1918. Within a short period the Central Rada dramatically transformed the Ukrainian political scene, and consequently that of the former Russian Empire as a whole.[195] Hrushevsky stated in his speech at a December 1917 session of the Rada, 'Beginning with the modest organization of cultural and professional Ukrainian organizations that gathered in one of the tiny premises of this building [the Pedagogical Museum in downtown Kyiv], we have turned ourselves into an organ of supreme authority recognized by all of Ukraine ... In the political sphere we have done a great deal. Circumstances were such that we have accomplished even more than we set out to do. We have stood and continue to stand for the principle of federation ... But circumstances are such that, as I said at the outset, Ukraine has in fact become a free and independent republic.'[196]

The Central Rada grew into the government of an autonomous and then an independent Ukraine as a result of intense competition with numerous rivals, including the Kyiv city council, the Kyiv Soviet, and the Provisional Government's military authorities. This happened in part because the Rada's leaders set themselves the clearly defined goal of securing Ukrainian statehood and evinced a strong desire to take on the task of governance. It is difficult, if not impossible, to overestimate Hrushevsky's role in keeping the Central Rada focused on the achievement of Ukrainian statehood, though his own path to the adoption of that goal was not a straightforward one. In 1914, at a meeting of the Society of Ukrainian Progressives with Pavel Miliukov, Hrushevsky emerged as the staunchest proponent of autonomy, which he placed on the agenda despite the displeasure of the leader of the Russian Constitutional Democrats. After the outbreak of the First World War, Hrushevsky made haste to Kyiv in hopes of reconstructing the Russian Empire on a federalist basis, but the government crackdown on the Ukrainian movement and the years he spent in exile apparently made him more cautious about promoting Ukrainian autonomy.

During the first days of the revolution, he was more than reluctant to raise the issue of autonomy, to say nothing of independence.[197] Like many Ukrainian activists of the pre–First World War era, Hrushevsky was unsure of what strategy to choose during the February days of 1917. Since the veterans of the Ukrainian movement initially viewed the revolution as a short-term disturbance, they did not want to compromise their political reputation in the eyes of the regime or jeopardize the future prospects of the Ukrainian cause. It was younger activists, not burdened with the previous experience of negotiating with the old regime, with no political capital to lose, who raised the Ukrainian banner during the first weeks of the revolution. Hrushevsky proceeded with extreme caution. He rejected a proposal to join the Moscow Duma as a representative of Ukrainian organizations, stating that after two years of exile he did not want to get involved in anything that might prevent his return to Ukraine. He also scorned the 'broad revolutionary perspectives' elaborated by younger members of the Ukrainian community in Moscow, pointing instead to the task of organizing schools and publishing books and newspapers, which he considered the agenda of the Ukrainian movement for the next decade. In a letter to Aleksandr Kerensky, then minister of justice in the Provisional Government and a politician whom he knew personally, Hrushevsky presented a list of Ukrainian demands limited to the return of the Galicians exiled to the interior of the Russian Empire during the war, the establishment of Ukrainian primary schools, the introduction of Ukrainian subjects in secondary schools, and the use of the Ukrainian language in the governmental institutions of Ukraine.[198]

There can be little doubt that Hrushevsky's return to Kyiv from Moscow, on the night of 12 March 1917, dramatically changed his attitude. In Kyiv, no longer concerned about an official prohibition on returning to Ukraine, Hrushevsky became much more adventurous than most of the 'old' Ukrainians and joined the younger generation in its push to deepen the revolutionary transformations. The very first public meeting that Hrushevsky attended after his return to Kyiv – the congress of cooperatives of Kyiv gubernia, held on 14 March – adopted a resolution calling for Ukrainian autonomy. On 19 March Hrushevsky addressed the first mass Ukrainian demonstration with a speech in which he called upon those present: 'Let us all swear at this great moment as one man to take up the great cause unanimously, with one accord, and not to rest or cease our labour until we build that free Ukraine.' He also invoked the authority of Taras Shevchenko, Mykola Kostomarov, Panteleimon Kulish, and the members of the SS. Cyril and Methodius Brotherhood, who had resolved, according to Hrushevsky, to liberate Ukraine from the Muscovite yoke and transform it into a free republic in a federation of Slavic nations. Hrushevsky declared that with the fall of tsardom, Ukraine was 'joining a free union of peoples of the Russian Federative Republic as a free member.'[199]

'A free Ukraine in a free Russia' and 'an autonomous Ukraine in a federal Russia' were the slogans of the day, and Hrushevsky invested a great deal of energy in convincing Ukrainian activists to abandon their old, mostly cultural, goals in order to support the demand for national and territorial autonomy. In his article 'The Great Moment,' written after the demonstration of 19 March 1917, Hrushevsky addressed the Ukrainian old guard with the following words: 'There can be no greater error at present than to pull out the old Ukrainian petitions and present them to the government afresh as our demands of the moment.'[200] Hrushevsky presented the new demands ten days later in the article 'There Is No Turning Back,' in which he reacted to a speech made by the head of the Provisional Government, Prince Georgii Lvov, who suggested that the granting of cultural-personal autonomy would solve the national question in Russia. Hrushevsky replied that the Ukrainian movement demanded broad territorial autonomy and the reconstruction of the former empire on a federalist platform.[201]

In the same article Hrushevsky raised the possibility of Ukrainian independence. At that point, he was using it as a threat against the Provisional Government in St Petersburg if it should refuse to grant Ukraine national-territorial autonomy. Hrushevsky wrote: 'The flag of independent Ukraine remains folded. But will it not be unfurled at the moment that the all-Russian centralists should wish to tear from our hands the banner of broad Ukrainian autonomy in a federative and democratic Russian republic?'[202] On the issue of the future status of Ukraine, Hrushevsky often found himself under attack by the radical supporters of Mykola Mikhnovsky, who advocated the immediate proclamation of independence and were especially popular among the military. Judging by Hrushevsky's memoirs, which were written in Soviet Ukraine in the mid-1920s, he was particularly hostile to the activities of Mikhnovsky's group, whose ideology he characterized as nationalist, militarist, and even fascist. Throughout most of 1917 Hrushevsky regarded demands for independence as counterproductive, probably because he did not believe that the Ukrainian movement was strong enough to acquire and sustain the independence of a state that had yet to be established. In his memoirs Hrushevsky made a very telling comment with regard to his own attitude toward autonomy and independence and that of his colleagues. 'If [we] were independentists awaiting the collapse of the old Russian Empire and the failure of its revolution, we could take malicious pleasure in such evidence of its poverty,' wrote Hrushevsky with regard to the Provisional Government's refusal to recognize Ukraine's right to autonomy in May and June 1917. 'But we had no hope of surviving on our own; we were more fearful that the gains of the revolution might perish beneath its [ruins].'[203]

As soon as the demands for autonomy and statehood became the principal slogans of the Ukrainian movement, the problem became one of attracting not only Ukrainians but also the other nationalities of Ukraine to that slogan. Hrushevsky did his best to persuade the minorities that they had no reason to fear Ukrainian autonomy. In March 1917 he addressed the issue of minority attitudes to Ukrainian autonomy in a number of articles that appeared in the newspaper *Nova Rada* (New Council), the mouthpiece of the Ukrainian movement at that time. In the first of them, titled 'To the Peoples of Ukraine,' Hrushevsky stated that Ukrainians were not struggling for their freedom in order to take away that of other peoples. On behalf of the Ukrainian movement, he declared that in an autonomous Ukraine, the minorities would receive proportional representation in government institutions; that in areas of compact settlement of a given nationality its language would be used in the school system and civil administration; that cultural institutions would be subsidized by the central government, and so on.

Short of territorial autonomy, Hrushevsky was offering the national minorities all the rights for which Ukrainians had struggled before the revolution. He also pledged to fight all manifestations of nationalism and chauvinism within the Ukrainian movement but asked in return that the minorities support the Ukrainian bid for autonomy: 'Those who stand resolutely, openly, and courageously by the Ukrainians at this decisive moment will establish a strong spiritual and cordial link between the Ukrainian people and themselves. Those who stand apart or remain hostile cannot, of course, expect particularly warm feelings from the Ukrainian side.'[204] The message was quite clear: stand with us and receive all the rights we can offer, or you are on your own. The date of Hrushevsky's article was highly significant: it appeared in the Easter issue of *Nova Rada* (New Council), a day traditionally known for pogroms against Jews. In his article Hrushevsky made special reference to the Jews, whom he called 'the most numerous of the non-Ukrainian nationalities of Ukraine, which by that token has the right to our particular attention.'[205] The Ukrainian leaders were especially eager to attract the Jews to their side, and their worst fear was that the Black Hundreds might provoke another anti-Jewish pogrom that would jeopardize the prospective alliance between Ukrainian and Jewish activists. Apart from Hrushevsky's article, the Easter issue of *Nova Rada* contained a special appeal to readers not to trust people with 'an angel's voice and a devil's soul,'[206] hinting at organizers of anti-Jewish pogroms.

In the course of 1917 the Jewish question became prominent in Ukrainian public discourse as never before. Hrushevsky's traditional sympathy for the plight of the Jewish population reinforced his hope, which materialized during the revolutionary days of 1917, that the Jewish community would endorse the Ukrainian cause. Its support – more specifically, that of the leadership of the Bund (General Jewish Workers' League) – indeed turned out to be crucial in Ukraine's bid for autonomy. In June 1917, after the publication of the Rada's first proclamation, which unilaterally proclaimed Ukrainian autonomy, members of the Provisional Government came to Kyiv to negotiate a compromise. When they insisted on the inclusion of representatives of the national minorities in the Central Rada, the position of the Jewish left was vital to working out an agreement. Taking into account the security concerns of the Jewish community, as well as Jewish social demands, the leaders of the Bund managed to find common ground with Ukrainian leftist parties in the Central Rada. 'Jewish s[ocial] democrats as allies of Ukrainian demands,' wrote Hrushevsky with regard to the Bund's resolution in support of Ukrainian autonomy, 'meant a great deal to the St Petersburg ministers, even though their motives were not so much of an all-state character, but rather inspired by self-defence, against pogroms ... '[207] There is little doubt that the policy of cooperation between the Ukrainian movement and the Jewish socialists adopted by the Central Rada under Hrushevsky's leadership was largely responsible for the fact that the Jewish population of Ukraine suffered no pogroms during the first months of the revolution.[208]

The increasing prominence of the Jewish question in Ukrainian politics could not, of course, reduce the traditional importance of the Russian and Polish questions to the Ukrainian cause. In his article 'To the Peoples of Ukraine,' Hrushevsky offered rights of cultural autonomy to members of both communities in Ukraine. Another article of his on the issue of national minorities titled 'Is Ukraine Only for Ukrainians?' dealt specifically with the Russian question. Hrushevsky condemned the efforts of some Ukrainians to force Russians out of Ukraine in order to take their posts for themselves. He was convinced that such efforts originated, more often than not, with those who had had no attachment to the Ukrainian movement before the revolution. Hrushevsky called on the progressive Russian elite to stay in Ukraine, maintaining that the country needed qualified cadres and that the leaders of the Ukrainian movement were prepared 'to leave every post in the hands of people sympathetic to us, in accord with us, who support the interests of this land and its people, recognizing the rights and needs of the Ukrainian majority while protecting the rights of the minorities.'[209] Loyalty to the territory and its people, not to Ukrainian nationality or ancestry, was proclaimed by Hrushevsky as the new government's principal requirement of the residents of Ukraine. With the declaration of that principle, Hrushevsky was laying the cornerstone of Ukraine's proposed relations with its national minorities.

When Hrushevsky almost single-handedly formulated the policy of the Ukrainian movement during the first weeks of the revolution, he was fully cognizant of the responsibility that he was taking on. With regard to his early pronouncements on the rights of the national minorities, he later wrote that he had attempted to calm those far removed from the Ukrainian movement 'with assurances that we would not allow the Ukrainian national movement to become nationalist and would ensure the free development of the non-Ukrainian population ... Who "we" were remained an enigma, and, in expressing my thoughts on the most immediate tasks and responsibilities of the Ukrainian citizenry so self-confidently, at my own risk and responsibility, I issued bonds that were guaranteed – guaranteed, it is true, completely and without reserve – by the new composition of the Central Rada.'[210]

While Hrushevsky strongly believed in the possibility of finding common ground between the Ukrainian and Jewish national movements and in the peaceful resolution of Russo-Ukrainian tensions, he was much more sceptical when it came to Polish-Ukrainian cooperation. Hrushevsky was adamant that the status of the Polish minority in Ukraine be resolved as part of the implementation of the policy of personal-cultural autonomy granted to all the peoples of Ukraine, not on the basis of any special arrangements. He remained extremely suspicious of Polish intentions vis-à-vis Ukraine, given the record of Polish rule over Ukrainians. Recalling the first Ukrainian demonstration in Kyiv in March 1917, he clearly welcomed the participation of the Ukrainian Poles but could not forget the history of Polish oppression in Ukraine. He wrote in his memoirs: 'Somewhere there was also a velvet banner with the Archangel Michael embroidered on it, made with love and enthusiasm out of some family raiment by "Ukrainian Catholic women," F. Volska and company, like a friendly hand extending from beneath the age-old incursions of Polish nobiliary faithlessness.'[211] In 1917, as during the Revolution of 1905, Hrushevsky continued to regard the Poles as the nationality that would suffer most from land redistribution. He feared that Polish national-cultural autonomy would create a basis for the consolidation of reactionary forces opposed not only to Ukrainian statehood but also to the social achievements of the revolution.[212] Hrushevsky's pessimism about the future of Ukrainian-Polish relations deepened with the renewed confrontation over the Kholm region, which was awarded to Ukraine at the insistence of Hrushevsky and the Central Rada delegation by the Treaty of Brest-Litovsk between Ukraine, Germany, and Austria-Hungary (1918).[213]

Adjusting the national and social demands of the Ukrainian parties and balancing them with the interests of the non-Ukrainian groups in the Central Rada was Hrushevsky's major challenge in his attempt to lead Ukraine toward national-territorial autonomy. In a speech to the Central Rada in mid-December 1917, Hrushevsky specifically mentioned complaints of non-Ukrainian members of the Rada that the debates were focusing mainly on issues of nation and state rather than social problems. In the spirit of the prevailing populist discourse, Hrushevsky responded by indicating the position of the representatives of the Ukrainian toiling masses, whom he thanked for their ability to balance social and national tasks, 'not allowing themselves to be distracted for an instant by any social intolerance or maximalism inappropriate to the moment or to be attracted to national chauvinism.'[214]

Hrushevsky's longevity as head of the Central Rada was based on his ability to stay (at least formally) above the squabbles between the Ukrainian parties and negotiate compromises between them. Another reason for his political success was that as the masses became radicalized, he was able to evolve with them. With the passage of time, Hrushevsky moved further and further left, despite objections from his old friends in the Society of Ukrainian Progressives. They resented Hrushevsky's closeness to the young radicals of the Ukrainian Party of Socialist Revolutionaries, who were prepared to go much farther along the road of social reform than their conservative predecessors, specifically on the question of land redistribution. Hrushevsky, for his part, no longer trusted the former progressives, who in his opinion had written him off during his exile of 1914–17. As Hrushevsky saw it, they did not want to compromise themselves by contacts with him during the war and summoned him back to Kyiv to chair the Central Rada only to help them deal with the rebellious youngsters.[215] When Hrushevsky's long-time supporter Ievhen Chykalenko, who (apart from the transfer of Hrushevsky's *Literaturno-naukovyi visnyk* to Kyiv) had financed numerous Ukrainian initiatives from the proceeds of his family estate before the revolution, told him that the Socialist Revolutionary approach to agrarian reform 'would make everyone who owned more land than the working norm into an enemy of the Ukrainian state, and one could not build the state on the basis of the proletarian class alone,' Hrushevsky replied that he would follow the majority in the Rada.[216]

If Hrushevsky had rejected the socialist program of land redistribution in his youth as contrary to the Gospel, he now embraced it as a reflection of the desires of the peasantry and the demands of the revolution. For good reason, given the demands of the moment, Hrushevsky was reviving his populist beliefs of the 1890s and dressing them up in new and fashionable socialist clothing (even the former progressives now called themselves socialists, renaming themselves the Ukrainian Party of Socialist Federalists in 1917). Although Hrushevsky long refused to join the Socialist Revolutionaries – the largest and most influential party in the Central Rada – he closely cooperated with its leadership, especially with those members of the party who were in charge of the Peasant Union, which constituted the backbone of the Rada's support in the countryside. He often advised the activists of the Ukrainian movement to listen to the people, respond to their demands, and not allow events to outpace them. The land issue, along with that of ending the war, was the crucial one in the Revolution of 1917, and Hrushevsky was determined not to lose the support of the peasantry at this new stage of development of the Ukrainian movement.[217]

During 1917 Hrushevsky produced a record number of articles and popular brochures on the history and current tasks of the Ukrainian movement. He also wrote new historical works and reissued old ones that advanced the Ukrainian cause. Many of Hrushevsky's works were printed in tens of thousands of copies and helped turn unprecedented numbers of 'Little Russians' into Ukrainians, as well as explain to their neighbours what the Ukrainian movement was about. First of all, Hrushevsky continued to educate the popular masses in the realm of Ukrainian history. In 1917 his *Illustrated History of Ukraine* saw its fourth edition.[218] His brief work intended for a peasant audience, *About Old Times in Ukraine*, first published in 1907, was reprinted three times in 1917.[219] Responding to the growing interest in the history of Russian-Ukrainian relations, especially the Pereiaslav Agreement of 1654 between Ukraine and Muscovy, Hrushevsky published a brochure on the subject that was issued twice.[220] He also reprinted some of his old articles on historical topics that he considered relevant to the new era,[221] as well a number of brochures that explained the origins of the Ukrainian movement and its goals. These included the essays *Who the Ukrainians Are and What They Want* and *Where the Ukrainian Movement Came From and Where It Is Going*. Both essays were issued twice in 1917.[222] A brochure explaining the main task of the Ukrainian movement – the achievement of autonomy (*What Kind of Autonomy and Federation We Want*) was issued four times.[223] There were two issues of Hrushevsky's brochure *On the Ukrainian Language and the Ukrainian School*, which was published for the first time in 1913.[224] Hrushevsky's newspaper articles from the first months of the revolution were reprinted in 1917 under the title *Free Ukraine*. That collection was also issued three times in the course of a year.[225]

How did Hrushevsky find time to publish, let alone write, all this material? Some of his critics implied that he was devoting too much attention to his own publishing projects. One of them, Volodymyr Vynnychenko – a prominent writer and prime minister of the government formed by the Central Rada – wrote in that regard: 'I have given all my attention throughout this year to the creation of a Ukrainian state, but I just do not have Hrushevsky's ability to use everything for my own good and proofread brochures while at the same time announcing the law of the Ukrainian republic.'[226] The secret of Hrushevsky's productivity did not, of course, lie in neglect of his duties at the Central Rada. Hrushevsky's energy and capacity for work had always amazed his contemporaries, but during the revolutionary months of 1917 he apparently outdid himself. In his memoirs Hrushevsky recalled those days as one of the happiest times of his life. 'Yes, the work was hard,' he wrote. 'But I considered myself happy, after several years of exile, in my pleasant office, amid the old Ukrainian art collected in it ... when I raised my eyes from the paper to find our Ukrainian sun looking in and a peaceful scene opening out on the Kyiv hills and in the Dnipro valley. I would rise early and work until noon, striving to receive no one and interrupting my work only for the telephone. From noon, of course, the whole time was taken up by all kinds of meetings. A great expanse of work unfolded, but there were few people [to do it].'[227]

If 1917 was one of the happiest years of Hrushevsky's life, 1918 turned to be one of the most difficult and tragic. It began with the Bolshevik advance on Kyiv and continued with the Central Rada's abandonment of its capital and retreat to the west. It witnessed the return of Hrushevsky and the Ukrainian government to Kyiv in March 1918, only to be deposed by a German military administration that installed the government of Hetman Pavlo Skoropadsky in April. Hrushevsky, who was elected president of the Central Rada, was forced into hiding. During the stormy winter and spring of 1918, a number of questions attracted Hrushevsky's particular attention. The most important of them was the issue of Ukrainian independence and relations with Russia. It was Hrushevsky who declared the de facto independence of Ukraine during the session of the Central Rada on 17 (30) December 1917. He was one of the authors of the Fourth Universal of the Central Rada of 12 (25) January 1918, which proclaimed Ukrainian independence de jure. It was also Hrushevsky who insisted on the proclamation of Ukrainian independence by the Central Rada, and not by the Ukrainian Constitutional Assembly in January 1918. What happened to Hrushevsky in the last months of 1917 to change his attitude toward independence in such a dramatic way? He himself indicated the new political circumstances. Both in the text of the Fourth Universal and in Hrushevsky's articles explaining it, independence was presented as an act forced upon the Central Rada by unfavourable circumstances. What were those circumstances? Judging by the text of the proclamation, the first one was the much-discussed issue of peace. The Bolshevik regime was dragging its feet on the issue of ending the war. To achieve the long-awaited peace, Ukraine had to declare its independence and become a subject of international law. The second reason was the state of war imposed on Ukraine by the Bolshevik government.[228]

In his speeches and published articles of the time, Hrushevsky often declared that the Ukrainian movement remained faithful to the idea of federalism and would return to it once unfavourable circumstances were overcome. He did not promise, however, that the return would be swift. In his article 'The Great Duty,' Hrushevsky wrote: 'The weighty word has been spoken! Ukraine has become a free and independent separate state. How long it will remain in this condition, that is, how soon an actual opportunity will present itself to establish a federal association with other republics, no one at this moment can say with certainty.'[229] Writing about a future federation, Hrushevsky stated that the time to seek partners would come when life had returned to normal and the social and national goals of the revolution had been secured. 'That will be the time to look about at the neighbours who organize themselves around Ukraine and consider with whom our peasant-worker-laborer People's Republic can walk a common path.'[230] Hrushevsky was in fact returning to the position that he had first expressed more than thirty years earlier in his gymnasium diary. Ukraine, he had written at that time, did not have to rush into a new federation. It should first organize its own affairs and only then look for partners. An important element of Hrushevsky's old/new attitude to federalism was that he did not view Russia as an obligatory partner in the new federal arrangement. He wrote that the Bolshevik leaders of Russia (Vladimir Lenin and Leon Trotsky) had discredited the federal principle by replacing it with the old Russian centralism and that it would be difficult for anyone to call himself a federalist in the near future.[231]

The Bolshevik offensive that triggered the proclamation of Ukrainian independence was viewed very differently in St Petersburg and Kyiv. If for the Bolsheviks it was an attempt to impose their proletarian rule on the territory of the former Russian Empire, crushing the resistance of the local 'bourgeoisie,' for Hrushevsky and most deputies to the Central Rada it manifested the revival of Russian imperialism. The Bolsheviks were discredited in the Fourth Universal and in Hrushevsky's numerous writings on a number of different levels. Apart from being exposed as pseudo-federalists, they were characterized as invaders who had come to Ukraine to take grain from the peasants. They were also denounced as traitors to democracy and revolution in general. 'Our struggle with Bolshevism,' wrote Hrushevsky, 'is simultaneously a struggle with counterrevolution, which concealed itself behind it [Bolshevism] and awaited the moment when, following in its tracks or advancing side by side with it, the revolution could be crushed.'[232] Hrushevsky believed that by invading Ukraine the Bolsheviks were realizing the dreams of the Russian bourgeoisie, which hoped that before destroying itself, Bolshevism would return Ukraine to Russian control.[233] For the first time since the onset of the revolution, Hrushevsky was prepared to separate the Ukrainian Revolution from the Russian one in his own mind and in the minds of his readers and followers. He regretted that the Ukrainian Revolution had long been obliged to develop within the bounds of the Russian Revolution, which 'dragged us through blood, through ruin, and through fire.'[234] Now he felt no obligation toward the Russian Revolution, as in his mind it had joined forces with the Russian counterrevolution in its offensive against Ukraine's national existence.[235]

The declaration of Ukrainian independence allowed the leaders of the Central Rada to treat the Bolshevik offensive in terms of international conflict. That interpretation gave the Central Rada additional means to discredit the Bolshevik intervention. Hrushevsky, for his part, claimed that after the declaration of Ukrainian independence no one could treat the Bolshevik conflict with the Central Rada as a mere skirmish between two political groups and declare neutrality. 'There is now a struggle between two states, Ukraine and Great Russia,' he wrote, 'in which all citizens of the Ukrainian Republic, all its residents, regardless of their views and convictions, are obliged to support the Ukrainian government.'[236] Hrushevsky also regarded the Bolshevik offensive as the aggression of one nation against another, denouncing it as such within the framework of nation-based discourse. He claimed that although the Bolshevik leaders avoided explaining their actions in national terms, the national character of the conflict was apparent on the ground. 'The motif of national struggle is perfectly apparent, in its most obvious and unadorned aspect, at least in the views and expressions of the rank-and-file masses,' wrote Hrushevsky in February 1918 after the exodus of the Central Rada and its government from Kyiv. 'For it, the purpose of this campaign is to "beat the topknots," who, after 250 years of enslavement, have dared to raise their heads and throw off the Muscovite yoke.'[237]

The moment of truth in Hrushevsky's thinking on Russo-Ukrainian relations came with the Bolshevik assault on Kyiv, which left his house in ruins; his library, manuscript collection, and Ukrainian artefacts burned; and his mother dead as a result of shock suffered during the Bolsheviks' deliberate bombardment of Hrushevsky's house. Hrushevsky was convinced that his personal ordeal and disenchantment with his old beliefs reflected the tragedy and reorientation of Ukraine as a whole.[238] In an article titled 'The End of the Muscovite Orientation,' he wrote: 'The first thing that I consider outworn and obsolete, something "that has burned in my office," is our orientation on Muscovy, on Russia, long and insistently imposed on us by force, and finally, as often happens, in fact accepted by a considerable portion of the Ukrainian citizenry.'[239] In attacking the traditional orientation of Ukrainian society on Russia, Hrushevsky built on arguments developed in his articles written at the time of the 1905 revolution. He condemned the sacrifices made by Ukrainians for the sake of the all-Russian cause, which, in his opinion, originated in the self-seeking motives of the Ukrainian elites, reinforced by the terror inflicted on Ukrainian society by the Russian authorities. Hrushevsky attacked the Muscovite orientation of Ukrainian society in the strongest terms, stating: 'I shall speak harsh but true words: this spiritual slavery; the truckling of a slave who has been beaten in the face so long that they have not only destroyed all vestiges of human dignity within him but made him a supporter of subjection and slavery, its apologist and panegyrist.'[240]

Hrushevsky took no prisoners in his campaign against Ukrainian servility, attacking even Nikolai Gogol, a sacred cow of Little Russian identity, whom he described as a product of the 'moral and political demoralization of Ukrainian society.' Russians and Ukrainians, he claimed, were 'akin by blood but opposed in spirit' and divided by historical, cultural, and psychological boundaries. Hrushevsky hoped that the Bolshevik assault would help Ukrainians recognize those distinctions. In his political writings of 1918, Hrushevsky in fact declared the Russians as much 'others' in relation to Ukrainians as were the Poles. If in his articles and brochures of the spring and summer of 1917 Hrushevsky blamed the Muscovite authorities and the oppressive tsarist regime for Ukraine's troubles, while stressing the revolutionary solidarity of all participants in the Russian Revolution and insisting on Ukraine's joining a federation of peoples led by Russia, he now defined his enemies not just as the Bolsheviks but as the whole Russian nation.

Hrushevsky was convinced that the flames that consumed his house had not only destroyed the old orientations of Ukrainian politics and culture but forged new ones as well. Rejecting the Ukrainian orientation on Russia in his writings of 1918, Hrushevsky indicated another, pro-Western, tradition in Ukrainian history. This was a politically expedient argument, readily understandable to his readers, given the de facto German occupation of Ukraine at the time. By highlighting the pro-Western tradition in the Ukrainian past, Hrushevsky was seeking to depict Ukraine as a European country and reinforce the historical and cultural boundaries between Ukraine and Russia. He viewed the Russians as a Westernized but still Eastern people, while representing the Ukrainians as a Western people that had been gradually Easternized in the course of its history. The gap between Russia and the West was fully demonstrated, in Hrushevsky's opinion, by the nineteenth-century Slavophiles, who, among other things, idealized the Russian soul and were convinced of Russia's moral superiority over decadent Western Europe. Commenting on the Slavophile idealization of elements of the Russian national character, Hrushevsky noted: 'Only it would be better not to endow these characteristics with fine names and idealize them, for they rarely attain the level of "God-bearing": lack of human dignity in oneself and disrespect for the dignity of others; lack of taste for a good, comfortable, well-ordered life for oneself and disrespect for the interests and needs of others in such a life and the achievements of others in that sphere; lack of will to establish an organized social and political life; a disposition to anarchism and even social and cultural destructiveness; a careless attitude toward cultural and social values and the vaunting of one's own lack of culture and organization with regard to such values; constant vacillation between social and moral maximalism and utter nihilism, which often descends to a complete loss of moral criteria – there is little to admire in all this, and in the face of all these flaws of social character, various good – even very good – traits of individual character recede into the background.'[241]

Hrushevsky's critical assessment of the Russian national character was strongly influenced by an intellectual tradition going back to Mykola Kostomarov and Volodymyr Antonovych. The positioning of Ukraine closer to the West than to the East in the East-West paradigm, a tradition in Ukrainian political thought that can be traced back at least to the writings of Mykhailo Drahomanov, helped Hrushevsky portray Ukrain-

ians not only as different from Russians but also as culturally superior
to them. He regarded Ukrainians as a people endowed with respect for
personal dignity and a love of established forms of life, good manners,
order, and beauty, which gave them a greater affinity for the West than
the Russians possessed.[242] In formulating the tasks of Ukrainian cultural development, Hrushevsky warned Ukrainian society against repeating the mistakes of the Russians, who had indeed enriched world
culture with the works of such titans as Fedor Dostoevsky, Ivan Turgenev,
Leo Tolstoy, and Peter Tchaikovsky, but failed to educate their masses.
The westward reorientation of Ukrainian political and cultural life advocated by Hrushevsky was not meant to lead from one extreme to
another. In his view, Ukrainians were to take the best from every culture
with which they came into contact, and Ukraine's future geopolitical
and cultural role was to be played out in the Black Sea region.[243] The
Ukrainians were faced with the task of transferring the 'culture of
beauty,' which Hrushevsky took to mean certain elements of artistic
culture, into the 'culture of life,' by which he meant the education of the
popular masses and the modernization of Ukrainian society.[244]

After the dissolution of the Central Rada by the German occupation
forces, Hrushevsky was forced to go underground. He returned to
active political life only with the collapse of the Skoropadsky regime in
late 1918. He welcomed the return to power of his former allies in the
Central Rada – representatives of Ukrainian populist and social-demo-
cratic parties – but times had changed. His former disciples became
political leaders in their own right. In 1919 Hrushevsky emerged as one
of the leaders of the centrist faction of the Ukrainian Party of Socialist
Revolutionaries, but the centre turned into the left when the original left
wing of the party split away, adopted the name 'Borotbists,' and eventually joined the Communist Party (Bolshevik) of Ukraine. With the
desertion of the left, Hrushevsky lost his struggle with the right-wingers
and had little choice but to leave the Ukrainian political scene. In late
March 1919 he left for Western Europe to attend the Congress of the
Socialist International as a delegate of the Ukrainian Socialist Revolutionaries. By that time his political career in Ukraine was all but over.
The common national front had dissolved, differences between parties
were increasing, and Ukrainian politics no longer called for a leader
who could negotiate among competing factions and serve as a symbol
of national unity. Conflict and confrontation were defining the new face
of the revolution. Bolshevik intervention and the resulting civil war
propelled to power military governments and leaders willing to take on

dictatorial powers, and Hrushevsky was no longer willing or able to adapt to the demands of the moment. The Ukrainian Revolution had long passed its parliamentary stage. He had to go.[245]

For most of Hrushevsky's life, up to the Revolution of 1917, the main source of his own and his family's income were the proceeds from numerous reprintings of his father's textbook of Church Slavonic. Hrushevsky called the book 'our source of nourishment over many years' and was involved in preparing a new edition of it as late as the end of 1916.[246] The revolution effectively removed Church Slavonic from the school curriculum in the former Russian Empire, putting an end to an era in which it symbolized the existence of a common all-Russian language and culture, and a book produced by a talented graduate of the Kyiv Theological Academy could be as much at home in Russia as in Ukraine. Mykhailo Hrushevsky turned out to be one of the most unrelenting critics and destroyers of that world – an activity that he helped finance with the proceeds from his father's textbook. Born and raised in the family of a government employee who made his living out of the Russification of the imperial borderlands, Hrushevsky rejected the all-Russian imperial identity and raised his father's subnational Little Russian consciousness to the level of a national one. The young Hrushevsky was motivated to embark on his Ukrainian journey by a deeply felt duty to his people. A romantic and ambitious youth, he wanted his life to matter and be remembered by history: as a mortal struggling to overcome his mortality, he was eager to devote himself to a cause larger than life. Faced with the dilemma of choosing between service to his people and service to God according to the all-Russian Orthodox tradition that he then embraced, Hrushevsky chose service to the people. It was a very personal choice, not imposed on him by family or circumstance, but made of his own free will. Still, Hrushevsky's experience helps reconstruct the larger picture of the Ukrainian 'awakening' of the nineteenth century, for he was not the only one who made such a choice.

   Hundreds, if not thousands, of members of the nineteenth-century Little Russian intelligentsia embraced the new Ukrainian identity, building, reconstructing, and reformulating it in the process. Why did they do so? Why did they decide to kill the goose that laid the golden egg, refusing to immerse themselves in the Russian cultural sea and share the spoils of empire with the Great Russians? There is little doubt that the rise of nationalism in late nineteenth-century Eastern Europe in

general and the Russian Empire in particular should be held responsible for the cultural rebellion of Hrushevsky and his generation. The
shell of all-Russian culture was dissolving before their eyes, with Great
Russian identity emerging as its most powerful successor, and the new
generations of Little Russians had to make a choice: either to follow the
mirage of all-Russian culture and turn themselves into Great Russians
or to overturn the old hierarchy of identities, ending the subordination
of the Little Russian identity to the all-Russian one, declare its independence, and draw a clear dividing line between that new national identity and its new 'other' – the Great Russians.

Like many but not most of his compatriots, Hrushevsky made the
latter choice. He was prepared and encouraged to make it by the example of two previous generations of Ukrainophiles – the romantics of
the 1840s and the populists of the 1860s. It was under the influence of
their writings, with Taras Shevchenko and Mykola Kostomarov standing for the first group and Volodymyr Antonovych and Mykhailo
Drahomanov representing the second, that Hrushevsky's assimilation
to Ukrainian identity took place. Hrushevsky entered Ukrainian political and cultural life during the 1890s in an atmosphere defined by new
views, ideas, and trends of social thought. Having been converted to
positivism during his years at Kyiv University, as a young professor he
witnessed the rise of idealism and neoromanticism. Having grown up
under the influence of moderate populism, he had to adjust to the
demands of social radicalism. Having been taught by his advisers and
by prevailing circumstances to confine his Ukrainian activism to the
sphere of cultural work, he confronted the rapid politicization of cultural life and the creation of national parties where earlier there had
been only small apolitical groups of Ukrainophiles terrified of official
persecution. These dramatic changes, which influenced the ways in
which national movements defined themselves and their leaders and
formulated their goals and strategies, were not limited to the Ukrainian
movement: they were also representative of Russian developments
and, to an even greater degree, of the Polish national revival of the
period.

The Poles, the traditional 'other' of Ukrainian cultural identity, were
fighting a campaign against the dominant Russian culture very similar
to the one being waged by the Ukrainians. In the course of the nineteenth century, the Ukrainian movement, like its Polish counterpart,
experienced romanticism, disappointment with romantic ideals, and a
retreat to positivism and cultural work, followed by an era of political

activism. While following a course parallel to that of the Polish national movement, the Ukrainian movement fought it every step of the way, first under the banner and cover of the all-Russian idea, as in the 1860s, and later under its own banners and slogans. Thus the Poles served as an example and an inspiration to the younger Ukrainian national activists. They were also adversaries of the Ukrainians in the Russian Empire and in the Habsburg Monarchy, where they exercised political, economic, and cultural dominance over the Ukrainian peasant majority and the weak Ukrainophile intelligentsia. Hrushevsky strongly believed that the Polish nation-building strategy resembled the Great Russian one, for it also depended on restricting Ukrainian culture to a prenational level of development and strove to exploit the Ukrainian ethnos as raw material for the construction of Polish national culture. In the two-way contest of Polish and Ukrainian projects for the nationalization of the 'Ruthenian' peasantry, the Ukrainian project was by far the weaker. Consequently, Hrushevsky did not hesitate to accept Russian help in fighting the Polish project, as in the case of the administrative separation of the Kholm region from the Vistula Land, or to play the Polish card – the strength of the Polish movement in the Russian Empire – to force the Russian authorities to make concessions to the national minorities, including the Ukrainians.

If fighting the Polish project was hard enough for the Ukrainian activists, confronting the Great Russian one was even more difficult. The 'othering' of the Poles did not constitute a major problem for the proponents of the Ukrainian movement, given the existence of a clear religious, linguistic, and cultural boundary between Poles and Ukrainians, which was deeply rooted in Ukrainian (Little Russian under the Romanovs; Ruthenian under the Habsburgs) historical tradition. There was little sense of such a boundary when it came to Russo-Ukrainian relations and historical narratives. The proponents of the two types of all-Russian identity – Little Russian in the East and Russophile in the West – worked hard to make the existing boundary between the two nationalities all but irrelevant for the purposes of the Great Russian nation-building project, which was still developing under the all-Russian banner. Hrushevsky entered the struggle under the all-Ukrainian banner. His goal was to reinforce the western boundary between Poles and Ukrainians, to establish a new border in the east, building on the foundations of the Little Russian identity, and to bridge the political, cultural, and historical gap that divided the two parts of the prospective Ukrainian nation: Habsburg Ruthenia and Romanov Little Russia. This was Hrushevsky's task both as a political and cultural activist and as a historian, one who saw in the past not only the answers to the concerns of the present but also the contours of the future.

The Revolution of 1905 in the Russian Empire, the lifting of the ban on Ukrainian-language publications, and the expansion of opportunities for political and cultural work made possible the progress of the Ukrainian movement in the Russian Empire from the stage of scholarly interest to that of mass propaganda (to cite Miroslav Hroch's formula). Hrushevsky had been working toward that goal since the late nineteenth century and was better prepared than anyone else to transfer the expertise accumulated by the 'Ukrainian Piedmont' (Galicia) to the fertile soil of Russian Ukraine. Populist and positivist by upbringing, he embarked on the project of developing a broad national identity by creating the image of an ancient and democratic Ukraine and disseminating it in hundreds of articles and historical works. This was a Ukraine oppressed by its social and national enemies but now risen from its knees and advancing to meet its destiny – the conquest of national freedom – under the leadership of the rebellious intellectuals who were her heroes.

The sowing of the seeds of national consciousness bore fruit with the outbreak of the 1917 revolution. The revolution liberated Hrushevsky and the whole Ukrainian movement from the internal exile of the first years of the war, propelling them to heights previously undreamt of. The idea of national-territorial autonomy – an old Ukrainophile slogan relentlessly propagated by Hrushevsky throughout the prerevolutionary years – was finally accepted by the masses, the new masters of the situation. Now that slogan was embraced by the Little Russian peasantry and the peasant-based military, who were being transformed into Ukrainians in the struggle for its implementation. Hrushevsky guided the process. Consolidating the strongest bloc of political parties in the Central Rada on the basis of his national platform, he accommodated the social demands of the masses while leading them toward Ukrainian autonomy and, eventually, independence. He published tens of thousands of copies of his popular brochures on Ukrainian history, culture, and politics, awakening the masses and turning fellow travellers of Ukrainian autonomy into enthusiastic supporters of the cause.

From his articles, public pronouncements, and memoirs, Hrushevsky emerges as a federalist by conviction who regarded Ukrainian independence as a temporary phenomenon dictated by prevailing circumstances; a transitional stage preparatory to Ukraine's entry into a federation with other democratic republics on the basis of complete equality. Probably the best way to define Hrushevsky's stand with regard to Ukrainian autonomy and independence would be to state that, without prejudice to his federalist convictions, Hrushevsky supported Ukrainian independence whenever he thought that the Ukrainian state could sustain it and the popular masses could benefit from it. If in the summer of 1917 he fiercely opposed the independentists in the Ukrainian ranks, considering their actions mere manifestations of nationalist ideology, he clearly changed his mind in late 1917 and early 1918, when Bolshevik Russia launched a military offensive against the Central Rada, and the only way to save Ukrainian autonomy and the gains of the revolution was to declare independence. With the proclamation of independence in January 1918, Hrushevsky developed a whole program to nationalize Ukrainian identity, for which he intended to marshal the resources of the newly established state. Despite Hrushevsky's later retreat from the principle of Ukrainian independence and his return to the idea of a federation with other nations, including Russia, his articles of 1918 completed a symbolically important transition in the development of the Ukrainian idea. With unprecedented authority and conviction, the leader of the Ukrainian nation had explicitly declared a complete break of the Ukrainian movement with Russia. For the Ukrainian national project, there was no going back.

Chapter 2

The Delimitation of the Past

In 1853, once the shock of the Revolution of 1848 and the 'spring of the nations' had receded in the Habsburg Monarchy, the Austrian historian and adviser to the imperial minister of education Josef Alexander Helfert undertook to formulate an official view of the meaning, role, and tasks of national history (*Nationalgeschichte*). In a pamphlet titled *On National History and Its Current State of Cultivation in Austria*, he wrote: 'It is true that mankind is divided into a great number of tribes that differ as to language and colour. But according to our ideas, national history is not the history of any such group defined by its racial origin. We think that national history is the history of the population of a territory that is politically united, subordinate to the same authority and living under the protection of the same law. For us, Austrian national history is the history of the Austrian state and people as a whole.'[1]

For the vast majority of nineteenth-century Russian historians, their national history was also defined not as the annals of a particular ethno-national group but of the state and those who had settled its territory. Although the latter was understood as the Russian people,[2] the notion of Russianness was quite broad and included the three 'Russian' tribes – the Great Russians, Little Russians (Ukrainians), and Belarusians. Ukraine was a special case in the changing imperial narrative of Russian history: depending on the dominance of the statist or nationalist element in that narrative at any given time, certain segments of Ukrainian history were either included in it or excluded from it. The Russian dynastic historical narrative, which was constructed in the course of the fifteenth and sixteenth centuries, had always been based on the foundations of Kyivan history. The incorporation of Kyiv and Left-Bank Ukraine into the Muscovite state in the second half of the seventeenth century further emphasized the role of Kyivan Rus' in the grand narrative. At that time, the old historical scheme of the sixteenth-century Muscovite scribes who linked Kyivan and Muscovite history by means of dynastic bonds was reinforced by the notion of ethnic affinity between Russia and Ukraine.[3] That view was popularized by the author of the Kyivan *Synopsis* (1674) – by far the most popular historical work to appear in the pre-nineteenth-century Russian Empire. The *Synopsis* identified Kyiv as the first capital of the Russian state and treated the history of Russia and Ukraine as that of one 'Slavic-Russian' people.[4]

A new stage in the development of the all-Russian historical narrative began with the publication of Nikolai Karamzin's *History of the Russian State* (1816–24). Karamzin, a founding father of modern Russian literature, focused his attention almost exclusively on the history of the Russian monarchy and the Russian state. He treated Kyivan Rus' as part of the Russian past, giving only occasional attention to subsequent periods of Ukrainian history as part of the annals of a more broadly conceived Russian 'fatherland.' There is little doubt that Karamzin did not discriminate consciously against Ukrainian history, but his focus on the development of the Russian state and the fact that his *magnum opus* did not go beyond the early seventeenth century left most of the Ukrainian past outside his grand narrative, relegating it to the history of the Polish and Lithuanian states – a development that was to have a profound impact on later Russian and Ukrainian historiography.[5]

The partial 'correction' of Karamzin's scheme on the imperial level and the reintegration of parts of Belarusian ('west Russian') and Ukrainian ('south Russian') history into the Russian imperial narrative was undertaken in the 1830s by Nikolai Ustrialov as a reaction to the Polish uprising of 1830–1 and the imperial effort to claim the territories formerly controlled by the Polish-Lithuanian Commonwealth for the 'Russian nationality.' Ustrialov's 'correction' of Karamzin's paradigm resulted in the further incorporation of the Russian (under the circumstances, all-Russian) national discourse into the imperial historical narrative, which had been founded on Russian monarchical mythology, and introduced elements of the post-Kyivan Ukrainian past into Russian history – a significant development based on the treatment of Ukrainians as part of one Russian people, the masters of the Russian Empire. Ustrialov's paradigm should be considered one of the factors that slowed the division of Russian and Ukrainian historiography into separate fields of scholarship. Ukraine and its history now came to be regarded as an integral part not only of the Russian imperial narrative but also of the emerging Russian national one. True, apart from the history of Kyivan Rus', it was assigned roles that were far from central to either of those narratives.[6]

By the turn of the twentieth century, Russian imperial historiography had managed to produce a historical narrative that combined elements of Russian statist and national discourses.[7] Throughout the nineteenth century it developed along two principal lines. One, reflected in the most popular textbooks – those of Ustrialov and, later, of Ilovaisky – responded to the practical needs of the empire and the increasing importance of the concept of official nationality by presenting significant parts of Ukrainian history in the context of the all-Russian historical narrative. The other tendency was represented by the authors of academic histories of Russia, including Karamzin and Vasilii Kliuchevsky, who focused predominantly on Great Russian history (with the usual exception of Kyivan Rus'). Either because of their statist approach or their genuine interest in Great Russian history, these writers inadvertently excluded the history of the other 'Russias' from the imperial narrative. Some Russian intellectuals even undertook a conscious attempt to expel the Ukrainians and their history from the old all-Russian historical narrative, a process best illustrated by Mikhail Pogodin's theory of the Great Russian origins and ethnicity of Kyivan Rus'.[8]

Russian and Ukrainian historians of the second half of the nineteenth century often found common ground in combating the Normanist theory or refuting Polish claims to cultural superiority and a *mission civilisatrice* in Eastern Europe but generally pursued these agendas on behalf of distinct historical paradigms. The works of Mykola Kostomarov and Hrushevsky's professor, Volodymyr Antonovych, may serve as examples of such cooperation between the two historiographies. Still, the continuing replacement of the all-Russian narrative with the Great Russian one in the works of Vasilii Kliuchevsky deepened resentment in Ukrainian ranks and increased pressure on Ukrainian historians of both the Ukrainian and the Little Russian persuasions[9] to renegotiate the status of the history that they were writing vis-à-vis the changing imperial narrative. These tensions became particularly apparent in the last decade of the nineteenth century and the first decade of the twentieth, when Mykhailo Hrushevsky took the helm of Ukrainian historiography.

As noted above, Hrushevsky's work on Ukrainian national history involved two interdependent processes, dismantling or 'deconstruction' of the imperial all-Russian historical narrative and the construction of the Ukrainian national one. This chapter will deal mainly with the first process but will also touch on elements of the second as it follows Hrushevsky's efforts to separate the historical narratives of Russia and Ukraine. The chapter begins with Hrushevsky's undermining of the imperial narrative by exposing the artificiality of its historical scheme and its inadequacy to the demands of modern scholarship. It continues with a discussion of Hrushevsky's attempts to claim for the Ukrainian narrative the most ancient period in the history of the Eastern Slavs and to exclude the Great Russians from historical developments on the territory of Ukraine. The cases of the Antes and the Normans serve as examples of Hrushevsky's treatment of the early ethno-political history of the region and elucidate his search for the origins of the Ukrainian people. The chapter concludes with a discussion of Hrushevsky's contribution to the best-known aspect of the Russo-Ukrainian historical debate – the contest for Kyivan Rus'. The Ukrainian claim to the Kyivan heritage, which until then had been the cornerstone of the Russian historical identity (in its dynastic, statist, and national incarnations), was the single most important step in the dismantling of the Russian historical narrative and the creation of a Ukrainian one, and as such receives special attention in this chapter.

Challenging the Imperial Narrative

In 1904 Mykhailo Hrushevsky published his by far most famous article, 'The Traditional Scheme of "Russian" History and the Problem of a Rational Organization of the History of the Eastern Slavs.' Conceived as a contribution to the proceedings of the Slavic Congress of 1903 in St Petersburg, it was published there in one of the collections of the Russian Academy of Sciences.[10] As one of Hrushevsky's biographers has noted, 'this brief essay was to revolutionize thought about Ukrainian history.'[11] If that was indeed the case, what was so revolutionary about that particular article?

The most obvious characteristic that distinguished the article from all other writings on Ukrainian history issued in the Russian Empire at the time was the simple fact that it was written and published in Ukrainian. As discussed above, since 1876 there had been a severe prohibition on the publication of virtually all categories of Ukrainian literature in the empire. It was the inclusion in the published proceedings of contributions in languages other than Russian by foreign participants in the Slavic Congress that facilitated the appearance of Hrushevsky's article in the otherwise prohibited language. Its novelty, however, went far beyond the language of publication. Hrushevsky used the issue of the 'rational' organization of Slavic history raised by the congress organizing committee to attack the traditional paradigm of 'Russian history.' His major charge against it was lack of rationality, a fatal flaw in the positivist world of Russian scholarship at the turn of the century. Indeed, Hrushevsky set out to deconstruct the historical grand narrative of the Russian Empire. He had actually embarked on that project long before, but the article of 1903 was the clearest, most eloquent, and most provocative presentation of his argument.

Hrushevsky characterized the traditional scheme as follows: 'The generally accepted presentation of Russian history is well known. It begins with the prehistory of Eastern Europe, usually with its colonization by non-Slavs, then the settlement of the Slavs and the formation of the Kyivan state. Its history is brought up to the second half of the twelfth century, and then it shifts to the Grand Principality of Vladimir; from here, in the fourteenth century, to the Principality of Moscow; then it follows the history of the Muscovite state and then of the empire.'[12] Hrushevsky asserted that this scheme amounted to little more than a continuation of the genealogies of the medieval rulers of Muscovy. Particularly questionable, in his opinion, was the link established by the old scheme between the history of the Kyivan state on the one hand and that of the Principality of Vladimir-Suzdal and the Tsardom of Muscovy on the other. Hrushevsky postulated that the Kyivan state was the creation of one nationality (Ukrainian-Ruthenian), while the principalities of Vladimir-Suzdal and Moscow, with their distinct law and culture, were products of the historical development of another (Great Russian) nationality (*narodnost'*).

Hrushevsky further argued that with the rise of scholarly interest in national histories, the traditional scheme of Russian history had been transformed into the history of the Great Russians. That process was abetted, in Hrushevsky's opinion, by the special importance ascribed to the development of the Muscovite state in the traditional scheme of Russian history, given that for centuries neither the Ukrainians nor the Belarusians had had states of their own. 'The unique and exclusive significance of the history of the Great Russian state in the current scheme of "Russian" history,' wrote Hrushevsky, 'is actually due to the replacement of the concept of the history of the "Russian people" (in the meaning of the Rus', East Slavic nationalities) by the concept of the history of the Great Russian people.'[13] Exposing the traditional imperial paradigm that had deprived the Ukrainians and Belarusians of a history of their own, Hrushevsky suggested the creation, on the ruins of the dismantled all-Russian narrative, of separate narratives for the Russian (Great Russian), Ukrainian, and Belarusian nationalities.

Did the historical paradigm described by Hrushevsky really exist, and, if so, who represented it at the turn of the twentieth century? It would be no exaggeration to state that in assaulting the traditional scheme of Russian history, Hrushevsky was declaring war on virtually all Russian historians of the period. Still, it is difficult to think of a better representative of the dominant historiographic trend than the dean of Russian historians at the time, Vasilii Kliuchevsky.[14] In 1904, the year in which Hrushevsky's ground-breaking article appeared, Kliuchevsky began the publication of his famous *Course of Russian History*, which was based on lithographic copies of lectures that he had delivered at Moscow University in the 1880s. That text was revised and brought up to date for publication at the turn of the twentieth century. Kliuchevsky's *Course* represented the most authoritative interpretation of Russian history produced by the Russian historical establishment of the late imperial era, and it was against this work that Hrushevsky and his scheme of Ukrainian history were often judged by the Russian educated classes of the first two decades of the twentieth century.[15]

What was the scheme of Russian history set forth by Kliuchevsky, and what place did he reserve in his narrative for the Ukrainian and Belarusian nationalities? Kliuchevsky's general outline corresponded fully to the traditional scheme of Russian history as summarized by Hrushevsky. It began with the history of the Kyivan state and proceeded to the development of the Vladimir-Suzdal principality, the Tsardom of Muscovy, and finally the Russian Empire. Kliuchevsky's scheme of Russian history serves as a perfect illustration of what Hrushevsky had in mind when he wrote about the transformation of the traditional, dynastically oriented narrative into a history of the Great Russian nation. In his *Course*, Kliuchevsky enjoined his students to recall how Russian history of the twelfth and thirteenth centuries had been taught in Russian gymnasiums. As he put it: 'Up to the mid-twelfth century (i.e., to Andrei Bogoliubsky), the student's attention is concentrated chiefly on Kyivan Rus', its princes, and the events that took place there, but from the middle or end of the twelfth century, your attention was abruptly shifted in a different direction, to the northeast, to the Suzdal Land, to its princes, and to the events that took place there. The historical scene was shifted almost too suddenly, without sufficient preparation of the observer for such a shift. Under the first impression of that change we cannot apprehend either where Kyivan Rus' disappeared or where the new upper-Volga Rus' came from.' Kliuchevsky proposed that the problem be resolved through research on the causes of this change, which he saw in the migration of the main mass of the 'Russian' population from the Dnipro to the Upper Volga region.[16] Thus Kliuchevsky recognized the problem inherent in the 'traditional' scheme of Russian history, but instead of challenging the old dynastic paradigm, he reinforced it with a new argument from the arsenal of national history.

For Kliuchevsky, state and nationality were the two main subjects of Russian history, while its periodization was based on the migrations of the broadly defined 'Russian nation.' Russian history began with the 'Dnipro period,' which lasted from the eighth to the thirteenth century. It was succeeded by the 'Upper Volga period' (from the thirteenth to the mid-fifteenth century), which in turn was followed by the 'Great Russian' period (from the mid-fifteenth to the early seventeenth century). The last element of Kliuchevsky's scheme was the 'all-Russian' period, which lasted from the seventeenth to the mid-nineteenth century. According to his scheme, the main actors of the first two periods of 'Russian' history were the Russian people in general. The formation of the Great Russian 'tribe,' which Kliuchevsky defined as a separate branch of the Russian *narod* (nation or people), took place in the third, 'Great Russian,' period, when the main mass of the 'Russian population' moved from the Upper Volga region to the Middle Volga and Don areas. It was then, according to Kliuchevsky, that the 'Great Russian tribe was united for the first time in one political entity under the authority of the Muscovite sovereign.' During the fourth period, the 'Russian people' expanded across the entire plain between the Baltic, White, and Black seas, and even moved beyond the Ural Mountains and the Caucasus. At that time, argued Kliuchevsky, all the components of the 'Russian nationality' were united under a single political authority.[17]

This was the periodization presented by Kliuchevsky in his lectures for the 1884–5 academic year. It remained intact in the 1904 edition of the lectures, although Kliuchevsky made a few minor additions to his original text, some of which are of special interest for the present discussion.[18] To his old definition of the fourth period as the one in which 'politically almost all parts of the Russian nationality are united under one authority,' Kliuchevsky added a new detail: 'One after another Little Russia, White Russia, and New Russia adhere to Great Russia, forming the All-Russian Empire.'[19] This was the first time that Kliuchevsky introduced the notions of Little Russia (Ukraine) and White Russia (Belarus) into his basic scheme of Russian history. He treated them not as names of national entities but as territorial designations, lumping them together with New Russia (Southern Ukraine). The only national entities with an active role in Kliuchevsky's scheme were the 'Russian' and Great Russian peoples. In 1904 as in 1885, Kliuchevsky subscribed to the view that treated Russian history as an account of the 'Russian' ('all-Russian') nation and state, presenting the Great Russians as the principal actors of that history.

As for the origins of the 'Russian' nationality, Kliuchevsky was rather vague and inconsistent in defining the period when it came into existence. He regarded early Kyivan Rus' as a 'Russian state' but not as a state of the 'Russian people,' which he did not consider to have existed in the tenth, eleventh, or even twelfth centuries. According to Kliuchevsky, in the mid-eleventh century there existed only certain 'ethnographic elements' that later formed the 'Russian nationality.' In his opinion the bond between the various Slavic tribes that inhabited the Kyivan state was mainly 'mechanical,' not spiritual. As proof Kliuchevsky cited the example of the Viatichians, who in the early twelfth century still did not accept Christianity.[20] He believed that in the Kyivan era national identity was only coming into existence, as it expressed itself not in loyalty to the nation (people) but to the Rus' Land in general.[21] This generally realistic assessment of the extent of national self-identification in the Kyivan state all but contradicted the logic of Kliuchevsky's general scheme of Russian history, according to which the 'Russian' nationality, in order to be divided after the decline of Kyivan Rus' and reunited in an 'all-Russian' state during the fourth period of 'Russian' history, had first to be formed during the Kyivan Rus' period.

Kliuchevsky placed special emphasis on the disintegration of the 'Russian' nationality in the additions that he made to the text of his *Course* prior to the publication of its first volume in 1904. In this slightly revised presentation of his general scheme of 'Russian' history, Kliuchevsky noted the 'general breakup and dispersion of the nationality' between the thirteenth and mid-fifteenth centuries.[22] Also added to the original text was Kliuchevsky's broad interpretation of the history of the 'Russian nationality.' 'The Russian nationality,' wrote Kliuchevsky, 'having been formed in the first period, was torn apart in the course of the second. The main mass of the Russian people, retreating before the insuperable external dangers from the southwestern Dnipro region to the Oka and upper Volga, gathered its shattered forces there, recovered in the forests of central Russia, saved its nationality and, arming it with the strength of a consolidated state, came back to the southwestern Dnipro region to rescue the weaker portion of the Russian people, which had remained there, from the foreign yoke and influence.'[23] To legitimize such a view Kliuchevsky needed to posit the existence of a 'Russian nationality' prior to the thirteenth century. The term *zaviazavshaiasia* (having been formed), employed by Kliuchevsky in the passage cited above with respect to the formation of the 'Russian nationality,' was apparently introduced in order to downplay the contradiction between the historian's earlier claim concerning the lack of a common national identity in the Kyivan period and his theory of the division of the 'Russian nationality' into two branches. Consequently, in another addition to the original text of the lectures, he introduced the notion of an 'initial Russian nationality' that allegedly began to divide into the 'two new branches' sometime in the thirteenth century.[24]

Kliuchevsky associated that division with the decline and alleged depopulation of the Kyivan Land in the thirteenth century, caused by the resettlement of the local population to the northwest (Galicia and Volhynia) and the northeast (the Suzdal principality).[25] His views on the issue were reminiscent of some elements of Mikhail Pogodin's theory, which claimed that the native population of the Kyiv area was Great Russian and had not migrated northward until the thirteenth century, whereafter it was replaced by the Little Russians. 'The Pogodin theory sought to erase that distinction by settling the Dnipro region with Great Russians in the tenth to twelfth centuries and subsequently making them emigrate from there in the thirteenth and fourteenth centuries, but I doubt that anyone would want to defend the old historical scheme today on the basis of that risky and almost completely abandoned theory,' wrote Hrushevsky in his article on the traditional scheme of 'Russian' history.[26] To be sure, Kliuchevsky's scheme was much more sophisticated than Pogodin's, although it was also based on the idea of the depopulation of the Kyivan Land and the migration of at least part of its population to the northeast.

Unlike Pogodin, though, Kliuchevsky did not believe in the existence of Great Russians and Little Russians in the tenth to twelfth centuries, preferring to discuss either prenational 'ethnographic material' or the 'initial Russian nationality.' Although Kliuchevsky dated the beginning of the depopulation of the Kyivan Land to the twelfth century and sought the origins of the division of the 'Russian' nationality in the migrations of the thirteenth century, he did not begin applying the terms 'Great Russian' and 'Little Russian' to groups of the East Slavic population until his account reached the fifteenth century. It was then, according to Kliuchevsky's scheme, that the Slavic population of the Upper Volga region moved to the area of the Middle Volga and Don, and the Great Russian period of 'Russian history' began. The formation of the Little Russian branch of the 'Russian' people was linked, in Kliuchevsky's opinion, with the resettlement of the Dnipro region by immigrants from Poland, Galicia, and Volhynia whose ancestors had allegedly left the Kyivan Land in the thirteenth century. He also suggested that Turkic nomads of the steppe area, who moved there after the decline of Kyivan Rus', participated in the formation of the 'Little Russian tribe.'[27]

Kliuchevsky's treatment of the various elements of Ukrainian history within the framework of the all-Russian paradigm also corresponded closely to Hrushevsky's description of the 'irrationalities' of the traditional scheme of 'Russian' history. In his article of 1904, Hrushevsky argued that in shifting the centre of attention from Kyivan Rus' to the Vladimir-Suzdal principality in the thirteenth century, the traditional Russian narrative showed no interest in the subsequent history of Ukraine and Belarus, making an exception only for a limited number of episodes that were included in the all-Russian narrative for a variety of reasons. 'As for the history of the Ukrainian-Rus' and Belarusian lands, that remained outside the boundaries of the Muscovite state,' wrote Hrushevsky. 'Certain of the more significant episodes are sometimes included (Danylo's state, the formation of the Grand Duchy of Lithuania and the union with Poland, the church union, and Khmelnytsky's wars) and sometimes not included at all, but in any case, with their annexation to the Russian state these lands cease to be the subject of that history.'[28]

Kliuchevsky treated the episodes of 'West Russian' history in a manner closely resembling the 'traditional' scheme of 'Russian' history as described in Hrushevsky's article. He began his narrative with the times of Jagiełło (Jogaila), discussed the consequences of the Union of Lublin (1569), which established the Polish-Lithuanian Commonwealth, moved on to the settlement of the Ukrainian steppe, and proceeded to consider the struggle of Cossackdom for the 'Russian faith and nationality.' He discussed all these developments at relative length, but only as background to the 'Little Russian question,' which emerged in Russian foreign policy in the mid-seventeenth century. Conceptually, he treated the 'Little Russian question' like any other 'question' of seventeenth-century Russian foreign policy, including the 'Baltic' and 'Eastern' ones.[29] Kliuchevsky attempted to legitimize this traditional approach of imperial Russian historiography by stressing the particular importance of the Great Russian nationality for 'all-Russian' history. To prove the point, he claimed that most of the 'Russian' population had assembled in the Upper Volga region following the decline of Kyivan Rus'. He also invoked the national factor, referring to the 'Russian forces' that found safe haven in the Finnish woods of the Oka and Upper Volga region: in Kliuchevsky's account, they took up and continued the 'defeated national cause of Kyivan Rus'.'[30] Kliuchevsky also stressed the importance of the Great Russians in 'all-Russian' history by claiming that they constituted more than two-thirds of the entire 'Russian' population of the empire, since there were three times as many Great Russians as Little Russians, and three times as many Little Russians as Belarusians.[31]

Preparing his lectures for publication in 1903–4, Kliuchevsky apparently felt obliged to pay more attention to the history of 'other Russians.' He significantly extended his discussion of the separation of the 'Russian people' into two branches and paid somewhat more attention to 'Little Russian' issues. The time that elapsed between the lithographic publication of Kliuchevsky's course in the mid-1880s and its appearance in print in the first decade of the twentieth century had placed the Ukrainian question on the scholarly agenda as never before, and Kliuchevsky now had to explain why he, a Russian national historian, had not covered other parts of the history of the 'Russian nation.' 'Having cast a cursory glance at the fate of Southwestern Rus' in the period under study,' wrote Kliuchevsky in one of his additions to the original text, 'we lost sight of it for a long time in order to concentrate all our attention on the northeastern half of the Russian land ... Such a limitation of our field of vision is an inevitable concession to the conditions of our study. We can follow only the dominant movements of our history and sail in its mainstream, so to speak, without deviating into offshore currents. From the thirteenth century, the strongest national forces concentrated in the Upper Volga region, and that is where we should seek the origin of the bases and forms of national life that later became dominant.'[32]

Symptomatic of the new political and cultural atmosphere in the Russian Empire was the fact that the explanations offered by Kliuchevsky could hardly satisfy either proponents of a separate Ukrainian history, like Hrushevsky, or moderate historians of the Little Russian persuasion, who, like Kliuchevsky himself, strongly believed in the existence of one Russian nationality. Whatever Kliuchevsky's assertions at the time, he was the first modern Russian historian to stress the profound differences between the Kyivan and Upper Volga periods of 'Russian' history – emphases that facilitated the interpretation of Kyivan Rus' history as the creation of a nationality distinct from the one that established the Upper Volga principalities.[33] Kliuchevsky's almost exclusive focus on Great Russian history, which he treated as the mainstream of Russian history in general, also helped undermine the legitimacy of the all-Russian narrative.

One of the moderate Ukrainian historians dissatisfied with the practice of reducing all-Russian history to that of Great Russia was Ivan Linnichenko. Like Hrushevsky, he was a student of Volodymyr Antonovych, but unlike his professor or his younger colleague, Linnichenko had little sympathy for the Ukrainian cause and believed strongly in the unity of the 'Russian' people.[34] Linnichenko expressed his dissatisfaction with the dominant trend of imperial Russian historiography in his inaugural lecture at Moscow University, the bastion of Kliuchevsky and his school, in 1897. 'In certain instances we repeat with pride,' stated Linnichenko in his lecture, 'that Rus' is everywhere, from the icy Finnish crags to flaming Colchis; from the White Sea all the way to the distant Carpathian Mountains. But as soon as it comes to defining the basic features of the Russian character and Russian national institutions, we immediately begin to throw overboard one group of Russians after another; we strike out one period of our history after another; and so we conclude by endlessly narrowing Rus', both territorially and historically.'[35]

Linnichenko's reference to the broad geographic definition of Rus' alluded to a well-known verse by Aleksandr Pushkin,[36] but it also was very close to Kliuchevsky's geographic description of Russia in his *Course*. Kliuchevsky could also be considered a target of Linnichenko's critique of those who defined the Russian national character and Russian national institutions on the basis of the character and institutions of only one part of the all-Russian people. In suggesting an alternative to this dominant scheme, Linnichenko did not want to discard the old imperial paradigm but rather to extend and broaden it so as to give greater prominence and attention to Ukrainian-Belarusian history. He demanded for Western (Belarusian) and Southwestern (Ukrainian) Rus' the same rights as those accorded to the history of Northern (Great Russian) Rus'. Linnichenko claimed that the history of the western and southwestern territories was not 'local' history, alluding to the term used to define particular regions of Great Russia, but part of 'all-Russian' history.[37]

Linnichenko's position was largely shared by another prominent Ukrainian historian, a Great Russian by origin, Aleksandra Efimenko.[38] In the preface to her survey *History of the Ukrainian People* (1906), Efimenko expressed her dissatisfaction with the dominant practice in the 'Russian scholarly literature' of treating 'Russian' history exclusively in terms of Northeastern Rus'. She believed that such an interpretation of 'Russian' history made for a 'historical understanding so one-sided as to verge in particular instances on the falsification of social self-understanding, though entirely involuntary and unconscious in most instances.'[39] Like Linnichenko, Efimenko believed that Russian history was composed of two parts: the history of Northeastern or Muscovite Rus' and that of Southern and Western, or Polish-Lithuanian Rus'. She justified that approach by the size of territory and population of Southwestern Rus', which she considered comparable to the territory and population of Northeastern Rus', as well as by the distinct nature of their respective cultures and histories. Efimenko treated the two parts of Rus' as equals. She tended, though, to equate the history of Polish-Lithuanian Rus' with that of Southern Rus'/Little Russia, claiming that only Southern Rus' 'lived its own political life, while Western Rus' – the Belarusian tribe – ended its political existence with its absorption by the Lithuanian state.'[40]

Efimenko stressed the importance of research on Southern Rus' for the advancement of general 'Russian' historical studies, addressing her argument first and foremost to the Russian 'Westernizers.' She asserted that the study of Polish-Lithuanian Rus' would alter prevailing views about the opposition between Russia and Europe and help 'establish a clear view of our genuine national particularities, our true difference from Europe, which is rooted not only in the relatively late conditions and particularities of Northeastern Rus'.'[41] Efimenko buttressed her argument by indicating the neglect of the history of Southwestern Rus', as demonstrated by the lack of general histories of Ukraine. In Efimenko's opinion it was only the events of 1904 (an apparent reference to the liberal policies of the new imperial minister of the interior, Prince Petr Sviatopolk-Mirsky) that served to legalize Ukrainian history, a development that she associated with the publication of Hrushevsky's *Survey*

History of the Ukrainian People in the same year. It is interesting to note that while criticizing the dominant paradigm of Russian history from a very moderate standpoint, Efimenko felt it necessary to defend herself against possible accusations of 'South Russian national subjectivism.' She did so by referring to her Great Russian origins and to the work she had accomplished in the field of Great Russian history.[42]

Efimenko's attempt to raise the profile of 'Southwestern Rus'' by incorporating the history of the Grand Duchy of Lithuania into all-Russian history was hardly an original undertaking. In his article on the traditional scheme of 'Russian history,' Hrushevsky noted similar attempts by the Russian historians Nikolai Ustrialov, Dmitrii Ilovaisky, and Konstantin Bestuzhev-Riumin, who 'tried to present in parallel fashion the history of "Western Rus'," that is, of the Grand Duchy of Lithuania, and of "Eastern Rus'," that is, of the Muscovite state.'[43] Among the most prominent adherents of that tradition was Kliuchevsky's student and successor in the chair of Russian history at Moscow University, Matvei Liubavsky. In his *Survey History of the Lithuanian-Russian State* (1910), Liubavsky complained, as Linnichenko and Efimenko had done before him, about the lack of scholarly interest in the history of 'Lithuania and Western Rus'.' In keeping with the spirit of post-1905 Russia, he attempted to interest his readers by drawing attention to the constitutional traditions of the 'Lithuanian-Russian' state. Liubavsky wrote that if the Muscovite state had evolved toward monarchical absolutism, 'The Grand Duchy of Lithuania developed in the direction of constitutionalism and political decentralization. Ultimately it issued in a kind of elective monarchy (within dynastic limits).'[44]

Liubavsky saw the Russian past as a history of two 'Russian' states, Muscovy and 'Lithuania-Russia,' and believed that the study of 'Lithuanian-Russian' history helped explain the Russian historical process as a whole. He asserted that not only the history of the Muscovite state but also that of the 'Lithuanian-Russian' state was, 'in a certain sense, a direct continuation, a further development of the history of Kyivan Rus'.' He even went so far as to argue that 'Lithuanian Rus'' had preserved many more Kyivan Rus' traditions than Suzdal Rus', which, 'having settled along the Upper Volga and its tributaries, established its existence there on new foundations, different from those of Dnipro and Dvina Rus'.'[45] Liubavsky believed that the Union of Lublin (1569), which marked the de facto abolition of the Grand Duchy of Lithuania as an independent political entity and incorporated the Ukrainian and Belarusian lands into the Polish-led Commonwealth, was 'an event of the first importance in all-Russian history.' According to him, the significance of that union lay in the fact that it associated Lithuania and Western Rus' much more closely with Poland, while separating and estranging them from Northeastern Rus'. In Liubavsky's opinion, the time had come for Lithuanian Rus', 'already united with Eastern Rus' for more than a century [as a result of the partitions of Poland], to become united with it in the scholarly sense as well.'[46] With regard to the timing of his enterprise, Liubavsky was clearly mistaken. The time for a scholarly and ideological undertaking of that kind was already past, and the 'unification' did not work either in political or in historiographic terms. In the latter case, the future belonged not to state-based paradigms but to nationally based ones, such as the historical scheme advanced by Hrushevsky.

It appears from Hrushevsky's article of 1904 that he was at least as dissatisfied with the 'traditional' scheme of 'Russian' history as Linnichenko, Efimenko, and Liubavsky. He wrote that 'one must bid farewell to the fiction that "Russian history," when at every step the history of Great Russia is substituted for it, is the history of "all Russia."'[47] But in seeking a solution to the problem, Hrushevsky proceeded in a direction entirely different from the one suggested by his colleagues, none of whom challenged the idea of all-Russian history per se, advocating instead the restructuring of the paradigm and giving greater prominence to the history of Southwestern Rus'. Hrushevsky, for his part, postulated the complete separation of Ukrainian history from that of Russia. If Liubavsky's and Efimenko's division of all-Russian history was informed by the statist approach, Hrushevsky based his outline of East Slavic history on the principle of nationality. For Hrushevsky, each of the East Slavic nationalities deserved a history of its own.

He claimed that 'indeed, there can be no "all-Russian" history, just as there is no "all-Russian" nationality.'[48] Consequently, he argued that the old 'Russian' history should be divided into three parts, not two, with the Russians, Ukrainians, and Belarusians all acquiring historical narratives of their own. Hrushevsky admitted that Belarusian history would be less rich in detail than that of Ukraine and proposed that numerous episodes traditionally viewed as belonging to all-Russian history be reassigned to the history of the Belarusians. He wrote in that regard: 'The Belarusian nationality fares even worse [than the Ukrainian] under this [traditional] scheme. It is completely obscured by the histories of the Kyivan state, the Vladimir-Moscow state, and even by the Grand

Duchy of Lithuania. Though nowhere in history does it clearly figure as a creative element, its role nonetheless is not insignificant. I shall limit myself to noting its importance in the formation of the Great Russian nationality or in the history of the Great Duchy of Lithuania, where the cultural role among the Slavic peoples, in relation to the much less developed Lithuanian tribes, belonged above all to the Belarusians.'[49]

In his deconstruction of the 'traditional scheme,' Hrushevsky indicated tendencies within Russian historiography itself that he found consonant with his own views and ideas. He assumed that even proponents of the traditional paradigm would recognize that its faults and errors were too significant to be ignored. Some of the most important ideas advanced in Hrushevsky's article of 1904 had been introduced in his earlier reviews of the works of Russian historians such as Pavel Miliukov, Nikolai Zagoskin, and Mikhail Vladimirsky-Budanov.[50] Miliukov, a student of Kliuchevsky and a rising star of Russian national historiography,[51] was singled out for praise by Hrushevsky, who reviewed all his major works of the 1890s. These included two volumes of *Essays on the History of Russian Culture* and the first and only volume of *Main Currents of Russian Historical Thought*.[52] In his review of *Main Currents*, Hrushevsky wrote: 'Professor Miliukov has taken a highly serious approach to his subject. Not content with published material, he also makes use of unpublished sources, studying the main currents of historiography in connection with cultural and spiritual tendencies in general. He evaluates them from a progressive scholarly viewpoint free of all official, chauvinist, and other conventions that are sometimes so deeply rooted in Russian historiography; hence we must recognize that Mr Miliukov's work constitutes a very serious contribution to the literature.'[53] In his review of the *Essays*, Hrushevsky criticized Miliukov for confusing 'Russia' with 'Great Russia' and writing essentially Great Russian history while using the term 'Russian' in the title of his book. Nevertheless, he considered the first two volumes of the *Essays* highly interesting in content and ideas.[54]

What did Hrushevsky find so valuable in Miliukov's works? His reviews provide part of the answer, while a comparison of Hrushevsky's views with Miliukov's on history in general and Russian history in particular sheds further light on the matter. First of all, Hrushevsky and Miliukov were shaped as historians by similar ideas. Both were positivists influenced by sociological thinking, which made them view the history of peoples and society, not that of heroes, states, and legal institutions, as the principal subject of new historical research.[55] Some

of Miliukov's views on specific issues of Russian history were consonant with Hrushevsky's own interpretation of the Russian and Ukrainian past.[56] Miliukov, for example, considered Kyivan Rus' separate
from later periods of Russian history 'not only chronologically but
actually.'[57] He also all but excluded the Kyivan Rus' period from his
discussion of Russian culture, for which he was criticized by Venedikt
Miakotin.[58] In Hrushevsky's opinion, Miliukov's discussion of the history of Russian culture was in fact limited to the evolution of Great
Russian or, more specifically, Muscovite culture.[59] Hrushevsky also
expressed the hope that in his *Main Currents*, Miliukov had 'consciously'
excluded the discussion of eighteenth- and nineteenth-century Ukrainian historiography from his survey.[60]

More importantly, it was none other than Miliukov who began the
process of dismantling the traditional scheme of 'Russian' history by
demonstrating that the basic elements of the Russian historical narrative put together by Nikolai Karamzin in the early nineteenth century
were initially formulated as a response to the immediate tasks of Muscovite foreign policy of the late fifteenth and early sixteenth centuries.
In analysing Karamzin's views in his *Main Currents*, Miliukov made a
brief excursus into the history of Muscovite political thought. He noted
how the idea of the direct responsibility of the princes for the division of
Rus' lands into appanages came into existence in the times of Ivan III
and how Muscovite diplomacy invoked the notion of the hereditary
rights of the Muscovite tsars to the Rus' lands under Lithuanian administration. He also traced the development of the notion that the power
of the Muscovite princes derived from Byzantine origins. According to
Miliukov, all these ideas had been employed as cornerstones of the
Russian historical scheme.[61]

There is little doubt that Miliukov's deconstruction of the Muscovite
historiographic scheme, especially its treatment of the role of the Kyivan
dynastic factor in Muscovite political thought, strengthened Hrushevsky's own critique of the traditional scheme of 'Russian' history. It
was under the influence of Miliukov's 'discoveries' that Hrushevsky wrote in his review of *Main Currents* (1898): 'The historical
scheme of Muscovite historiography of the sixteenth and seventeenth
centuries, its officious and utilitarian character had their influence on
Russian historiography of the eighteenth and even nineteenth centuries.'[62] He stressed this point again in his article of 1904 on the traditional scheme of 'Russian' history: 'This is an old scheme that has its
beginnings in the historiographic scheme of the Muscovite scribes, and

at its basis lies a genealogical idea – the genealogy of the Muscovite dynasty. With the beginning of academic historiography in Russia, that scheme became the basis for the history of the "Russian state."'[63] In the late nineteenth and early twentieth centuries, both Hrushevsky and Miliukov were involved in the deconstruction of the old imperial paradigm of Russian history. Neither shared the fascination of the previous generation of Russian historians with issues of political and legal history, and both welcomed the advance of the new paradigm of national history.[64]

Hrushevsky thought that Russian historians had already done a good job of developing a new scheme of Great Russian history by 'cleansing' the 'all-Russian' narrative of episodes properly belonging to Ukrainian and Belarusian history. By far the most important episode of the Ukrainian past artificially attached to that of the Great Russian nationality, in Hrushevsky's opinion, was the history of Kyivan Rus'. That is why he welcomed the penetration of the 'national' paradigm into Russian historiography of the Kyivan state. Here again, as elsewhere, Miliukov's contribution cannot be overlooked. There is little doubt that Miliukov's interpretation of Kyivan Rus' ethnic history was much closer to the views of Hrushevsky than to those of his former professor, Vasilii Kliuchevsky. By virtue of his acceptance of Pogodin's theory of the depopulation of the Kyivan Land in the thirteenth century, Miliukov also subscribed to Pogodin's thesis that the history of the Rus' nationalities could be traced back to the times of Kyivan Rus'. If Kliuchevsky found it appropriate to speak of the Great Russian and Little Russian nationalities only from the fifteenth century on, Miliukov believed that the 'Russian dialects' took shape long before evidence of them became available in historical sources. He also strove to associate the 'North Russian' and 'South Russian' (Little Russian) 'dialects' with particular East Slavic tribes. Miliukov traced the 'Little Russian dialects' back to the White Croats of Galicia and the Volhynians, frequently employing the terms 'Ukrainian' and 'Ukrainians' in his analysis. He also linked the Belarusian dialects with the Krivichians but was more cautious in associating other tribes with either North Russian or South Russian 'dialects.'[65]

A Russian historian whom Hrushevsky particularly praised for his interpretation of the history of Kyivan Rus' was Vasilii Storozhev, who viewed Dnipro (Kyivan) Rus' and Northeastern Rus' as products of the historical activity of two different parts of the Russian nationality. In his article on the traditional scheme of 'Russian' history, Hrushevsky noted that it would be preferable to treat these two parts as separate nationalities but generally praised Storozhev's approach.[66] Hrushevsky's high opinion of Storozhev's views was also expressed in his earlier review of a collection of articles on Russian history published by Storozhev in 1898. There, apart from lauding Storozhev's analysis and expressing his opinion of the need to treat the two branches of the 'Russian' nation as separate nationalities, Hrushevsky noted that Great Russia was influenced in its evolution by the political and cultural heritage of Kyivan Rus' but compared the relation between the principalities of Kyiv and Suzdal-Vladimir to that between Rome and barbarian Gaul.[67] Hrushevsky later used this comparison in his article on the traditional scheme, where he wrote: 'The Vladimir-Moscow state was neither the successor nor the inheritor of the Kyivan state. It grew out of its own roots, and the relation of the Kyivan state toward it might more accurately be compared, for instance, to the relations between the Roman state and its Gallic provinces than described as two successive periods in the political and cultural life of France.'[68] Another Russian scholar whose contribution to the field of East Slavic history Hrushevsky noted in his article of 1904 was Dmitrii Korsakov, the author of a book on the history of the Rostov principality.[69] Hrushevsky treated Korsakov's work as an attempt to discover the origins of Great Russian history in the history of Northeastern Rus' – a development that he obviously welcomed.

Whatever the contributions of these Russian historians to Hrushevsky's deconstruction of the imperial Russian narrative, it is clear that by introducing the concept of a distinct Ukrainian national narrative he took their conclusions several steps farther, reaching a qualitatively new stage in the development of East European historiography. How did Russian historians respond to his challenge? Judging by the reaction in Russian scholarly publications, Hrushevsky's critique of the traditional scheme of 'Russian' history did not go unnoticed, but we know relatively little about the response of those historians whose works Hrushevsky mentioned in his article of 1904.

Little is known about Miliukov's reaction to Hrushevsky's interpretation of his views and his deconstruction of the traditional scheme, except that, as mentioned earlier, Miliukov regarded Hrushevsky's attempts to establish an unbroken Ukrainian presence in the Kyiv region as a continuation of the 'Ukrainophile' tradition.[70] The friendliest and most supportive of the Russian historians appears to have been Storozhev, whom Hrushevsky first met during his archival trip to Moscow in 1892.[71] Storozhev's attitude to Hrushevsky's article on the traditional scheme of 'Russian' history can be reconstructed on the basis of his general appraisal of Hrushevsky's *Survey History of the Ukrainian People*, which developed many of the ideas presented in the article. In a letter of January 1905 to Hrushevsky, Storozhev expressed enthusiasm for the *Survey*. Addressing Hrushevsky's apparent concern that some Russian scholars might consider the book rather partisan, Storozhev wrote: 'You write that I am "a man free of various nationalist prejudices." That is not entirely true: You could freely write that I am an ardent hater of those prejudices. Having read your book, I would not say that even a single page was offensive to me by virtue of its tendentiousness. Your book contains only that "goodly share of tendentiousness" that adorns every vital piece of work.'[72] We know very little about the response to Hrushevsky's article on the part of Korsakov, who reviewed the second edition of the *Survey History* (1906) and generally praised it but apparently was uneasy about Hrushevsky's 'Ukrainization' of Kyivan Rus'.[73] Korsakov and Hrushevsky later maintained good relations: in 1913, for example, Hrushevsky contributed to a festschrift for Korsakov.[74] The latter thanked his younger colleague for his contribution and wrote that he welcomed cooperation between 'Great Russian' and 'South Russian' historians, which had developed 'in spite of self-styled representatives of true Russian people, those epigones of Katkovian phantasmagorias.'[75]

Storozhev and Korsakov were clearly among those Russian historians who were prepared to judge Hrushevsky's contribution to the field on the basis of its scholarly merit, irrespective of the political ramifications of his theories. There is good reason to believe, however, that most Russian historians not only did not welcome Hrushevsky's deconstruction of the imperial narrative but were hostile toward it. One such historian was a Ukrainian by birth, Ivan Filevich, who was then teaching at the University of Warsaw. As noted earlier, in 1892 he was among those who welcomed the publication of Hrushevsky's book on the history of the Kyivan Land and gave it a highly positive assessment.[76] Ten years later, in 1902, Filevich published a brochure in Lviv attacking Kostomarov's theory of the two Rus' nationalities. He singled out Hrushevsky as a scholar who had applied that theory, contrary to historical fact, in order to establish the distinctive character of Ukrainian history.[77]

Judging by the scant evidence available on the response to Hrushevsky's article in the Russian Empire, the clash between proponents and opponents of Hrushevsky's views took place mainly in Ukraine. A good indication of its character is given by the debates conducted on the issue at the Historical and Philological Society of the University of New Russia in Odesa. The initiative to hold a discussion on Hrushevsky's article came from the head of the society, the philologist Vasilii Istrin.[78] Petro Klymovych, a lawyer and active member of the Odesa Ukrainian Hromada, gave a paper based on the article. Writing to Hrushevsky in March 1905, Klymovych described the reaction of the audience to his presentation: 'There was hot debate: the *moskali* [derogatory term for Russians] (and our university is "swarming" with them) attacked strongly ... I was supported by only two of our countrymen, and weakly at that, while the *moskali* turned on me in droves as I defended your tenets.' Istrin, who, judging by Klymovych's letter, was wounded by Ivan Franko's critique of his work and called him a 'zealous *khokhol* [derogatory term for Ukrainians],' was reluctant to allow Klymovych to give a new paper based on another article of Hrushevsky's about old Rus' ethnography published in the same collection as the article on the traditional scheme of 'Russian' history. Eventually Klymovych was allowed to deliver his paper, but a presentation by an opponent of Hrushevsky's, the philologist Boris Liapunov, was scheduled for the same day.[79]

It was also the Odesa milieu that produced the first (and only) substantial response to Hrushevsky's article of 1904, although it was delayed for more than a decade. The response appeared in the revolutionary year of 1917 under the title *The Little Russian Question and the Autonomy of Little Russia: An Open Letter to Professor M.S. Hrushevsky*. Its author was Ivan Linnichenko, well known to us from the discussion above, who spent most of his career teaching at Odesa University. Linnichenko's brochure contained a critical review of Hrushevsky's article of 1904, as well as Linnichenko's arguments against the autonomization of Ukraine in 1917. According to Linnichenko, the first part of his brochure was written soon after the publication of Hrushevsky's article on the traditional scheme of 'Russian' history, but its publication was delayed because, under prevailing circumstances, Hrushevsky would have had no opportunity to respond to Linnichenko in the public press with 'full freedom and sincerity.'[80]

The 'lenient' treatment of Hrushevsky by his Russian and Little Russian opponents before the Revolution of 1917 was later regretted by another historian of the Little Russian persuasion, Andrei Storozhenko. Writing after the revolution under the pseudonym 'A. Tsarinny,'[81]

Storozhenko expressed his dissatisfaction that Russian academics had spared Hrushevsky from criticism before the revolution. In that context, Storozhenko mentioned the name of Aleksei Shakhmatov and complained that Kharkiv University had awarded honorary doctorates to Hrushevsky and Ivan Franko at the initiative of the 'Ukrainophiles' Dmytro Bahalii and Mykola Sumtsov. The reason for such appeasement of Hrushevsky, according to Storozhenko, lay in his revolutionary political convictions. Storozhenko expressed the hope that someday someone would write a whole volume exposing Hrushevsky's 'distortions, misrepresentations, and arbitrary fabrications.'[82]

There are no grounds to question the sincerity of Linnichenko's statement that he initially spared Hrushevsky from public criticism because of the latter's lack of opportunity to respond to him in kind or to deny the existence of a certain degree of solidarity among liberal-minded Russian scholars. There is, however, sufficient proof that not all of Hrushevsky's opponents were as protective of him as Linnichenko when political persecution was at issue. The collection of articles published in Kyiv in 1908 to prevent Hrushevsky's election to the chair of history at Kyiv University indicates that there was no lack of political denunciators.[83] Still, it was only the Revolution of 1917 that turned the Ukrainian movement into an unprecedented threat to proponents of the 'all-Russian' identity and created a demand for the examination and critique of the historical views of its leader, Mykhailo Hrushevsky. Symptomatic of the new atmosphere was the stand taken by Aleksei Shakhmatov toward the Ukrainian movement. Shakhmatov, who was instrumental in the lifting of the official ban on Ukrainian-language publications in 1905 and helped ease restrictions imposed on Hrushevsky during his exile in Simbirsk in 1914, took a very different approach to the 'Ukrainian question' on the eve of the 1917 revolution. He allegedly told one of the leaders of the Ukrainian movement in St Petersburg (Petrograd), Oleksander Lototsky: 'Until now I was with you. However, when it comes to autonomy for Ukraine, I fasten all my buttons. For this involves the most vital interests of the Great Russian nation, which you are separating from the warm [Black] sea.'[84] The outcome of the revolution made the proponents of the all-Russian idea much more aggressive. Telling in that regard is the fact that Storozhenko wrote his *Ukrainian Movement* in response to a request published in an émigré Russian newspaper for a survey history of the Ukrainian movement.[85] The author of another anti-Ukrainian work that employed quotations from Kliuchevsky to refute Hrushevsky's views, Prince Aleksandr Volkonsky, wrote his *Historical Truth and Ukrainophile Propaganda* in 1920 in order to counter Ukrainian publications distributed in Western Europe and persuade the Entente to deny political support to an independent Ukraine.[86]

What were the arguments leveled against Hrushevsky by his opponents? Linnichenko's brochure offers the most comprehensive answer to this question, as it was by far the most scholarly and professional treatment of the controversy over the traditional scheme of 'Russian' history and Hrushevsky's views in general. Linnichenko's views on the issue were generally in accord with those of other Great Russian and Little Russian critics of Hrushevsky. As noted earlier, Linnichenko was an imperial Russian historian of Ukrainian origin who became dissatisfied quite early in his career with the lack of attention to 'South Russian' history within the 'all-Russian' paradigm and demanded greater attention to the history of that region. He claimed that Hrushevsky's article of 1904 also addressed the problem he had indicated in his lecture of 1897 at Moscow University, but from a different perspective – one that Linnichenko considered unacceptable. Linnichenko quoted from Hrushevsky's article at length, giving excerpts in Russian translation and presenting a generally accurate account of Hrushevsky's views.[87]

The main point of Hrushevsky's interpretation of East Slavic history with which Linnichenko could not agree was his treatment of the historical role of state and nationality. Linnichenko perceived a major 'contradiction' in Hrushevsky's injunction to study the history not of the Russian state but of the Ukrainian nationality, 'which,' added Linnichenko, 'never possessed independent statehood.' According to Linnichenko, Hrushevsky went too far in seeking to shift the focus of historical research from the history of the state to that of people and society. In separating the state from the people, he allegedly followed the 'old Slavophiles,' who viewed state and people as independent entities and confused the state with the government. Proposing to define the state as the product of a social union, Linnichenko claimed that it was impossible to study the history of society without studying the history of the state, which alone could serve as the focal point of any historical narrative.[88]

Not surprisingly, Linnichenko believed that Hrushevsky grossly underestimated the role of the state as a general factor in history. He quoted Hrushevsky's assessment of the role of the state from his article of 1904 ('The political and state factors are important, of course, but in addition there are other factors, economic and cultural, that may be of greater or lesser significance than the political one, but in any event should not be overshadowed by it'), concluding that Hrushevsky did not fully appreciate the importance of the state, which exercised a dominant influence on the cultural development of society.[89] Linnichenko claimed that because Ukraine (Little Russia) lacked an independent state, it never developed its own independent culture, being influenced instead either by Polish or by Great Russian culture.[90] He supported his argument about the historical absence of Ukrainian statehood by invoking the authority of Professor Volodymyr Antonovych, who had supervised both Hrushevsky's work and his own. It was Antonovych, noted Linnichenko, who expressed the opinion that the Little Russians had not created a state of their own in the seventeenth century, as they were a 'stateless' people.[91]

In his polemic with Hrushevsky, Linnichenko made a spectacular reversal of the views expressed in his lecture of 1897 at Moscow University. If originally he had protested the neglect of the history of Southwestern Russia that resulted from the old historical paradigm of Russian history and challenged the definition of its history as 'local,' he now did the exact opposite, defending the Kliuchevskian focus on Great Russian history. Linnichenko wrote in his brochure of 1917: 'Mr Hrushevsky seems to assume that the particular attention devoted by our historians to the history of the Great Russian state is an evil intention, a bureaucratic intrigue – the substitution of the notion of "Great Russian" for that of the "Russian people." But in his enthusiasm for narrow national sympathies, Mr Hrushevsky is unwilling to comprehend that a historian comes to know the truth by studying the past and, if he discovers in it an agent of great creative power, then, naturally, he focuses attention on it; and even he will not deny that the creative agent in the establishment of the contemporary Russian state as an integral whole was predominantly the Great Russian nationality.'[92] Thus, Linnichenko justified the special focus on Great Russian history against which he had earlier protested by indicating the special role of the Great Russians in the formation of the 'all-Russian' state. For Linnichenko the state remained the alpha and omega of historical research, and he accused Hrushevsky of seeking to replace history with ethnography.[93] In countering Hrushevsky's strategy of deconstructing the old imperial historical narrative by means of the nation-based approach, Linnichenko ultimately fell back on the old-fashioned statist argument.

If the intellectual response to Hrushevsky's effort to deconstruct the imperial historical narrative and replace it with three national narratives was delayed by thirteen long years, the political consequences of the rejection of his views by most of his Russian and Little Russian colleagues were felt almost immediately. Hrushevsky's new scheme, especially its implementation in the *Survey History of the Ukrainian People* (1904), helped establish his reputation in Russian scholarly circles as a leader of 'Ukrainian separatism.' Hrushevsky wrote in his autobiography that 'the enemies of the Ukrainian movement justly perceived [in the *Survey*] a historical justification of Ukrainian national strivings and of the program of Ukrainian autonomy.'[94] The same forces prevented Hrushevsky's appointment to the chair of Russian history at Kyiv University in 1908.[95]

The Search for Origins

It would be difficult to overstate the importance of the myth of origins for any national narrative. One of the absolute requirements of national mythology and national historiography (to the degree that the two overlap) is that every nation must have its own myth of origins, which cannot be shared with any other nation. Otherwise, the myth could not fulfill its main function – that of legitimizing the existence of a given nation by endowing it with an ancient and preferably glorious past. National narratives of suppressed nations could not therefore share the founding myths underlying the narratives of imperial nations: new ones had to be produced or, failing that, parts of the imperial narrative had to be appropriated. The national 'awakeners' of the nineteenth and early twentieth centuries were fascinated by the mysterious origins of their respective nations, which helped turn the fathers of modern nations into historians and vice versa.[96]

Hrushevsky's search for the origins of the Ukrainian nation took place at a time when many of his colleagues in Central and Western Europe were busy establishing the prehistoric origins and early historical roots of their own nations. In his *History*, Hrushevsky commented specifically on one such attempt undertaken by the German scholars Matthäus Much and Gustaf Kossinna, who argued in favour of Germany as the ancestral homeland of the Indo-Europeans and presented the Germans as direct heirs of Indo-European culture. Hrushevsky noted that the theories of those two authors 'coincided with the aspirations of German society and gained a large number of supporters,' but dismissed them as 'pure fiction.'[97] He took care to ensure that his own search for the origins of the Ukrainian nation was based on the solid foundations of historical sources and scholarly literature.

Below I shall examine Hrushevsky's attempt to claim for the Ukrainian national narrative the most ancient parts of the historical and prehistoric past that had previously been taken to belong to Russian history. I shall discuss his interest in the pre-Slavic history of Southern Ukraine, the region in which imperial art museums harvested numerous masterpieces of Scythian gold; his attempts to find ancestors of the Ukrainian nation among tribes earlier considered proto-Russian, or at best East Slavic; and, finally, his interpretation of one of the most controversial problems in East Slavic history – the origins of the Rus' state.

In 1922 Oxford University Press published a book by a distinguished scholar of the ancient world, a native of Kyiv and a graduate of Kyiv and St Petersburg universities, Michael Rostovtzeff (Mikhail Rostovtsev), titled *Iranians and Greeks in South Russia*. Adapted from Rostovtzeff's Russian-language monograph *Èllinstvo i iranstvo na Iuge Rossii* (1918), the work was augmented with an excursus on the history of Kyivan Rus'. The latter was based on Rostovtzeff's French-language essay about the origins of ancient Rus' that subsequently appeared in the *Revue des études slaves*. In his new book, Rostovtzeff treated the Russian past as the history not of a state or a nation but of a territory. He explained his approach as follows: 'The history of Russia as an economic and political organism is much more ancient than the earliest references to the Slavonic race ... We must therefore treat the history of Russia not as the history of the Slavonic race but as the history of the country of Russia.'[98]

In applying this method to his account of Russian history, Rostovtzeff was primarily concerned with establishing connections between the pre-Slavic and Slavic history of the Kyivan Rus' lands. He considered this a novel approach to the history of 'Southern Russia' and criticized his predecessors for failing to see any connection between the history of the pre-Slavic and Slavic histories of the region. Rostovtzeff specifically mentioned Vasilii Kliuchevsky and Sergei Platonov as representatives of the 'view which denies the existence of any link connecting the history of Slavonic and the history of pre-Slavonic Russia or rather the possibility of finding such links.' He also noted the work done in that area by the 'archaeologists' Ivan Zabelin and Nikodim Kondakov, who allegedly were 'the only scholars who have felt (rather than proved) this connection.' Dmytro Bahalii and Mykhailo Hrushevsky were characterized by Rostovtzeff as scholars who treated the history of the two periods not in conjunction but in opposition.[99]

Rostovtzeff, a noted specialist and professor of the history of the ancient world at St Petersburg, Wisconsin (Madison), and Yale Universities, unfortunately was all but a dilettante in the field of Slavic history. The connection between the pre-Slavic and Slavic history of the region that he called Southern Russia had been studied by historians of Ukraine long before the publication of Rostovtzeff's book in 1922. As early as his inaugural lecture of 1894 at Lviv University, Hrushevsky had indicated the link between the pre-Slavic and Slavic history of Ukraine: 'Archaeological studies do not discover the Rus' peoples in their contemporary settlements only in a state of notably high culture. In these settlements they had predecessors in the cultural lives of other peoples, of other races, who experienced a long period of elementary culture that goes back to the earliest times, the times of the early Stone Age (Paleolithic period). That ancient race did not disappear; it lived together with the Slavic migrants and merged into one nation with them.'[100] Thus, in a review of Rostovtzeff's works written in 1925, Hrushevsky questioned the novelty of Rostovtzeff's approach, pointing out that the influence of pre-Slavic cultures on later Slavic settlements had been clearly identified in earlier studies by Ukrainian historians. He referred to the work done by Kyiv historians in the 1880s and 1890s, noting that Antonovych, in his lectures of 1893, inspired by the archaeological discoveries of Vikentii Khvoika, had demonstrated the intermingling of historical cultures and races in the Kyiv region. 'In the first volume of my *History of Ukraine*,' wrote Hrushevsky, 'I attempted to do the same for Ukraine as a whole.'[101]

Indeed, Hrushevsky's search for the origins of Ukrainian history took him back to pre-Slavic and prehistoric times. In the opening chapters of volume 1 of his *History of Ukraine-Rus'*, Hrushevsky interpreted the Ukrainian past as the history of the territory settled by Ukrainians by the end of the nineteenth century. 'The history of our country as a territory ... begins with the most recent geological formations,' wrote Hrushevsky in the opening paragraph of the second chapter (that is, the first, if one excludes introductory remarks) of volume 1 of the *History*.[102] He gave considerable attention to archaeological findings on the territory of Ukraine pertaining to Paleolithic and Neolithic cultures, as well as to the copper, bronze, and iron ages. One chapter was devoted to the history of the Greek colonies in the northern Black Sea region, as well as of the Cimmerians, Scythians, Sarmatians, and other peoples who populated the territory of Ukraine. Hrushevsky did thorough research on these subjects, whose treatment underwent significant revision in the second and third editions of volume 1 of the *History*.[103] He was resolute, however, in including the ancient history of the territory eventually settled by Ukrainians in their national narrative.

If the history of Ukraine began for Hrushevsky with the history of geological formations, his starting point for the history of the Ukrainian people was the Slavic settlement of Eastern Europe. Being a primordialist par excellence, Hrushevsky was prepared to look much farther back in time than Kyivan Rus' for the origins of his people. At the same time, he showed great caution in making use of archaeological and anthropological material to define the Ukrainian physical type according to the latest scholarly trends.[104] 'This work seeks to trace the historical development of the life of the Ukrainian people or of those ethnopolitical groups that form what we think of today as the Ukrainian people,' wrote Hrushevsky in his introductory remarks to the third edition of volume 1 of the *History*.[105]

Hrushevsky strongly believed that Ukrainian territory constituted part of the ancient 'homeland' of the Slavs. In his opinion that homeland was located between the Carpathian Mountains in the west and the Valdai Hills in the east, a view shared by most Slavists of the late nineteenth and early twentieth centuries.[106] By placing the Slavic homeland in that area, Hrushevsky rejected the theory that limited it to Sub-Carpathia. The latter theory, especially popular among Russian historians from Nikolai Nadezhdin to Vasilii Kliuchevsky, was based on the argument that Slavic linguistic elements were better preserved in the toponyms of Galicia and Volhynia than anywhere else. It made Ukraine the earliest homeland of all the Slavs and was thus in accord with Hrushevsky's search for Ukrainian ancestry among the first Slavic tribes. Nevertheless, Hrushevsky rejected it, as he believed that conclusions drawn on the basis of toponymical material were not supported by evidence from other sources.[107] Hrushevsky the scholar was clearly contradicting Hrushevsky the nation-builder, rejecting on scholarly grounds a theory that would have given Ukraine the exclusive right to call itself the cradle of Slavic civilization.

Hrushevsky believed that in the fourth century A.D. Slavic colonization had extended across most of Ukrainian territory. In his opinion it was the advance of the Slavic tribes all the way to the northern Black Sea region that brought together the ethnic and territorial factors of Ukrainian history, initiating the formation of the Ukrainian nation. In the first volume of his *History of Ukrainian Literature* (1923), Hrushevsky wrote: 'At this moment the southeastern, Ukrainian branch [of Slavdom] takes over the territory destined for it by fate as its historical workshop.

Until now the history of this territory had followed its own separate paths, independently of the history of the future Ukrainian population. From this time forward, these two elements become indissolubly bound together, and there begins the process of national formation – the transformation of the population into a national community on its national territory under the influence of the circumstances afforded by this territory.'[108]

Hrushevsky's search for the ancestors of modern Ukrainians among the Slavs led him to believe that the first 'ethno-political group' that should be viewed as a direct ancestor of the Ukrainian tribes was the Antes (Antae). This was a tribal alliance that occupied the northern Black Sea region from the Danube in the west to the Sea of Azov in the east between the fourth and seventh centuries A.D. It is known that in 385 the Antes were defeated by the Goths. They were known to Byzantine authors of the sixth and seventh centuries as one of the barbarian peoples in the northern borderlands of the empire. The Antes disappeared from Byzantine view in the early seventh century and were most likely wiped out by the Avars, who established their rule over the territory in the seventh century.[109]

Discussions concerning the ethnicity of the Antes continue to this day, with some authors arguing their Alano-Iranian or Gothic descent. Nevertheless, as in Hrushevsky's time, most scholars believe that the Antes were of Slavic origin.[110] The strongest support for that theory comes from the first direct reference to the Antes in historical sources. Jordanes, the author of *De origine actibusque Getarum* (551), referred to the Antes as an entity that together with the Sclaveni constituted a *natio* called the Veneti, a name that at the time was reserved for the Slavs.[111] In the 1830s a German scholar, Kaspar Zeuss, proposed a hypothesis according to which the Sclaveni of Jordanes were regarded as Western Slavs, while the Antes were considered to be a combination of Eastern ('Russian') and Southern Slavs.[112] Between the 1860s and 1880s, a number of Russian scholars attempted to link the Antes with one of the East Slavic tribes. Aleksandr Gilferding, Iosif Pervolf, and Dmitrii Ilovaisky all saw the Antes as ancestors of the Viatichians,[113] a northeastern East Slavic tribe that settled the basin of the Oka River. Evgenii Golubinsky considered them ancestors of the southern tribes of Ulychians and Tivertsians.[114] These hypotheses were criticized by a German scholar, Gregor Krek, who 'improved' Zeuss's old theory by suggesting that the Antes were Eastern ('Russian') Slavs.[115] Some scholars regarded the Antes primarily as a political as opposed to an ethno-political alliance.

This view, first introduced in the 1870s by the Russian historian Arist Kunik, met with little support, mainly because Kunik's speculation that the Antes were an Asian dynasty was based on no evidence at all.[116]

Hrushevsky was well versed in the historiography of the Antes problem and presented his views on it in an article titled 'The Antes' (1898) and in volume 1 of his academic *History*.[117] He rejected Kunik's theory as contradicting the account of Prokopios, who claimed that the Antes were governed not by authoritarian rulers but by a popular assembly. He also rejected a linguistically based hypothesis that linked the Antes with the Viatichians, as he found its argument questionable. Instead, as a starting point for his discussion, Hrushevsky accepted the view advanced by Krek, who regarded the Antes as Eastern Slavs. Hrushevsky found Krek's hypothesis particularly convincing, given that the Southern Slavs of Moesia and Pannonia were known as 'Sclaveni' and could not have belonged to the Antes group. 'Therefore, the Antes could only have been the eastern group, though not necessarily all of it, since we do not know how far north the Antes name reached,' wrote Hrushevsky. 'In theory, it may have encompassed all the East Slavic tribes, but in our references we encounter the name only in connection with events and circumstances that bear on the southern, Black Sea colonization of the East Slavic branch.'[118]

This conclusion of Hrushevsky's, based on the accounts of Byzantine authors, who indeed reported on activities of the Antes only in the Black Sea region, corresponded to Pavel Šafařík's earlier observation that it was unknown how far north the territory of the Antes extended and came very close to Golubinsky's theory that the Ulychians and Tivertsians were descended from the Antes. Hrushevsky referred to Šafařík's observation in his discussion of the issue but rejected Golubinsky's theory as unsubstantiated, noting the lack of evidence that Ulychian and Tivertsian settlements had covered the whole area originally populated by the Antes. In his article of 1898, Hrushevsky asked: 'Why was it these two particular Rus' peoples that joined together under one general name?' For Hrushevsky, the Ulychians and Tivertsians alone made little sense as descendants of the Antes but could be viewed as such in conjunction with the Siverianians.[119]

Why, we may ask in turn, did this combination of tribes make more sense to Hrushevsky than the two tribes suggested by Golubinsky? The answer to this question was provided by Hrushevsky in the following statement: 'The Antes are not the northern-eastern-southern branch of Slavdom but the southern part of its north-eastern division – those tribes that comprised the ethnic group known today as the Ukrainian-Rus' people.'[120] Apparently, in Hrushevsky's opinion, the Siverianians, Ulychians, and Tivertsians had more reason to be together as the nucleus of the future Ukrainian nation than the Ulychians and Tivertsians on their own. The essence and novelty of Hrushevsky's approach to the Antes issue was his introduction of the national factor into the discussion. According to his logic, not only did the national narrative of Ukrainian history find its starting point in the Antes union, but the composition of the union could be defined on the basis of subsequent ethnic affinity. Siverianians and other 'proven' ancestors of the Ukrainians had to be counted in, while the Viatichians, as 'proven' ancestors of the Russians, had to be excluded from the union.

Why, then, one might ask, did Hrushevsky leave other proto-Ukrainian tribes out of the list of direct heirs of the Antes, limiting it to the Ulychians, Tivertsians, and Siverianians? An answer to this question may be found in the fact that the settlements of most other proto-Ukrainian tribes were too far north and west to be considered parts of the area originally inhabited by the Antes. The Polianians, who settled southwest of the Siverianians, constituted the only exception but were excluded from Hrushevsky's list, apparently because their 'Ukrainian' character was disputed at the time by some Russian scholars. In new editions of the first volume of the *History*, as opposed to his article of 1898, Hrushevsky felt it best not to name specific tribes at all, presenting the Antes as ancestors of Ukrainian tribes in general.[121] He summarized his argument as follows: 'Everything points to this identification of the Antes with the ancestors of our people and endows it with a probability that verges on certainty.'[122]

Not surprisingly, Hrushevsky's attempt to claim the Antes exclusively for Ukrainian history provoked strong criticism on the part of Russian scholars. The earliest reaction to Hrushevsky's 'Ukrainization' of the Antes came from Aleksandr Pogodin, whose study *From the History of Slavic Migrations* (1901) advanced the theory of the East Slavic origins of the Antes.[123] Pogodin's interpretation of the ethnic origins of the Antes was followed by Aleksei Shakhmatov, who discussed the issue in the context of his search for the ancestral homeland of the Slavs in general. In his *Introduction to a Course on the History of the Russian Language* (1916), Shakhmatov stated that 'Sclaveni' was a term traditionally applied to the Southern Slavs, while the Eastern Slavs (he used this term interchangeably with 'Russians') were known to Byzantine authors as the Antes. Shakhmatov offered no specific argument to support his treatment of the Antes as Russians. Instead, after a two-paragraph review of what was known about the Antes from historical sources, he made the following assertion: 'The relation of the Slovenes to the Antes, their mutual geographic location, common descent, and subsequent dispersion – all this seems to me to provide irrefutable proof of the above-mentioned identification of the Slovenes with the ancestors of the Southern Slavs and of the Antes with the ancestors of the Eastern Slavs, that is, the Russians. The history of the Russian people should therefore begin with the sparse data preserved for us by the historical sources about the Antes.'[124]

In effect, Shakhmatov accepted Hrushevsky's 'nationalization' of the Antes but did so on behalf of the 'all-Russian' nation, not the Ukrainian one. If Hrushevsky treated the history of the Antes as the starting point of the history of the Ukrainian people, Shakhmatov regarded it as the beginning of 'Russian' (East Slavic) history. This approach was developed in his subsequent publications. In his monograph of 1919, *The Most Ancient Destinies of the Russian Tribe*,[125] Shakhmatov disagreed with Hrushevsky's interpretation of the Antes' history, claiming that the division of the 'Russian tribe' had occurred not before but after the Antes' arrival in 'Southern Russia.' He continued to regard the Antes as 'ancestors of the Russian tribe as a whole.' Responding to this argument in 1926, after Shakhmatov's death, Hrushevsky presented it as an example of a priori thinking. He noted Shakhmatov's treatment of his own hypothetical suggestions as established facts and commented: 'Being familiar with the late scholar's professional style, exceedingly rapid in proposing scholarly hypotheses and in unceasingly reworking and changing them in connection with the new ideas produced by his prolifically creative intellect, one might think that over the seven or eight years that have gone by since the publication of these works, he himself would have made a variety of changes to them.'[126]

Hrushevsky believed that one of the requirements for the formation of a people was its settlement and continuing existence on a compact territory. He was therefore especially (and critically) attentive to Shakhmatov's attempts to identify such a homeland for the 'all-Russian' people. He claimed that Shakhmatov had developed his hypothesis on Slavic migration under the influence of the events of the First World War, with an eye to the theory of the existence in ancient times of a united Russian people and one Russian statehood. Hrushevsky ridiculed Shakhmatov's theory of Slavic migration, pointing to its hidden agenda of carving out a separate homeland for the Eastern Slavs:

'That is why [Shakhmatov] conjures up the fantastic journey of this
Russian people around Kyiv (from the Baltic Sea to the mouth of the
Danube, from there to Volhynia, from Volhynia to the Dnipro, and from
beyond the Dnipro back to the Baltic region), which resembles nothing
so much as the wanderings of the Hebrew people in the Arabian desert
under the leadership of the prophet Moses.'[127]

Shakhmatov's interpretation of the Antes issue was rejected not only
by Hrushevsky but also by one of the foremost authorities in Slavic
history and ethnology, the Czech scholar Lubor Niederle. In 1910
Niederle published an article on the history of the Antes that became
the basis for his discussion of the Antes problem in his later studies on
the history of the Slavs. These included the first volume of Niederle's
Manuel de l'antiquité slave (1923) and the volume of his *Slavic Antiquities*
devoted to the history of the Eastern Slavs (1924). In the dispute between Hrushevsky on the one hand and Pogodin and Shakhmatov on
the other, Niederle took an intermediate position. He claimed to reject
both Pogodin's and Shakhmatov's views of the Antes as Eastern Slavs
in general and Hrushevsky's treatment of the Antean state as a precur-
sor of Kyivan Rus'. Niederle believed that the Antes constituted a
temporary political union of a number of 'South Russian' tribes. His
position was identical to the one developed by Hrushevsky, the sole
exception being that Niederle refused to identify the Antes with the
ancestors of the Ukrainians. In his *Manuel de l'antiquité slave*, Niederle
underscored this view by asserting that the Antes were not Ukrainians, as no such people had existed between the fourth and eleventh
centuries.[128]

A year later, in the volume of *Slavic Antiquities* specifically devoted to
the history and ethnology of the Eastern Slavs, Niederle advanced this
argument even further, but this time he limited the period in which a
separate Little Russian/Ukrainian people could not exist to the fourth-
seventh centuries. 'This was not a distinct Slavic people, "Little Russian" or "Ukrainian" in the sense of the more recent Ukrainian theories,'
wrote Niederle. 'Between the fourth and seventh centuries, there was as
yet no such people here. There were only a few South Russian tribes
associated for some time as a political entity. The Antean alliance cannot be considered Little Russian in the national sense of the word, as we
do not know whether all of Shakhmatov's[129] Little Russian branch
constituted it, and, in the second place, this was only a temporary
political alliance ... of South Russian tribes grouped around a large
centre comparable to the one that was beginning to be established in

Novgorod the Great in the north, in Halych (among the Croats) in the west, and on the Oka in Riazan.'[130]

In reacting to this critique, Hrushevsky maintained that Niederle's interpretation of the Antes issue in his article of 1910 introduced no new elements that could challenge his own account of Antean history. Hrushevsky also believed that Niederle took essentially the same position on the composition of the Antean union (limiting it to the southern branch of the East Slavic tribes) as he did and that Niederle's critique of his reading of the issue was little more than a misunderstanding.[131] Indeed, Niederle's critique of Hrushevsky did not challenge the core of his scholarly argument. Niederle's characterization of Hrushevsky as a proponent of the idea that Kyivan Rus' was in fact an Antean state was based on a passing remark of Hrushevsky's in the conclusion to his article of 1898. There Hrushevsky indeed referred to Kyivan Rus' as a state of the Antes while making a point about the continuity of international politics in the area.[132] This was clearly an overstatement, and Hrushevsky not only avoided such comparisons in his subsequent publications but also claimed that he had never considered the Antes anything but a pre-Kyivan entity.[133]

Apparently in order to avoid provoking his critics even further, in his Russian-language publications Hrushevsky replaced references to the Antes as Ukrainian tribes with references to them as South Russian tribes. That was the case with the Russian translation of the first volume of Hrushevsky's *History*, published in 1911 under the title *Kievskaia Rus'*. There Hrushevsky removed all references to the Antes as ancestors of the Ukrainians, replacing the terms 'Ruthenian' and 'Ukrainian' with 'South Russian' and 'Southern East Slavic.' As a result, the passage that in volume 1 of the *History* read 'All this, I say, makes it certain, it might be said, that in the Antes we have the ancestors of the Ukrainian tribes' was rendered in Russian translation as 'All this, I repeat, makes it certain, it might be said, that in the Antes we have the ancestors of the later South Russian tribes.' The passage 'The identity thus established between the Antes and the Ukrainian tribes reveals to us a number of facts about the earliest history of their colonization' from the *History* was rendered as 'The identity thus established between the Antes and the southern East Slavic tribes reveals to us a number of facts about the history of their early colonization.'[134]

Indeed, there was no difference between Niederle's approach and Hrushevsky's interpretation of the Antes issue in his Russian-language book on Kyivan Rus', but Niederle, who knew and cited that book, preferred to overlook this change in terminology and continued to criticize Hrushevsky instead of admitting the latter's priority in identifying the Antes as southern tribes of East Slavic origin. Hrushevsky believed that Niederle's critique of his interpretation of Antean history was politically motivated. In his critical review of Niederle's *Manuel de l'antiquité slave*, Hrushevsky presented Niederle's position on the Antes issue as a manifestation of his concern about 'the undermining of Russian unity.' He supported this statement with a reference to the concluding remarks of Niederle's book, in which the author claimed that Great, Little, and White Russia had always been and still remained parts of one nation, and even if they were to become autonomous in the future, they would still remain constituents of a single nation and, it was to be hoped, of a united Russian state.[135]

After 1917 Hrushevsky's critique of Niederle's political viewpoint provoked a response from Russian émigré circles. An author known only under the initials E.K. published an article in the Russian émigré newspaper *Vozrozhdenie* (Rebirth) titled 'M. Hrushevsky versus L. Niederle,' in which he branded Hrushevsky a 'headlong separatist' whose attack on the 'great Slavist' Niederle was termed 'the extreme of crudity and savagery.' The anonymous author characterized Niederle's concluding passage on the unity of the three East Slavic peoples as 'words to which a Russian has decidedly nothing to add.'[136] In 1925, reviewing Niederle's *Slavic Antiquities*, Hrushevsky responded to this Russian émigré attack as follows: 'I consider it superfluous to justify my right to make a critical assessment of the research of a Czech Slavist whose work I have followed closely for thirty years, and it is highly likely that I can assess its strong and weak points no worse than the anonymous author. But I think it impossible to overlook this small but characteristic illustration of where Professor Niederle's all-Russian declarations find their supporters – declarations with which he spoils his scholarly works in the eyes of every serious scholar and with which he has been unable to dispense in this new book of his.'[137] In his review Hrushevsky specifically mentioned Niederle's statement that in his opinion, Ukraine and Russia would remain united in the future, and those who wanted to divide the two 'Russian' peoples would also seek to divide the Czechs and Slovaks. 'This may be a highly apt ad hominem argument to use on the Czech reader – if he recognizes Ukraine's right to self-determination, then by the same token he must recognize it for Slovakia – but such politicking creates an unpleasant impression in a book that aspires to take the place of Šafařík's great work for present-day Slavdom,' wrote Hrushevsky.[138]

Returning to his differences with Niederle in an article of 1926 on the early history of the Kyiv region, Hrushevsky once again stressed the similarities between his and Niederle's approaches to the history of the Antes. 'Whether one calls it "Ukrainian," "Little Russian," or "South Russian,"' wrote Hrushevsky in regard to their disagreements, 'is a matter of taste, for all the names are anachronistic. In calling it "South Russian," Niederle also falls into anachronism, as he considers the name of Rus' to be no older than the ninth century in Ukraine.'[139] As is apparent from this quotation, Hrushevsky remained a staunch opponent of Shakhmatov's efforts to characterize the Antes as representatives of one 'all-Russian' people and continued to view them as ancestors of the Ukrainian nation, but the admission that calling the Antean union 'Ukrainian' was as much an anachronism as their identification with the 'South Russians' was an indication of Hrushevsky's increasing caution on the issue.

The development of the debate on the ethno-cultural identity of the Antes after the publication of Hrushevsky's article of 1898 was profoundly influenced by early twentieth-century political polemics between proponents of 'all-Russian' and Ukrainian identity. It was also informed by conflicting views on whether one 'all-Russian' nationality or separate 'Great Russian' and 'Little Russian' ones took historical precedence in East Slavic history. Moreover, the demarcation of national histories was based not only on debates over the inclusion of particular episodes in the historical narrative of one nation or another but also on efforts to exclude or marginalize such episodes, or indeed whole epochs in the histories of peoples or ethnic groups, when constructing national paradigms. If Hrushevsky's position on the ethnic origins of the Antes represented a case of inclusion, his stand on the role of the Normans/Norsemen/Varangians represented a case of exclusion of a major historical actor from (or, more precisely, marginalization within) the national historical paradigm.

The issue of the origins of the Rus' state was one of the most important problems discussed in Russian historiography of the eighteenth and nineteenth centuries. Was the Rus' state and dynasty 'Russian' or Varangian, meaning 'Germanic'? It was in debates on these questions that imperial historiography first acquired national characteristics and began to construct its narrative in opposition to the West. As the concept of modern national identity challenged the imperial Russian narrative, it became necessary to revisit the Varangian issue. For Hrushevsky, the answer to this 'accursed' question of Russian history was no longer limited to the 'Russian' and 'Germanic' options but included a Ukrainian option as well. The Ukrainian national narrative inherited the Varangian problem from the Russian imperial narrative and responded to it within the framework created by its predecessor. The choice between foreign and native founders of Rus' pitted Normanists against anti-Normanists, and Hrushevsky made a clear choice in favour of the natives, whom he took to be Ukrainians. Thus he emerged in his scholarly works as a staunch anti-Normanist. By taking a stand on the Varangian issue, Hrushevsky was entering an already crowded field of historical polemics between the Normanists and the anti-Normanists – those who believed in the Norman origins of the Rus' princely dynasty and credited the Norsemen with the creation of the Rus' state and legal system and those who denied them such a role, arguing the local origins of the dynasty, state, and name of the nation.

The origins of the Normanist controversy, which are closely associated with the origins of historical scholarship in the Russian Empire, go back to the eighteenth century. Gottlieb Siegfried Bayer, a founder of Russian historiography as a scholarly discipline, is also considered the father of Normanism. His views on the role of the Normans in early Rus' history were accepted and further developed by a number of scholars, mostly of Central European origin, who belonged to the Russian Academy of Sciences. Among them were Stroube de Piermont, G.F. Müller, and August Schlözer. A paper on old Russian history read by Müller in 1749 provoked a strong critical response from a scholar of Russian origin, Mikhail Lomonosov. From that time the discussion of the role of the Norsemen in the history of Rus' has had clear political overtones, since Russian scholars have viewed it as a struggle against the alleged attempts of Western scholars to deny Russians/Eastern Slavs credit for creating their own state. That tendency in the interpretation of the role of the Normans in Russian history became firmly established in Russian scholarship, notwithstanding the fact that such prominent Russian historians as Karamzin and Mikhail Pogodin supported the Normanist theory, while such non-Russian scholars as Gustav Ewers were among its staunchest opponents.[140]

Among Ukrainian historians the first to take part in the Normanist debate was Mykhailo Maksymovych, followed by Mykola Kostomarov. Both were anti-Normanists in the sense that they believed in the Slavic origins of the Rus' state. For both of them, as for all anti-Normanists, one of the most difficult aspects of the problem was the interpretation of the account in the Primary Chronicle (the earliest of the Rus' annals) of the invitation issued to the Varangians by the Novgorodians in the ninth century and the chronicler's belief in the Varangian origins not only of the Kyivan dynasty but of the Rus' name itself. References to the chronicle account were among the arguments most often employed by the Normanists, and opponents of their view had to deal with that account in one way or another. Maksymovych and another scholar of Ukrainian origin, Iurii Venelin (Gutsa), questioned the Scandinavian ethnic origin of the Varangians of the Primary Chronicle, arguing that the Varangians invited by the Novgorodians were in fact Baltic Slavs.[141] Kostomarov, for his part, traced the origins of the Rus'/Varangians to Lithuania but later abandoned that theory.[142]

Given the position taken in the Normanist debate by Maksymovych and Kostomarov, one might claim that Hrushevsky continued the established tradition of Ukrainian historiography, although he did so in a new and much more sophisticated way. In his interpretation of the origins of the Kyivan state, Hrushevsky subscribed in many respects to the theory advanced in the 1870s by none other than Dmitrii Ilovaisky, whose textbooks on Russian history were among the most important vehicles promoting the idea of the unity of the 'Russian' people. In the 1870s, Ilovaisky published a number of anti-Normanist articles. He pressed the attack in his later publications, as well as in his general course on Russian history.[143] Hrushevsky, while sharing Ilovaisky's general approach to the issue, was quite critical of his scholarly qualifications, considering him rather superficial in argumentation. 'To be sure,' wrote Hrushevsky, 'the anti-Normanists may often have wished for a less energetic but more cautious advocate. The philology with which Ilovaisky hoped to counter the Normanists' philology was often appalling, his research methods were very weak, and he slashed through rather than resolved questions.'[144]

Nevertheless, Ilovaisky introduced two important elements into the Normanist dispute that were later followed up and developed by Hrushevsky. The first was Ilovaisky's rejection of the Primary Chronicle's account of the invitation to the Varangians as unreliable. The second was the development of a theory according to which the name of Rus' belonged not to the Varangians but to the Kyivan Polianians, who established the Rus' state and gave their name to it, as well as to its population. In the first instance, Hrushevsky gave Ilovaisky full credit, also noting the influence on his writings of ideas initially expressed by Mikhail Kachenovsky and Stepan Gedeonov.[145] In the second case, Hrushevsky avoided mentioning Ilovaisky, although his own interpretation of the history of Kyivan Rus' as a state built by the Polianians closely resembled Ilovaisky's views. Hrushevsky's silence on the matter is at least partly to be explained by the fact that he used his hypothesis about the dominant role of the Polianians as a basis for advancing an exclusive Ukrainian claim to the history of Kyivan Rus' – a claim that challenged and deconstructed Ilovaisky's vision of the Russian past as the history of one Russian people.[146]

Hrushevsky gave an extensive historiographic survey of the Normanist dispute in one of the excursuses to the text of volume 1 of his academic *History*. There Hrushevsky analysed the pros and cons of the Normanists' arguments. He explained away the Varangian origins of the names of Rus' warriors by accepting that there were indeed many Varangians in the service of the Rus' princes and among the Rus' merchant class. In Hrushevsky's opinion it was those newcomers to the Rus' lands who could easily create the impression among neighbouring peoples that the Rus' were generally of Swedish origin. That is how he explained the reference to the Swedish origins of the Rus' in the Annales Bertiniani, the Norse origins of the Rus' names of the Dnipro Rapids recorded by Constantine Porphyrogennetos, and the Scandinavian origin of the names of Rus' representatives listed in their treaties of 911 and 944 with Byzantium. Hrushevsky considered the origins of the name 'Rus" to be the Achilles' heel of the Normanist theory. He ridiculed the notion that the Swedes, known to the Finns as 'Ruotsi,' would abandon their own name and accept someone else's appellation as their own. He also claimed that the Kyiv area was known as 'Rus" long before Riurik was even born.[147]

Especially important for Hrushevsky's anti-Normanist argument was his research on the composition and textual history of the Primary Chronicle – a subject to which he devoted the second of the two excursuses to volume 1 of his *History*. There Hrushevsky drew inspiration and critical zeal from the works of Aleksei Shakhmatov, the leading authority on the study of the Rus' chronicles and a Normanist par excellence. Shakhmatov revolutionized the study of the Primary Chronicle by reconstructing its oldest version from the text of the second redaction of the Novgorod I Chronicle.[148] This and other discoveries and hypotheses of Shakhmatov's profoundly affected Hrushevsky's own research on chronicle-writing in Rus', regardless of whether he followed Shakhmatov's lead or rejected it. One of Shakhmatov's theories that met with criticism from Hrushevsky was his assumption that the 'Oldest Kyivan Compilation,' which allegedly served as the basis for the earliest accounts in the Primary Chronicle, came into existence

ca. 1037. Hrushevsky noted the problems associated with that particular interpretation of the chronicle text and suggested that the earliest
redaction of the Primary Chronicle stopped before 1037. He also disagreed with Shakhmatov's identification of Nestor the Chronicler with
Nestor the Hagiographer and suggested the important role played in
the editing of the chronicle by Sylvestr, the hegumen of the Kyiv
Vydubychi Monastery.[149] Major points made by Hrushevsky undermined the Normanists' acceptance of the Primary Chronicle as a reliable historical source. They also proved valid from the scholarly
viewpoint, as many of them were further developed by students of
Kyivan chronicle-writing in the 1920s and 1930s.[150]

One of the main hypotheses proposed by Hrushevsky in the course of
his research on the Primary Chronicle was his suggestion that the
chronicle was composed by a number of authors/editors over a period
of some sixty years and had undergone a number of revisions in the
process. Not by accident, Hrushevsky used the Primary Chronicle's
account of the invitation to the Varangians to explain the nature of those
revisions. 'The story of the invitation of the Varangian princes to Rus',
as compared with the short account in the older redaction,' wrote
Hrushevsky, 'has been expanded to support the Normanist theory – for
example, after the words "they went overseas to the Varangians," the
chronicler added, "For it is so that these Varangians were called Rus', as
[now] others are called Swedes, and others Northmen ..." etc., as well
as the very telling addition, "they took with them all the Rus'."'[151]
Hrushevsky also noted several more instances, indicating that the original version of the chronicle was subsequently revised to support or
accommodate the theory of the Norman origins of the Kyivan princely
dynasty. The message to the reader was very clear: the Primary Chronicle
in general and its account of the invitation to the Varangians was a
construct of later times, and arguments advanced by proponents of the
Normanist theory based upon it could not be taken at face value. Thus
Hrushevsky sought to establish 'reasonable doubt' about the chronicle
version of the Varangian story.

In volume 1 of his academic *History*, Hrushevsky presented the
Normanist theory of the origins of the princely dynasty as only one of
the many legends that circulated in Kyiv around the time of the composition of the Primary Chronicle. Competing with that legend, in
Hrushevsky's opinion, was a story about the founding of Kyiv by the
three Polianian brothers Kyi, Shchek, and Khoryv and their sister Lybid;
the story about Kyi's ferry on Dnipro, which allegedly gave its name to

the city; and the Novgorodian legend based on the story of the conquest of Kyiv by the Novgorod Varangians, which served the purposes of advancing Novgorodian interests and defending Novgorod's autonomy within the Kyivan state. In Hrushevsky's opinion there were several factors that facilitated the rise to prominence of the Varangian theory over all other Kyivan legends. These included the tradition of the Varangian conquest in Northern Rus', the prominent role played by the Varangians in Kyiv in the tenth and eleventh centuries, and the early acceptance by the Varangians of the local name of 'Rus'.'[152]

Many of the points made by Hrushevsky in his attack on the Normanist theory proved valid and were accepted by the new generation of students of Kyivan Rus'.[153] The survey of the Normanist controversy that appeared as an excursus in volume 1 of his *History* was particularly useful, as it summed up the Normanist debate at a time when historical and linguistic arguments were giving way to arguments based predominantly on archaeological material.[154] But not all of Hrushevsky's assumptions stood the test of time. Among the latter was Hrushevsky's belief in the Slavic origins of the names of some of the first Kyivan princes, including Princes Oleh and Ihor and Princess Olha. Hrushevsky rejected the Normanist identification of these names with the Scandinavian names Helgi, Inger, and Elga, but his own attempts to find Slavic roots for them were less than successful. In his excursus on the Normanist theory, Hrushevsky simply avoided the issue. Commenting on the origins of the names of Rus' representatives listed in the diplomatic treaties with Byzantium, he wrote: 'The names in the treaties attest that in the first half of the tenth century, in particular, there were very many Varangians in the prince's senior retinue. The names of the Kyivan princes present a somewhat less clear picture. The Normanists derive them from Scandinavian roots, but their Scandinavianism is not so certain.'[155]

Hrushevsky's attempt to derive the names of the first Kyivan princes from Slavic roots met with strong opposition from the Polish philologist and cultural historian Aleksander Brückner, who reviewed the German translation of volume 1 of the *History* (1906).[156] Brückner was a convinced Normanist, and while lauding Hrushevsky's historical erudition, he severely criticized the latter's arguments against Normanism. In his critique of Hrushevsky, Brückner often assumed a paternalistic and condescending tone, deriding the anti-Normanist scholarly trend as a 'heresy.' He described Lomonosov, Ilovaisky, and Hrushevsky (all anti-Normanists) as philological dilettantes and characterized the philology of Ilovaisky and Kostomarov as 'Mongol-Cossack.' To be fair to Brückner, it should be noted that he meted out similar treatment to some proponents of the Normanist theory. Mikhail Pogodin, for example, was characterized as an individual 'from under a dark star, in whom only *reliability* [loyalty to the regime] functioned instead of a brain.' As an authority on Slavic literature and linguistics, Brückner focused his main attention on the linguistic side of the Normanist debate. 'If Swedish names appeared only among the retinue, we could still manage to reckon with that subterfuge,' wrote Brückner about Hrushevsky's claim that the Norse names of Rus' warriors were to be explained by the large number of Varangians in the service of the Kyivan princes, 'but what are we to do with the fact that the princes themselves, from Riurik to Ihor, all have Swedish names – or were they, too, in the service of the Slavs? Naturally, in the face of this fact, all subterfuges are useless, and nothing remains but to deny the fact itself and assert that the names of the ruling princes are not Swedish. Here the author comes to grief because he is not a philologist.'[157] When it came to history, Brückner was a specialist neither in Kyivan Rus' in general nor in the Normanist issue in particular. Consequently, he tended to counter Hrushevsky's arguments not with conclusions based on his own research but with standard Normanist postulates and clichés.

Why did Hrushevsky put his scholarly reputation on the line in order to defend some of the most controversial elements of the anti-Normanist view, and why did he join the anti-Normanist camp in the first place? The answer to the latter question was provided by Hrushevsky himself in his excursus on the Normanist theory. There he wrote: 'Yet, whereas accusing the Normanists of a "German plot" is absurd, the charge that Normanism was harmful to the investigation of Rus' history is quite just. The "clear and simple" Normanist legend obscured the beginnings of the sociopolitical life of Rus' before 862. It relieved the historian of the need to search for traces of social evolution within the people themselves, because history began "in a vacuum" – from the arrival of the Northmen.' 'These distortions,' continued Hrushevsky, referring to the impact of the Normanist theory on Russian historiography, 'went much deeper – to the very heart of things. Given its unprecedented beginnings, the history of Rus' differed fundamentally from the history of other peoples. Universal laws of evolution could not be applied to Rus', as M. Pogodin clearly stated in the introduction to his *Drevniaia rossiiskaia istoriia do Mongol'skogo iga* ([Ancient Russian History to the Mongol Yoke], 1871). This gave birth to the Slavophile theory that political rights had been renounced and that there had been no struggle in the history of Rus', the theory of the age-old passivity of the Slavic ethnos and its need for foreign creative elements.'[158]

As a strong proponent of the study of the socio-political history of the Rus', Hrushevsky needed no deus ex machina to explain the origins of the Rus' state, law, and social order. He also believed in the applicability of universal laws to Rus' history and did not consider the Slavs inferior to their western and northern neighbours. There was also another factor that could not but influence Hrushevsky's stand on the Normanist issue. That factor was Hrushevsky's own scheme of Ukrainian history, which began with the history of the territory, proceeded to the history of the Antes as the first Ukrainian ethnic and political entity, and then turned to the history of the Kyivan state, created by the Ukrainian tribe of the Rus'/Polianians. There was no place in that nationally inspired narrative for the Varangians or for a state established by them.

As noted earlier, Hrushevsky's treatment of the Polianians as the original bearers of the name of Rus' and as founders and masters of the Rus' state finds parallels in the views of another prominent anti-Normanist, Dmitrii Ilovaisky. The latter's anti-Normanism was also inspired by the belief that the Eastern Slavs needed no northern assistance in the development of their state, society, and culture. As Ilovaisky himself noted in that regard, 'It was not from impoverished, half-savage Scandinavia that the seeds of civilization penetrated Russia at the time, but rather the other way around, from Rus' into Scandinavia.'[159] Ilovaisky's belief in the special role of the Polianians in establishing the Kyivan state fitted well into his general scheme of the Russian past as a history of the tripartite Russian nation. It fitted Hrushevsky's paradigm of Ukrainian history even better. The difference between Hrushevsky's and Ilovaisky's approaches lay in the fact that while agreeing to elevate the Polianians to the status of creators of the Kyivan Rus' state, they could not agree on which nation should be credited for that accomplishment, the tripartite Russian people or the Ukrainians.

The Contest for Kyivan Rus'

The question of who had the better claim to Kyivan Rus', the Russians or the Ukrainians, was crucial to Hrushevsky's attempt to deconstruct the Russian imperial paradigm. In many ways, Hrushevsky's answer to that question defined his image and that of his historical paradigm in the eyes of his contemporaries, and even more so in the eyes of future generations of scholars. It should be noted nevertheless that Hrushevsky was a relatively late arrival to a debate that had originated in the mid-nineteenth century.[160]

The debate itself began as a reaction to the writings of Mikhail Pogodin, the author of the theory of Great Russian outmigration from the Kyivan Land to the northeast in the aftermath of the Mongol invasion. In the 1840s Pogodin accepted the view advanced by Mykhailo Maksymovych that treated the Polianians as a Little Russian tribe.[161] As a result Pogodin regarded Kyivan Rus' history and culture as essentially 'Little Russian,' a designation he also applied to the Riurikid dynasty of the Kyivan period. He even declared the twelfth-century prince of Suzdal-Vladimir, Andrei Bogoliubsky, a 'Little Russian,' an assertion that drew critical remarks from none other than Maksymovych himself.[162] Indeed, Pogodin not only embraced the 'national' approach to the history of Kyivan Rus' but was prepared to advance the Ukrainian claim to its history further than the Ukrainians themselves. All that was about to change with the onset of official repression against the members of the Brotherhood of SS. Cyril and Methodius, which signalled the end of Pogodin's superficial Ukrainophilism.[163]

In the 1850s, while furthering his new political agenda of Rus' unity, Pogodin accepted a theory advanced by the philologists Izmail Sreznevsky and Petr Lavrovsky, who claimed that Kyivan Rus' literary monuments were written in a language much closer to Great Russian than to Ukrainian (Little Russian).[164] In a letter to Sreznevsky written in 1851 and published in 1856, Pogodin suggested a theory that would later bear his name. According to this theory, the Kyivan Land was originally populated by Great Russian tribes that migrated to the northeast after the Mongol invasion, taking with them their language, culture, and political system, while the Kyiv region was later repopulated by Little Russian migrants from the west.[165] Pogodin's hypothesis drew an enthusiastic response from Russian scholars and literary figures, including Ivan Aksakov, who wrote to Pogodin: 'I have thought much the same about the Little Russians for some time, though I trace the origins of the *khokhols* [Ukrainians] to Tmutarakan.'[166] It was more difficult to prove the soundness of Pogodin's theory to the *khokhols* themselves. The first to protest against Pogodin's attempt to deny Ukrainians all rights to Kyivan Rus' was his friend of many years, Mykhailo Maksymovych.[167] As Pogodin's theory was based primarily on a linguistic argument, linguistics along with history became the major battleground between Pogodin and his supporters on the one hand and Maksymovych and his followers on the other. Eventually, in order to shield himself from Maksymovych's criticism of his linguistic argumentation, Pogodin was obliged to admit that he was not a specialist in philology. At the same time, he was unable to come up with enough evidence to support his historical argument.[168]

The discussion unexpectedly gained a new stimulus in the 1880s, with the prominent Russian philologist Aleksei Sobolevsky raising his voice in defence of Pogodin's theory.[169] Almost immediately, Sobolevsky was countered by a number of Ukrainian historians and philologists who claimed that Pogodin's theory was mistaken, as there was little if any historical or philological evidence to support it.[170] The confrontation between proponents and critics of the Pogodin theory took the form of an exchange of papers at meetings of the Kyiv Historical Society of Nestor the Chronicler. Summaries of these papers, originally delivered in 1882, were published in Kyiv in the late 1880s, when Hrushevsky was beginning his scholarly career at Kyiv University under the supervision of Volodymyr Antonovych, who had participated in the debates.[171] It was on Antonovych's advice that Hrushevsky decided to work on the history of the Kyivan Land from the eleventh to the fourteenth century, a period exceptionally important for the debate on the Pogodin theory. As noted earlier, the work grew eventually into Hrushevsky's first monograph, *A Survey History of the Kyivan Land* (1891),[172] which established his name in Ukrainian and Russian scholarly circles. Thus Hrushevsky entered the historical profession in the ranks of the opponents of Pogodin's theory.

What were Hrushevsky's views concerning Pogodin's hypothesis, and what was his contribution to a scholarly debate that had been going on for more than thirty years, engaging some of the best names in the field, by the time Hrushevsky's first monograph was published? It should be noted that Hrushevsky discussed various aspects of the Pogodin theory not only in his *Survey History of the Kyivan Land* but also in a number of articles and reviews, as well as in volumes 1 and 3 of his academic *History*. Taken together, all these works give a good idea of the nature of Hrushevsky's contribution to the debate and make it possible to follow the evolution of his views on different aspects of the problem. Hrushevsky's contribution was most substantial in the historical discussion of Pogodin's hypothesis rather than in linguistic analysis, where he relied mainly on research done by others. As proponents of the Pogodin theory claimed that the language of the literary monuments of the Kyivan era was almost entirely free from the influence of Ukrainian dialects, Hrushevsky countered those statements with references to research suggesting that Kyivan literary works written in the eleventh century and later constituted a separate, Eastern Ukrainian corpus of East Slavic literature. Hrushevsky also suggested that the 'Kyivan literary school was not local in character, but one that encompassed people from various other centers, resulting in the emergence of a kind of common language, similar to the Greek koine.'[173]

Hrushevsky's historical critique of the Pogodin theory addressed three major issues. One was the question of the ethnic origins of the Rus' tribes of Polianians and Siverianians, who constituted the core of the Kyivan state. Another issue was the extent of Mongol destruction of the Kyivan Land, and whether it was severe enough to cause the depopulation of the area. The third question concerned the alleged exodus of population from the Polianian Land immediately after the Mongol invasion and its replacement at some later point by migrants from Western Ukraine.

When it comes to the ethnic origins of the Polianian and Siverianian tribes, Hrushevsky became a participant in the ongoing discussion of this issue in a somewhat unexpected manner. In the late 1890s he was asked his opinion about the ethnic origins of the Polianians by the Croatian philologist Vatroslav Jagić, a professor at the universities of St Petersburg and Vienna[174] and one of the best-qualified critics of Sobolevsky's theories. Jagić published Hrushevsky's response in one of his articles in which he asserted that there were no grounds to believe that the Polianians belonged to the Great Russian linguistic group. The essence of Hrushevsky's argument in his letter to Jagić was that the Polianians could not belong to an ethnic and language group different from that of the population that surrounded them in Right-Bank Ukraine.[175] Hrushevsky believed it was Jagić's stand that convinced his student Aleksei Shakhmatov, who had originally held that the Derevlianians, Polianians, and Siverianians were Great Russians, to drop the first two tribes from his list of speakers of Great Russian dialects.[176] Indeed, Shakhmatov's decision to abandon the theory of the Great Russian character of the Polianians spelled the end of one of the most powerful arguments advanced by proponents of the Pogodin theory. The battle was won but the war was far from over, as the question of the ethnicity of the Polianians' neighbours to the north and east, the Siverianians, soon became a major bone of contention between the two scholarly camps.

The hypothesis concerning the Great Russian origins of the Siverianians was supported by the authority of the same philologists who admitted the Ukrainian/Little Russian origins of the Polianians, namely, Jagić and Shakhmatov. The idea was first advanced by Jagić in the same article in which he accepted Hrushevsky's argument against the Great Russian character of the Polianians. As Jagić provided no evidence in support of his assertion, Hrushevsky believed, apparently not without reason, that Jagić was merely offering a compromise solution to proponents and opponents of the Pogodin theory. He was depriving the former of the Polianians while proffering them the Siverianians, who were also claimed by the latter. The Dnipro would emerge in this scheme of Jagić's as a boundary between the Great Russian and Ukrainian tribes.[177] Shakhmatov, who, as noted earlier, was among those who accepted Jagić's compromise, tried to provide at least some argumentation in support of the new theory. One of the arguments that he advanced was based on the troublesome history of relations between Kyiv and Chernihiv, the respective centres of the Polianian and Siverianian territories, which also served as centres of separate principalities. Shakhmatov believed that relations between Chernihiv and Kyiv were so troublesome because one was the centre of a Little Russian tribe and the other of a Great Russian one.[178]

Hrushevsky considered this argument of Shakhmatov's poor evidence of any ethnic differentiation between the Polianians and the Siverianians. He made reference to the history of Pereiaslav, another centre of the Siverianian Land that was often at odds with Chernihiv not because of ethnic animosity but because the Pereiaslav princes sought special relations with the Suzdal principality in their attempts to remain independent of Chernihiv. Hrushevsky's conclusion was that political divisions did not coincide with ethnic ones, as political considerations often contributed to carving separate entities out of ethnically homogeneous territories. Hrushevsky also countered Shakhmatov's 'political' argument with archaeological and linguistic data, asserting that the Polianian and Siverianian burials were barely distinguishable one from another, while there were significant differences between the burial types of the Siverianians and the Viatichians, ancestors of the Great Russians. Hrushevsky also supported his argument by noting the existence of archaic Ukrainian dialects in the Desna region, a territory settled by the Siverianians. Moreover, he rejected another of Shakhmatov's hypotheses that explained the Ukrainian presence in traditional Siverianian territories by the possible migration of the Right-

Bank Ukrainian population to that area. In an article of 1904, 'Contested Issues of Old Rus' Ethnography,' Hrushevsky demonstrated that there was no evidence whatever to support Shakhmatov's hypothesis.[179] Indeed, Shakhmatov eventually accepted most of Hrushevsky's arguments in one form or another. He first dropped his support for the theory of the Great Russian origins of the Siverianians (1907),[180] and then, in his *Introduction to a Course on the History of the Russian Language* (1916), identified the Siverianians as part of the 'southern group' of East Slavic tribes, assigning them a territory south of the Desna.[181]

In his article 'Chernihiv and the Siverian Land in Ukrainian History' (1927), Hrushevsky still disagreed with some of Shakhmatov's assertions and hypotheses, including the latter's belief that the Don region was originally settled by the Viatiachians, while territories to the north of the Desna were settled by the Derevlianians, but generally he celebrated a victory over his opponent on the issue of the ethnic origins of the Polianians and Siverianians.[182] Hrushevsky wrote about the problem as follows: 'Hypotheses on the Siverian Land's standing apart from the southern group of East Slavic tribes may be considered relegated to the archives since the appearance of Shakhmatov's above-mentioned book [the *Introduction*]. Just as in the late 1890s the new edition of his *Survey* meant the complete renunciation of the theory of Kyivan Great Russians, so this course of 1916 means the liquidation of the Great Russians of Chernihiv. Today the membership of the Siverian Land in the Ukrainian group no longer encounters any serious objections; the polemics of the 1900s have placed a cross over them, and any current doubts are a belated echo of an argument that is dead and buried.'[183]

The 'doubts' mentioned by Hrushevsky did not, of course, disappear overnight, as was apparent from Niederle's *Manuel de l'antiquité slave*. There Niederle counted the Polianians among the ancestors of the 'Little Russians,' while listing the Siverianians among the ancestors of the Great Russians. He made reference in that regard to Shakhmatov's article of 1899. Although Niederle noted that the Russian scholar had changed his mind and now regarded the Siverianians as part of the southern group of East Slavic tribes, he himself refused to change his position.[184] Some questions concerning Hrushevsky's theory were also raised by the Ukrainian scholar Volodymyr Parkhomenko, who reviewed his article of 1927 on the history of Chernihiv and the Siverian Land. Parkhomenko believed that the Polianians had come to Kyiv from the area north of the Sea of Azov and questioned anything that was not in accord with his view of the issue.[185] Basing his argument on

Hrushevsky's own observations concerning the rivalry between Chernihiv and Pereiaslav, he raised the question of whether Pereiaslav could have been settled by a tribe other than the Siverianians, indicating the possibility of Polianian settlement of the area. Parkhomenko also asked why scholars invariably linked Ukrainian dialects of the Desna area with Siverianian settlement when they could be linked with the Derevlianians.[186] In essence, Parkhomenko's questions challenged some of the premises of Hrushevsky's argument against Shakhmatov but did not undermine its basic rationale. The course of the discussion generally vindicated Hrushevsky's position: by the end of the 1920s theories of the Great Russian ethnicity of the Polianians and Siverianians had all but vanished.

As noted earlier, the second basic premise of the proponents of the Pogodin theory was a belief in the severe destruction of the Kyivan Land at the time of the Mongol invasion (1240), a development that allegedly caused the depopulation of the region and the migration of its inhabitants to the northeast. This belief in the devastation of the Kyivan Land to an extent unknown in other Rus' territories was first questioned and successfully refuted by Mykhailo Maksymovych. He challenged the relevance to the subject of two sources used by Pogodin to support his hypothesis. One was the account of the devastation of Ukrainian territories recorded by the author of the Suzdal Chronicle; the other consisted of the notes of Giovanni da Pian del Carpini, the pope's emissary to the Mongols, who visited Ukraine in 1245 and 1247.[187] In Maksymovych's opinion these accounts said nothing about outmigration, and while they indeed conveyed a picture of Mongol devastation of the area, there were no grounds to assert that it was more severe than that caused by the Mongol invasion of northeastern Rus', or that the towns destroyed by the invaders were not rebuilt in southern Rus' as they had been in the north-eastern portion of the former Kyivan state.[188]

Maksymovych's critique of Pogodin's historical argumentation was further developed by Antonovych. In his article of 1882 on the history of Kyiv between the fourteenth and sixteenth centuries, Antonovych devoted particular effort to a critical analysis of the reports on the Mongol invasion in the Rus' chronicles. After comparing the accounts in the Hypatian and Laurentian codices and the Voskresensk and Hustynia chronicles, as well as the description of the Mongol sack of Kyiv in the Kyivan *Synopsis* (1674), he concluded that the scope of the Mongol devastation had been vastly exaggerated by the authors and editors of the Rus' chronicles and other historical writings. Antonovych also noted the information provided by the same chronicles on the continuity of political, religious, and social life in Kyiv and the surrounding area in the decades following the invasion. He admitted the decline of Kyiv's political importance in the Mongol period but not the exodus of the Kyivan population – the crucial component of the Pogodin theory.[189]

When Hrushevsky entered the Pogodin debate with the publication of his book on the history of the Kyivan Land (1891),[190] he faced the very specific task of countering the arguments marshalled in defence of the Pogodin theory by one of its most outspoken and talented proponents, Aleksei Sobolevsky.[191] This linguist's numerous works on the ethnic origins of the Kyivan population appeared after the publication of Antonovych's essay of 1882 on the history of Kyiv, and it fell to Hrushevsky to respond to Sobolevsky's arguments. In his book Hrushevsky offered a brief review of Sobolevsky's linguistic hypothesis and made a number of critical comments about it but focused attention on Sobolevsky's historical arguments. In countering them, Hrushevsky divided the question of the Mongol devastation of the Dnipro region into two parts: the sack of the city of Kyiv and the alleged devastation of the Kyivan Land. Hrushevsky took the view that if the extent of Kyiv's destruction was arguable, there was no evidence whatever to suggest that the land as a whole had been so devastated as to prompt outmigration on a mass scale. In Hrushevsky's opinion, even the devastation of the city of Kyiv as a result of the invasion was grossly exaggerated by proponents of the Pogodin theory.

The sources most often cited by those proponents to establish the devastation of the Kyivan Land were the notes of Carpini and the Life of St Mykhail of Chernihiv, neither of which, in Hrushevsky's view, sufficed to prove their contention. Hrushevsky demonstrated that Carpini's account of Mongol destruction was in fact related not to the Kyivan Land but to Volhynia, while the picture of devastation presented by the author of the Life St Mykhail made no specific reference to the Kyivan Land but pertained to the general situation in all the Rus' lands attacked by the Mongols. Hrushevsky also objected to Sobolevsky's interpretation of the chronicle account of the return of Prince Mykhail from Poland to the Kyiv region after the Mongol attack and his subsequent stay on one of the islands in the vicinity of Kyiv. Sobolevsky treated that information as proof that Mykhail had nowhere to stay in Kyiv, as it had been completely destroyed. Hrushevsky responded that at least two earlier Kyivan princes had built their palaces on islands in the Kyiv area, as Prince Mykhail might also have done. Hrushevsky also rejected another argument adduced by Sobolevsky to demonstrate the complete devastation of Kyiv after the Mongol sack of the city. That argument was based on the chronicler's account of the Mongols sparing the life of the voevoda Dmytro (who was in charge of the defence of Kyiv) as an indication that all other inhabitants of Kyiv were massacred. With reference to Carpini's evidence, Hrushevsky argued that the Mongols generally killed all nobles and that the simple fact of their having spared Dmytro's life was worth noting by the chronicler, regardless of the fate of the rest of the Kyivan population.[192]

Even less credible, in Hrushevsky's opinion, was Sobolevsky's attempt to prove the alleged devastation of the whole of the Kyivan Land. Hrushevsky argued that none of the chronicles provided any information about its devastation, while the Volhynian Chronicle account held that after the sack of Kyiv the Mongols, led by Batu Khan, did not stay in the area but proceeded westward. Nor did Hrushevsky agree with Sobolevsky's suggestion that the Kyivan Land had suffered more from the invasion than the northeastern part of the Rus' realm. Sobolevsky made this claim on the basis that the population of the northeast could take shelter from the Mongols in the surrounding forests and found support for his hypothesis in chronicle accounts of the rapid revival of the Rostov territory after the Mongol invasion. Hrushevsky responded by pointing out that there was hardly any lack of forests in the Kyiv area and that there was no reason to consider the population of that territory any less resistant to the attacks of the Mongols than the population of the northeastern region.[193] The true reason for the lack of historical information on the return to normality in Kyiv and the surrounding area in the wake of the invasion was, in Hrushevsky's opinion, not the devastation of the land but the lack of a local chronicle recording developments in the region and taking note of the obvious political decline of Kyiv, which had begun long before the Mongol attack. According to Hrushevsky, the Mongol invasion disrupted links among the major centres of Kyivan Rus'. This led political centres that maintained their chronicle-writing to lose interest in Kyiv and the surrounding area, creating gaps in the accounts of its history.

Hrushevsky revisited the debate over the alleged devastation of the Kyivan Land in the third volume of his academic *History*, which was first published in 1900 and appeared in a second edition in 1905. There his treatment of the issue was less polemical, as he no longer considered it his major task to respond to the specific arguments made by Sobolevsky. He focused instead on a general discussion of the issue based on an analysis of the narrative sources, particularly the Rus' chronicles. Continuing the research begun by Antonovych, Hrushevsky critically assessed the chronicle accounts, paying special attention to their data on the continuty of social organization in the Kyiv area following the Mongol invasion. In assessing the impact of the invasion on the lands of the Middle Dnipro, Hrushevsky wrote as follows: 'Our sources are not lacking in very powerful images of the devastation of these lands ... But on obtaining more detailed reports about these lands, we conclude that in fact things were not so terrible as one might think from the words of the chronicler.'[194] He believed that the population of the Kyivan Land was accustomed to constant raids by the steppe no-mads and could easily survive the Mongol attack by retreating into the forests. 'There can be no lack of certainty,' he wrote, 'that the old, pre-Tatar population was completely preserved in the forest belt of Ukraine – in Polianian, Derevlianian, and Siverianian Polisia.'[195]

In his book of 1891 on the history of the Kyivan Land, Hrushevsky paid special attention to the issue of the 'restructuring of political and social relations' in Ukraine under the influence of the Mongol inva-sion.[196] He argued that after the invasion, the Kyiv region witnessed the disappearance of princely rule as many of its cities and towns came under Mongol administration in one way or another. Hrushevsky was convinced that this shift had inaugurated a period of communal rule in Eastern Ukraine as the city and village communes broke away from the authority of their princes and conducted their internal affairs indepen-dently, under the nominal control of the Mongols. Hrushevsky found the embodiment of this free communal life in the history of the Bolokhiv Land in the upper Boh area. For the most part, Hrushevsky welcomed the desire of the Bolokhovians and other 'Tatar people,' as the Ukrain-ian population under Mongol control was known to the author of the Galician-Volhynian Chronicle, to resist the reimposition of princely control over their affairs, because such resistance corresponded to his populist-inspired views on the role of communities in Ukrainian his-tory in general.[197]

In 1892, under the pseudonym 'Serhiienko,' Hrushevsky published an article devoted to the history of Ukrainian communal life under Tatar rule.[198] There he reinforced many of the points originally made in his monograph of 1891. He praised the resistance of the Bolokhovians and other 'Tatar people' to the attempts of Prince Danylo of Galicia-

Volhynia – one of the major heroes of the Ukrainian historical narrative, including Hrushevsky's own works – to regain control over those communities under the banner of the anti-Mongol struggle. The article had a mixed reception. Hrushevsky's professor, Volodymyr Antonovych, reacted very favourably, as the article reflected many of his own populist ideas. By contrast, from his exile in Bulgaria, Mykhailo Drahomanov severely criticized Hrushevsky's position. Drahomanov attacked the very idea of counterposing state and community in Ukrainian history, a tendency that in his opinion was inspired by the Russian scholarly tradition and promoted the separation of Rus' history from that of Europe. He also regarded the confrontation between Danylo and the Bolokhiv communities as one between different states and gave a negative assessment of the 'Tatar people's' actions, as they prevented Danylo from waging an effective struggle against the Mongols.[199] Hrushevsky was familiar with Drahomanov's critique and apparently agreed with some of the points made by the patriarch of the Ukrainian movement. He presented a much more balanced treatment of the 'Tatar people' issue in the second edition of volume 3 of the *History*. Now he was not so enthusiastic about the democratic nature of the 'communal movement,' paid less attention to its history, and noted much more clearly than before that the whole movement benefited the Mongols.[200]

The 'Tatar people' controversy was all but forgotten when Hrushevsky made reference to his article of 1892 in his revolutionary-era political pamphlet on the current tasks of the Ukrainian Party of Socialist Revolutionaries (1920), in which he was a leading figure. Hrushevsky recalled the controversy surrounding the article and the support expressed for it by Antonovych in order to make the point that there had always been a strong populist and anti-state tradition in the Ukrainian national movement. The reference to the 'Tatar people' also served another purpose: Hrushevsky strained to convince his readers that, given the new political circumstances, his party should not pursue the mirage of independent statehood but draw closer to the masses and return to Bolshevik-occupied Ukraine, as the 'Tatar people' of the thirteenth century had returned to the Mongol-controlled territories in order to escape the authority of the princes.[201] Hrushevsky's references to the episode of the 'Tatar people' provoked a sharp and effective critique by other leaders of the Ukrainian movement, including the historians Viacheslav Lypynsky and Dmytro Doroshenko. The latter accused Hrushevsky of neglecting the history of Ukrainian statehood in his scholarly work and of opposing Ukrainian statehood in general. The point completely overlooked by Hrushevsky's critics, however, is that his interpretation of the 'Tatar people' was not only influenced by his views on the role of the state and the people in history but was also a major argument in his polemic with proponents of the Pogodin theory. Hrushevsky viewed the history of the princeless communities in Mongol-ruled Ukraine as a crucial piece of evidence supporting his theory of the survival of the Kyiv-area population after the Mongol invasion. Thus, in the 'Tatar people' Hrushevsky found not only the embodiment of his social ideals but also proof of a continuous Ukrainian presence in the region.

The third major element of the Pogodin theory on which both its proponents and opponents continually focused was the issue of the migration of peoples in the Middle Dnipro region. This postulate consisted of two parts – the outmigration of the population in the wake of the Mongol invasion and the subsequent resettlement of the region by new immigrants in the centuries following Mongol rule. Proponents of the Pogodin theory tried to prove that both migrations had actually taken place, while its opponents indicated the lack of any conclusive data in that regard. In this instance the opponents had a much easier task than in other cases, as there were indeed few if any traces of such migration in the area.

It was Maksymovych who first pointed out to Pogodin that he was unable to provide any reliable evidence of outmigration of the Polianians to the north. He commented specifically on the account of the emigration to Muscovy in 1332 of the Kyiv noble Rodion Nesterovych, a case used by Pogodin to support his hypothesis that there had indeed been such a migration. Maksymovych argued that Nesterovych's emigration occurred long after the Mongol invasion, and according to the Pogodin theory, anyone emigrating to Muscovy at that time had to be a Great Russian, not a Little Russian. Maksymovych also maintained that the number of people accompanying Nesterovych on his journey to Muscovy (1,700) suggested, if anything, the existence of a large population in the Kyiv region.[202] He proceeded to ridicule Pogodin's argument by asking why the latter thought that the new migrants from the Carpathians would want to subject themselves to Mongol rule when the Polianians were fleeing it. 'And what sort of historical evidence do you have of this resettlement of Little Russians from the Carpathians to the Dnipro in the Tatar era?' continued Maksymovych. 'You have not presented me even with a historical hint of this resettlement. And is not this as arbitrary an invention of yours as the invention by others of the settlement of an abandoned Ukraine by "Lithuanian refugees"?'[203]

The subsequent studies of Volodymyr Antonovych and Mikhail Vladimirskii-Budanov devoted to the settlement of Dnipro Ukraine established the correctness of Maksymovych's postulate that there was no noticeable migration to that area from Galicia or Volhynia. Only in the fifteenth and sixteenth centuries did new migrants move there, not from the west but from the Prypiat forests and marshes to the north. Hrushevsky used the research of these scholars as a prominent argument in his critique of the Pogodin resettlement theory. He also brought a socio-economic factor into the discussion. In countering Sobolevsky's view that the Kyivan Land was resettled by migrants from the west, he suggested that the mass outmigration of the Volhynian population in the sixteenth century was caused by the growing power of the landlords and an increase in peasant labour obligations, a development that did not occur in Volhynia in the fourteenth and fifteenth centuries. Hrushevsky also pointed out that in the mid-sixteenth century Volhynian landlords were complaining about the escape of their serfs to the west, especially to Poland, not to the east.[204] Furthermore, Hrushevsky developed Maksymovych's critique of Pogodin's argument regarding the emigration to Muscovy of Rodion Nesterovych in 1332. Indicating the unrealistically high number of people whom Nesterovych was said to have brought with him to Muscovy, Hrushevsky considered the whole account, which was preserved in the family chronicle of the Kvashnins, a Muscovite boyar family, to be a legend. He interpreted the incident as proof of outmigration to the north not by the population at large but by members of the local elite – a phenomenon caused by the political decline of Kyiv. The main mass of the population, in Hrushevsky's opinion, retreated to the forest areas of northern Ukraine and survived the Mongol invasion there.[205]

Hrushevsky was so convinced of the strength of the scholarly arguments against the Pogodin theory that in his article of 1904 on the traditional scheme of 'Russian' history he expressed doubt whether anyone was still prepared to defend the old hypothesis.[206] His attitude proved too optimistic: as noted earlier, some elements of the Pogodin theory were revived by Vasilii Kliuchevsky in his *Course*. Kliuchevsky believed that outmigration from the Kyiv area began before the Mongol invasion, which only intensified it. He repeated the standard arguments employed by proponents of the Pogodin theory about the devastation of the Kyivan Land and found proof of northward Kyivan migration in the hydronyms and toponyms of Suzdalian Rus', which indeed often resembled those of the Kyivan region. Kliuchevsky found further support for his hypothesis in the popularity in the Russian North of the *byliny* of the Kyiv cycle, a folk tradition that was lost in the Kyiv region itself. He dated the beginning of the alleged resettlement of the Middle Dnipro region to the fifteenth century, viewing it as a movement of population from west to east. In Kliuchevsky's opinion, that movement was prompted by two factors – on the one hand, the disintegration of the Golden Horde and the strengthening of the Muscovite state and, on the other, the introduction of serfdom in the Polish state.[207]

In the third edition of volume 1 of the *History* (1913), Hrushevsky characterized Kliuchevsky as a 'resolute defender' of the Pogodin theory.[208] In reality, though, Kliuchevsky subscribed only to some elements of Pogodin's hypothesis. As noted earlier, he believed that the Polianians migrated both north and west and that their descendants allegedly resettled the Kyiv region from the west after the end of Mongol rule. Kliuchevsky's theory of the outmigration of the Kyivan population in two directions had scant support in the historical sources and was little more than an attempt to find a compromise solution to the Pogodin-Maksymovych controversy. His hypothesis 'established' the Great Russian link with Kyivan Rus' without denying such a link to the Ukrainians. In essence, Kliuchevsky's view resembled the theory of the division of Kyiv's political power between Suzdal and Halych postulated by Maksymovych back in the 1830s.[209]

Kliuchevsky's hypothesis was briefly criticized by Hrushevsky in a footnote to the second edition of volume 3 of the *History*. The volume appeared in print in 1905, the year following the publication of the first volume of Kliuchevsky's *Course*, and Hrushevsky, who referred to the latter as a recent contribution, apparently added this note at the last moment. Hrushevsky considered Kliuchevsky's evidence weak and inconclusive. 'These indications,' he wrote, 'aside from being rather weak in general, say nothing about emigration from the Dnipro region after the Tatar devastation – they speak of an earlier colonization, in the tenth to twelfth centuries (and sometimes not even about colonization, for example, the establishment of direct communication between the Ukrainian Dnipro region and the Volga region; the building by princes of towns whose names were borrowed from Ukraine; or the preservation of the Kyiv *bylina* cycle in the North – all these are facts that have other explanations, not only migration).'[210] If in 1905, when sending the second edition of volume 3 of his *History* to print, Hrushevsky did not have enough time or space to react to Kliuchevsky's theories at length, it appears that subsequently he did not consider Kliuchevsky's views important enough to warrant a special response. In a note to the third edition of volume 1 (1913) of the *History*, he simply cited an article by Aleksandr Spitsyn that examined and criticized Kliuchevsky's argument about the migration of the Kyivan population.[211]

In hindsight, Hrushevsky's lack of interest in and disregard of Kliuchevsky's theories proved a tactical error. While Hrushevsky may have won the scholarly argument, the battle to shape the public perception of the history of Kyivan Rus' and the ethnicity of its core population still lay ahead. Kliuchevsky's views on the depopulation of the Kyiv region, for all their speculative nature, gained currency among the Russian public at large, first and foremost because of the popularity of Kliuchevsky in general and his *Course* in particular. They also made their way into Russian émigré and Soviet historiography, thereby profoundly influencing the treatment of the issue in Western historiography as well.

Mykhailo Hrushevsky became involved in the scholarly debate on the historical legacy of Kyivan Rus' at a relatively young age, and as the debate wore on he shifted position: from a faithful continuator of the Maksymovych tradition, which saw the debate as hinging on the issue of which of the Russian nationalities had a better claim to Kyiv, he developed into a national historian who posed the same question with reference not to nationalities but to separate nations. It would appear that Hrushevsky was still a follower of Maksymovych when he wrote his award-winning book on the history of Kyivan Land and even when he came to Lviv in 1894. In his inaugural lecture at Lviv University Hrushevsky still spoke about Kyivan Rus' as a federation held together by the unity of the Rus' people.[212] Only later, at the turn of the twentieth century, did he emerge as one of the boldest promoters of the new scheme of Ukrainian history, which was based on the assumption that no such coherent ethnic group had ever existed.

Hrushevsky's well-grounded claim to Kyivan Rus' history on behalf of the Ukrainian national narrative marked the turning point in the separation of Ukrainian history from Russian. His name became closely associated with that revolution in East Slavic history and with the scheme of Ukrainian history that began with the period of Kyivan Rus'. But how novel was the idea of starting Ukrainian history with the Rus' era? There have been recent attempts to answer this question by putting Hrushevsky's contribution to the debate on the legacy of Kyivan Rus' into a broader historiographic context. Some historians have noted the contribution of Hrushevsky's predecessors, including Maksymovych and Antonovych, to the formulation of the Ukrainian claim to the Rus' era.[213] Others, in defining the essence of Hrushevsky's 'conceptual revolution,' tend to exclude from it any direct reference to his claim to Kyivan Rus'.[214] Nevertheless, Hrushevsky is known to broader historical circles in Eastern Europe first and foremost because of his 'appropriation' of Kyivan Rus' for the Ukrainian historical narrative. Representative of that view is the assessment of Hrushevsky's contribution to Ukrainian history made by his older colleague Dmytro Bahalii. In the 1920s Bahalii pointed out that the historical scheme employed by Hrushevsky was not entirely of his own making but continued to associate that scheme with Hrushevsky's name and reaffirmed his own adherence to the 'Hrushevsky scheme' despite attacks from Marxist critics and pressure from the authorities.[215]

Given these contrary opinions, how should one define Hrushevsky's actual contribution to a debate that began long before his birth? One may argue that it was at least twofold. In the first place, Hrushevsky's claim to the Kyivan Rus' period was an exclusive one. Unlike his predecessors, he was not satisfied with part of the Kyivan heritage but wanted it all: for Hrushevsky, the Rus' period was no longer a portion of the all-Russian narrative but constituted a separate narrative in its own right. Second, Hrushevsky was a recognized authority in the field of early Rus' history whose expertise surpassed that of all contemporary authors of general surveys of Russian history. Given Hrushevsky's preeminent status, his conclusions could not easily be ignored or dismissed.

Hrushevsky's exclusive claim to Kyivan Rus' on behalf of Ukraine left Russian history without its starting point, and it was this attempt to remove the keystone from the arch of the Russian imperial paradigm that drew most fire from Hrushevsky's critics. Exceptionally important in the rejection and discreditation of Hrushevsky's paradigm of East Slavic history was the role of Ukrainian historians of the Little Russian persuasion. Such scholars as Filevich, Linnichenko, and Storozhenko were in the forefront of the historiographic and political debate initiated by Hrushevsky, which raises the question of whether the whole controversy was an internal Ukrainian problem. To the degree that the historiographic debates reflected the split within the Ukrainian intelligentsia over the choice of modern national identity, it was indeed a Ukrainian problem. But it was a major Russo-Ukrainian problem as well. Among the initiators of the historiographic controversy were such Russian scholars as Pogodin and Sobolevsky, and among Hrushevsky's opponents in the late nineteenth and early twentieth centuries were such representatives of Russian scholarship as Florinsky, Liapunov, and Shakhmatov. Indeed, the Russo-Ukrainian aspect of the controversy overshadowed the internal Ukrainian one, since the debate on the 'all-Russian' historical narrative went to the core of both Russian and Ukrainian identity.

At least two major tendencies were apparent among the Russian participants in the discussion. The first tendency coincided with the growth of the modern Russian national identity, reflecting the growing interest of Great Russian society at large in Great Russian history. It was this tendency that Hrushevsky tried to enlist in support of his deconstruction of the traditional scheme of 'Russian' history. This tendency was opposed and eventually defeated by those historians who adhered to the Russian imperial narrative or regarded the Russian national narrative as composed of the histories of all three 'Russian tribes': Great Russians, Little Russians, and White Russians. As noted earlier, the Ukrainian revival and struggle for independence from Russia during and after the Revolution of 1917 brought home the threat posed by Hrushevsky's scheme to the idea of Russian unity not only to proponents of the all-Russian idea in Ukraine but also to historians in Russia itself. Prior to the Revolution, only one major Russian historian, Aleksandr Presniakov, the author of a monograph on the foundations of the Great Russian state, admitted to being somewhat influenced by Hrushevsky's scheme. As a result he traced the origins of Great Russian history to Northeastern and not Southeastern Rus'.[216] Among other eminent Russian historians whose views were influenced in one way or another by Hrushevsky's works, one might name Matvei Liubavsky and Sergei Platonov.[217] Their major works (including Presniakov's book on Great Russian statehood) were written prior to the Revolution of 1917, reflecting the significant degree of tolerance toward the Ukrainian project that then prevailed in Russian academic circles. That attitude perished in the flames of the revolution.

Representative of the new tendency in Russian scholarship was the position taken by Michael Rostovtzeff with regard to Hrushevsky's interpretation of Kyivan Rus'. In the above-mentioned French-language article of 1922 on the origins of Rus', he made extensive use of

Hrushevsky's *History of Ukraine-Rus'* but severely criticized its author for his attempt to separate Russian and Ukrainian history and to assign the Kyivan period exclusively to the history of Ukraine. He noted that Hrushevsky's key concepts, namely 'the complete separation of Russian and Ukrainian history and the exclusive claim to Kyivan history for the latter make the reading of the book a painful task.' 'This is all the more regrettable,' added Rostovtzeff, 'as the author's erudition is great.'[218] Hrushevsky responded to Rostovtzeff's critique by stating in his 1925 review of Rostovtzeff's works: 'unfortunately, in spite of the decentralizing tendencies of the revolution, Ilovaisky's old scheme finds new defenders among scholars of whom something better might have been expected.'[219]

After 1917, with Hrushevsky's scheme making impressive headway in Soviet Ukraine, it was no longer possible to ignore the Ukrainian challenge to Russian historiography and reject Hrushevsky's claim to Kyivan Rus' out of hand. Traditional Russian historiography looked in several directions for a solution to the 'Ukrainian problem.' It took notice of the complaints and proposals of Liubavsky, Linnichenko, and Efimenko, who wanted a new paradigm of Russian history including as much as possible of the history of Western and Southwestern Rus'. The multivolume *History of Russia* produced by George Vernadsky, the scion of the Russian imperial historiographic school and the protégé of Rostovtzeff at Yale University, may be regarded as a contribution to the creation of such a paradigm. In his Russian history courses Vernadsky paid unprecedented attention to the history of Ukraine.[220] In 1941 he wrote an introduction to the English translation of Hrushevsky's *Illustrated History*, praising its author as 'the leading Ukrainian historian, whose authority has been widely recognized both in and outside of his country.'[221] Without criticizing Hrushevsky's appropriation of Kyivan Rus', Vernadsky presented it as the common inheritance of Russians and Ukrainians.[222]

Vernadsky was among the most prominent of the Russian émigré 'Eurasianists,' a group of intellectuals who placed special emphasis on Russia's Asian connection and considered the Russian Empire the direct heir not of Kyivan Rus' but of the Mongol Empire. That approach removed Kyivan Rus' from the centre of the Eurasianists' attention but did little to change their general interpretation of Ukrainian history as part of the all-Russian narrative.[223] In discussing the history of Russo-Ukrainian relations, one of Vernadsky's fellow Eurasianists, Prince Nikolai Trubetskoi, invariably referred to the notion of a common Russo-

Ukrainian high culture advanced at the beginning of the twentieth century by Petr Struve.[224] But it was the ideas and approaches first suggested by Vasilii Kliuchevsky that were by far the most influential in shaping the Russian response to the Ukrainian historiographic challenge. In his above-mentioned political pamphlet, *Historical Truth and Ukrainophile Propaganda* (1920), Prince Aleksandr Volkonsky quoted whole passages from Kliuchevsky's *Course* to prove the migration theory. He explained his fascination with Kliuchevsky as follows: 'All that we have said so far about the Little Russians has been copied word for word, or almost word for word, from Professor Kliuchevsky's course. We have consciously resorted to such a simplified method of exposition. The Ukrainophile party freely accuses its opponents of lying and juggling with the facts. Let it reckon not with me but with Professor Kliuchevsky. There are those among the dead who are more difficult to defame than the living.'[225]

While Ukrainian historiography, beginning with Hrushevsky, has had no difficulty in rejecting Kliuchevsky's approach, that approach gained numerous supporters in the ranks of Russian and then Soviet historians. Kliuchevsky's interpretation of Kyivan Rus' history as the product of a single all-Russian nationality offered a convenient resolution to the old debate on the Pogodin theory, which was reinvigorated in the twentieth century by the construction of the Ukrainian national narrative. If one were to consider Pogodin's exclusive claim to Kyivan Rus' on behalf of the Great Russians the original thesis, then Hrushevsky's attempt to claim it for the Ukrainians alone could be considered the antithesis. The Kliuchevsky-inspired compromise gave both sides a claim to the Kyivan legacy, based on the theory of a single 'old Russian' nationality that allegedly existed in the times of Kyivan Rus'. That compromise solution, which was fully developed by Soviet historiography, continues to dominate scholarly attitudes toward Kyivan Rus' history. It also establishes the Rus' era as the only safe haven of the nineteenth-century concept of all-Russian nationality, which dominated all periods of East Slavic history in pre-revolutionary historical writing.

Chapter 3

The Construction of a National Paradigm

Not unlike the old scheme attacked by Hrushevsky, his own outline of Ukrainian history was rooted in the historiographic tradition of the medieval and early modern chronicles. Indeed, the tradition of treating the Principality of Galicia-Volhynia as the successor to Kyivan Rus' was initiated by the compilers of the Hypatian Codex and the authors of the Galician-Volhynian Chronicle, a portion of the codex that was written at the end of the thirteenth century and covered events from 1201 to 1292.[1] This scheme was later employed by Ukrainian chroniclers of the early modern period, especially Feodosii Sofonovych,[2] and was followed and further developed by Ukrainian historians of the nineteenth century. The latter brought about a confluence of the two main currents of early modern Ukrainian historiography: that of the church historians, who saw the history of Rus' in its various political and cultural incarnations as the main subject of their narration, and that of Cossack historiography, which focused on the glorious deeds of the Cossacks and their leaders. These two trends merged in the 'Little Russian' narrative of Ukrainian history, which united interest in Rus' history and in the exploits of the Cossacks, focusing on the development of Little Russia – the Rus' territory settled by the Cossacks.

Modern Ukrainian historiography began its development in response to the publication of Karamzin's *History of the Russian State*. The rise of Karamzin's star in imperial Russian historiography coincided with the demise of the common all-Russian high culture that was constructed in the late seventeenth and early eighteenth centuries with the active participation of the Ukrainian secular and religious elites. The spectacular progress of Great Russian high culture and its efforts to supplant the all-Russian cultural construct of the eighteenth century were among the major factors that led to the disintegration of the old all-Russian historical narrative. The development of linguistics and the onset of romanticism in the early nineteenth century turned the attention of the scholarly community to the existence of separate languages and peoples, inspired historians to search for ethnic origins, and led to debates over which nation had the best claim to particular parts of the all-Russian historical construct. The rise of anthropology and the development of archaeological research in the second half of the nineteenth century advanced the national projects even further, triggering a search for ethnic anthropological types in prehistoric times.

As Karamzin's narrative failed to include significant parts of Ukrainian history, Ukrainian authors of the first half of the nineteenth century sought to redress this perceived anomaly, attempting to secure a place for the history of their homeland in the imperial narrative. The anonymous author of the *History of the Rus'*, which began to circulate in manuscript in Ukraine after the publication of Karamzin's *History*, identified the Little Russians rather than the Great Russians as the true heirs of the Kyivan legacy and claimed pride of place in Russian history for his compatriots. Dmitrii Bantysh-Kamensky, the author of the *History of Little Russia* (1822), sought to correct Karamzin's 'error' by reintroducing 'Little Russian' history into the imperial narrative. His attempt was only partly successful. Ironically, it was the critique voiced by the Russian journalist and historian Nikolai Polevoi, who attacked Bantysh-Kamensky's *History* for narrating the Ukrainian past as the history of a mere Russian province and not of a separate entity, that set off the Ukrainian search for a distinct historical paradigm. That search began with the publication in 1842–3 of the *History of Little Russia* by Mykola Markevych. The work, written in the tradition of the eighteenth-century Cossack chronicles, reintroduced many 'peculiarities' into Ukrainian history but still viewed it as part of the all-Russian historical narrative. As Zenon Kohut has noted, 'in essence, Markevych and the other historians of the early nineteenth century wanted Ukraine to have its proper place within the history of this [Russian] monarchy and state.'[3]

The transformation of the Little Russian subnational narrative into the Ukrainian national one began with the works of the first rector of Kyiv University, Mykhailo Maksymovych. In his polemics with Mikhail Pogodin, Maksymovych laid claim to the Kyivan Rus' heritage on behalf of Ukraine and defended the distinct character of Ukrainian history in polemics with Polish historians. Still, not unlike his Cossack predecessors, Maksymovych used the term 'Ukraine' mainly in reference to the Dnipro region and focused his research on it. The break with the Cossack historiographic tradition occurred in the works of Panteleimon Kulish, Osyp Bodiansky, and Mykola Kostomarov, who argued for expanding the Ukrainian narrative in chronological, geographic, and social terms. In the second half of the nineteenth century, Ukrainian historiography was often confined to a supporting role in the imperial Russian response to Polish claims to Right-Bank Ukraine, but Mykhailo Maksymovych, Mykola Kostomarov, and Volodymyr Antonovych managed to lay the foundations for a new synthesis of Ukrainian history. The concept of East Slavic unity was questioned and the continuity of Ukrainian history asserted; attempts were made to include lands as geographically remote as Galicia in the new narrative.[4] Still, none of these theses was fully developed in scholarly terms, and Ukrainian history was not considered an academic subject in its own right.

It fell to Mykhailo Hrushevsky to continue the research conducted by the founding fathers of Ukrainian historiography and address the challenges it faced in the age of national 'awakening' by creating a national narrative of Ukrainian history. This chapter discusses the process, principles, and methods of construction of the Ukrainian national narrative. Its first section examines the conditions in which that project developed at the turn of the twentieth century – the obstacles that it encountered in Russian Ukraine and the circumstances that favoured its development in Galicia. The second section considers the compound term 'Ukraine-Rus',' which was used to define the Ukrainian national narrative at its inception. It investigates the ways in which the continuity of Ukrainian history was established and how the structuring of the new narrative developed in the course of debates on the periodization of the Ukrainian past. The third section deals with Hrushevsky's development and implementation of a historical paradigm that allowed him to turn Ukrainian history into a national grand narrative – the story of the rise, decline, and resurgence of a nation. The fourth and last section discusses Hrushevsky's treatment of the history of the Ukrainian Cossacks, showing how premodern historical mythology was adapted to serve the purposes of the national narrative.

Toward a New Narrative

After Mykola Markevych, Ukrainian historians refrained from writing general surveys of Ukrainian history. One reason for this was the preoccupation of many Ukrainian authors (shared by a significant number of their West and Central European colleagues) with the task of uncovering and publishing historical sources, often at the expense of their interpretation. Mykhailo Drahomanov voiced a conviction of many of his Ukrainian colleagues of the 1870s when he stated that the Ukrainian nation and its history would be acknowledged by others once the wealth of documents pertaining to that history was published.[5] Volodymyr Antonovych's activities in the Kyiv Archaeographic Commission, which produced the multivolume documentary series *Archive of Southwestern Russia*, clearly helped achieve that goal.[6] But times were changing, and by the early 1890s the leaders of the Ukrainian movement were coming to realize that what they needed at that new stage of the movement's development was not just new collections of documents but a new synthesis of Ukrainian history.

The same Drahomanov now criticized Antonovych and his school for avoiding any assessment of historical facts in their works and called for a synthesis that would not focus on the Cossack era alone but present the Ukrainian past in the context of European history.[7] He further maintained that the new narrative should go beyond national and confessional paradigms – a reference to the dominant interpretation of Ukrainian history as a struggle between Orthodox Rus' and Catholic Poland – to address a broad spectrum of issues. Drahomanov wrote: '... Our history must be examined as a whole in all its eras: princely, feudal Lithuanian, lordly Polish, Cossack, and tsarist Russian (along with the imperial and constitutional Austrian period), and in each of these eras we must pay attention to the growth or decline of population, the economy, mores and ideas in the community and the state, education, and the direct or indirect participation of Ukrainians of all classes or cultures in European history and culture.'[8]

The need for a new synthesis of Ukrainian history was also obvious to members of Antonovych's circle, although they placed less emphasis on the European context. Antin Syniavsky, an exiled student of Antonovych's whose political convictions were inspired by Drahomanov, and who played a leading role in 'recruiting' Hrushevsky into the Ukrainophile movement in the late 1880s, wrote in the Lviv newspaper *Zoria* (Star) in 1891: 'We lack a complete history of the Rus'-Ukrainian people; of all its lands – Ukraine, Galicia, Bukovyna, and Hungarian Rus'. It must correspond to the current growth of national self-knowledge and tell us about the fates of our people from our own viewpoint. At present, the majority must examine its history through tendentious

Polish and Russian glasses.'[9] Drahomanov's opponent of the time, Borys Hrinchenko, also called for a survey of Ukrainian history, stressing the national awakening of the popular masses. Commenting on the national identity of the Ukrainian peasant, he wrote: 'He does not know his history, nor can he know it: to this day our patriots have not managed to write it, and oral narratives themselves are lacking, and even those we have are already being forgotten, and in places they have indeed been forgotten entirely. Consequently, our peasant does not even know his national name.'[10]

Whatever the Ukrainian activists' conceptions of the new historical narrative, all agreed on the need to create one. The task fell to Antonovych and his circle, more precisely on the shoulders of its younger generation, including Antonovych's most talented student, Mykhailo Hrushevsky. In Hrushevsky's own words, the production of a complete history of Ukraine was 'a matter of honour not only for me but for my whole generation.'[11] In December 1895 the editorial board of the Ukrainophile journal *Kievskaia starina* announced a competition for writers willing to produce a survey of Ukrainian history.[12] Although the winner was Aleksandra Efimenko, it was Mykhailo Hrushevsky – probably considered too young and inexperienced at the time – who first responded to the challenge faced by Ukrainian historiography of the day. In 1898 Hrushevsky published the first volume of his academic *History of Ukraine-Rus'*, and in 1904 he not only presented an outline of Ukrainian history as a national narrative in his article on the traditional scheme of 'Russian' history but also convinced the Russian authorities of the need to publish his *Survey History of the Ukrainian People*, which presented a coherent narrative of the Ukrainian national past.

Even though all three of the above-mentioned appeals for the creation of a Ukrainian historical narrative came from activists of Eastern Ukrainian origin, they were published in the Ukrainian media in Austria (Drahomanov's and Syniavsky's in Galicia and Hrinchenko's in Bukovyna), and the narrative itself was created by another representative of Dnipro Ukraine who held a teaching position at an Austrian university. These facts suggest that the creation and publication of such a narrative was all but impossible in the Russian Empire (prior to 1904, at least). It was not only the intellectual reservations of Antonovych and his associates that prevented them from creating a national narrative of Ukrainian history, but also political conditions prevailing in the Russian Empire from the official persecution of the SS. Cyril and Methodius Brotherhood in 1847 up to the relative relaxation of Russian censorship on the eve of the Revolution of 1905. As late as 1904 Hrushevsky encountered numerous obstacles to the publication of his work in Russia. Judging by his autobiography, Russian publishers were more than reluctant to issue his *Survey*. 'One of the most liberal publishers declined,' wrote Hrushevsky, 'fearing that an account of Ukrainian history that differed sharply from the accepted account of Russian history (that is, the inclusion of ancient Rus') would bring down an unfavourable judgment on the book from Russian scholarly circles.'[13] The precedent created by the publication of Hrushevsky's survey and, more importantly, the revolutionary events of 1905 made it possible for other authors to publish surveys of Ukrainian history. Not only did Aleksandra Efimenko finally publish her *History of the Ukrainian People* in 1906, but her work was soon followed by the appearance of a *History of Ukraine-Rus'* (1908) by Mykola Arkas.[14]

The long absence of general accounts of Ukrainian history was lamented in introductions to these publications. 'There is no comprehensive Russian-language survey of the history of the Ukrainian people, although the need for one is apparent, if only from the success of the recently reprinted old *History of Little Russia* by Bantysh-Kamensky, which is being bought avidly thanks to its title alone,'[15] wrote Hrushevsky. Efimenko also regretted the long absence of systematic accounts of Ukrainian history, noting the reissue of Bantysh-Kamensky's survey as an indication of the lack of modern interpretations of the history of 'Southern Rus'.' 'For anyone interested in gaining a general idea of the history of this half of Rus',' wrote Efimenko, 'nothing remains but to turn to the works of Bantysh-Kamensky and Markevych, which go back to the thirties and forties of the past century. Those works under the title *History of Little Russia* indeed constitute a systematic survey of the subject. But both those works have become so dated in their methods, suffer so much from the lack of historical criticism, and have fallen so far behind in relation to their sources that by now their significance is merely bibliographic: they offer nothing either to historical scholarship in the strict sense or to the public.'[16] The problem, though, lay not only in the failure of the old narratives to meet the demands of modern scholarship in terms of their treatment of sources, as noted by Efimenko, but also in their incompatibility with new ideological and historiographic trends. Both Bantysh-Kamensky's and Markevych's histories were written within the framework of the Russian state-based paradigm, while Efimenko herself was writing the history of a people, not of a state.

Surprisingly at first glance, none of the surveys of Ukrainian history published in the Russian Empire was written by a scholar holding an appointment at a Russian university. Hrushevsky was a professor in an Austrian university, while Efimenko never received even a master's degree (only in 1910 did Bahalii, then rector of Kharkiv University, succeed in granting her a doctorate in Russian history honoris causa) and never taught at a university. Also lacking a historical education was Mykola Arkas, a navy officer and a prominent bureaucrat in the Kherson province of Southern Ukraine.

The lack of professional historians from the Russian universities among the authors of the first surveys of Ukrainian history reflected the lack of university courses covering Ukrainian history as a whole. This in turn was a product of the anti-Ukrainian attitudes that persisted in Russian universities in Ukraine into the first decade of the twentieth century. A vicious circle developed: political pressure precluded the introduction of a general course of Ukrainian history, making it unnecessary to produce a survey of the subject, and the lack of a survey hindered the introduction of Ukrainian history into the university curriculum. The political factor was paramount in that process, as shown by the situation prevailing in Russian universities in Ukraine after the Revolution of 1905. Surveys were published and professors prepared to teach Ukrainian history were available, but the courses were not offered because of interference from the university administration.

What academics could do, however, was discuss particular topics or periods of Ukrainian history in general courses on Russian history, or offer them as subjects of special courses dealing with local history. That solution did not undermine the validity of the all-Russian narrative and was tolerated by the university administrators. As a result, Volodymyr Antonovych tried to infuse his lecture courses on Russian history with as much Ukrainian content as possible. His course on 'Russian' history, which he taught in collaboration with Vladimir Ikonnikov, would begin with the history of Kyivan Rus' and then separately consider its two successors, Southwestern Rus' and Northeastern Rus', before 'reuniting' them in the historical account of imperial Russia.[17] That was Antonovych's answer to the problem posed by the traditional scheme of 'Russian' history, especially its neglect of 'Southwestern Rus'.' The same approach was taken by Antonovych's student and professor of Russian history at Kharkiv University, Dmytro Bahalii, in his courses on Russian history.[18] Oleksii Markevych, who taught at Novorossiisk (Odesa) University between 1880 and 1895, offered a special course every semester on the history of 'Southern Russia,'[19] but at Odesa University, as elsewhere, there were no general courses in Ukrainian history and, as a result, no surveys or textbooks on the subject were produced.[20]

This is not to say that Ukrainian historians wrote no surveys at all, only that such works were not surveys of Ukrainian history. Instructive in this regard is the case of Hrushevsky's older colleague Dmytro Bahalii. The fact that Bahalii did not produce a survey of Ukrainian history prior to the revolution and busied himself with writing textbooks on Russian history, even at a time when Hrushevsky and Efimenko were concerned with responding to the growing demand in Ukrainian circles for a separate historical narrative, can be explained only in part by the demands of his successful administrative career. Bahalii was rector of Kharkiv University, later a member of the State Council of the Russian Empire, and finally head of the Kharkiv city council, which made considerable demands on his time and energy, yet he still found time to work on his Russian history textbooks.[21]

Probably a more important factor accounting for Bahalii's reluctance to produce a survey of Ukrainian history was the atmosphere of hostility toward Ukrainian scholarship in the Russian universities of Ukraine. Scholars who focused on topics in Ukrainian history and literature, or who were suspected by the authorities of sympathy for the Ukrainian national movement, encountered difficulties in obtaining positions, receiving tenure, and getting promotions. The only way to pursue a university career and carry out research in Ukrainian studies was to present them as part of Russian studies, an exercise in which both Antonovych and Bahalii proved successful, holding positions in Russian history at Kyiv and Kharkiv universities, respectively.[22] Thus, Bahalii was one of the Ukrainian historians who continued to work within the all-Russian historical paradigm. Apart from his predominant concentration on topics related to the history of Ukraine, Bahalii's self-identification as a Ukrainian historian was demonstrated by his continuation of Kostomarov's federalist approach to Russian history and by his adherence to the regional (*oblastnicheskaia*) school of Russian imperial historiography associated with the names of Afanasii Shchapov and Volodymyr Antonovych, as opposed to the 'centralist' school, which was represented by Sergei Soloviev and, in relation to Ukrainian history, Soloviev's student Gennadii Karpov.[23]

It is fair to assume that, had it been possible freely to teach courses in Ukrainian and publish textbooks on the subject, the creation of a Ukrainian national narrative would have been much easier, and the separation of the Russian and Ukrainian historical narratives would have proceeded more quickly. On the other hand, one should not assume that, given such conditions, Ukrainian historians would necessarily have produced a national narrative. After all, Efimenko's survey shows that even after the publication of Hrushevsky's work, Ukrainian history could still be presented as part of an all-Russian narrative. Despite the title of her book, the *History of the Ukrainian People*, Efimenko regarded Ukrainian history as a chronicle of Southern Rus' and considered it part of all-Russian history. She used 'Ukraine' mainly to designate the Eastern Ukrainian Cossack territories and regarded the Ukrainian language as a simple folk (*prostonarodnyi*) dialect. She also claimed that the South Russian question could have been resolved as early as 1655, when the 'Russians' (the term encompassed both Muscovite and Cossack detachments) took control of Lithuania and 'Southern Rus'' as far as Lviv and Lublin.[24] In many ways, Efimenko continued Mykola Kostomarov's tradition of designating Ukrainians as Southern Russians, and in terms of the 'Ukrainization' of the Ukrainian past she was far behind Antonovych and his school.

The political freedom that Hrushevsky exercised in Austria-Hungary was one of the crucial factors allowing him to develop a paradigm that presented Ukrainian history as a separate field of study, not only equal in significance and importance to Russian history but also independent of it. It is equally apparent that his task was eased not only by the absence of Russian censorship in Austrian Galicia but also by the rise of the mass Ukrainian movement there and its earlier attempts to create a Ukrainian historical narrative wholly distinct from the history of Russia.

In the second half of the nineteenth century conditions in Galicia and Bukovyna were much more favourable to the Ukrainian national movement in general and its historical project in particular than in the Russian Empire. Still, even there, the Ukrainian movement had to confront proponents of the pan-Russian national project. With its rise in the 1860s and 1870s, the Ukrainian movement in Galicia was faced with the already well-developed ideology of the Russophile movement (Muscophiles, 'Old Ruthenians'),[25] which was busy transferring the pan-Russian project of the Romanov Empire to Galician soil. In the realm of historiography, this was done by one of the forerunners of the Russophile movement, Denys Zubrytsky, the author of *The History of the Ancient Galician-Russian Principality* (1852–5).[26] As Zubrytsky explained the mission of his history in a letter of 1852 to Mikhail Pogodin, his 'main intention in writing it was to acquaint Galicians both with

Russian history and, to the extent possible, with the Russian language.'[27] The all-Russian interpretation of history was further advanced by Izydor Sharanevych in his *History of Halych-Volodymyr Rus' from the Earliest Times to 1453* (1863).[28] The author of the first Galician historical synthesis was the Russophile Bohdan Didytsky, who published a *People's History of Rus'* in 1871.[29] Didytsky's history was followed by the *Illustrated People's History of Rus'* (1890), written by another Russophile, Teodor Ripetsky.[30]

For some time, proponents of the Ukrainian movement ('Young Ruthenians' or 'populists' in the terminology of the day) failed to produce a counterpart to the Russophile interpretation of the history of their homeland, and the Ukrainian movement in Galicia long relied mainly on the publication in Galician periodicals of popular historical essays written by Ukrainian activists from Russian-ruled Ukraine.[31] The major obstacle to the creation of a Ukrainian historical narrative in Galicia was the distaste for the romantic interpretation of the Ukrainian past – especially the glorification of princes, hetmans, and other heroes of traditional historiography, without whom the construction of the new national narrative would have been all but impossible – that ran deep in the psyche of the Galician populists. In 1863 one of the early activists of the Ukrainian movement in Galicia, Danylo Taniachkevych, gave a rather pessimistic assessment of the social role of history: 'The days of the boyars have passed and unruly Cossackdom has become extinct, and perhaps God is to be praised for that ... There is no trace in history of the building of new fortresses and castles upon the great ruins: the hand of the farmer is sowing God's seed here! Nor is there any reason for heartfelt pining and looking back there, for it is not a paradise that we have lost. And that happy paradise is more probably ahead of us, only we do not know how to find it.'[32] In 1876 the Ukrainophile Prosvita Society refused to publish a biography of Bohdan Khmelnytsky on the grounds that it portrayed an individual, not the people in general, as the protagonist of history.[33] 'Why the devil have you sent me an article about hetmans?' wrote one of the leaders of the Ukrainian Radical Party, Ivan Franko, to another populist leader, Mykhailo Pavlyk, in 1878. 'Do you really think there is nothing better to print here than such swill?'[34]

Another reason for the relatively long absence of a Ukrainian historical narrative in Galicia was the simple lack of scholarly expertise. As Taniachkevych asserted in 1863, the study of history called for high qualifications and strong devotion. He advanced the idea of establishing a chair of 'our history in our native tongue' at Lviv University, to which he proposed to invite Mykola Kostomarov.[35] The project never materialized, and the first serious attempt at a Galician-Ukrainian synthesis of Ukrainian history came only in the late 1870s with the publication of a Polish-language polemical tract, *The Policy of the Poles toward Rus'*, by the Ukrainophile Stefan Kachala.[36] Kachala's work was influenced by the writings of Panteleimon Kulish and found understanding and appreciation in Dnipro Ukraine, where excerpts from it were translated into Russian and published in the Ukrainophile journal *Kievskaia starina*.[37]

The demand for a new synthesis of Ukrainian history, which was strongly felt in Galicia, was partly met by the compilation of a multivolume anthology on the subject. The idea of publishing such an anthology occurred to a Galician activist, Oleksander Barvinsky, who later became a moving force behind the establishment of a chair of Ukrainian history at Lviv University and the invitation to the young Kyivan Mykhailo Hrushevsky to accept the position.[38] Barvinsky regarded the planned anthology of works on Ukrainian history as a means of raising the level of national consciousness among the Ukrainian intelligentsia – a clear departure from the nihilistic view of Ukrainian history expressed in the early 1860s by Taniachkevych. In his memoirs (1913), Barvinsky explained his decision to publish the anthology as follows: 'The experience gained up to that point on the basis of the activity of the Prosvita and Ruthenian Discourse branch in Ternopil, as well as the establishment of reading rooms in Podilia and the popular lectures and evening programs held there, convinced me that the educated stratum of our society also required a deepening of its national consciousness, and that could be achieved with the help of a fundamental acquaintance with our past. My popular little books on the *History of Rus'* published by the Prosvita Society could not, in my view, satisfy that need; they could not give our intelligentsia fundamental historical knowledge, and at that time we had no complete picture of the history of Ukraine-Rus' for the educated stratum of our society.'[39]

In 1886, in order to present a 'complete picture' of national history, Barvinsky began to publish the Ruthenian Historical Library. In order to determine the content of volumes in the series, which were to be translated from Russian and Polish (very few historical works were then available in Ukrainian), Barvinsky visited the dean of Ukrainian historians, Volodymyr Antonovych, in Kyiv. The latter supported Barvinsky's initiative as an effective way of raising national consciousness and gave his recommendations concerning texts to be included in Barvinsky's historical library. He suggested that the series begin with a Ukrainian translation of Stefan Kachala's general survey of Ukrainian history, to be followed by individual monographs on the subject from the princely era to modern times. These would include works by Antonovych himself, as well as numerous studies on Ukrainian history by Mykola Kostomarov.[40]

The publication of the Ruthenian Historical Library proved an unqualified success. In all, between 1886 and 1904, twenty-four volumes of the Library appeared in print.[41] Apart from the works of well-known Ukrainian historians, the series included the writings of opponents of the Ukrainian idea, including studies by Dmitrii Ilovaisky (on the history of Kyivan Rus' and the Grand Duchy of Lithuania) and Ivan Linnichenko (on the social structure of Galician Rus').[42] Thus, when it came to bringing some of Ilovaisky's ideas into the mainstream of Ukrainian historical writing, Barvinsky, by all accounts, was a forerunner of Hrushevsky. This applied particularly to Ilovaisky's anti-Normanist views, as one of the volumes of the Ruthenian Historical Library included translations drawn from a collection of his articles, *Researches on the Origins of Rus'*.[43] Barvinsky's popularization of anti-Normanist ideas in the publications of the Ruthenian Historical Library provoked a negative response from some activists of the Ukrainian movement. One of the reviewers of the Library, Omelian Kalytovsky, considered anti-Normanism contrary to the goals of Ukrainian historiography. Kalytovsky's position becomes clearer in light of the views of another Ukrainian activist, Omelian Partytsky, who believed that Normanism supported the assertion of Ukraine's distinct historical character.[44] If in Eastern Ukraine anti-Normanism had become part of the Ukrainian historiographic tradition long before the turn of the twentieth century, in Western Ukraine it was considered a new, controversial, and potentially harmful deviation. Generally speaking, the publication of the Library proved an important episode in the development of Ukrainian historiography, as it created a new historiographic canon that included Ilovaisky and Linnichenko along with Kostomarov and Antonovych.

Barvinsky tried his hand not only at publishing the Ruthenian Historical Library series but also at compiling the first Ukrainophile survey of Ukrainian history to be published in Austria-Hungary. The efforts of the Galician Ukrainophiles to create their own narrative were finally crowned with success in 1890, when the Ukrainophile Prosvita Society published Barvinsky's *Illustrated History of Rus'* in Lviv.[45] The book covered the history of Ukraine (both Russian and Austrian parts) up to the second half of the nineteenth century. The narrative was divided into three periods: before the Lithuanian conquest, under Lithuanian and Polish rule, and from the Cossack era to the nineteenth century. Barvinsky's Ukrainophile narrative clearly benefited from its Russophile forerunners, who stressed the independence of Rus' history from the Polish narrative – a tenet shared by the Ukrainophile authors.

Although the Russophiles presented the history of Galicia as part of all-Russian history, in many cases their reading of the Galician past foreshadowed the interpretation of Galician history developed by the Ukrainophiles. That was true of the special emphasis placed by representatives of both historiographic trends on the Galician-Volhynian principality. In the eyes of both Russophiles and Ukrainophiles, its history was an important link with the all-Russian past – the history of Kyivan Rus'. Interest in that era was also regarded with favour by the authorities, as the incorporation of Galicia into the Habsburg Monarchy was officially justified by the dynastic rights of the Habsburgs, allegedly rooted in medieval Rus' history. Another important element of the Russophile historiographic approach, shared with their Ukrainophile adversaries, was their interpretation of the era of Polish rule over Galicia as a 'dark age' in its history. In time, the Russophile historiographic scheme, which initially included lengthy segments of the history of Russia, evolved into an outline fairly similar to the one eventually constructed by the Ukrainophiles. That process was best reflected in the writings of Teodor Ripetsky. In his *Illustrated People's History of Rus'*, the latter limited his coverage of Russian history to the absolute minimum, drawing his narrative line from Kyivan Rus' through the Galician-Volhynian principality to the history of the Cossacks.[46]

Barvinsky's history soon emerged as the most popular historical work in the Galician village reading clubs and maintained that status until the publication of Hrushevsky's *Illustrated History of Ukraine* in the second decade of the twentieth century.[47] The publication of Barvinsky's *Illustrated History of Rus'* was also welcomed by historians from Dnipro Ukraine. One of them, Antin Syniavsky, published a review in which he called it 'a valuable gift to Ruthenian-Ukrainian society that we do not have with regard to our history and that should be in every Ruthenian-Ukrainian family. This is all the more reason to regret that this history of Rus' is not permitted to see Ukraine.'[48] The leitmotif of Syniavsky's review, however, was not praise for Barvinsky but insistence on the need for a full scholarly narrative of Ukrainian history, not just a brief popular historical survey. What did Antonovych's student find wanting in Barvinsky's pioneering work? To begin with, he did not approve the distribution of the material or the periodization. He was also concerned that Barvinsky did not know the most recent literature, used a good deal of legendary and unverified data, and either remained aloof from scholarly debates that were extremely important to scholars from Dnipro Ukraine or took the wrong side in such debates. One of them concerned the ethnic origins of the Ukrainian people and the formation of the Belarusian, Great Russian, and Ruthenian-Ukrainian 'tribes.' Another was the issue of the devastation of Kyiv after the Mongol invasion. Barvinsky's offhand remark that Kyiv had been reduced to ruins flew in the face of the efforts of Antonovych's circle to prove Mikhail Pogodin and his followers wrong. Nor was Syniavsky entirely satisfied with Barvinsky's treatment of social factors in history.

Syniavsky began his review by claiming rather undiplomatically that Barvinsky was free to follow those Polish historians who wrote that the Poles did not have a written record of their own history and say the same about the Ukrainians. He concluded with the hope that Barvinsky would find time to write a 'complete' history of Ukraine. The Dnipro Ukrainians wanted a history written on the same scholarly level as the Russian and Polish narratives. They wanted that narrative to reflect their interest in the origins of nations and to present all aspects of the history of their people and society, not only political developments. Last but not least, they wanted it to address the most contentious issues of Russo-Ukrainian relations, including the problem of Kyivan Rus'. The Galicians were well aware that they could not produce such a narrative, given their lack of professionalism at a time when history was coming to be regarded less as an art than as a science.

That realization was at least partly responsible for Barvinsky's own efforts to establish a chair of Ukrainian history at Lviv University and to invite a scholar from Dnipro Ukraine to fill it. Hrushevsky, who was appointed to the chair, fully addressed the scholarly interests of his Kyiv mentors and colleagues in his works, but he was probably no less attuned to the concerns of his Galician forerunners.

Structuring the Past

Galician realities of the late nineteenth century found expression, among other things, in the title of Hrushevsky's magnum opus, the *History of Ukraine-Rus'*. What was the origin and significance of that compound term, which already seemed outdated and inadequate to Hrushevsky's Eastern Ukrainian contemporaries in the first decade of the twentieth century? Its origins were directly related to the development of the Ukrainian historical project in Galicia. The massive translation effort undertaken by the publishers of the Ruthenian Historical Library concentrated attention on the need for a Ukrainian scholarly terminology, first and foremost the selection of a suitable term to denote the Ukrainian people and their territory. The problem was not so simple as it might appear at first glance. The terms 'Ukraine' and 'Ukrainian,' which were adopted by the Ukrainian national 'awakeners,' had both advantages and drawbacks. Ironically, back in the early nineteenth century, the leaders of the Ukrainian national movement in the Russian Empire had chosen for themselves and their land names that were as little established in their country's intellectual tradition as they were among the common people. During the princely era, the term 'Ukraine' was used by the Rus' chroniclers to define the borderland of the settled area. In the early modern period, it was applied to the middle Dnipro territories, the cradle of Ukrainian Cossackdom. Not until the nineteenth century was it employed to define the Ukrainian ethnos or its ethnic territory as a whole. The choice of the nineteenth-century national awakeners was apparently influenced by two major considerations. First was the desire to stress their links with the glorious Cossack tradition, as Ukraine – the middle Dnipro region – was above all the homeland of Cossackdom, and second was the imperative of drawing a clear distinction between their own land and people and those of Russia. The existing tradition of using ethnonyms and toponyms derived from 'Rus'' – 'Ruthenia(n)' in Western Ukraine and 'Little Russia(n)' in Eastern Ukraine – implied too close an association with Russia to allow Ukrainian activists of the early nineteenth century to make a plausible case for the distinctive character of their Little Russian/Ruthenian people.[49]

Besides offering solutions, the term 'Ukraine' created difficulties. One of the many problems with the terms 'Ukraine' and 'Ukrainian' was that they introduced even more discontinuity into the history of Ukraine, which, from the viewpoint of any traditional-minded historian, was already full of discontinuities, given the long centuries of absence of a state ruled by local elites. The first cautious attempts at the Ukrainization of the 'Little Russian' past by proponents of the Ukrainian movement in the early nineteenth century had already met with protests on the part of the anonymous author of the *History of the*

Rus', a forerunner of Ukrainian national historiography. In the introduction to his work, he attacked those who were beginning to apply the terms 'Ukraine' and 'Ukrainian' to the history of the Dnipro region. For the author of the *History of the Rus'*, that land was Little Russia. He claimed that the inhabitants of Little Russia were the true Rus' people and denounced the whole 'Ukrainization' project as a Polish intrigue.[50] The terms 'Ukraine' and 'Ukrainian' were even more difficult to popularize in Western Ukraine. In Habsburg-ruled Galicia and Bukovyna, popular historical memory had no particular attachment to the Cossack past, and the terms 'Rus'' and 'Ruthenian' served reasonably well to distinguish the local population from the dominant Polish minority and the Austrian ruling elite.

A solution was eventually found in the introduction of the term 'Ukraine-Rus'' into political and scholarly discourse in the last decades of the nineteenth century. It resulted from a conscious effort to overcome the terminological differences between the Russian and Austrian branches of the Ukrainian national movement. Judging by Barvinsky's memoirs, that term was suggested by Antonovych in the course of their discussion of the Library project. As Barvinsky wrote in 1913, 'it was also necessary to establish an expression in relation to the name of our land and people as opposed to Muscovy, and on Antonovych's advice the adjective "Ukrainian-Rus'" (*ukraïns'ko-rus'kyi*) was adopted as opposed to "Great Russian" (*velyko-rus'koho*), and the noun "Ukraine-Rus'" (*Ukraïna-Rus'*) as opposed to "Muscovy."'[51] It is thus quite obvious that in Barvinsky's eyes the use of the new term was justified by the need to distinguish Ukraine clearly from Russia. One might also assume that Antonovych hoped the new term would eventually replace another compound ethnonym, 'Little Russian,' opening the way to a gradual change of popular self-identification. If that was indeed the plan, then it was never realized in Eastern Ukraine, where the compound 'Ukraine-Rus'' failed to gain any noticeable popularity, even among the intelligentsia. It proved much more successful in Galicia and Bukovyna, where, once accepted, it dominated public discourse for more than a quarter-century. The success of the term in the Habsburg Monarchy can be explained by its capacity to bridge the gap between the two parts of the Ukrainian national movement, 'Great Ukrainian' and Galician, whose representatives – even in Barvinsky's own memoirs – were respectively termed 'Ukrainians' and 'Ruthenians' on numerous occasions.

In both parts of Ukraine, the introduction of the term 'Ukraine-Rus'' obviously helped bridge the gap between the new national movement and the Ukrainian historical tradition. Writing in 1913, Hrushevsky explained the use of the term by the need to bring together the new Ukrainian movement and historical Ukraine: 'As awareness of continuity and uninterruptedness of ethno-national Ukrainian life grew, the Ukrainian name came to encompass the entire history of the Ukrainian people. In order to underscore the link between modern Ukrainian life and its ancient traditions, the name was also employed (during the final quarter of the last century) in the compound forms "Ukraine-Rus'" and "Ukrainian-Ruthenian," wherein the old traditional name was combined with the new term representing national rebirth and the national movement.'[52]

Barvinsky's series, which maintained its original title of Ruthenian Historical Library, included volumes that popularized the compound ethnonym, such as the translation of excerpts from Ilovaisky's works titled *The Princely Period in the History of Ukraine-Rus'*. As the term gained currency among the population at large, it lent momentum to the project of raising the national consciousness of Ukrainians in Galicia and Bukovyna. Peasant readers of Barvinsky's Library thanked him for his work in the following words: 'Accept these few simple words of thanks for such great efforts on your part for the good of your people. As far as we have acquainted ourselves with the *History of Ukraine-Rus'*, it is a work of great significance that encompasses our past, showing the tracks followed by our ancestors, where they slipped, and where we should tread today so as not to perish without trace and attain some position in the world ... [The Library] is our bible and law, which should be in every home, and we would then be a people like others, for then we would know ourselves.'[53]

The compound term 'Ukraine-Rus'' proved transitional in Hrushevsky's usage, employed at a certain point in his career and all but abandoned later. In his work of 1891 on the history of the Kyivan Land, published in Russian, Hrushevsky used the term *russkii* (Russian) in relation to the Ukrainian population of the princely era. In 1894, discussing the early history of Ukraine in his inaugural lecture at Lviv University, he used the term *rus'kyi* (Ruthenian) in the same way as *russkii* in his Russian-language publications. This proved an exception to Hrushevsky's practice in Galicia. In his Ukrainian-language publications there, beginning with his article of 1892 in the *Memoirs of the Shevchenko Scientific Society*, Hrushevsky made almost exclusive use of the compound 'Ukraine-Rus'.' He also employed it in the series title of the *Sources on the History of Ukraine-Rus'*, initiated in 1895, and in the title of his academic *History of Ukraine-Rus'*, the first volume of which was published in 1898.[54] The compound also appeared in Hrushevsky's famous article on the traditional scheme of 'Russian' history (1904), but that was one of its last occurrences in his work. In his Russian-language *Survey History of the Ukrainian People*, published in the same year as his programmatic essay, Hrushevsky abandoned the compound and switched to the simple 'Ukraine.' He followed the same policy in his Ukrainian-language *Illustrated History of Ukraine* (1911). As early as 1913, upon issuing the third edition of volume 1 of his academic *History*, Hrushevsky noted that the compound 'Ukraine-Rus'' was now all but supplanted in the scholarly literature by the term 'Ukraine.' The outdated term nevertheless remained in the title of Hrushevsky's major work, whose consecutive volumes, the last of which appeared in print in 1936, served as a reminder of those not so distant times when the term 'Ukraine' still needed additional components in order to root the nationalization project in the historical past and extend it beyond the boundaries of Dnipro Ukraine.

Hrushevsky's gradual but decisive switch from 'Rus'' to 'Ukraine' in writing the history of Kyivan Rus' drew a barrage from both the Polish and the Russian/Little Russian camps. In 1913, reviewing volumes 4, 5, and 6 of Hrushevsky's *History*, the Polish historian Ludwik Kolankowski wrote that he would not use the term 'Ukrainian' in his discussion of the work. He maintained that even if the 'Ruthenians' accepted the term, the Poles should continue to use their own historical terms, *Ruś* and *ruski*.[55] The same position was taken in 1917 by a reviewer of one of Hrushevsky's German-language brochures, Czesław Frankiewicz, who stated that the term 'Ukrainian' was ill-suited to the discussion of Rus' history and that Polish scholarship had to continue employing terms endowed with historical legitimacy, namely, *Ruś* and *ruski*.[56] Also extremely critical of the term 'Ukrainian' (instead of 'Ruthenian') was Hrushevsky's arch-enemy, Franciszek Rawita-Gawroński.[57] It was only after Hrushevsky's death that one of the Polish reviewers of his works, Adrian Kapystiański, effectively accepted Hrushevsky's terminological innovation by using the terms 'Ruthenian,' 'Ukrainian-Ruthenian,' and 'Ukrainian' interchangeably in the course of assessing the historian's scholarly legacy.[58] Ironically, some Little Russian authors, such as Andrei Storozhenko, who was highly critical of Hrushevsky's use of 'Ukraine,' discerned a Polish 'intrigue' in the introduction of the term.[59] In reality, what united representatives of both the historiographic traditions once dominant in the Ukrainian lands was their determination to stop the 'nationalization' of Ukrainian history. One way of doing so was to deny it the right to use a name different from the ones established in both dominant historiographic traditions.

Establishing the continuity of Ukrainian history was an important element of Hrushevsky's project, and the title of his *History* was only its most obvious manifestation. The actual 'glue' with which Hrushevsky intended to piece together the various periods of Ukrainian history in order to produce a continuous account was the history of the people (*narod*). That historiographic approach was most eloquently expressed by Hrushevsky in his inaugural lecture at Lviv University (1894). There he asserted: 'I have gone beyond the bounds of my chronological course in order to show how closely and indivisibly all periods of Rus' history are connected with one another, how one and the same popular striving, one and the same leading idea extends across that whole row of centuries amid such different political and cultural circumstances. Only from that viewpoint do this link and this unity become clearly discernible, supplanting the mechanical coupling of distinct periods. The people, the popular masses, bind them into a whole and are and ought to be the alpha and omega of historical research.'[60]

From the very start of his scholarly career, Hrushevsky put the people at the centre of his historical writings. In political terms, his focus on the people reflected the views of Kyivan populist circles of the second half of the nineteenth century. In purely scholarly terms, it can be traced back to the works of Mykola Kostomarov, which stressed the importance of the ethnographic approach to the writing of history.[61] Both tendencies combined and reinforced each other in the circle established by Volodymyr Antonovych and his students at Kyiv University, which served as Hrushevsky's intellectual cradle.

It comes as little surprise that the two major subjects of Hrushevsky's inaugural lecture at Lviv University echoed central themes presented in Antonovych's own inaugural lecture at Kyiv University (1870), as well as in the latter's introductory lecture to a course on the history of Galician Rus' and Ukrainian Cossackdom delivered in the early 1870s. Like Antonovych before him, Hrushevsky believed that the historian's task was to study the history of the people as opposed to that of the state and placed special emphasis on the importance of scholarly objectivity in historical research.[62] Among the views expressed by Antonovych that influenced Hrushevsky's interpretation were the understanding of the Ukrainian past as a continuous process from ancient times to the present; the view of Kyivan Rus' history as a product of the interaction of princes, their retinues, and popular communes; the positive assessment of the Lithuanian period of Ukrainian history; and an extremely negative attitude toward Polish rule in Ukraine.[63]

Under the influence of Antonovych, Hrushevsky became a strong believer in and adherent of populist ideology, but with the passage of time he adopted a broader national approach – a process reflected in his use of the fundamental term *narod*. Slowly but surely, its meaning changed in Hrushevsky's writings during the last decade of the nineteenth century and the first decade of the twentieth. If at first he used it as a synonym of 'popular masses,' he gradually came to regard it as the equivalent of 'nation.' In his inaugural lecture at Lviv University in 1894, Hrushevsky asserted that the history of the state or of culture should interest the historian only to the degree that it reflected and influenced the life of the people or, on the contrary, was itself influenced by it.[64] With the passage of time, this strict interpretation of Ukrainian history as a predominantly 'populist' account made way in Hrushevsky's thinking for a more inclusive national project, which, while remaining attentive to the history of the popular masses, did not disregard or marginalize the history either of the state or of culture. As discussed earlier, in his article of 1904 on the traditional scheme of 'Russian' history, Hrushevsky placed nationality (*narodnist'*) at the centre of his scheme of Ukrainian history. His transformation from 'populist' into broadly defined national historian was all but complete by the First World War. Presenting his new understanding of the Ukrainian historical process in the introduction to volume 1 (third edition) of his academic *History* (1913), Hrushevsky not only switched to a new use of the term 'people' (in the sense of 'nation') but also introduced culture (along with the social factor) as one of the two paramount elements in the historical experience of the Ukrainian people (nation) after the collapse of Ukrainian statehood. The view that the history of the state was only partly relevant to the history of the people, which Hrushevsky had asserted in his inaugural lecture of 1894, was limited in his work of 1913 to the role of non-Ukrainian states in Ukrainian history.[65]

Hrushevsky expressed his new credo in the following words: 'Thus, social and cultural processes constitute the leitmotif that leads us through all the fluctuations of political life, through all the stages of its rise and decline, and unifies into a single whole the history of Ukrainian life, regardless of the various upheavals, even catastrophes, that it experienced. Historians have usually taken the opposite approach. Tracing the history of political organizations, they tacked on parts of the history of the Ukrainian people to that of the Polish or of the Russian state, so that this history disintegrated into a series of disjointed episodes lacking all connection and continuity. When, however, Ukraine's social and cultural processes are viewed as the foundation, that history becomes an organic whole, a whole in which continuity has never been broken and in which even the most dramatic changes occurred on an ancient and stable foundation, which changed very slowly under their impact.'[66]

As Hrushevsky's outline of Ukrainian history attests, he did not rely on a purely populist approach for too long. In his article of 1904 on the traditional scheme of 'Russian' history, he suggested that the line of Ukrainian historical development proceeded from the Kyivan period to the Galician-Volhynian one, and subsequently to the Lithuanian-Polish era. The construct of Ukrainian history suggested by Hrushevsky, like the old scheme of 'Russian' history that he criticized, was based on the statist approach. It also included at least one major geographical shift, from the Kyivan Land in the twelfth century to the Principality of Galicia-Volhynia in the thirteenth. But there were also major differences between these two approaches. Unlike Pogodin and Kliuchevsky, Hrushevsky did not believe in mass eastward or westward migrations of population from the Kyivan Land. His rationale was of a different kind. Hrushevsky viewed both the Kyivan Rus' state and the Principality of Galicia-Volhynia as products of the historical activity of one and the same Ruthenian-Ukrainian nationality.[67] Hrushevsky's emphasis on the history of the people and his later fascination with the social and cultural life of the nation proved crucial for establishing the continuity of the Ukrainian historical experience and served as the framework for the new national paradigm of Ukrainian history.

In his critique of Hrushevsky, Linnichenko suggested that 'Mr Hrushevsky's new scheme is very old news.'[68] Although it is not entirely clear what Linnichenko meant, there can be little doubt that in a number of ways, the scheme of Ukrainian history employed by Hrushevsky completed the preparatory work accomplished by a score of Ukrainian historians of the populist orientation, including Mykhailo Maksymovych, Panteleimon Kulish, Mykola Kostomarov, and Hrushevsky's own professor, Volodymyr Antonovych. While none of them produced a major synthesis of Ukrainian history, their research on particular topics not only challenged the dominant imperial historical paradigm but also laid the foundations for Hrushevsky's interpretation.[69] Hrushevsky's own scheme of Ukrainian history (as presented in his article of 1904 and his *Survey History of the Ukrainian People*) closely resembled the outline of a series, 'Essays on the History of Little Russia,' suggested in December 1895 by the editorial board of the journal *Kievskaia starina*. The outline was drafted with the active participation of Volodymyr Antonovych and followed by Aleksandra Efimenko in her *History of the Ukrainian People* (1906). It began with prehistoric times and proceeded to the history of the Kyivan principality and the appanage period in 'Southern Rus'' (with special emphasis in Efimenko's survey on the history of the Galician-Volhynian principality). Apart from the Antonovych-Efimenko scheme, Hrushevsky's outline of Ukrainian history had much in common with the outlines presented in Oleksander Barvinsky's *Illustrated History of Rus'* and the review of that work by Antin Syniavsky.[70]

The historical paradigm sketched by Hrushevsky in his article on the traditional scheme of 'Russian' history and further developed in his *Survey, Illustrated History of Ukraine,* and the academic *History of Ukraine-Rus'* not only manifested a continuation of the Ukrainian historiographic tradition but also incorporated a number of innovations. These become particularly apparent when one considers the differences between Hrushevsky's periodization of Ukrainian history and the scheme adopted by Efimenko in her *History of the Ukrainian People*. With regard to the princely era, the salient difference was Hrushevsky's introduction of the state factor as a major criterion for the periodization of the Ukrainian past. The first chapter of Efimenko's course, titled 'The Prehistoric Era,' corresponded in Hrushevsky's *Illustrated History* to a section titled 'Before the Founding of the Kyivan State.' The period from the tenth to the fourteenth century, covered by Efimenko in a chapter on the origins of the land of Rus' and one titled 'The Appanage Era,' was rendered by Hrushevsky in a chapter titled 'Statehood.' In his *Illustrated History*, Hrushevsky not only stressed the role of the state in the first centuries of Ukrainian history but also used the state factor to link two areas of Ukraine, the Dnipro region (including Kyiv) and Galicia.

Presenting the history of different Ukrainian lands as the past of a single national entity was one of the major challenges and objectives of Hrushevsky's narrative. He dealt with the problem not only in his definition of the Kyivan-Galician period of Ukrainian history but also in establishing the chronological scope of the following period, which in his account covered the Ukrainian past from the mid-fourteenth to the end of the sixteenth century. Both in his article on the traditional scheme of 'Russian' history and in his *Illustrated History of Ukraine*, Hrushevsky called this the Lithuanian-Polish period.[71] In Efimenko's survey that era was covered by a chapter on Southern Rus' within the Lithuanian state (with a subsection on the history of Galician Rus') and another chapter on the history of Southern Rus' under Polish rule from the Union of Lublin (1569) to the Khmelnytsky Uprising (1648).[72] In general terms, Efimenko's outline (and the one developed by Antonovych on which it was based) followed the scheme developed by Mykhailo Maksymovych. In his article of 1857 on the history of Polish-Ukrainian antagonism, Maksymovych divided post-Kyivan Ukrainian history into a number of periods. The first of these was the era of Tatar control. The second period, 'The Era of Lithuanian Rule,' covered Ukrainian history from 1320 to 1569. The third period, termed 'The Era of Polish Rule,' extended from 1569 to 1648 and thus corresponded exactly to the analogous chapter of Efimenko's work.[73]

Why did Hrushevsky not follow Maksymovych and Efimenko in designating the period between the Union of Lublin and the Khmelnytsky Uprising as a separate era of Ukrainian history? Part of the answer is to be found in Hrushevsky's desire to produce a historical scheme that would fit the history of Eastern and Western Ukraine alike. Hrushevsky could not follow Maksymovych's example, because the latter's periodization of Ukrainian history applied first and foremost to 'Ukraine' as that term was understood in the mid-nineteenth century, that is, the Dnipro region, leaving Galician history out of account. The division of Ukrainian history into Lithuanian and Polish periods also separated late medieval Galician history from that of the rest of Ukrainian territory, for Galicia became part of the Polish state in the mid-fourteenth century, while Ukrainian lands to the east were under the tutelage of Lithuanian princes. By introducing the notion of a 'Lithuanian-Polish' period, Hrushevsky was able to treat both Western and Eastern Ukrainian lands prior to the Union of Lublin as an entity. In so doing, he followed the periodization employed by his fellow Galician Barvinsky and effectively rejected Syniavsky's critique of that approach.[74] Another important element in Hrushevsky's definition of the 'Lithuanian-Polish' period was its choronological extension to the end of the sixteenth century. After that point, according to Hrushevsky, Ukrainian history entered a new period of its development, the Cossack era, which covered almost the whole of the seventeenth and eighteenth centuries. By introducing this dividing line between the Polish-Lithuanian and Cossack periods of Ukrainian history, Hrushevsky was refusing, in effect, to treat the state factor, which was crucial to his definition of the first period, as a guiding principle for the periodization of Ukrainian history after the decline of Ukrainian statehood.[75]

Thus, Hrushevsky's scheme of Ukrainian history took account of several important factors and addressed a number of concerns expressed in Ukrainian historiography of the turn of the twentieth century, both in Galicia and in Dnipro Ukraine. These included the issue of the unity of the Ukrainian lands (implying the unity of the Ukrainian national narrative), as well as the role of the state and the significance of social and national factors in Ukrainian history. Despite all the criticism of his scheme from enemies and well-wishers alike,[76] Hrushevsky managed to include all these factors in his paradigm and arrange them in a balanced manner to produce a national narrative of Ukrainian history – a historiographic product qualitatively different from all previous narratives of the history of Ukraine. At the core of this new narrative lay the story of the Ukrainian nation.

The Story of a Nation

Hrushevsky strongly believed in the distinct character of the Ukrainian nation, which he regarded not so much as the product of any racial distinctiveness (he believed that the Ukrainian nation was racially mixed) as of long historical evolution. In that respect, Hrushevsky followed scores of nineteenth-century activists and theoreticians of the national movement, including the enormously influential Mykhailo Drahomanov.[77] In the introduction to the third edition of volume 1 of his academic *History* (1913), Hrushevsky wrote: 'The Ukrainian population differs from its closest neighbours both in anthropological characteristics – i.e., in body build – and in psychological features: in individual temperament, family and social relationships, way of life, and in material and spiritual culture. These psychophysical and cultural characteristics, some of which emerged earlier than others, are all the result of a lengthy process of evolution and quite clearly unify the individual groups of the Ukrainian people into a distinct national entity that differs from other such national entities and possesses an unmistakable and vital national personality – that is, comprises a separate *people* with a long history of development.'[78]

In the last decade of the nineteenth century and the first years of the twentieth, as Hrushevsky's focus shifted from the people as the embodiment of the popular masses to the people as constituents of a nation, his history became more and more national in character. It acquired its own logic and rhythm that influenced the periodization established by Hrushevsky in the earlier stages of work on his academic *History*. In this respect, as in others, the national factor in Hrushevsky's interpretation of the Ukrainian past showed to best advantage in his writings of the period following the Revolution of 1905. To show how Hrushevsky's national paradigm of this period accorded with his general scheme of Ukrainian history, I shall turn again to his introduction to the third edition of volume 1 of the academic *History* (1913).

There, Hrushevsky divided Ukrainian history into four major periods. The first, the 'princely era,' which was dominated by the activities of Ukrainian principalities, was followed in Hrushevsky's scheme by the 'transitional' period, which began in the mid-fourteenth century and was characterized in political terms by the dominance of the Lithuanian and Polish states. The third period covered the 'popular' or Cossack era, and the fourth, with a survey of which Hrushevsky intended to conclude his academic *History*, was termed the 'era of Ukrainian national revival' and covered the developments of the nineteenth century.[79] Hrushevsky viewed that period as the apotheosis of Ukrainian history. He wrote: 'If we were to apply the old historiographic terminology, the two periods in which Ukrainian political life flourished – the ancient princely era and the more recent populist (Cossack) age – could be regarded as the thesis and antithesis, which reach their synthesis in the century of Ukrainian rebirth. Popular aspirations are reemerging and becoming enlightened by progressive European thought, and they are being adopted by the new intelligentsia that has emerged on this ground under the impact of progressive ideas.'[80]

By 'the old historiographic terminology,' the historian obviously meant the Hegelian triad, a product of the romantic age perceived by Hrushevsky and his contemporaries as somewhat outdated in the era of positivism. Nevertheless, Hrushevsky the historian-sociologist, as he often referred to himself, badly needed that outdated terminology to formulate his essentially romantic national paradigm of Ukrainian history. At the centre of that paradigm was the concept of the rebirth/ revival of the Ukrainian nation. That concept can be traced back to the first document of modern Ukrainian political thought, Kostomarov's *Books of the Genesis of the Ukrainian People*, which are clearly marked by the Polish messianism of Adam Mickiewicz.[81] Hrushevsky's paradigm also reflected the influence of sociological concepts popular at the turn of the twentieth century that drew on the biological sciences, regarding societies as organisms subject to cycles of growth, competition, and decline.[82]

Apparently, Hrushevsky was so fascinated with the tripartite paradigm of national history that he applied it not only to the 'long' history of Ukraine – from prehistoric times to his own day – but also to its short variant, from the times of Kyivan Rus' to the end of the Cossack era, with the late sixteenth and seventeenth centuries also figuring as a period of national revival. Thus Hrushevsky's historical scheme, as it evolved over time, comprised two declines and two revivals of Ukrainian national life. The first decline took place after the last of the Ukrainian states lost its independence in the mid-fourteenth century and continued until the end of the sixteenth century. It was succeeded by the resurgence of the late sixteenth century, which found expression in the rise of the Ukrainian national and cultural movement and the growth of Cossackdom. The second decline took place in the second half of the eighteenth century with the abolition of the Ukrainian Cossack state (the Hetmanate) and the Zaporozhian Sich. That decline was followed by the Ukrainian national revival of the nineteenth century. The complexity of the scheme forced Hrushevsky to adopt such terms as 'first revival' and 'second revival,' which he frequently used in the 1920s.[83]

Let us consider in greater detail how Hrushevsky applied his national paradigm to the first 'cycle' of his academic *History*, covering the three periods from Kyivan Rus' to the 'first' revival of the late sixteenth and early seventeenth centuries and analysed in the prerevolutionary volumes of his magnum opus. Hrushevsky gave his most comprehensive characterization of the first period – the 'princely era' – in the introduction to the third edition of volume 1 of his *History* (1913). In his view the first period was shaped politically by the Rus' state. The inclusion of all branches of the Ukrainian people in a single state helped develop common cultural and social characteristics. Hrushevsky made specific reference to the introduction of Christianity, which entailed the influence of Byzantium, and the spread of Kyivan law throughout the Rus' lands. In social and economic terms the period was characterized, in Hrushevsky's opinion, by the dichotomy between the princely retinue and the popular masses, as well as by the emergence of the merchant-boyar stratum.[84]

Hrushevsky treated the rule of Volodymyr (Vladimir) the Great (978–1015) as the pinnacle of Ukrainian history in the princely era. Ever since the Primary Chronicle, Volodymyr and his age had been especially important to historians of the Rus'. The authors of the first chronicles and compilations based upon them singled out Volodymyr from a score of other famous Kyivan princes (including his father, Sviatoslav, and his son Iaroslav the Wise) primarily because of his role in the Christianization of Rus', which began ca. 988 and continued with Volodymyr's strong support until the end of his reign. The tradition of eulogizing Volodymyr was also strong in the early modern Ukrainian historiographic tradition. In the *Synopsis* (1674), the Kyivan monks presented Volodymyr as the first Russian (*rossiiskii*) monarch. The monks had more than enough reason to glorify Volodymyr the Great, who as a venerated Orthodox saint enhanced the importance of Kyiv and its brand of Christianity in the Romanov realm.[85] But what was Hrushevsky's basis for considering Volodymyr and his era the summit of Kyivan Rus' history? Indeed, why did Hrushevsky esteem Volodymyr more highly than Sviatoslav or Iaroslav the Wise?

Hrushevsky's own answer to this question is to be found in the first edition of his *Survey History of the Ukrainian People* (1904), where he wrote: 'The time of Volodymyr the Saintly or the Great was the culminating point in the formation of the Kyivan or Rus' state, in the mechanical process, so to speak, of its evolution.'[86] After that, in Hrushevsky's opinion, the Kyivan state declined steadily, with Iaroslav the Wise presiding over the initial stage of the process. According to Hrushevsky, the decline was all but complete by the mid-thirteenth century, and only the rise to prominence of the Galician-Volhynian principality ensured the continuity of Ukrainian statehood.[87] Hence, in 1904 Volodymyr and his era were important to Hrushevsky first and foremost as a reflection of the high point in the development of the Ukrainian state. As compared with Hrushevsky's inaugural lecture at Lviv University, that judgment signified a major shift in his interpretation of Ukrainian history and was a far cry from the populist principles he had declared ten years earlier.[88]

Although Hrushevsky did not entirely abandon the populist views of his youth, he was clearly prepared to make significant changes of emphasis in his interpretation of the princely era. In 1894 he did not distinguish between the role of the native and the foreign state, asserting that 'whether native or foreign, it [the state order] was never, or hardly ever, created according to their wishes [that is, those of the popular masses], and the community and the state stood opposed to each other not only in the ancient period.'[89] By 1912 Hrushevsky drew a clear distinction between the control exercised over the popular masses by native and foreign states. 'From the national standpoint,' wrote Hrushevsky in the *Illustrated History of Ukraine*, 'it meant a great deal that this sovereign independence [of Ukraine] protected our people from enslavement by other peoples and from the exploitation of our economic and cultural forces for the development and strengthening of the culture of some other sovereign ruling nationality.'[90] Hrushevsky now believed that as long as the state remained in the hands of local elites, they used the available resources, among other things, to develop national culture, which also served the interests of the popular masses.[91] Thus, by adopting a national standpoint, Hrushevsky managed to reconcile (if not completely harmonize) some of the conflicting interests of the elites and the masses, as well as to rehabilitate the state within the framework of populist discourse as an institution that served the interests of the masses by defending them against foreign oppression and developing national culture.[92]

Hrushevsky's new emphasis on the role of the national factor in Ukrainian history helped make Volodymyr the Great an even greater hero of his nationalized historical narrative, for he could now be presented as a builder not only of the state but also of the nation. In Hrushevsky's opinion, Volodymyr was able to consolidate the various parts of the vast Kyivan state, originally assembled by mere force of arms, through the use of political, legal, and cultural ties. The new elements that Volodymyr introduced into the political and cultural life of Kyivan Rus' in order to strengthen its unity were a princely dynasty, with Volodymyr's sons ruling major parts of the Kyivan state, the establishment of the Rus' law throughout the state, and the introduction of a common Christian culture promoted by the Orthodox Church and based on the cultural accomplishments of Byzantium.[93] 'A variety of lands and tribes,' wrote Hrushevsky, 'were bound together not only by the dynastic link – common princely descent and a common stratum of retainers that spread from Kyiv across all those lands, and with it the common Kyivan law and order that was propagated and established throughout the lands by princely governors, officials, and judges. They were also bound together by a common faith and church, as well as by a common hierarchy (priesthood) subordinate to the Kyivan metropolitan, by literature and education strongly tinged with an ecclesiastical coloration, and by art.'[94]

Hrushevsky was generally successful in accomplishing the transformation of Vladimir the Great, the Orthodox saint and one of the leading ideological symbols of the Russian Empire, into Volodymyr the Great, a Ukrainian national hero. (That transformation must have had special meaning for Hrushevsky, given his attachment to Kyiv, with its statue of the famous prince and baptizer of Rus' on the hills sloping down to the Dnipro, as well as the historian's *alma mater* bearing his name.) Hrushevsky presented Volodymyr as a positivist hero, a builder of state and nation. He was also inclined to retain the traditional image of Volodymyr as baptizer of Rus', for he was much less sceptical with regard to the Primary Chronicle's account of the baptism of Rus' than were other students of the chronicle.[95] No other Rus' prince could rival Volodymyr in Hrushevsky's narrative. The only comparable figures in his *History* were those of the Galician-Volhynian princes Roman and Danylo, builders of another medieval Ukrainian state. Hrushevsky admired them both and depicted them more as romantic than as positivist heroes, distinguished by their energy and, in the case of Danylo, by the popularity he enjoyed among the population at large.[96] Given Hrushevsky's populist beliefs, Danylo was in many ways an ideal ruler, as he was known for mustering the support of the people in the struggle against the boyar elites, but even he did not outshine the nation-builder Volodymyr. Danylo's failing, apparently, was that the Galician-Volhynian state he helped strengthen proved incapable of gathering all the Ukrainian lands, as had the Kyivan state of Volodymyr the Great, even though it prolonged the period of Ukrainian sovereignty.[97]

Hrushevsky strongly believed that Volodymyr's reforms helped reduce the importance of boundaries between different Ukrainian tribes, establishing national links that outlived the Kyivan state itself. He did not, however, seek to assert that those changes affected only the Ukrainian tribes. Not only in his academic *History* but also in his popular works, including the Russian-language *Survey History of the Ukrainian People* and the Ukrainian-language *Illustrated History of Ukraine*, he pointed out that the Kyivan era helped draw together Ukrainian, Belarusian, and Russian territories.[98] In his Russian-language publications Hrushevsky continued to use the term 'Russian' in relation to the Kyivan state.[99] He clearly did not want to frighten away his Russian readers by mentioning Ukraine in the same breath as Kyivan Rus', which lay at the foundations of Russian historical consciousness. At the same time, Hrushevsky remained true to his principal thesis that Kyivan Rus' was a creation of the Ukrainian nationality and found it frustrating that his interpretation of Kyivan Rus' history was far from generally accepted. As he noted in the *Survey*: 'Only with difficulty and very slowly is the scholarly literature becoming cognizant of the clear and perfectly obvious fact that the Kyivan state, its laws, everyday existence, and culture were the product of the Ukrainian nationality, and its laws and culture in the Great Russian nationality constitute almost the same kind of reception as Byzantine or, for example, Polish law and culture in the life of the Ukrainian people in the seventeenth and eighteenth centuries.'[100]

As noted earlier, in Hrushevsky's historical scheme the era of national decline was assigned to the 'transitional' period that lasted from the mid-thirteenth to the end of the sixteenth century. Hrushevsky's original account of this period of Ukrainian history exemplifies the development of some of the most effective methods of constructing national identity – seeking external causes for the nation's woes, defining the enemy in ethnic/national terms, and blaming that enemy for the hardships besetting the historian's own people. Hrushevsky believed that the dramatic decline of Ukrainian national life was caused not only by prevailing circumstances but also by a very specific enemy with a clear national identity. That enemy, in Hrushevsky's eyes, was Poland. In volume 4 of his academic *History* (1903, 2d ed. 1907), he rendered the following assessment of the Polish factor in the 'transitional' centuries of Ukrainian history: 'Having brought the Ukrainian lands under its rule, it [Poland] sought to reduce Ukrainian life to its Polish design. This was a process of bending and breaking historically developed Ukrainian forms in the social, political, and cultural spheres to fit the Polish mould. A process of enslaving the Ukrainian people to the Polish nationality, not only in the cultural or political sphere but also in the social and political one – returning the Ukrainian populace to the condition of a servile, subject, exploited nationality. And the lack of strong and sharp opposition to this process on the part of Ukrainian society, on the part of the Ukrainian people, endowed this fatal process, these lethal Polish efforts, endowed these times with the character of a period of decline not only of the political but also the social forces of the Ukrainian people.'[101]

In 1913, in his introduction to volume 1 of the *History*, Hrushevsky broadened his approach to the assessment of the 'transitional' period of Ukrainian history presented only a few years earlier. In political terms, Hrushevsky now characterized that period as a time of Lithuanian and Polish control over the Ukrainian lands. In cultural terms, he saw it as an era of the decline of the Byzantine legacy and the growth of Western influences. In social terms, it was a period of growing antagonism between masses and elites, and in the national sphere it was a time when social antagonisms acquired a national and religious colouring, and Ukrainian society began to take cognizance of the 'threat of impending national death.'[102] Despite this much more balanced account of the 'transitional' period of Ukrainian history, Hrushevsky's negative view of the Polish factor in Ukrainian history remained one of the main features of his general interpretation of the Ukrainian past.

The problem that Hrushevsky faced in relating his Ukrainian historical paradigm to the Polish one was different from the challenge posed by the imperial Russian narrative. In the latter case, Hrushevsky's main task was to delimit the past and establish a Ukrainian claim to many significant episodes of the imperial historical narrative. With regard to Poland, the task was not so much one of presenting Ukrainian history as a distinct process, separate from the Polish grand narrative (this had already been achieved by his predecessors), as of giving the Ukrainian nation a sense of equality in relations with its historically dominant and culturally much more Westernized counterpart, which was also far more advanced in terms of nation-building. In dealing with this problem, Hrushevsky found himself following in the footsteps of a number of nineteenth-century Ukrainian historians.

The origins of the Ukrainian response to Polish theories about the benefits of Poland's rule over Ukraine can be traced back to the anonymous author of the *History of the Rus'*, who argued that the Cossacks were not organized by the Poles and that the Dnipro area was settled not by the Poles but by the Rus'.[103] Another Ukrainian historian who took an active part in historiographic discussions with Polish scholars was Mykola Kostomarov. He not only rejected the claims of Polish authors who asserted that the Ukrainians (Ruthenians) belonged to the same nation as the Poles[104] but was also very critical of the suggestion that Polish rule had benefited Ukraine, claiming that it had not improved the condition of the popular masses in any way.[105] Volodymyr Antonovych was also a strong opponent of the interpretation, popular among Polish historians, of Polish-Ukrainian relations as an encounter of the civilized and tolerant Polish state with the uncouth and brutal Ukrainian peasant who refused to acknowledge how much he owed to the benevolent rule of his masters.[106] But by far the most important of Hrushevsky's forerunners in the critique of Polish historical myths was Mykhailo Maksymovych, the original critic of the Pogodin theory.[107]

In his open letter of 1857 to the renowned Polish historian Michał Grabowski, Maksymovych polemicized with the latter's assertion that it was the Polish authorities who settled the Ukrainian territories laid waste by the Tatar invasion. Maksymovych suggested that the Polish period in the history of Ukraine (as noted earlier, in his usage the term referred only to the Dnipro region) had been relatively short, lasting only eighty-five years, from the Union of Lublin (1569) to the Pereiaslav Agreement (1654). Thus, argued Maksymovych, many accomplishments attributed by Grabowski to the Poles could not in fact be laid to their account. Second, Maksymovych rejected the theory of the depopulation of Ukraine after the Tatar invasion, citing numerous indications of the continuity of organized life in the middle Dnipro region. Thus, in his letter to Grabowski, Maksymovych fought against the historical assumption (of the depopulation of Ukraine after the Tatar invasion) that served as the basis for Russian and Polish claims to the area.[108]

Maksymovych countered Grabowski's assertion about the just and tolerant character of Polish rule in Ukraine, noting the numerous Cossack uprisings provoked by that regime. In refuting Grabowski's thesis that the Polish government had no conscious plan to oppress Ukraine, Maksymovych referred to its consistent support for the church union and the officially sponsored persecution of Orthodox Ukrainians. Maksymovych also argued against Grabowski's thesis of a significant Polish influence on the origins and organization of the Zaporozhian Cossacks. He pointed out that Cossackdom had become established in Ukraine in the first half of the sixteenth century, prior to the Polish incorporation of the area, and that the first Cossack leaders were not Poles but 'Orthodox Ruthenians.' Among other things, Maksymovych criticized Grabowski's assertion that the Cossack uprisings were little more than soldiers' uprisings, revolts of the rabble, and manifestations of civil strife, since the leaders of Ruthenian nation ignored them and remained on the side of the Polish government. The Ukrainian historian countered his opponent's argument by citing numerous actions of Ukrainian nobles who either defended the interests of the outlawed Orthodox Church or joined the Cossack Host in the times of Bohdan Khmelnytsky.[109]

Hrushevsky thought highly of Maksymovych's critique of Polish historical mythology with regard to Ukraine. In volume 3 of his academic *History*, he noted that Maksymovych had made a number of very important observations concerning the Polish theory of the resettlement of the Ukrainian steppe in the sixteenth and seventeenth centuries. Hrushevsky regarded Grabowski's article, to which Maksymovych had taken exception, as a manifestation of the historical theory that 'has become a commonplace since the mid-nineteenth century, when stress began to be placed in Polish historiography and literature on the Polish cultural mission and its achievements on behalf of universal culture: allegedly, Poland collapsed for no other reason than exhaustion from its striving for those lofty goals.'[110]

Hrushevsky was generally rather sceptical with regard to the positive impact of Polish culture in Ukraine. In volume 6 of the *History* (1907), he wrote that prior to the second decade of the sixteenth century, Poland had very little to offer Ukraine in the realm of culture, since it was itself a 'hinterland' of Western Europe. Until then, argued Hrushevsky, if the Polish cultural element maintained superiority over the Ruthenian one, it was only because Polish culture was supported by the Polish state. That situation changed only in the course of the sixteenth century, when the Polish social and cultural movement inspired by the Reformation began to exercise a major influence on Ukrainian cultural life. But even then, in Hrushevsky's opinion, that influence was more negative than positive, for in the competition between Polish and Ruthenian culture, the new Polish movement 'sharply and strongly tipped the balance in the Polish direction.'[111] Hrushevsky clearly viewed Polish cultural influences in Ukraine through the prism of the struggle between the Ukrainian people and its most powerful oppressor at the time.

Hrushevsky sought the origins of Polish-Ukrainian antagonism in the medieval contest between the two nations for control of the borderland.[112] He supported his argument by quoting the words of the eleventh-century Prince Vasylko of Terebovlia, who justified his war against the Polish princes in national terms: 'I thought of the Liakh land: I shall advance on it over the summer and winter; I shall destroy the Liakh land and avenge myself upon it for the Rus' land.'[113] By asserting that the Polish-Ukrainian antagonism of the medieval era was rooted in national differences, Hrushevsky challenged the interpretation of the dean of Galician Russophile historians, Denys Zubrytsky, and Hrushevsky's own frequent opponent, Ivan Linnichenko, who believed that during the princely era wars between the Polish and Galician-Volhynian princes had resulted from dynastic conflicts, not national ones. Hrushevsky ridiculed that notion, stating that for all practical purposes, Linnichenko accepted Taras Shevchenko's romantic interpretation of the Polish-Ukrainian conflict, according to which it was 'insatiable priests and magnates' who instigated the quarrel between the two peoples. The only difference between the two interpretations, noted Hrushevsky, was that Shevchenko dated the conflict from the sixteenth

century, while Linnichenko moved its origins back to the fourteenth
century, when Poland conquered Galicia. Hrushevsky was convinced
that the Polish takeover of Galicia in the mid-fourteenth century did not
initiate mutual animosity between the Poles and Ukrainians, as
Linnichenko claimed, but transformed the sporadic conflicts between
them into a permanent confrontation.[114]

Hrushevsky's almost exclusively negative assessment of the role
played by the Polish element in Ukraine contrasted sharply with his
much more balanced interpretation of the role of the Lithuanian factor
in Ukrainian history. The Lithuanian state took control of most of the
Ukrainian lands in the mid-fourteenth century and maintained its presence there until the Union of Lublin (1569). It was in this period that the
remnants of Ukrainian political autonomy were eliminated and the
Catholic offensive on Orthodox Rus' began. While Hrushevsky regretted all these developments, he was much more forgiving in his assessment of Lithuanian policy toward Ukraine than in his attitude to Poland.
Part of the explanation for this anomaly may lie in Hrushevsky's view
of the Ukrainian record from the fourteenth to the sixteenth century as
'the history of the enserfment of the Ukrainian land and the Ukrainian
people by neighbouring states, whose gains were ultimately gathered
almost completely, without exception, by the Polish state.'[115] Another
reason for Hrushevsky's differential treatment of Polish and Lithuanian
rule in Ukraine probably lay in the political circumstances prevailing at
the turn of the twentieth century, as the Lithuanians posed no threat to
the Ukrainian revival of that period, while the Polish national elite in
Habsburg Galicia did everything in its power to hinder the development of the Ukrainian national project.

There were also important historiographic factors that influenced
Hrushevsky's interpretation of Lithuanian-Ukrainian relations in the
late medieval and early modern periods. Some of them derived from
the common tradition of nineteenth-century Russian and Ukrainian
historiography, which viewed the Grand Duchy of Lithuania as a
Lithuanian-Russian/Ruthenian, Russian/Ruthenian-Lithuanian, or simply West Russian/Ruthenian state. That tradition was based on the
historical record of the Grand Duchy, in which Ruthenian (Ukrainian-
Belarusian) elites often played a major role in decision-making and in
the governance of the state. Hrushevsky's interpretation of the history
of the Grand Duchy of Lithuania continued that tradition, and many of
his views on the 'Lithuanian' period of Ukrainian history can be traced
back to the writings of Maksymovych, Antonovych, and a student of

Ukrainian and Belarusian law, Mikhail Vladimirsky-Budanov. Not unlike his predecessors, Hrushevsky regretted the ease with which the Ruthenian elites of the fourteenth century surrendered their independence to the Lithuanian princes but found compensation for it in the latter's willingness to adopt the local political tradition, religion, language, and culture. Hrushevsky claimed that Ruthenian became the official language of the Duchy, while a significant part of the Lithuanian ruling elite accepted Orthodoxy, married into Ruthenian families, and regarded their state as a Lithuanian-Ruthenian polity, perceiving themselves as continuators of the political tradition of Kyivan Rus' and engaging in competition with the Grand Principality of Moscow for the territories of the former Kyivan state.[116]

A tendency in the political life of the Grand Duchy of Lithuania that met with Hrushevsky's strong disapproval was its ever-growing dependence on the Kingdom of Poland. That process was initiated by the union of Poland and Lithuania concluded in Kreva in 1385, which culminated in the complete incorporation of the Lithuanian state into the Polish-led Commonwealth as a result of the Union of Lublin (1569). Hrushevsky viewed this gradual incorporation of the Grand Duchy into the Polish state as the single most important factor in the political life of the Ukrainian lands between the fourteenth and sixteenth centuries. He maintained that from the very beginning of that process, the Polish ruling circles set themselves the goal of the complete incorporation of the Grand Duchy into the Kingdom of Poland. In Hrushevsky's opinion, the Union of Kreva put an end to the Ruthenization of the Lithuanian state. Among the conditions of that union was the acceptance by the Lithuanian nobles, hitherto mostly pagan, of the Catholic faith, and the extension to this newly Catholic elite of the privileges enjoyed by the Polish nobility. The members of the Orthodox Ruthenian elite were left out of that process. In Hrushevsky's opinion, the division of the ruling elite of the Grand Duchy of Lithuania into two competing groups, Lithuanian and Ruthenian, had the effect of weakening the state, creating conflicts between the two ruling groups, and forcing the Lithuanian magnates to look for support to Poland, while the Ruthenian nobles were encouraged to seek help from Muscovy.[117]

In Hrushevsky's view the Union of Lublin, which, among other things, incorporated all the Ukrainian lands directly into the Kingdom of Poland,[118] had two major consequences for Ukraine. First, it established closer links between Galicia, already under Polish control since the mid-fourteenth century, and the central and eastern Ukrainian territories, which until then had been ruled by Lithuania. These territories were now encompassed by the borders of a single state – a development clearly welcomed by Hrushevsky. Second, by annexing Central and Eastern Ukraine to the Kingdom of Poland, the Union of Lublin opened it up to Polish political, social, cultural, and religious influence – an absolute evil in Hrushevsky's belief system. He stressed the negative character of that development as follows: 'Ukrainian life was broken to fit Polish patterns and Polonized. This was a complete restructuring from top to bottom that left not one stone upon another in Ukrainian life. It transformed that life according to Polish patterns, pushing the Ukrainian populace, which clung to its Ukrainian nationality, to the very bottom.'[119] The results, in Hrushevsky's opinion, were disastrous for every sphere of Ukrainian life.

Hrushevsky believed that social and economic relations were the proper focus of historiography dealing with the era of the gradual decline of the Ukrainian nation. In line with that thesis, he devoted more than half of volume 5 of his academic *History* to a discussion of the structure of Ukrainian society from the fourteenth to the sixteenth century, and almost half of volume 6 to an analysis of Ukrainian economic life of that period. As a national historian, Hrushevsky did not have to pay such scrupulous attention to the economic or social history of Ukraine at the time of its political decline, but, in the tradition of populist historiography, he strongly believed that those aspects of Ukrainian life had more to say about the people's existence than did political history. Generally speaking, in the 'Lithuanian-Polish' volumes of the *History* Hrushevsky was able to complement his populist views with a national outlook. His general conclusions about the socioeconomic development of Ukraine during that period supported his thesis about the negative impact of Polonization on all aspects of Ukrainian life. It was Polonization that, in Hrushevsky's opinion, spread unruliness among the nobility, subordinated urban life to nobiliary control, ruined the culture and economy of the towns, and promoted the enserfment of the peasantry.[120] Particularly unbearable to Hrushevsky was the condition of the Ukrainian peasantry, which worsened as a result of the growing demand for grain on international markets, a development that increased the exactions of corvée labour.[121]

Like Maksymovych before him, Hrushevsky gave the Polish government very little credit for the colonization and settlement of Eastern Ukraine. Unlike Maksymovych, though, he believed that social and national factors were closely intertwined in the fabric of Polish-Ukrainian antagonism and that the Polish oppression of Ukraine had not only a national but also a social character. It was the overburdened and disillusioned peasants who, in Hrushevsky's opinion, set off the colonization drive from the settled areas of Ukraine to the steppe borderlands along the Dnister and Dnipro rivers. The nobility, for its part, benefited from that movement of peasants into the eastern territories, as it acquired rights from the Polish kings to lands already settled by peasants fleeing enserfment or about to be settled by them. Hence, in Hrushevsky's opinion, the settlement of Eastern Ukraine was the result of the colonizing movement of the Ukrainian peasantry.[122] In volume 7 of the *History* he strongly disputed the view presented by one of the most authoritative students of Ukrainian colonization, the Polish historian Aleksander Jabłonowski. The latter, in line with the Polish historiographic tradition, attributed the growth of the settlement of southern Ukraine to the activities of the Polish nobility, which allegedly became interested in the colonization of the region after the Union of Lublin. Hrushevsky believed that the Polish nobiliary role was secondary to that of representatives of Ukrainian princely families, who came to the area not because of the political consequences of the Union of Lublin but because of the success of the popular colonization of steppe Ukraine.[123]

Why did Hrushevsky take such a strong anti-Polish stand in his interpretation of early modern Ukrainian history? However much he may have sought to 'other' Ukraine's western neighbour, there is no evidence to suggest that Hrushevsky consciously manipulated his evidence to that end.[124] Moreover, the events of the late sixteenth and early seventeenth centuries, which Hrushevsky began to discuss in volume 6 of his academic *History*, were full of examples of strong Ukrainian-Polish antagonism and of the repressive role played by the Polish-dominated Commonwealth in relation to its Ruthenian subjects. There are, of course, also other factors that should be taken into account in assessing Hrushevsky's interpretation of Polish-Ukrainian relations. One of them was the Ukrainian historiographic tradition, which could not but shape some of Hrushevsky's attitudes. Hrushevsky's hostility to Poland directly echoed the sentiments expressed by the authors of the clerical chronicles of the seventeenth century and the Cossack chronicles of the eighteenth century, who saw the Catholic Poles as their main enemies. That attitude was also encouraged by the Russian imperial authorities, beginning with Peter I, and further strengthened by the nineteenth-century Russian-sponsored ideological campaign against Polish claims to Right-Bank Ukraine. This was the atmosphere in which

Antonovych's documentary school was allowed to flourish, making it possible for Antonovych and his students to build the foundations of Ukrainian national historiography, since they claimed Right-Bank Ukraine not so much for the Russian Empire as for their own Ukrainian project. Numerous students of Antonovych's were countering the belief of Polish scholars in their country's civilizing mission in Eastern Europe, which was inspired by nostalgia for and idealization of Poland's lost statehood and by the powerful influence of European imperialism.

Hrushevsky wrote most of his academic *History* at a time of severe crisis in Ukrainian-Polish relations in Galicia. That circumstance could not but affect his account of the 'transitional' era in Ukrainian history. The potential for cooperation between the two oppressed nations, Polish and Ukrainian, in the struggle against their common enemy – Russian imperial rule – never materialized, notwithstanding the fact that the Polish national movement not only combatted its Ukrainian counterpart but also profoundly influenced it in the course of the nineteenth and early twentieth centuries. This situation was also reflected in the relation between the two historical narratives. After all, it was the doyen of Polish historiography, Joachim Lelewel, who opened the door to Hrushevsky's deconstruction of the Russian imperial narrative by stating in 1839: 'The greatest of all the legends, lies, and mistakes with which the history of Rus' [Ukraine and Belarus] is filled is [the notion] that this history is synonymous with Muscovite and Russian history and the history of the tsars and emperors.'[125]

How did Polish historians react to Hrushevsky's interpretation of the history of Polish-Ukrainian antagonism? Probably the best summary of Polish views on the issue is to be found in Ludwik Kolankowski's lengthy review of volumes 4–6 of Hrushevsky's *History*, published in 1913 in the Lviv *Kwartalnik Historyczny* (Historical Quarterly).[126] Like most Polish reviewers of Hrushevsky's works, Kolankowski acknowledged Hrushevsky's extraordinary erudition but considered his interpretation of Poland's role in Ukrainian history extremely biased. Not without reason, he believed that Hrushevsky's anti-Polish prejudice was rooted in the current status of Polish-Ukrainian relations in Galicia. 'The strained Polish-Ruthenian relations of the present age,' wrote Kolankowski, 'have made a highly deleterious impression on Hrushevsky, with the result that this extraordinarily industrious, simply tireless researcher, in his work, which has all the external characteristics of a scholarly product, yields passages and entire chapters worthy at best only of a poor publicist.'[127]

Kolankowski quoted at length from Hrushevsky's *History* in order to show how negative it was toward Poland and its policies. Many of Hrushevsky's statements were reproduced without comment, as if Kolankowski were convinced that their tendentiousness was too obvious to require elaboration. In those cases when Kolankowski commented on Hrushevsky's position, he did not deviate significantly from the standard Polish line as presented by Michał Grabowski in his article of 1857. Kolankowski criticized numerous aspects of Hrushevsky's interpretation of Polish-Ukrainian relations, presenting factual arguments with regard to three of them: the religious policy of King Kazimierz the Great toward the Orthodox Church of Galicia in the second half of the fourteenth century; the consequences of the Union of Lublin for the Ukrainian lands; and the role of the Polish government in the settlement of Eastern Ukraine.

Kolankowski ended his review by summarizing Hrushevsky's opinions on the role of the Polish factor in the conclusion of the Union of Brest (1596) but did not comment on them, probably assuming that the mere presentation of Hrushevsky's position on the issue was sufficient to convince the Polish reader of the artificiality of the latter's assessments. What were those assessments? The issue of the religious policy of the Polish government in Ukraine, especially the role of the Polish authorities and the Catholic Church in the introduction of the church union at the end of the sixteenth century, had been one of the most sensitive topics in Polish-Ukrainian debates ever since the religious polemics of the late sixteenth and early seventeenth centuries. The nineteenth century brought into the ongoing discussion the idea of Polish religious tolerance and the absence of any deliberate plan on the part of the Polish authorities to persecute the Orthodox Church. That idea was presented, among other works, in Michał Grabowski's article (severely criticized by Maksymovych in 1857) and in Kolankowski's review of volumes 4–6 of Hrushevsky's *History*. It was this interpretation of Polish-Ukrainian religious relations that Hrushevsky countered in his own writings on the history of religious and national life in early modern Ukraine.

Hrushevsky viewed the expansion of Catholicism and the subsequent church union in the Ukrainian lands as a form of Polonization of the Ukrainian people and condemned it as such. At the same time, he was careful not to ascribe to the religious factor an exclusive role in the development of Polish-Ukrainian antagonism, as he believed that with the passage of time, the ethnically based conflict between Poles and Ukrainians in the border areas superseded the religious one. In Hrushevsky's view, however, the opposing religious affiliations of the Catholic Poles and the Orthodox Ukrainians gradually lent a religious coloration to the Polish-Ukrainian conflict. 'With the Polish occupation of Western Ukraine in the second half of the fourteenth century,' wrote Hrushevsky, 'there were no longer episodic and sporadic encounters and conflicts with a foreign nationality and religion, but all along the line the Ukrainian nationality and its "Ruthenian faith" encountered the privileged nationality and the state Polish Catholic religion. At every turn, especially after the transitional period of the occupation itself, the local Ruthenian had occasion to feel that he was a schismatic, almost a heathen; he had to defend his ancestral faith against plans to supplant it with the Catholic Church, and himself against a variety of dues for the benefit of the latter.'[128]

Hrushevsky (himself a devout Orthodox Christian) treated the history of the Orthodox Church in Ukraine as a Ukrainian national phenomenon. He viewed the support given by the princes, nobility, burghers, and Cossack leaders to that church as an endorsement not only of the religious agenda but also of the national one. During the early decades of the seventeenth century, wrote Hrushevsky, 'the circumstances of Ukrainian life ... led to the concentration of national interests, national aspirations, and national struggle in the defense of the existence of the Orthodox Church.'[129] It was with this thought in mind that Hrushevsky presented in his academic *History* a detailed discussion of the brotherhood movement, the revival of Orthodox learning and the founding of the Ostrih Academy by Prince Kostiantyn Ostrozky, and the rise of a Ukrainian polemical literature arguing for and against the church union. In Hrushevsky's view, these developments marked the beginning of the Ukrainian national revival. In his study of *The Cultural and National Movement in Ukraine*, published in 1908, Hrushevsky wrote that the idea of nationality was a creation of relatively recent times and that earlier it had taken the form of ideas of political, social, religious, geographic, and cultural loyalty.[130] This definition of national identity (which may strike some as unexpected from a leader of the Ukrainian national 'awakening' and the author of the first complete history of the nation) gave Hrushevsky a unique opportunity to analyse numerous forms of early modern political, cultural, and religious life within the context of the Ukrainian revival.

The Cossack Mythology

After the Revolution of 1905 in the Russian Empire, when Hrushevsky began work on the Cossack-era volumes of his academic *History*, his scholarly interest did not focus primarily on the history of the popular masses as such but on the Ukrainian national 'awakening' of the late sixteenth and early seventeenth centuries. In the preface to the seventh volume of his *History*, Hrushevsky characterized the Cossack era as a period in which 'for the first time in historical memory, the Ukrainian nation came forth actively as the architect of its own destiny and life, rising to a life-or-death struggle for the realization of its dreams and desires; but, after age-old strivings, bleeding and exhausted in the struggle against insurmountable obstacles, it fell on the battlefield, its hopes and dreams shattered. Since this is the most vivid and interesting period of Ukrainian life from the viewpoint both of the Ukrainian descendant of those generations of Ukrainian fighters and of the outside researcher, the historian-sociologist, it has long been treated separately in the history of the Ukrainian nation as a self-contained unit.'[131]

In volume 7 of the *History*, Hrushevsky clearly drew a parallel between the contemporary 'awakening' of the Ukrainian nation, for which he had worked so intensively, and the Cossack period, which he regarded as an important factor in the seventeenth-century 'revival' of the Ukrainian nation. This parallel established the Cossack past in the eyes of the Ukrainian intelligentsia as Ukraine's 'golden age,' replete with heroes whose daring exploits were to serve as a source of inspiration for Hrushevsky's contemporaries. Cossack history had acquired many characteristics of a Ukrainian 'golden age' long before Hrushevsky's day,[132] providing a foundation for one of the myths that John A. Armstrong, in his pioneering study on the role of historical mythology in the evolution of Ukrainian national consciousness, defined as 'the integrating phenomenon through which symbols of national identity acquire a coherent meaning.'[133]

The transformation of the Cossack image into an icon of Ukrainian historical identity apparently began in the early eighteenth century within the boundaries of the Hetmanate. As Zenon Kohut argues, the ruling elite of the Hetmanate needed the Cossack past and Cossack history to justify and defend its privileges against advancing Russian absolutism.[134] The need to record the Cossack past became especially urgent after the defeat of Hetman Ivan Mazepa at Poltava in 1709 and the abolition of the hetmancy by Peter I in 1722. Around the same time, fundamental works of Cossack historiography were produced by Hryhorii Hrabianka and Samiilo Velychko, and Cossack history was substantially introduced into Ukrainian historiography (the most important work of pre-Cossack Ukrainian historiography, the *Synopsis*, almost completely ignored the Cossack past). This newly conceptualized Cossack history also provided the emerging Ukrainian nation with its first Cossack hero, Hetman Bohdan Khmelnytsky, whose cult played an important role in the formation of modern Ukrainian consciousness.[135]

Ukrainian authors of the nineteenth century helped disseminate Cossack-related historical memory far beyond the boundaries of the Hetmanate. The new, romantic image of the Cossack past was presented in the writings of the Ukrainian national poet and 'father' of the Ukrainian nation, Taras Shevchenko. Through the medium of Shevchenko's poetry, the main elements of Cossack 'mythology' were disseminated throughout Ukraine and provided the 'awakening' nation with the sense of a shared glorious past. Cossack history thus played an important role in shaping modern Ukrainian national identity.[136]

The significance of the Cossacks in early modern Ukrainian history was very special indeed. Although Cossackdom as a way of life was not limited to Ukrainian territory and represented a historical phenomenon shared by Ukrainians and Russians, the roles played by Cossacks in the history of these two peoples were profoundly different. In Russia the Cossacks remained a marginal factor in national history, border warriors who challenged the Russian state on a number of occasions but eventually were defeated by it. In Ukraine the Cossacks were those who took upon themselves the difficult task of defending the national religious and cultural tradition against the attacks of foreign states, which culminated in the creation of a polity of their own. The Ukrainian Cossacks were able to extend their rule and spread their political culture across the vast territories of Dnipro Ukraine, thereby becoming one of the most important factors in the formation of the modern Ukrainian nation.[137]

Mykhailo Hrushevsky was fully aware of the importance of the Cossack period in Ukrainian history and largely shared the general fascination of Ukrainian patriots with the Cossack past. In his autobiography Hrushevsky noted that discussions of the origins of the Ukrainian

Cossacks in Ukrainian and Russian periodicals of the 1880s figured among the intellectually challenging topics that prompted him (then a gymnasium student in Tbilisi) to choose Ukrainian history as his future field of specialization.[138] Nevertheless, at the beginning of his academic career, Hrushevsky was more than sceptical about the role of Cossackdom in Ukrainian history, seeing the Cossacks as antagonists of the popular masses. Hrushevsky's original lack of enthusiasm was shared by many Ukrainian populist leaders of the second half of the nineteenth century. Unlike the romantics of the first half of the century, the new generation of Ukrainian activists was highly dubious about many traditional elements of the Cossack historical myth.[139]

Hrushevsky's early views on the historical role of the Cossacks were fairly close to those held by Orest Levytsky, an older colleague of Hrushevsky's, and like him a student of Volodymyr Antonovych. Levytsky expressed the populist credo of contemporary Kyiv historians in his doctoral dissertation (1875), in which he claimed: 'Whenever the Cossacks, relying on the popular masses, succeeded with their help in overcoming circumstances disadvantageous to themselves, they would immediately manifest a tendency to lock themselves in a separate estate and take hold of certain rights, without allowing the people to participate in them and, in general, abandoning their loyal ally to his fate.'[140] Hrushevsky quoted that extract from Levytsky's dissertation in volume 9 of his academic *History* in order to illustrate the views of Volodymyr Antonovych and his school on Cossack history, which he no longer shared.[141]

If in 1898, in his article on Bohdan Khmelnytsky and his era, Hrushevsky presented Cossackdom as a stratum that betrayed the interests of the peasant masses,[142] in his *Survey History of the Ukrainian People* (1904), written with an eye to boosting Ukrainian national consciousness and presenting the Ukrainian historical record to imperial Russian society, Hrushevsky completely abandoned Levytsky's approach and gave a highly positive assessment of the Cossacks. He also excluded the issue of social differentiation within the Cossack ranks from his discussion of the Khmelnytsky era. He claimed that, while differences between the Cossack officers and the rank and file (*chern'*) were discussed in the sources soon after the death of Khmelnytsky, the Cossack officers did not consolidate as a distinct stratum until the end of the seventeenth century.[143] Hrushevsky further modified his views on the issue in volume 7 of his academic *History* (1909), where he successfully elevated Cossackdom to the status of chief protagonist of Ukrainian history, representing the desires of the popular masses. He achieved this transformation by dividing the Cossacks into poor rank-and-file soldiers and well-to-do officers. In his narrative Hrushevsky sided with the Cossack *chern'*, which he treated as part of the populace.[144] If in his introduction to the second edition of volume 1 of the *History* (1904), Hrushevsky, in complete accord with populist ideas, characterized the seventeenth and eighteenth centuries in Ukraine as a period of 'popular struggle aimed at toppling a hostile socio-economic order and reforming social relations so as to conform to the national ideals of justice,'[145] five years later, in the preface to volume 7 of the *History*, he had clearly changed his mind. He went out of his way to state that the volumes covering the third period of Ukrainian history would be 'devoted to the history of the national revival, carried out with the aid of a new socionational agent (factor) – Cossackdom. The cycle will be primarily a history of this new national force and, furthermore, a history of its struggle against the hostile Polish regime; of the revival of cultural and national forces; of the efforts to rebuild social and national relations with the assistance of the Cossack forces and under their protection, according to the wishes and ideals of society.'[146]

One of the problems that most interested Hrushevsky in his work on the early history of the Ukrainian Cossacks was that of continuity in Ukrainian history. In the preface to volume 7 of the *History*, Hrushevsky stressed that the Cossack period 'must be meticulously examined for links with the previous stages, for the organic connectedness and continuity of a people's life are never totally broken by any change or turning point as long as that people lives.'[147] He thus confirmed his loyalty to the principles declared in his inaugural lecture of 1894, where he claimed that the popular masses constituted a natural link between different periods of Ukrainian history.[148]

Hrushevsky selected his epigraph for the seventh volume of the *History* from the text of the 'Protestation' (1621), an Orthodox document that depicted the Cossacks as noble warriors whose roots went back to the times of Kyivan Rus' itself. The 'Protestation' claimed that the Cossacks were an integral part of the Rus' nation, fought for Rus' under Prince Oleh, and accepted Christianity at the time of Prince Volodymyr.[149] The epigraph must be treated more as an attempt on Hrushevsky's part to convey a sense of the continuity of the Ukrainian past than as evidence of such continuity. Hrushevsky went on to address the issue in a strictly academic manner in the text of the volume.

In a thorough analysis of the writings of his predecessors and contemporaries, Hrushevsky divided all theories regarding the origins of the Cossacks into two major groups: those that sought the roots of Cossackdom in the history of Kyivan Rus' and those that linked their origins to the Circassians. Hrushevsky dismissed the 'Circassian' theory, which had been developed by a number of prominent historians, including the Russians Ivan Boltin, Mikhail Pogodin, Sergei Soloviev, and Mikhail Vladimirsky-Budanov and the Ukrainians Panteleimon Kulish and Mykola Kostomarov. He argued that the whole historiographic tradition was based on a confusion created by the author of the Voskresensk Chronicle, who regarded the Ukrainian Cossacks (the *cherkasy* of contemporary Muscovite documents) as descendants of the non-Slavic Circassians.[150]

Hrushevsky paid significantly more attention to the analysis of theories that associated Cossack origins with the princely era. The idea of the existence of a strong link between Cossack social institutions of the late fifteenth and early sixteenth centuries and the Kyivan Rus' communes of the twelfth and thirteenth centuries was introduced into modern Ukrainian historiography by the writings of the young Mykola Kostomarov (who later sided with supporters of the 'Circassian' theory), Mykhailo Maksymovych, and Volodymyr Antonovych. The latter supported the so-called princely theory of Cossack origins.[151] Hrushevsky dismissed the argumentation of proponents of all the 'Kyivan Rus'' theories, claiming that the historians who developed them compared the institutions of Kyivan Rus' to those established by the Cossacks around the turn of the seventeenth century. He was convinced that the beginnings of Cossack social organization had been shaped by the specific circumstances of their life in the steppe and by government regulation of the Cossack stratum much more than by the legacy of Kyivan Rus'. In his approach to the problem, Hrushevsky strongly committed himself to the study of the Cossacks as a distinct social stratum, noting the lack of evidence of such group identity before the late sixteenth century.[152]

The obvious danger of such an approach for a scholar who had undertaken to write the national history of Ukraine lay in the fact that it effectively cut off Cossack history from the pre-Cossack Ukrainian past, thereby undermining Hrushevsky's most important historiographic objective – that of establishing the continuity of Ukrainian history. Hrushevsky avoided the possible conflict between the two approaches by treating Cossackdom as a two-dimensional phenomenon. According to him, the history of the Cossacks as a social formation began in the late sixteenth century, but Cossackdom as a way of life could be traced back as far as the times of Kyivan Rus'. Hrushevsky made the point as follows: 'As a way of existence, the features of Ukrainian life that become known to us in the sixteenth century under the specialized term 'Cossackdom' (kozatstvo) are as old as Ukraine. This was the result of an age-old struggle between the sedentary, agricultural way of life and the rapacious, nomadic robber population of the steppes, a struggle that continued for centuries in constantly new and changing forms and variants on the same territory of Ukraine.'[153]

In his study of the early forms of Cossack social organization, Hrushevsky found himself situated between two established historiographic traditions. One was represented by Mykola Kostomarov and Volodymyr Antonovych, who, as mentioned earlier, sought the origins of Cossack social institutions in the times of Kyivan Rus'. The other, associated mostly with the names of Marian Dubiecki, Panteleimon Kulish, and Andrei Storozhenko, tended to view the Cossacks as unruly warriors incapable of establishing any form of social organization on their own and benefiting in that respect from the innovations of outsiders.

Writing in the tradition of Polish historiography, with its belief in the civilizing mission of the Polish element in Eastern Europe, Dubiecki argued that the Ukrainians (lud rusiński) could not have created on their own the forms of social organization that existed in Zaporizhia. He also claimed that Zaporozhian society was organized by the Polish leaders of the Cossacks on the models provided by Western religious brotherhoods. Commenting on Dubiecki's views, Hrushevsky questioned the Polish ethnic origin of such Cossack leaders as Ostafii Dashkovych and Dmytro Vyshnevetsky, pointing out that others, like Przecław Lanckoroński and Samiilo Koretsky, had nothing to do with the early history of Zaporizhia. In Hrushevsky's opinion, 'Polish "knightly" circles could have grafted onto Cossackdom and Zaporizhia only what they had – anarchy, disrespect for law and government, lack of discipline, disrespect for society and other people's property and labor – and graft them indeed they did. On the other hand, the Zaporozhians' strict simplicity, discipline, and disinclination to sybaritism and to excess could have formed only independently of Polish influences.'[154]

Hrushevsky argued that the Zaporozhian Host – the Cossack military organization – took shape in the Lower Dnipro area, which served as the true cradle of Cossackdom. It was there, in his opinion, that the Cossacks first established themselves as a social group. Only later did they manage to form a distinct stratum in the settled area, where the control of the nobles and local authorities over the populace was too severe to permit the existence of a Cossack order before the imposition of government regulation.[155] In general, Hrushevsky tended to minimize the impact of such government officials as the border starosta Ostafii Dashkovych and others on the early history of Cossackdom. In discussing the conflicts between Dashkovych and the population of the borderlands, Hrushevsky clearly took the side of the 'people.' He argued that nobles who headed Cossack expeditions against the Tatars were not the true organizers of Cossackdom and even tried to conceal from the central government the extent of their actual links with the Cossacks.[156]

At the same time, Hrushevsky was convinced that the formation of a Cossack stratum was closely associated with the attempts of the Polish government to hire Cossacks for military service. Members of Cossack detachments recruited by the government were exempt from the jurisdiction of the local authorities and subject to the military administration. That innovation was introduced by the government in the 1570s and reinforced by King Stefan Batory's regulations of 1582. Hrushevsky argued that before this type of Cossack immunity was put in place by the authorities, 'the overwhelming majority of Cossacks was concealed in other social strata. The Cossacks did not set themselves apart within such strata, because it was not in their interest to declare or manifest Cossackdom as their status in society.'[157] With the introduction of Cossack immunity from the local authorities, the new social status became very attractive not only to actual Cossacks, who began to claim membership in the Cossack stratum, but also to members of other strata, especially peasants and burghers.

Hrushevsky also carefully studied the role played by government regulations in shaping Cossack organization. According to him, those regulations imposed a new structure on the basic social nucleus that already existed in the steppe, namely the military and commercial company headed by the *otaman*. Recognizing the role of government in the organization of the Cossack Host in the settled area, Hrushevsky refused to admit the same role with regard to the Lower Dnipro (Zaporizhia) Cossacks. In that instance, Hrushevsky remained faithful to the basic principle of his populist outlook, maintaining his belief in the creativity of the popular masses in general and the Ukrainian Cossacks in particular. In Hrushevsky's opinion, the governmental reforms provided only an impulse toward the transformation of the Cossacks into a new social stratum, while the actual transformation was accomplished by the Cossacks themselves.[158]

For Hrushevsky, Ukraine's interaction with the steppe was one of the most important factors that influenced the history of the Ukrainian people and certainly the most important factor in the history of Cossackdom. Hrushevsky wrote at length about the impact of the steppe on Ukrainian history in the introduction to volume 1[159] and discussed the colonization of the steppe areas in volumes 5, 6, and 7 of the *History*. He produced a thoroughly researched account of the Ukrainian movement into the steppe and presented the early history of the Cossacks as an integral part of that process. Although Hrushevsky paid close attention to official efforts to secure the steppe border against the Tatars, his main interest lay in the history of the popular colonization of Southern Ukraine. As for the nature of colonization and the role of various social groups in that process, Hrushevsky believed that it was the success of popular colonization that made possible the transformation of the uninhabited steppe into a settled area. In the 'Cossack' volumes of the *History*, he developed some of the opinions expressed in the volumes on the Lithuanian-Polish period.

With the advance of colonization in Dnipro Ukraine in the second half of the sixteenth century, which brought a huge influx of newcomers to the steppe areas, the Ukrainian Cossacks rapidly grew in numbers. According to Hrushevsky, the new Cossacks were recruited from the ranks of peasants who were forced to leave their villages because of growing economic pressure from the nobility. Another important factor that brought newcomers to the steppe was Cossack status itself – the fact that the Cossacks as a distinct social stratum were exempted from the jurisdiction of the local authorities. Hrushevsky argued that the growth of colonization changed the very nature of Cossackdom. Apart from the Cossacks, who continued to regard military expeditions into the steppe as their main occupation, there appeared another expanding group that availed itself of Cossack status in order to evade nobiliary control and government taxation while tilling the land. The two groups supported each other, combined into a single stratum, and mutually benefited from their activities.[160] Apart from the division of Cossacks into 'warriors' and 'plowmen,' Hrushevsky discussed the division between the wealthy and the poor, which he employed in order to explain the nature of the conflicts between various Cossack groups in the late sixteenth and early seventeenth centuries.[161] The settled Cossack areas were generally strongholds of the well-to-do Cossacks, while the Lower Dnipro area, especially Zaporizhia, tended to attract poorer elements.

In Hrushevsky's opinion, the government's introduction of the Cossack register helped draw a legal distinction between well-to-do Cossacks and poor ones. He pointed out that the registered Cossacks were not only supposed to perform their military duties in time of war but also to police the rest of the Cossacks in peacetime. In general, Hrushevsky did not overestimate the importance of the register, noting that after its introduction in Ukraine in the sixteenth century, there were long periods when there were no registered Cossacks at all. The Polish government simply had no need to hire Cossack detachments, nor could it afford their services.[162] For the most part, Hrushevsky remained loyal to the dominant trend of Ukrainian nineteenth-century historiography, which viewed the growth of Cossackdom as a response of the Ukrainian population to the advance of Polish government offices and institutions into Ukraine. For Hrushevsky, the Cossacks represented the spirit of freedom, which contrasted with the growing enslavement of the popular masses outside Cossack territory. Consequently, the population of the borderlands, which came from every social background, was able to defend itself not only against Tatar raids but also against the claims and abuses of government officials.[163]

Nowhere is Hrushevsky's interest in the 'golden age' of Cossackdom so clearly stimulated by his role as a national awakener of Ukraine as in his treatment of the Cossacks' association with the Ukrainian cultural revival of the first decades of the seventeenth century. Hrushevsky rightly saw the Cossacks as closely related to the revival and as the stratum that took upon itself the defence of the national interests of the Rus'. The event that most attracted Hrushevsky's attention was the participation of the Cossacks led by Hetman (at that time Colonel) Petro Konashevych-Sahaidachny in the consecration of a new Orthodox hierarchy in the autumn of 1620. The ceremony was performed by Patriarch Theophanes of Jerusalem against the will of the government and could be carried out only thanks to the protection offered by the Cossacks.

Hrushevsky presented Cossackdom as an ethnically and culturally Ukrainian phenomenon, emphasizing the growth of the Dnipro Cossacks as part of the development of the Ukrainian nation. He did not comment on the statements of the Polish authorities, who claimed in their attempts to avoid responsibility for Cossack attacks on the Ottoman domains that the Cossacks were not really subjects of the Polish king and came from various ethnic backgrounds. Instead, Hrushevsky attempted to reconstruct the ethnic composition of the Cossack Host on the basis of the 1581 census of a Cossack detachment that took part in the Livonian War (1558–83). He explained the presence of a large number of Cossacks from Belarus and Muscovy in that detachment by pointing out that the regiment had been involved in military operations on those territories and thus necessarily included a significant number of local recruits. Having analysed the composition of the rest of the detachment, Hrushevsky concluded that most of the Cossacks were of Ukrainian background.[164]

The discussion of Cossack involvement in church affairs during the 1620s presented Hrushevsky with an opportunity to discuss the issue of their general religiosity.[165] In the historiographic discussion of the issue, which can be traced back to the writings of Mykola Kostomarov and Panteleimon Kulish, Hrushevsky, as was often the case, sided with Kulish. He accepted Kulish's argument that Kostomarov and his followers had exaggerated the religiosity of the Zaporozhian Cossacks in the sixteenth and early seventeenth centuries by attributing to that period information taken from eighteenth-century sources. Hrushevsky disagreed with Platon Zhukovich, who saw proof of the existence of chaplains in the Cossack Host in the newly discovered 'Protestation' of the Orthodox hierarchs. He treated that document more as proof of the existence of a strategic alliance between the Cossack officers and the Orthodox hierarchy than as evidence of general Cossack religiosity.[166]

The point on which Hrushevsky disagreed with Kulish was the Cossack role in the consecration of the new Orthodox hierarchy. Kulish argued that the Cossacks were not really interested in church affairs and that it was Patriarch Filaret of Moscow and his circle who initiated the consecration of the new hierarchy by Patriarch Theophanes of Jerusalem.[167] Hrushevsky replied that Theophanes consecrated the new bishops at the insistence of the local Orthodox clergy and laity, against the wishes of the Polish king. The consecration, which gave a new impulse to the religious struggle in Ukraine and contributed immensely to the religious polemic and the development of Ukrainian religious, political, and social thought, would have been impossible without the assistance of the Cossacks, who offered protection against government sanctions both to the patriarch and to the newly consecrated hierarchy.[168]

Hrushevsky viewed the Cossack-Orthodox alliance as one forged 'on the basis of a Ukrainian national platform in the name of what then amounted to a national postulate.'[169] He referred to the Orthodox hierarchy that was consecrated under Cossack protection in 1620 as the

'Ukrainian intelligentsia,' observing: 'The Cossacks proclaimed their solidarity with the Ukrainian intelligentsia in its religious and national aspirations, and from that time on, for more than a century, the story of Cossackdom became central to Ukrainian life.'[170] The forging of an alliance between the intelligentsia and other strata of society on the basis of a 'Ukrainian national platform' was a crucial issue for the Ukrainian intelligentsia both in Galicia and in Dnipro Ukraine at the time of the 1905 revolution. Hrushevsky interpreted the events of the 1620s as a successful example of such an alliance.

In Hrushevsky's view, the early modern 'Ukrainian intelligentsia' included, apart from the Orthodox hierarchy and clerics, representatives of the Ukrainian nobility and burghers as well. He viewed the alliance of Cossackdom with the nobility and burghers as a union of otherwise mutually hostile social elements. In his opinion, Cossackdom as a social stratum had much more in common with the peasantry, and by establishing close links with the 'intelligentsia' (the leaders of the Orthodox clergy and nobility), the Cossacks positioned themselves between those two major social forces of early modern Ukraine. As Hrushevsky put it: 'From a general national viewpoint, the fact that between the two polarities of the Ukrainian element, which were separated by socioeconomic interests – that chasm of Polish nobiliary law – there appeared a specific unifying factor in the form of Cossackdom, which bound the disunited Ukrainian nationality with a new bond, could also be considered advantageous.'[171]

Hrushevsky the 'national awakener' clearly welcomed the alliance of the Cossacks with the Ukrainian nobility, but Hrushevsky the populist was uneasy about it, reproaching the Cossacks for their inability to part ways with the upper classes and take a more decisive stand in defence of the social interests of the peasantry. Hrushevsky wrote with obvious regret that 'Cossackdom's attitude to the socioeconomic demands of the masses did not go beyond the stage of a certain consonance, a certain sympathy or union of interests.'[172] Hrushevsky believed, though, that the involvement of the Cossack officers in church affairs was greeted with sympathy by the rank-and-file Cossacks. To quote him, 'Yet we know of the Cossacks' inclination to cloak their border hunt for booty in the idealistic garb of a struggle "against the enemies of the "Holy Cross." Thus we can understand that even a wild freebooter who, when the need arose, would be equally unsparing of his coreligionist, an Orthodox Muscovite or Belarusian, as of a Muslim, found it pleasant to sense a higher mission in Cossack life, to have some ideological framework for his rampages in the steppe borderland.'[173]

Hrushevsky's study of the early history of the Ukrainian Cossacks presented him with a unique opportunity to revisit the old historical narrative created by the authors of the eighteenth-century Cossack chronicles. An element of the narrative that no longer met the demands of modern scholarship was the early history of the Zaporozhian hetmans. A list of hetmans reaching as far back as the early sixteenth century was often included in the Cossack chronicles of the eighteenth century, when the institution of the hetmancy was under constant threat of abolition by the Russian authorities. Under those circumstances, the list served as an important argument in the Cossack officers' bid to defend their traditional rights. Hrushevsky traced the history of the list in historical writings of the eighteenth and nineteenth centuries. On the basis of his research, he concluded that Ostafii Dashkovych and Przecław Lanckoroński, often identified as the first Cossack hetmans, were not in fact the first organizers of Cossackdom; rather, they played a role similar to that of such border officials as Iurii Pats, Senko Polozovych, and Biernat Pretwicz.[174]

Hrushevsky gave his most enthusiastic approval to the activities of another legendary hetman, Prince Dmytro Vyshnevetsky. Contrary to his treatment of Pats, Polozovych, Dashkovych, and Lanckoroński, Hrushevsky considered Vyshnevetsky a true leader of emerging Cossackdom – above all, a forerunner of the Zaporozhian Host. Although Vyshnevetsky's activity beyond the Dnipro Rapids was short-lived and not very successful (Vyshnevetsky and his Cossacks were forced by the Tatars to abandon their newly built fortress in 1557), Hrushevsky discerned the beginnings of the Zaporozhian Host in this expedition. He saw it as another important achievement that Vyshnevetsky introduced Cossackdom to the world of international politics and made, or attempted to make, alliances with Muscovy, the Ottoman Empire, and Moldavia. Hrushevsky disagreed with those of his predecessors who saw Vyshnevetsky's actions mainly as the 'aimless movements of a restless spirit.' 'But even in the worst case,' wrote Hrushevsky, 'even if that opinion were justified, the phenomenon was still so extraordinary and glamorous against the background of the immobile, routine life of our Ukrainian magnates that it must attract the attention of any student of life in those times.'[175] In 1909, the year in which volume 7 appeared in print, Hrushevsky published a study of the image of Dmytro Vyshnevetsky in Ukrainian folklore, arguing that the prince was depicted in one of the Ukrainian epic songs (*dumy*) under the name of Baida.[176]

Along with the history of the first Cossack hetmans, a significant part of the eighteenth-century historical narrative reexamined by Hrushevsky was the history of the 'Batory reform.' He was not the first historian to challenge the eighteenth-century chroniclers' claim that it was King Stefan Batory of Poland who had created the six-thousand-strong Cossack army, divided it into six regiments, and established Cossack ranks. In questioning the Batory legend, Hrushevsky followed Panteleimon Kulish and Aleksander Jabłonowski, while opposing Mykola Kostomarov, Volodymyr Antonovych, and Dmytro Iavornytsky. At the same time, he criticized the views of Włodzimierz Jarosz[177] and Andrei Storozhenko, who maintained that Batory's regulations had no major impact on Cossack organization and social life. Hrushevsky viewed those regulations as an important step toward establishing Cossackdom as a distinct social group.[178] His analysis of the issue effectively put an end to the popularity of the Batory legend in Ukrainian historiography.

Another important element of the old historical narrative questioned by Hrushevsky was the belief in the anti-Uniate character of the first Cossack movements led by Khrystofor Kosynsky and Severyn Nalyvaiko. Polish authors of the first half of the seventeenth century referred to the Orthodox in general as 'Nalyvaikoites' and called Orthodoxy 'the Nalyvaiko faith.' The Ukrainian historiographic tradition that began with Hryhorii Hrabianka and ended with the anonymous author of the *History of the Rus'* presented both Cossack leaders as martyrs for the Orthodox faith who rebelled against the introduction of the church union at the Synod of Brest (1596). According to the story recounted by the author of the *History of the Rus'*, Hetman Kosynsky (who in fact died in 1593) was arrested at the Brest synod, 'immured in a stone pillar at a monastery and starved to death.'[179] Commenting on the popularity of this legend, Hrushevsky noted in the *History*: 'Such was this story, repeated widely in textbooks and popular books. When I was a small boy, it made my heart, too, cringe in sorrow and anger.'[180] Hrushevsky not only rejected the idea of Kosynsky's involvement in church affairs on the side of the Orthodox but also questioned the motives of Nalyvaiko's intervention in that struggle. He believed that Nalyvaiko's attack on the possessions of an initiator of the church union, Bishop Kyrylo Terletsky, was prompted more by personal considerations than ideological ones. Hrushevsky also concluded that Nalyvaiko's detachments became involved in the religious conflict only accidentally, as they had never pursued any religious or national goals.[181]

Hrushevsky declined to interpret the Cossack revolts led by Kosynsky and Nalyvaiko as anything but a manifestation of Cossack 'unruliness.' He disagreed with Kulish and Iavornytsky, who considered that the main goal of those movements had been to end Polish rule in Ukraine. Hrushevsky did not trust contemporary Polish statements on the matter and saw no evidence of such ideas in the Cossack documents. He treated the Cossack disturbances of the period as a series of unrelated outbursts that lacked a definite program,[182] characterizing them as 'mischiefs,' 'conflicts,' 'wars,' and 'movements,' but never as 'uprisings' or 'revolts.' Hrushevsky reserved the latter terms for the Cossack rebellions of the seventeenth century. According to him, the two main areas in which the Cossacks played an important role were seventeenth-century social movements and the Ukrainian cultural revival of the period.[183]

Hrushevsky was not the first historian to question or criticize many components of eighteenth-century Cossack historiography, but he was the first to do so systematically and consistently. His 'demythologization' of Cossack history allowed him to present a scholarly account of the Cossacks that met the needs of the Ukrainian cultural revival. Hrushevsky demonstrated that the old historiographic tradition, which depicted the Cossack leaders of the late sixteenth century as defenders of the Orthodox faith and the Ukrainian nation, was sharply at odds not only with historical reality but also with the national paradigm of Ukrainian history. Not without irony, Hrushevsky wrote, 'Now we know very well that "Kosynsky's uprising" was at the outset nothing more than a clash between a Cossack chieftain, perhaps one not even Ukrainian or Orthodox by origin, and the pillar of Orthodoxy and Ukrainian identity at the time, Kostiantyn Ostrozky.'[184] The old Cossack mythology fell victim to the new paradigm of Ukrainian national history. Those elements that did not promote the new ideology of the national 'awakening' were either dropped entirely or reshaped to meet the new standards of national myth-making.

Hrushevsky devoted more than half of his academic *History* to Ukrainian Cossackdom. Some critics and reviewers of Hrushevsky's magnum opus, including Dmytro Bahalii, even argued that he overemphasized the role played by the Cossacks in Ukrainian history, and, beginning with the seventeenth century, all but replaced the history of Ukraine with that of the Cossacks.[185] One might add that if Hrushevsky's *History* had not ended where it did (in the mid-seventeenth century), he would have devoted even more attention to Cossackdom. In accounting for this fascination of Hrushevsky's with the history of the Cossacks, it is hard to overlook the direct impact on him of the Cossack chronicles and of the tradition initiated by the author of the *History of the Rus'*, for whom nine-tenths of his subject was Cossack history. It is also difficult to overstate the significance of historical mythology in the nationalization of the East European historical past in the nineteenth and early twentieth centuries. The father of Czech national historiography, František Palacký, with whom Hrushevsky has often been compared, built his grand narrative of the Czech past around the Hussite movement.[186] Hrushevsky accomplished the same task with regard to Ukrainian history by first rehabilitating and then fully utilizing the myth of Ukrainian Cossackdom for the purpose of constructing Ukrainian nationhood. He was more than successful in turning the Cossacks from Little Russians (as most earlier Ukrainian historians had defined them) into Ukrainians and presenting them not only as representatives of the Ukrainian popular masses but also as exemplars of the Ukrainian nation at large.

Hrushevsky's paradigm of the Ukrainian past as the history of the rise, fall, and resurgence of the Ukrainian nation conformed closely to the general scheme applied by the national 'awakeners' of the nineteenth century to the history of Central and East European nations in general. The belief that once glorious nations had fallen asleep at some point and needed to be awakened was widespread among the leaders of the European national movements. Still, Hrushevsky's application of this paradigm to the 'long' and 'short' (that is, until the end of the eighteenth century) narratives of Ukrainian history was influenced not only by the prevailing trends of the time but also by the Ukrainian historiographic tradition that preceded Hrushevsky by centuries. The focus of the historical narrative on the glorious deeds of the Kyivan princes can be traced back to the earliest Rus' chronicles. Hrushevsky's identification of the period of Polish rule as a period of darkness and his focus on the history of the Dnipro Cossacks, with its well-developed mythology, can be traced back to the traditions established by the Cossack chroniclers.

But it was in Hrushevsky's writings that those features of earlier narratives acquired most explicit articulation and new meaning. Providing Ukrainian history with the most ancient beginnings imaginable, he established its continuity over a period of some 1,500 years and extended his narrative to cover all of Ukrainian ethnic territory, from Transcarpatia and Galicia in the west to the Azov steppes and the

Kuban peninsula in the east. Hrushevsky's narrative did not neglect the history of the state or the elite and its culture, but its principal subject was the people, whose evolving story ensured the continuity of the narrative itself. Although the meaning of the term 'people' gradually changed in Hrushevsky's usage from 'popular masses' to 'nation,' he always held the masses in high regard, which prevented him from developing such figures as Kostiantyn Ostrozky and Bohdan Khmelnytsky into full-fledged heroes in his account.

Hrushevsky's appropriation of essential episodes of the Russian historical narrative to construct his account of Ukrainian history, establishing it as a subject of study separate from Russian history (in its imperial statist or national populist incarnations), created a great stir in scholarly circles and in public opinion. Nevertheless, Russia never figured in Hrushevsky's prerevolutionary historical writings as the major 'other' of Ukraine. That role was clearly reserved for the Poles, who emerged as the major villains in the story of the Ukrainian nation.

Hrushevsky clearly believed that his scheme of Ukrainian (and, by extension, East Slavic) history offered a much more accurate interpretation of the historical process than did the traditional scheme of 'Russian' history. That belief came to be shared by a whole generation of Ukrainian historians. The historical narrative created by Hrushevsky almost immediately became the master narrative of Ukrainian history and of the development of the nation. Hrushevsky was not the first to suggest a comprehensive scheme of Ukrainian history. He was, however, the first to implement a distinct Ukrainian historical scheme consistently in his prolific writings. He endowed that scheme with scholarly credibility and authority, closely associating it in the process with his own name and historiographic legacy.

What of the public response to Hrushevsky's work? Did general readers note the emergence of a Ukrainian national narrative in Hrushevsky's writings and, if so, how did they understand it? What aspects did they accept and reject? What difference did their reading of Hrushevsky make to their understanding of Ukrainian history? It is generally difficult, if not impossible, to answer questions about popular reaction and attitudes toward changes in intellectual paradigms. The main problem here is the lack of sources reflecting such attitudes. In Hrushevsky's case, we are in a somewhat better position to deal with these questions. Since he presented and developed his views in numerous popular writings, some of his nonacademic readers made the effort to write to him or to his colleagues in order to express their views. Letters of this kind have been preserved in Hrushevsky's personal archive, giving us an opportunity to explore the questions formulated above.

Judging by the available correspondence, the lifting of the official ban on the import of the first volumes of the *History of Ukraine-Rus'* aroused interest in Hrushevsky's work among nonhistorians, who wrote to him about acquiring copies of the multivolume edition.[187] As might be expected, however, it was the publication of the *Illustrated History of Ukraine* that produced a much more profound impact on general readers. Its first edition appeared in 1911, followed by a revised version in 1912. It is apparent from the letters that the *Illustrated History* was especially popular among the nationally conscious Ukrainian intelligentsia and workers of the Russian Empire. The fact that these letters were written in Ukrainian indicates that their authors were already active in the Ukrainian revival, with which they closely associated themselves. A letter written to Hrushevsky in August 1912 by a teacher from Tarashcha, O. Hrunko, shows that those who read the *Illustrated History* were eager to acquire the academic *History* as well. But it also appears that the Ukrainian intelligentsia in the provinces could not afford the outlay required to buy all the published volumes.[188] Letters to Hrushevsky from Siberia attest that it was financially difficult for political exiles there to buy even the one-volume *Illustrated History*.[189]

What were the expectations of those who wanted to acquire Hrushevsky's book, and what was the reaction of those who actually read it? The first group was alerted to Hrushevsky's work either through publications in the Russian press or by word of mouth and regarded the book as a revelation of the Ukrainian national past. Hryhorii Porevych, a political exile who wrote to Hrushevsky from Ust-Sysolsk, stated: 'Your work is so popular and substantial that it is my heart's desire to obtain it.' He added that his 'great desire to take cognizance of our historical life' had caused him to write to Hrushevsky with a request for a copy of the book.[190] Such expectations were heightened by the comments of those who had read the *Illustrated History*. The above-mentioned Hrunko from Tarashcha confided to Hrushevsky: 'This year, with great difficulty, I managed to obtain a copy of your *Illustrated History of Ukraine*, which I read with ardour, heatedly, without even stopping to take a breath. There I learned certain things about Ukraine that conventional Russian textbooks did not offer.'[191]

Excitement on learning the 'truth' about Ukraine that had been concealed by official Russian historiography is particularly strong in a letter from F. Iaronovetsky, a Ukrainian worker in Siberia, who corresponded with Lev Iurkevych, a Ukrainian political activist in Lviv with whom Hrushevsky was acquainted. Thanking Iurkevych for sending him some Ukrainian books, including Hrushevsky's *Illustrated History*, Iaronovetsky wrote: 'And I thank you again for the books, which are of very great value to me, for I have never yet read such books in my life, and until now I used to think that our Ukraine had no significance in its life in relation to other states; and now, having read these books, I learned that Ukraine was far from what Russian patriots consider it to be!'[192]

Iaronovetsky's letter is particularly significant not only because it was never intended to be seen by Hrushevsky, and thus offers a candid reaction to the book, but also because it reports precisely what impressed this reader in Hrushevsky's work and how he understood its content. The 'truth' about Ukraine that Iaronovetsky gleaned from the *Illustrated History* had to do first and foremost with the struggle against the Ukrainian inferiority complex and the project of endowing Ukraine with a glorious past, including a record of statehood, military victories, and cultural achievement. Iaronovetsky wrote that after reading the books sent to him by Iurkevych (the context suggests that he was referring particularly to Hrushevsky's work), he learned that Ukraine 'had priority in culture over Russia, and that it was the same kind of state as others, and gained glory through its army just like other states, and in addition it has its own ancient language and writing.' Also not lost on Iaronovetsky was Hrushevsky's paradigm of the rise and decline of the Ukrainian nation. Referring to the demise of Cossack statehood as discussed by Hrushevsky, Iaronovetsky wrote: 'And now I know how it [the Ukrainian state] fell and was destroyed.'[193] Clearly, the 'nationalization' of the old populist narrative of Ukrainian history undertaken by Hrushevsky at the turn of the twentieth century was finding a positive response among readers.

There were two events in Ukrainian history that particularly attracted Iaronovetsky's attention: Khmelnytsky's 'error,' meaning the Pereiaslav Agreement of 1654, and the alleged visit of Peter I to Pavlo Polubotok, the acting hetman of Ukraine, whom Peter imprisoned for defending Ukraine's freedoms. These key episodes, which took place at critical junctures in Russo-Ukrainian relations – the mid-seventeenth century and the early eighteenth – clearly did not leave the reader indifferent. Iaronovetsky was obviously excited by the legend of Peter's visit as retold by Hrushevsky, believing that the powerful tsar had indeed gone to his victim to ask forgiveness. In Iaronovetsky's mind, the scene symbolized the admission of wrongs done to Ukraine by Russian rulers. Ukraine emerges from Iaronovetsky's letter as a country with its own glorious history, more a result of the joint efforts of its people than of its individual representatives. While Polubotok could clearly be regarded as one of the 'heroes' of the Ukrainian narrative, Iaronovetsky does not comment on him at all and mentions Khmelnytsky only in connection with his 'error' at Pereiaslav. It is hard to say how many readers were as alert and receptive to Hrushevsky's views as Iaronovetsky, but the fact that there were such people indicates that the historical narrative he created was playing its part in the formation of modern Ukrainian national identity.

Some of the secret police reports of the period indicate that Hrushevsky's narrative was contributing not insignificantly to the parallel project of politicizing Ukrainian identity. In November 1913 a secret police agent code-named 'Gogol' (apparently to underline the Little Russian character of his views and loyalties) reported to his handlers about a meeting of a clandestine Ukrainian student group in Kharkiv: 'Extracts from the *History of Ukraine* were read (according to Hrushevsky), and it was emphasized in Bazhanov's lecture that ... all the events up to Volodymyr and after Volodymyr concerning Kyiv and Volhynia were events not of Russian but of Ukrainian history.'[194] The students present at the meeting were 'technologists,' indicating that interest in the new paradigm of Ukrainian history was spreading beyond the ranks of historians and specialists in the humanities to embrace wider circles of the young Ukrainian intelligentsia as far east as Kharkiv. The thesis itself, as advanced by Bazhanov on the basis of Hrushevsky's writings, was evidently considered politically dangerous by 'Gogol' and his superiors. Indeed, it would appear that whether Hrushevsky was prepared to admit it or not, his historical paradigm was undermining not only the imperial historical narrative but also the foundations of the state that the narrative was designed to legitimize.

Part 2

Nation and Class

The Revolution of 1917 in the Russian Empire was a turning point in the unmaking of imperial Russia. It redefined relations between the all-Russian, Great Russian, and Ukrainian projects, as well as between dominant discourses on the one hand and historical paradigms and narratives on the other. Among the main victims of this restructuring was the all-Russian project, as the Bolsheviks – the new masters of the former Russian Empire – came to accept, not only in theory but also in practice, the division of the all-Russian nationality into three separate nations: Russian, Ukrainian, and Belarusian.

As the Russian imperial discourse, based on the paradigm of an all-Russian nationality, was discarded along with the now defunct empire, it was replaced by a nation-based anticolonial discourse that stressed the rights of the formerly oppressed nationalities vis-à-vis the formerly dominant ones, as well as by a class-based discourse that emphasized class interests and class struggle. The concepts of class and nation defined the formulation, articulation, and presentation of Bolshevik policy toward the nationalities at every significant juncture of Soviet history. In the final analysis, it was the primacy of class over nation in the official hierarchy of discourses that allowed the Bolsheviks to formulate their new empire-saving project – a policy designed to keep the non-Russian nations of the USSR under Moscow's control.

Not surprisingly, it was the Great Russian project that emerged as the main beneficiary of Bolshevik efforts to save the empire. Around this core nation, they sought to mobilize the non-Russian subjects of the former empire in the 1930s. The Russians returned to the centre of nation-based political discourse, although they were dramatically different from the Russians of the recent imperial past. The Ukrainians and Belarusians were no longer part of the dominant Russian nation, and in that sense prerevolutionary imperial Russia ceased to exist. In the minds of the peoples of the former empire, and then of the world at large, it was replaced slowly but surely by the notions of a new Soviet polity and a new Russian identity.

The path toward the formulation of a model for the 'solution' of the national question in the USSR, as well as toward the establishment of a balance between class and national discourses intended to legitimize that model, was neither simple nor straightforward. The task of unmaking the old imperial structures and identities and the concomitant development of post-imperial national ones brought together the Bolshevik authorities and the leaders of the Ukrainian national movement, making possible Hrushevsky's return to Ukraine in 1924. Thus, Hrushevsky's life and work in the USSR from 1924 until his death in 1934 affords a unique opportunity to examine the interrelation between competing national projects, dominant discourses, and historical narratives in Soviet Ukraine and the USSR during the first postrevolutionary decades. It shows how and under what circumstances cooperation between the Bolshevik regime and the activists of the Ukrainian national movement became possible, what impact it had on their political positions and, finally, how their uneasy compromise shaped the historical narratives produced by both sides. A close reading of Hrushevsky's writings of the period also helps establish the degree to which the dominant narrative created by Soviet historiography in the 1920s and early 1930s was influenced by national interpretations of East Slavic history, and vice versa. Ultimately it also helps explain the formation of Soviet nationalities and national loyalties, as well as the role of the communist experience in producing separate Russian and Ukrainian national identities.

Chapter 4

Negotiating with the Bolsheviks

In March 1924 Mykhailo Hrushevsky and his family returned to Kyiv from their period of emigration in Central Europe.[1] Seven years had passed since Hrushevsky's return to Kyiv from exile in Russia in March 1917. In retrospect, the difference between the two returns was enormous. If in 1917 Hrushevsky made his way to Kyiv to lead the Ukrainian Revolution, in 1924 he came back as a symbol of the defeat of the Ukrainian cause in that same revolution. From the very beginning, Hrushevsky's return to Ukraine was a matter of political contention. His former colleagues in the Ukrainian Party of Socialist Revolutionaries, such as Mykyta Shapoval, viewed it as an act of treason that turned Hrushevsky into a 'political corpse, going past which Ukrainians should hold their noses.'[2] Kyiv students, by contrast, saw Hrushevsky's return as an attempt on the part of the Ukrainian political emigration to shift the centre of anti-Bolshevik resistance to Ukraine.[3] The Bolshevik regime, for its part, viewed Hrushevsky's return as a major propaganda coup. He was treated by the authorities as a representative of the *smena vekh* (change of landmarks) movement – the return to the USSR of exiles who had initially opposed the revolution.

How did Hrushevsky, a leader of the Ukrainian Revolution, consent to be treated as its opponent? How was it that he – the head of the independent Ukrainian state who announced in January 1918 that the Bolshevik war on Ukraine marked the end of the Ukrainian orientation on Russia – could agree to recognize the legitimacy of a party that he considered a mere regional branch of the Russian Bolsheviks? Exploring these questions is essential to understanding relations between the communist and national projects in the USSR and the uneasy process of "negotiation" between them. Answering them requires a consideration of several related questions: when and under what circumstances cooperation became possible; whether a compromise was reached and, if so, under what conditions; and who the ultimate beneficiary of the arrangement was. These were the questions that guided my research into the last decade of Mykhailo Hrushevsky's life.

The Return to Ukraine

The question of why Hrushevsky returned to Ukraine was first posed by the Soviet Ukrainian scholar Fedir Shevchenko in 1966 in an attempt to 'rehabilitate' the historian and his writings in the Ukrainian Soviet Socialist Republic (Ukrainian SSR). Shevchenko answered this question by indicating Hrushevsky's leftist leanings and claiming that he recognized the achievements of the Bolshevik Party in the socialist revolution. Hrushevsky's goal, claimed Shevchenko, was not to foment an insurrection against Soviet rule but to continue serving his people.[4] For all the restrictions imposed on historical scholarship by the Soviet regime, Shevchenko was able to give a generally correct answer to the question that he posed. At the time of his return to Ukraine, Hrushevsky indeed acknowledged the leading role of the Bolshevik Party in the socialist revolution and was prepared to cooperate with the authorities in promoting socialist construction in Ukraine. What remains unexplained, however, is the change in Hrushevsky's views between early 1918 and early 1924 that led him to adopt such an attitude.

There can be little doubt that any search for an answer to this quandary should start with the coup d'état arranged by the German high command in April 1918, which removed the Central Rada, its president, and government from power and installed the regime of Hetman Pavlo Skoropadsky. It would be difficult to exaggerate the impact of the events of April 1918 on Hrushevsky. On the personal level, the coup turned Hrushevsky from a head of state into a fugitive. On the political level, it shattered the united front of Ukrainian political organizations that Hrushevsky had managed to build, splitting the allegiances of Ukrainian activists along social policy lines. Many of Hrushevsky's prerevolutionary friends from the Society of Ukrainian Progressives, from whom he had distanced himself in 1917, now supported the new regime, which not only had the backing of the German military but was also endorsed by the Ukrainian landowning class. Such old acquaintances of Hrushevsky's as Dmytro Doroshenko and Oleksander Lototsky even held ministerial posts in the hetman's government. Hrushevsky, for his part, refused to cooperate with the new regime. He continued to regard the Ukrainian Revolution as a process that would bring the Ukrainian people not only national but also social liberation. For a while, Hrushevsky abandoned politics and even went into hiding. On the one hand, he wanted nothing to do with the conservative forces that had set themselves against the redistribution of land and thus the revolution in general. In Hrushevsky's opinion, they had hijacked the Ukrainian state-building project and were exploiting the achievement of Ukrainian independence to stop the revolution, denying the Ukrainian peasantry its long-awaited emancipation. On the other hand, Hrushevsky did not join the Ukrainian Socialist Revolutionaries and Social Democrats in preparing an armed insurrection against Skoropadsky in the last months of 1918. He returned to the political arena only in the aftermath of the insurrection.[5]

Hrushevsky's experience under the hetman's regime brought him closer to the Bolsheviks than he could ever have imagined. At the Ukrainian Labour Congress, which was summoned in January 1919 to replace the Central Rada and legitimize the new government, known as the Directory, Hrushevsky found himself at the head of a small group of delegates who advocated the Soviet system of government in Ukraine. He claimed that the Soviet system was not the invention of the Bolsheviks but that they had taken it over from the Mensheviks in the course of the revolution. Although Hrushevsky stopped short of supporting the left wing of the Ukrainian Party of Socialist Revolutionaries (UPSR), which advocated an alliance with the Bolsheviks, he argued that the Ukrainian Socialist Revolutionaries should support the Soviet system as a temporary measure. Very soon, that position cost Hrushevsky his political career. In the spring of 1919, when the leaders of the Directory accused him of involvement in a conspiracy to carry out a leftist coup d'état, Hrushevsky left for Western Europe as head of the Foreign Delegation of the UPSR to a conference of the Second International. Exiled in Vienna, he and his colleagues in the delegation went through a number of stages in defining their attitude toward the Bolshevik regime, evolving slowly but steadily toward the recognition of Bolshevik rule in Ukraine.[6]

In February 1920, a conference of the UPSR in Prague approved positions very close to those of Hrushevsky and the Foreign Delegation, adopting a resolution favouring the creation of a Ukrainian coalition government composed of Bolsheviks and Socialist Revolutionaries.[7] In the same month, the Central Committee of the UPSR condemned the military struggle against the Bolshevik regime and allowed party members to accept appointments to the Soviet government of Ukraine.[8] In April of the same year, the second conference of Socialist Revolutionaries abroad decided to recognize the legitimacy of the Soviet government of Ukraine on condition that it truly represent the 'national, social, and statist interests of the Ukrainian toiling masses organized in the sovereign socialist soviet republic.' As the term 'sovereign' did not necessarily mean 'independent' in that particular context, the Bolshevik regime fit the description of the 'soviet' government that the Socialist Revolutionaries were prepared to recognize, dropping their previous demand for a coalition. At the same time, the conference condemned the Ukrainian governments of Symon Petliura, Isaak Mazepa, and Ievhen Petrushevych for violating the national, social, and state interests of the Ukrainian people and allying themselves with international capital and the Polish and Romanian nobilities.[9] In May 1920, the third conference of the UPSR and its Foreign Delegation issued a joint statement condemning Petliura for undertaking a military campaign against the Soviet regime together with the Polish forces of Józef Piłsudski.[10] In July 1920, Hrushevsky wrote to the secretary of the Central Committee of the Bolshevik Party in Ukraine, Stanislav Kosior, whom he addressed as 'comrade,' to express his support and that of his colleagues (not without reservations) for the socialist transformations in Ukraine and Bolshevik efforts to take control of Western Ukraine.[11]

The attempts of Hrushevsky and his followers to find common ground with the Bolsheviks proceeded from the simple fact that by 1920 the Bolsheviks had emerged as masters of Ukraine, while the UPSR was all but annihilated. Its left wing established a separate Borotbist Party that joined the Bolsheviks, ensuring their victory in Ukraine. If Hrushevsky and his colleagues wanted to return and continue their political work, they needed Bolshevik approval. Another factor that clearly influenced Hrushevsky's attitude toward the Bolshevik regime was the change in its nationality policy. By the 1920s the Bolsheviks, learning from their mistakes, had stopped their persecution of all manifestations of Ukrainian cultural life and were even trying to encourage the linguistic Ukrainization of the local party and government apparatus.[12] The Bolshevik conflict with the resurgent Polish state for control of Ukraine also helped Hrushevsky and his group find common ground with Moscow. Hrushevsky continued to see the Poles as the main threat to Ukraine and categorically opposed any new partition of Ukrainian lands between the Russian Federation and the Second Polish Republic.

Last but not least, in political terms Hrushevsky found much more in common with the Bolsheviks than with the Poles or the Ukrainian government of Symon Petliura. What the Socialist Revolutionaries shared with the Bolsheviks was not only support for the Soviet form of government but also belief in socialist revolution.

Not surprisingly, in Hrushevsky's writings and statements of this period, class-based socialist discourse replaced the nationalist discourse of early 1918, helping him and his colleagues justify their change of heart with regard to the Bolsheviks. If in 1918 Hrushevsky portrayed the Bolsheviks as representatives of the old Great Russian centralism and chauvinism, denouncing them as tools in the hands of the Russian bourgeoisie, he now regarded them as leaders of the socialist revolution. In June 1920 Hrushevsky explained the change in his attitude as follows: 'Indeed, from the uncertain adventurists dominated by all the sins of Muscovite chauvinism and imperialism that they may have seemed at the outset, the Russian Bolsheviks have developed in the course of these three years into leaders of the world socialist movement to whom the whole labouring world, all those wronged and swindled by the contemporary capitalist regime, look with faith and love. Whatever the errors of the Bolshevik leaders in their policy toward Ukraine, however trying the activity of their agents in Ukraine may be to Ukrainians, every effort must be made to avoid conflict with Bolshevism out of respect for the significance to all humanity of the socialist revolution that it is leading.'[13] Hrushevsky condemned any attempt to fight Bolshevism at a time when it was beating back an offensive of 'world capitalism and its hirelings.'[14] He claimed that every time reactionary forces threatened to take over Ukraine, the popular masses looked to the Bolsheviks as the most uncompromising fighters against the bourgeoisie. Hrushevsky welcomed Bolshevik attempts to support Ukrainian cultural aspirations, while remaining extremely critical of Bolshevik intolerance toward other pro-Soviet socialist parties and the growing centralism of Moscow in the political and economic arena.[15]

Hrushevsky also strongly believed in the future of the Ukrainian Party of Socialist Revolutionaries and opposed its dissolution – a prospect that became a reality when some members lent their support to the Petliura camp, while the leftist Borotbists joined the Bolsheviks en masse. According to Hrushevsky, the Socialist Revolutionaries had a revolutionary mission to achieve something that no one had done before them: to win over the peasantry to the socialist cause and turn

Ukraine from an obstacle on the path to world revolution into its springboard. Hrushevsky discussed the mission and specific objectives of the UPSR in an article titled 'The Ukrainian Party of Socialist Revolutionaries and Its Tasks,' written in June-July 1920 and published in the first issue of the journal *Boritesia – poborete!* (Struggle – You Shall Overcome!), issued by the party's Foreign Delegation.[16] In it Hrushevsky developed some of the ideas expressed in his earlier writings. Among the new elements was his discussion of the role of tradition in party activity. Hrushevsky traced the ideological roots of socialist-revolutionary doctrine back to the SS. Cyril and Methodius Brotherhood, established by Kyivan Ukrainophiles of the 1840s. He also commented on the views of Taras Shevchenko and Mykhailo Drahomanov, going on to consider elements of social radicalism in the writings of Mykola Kostomarov, Volodymyr Antonovych, and Oleksander Lazarevsky.

In fact, Hrushevsky was claiming for his party the major part of the all-Ukrainian cultural and political heritage, most notably the well-developed cult of Taras Shevchenko. The article was followed by an appendix titled 'Shevchenko as Leader of the Social Revolution' in which Hrushevsky presented the celebrated father of the Ukrainian nation as a prophet of socialist ideology.[17] Hrushevsky claimed that in 1917 it was the young Socialist Revolutionaries who had taken the trail blazed by Shevchenko, while the older generation of Ukrainian activists, especially his former friends and colleagues from the Society of Ukrainian Progressives (later the Ukrainian Party of Socialist Federalists) had chosen the path of Panteleimon Kulish. Hrushevsky presented the latter as Shevchenko's antipode who had betrayed the interests of the Ukrainian masses. According to Hrushevsky, the older generation of the Ukrainian intelligentsia had transferred power to the bourgeoisie in order to suppress the revolution in Ukraine on condition that Ukrainian cultural needs be satisfied.[18] Clearly, what Hrushevsky had in mind was the support rendered by the Socialist Federalists to the regime of Hetman Pavlo Skoropadsky. More generally, by reinterpreting the tradition of the Ukrainian national movement in general, Hrushevsky opened the door to the Bolsheviks' subsequent adoption of certain elements of the Ukrainian national narrative.

Central to Hrushevsky's discussion of the Ukrainian political and social tradition was the issue of relations between the state and the masses, involving the right of the masses to rebel against the government if it did not represent and protect their interests. That set of issues was particularly important to Hrushevsky and his supporters in the

UPSR, given that more than once they had broken the bonds of national solidarity and rebelled against Ukrainian governments for the sake of socialist revolution. That was the case with the uprising against the hetman in late 1918, the alleged coup attempt against the Directory in 1919, and the condemnation of the Petliura government in 1920. Hrushevsky was clearly seeking to legitimize those acts not only in social terms but also within the context of national discourse, and the easiest way of doing so was to provide an appropriate reinterpretation of the Ukrainian political tradition. To make his point as convincing as possible, Hrushevsky recalled an episode from his own academic career – the publication in 1892, in the first issue of the *Memoirs of the Shevchenko Scientific Society*, of an article titled 'The Communal Movement in Ukraine-Rus' in the Thirteenth Century.'[19] The article dealt with the Mongol invasion, interpreting the conflict between Prince Danylo of Galicia-Volhynia and the local communities that accepted the rule of the Mongol khans, while resisting Danylo's attempts to reimpose his jurisdiction over them, as a conflict between communes and princes in general. Writing in the tradition of Ukrainian populist historiography, Hrushevsky took the side of the communes. As discussed in chapter 2 of this book, the article was criticized by Drahomanov but enthusiastically supported by Antonovych, who, as Hrushevsky wrote, 'was imbued with principled sympathy for all opposition and active struggle against the oppressive power of the state.'[20] In 1892 Hrushevsky apparently shared these views of his professor. He went much farther in 1920, drawing a clear parallel between Prince Danylo (whom he had presented as a national hero during the prerevolutionary era) and the Ukrainian 'bourgeois' governments on the one hand and the princeless communities and the popular masses on the other. He even called the members of those princeless communities 'Bolshevized Ukrainians.'[21]

Hrushevsky discussed the circumstances surrounding the publication of his article of 1892 in order to demonstrate the traditional strength within the Ukrainian movement of those factions that 'promoted social interests before national ones, going so far as to struggle against their state in defending the communal interests infringed by it.'[22] Writing about the Ukrainian populists of the late nineteenth century, Hrushevsky noted 'the antipathy with which these circles treated the efforts of the Ukrainian bourgeoisie to build a class-based national state, contrary to the socialist dreams of the masses.'[23] If Hrushevsky, having adopted a national platform between the revolutions of 1905 and 1917, was highly critical of Antonovych and his circle, he now praised Antonovych's populism and found much in the antistatist opinions of his teacher that was consonant with his own views. In order to make his point, however, Hrushevsky was clearly stretching his evidence. While Antonovych had indeed been critical of the state and its attributes, it was an exaggeration to take his favourable reaction to Hrushevsky's article as indicating that Antonovych or his followers had gone 'so far as to struggle against their state in defending the communal interests infringed by it.' Equally questionable was Hrushevsky's new interpretation of the course taken by the Ukrainophile journal *Kievskaia starina*, which, under the leadership of Oleksander Lazarevsky, had allegedly engaged in 'drawing up a bill of indictment of that bourgeoisie [the Cossack officer stratum] for its transgressions against the toiling populace.' Hrushevsky's statement in that regard was an oversimplification at best.

Ironically, Hrushevsky was paid back in kind by his opponents from the camp of Skoropadsky's supporters, Dmytro Doroshenko and Viacheslav Lypynsky. They exploited his politically motivated argument in support of the masses' right of rebellion to argue that Hrushevsky was an avowed antistatist who minimized the role of the state in Ukrainian history.[24] Quite shocking to Hrushevsky's former supporters of 1917 and early 1918 was his treatment of Ukrainian independence exclusively as an act forced upon Ukraine by unfavourable circumstances and his pledge of loyalty to the old federalist ideals. Hrushevsky stopped short of denouncing independence as such – as he saw it, that ideal, for which good and honest sons of Ukraine had spilled their blood, was irrevocable. He claimed nevertheless that the slogan of Ukrainian independence had been appropriated by the worst elements of Ukrainian society – bandits, organizers of anti-Jewish pogroms, warlords, and the like – who had turned it into an instrument of struggle not only against Soviet Russia but against socialism itself. Hrushevsky maintained that Ukraine had to reach an understanding with Soviet Russia.

Denouncing military struggle against the Bolsheviks, he insisted that the realities of the current situation and the threat of resurgent Russian imperialism obliged the Ukrainian political parties to reach an agreement with the Bolsheviks, even at the price of certain concessions. According to Hrushevsky, the solution to the Russo-Ukrainian problem lay in an economic and military alliance between the two states, leaving in abeyance the question of future federative or confederative ties. He hoped to see Russia and Ukraine enter an all-European/world federation of socialist republics as equals. 'I do not expect,' wrote Hrushevsky, 'that the Russian communists would want to insist that even in this world federation Ukraine should play the role of some adjunct to Russia ... But if such a plan should arise, it would be nothing other than a survival of the old Russian imperialism, not motivated by any interests of socialist revolution but, on the contrary, opposed to them and counterrevolutionary, for such tendencies would have to evoke a national reaction in Ukraine with renewed force.'[25]

Hrushevsky was quite critical of actual Bolshevik policy in Ukraine. He expressed his reservations not only in his articles, including the one on the tasks of the UPSR, but also in his letter of July 1920 to the secretary of the Bolshevik Central Committee in Ukraine, Stanislav Kosior. There Hrushevsky tried to find common ground with the Bolsheviks, citing the common interests of the world revolution. Indicating to Kosior that Ukraine, with its large peasant class, had become a stumbling block rather than an asset to the world revolution, Hrushevsky offered the services of the UPSR to involve the Ukrainian peasantry in the socialist cause. He claimed that his party had called off its struggle against Soviet Russia and was denying support to nationalist forces eager to continue that struggle with the help of the European bourgeoisie. The basis for the proposed agreement between the Bolsheviks and the UPSR, argued Hrushevsky, was his party's acceptance of the platform of the Third (Communist) International and Bolshevik support for the principle of national self-determination. As before, Hrushevsky saw an obstacle to the development of the socialist revolution in Ukraine in the centralist policies of the Bolshevik leadership in Moscow. Once again, Hrushevsky lent his support to the idea of a federation of Soviet republics but objected to any federation in which Ukraine would be linked more closely to Russia than to any other member state. In Hrushevsky's view, the federation of Russia and Ukraine proclaimed by the Bolsheviks in February 1920 was a major political error. As Bolshevik power was limited to the cities, and the Soviet system was making little progress in the Ukrainian countryside, Hrushevsky proposed to Kosior that cooperation be established between the Bolsheviks and pro-Soviet Ukrainian parties. He wrote: 'The CP(B) [Communist Party (bolshevik)] should strive to transfer power in the Ukrainian SSR to the Soviet Ukrainian parties with all possible speed.'[26]

Did Hrushevsky mean what he was suggesting to Kosior? Did he consider it possible that the Bolsheviks would indeed hand over power to the parties whose government they had just defeated on the battlefield? Or was this just a bargaining strategy intended to promote a more modest goal – the legalization of the UPSR in Ukraine? The latter was indeed a much more realistic objective. In fact, the year 1920 saw the legalization of the Central Committee of the UPSR in Ukraine. The Bolsheviks also allowed the return of the former head of the Central Rada government and a Social Democratic member of the Directory, Volodymyr Vynnychenko, who was appointed deputy head of the Bolshevik government in Ukraine but excluded from the Bolshevik Politburo and Central Committee – the true centre of power under the communist regime. The policy of cooperation with the Bolsheviks seemed to be bearing its first fruits, and Hrushevsky may indeed have had inflated expectations concerning its further course.

Any such hopes were dashed by the events of the summer and autumn of 1920. The changing fortunes of the Bolshevik war with Poland brought the Piłsudski-Petliura forces back to Ukraine, and many members of the UPSR who had earlier cooperated with the Bolsheviks now changed sides. The Bolsheviks, who had never completely trusted the Socialist Revolutionaries in any event, arrested the members of the UPSR Central Committee. Disappointed with the Soviet regime, Vynnychenko returned to Central Europe and became an ardent foe of all cooperation with the Bolsheviks.

The Bolsheviks, for their part, were sending mixed signals to Hrushevsky and his group. The situation was aggravated by the public trial in May 1921 of the UPSR Central Committee members arrested by the Bolsheviks in the previous year. The trial, at which the leaders of Hrushevsky's party were 'unmasked' as enemies of the toiling masses, was a grave setback to Hrushevsky and other Socialist Revolutionaries who wanted to resume their political work in Ukraine. Hrushevsky and his group issued a statement condemning the trial and terming it an error that hindered the cause of the socialist revolution. The statement accused the Bolshevik government of introducing a one-party dictatorship in Ukraine.[27] Hrushevsky also noted the intolerance of the Bolshevik regime toward other political parties in April 1921 in his article commemorating the fiftieth anniversary of the Paris Commune. There he wrote that the Bolsheviks' 'sectarian exclusiveness and intolerance of non-communist socialist parties weakens the achievements of communism more than does the diversity of ideas in the Paris Commune.'[28] For all his harsh statements, Hrushevsky clearly had not given up hope of finding common ground with the Bolsheviks. He and his Vienna group of Socialist Revolutionaries continued their attempts to establish a dialogue with the Bolshevik masters of Ukraine.[29] Not surprisingly, Hrushevsky's attitude led to a split in the Socialist Revolutionary organizations abroad. Part of the membership, led by Mykyta Shapoval, joined Vynnychenko in opposing cooperation with the Bolsheviks. Shapoval, who resided in Prague, managed to create an alternative party centre that gained the support of Socialist Revolutionary organizations in Poland and Galicia, outflanking Hrushevsky's Foreign Delegation in Vienna. The split became public at the fourth party conference, which took place in Prague in January 1921, and gathered momentum in the spring and summer of that year.[30]

Hrushevsky and his group, which advocated further negotiations with the Bolsheviks even after the trial of the Central Committee members, found themselves in a very precarious situation. They either had to demonstrate that negotiations with the Bolsheviks could bring results or join the UPSR majority, which, given the circumstances of the conflict, was hardly feasible, for relations between the two émigré groups had become very hostile indeed. Not surprisingly, Hrushevsky decided to go ahead with the negotiations. In May 1921 Oleksander Zhukovsky, his close associate and secretary of the Foreign Delegation, visited Riga and sent a telegram and a note to Kharkiv, the capital of Soviet Ukraine, asking for the legalization of the UPSR in Ukraine. In June another member of the Foreign Delegation, Mykola Chechel, left for Moscow to take part in the Congress of the Third (Communist) International and meet with the Ukrainian communist delegation. In July Chechel met with Oleksander Shumsky (a former Socialist Revolutionary and Borotbist who now headed the Ukrainian delegation at the Soviet-Polish peace talks in Riga)[31] in Moscow and then travelled with him to Kharkiv, where he had meetings with the head of the Soviet Ukrainian government, Khristian Rakovsky, and the influential party leader Dmytro Manuilsky. Chechel also met the imprisoned members of the UPSR Central Committee, who at his urging supported the Foreign Delegation's policy of negotiations with the Bolsheviks.[32]

How did the Bolsheviks respond to all these efforts to establish a dialogue? Judging by the minutes of Ukrainian Politburo meetings, which are now available to scholars, between January and June 1921 the supreme party organ in Ukraine discussed the issue of Hrushevsky and his colleagues at least four times. Eventually the Politburo confirmed its opposition to the legalization of the UPSR but decided to allow individual party members to return to Ukraine on condition that they leave the party and condemn its activities.[33] Hrushevsky's emissary, Mykola Chechel, learned of the Politburo decision from Oleksander Shumsky at their meeting in Moscow in July 1921. According to Shumsky, the decision was made in May in response to information supplied to Kharkiv by Oleksander Zhukovsky.[34]

Given the Politburo's previous refusals to permit Hrushevsky's return to Ukraine, its decision of May–June 1921 should be considered a victory for those forces in the Bolshevik leadership that favoured his return. From the viewpoint of Hrushevsky himself, who was pushing for the legalization of his party in Ukraine, it was a clear disappointment. All his arguments in favour of legalization, carefully crafted within the context of revolutionary discourse, were bluntly rejected by the Bolsheviks. The position of the Bolshevik leadership was presented most explicitly by Shumsky at his meeting with Chechel in Moscow in July 1921. According to Shumsky, the Bolshevik leadership believed that the Hrushevsky group was sincere about wanting to promote the Soviet cause in Ukraine. Nevertheless, it was convinced that the legalization of the UPSR would have rather negative consequences. Apparently in response to Hrushevsky's claim that the Socialist Revolutionaries could win the Ukrainian peasantry over to socialism, Shumsky stated that broadening the social base of the dictatorship of the proletariat in such a manner was not in the Bolsheviks' best interests, as it would corrupt the regime by bringing in the influences of the petty bourgeoisie. The Bolsheviks equated the dictatorship of the proletariat with that of their own party, argued Shumsky, and were averse to sharing power with other parties. Thus the legalization of the UPSR would inevitably create a rallying point for opposition forces, first and foremost the petty bourgeoisie, which Shumsky characterized as the Communist Party's main enemy at that moment.[35] The common ground on which Hrushevsky wanted to initiate a dialogue and build a relationship with the Bolsheviks – the cause of world socialist revolution – was not regarded by his intended counterparts as sufficient reason to allow the legalization of any noncommunist party.

The Bolshevik leadership agreed to Hrushevsky's return to Ukraine, not as a political leader but as a private citizen who could lend badly needed recognition and legitimacy to the regime. Hrushevsky refused. In his open letter of 15 November 1921 to the head of the Soviet Ukrainian government, Khristian Rakovsky, he expressed his dissatisfaction with the communist regime's decision to deny legalization to the UPSR and stressed that by dispensing with the cooperation of noncommunist parties, the Bolsheviks were endangering the cause of the socialist revolution in Ukraine. Among the threats to the regime, he indicated its growing bureaucratization and the penetration of its apparatus by individuals who harboured Ukrainophobic prejudices and were unsympathetic, if not overtly hostile, to socialist ideals. Claiming that those elements had effectively alienated the Ukrainian population from the regime, Hrushevsky once again offered his party's cooperation in bringing the people closer to the Bolshevik government and warding off imminent peasant uprisings. The actual reason for the refusal to legalize his party in Ukraine, asserted Hrushevsky, was that such legalization would contradict the existing system of government in principle. He called on Rakovsky to change the system: 'As one socialist to another, in the name of the common interests of the socialist revolution,' wrote Hrushevsky, '... I have resolved to address this appeal of mine ... to your party, to those on whom the direction of your policy depends ... [C]asting aside exclusiveness of party, it is necessary to apply the joint forces of all to strengthen Soviet construction and fill it with vital content and vital forces capable of protecting it against the threat of cataclysms and shocks on the part of all sinister forces, both internal and external.'[36]

For all its criticism of Bolshevik policy toward Ukraine, Hrushevsky's letter to Rakovsky did not affect the government's stand on the desirability of Hrushevsky's return to Ukraine as a private citizen. In January 1922 the Politburo once again asked Rakovsky to look into the issue of admitting Hrushevsky and his group of Socialist Revolutionaries to Ukraine.[37] In April of the same year Hrushevsky was invited to attend a scholarly congress in Kharkiv. He did not go but sent his close associates, Chechel, Zhukovsky, and Volodymyr Zalizniak, as representatives of the Ukrainian Sociological Institute, a scholarly institution founded by Hrushevsky in Prague in 1919 and then moved to Vienna.[38] Apparently, Hrushevsky was not prepared to travel to Ukraine without securing concessions from the Bolsheviks. That, after all, was the essence of his criticism of Vynnychenko's return to Ukraine in 1920.[39] Nevertheless, Hrushevsky was already contemplating a return to Kyiv and even beginning to make preparations for it. As early as April 1922, in a letter to Kyrylo Studynsky, Hrushevsky asked his former colleague at Lviv University to take care of the publication and sales of his books in Lviv, 'especially if I return to Kyiv, from where I will be unable to monitor either sales or prices or printing.'[40]

The difficult financial situation in which Hrushevsky found himself in Vienna also obliged him to think about his future. In September 1922 he wrote Studynsky that he was seriously considering a return to Ukraine – if not a permanent one, then at least a short-term visit or a fact-finding mission – but realized that conditions were not yet ripe. Among the reasons that made his return pointless, he cited general apathy in society and disorientation in government circles caused by the bad harvest and famine. Neither government nor society could muster sufficient resources for cultural work, argued Hrushevsky, hence his relocation to Ukraine made little sense.[41] Working conditions in Vienna were, however, also far from ideal. Hrushevsky and his family supported themselves through the sale of his works, which he was actively reprinting at the time, but sales were declining, and in October 1922 Hrushevsky confessed in a letter to Studynsky: 'It is simply terrifying to think what will happen if we are unable to return next autumn.'[42] The following month Hrushevsky formally resigned his post in the Foreign Delegation. The road to Ukraine was now open.

It was not only Hrushevsky who was thinking of a return to Ukraine but also his younger colleagues in the Vienna group of Socialist Revolutionaries. After some debate it was decided that they would return not as a group but individually.[43] In the spring of 1923 Hrushevsky's close collaborator Chechel was already in Kharkiv, and it was through him that Rakovsky extended another official invitation to Hrushevsky to return to Ukraine. The terms were the same as those offered by the authorities in 1921: Hrushevsky was to devote himself to scholarly work in the Ukrainian Academy of Sciences.[44] In May 1923 Hrushevsky received a private letter from the academy asking whether he would agree to be elected as a member. He hesitated at first, but in August 1923, upon receiving an official request from the academy, he gave his consent. He did not want to become a government employee, but the academy remained at least pro forma a nongovernmental institution, and a position there could give Hrushevsky some measure of independence.[45] In November the Ukrainian Politburo adopted a resolution permitting Hrushevsky's return to Ukraine.[46] Following his election to the Academy of Sciences in December 1923, that institution began the process of obtaining an official letter from the government granting Hrushevsky immunity from political prosecution – one of the conditions of his return to Kyiv.[47]

The financial difficulties that Hrushevsky and his family experienced in the emigration were certainly a factor in his decision to return, but not the main one. There is no reason to disbelieve Hrushevsky's statement in a letter written from Kyiv to one of his American correspondents: 'You are mistaken in having gained the impression that I regret my return and that I returned merely because of material need.'[48] It should be mentioned that apart from an offer Hrushevsky received from Ukraine, there were other options for him to consider at the time. For a short period he even contemplated the idea of going back to Lviv, where he still had a house, but he did not think that the Polish authorities would admit him or that it would be possible to work in Lviv without 'humiliation.'[49] Prospects of teaching at Oxford or Princeton were discussed as well, but for a number of reasons were not high on his list of priorities. Hrushevsky wanted to stay as close to Ukraine as possible and wrote that he would go to the United States only if he had to 'avoid starving to death.'[50]

Hrushevsky gave much more consideration to an offer from the Ukrainian Free University in Prague and the Economic Academy in Poděbrady. He had been corresponding with the Prague Ukrainians about teaching there for most of 1923. In October of that year Hrushevsky was still hesitating whether to go to Prague or Kyiv.[51] In mid-November 1923 he finally decided in favour of Kyiv, probably as a result of the Politburo resolution permitting his return to Ukraine. The formal reason for turning down the Prague offer was that Hrushevsky and his counterparts there could not agree on a salary, but no less important was Hrushevsky's unwillingness to accept an offer from circles close to Mykyta Shapoval, his archenemy in the ranks of the Socialist Revolutionary Party. The party leaders did not want Hrushevsky to go to Ukraine, as they believed that his return would compromise the UPSR and the Ukrainian cause in general, but failed to convince Hrushevsky of this.[52] In November 1923, when he had already made his decision to return to Ukraine, Hrushevsky wrote to Kyrylo Studynsky: 'In moral terms, it would be very unpleasant for me to go to Prague. Shapoval and Co. have probably resorted to intrigue (in which they are great masters!) to compromise me as much as possible in all respects; there I would have no opportunity either to live peacefully or to work, but only to be constantly on the lookout for various intrigues – and who knows whether I could manage to overcome them!'[53]

The Bolshevik authorities were eager to exploit Hrushevsky's return to boost their political image even before he crossed the border. One of the Kharkiv newspapers published a cartoon depicting Hrushevsky as an old man pulling a cartload of his books back to Ukraine.[54] While still in Vienna, Hrushevsky had to protest through his colleagues in Kharkiv and Lviv against a statement made by Mikhail Frunze, at that time one of the top communist leaders in Ukraine, to the effect that Hrushevsky had written a letter of repentance asking the Bolshevik authorities to allow him to return. What made Hrushevsky choose Kyiv despite all his concerns regarding his Bolshevik counterparts? As Hrushevsky's letters attest, he was arranging all his affairs in Central Europe as though setting out for a land of no return.[55] An important reason for his decision to risk the return, disregarding warnings from friend and foe alike, was expressed in a letter to one of his American correspondents: 'I have come to the conclusion that work abroad is becoming ever less productive and useful from the national standpoint and that it is now possible to work more usefully in Ukraine.'[56] Hrushevsky believed that the true task at hand was not to lobby foreign governments abroad and become involved in émigré politics but to conduct cultural work at home, where political conditions had become favourable to such activity. In the same letter Hrushevsky stressed his commitment to cultural work as an important factor in the construction of national identity: 'You justly lament the lack of national consciousness among emigrants from Ukraine. But what can instill such consciousness if not cultural work? It did not exist; it could not exist under the tsarist regime!'[57]

During the last months of his stay abroad, Hrushevsky was clearly searching for elements of Bolshevik policy that could justify the decision he had already made. He enthusiastically welcomed the comments of a Socialist Federalist who told him that the Bolsheviks were performing a great service for Ukraine by destroying Russian power there. Hrushevsky even believed that they were doing so much more radically than the Ukrainians themselves.[58] 'For your information,' he wrote to Studynsky, 'I consider that in the given situation, in which I foresee no imminent change, we can liberate Western Ukraine and defend ourselves against the Muscovite onslaught only with the help of the Bolsheviks; our own forces, on which we should orient ourselves above all, are insufficient for that purpose, for we are undergoing a period of weakness.'[59] He also wrote to Studynsky that one of his reasons for going back was to organize a scholarly response to proponents of the 'all-Russian' idea who were now scattered throughout the world, busily discrediting the Ukrainian cause in scholarly circles.[60]

It is interesting that in his letters to Studynsky, whom he addressed as 'comrade' more often than not, Hrushevsky never tried to legitimize his return to Ukraine within the framework of socialist discourse. Nor did he ever refer to the interests of the world revolution and the advancement of socialism in Ukraine – motifs dominant in his letters to Bolshevik officials in 1920 and 1921. The same holds true for his letter to his American correspondent Tymotei Pochynok, whom he also addressed as 'comrade.' Among Ukrainians, Hrushevsky employed only national discourse to legitimize his return to Ukraine. He was accepting a compromise with the Bolsheviks not for the sake of socialist revolution but for the benefit of the Ukrainian cause.

The Soviet Academician

Hrushevsky returned to Ukraine at the invitation of the Ukrainian Academy of Sciences, with which he maintained close connections until the last days of his life. Hrushevsky's work in Soviet academic institutions impinges on a number of questions that go beyond his own scholarly activity and the evolution of his political views. They include the role of the Ukrainian Academy of Sciences in undermining the all-Russian national project and advancing the Ukrainian one, as well as the policy adopted toward the academy and academic life in general by the Soviet authorities in Moscow and the Ukrainian Bolshevik leadership in Kharkiv. Did the authorities welcome the participation of old-school academicians in public debates? To what extent was the academy autonomous of the state during the first two decades of Soviet rule? What were the academic establishment's motives for cooperation with the regime, and how far was it prepared to go in order to secure official support?[61] These are the questions I had in mind while following the ups and downs of Hrushevsky's career in the Soviet academic establishment prior to his arrest and de facto exile to Moscow in the spring of 1931.

Our saga begins with the first day of Hrushevsky's return from the emigration. A few hours after his arrival in Kyiv in March 1924, Hrushevsky was invited to attend a meeting of the sociology section of the Ukrainian Academy of Sciences. No sooner had he come in than he was elected to the academy's chair of sociology. For a scholar who had long regarded himself as a 'historian-sociologist,' founded the Ukrainian Sociological Institute in Vienna, and dreamt of transferring its activities to Ukraine, that election should have been a major triumph or, at the very least, a step in the right direction.[62] Hrushevsky nevertheless refused to accept the honour, claiming that he had returned to Ukraine primarily to continue his historical projects and would not have time to supervise the sociological section of the academy. Why was he so uncooperative and even ungrateful in responding to the offer from the institution that had made possible his return to Ukraine?

Hrushevsky's problems with the academy and its leadership went back to its inception in 1918 by the government of Hetman Pavlo

Skoropadsky. At that time Hrushevsky opposed its founding for both political and ideological reasons. On the one hand, he did not want to support a project initiated by the hetman; on the other, he had his own concept of the academy that differed significantly from the one advanced by the government. Hrushevsky envisioned the Ukrainian Academy of Sciences as an institution focused primarily on the humanities – disciplines directly related to Ukrainian studies and thus to Ukrainian nation-building. Instead, the academy was established along the lines suggested by its first president, the natural scientist Vladimir (Volodymyr) Vernadsky. In 1919, after the fall of the hetman's regime, Hrushevsky even advocated the abolition of the academy in its current form, but it survived, partly reorganized and somewhat Ukrainized.[63] Soon, with the support of the Bolshevik government, it appropriated the Ukrainian Scientific Society – Hrushevsky's scholarly base in Kyiv, which he had regarded, along with the Shevchenko Scientific Society, as the nucleus of a future Ukrainian Academy. Like Ukrainian statehood itself, the idea of the Academy of Sciences, on which Hrushevsky had worked so hard prior to the revolution, was hijacked by the hetman's government, and Hrushevsky could hardly reconcile himself to that.[64]

The report filed by Main Political Directorate (GPU) agents on 15 March 1924 – a mere week after Hrushevsky's arrival in Kyiv – presented the whole affair of Hrushevsky's election to the chair of sociology as an intrigue of his enemies at the Academy of Sciences. According to the report, some of the academicians had initially planned to offer Hrushevsky the post of president in order to ensure his participation in a united front against the authorities but eventually decided on the tactic of keeping him away from the management of the academy. The leadership of the academy, represented among others by its vice-president, the literary scholar Serhii Iefremov, and its academic secretary, the renowned Orientalist Ahatanhel Krymsky, wanted to marginalize Hrushevsky by denying him the academy's chair of Ukrainian history.[65]

Whoever informed the GPU on the situation in the academy apparently had first-hand knowledge of what was happening in its top echelons. The private diaries of one of the leaders of the anti-Hrushevsky group, Serhii Iefremov, indicate that from the very beginning he had serious reservations about Hrushevsky's return to Kyiv and his work at the academy.[66] Hrushevsky, who had supporters at the academy, was well aware of the difficulties awaiting him there and prepared to wage a lengthy positional war with his enemies. On the personal level, there was no love lost between Hrushevsky and his academic opponents,

Iefremov and Krymsky. But there were also important ideological reasons for their mutual animosity. Although Krymsky's and Iefremov's personal Ukrainian credentials were scarcely less impeccable than Hrushevsky's, both stood to the right of Hrushevsky on social issues. Iefremov was a former member of the Ukrainian Party of Socialist Federalists, which had supported the hetman's regime, and both he and Krymsky cooperated closely with the socially conservative academy members. On top of that, Hrushevsky regarded Krymsky as the dictator of the academy who kowtowed to the authorities and suspected Krymsky and his supporters of delaying his election to the academy in the second half of 1923.[67] Hrushevsky's opponents, for their part, doubted the sincerity of his leftist convictions and believed that he was compromising the autonomy and relative independence of the academy vis-à-vis the state and party apparatus by cooperating with the authorities. They also had serious reservations about his character.[68]

Whatever the negative effects of the internal bickering in the academy, Hrushevsky soon managed to establish a large-scale research and publishing program whose like the academy had never experienced. He was elected chairman of the academy's department of Ukrainian history, responsible among other things for the training of graduate students. Within a relatively short period, Hrushevsky attached a vast network of 'historical institutions' to that department, including a historical section of the former Ukrainian Scientific Society and numerous scholarly commissions. By the mid-1920s Hrushevsky's 'historical institutions' had become the most important centre of historical research in Ukraine, setting an example for other academic centres and Marxist scholarly institutes to follow. As always, Hrushevsky was tireless when it came to his scholarly projects. He resumed work on the *History of Ukraine-Rus'* and served as editor in chief of the scholarly journal *Ukraïna*. He also edited numerous collections of articles on Ukrainian culture, literature, political thought, and history published by various sections of his academic 'empire.' Hrushevsky performed miracles in adapting to the new conditions of scholarly work in Soviet Ukraine, which was financed and controlled by the Bolshevik bureaucracy. An accomplished scholar accustomed to the atmosphere of imperial Russian and Austrian universities and privately funded scholarly associations, he turned into a skilful Soviet-era administrator capable of extracting additional funding, positions, and office space by lobbying the communist authorities. In so doing, he would often negotiate with the authorities in Kharkiv, bypassing the president and official leadership of the academy. No doubt, that tactic created even more friction in Hrushevsky's relations with the academy.[69]

What impact did Hrushevsky's experience in Soviet Ukraine have on his political opinions and attitudes? The question is complicated by the fact that under the conditions of the Bolshevik regime, Hrushevsky had very little opportunity to express his views openly. Nevertheless, the task of answering this question does not seem entirely impossible. Letters to his foreign correspondents offer some information in that regard. Another source of information on Hrushevsky's attitudes during the last decade of his life are the reports of those from whom he sought to conceal his actual views – the informers and secret agents of the GPU. Information drawn from these two very different sources makes it possible to reconstruct Hrushevsky's political views of that period with considerable accuracy.

During the first months after his return to Ukraine, Hrushevsky was trying to persuade his correspondents that he did not regret his decision to come back to Kyiv and wanted them to disregard any rumours suggesting otherwise. That was the case with his letter to Pochynok. It was also the burden of Hrushevsky's numerous letters to Studynsky.[70] Hrushevsky welcomed the policy of Ukrainization, which, as he wrote to Studynsky, 'is being implemented rather firmly and is making its way forward, though with great difficulty.'[71] Ukrainization, formally adopted by the Ukrainian communists in April 1923 in an attempt to strengthen the Bolshevik regime in Ukraine, made possible the intensification of cultural work, which Hrushevsky viewed as crucial to the success of the Ukrainian nation-building project. He was prepared to take full advantage of the new opportunities presented by that policy, which he treated as a joint effort of the government and Ukrainian society. Informing Studynsky about the current situation in Ukraine, Hrushevsky suggested: 'One must think how to avoid allowing cultural life to backslide. So far, both government and society are holding their own. The Soviet republic is becoming visibly stronger, not weaker. All are interested to see what will happen on 1 August [1924] – the deadline for officials to learn the Ukrainian language and go over to conducting official business in Ukrainian.'[72]

Should one trust these statements of Hrushevsky's in letters addressed to correspondents abroad? He himself clearly expected that his letters would be read by the authorities and took the necessary precautions. For example, in a letter to Studynsky from Kyiv dated 22 May 1924, Hrushevsky conspicuously avoided mentioning the title of his book *From the History of Religious Thought in Ukraine,* which was then being published in Lviv, as he assumed that the authorities would not approve of a work on a religious topic.[73] Still, there is good reason to believe that the vast majority of those statements were genuine and reflected Hrushevsky's actual thoughts and feelings. As a rule, they not only correspond to the general trend of Hrushevsky's thinking prior to his departure for Kyiv but also do not contradict statements made in private and recorded by agents of the Bolshevik secret police. According to those reports, immediately after his return to Ukraine, Hrushevsky tended to be more positive than negative in his assessment of Soviet reality. In April 1924, meeting with his former UPSR colleagues Vsevolod Holubovych and Ivan Lyzanivsky, Hrushevsky allegedly blamed the wartime devastation of Ukraine not only on the Bolsheviks but also on the Ukrainian revolutionary governments, the White armies, and the Poles. At the same time, he was critical of the 'petty despotism' of the Bolsheviks and their refusal to legalize other parties. He believed that the national question in Ukraine was only half-resolved and expressed his scepticism about the Ukrainization of higher education.[74]

Secret police reports suggest that the unification of the Ukrainian lands in the context of a future struggle with Poland remained on Hrushevsky's political agenda after his return to Ukraine and, as before the revolution, he did not hesitate to seek Russian support to that end. The formation of the Ukrainian Socialist Soviet Republic (as it was known until 1937, when 'Soviet' preceded 'Socialist') and, later, of the USSR created much better conditions for achieving that goal than those prevailing under the tsarist regime. Consequently, Hrushevsky's attitude toward the USSR was quite positive. Discussing the future of Ukraine after the celebration of his jubilee, which took place in October 1926, he allegedly stated: 'I consider the USSR not only necessary but in fact vital to Ukraine, for we will only be able to combat Russia when all the Ukrainian lands are united. How is that to be accomplished? Only by involving the USSR in a war with Poland, and that war will take place. The inevitable development of events is leading us toward that war, and on the backs of the Russians, at the cost of sacrifices on the part of Great Russia, we shall obtain a united Ukraine.'[75]

When it came to Ukraine's relations with the all-Union authorities, Hrushevsky, judging by GPU reports, suggested supporting those Communist Party and government leaders who favoured administrative decentralization. He considered it futile for former Socialist Revolutionaries to contend for positions in the Soviet Ukrainian apparatus as long as the true centres of power – the Central Committee and the GPU – remained in Moscow. Instead, he proposed to ignore the all-Union structures. 'Better,' stated Hrushevsky, according to a secret police report, 'not to interfere with the USSR and live independently, in a cultured manner, but "unobtrusively," quietly and peacefully. Ignoring the authorities, the Ukrainian element is developing its national feeling, but by no means in conflict with the USSR. No, we are loyal to the USSR, so loyal as to make the GPU gnash its teeth.'[76]

These views, though expressed privately by Hrushevsky, became known to the authorities. In February 1927 the head of the Ukrainian GPU, Vsevolod Balytsky, quoted them in his report to Lazar Kaganovich, the general secretary of the Ukrainian party organization, and a member of the Ukrainian Politburo, Volodymyr Zatonsky. For a time such views were welcomed by the authorities, as they differed drastically from those of more conservative members of the Ukrainian intelligentsia. On the other hand, the authorities never trusted Hrushevsky, seeing him first and foremost as the former head of the Central Rada – their main enemy in late 1917 and early 1918, the crucial period in the development of the Bolshevik Revolution. The official attitude to Hrushevsky was well expressed in a comment by Vlas Chubar, who headed the Council of People's Commissars of Ukraine in 1923–34. In response to Hrushevsky's attempt to secure additional funding for one of his scholarly projects, Chubar allegedly stated: 'Why has the Central Rada bestirred itself?'[77] Some GPU assessments of Hrushevsky's political views – especially those dating from 1924–5, before Ukrainization was implemented on a large scale – were even less favourable to him. The GPU opened a file on Hrushevsky on 20 March 1924, almost immediately after his return to Ukraine. He was often followed by GPU agents,[78] who classified him as a Ukrainian counterrevolutionary of a leftist orientation. They characterized him as an 'avowed independentist' and gave a generally accurate assessment of the stability of his political views: 'He changes neither his political views nor his orthography; he bends but does not break.'[79]

Still, the authorities considered Hrushevsky a lesser evil than the group headed by Iefremov and Krymsky. As noted above, in the mid-1920s Hrushevsky and his supporters in the academy were seen by the authorities as representatives of the *smena vekh* (change of landmarks) movement, while his opponents were considered outright enemies of the Soviet regime. In his speech at a meeting of the Central Committee of the Communist Party of Ukraine in February–March 1927, Lazar

Kaganovich mentioned Hrushevsky among the 'former *smenovekhovtsy*' who continued to hold 'liberal-socialist-revolutionary' views. That group, in Kaganovich's opinion, posed little if any danger to the regime. Instead, he saw the main danger in groupings of Russian and Ukrainian academics who adhered to the constitutional-democratic ideology. Kaganovich specifically mentioned Iefremov as the leader of the academic group overtly hostile to the regime.[80] His assessment of the political situation in the Academy of Sciences explains why for the time being party officials not only supported Hrushevsky and his followers but also wanted him to become president.

Hrushevsky was first considered for the presidency at the time of the academy's inception in 1918. The offer came from Hetman Pavlo Skoropadsky, and Hrushevsky responded to it with a categorical 'no.'[81] In 1923, at the time of Hrushevsky's election to the academy, there was a faction that advocated his election as president. Hrushevsky was even privately informed by his supporters of such a possibility.[82] In November 1923 Volodymyr Zatonsky, a member of the Ukrainian Politburo, asked a Ukrainian official in Prague, Mykhailo Levytsky, to hint to Hrushevsky that if his candidacy were proposed, the authorities would support him.[83] Upon Hrushevsky's return to Kyiv, the local GPU suggested to its headquarters in Kharkiv the idea of promoting Hrushevsky for the presidency. The GPU officers believed that no academician would dare to vote openly against Hrushevsky. Another option suggested by the Kyiv agents was that of surrounding Hrushevsky with informers and secret agents who would exploit his authority to carry out tasks on behalf of the GPU.[84] Kharkiv headquarters responded that there was no point in promoting Hrushevsky as president, for he would not follow GPU instructions, and if the party authorities were to ask him to support their policies, he would probably want to be elected to the Central Committee, which the GPU considered impossible. For the time being, headquarters also did not encourage the idea of planting agents in Hrushevsky's entourage, asking the Kyiv office to focus its attention on Iefremov instead. The main task of the secret police at the time was to encourage conflicts within the academy. In the eyes of the Kharkiv authorities, there was no need to promote Hrushevsky for the presidency in order to achieve that goal.[85]

The situation changed quite dramatically over the following two years. In the spring of 1925 the newly appointed general secretary of the Central Committee of the Communist Party of Ukraine, Lazar Kaganovich, visited Kyiv and met separately with the leaders of the opposing factions in the academy, Krymsky and Hrushevsky.[86] Upon Kaganovich's return to Kharkiv, the Ukrainian Politburo discussed the issue of party work among the intelligentsia. The communist authorities were concerned about the relative independence of the academy and wanted to reform it with a view to increasing their influence there and among the Ukrainian intelligentsia in general. The specific reference to Hrushevsky in the Politburo resolution on that matter permits the suggestion that Hrushevsky's candidacy for the presidency of the academy may have been discussed on that occasion.[87] In early January 1926 the Politburo returned to the issue of the academy. On its agenda were the impending academic elections and the choice of a new president. Hrushevsky clearly emerged as the front runner for the office, but the authorities wanted a statement of political loyalty from him. The head of the Ukrainian government, Vlas Chubar, was authorized by the Politburo to work with Hrushevsky on such a statement.[88] Although there are indications that Hrushevsky never produced a statement completely satisfactory to the authorities,[89] by April 1926 the Politburo had already decided to support Hrushevsky's candidacy for president of the Academy of Sciences.[90]

That decision was made possible in part by the new strategy that Hrushevsky adopted at the beginning of 1926, allowing for limited cooperation with the regime on a number of political issues. In January 1926 Hrushevsky made an important speech at a session of the Directorate for the Development of Scholarship (Holovnauka) held to discuss the organization of scholarly work in Ukraine. In his presentation Hrushevsky stressed the role of the Soviet government in developing the Academy of Sciences, noting, however, that official support for the academy had helped legitimize Soviet power in the eyes of Ukrainian society. The authorities greeted this speech with enthusiasm, and its text was published in the newspapers.[91] During his trip to Kharkiv in early April 1926, Hrushevsky agreed to make a statement condemning the organizers of the Congress of Ukrainian Studies to be held in Prague. At the initiative of the authorities, Hrushevsky also agreed to convene a meeting at the academy to denounce the congress. His promises were fulfilled. In an interview with the newspaper *Proletars'ka pravda* (Proletarian Truth), Hrushevsky claimed that the congress was nothing but a political demonstration convened to undermine actual scholarly work being conducted in Soviet Ukraine. He also attacked the position of the Czechoslovak government, which supported the congress. Not without sarcasm, Hrushevsky stated that it would be better if the congress were organized not in Prague but in Transcarpathia, whose Ukrainian population was being subjected to Czechization.[92]

In a letter to Studynsky, Hrushevsky offered an explanation of his actions. He claimed that he was particularly exasperated by the Prague group's attempt to play the role of an all-Ukrainian scholarly centre.[93] In another letter to the same address whose content became known to the GPU, Hrushevsky wrote: 'I value the scholarly work being done abroad but resolutely condemn any political intrigue in it directed against the Ukrainian Soviet Republic, with which our scholarly future is associated. The Czech government is feeding the Ukrainian emigrants in Prague and is not allowing them into Subcarpathian Ukraine (where Ukrainian forces and schools are particularly needed), so that they do not interfere with the Czechization and Russification of that unfortunate land, and the emigration is lauding the Czech government, exalting it as a great protector of Ukrainian culture and deliberately concealing from the world the Czech double-dealing with regard to Subcarpathian Ukraine and the injustice being done to its people.'[94] There is little doubt that Hrushevsky's old disagreements with the Prague émigrés and annoyance with their scholarly pretensions influenced his decision to cooperate with the authorities in denouncing the Prague Congress. The authorities, for their part, expected to reap major political dividends from Hrushevsky's statement. Indeed, his position in the academic world and his close contacts with Studynsky, who then headed the Shevchenko Scientific Society in Lviv, helped prevent that organization from participating in the congress, but in Ukraine, the Ukrainian intelligentsia largely ignored Hrushevsky's statement. It was generally believed that he had been forced to make it under official pressure.[95]

Hrushevsky's public statements in support of government policy on academic matters and against the Prague Congress, made in the first months of 1926, introduced him to the sphere of Soviet public life, to which he had apparently aspired ever since his return to Ukraine. Soon after his arrival, Soviet officials had promised Hrushevsky that he would be consulted on a number of policy-related matters, including the drafting of the republican budget, the construction of the Dnipro hydroelectric power station near Zaporizhia, and other issues of public interest.[96] Hrushevsky's activities immediately after his return to Ukraine made some of his opponents in the academy suspect that his plans extended far beyond the limits of pure scholarship and had much to do with politics. The official support that he received in Kharkiv from some former Borotbists who had joined the Bolsheviks, as well as the Communist Party decision to support his candidacy for the presidency of the academy, also must have created the impression that Hrushevsky's public career, if not his political one, was still a going concern.[97]

In the summer of 1926, when Hrushevsky's relations with the authorities were particularly close, he made an attempt to enter the public arena on his own terms by submitting an article on cultural policy in Ukraine to the journal *Ukraïna*, which he edited. The article, titled 'In Shameful Memory,' marked the fiftieth anniversary of the Ems Ukase of 1876, which had effectively banned Ukrainian-language publications in the Russian Empire.[98] In his article, Hrushevsky stated that although the 'bell of 1876' had sunk, one could still hear it resounding from beneath the waves.[99] What Hrushevsky had in mind was that while the restrictions imposed on the Ukrainian national movement by the Ems Ukase were long gone, the policy aimed at subordinating Ukrainian culture to Russian still had its supporters and promoters in the USSR. Hrushevsky claimed that proponents of Russian 'great-power chauvinism' wanted to secure dominant status for the Russian language, culture, and history in the school curricula of Ukraine. He also noted attempts by the central authorities to curb translations from West European languages into 'provincial' languages so as to preserve the role of Russian culture as a 'window on Europe' for the non-Russian cultures of the USSR. He went on to discuss the attempts of 'pan-Russians' to hinder the development of high culture among the non-Russian nationalities and restrict the use of local languages to the family sphere. Hrushevsky then attacked the all-Union authorities for diverting resources from the republics to the centre in order to develop all-Union institutions, which in fact remained Russian in character. In his article, Hrushevsky presented not only his critique of what he considered remnants of Russian great-power nationalism but also his positive program for the development of Ukrainian culture. He declared as his goal the elevation of the Ukrainian language and culture in Ukraine to the same level as its Russian counterpart in Russia.

There is no doubt that Hrushevsky was addressing himself to a much wider audience than the regular readership of *Ukraïna*. His article was intended as a contribution to the larger discussion on the future of national cultures in the USSR that was then under way, involving party members and Soviet functionaries at the republican and all-Union levels.[100] In entering the Soviet public sphere, Hrushevsky was also adopting the vocabulary and rules of the dominant Soviet political discourse. By asserting that the motives of the new 'pan-Russians' were not very different from those responsible for the tsar's prohibition of the Ukrainian language and culture in 1876, Hrushevsky directly linked the policies of his opponents with those of tsarist officialdom, effectively delegitimizing them within the framework of the dominant discourse.

In attacking the proponents of Russian cultural dominance in Ukraine, Hrushevsky stated that the resumption in the USSR of a cultural struggle whose outcome was to be determined by the strength or weakness of a given nationality would compromise the very idea of a union of Soviet republics. He went on to say that preventing the Ukrainian nation from attaining the level of cultural development that it could achieve under capitalism would discredit the construction of socialism in the Soviet Union. Hrushevsky also maintained that granting Russian culture dominant status in the USSR would limit the Soviet Union to the boundaries of the former Russian Empire and jeopardize its chances for future expansion. Any appeasement of Russian 'great-power nationalism' by the authorities would only provoke outbursts of Ukrainian nationalism, which, in the historian's opinion, was little more than the reaction of an oppressed culture to the advance of the dominant one. While indicating the danger of resurgent Ukrainian nationalism, Hrushevsky suggested that the communist government had to wage a war on two fronts, counteracting the imperialist aspirations of Russian, Polish, Czech, and other great-power nationalisms on the one hand and opposing Ukrainian nationalist 'exaggerations' on the other.

In making these arguments, Hrushevsky invoked a number of major ideological paradigms of the hegemonic Soviet discourse. Among them was the officially proclaimed thesis of the equality of all the nationalities of the USSR, irrespective of their numerical strength, as well as the Soviet claim that only socialism could guarantee minority cultures their highest level of development. That postulate of official propaganda was of special importance to Ukraine, whose western territories were divided among the 'bourgeois' states of Poland, Romania, and Czechoslovakia. Hrushevsky also played on communist hopes for world revolution and the eventual adherence of other revolutionary nations to the USSR. The formula of struggle on two fronts against Ukrainian nationalism and Great Russian chauvinism was quite popular in official communist circles at the time, and Hrushevsky took it directly from the writings of party ideologists.

Hrushevsky also proclaimed his full support for the policy of Ukrainization. According to him, the wise and resolute nationality policy

adopted by the Communist Party and the Soviet government and conducted in the interest of a rapprochement between town and village
was more effective in neutralizing the 'elevated emotions of Ukrainian
society' than some of the writings of Mykhailo Drahomanov. That
argument was based on the official interpretation of Ukrainization as a
process intended to strengthen the link between the Russian-speaking
city and the Ukrainian-speaking village so as to draw the working class
and the peasantry closer together. But not all the officially accepted
clichés that found their way into Hrushevsky's article were the product
of its author's attempt at political mimicry. Hrushevsky shared many of
the views of his former colleagues from the Ukrainian Party of Socialist
Revolutionaries who had joined the communists in the early 1920s with
the intention of building a peasant-worker socialist Ukraine. At the
same time, there can be little doubt that the politically loaded vocabulary employed by Hrushevsky was deliberately chosen to help legitimize his views in the thoroughly controlled public sphere.[101]

In entering the discussion on the future of national cultures in the
USSR, Hrushevsky lent his support to those Soviet Ukrainian leaders
who favoured Ukrainization. He expressed alarm that the voices of
proponents of Great Russian chauvinism and great-power arrogance
were being raised not only in private conversations in the USSR and in
White émigré publications abroad but also in the All-Union Central
Executive Committee. He specifically attacked the high-ranking Moscow bureaucrats Iurii Larin and Avel Enukidze, who had criticized
nationality policy in Ukraine when speaking at a committee session in
April 1926. Arguing in favour of Ukrainization and against the dominance of Russian culture in Ukraine, Hrushevsky made arguments that
were neither new nor entirely original. Some of them were much more
forcefully presented by the communist writer Mykola Khvyliovy.[102]
The speeches of Larin and Enukidze were also criticized by Ukrainian
communist leaders, including Mykola Skrypnyk, then People's Commissar of Justice in the Ukrainian government.[103] In presenting his
views on Ukrainian cultural development, Hrushevsky probably expected his voice to be heard and supported by the Ukrainian communist leaders committed to the policy of Ukrainization, whom he himself
endorsed in the all-Union discussion on the direction of cultural policy.[104]
If that was indeed the case, then he was badly mistaken.

Soon after its publication, Hrushevsky's article was attacked by a
former member of the Central Rada and ideologue of the independent
Ukrainian Communist Party, Andrii Richytsky (Anatolii Pisotsky), who

dismissed Hrushevsky's worries about the future of Ukrainization. He claimed that the bell of Russian great-power chauvinism could not toll, as it had been shattered by the October Revolution.[105] The leaders of the ruling Bolshevik Party were no more sympathetic. The major rebuke to Hrushevsky came in November 1926 in a speech by the Ukrainian People's Commissar of Education, Oleksander Shumsky.[106] The speech was primarily devoted to a critique of Mykola Khvyliovy and the neoclassicist Ukrainian writers.[107] As for Hrushevsky's article, Shumsky maintained that its author should have limited his discussion to the tsarist prohibition of Ukrainian culture and his own struggle against it. In Shumsky's opinion, Hrushevsky had no right to draw a line of continuity between the policy of tsarist Russia and that of the Soviet government in Moscow. In so doing, he was allegedly thrusting aside the sympathies of Soviet Ukraine for Moscow, the capital of the Union and the centre of the world proletarian movement. Denouncing Hrushevsky's article as a 'defamation of Soviet power intended to discredit the Union and break up the brotherhood of peoples,' Shumsky questioned the sincerity of Hrushevsky's 'willingness to work for the cause of the socialist construction of our homeland.'[108]

It is hard to say to what degree Shumsky himself believed the accusations that he levelled against Hrushevsky. After all, in November 1926 Shumsky was already on his way out as chief communist ideologue of Ukraine, having been accused by Stalin himself of nationalist deviation from the party line. Shumsky's attacks on Khvyliovy, whom he had earlier defended against political accusations by his party comrades, and his critique of Hrushevsky should be regarded in this context as one of his last attempts to prove his loyalty to the party. Judging by the comments on Shumsky's speech by his successor as People's Commissar of Education, Mykola Skrypnyk, Shumsky failed to convince his enemies in the party leadership that he was a sincere opponent of Ukrainian nationalism.[109] Whatever the true thoughts and aspirations of Shumsky, whom Hrushevsky considered a personal enemy,[110] his argument against Hrushevsky adhered to one of the main rules of party propaganda of the day – the replacement of national categories with class-based ones. The canon that called for treating Moscow, the new centre of the former empire, not as the capital of Russia but as the epicentre of the world proletarian movement was introduced into Ukrainian political discourse by Joseph Stalin in his letter of April 1926 to the Ukrainian Politburo in connection with Khvyliovy's 'transgressions' and then repeated in the resolutions of the May 1926 session of the Central Committee of the Communist Party of Ukraine.[111] Shumsky adopted Stalin's logic when he wrote: 'Red Moscow has also been created by the will, effort, and blood of Ukrainian workers and peasants. Moscow is the capital of our Union. Moscow is the centre and brain of the proletarian cause throughout the world. This is our Moscow.'[112] Thus, the national paradigm was effectively replaced with a class-based internationalist one. The idea of reorienting Ukrainian culture from Moscow to Europe was now viewed as a rejection of proletarian culture for that of the bourgeoisie. This paradigm made it possible to justify the strengthening of Moscow's control over Ukraine and the maintenance of the dominant role of Russian culture in class terms rather than national ones.

Shumsky's speech once again reinforced the party message to the 'bourgeois' intelligentsia that despite all its efforts to adopt the vocabulary and norms of the hegemonic Soviet discourse, it was not welcome to participate in public life.[113] According to the logic adopted by Shumsky, which reflected the attitude of party cadres in general, representatives of the nationalist camp had no right to interfere in political discussions, for those were the exclusive preserve of the party. Shumsky claimed that the true goal of Hrushevsky's intervention in the party discussion was not to promote socialist construction but to exploit disagreements among Bolsheviks in order to foment animosity between ethnic groups. Shumsky stated that, together with Comrades Larin and Enukidze, he would merely have laughed off Hrushevsky's avowed support for his position were it not for Khvyliovy and his deviations. He attacked Khvyliovy as a party member who 'erred' and 'played into the hands' of 'the whole nationalist camp, from Academician Hrushevsky at its head all the way to [Dmytro] Dontsov.' For Shumsky, Khvyliovy's case was profoundly different from Hrushevsky's, as it involved a fellow communist who had allegedly become disoriented in the course of the ideological struggle, so much so as to abandon the proletarian camp. If Hrushevsky was beyond redemption in Shumsky's eyes, Khvyliovy was still worth saving for the communist cause.

In September 1926, two months prior to Shumsky's attack on Hrushevsky, the Ukrainian Politburo discussed the party's position on Hrushevsky's impending jubilee – his sixtieth birthday and the fortieth anniversary of his scholarly career.[114] The Politburo's main concern was that the occasion not take on the characteristics of a Ukrainian national celebration.[115] Thus, a special commission of the Politburo, including Volodymyr Zatonsky, Fedor Korniushin, Oleksander Shumsky, and

Panas Liubchenko, was created to deal with the matter. It was decided that the journal *Zhyttia i revoliutsiia* (Life and Revolution) would publish two articles to mark the jubilee, one dealing with Hrushevsky's scholarship and the other with his political activities. The members of the Politburo wanted to gain political points by exploiting the fact of Hrushevsky's return to Ukraine. Accordingly, they recommended that the prospective author of the article on Hrushevsky's political activities present him to the public as a politician who had no prospects as long as he was guided by the ideology of petty-bourgeois nationalism. For all his errors, Hrushevsky had found the strength to recognize the positive changes introduced by the proletarian revolution. The future author was also advised to stress, 'despite the actions of Hrushevsky himself,' that he had abandoned his former views.[116]

Characteristic of the party's new attitude to the policy of Ukrainization was the Politburo's recommendation to the author of the article to emphasize that it was not the Bolsheviks who came to Hrushevsky, but Hrushevsky himself, 'a custodian of the continuity of Ukrainian cultural development,' who had come to the Bolsheviks. In this case, the Politburo was clearly countering the earlier argument advanced by Hrushevsky, who claimed that the official policy of Ukrainization signalled the regime's rejection of its former anti-Ukrainian orientation and constituted an attempt to legitimize itself by taking over the nation-building platform of the Ukrainian national parties. In the above-mentioned speech delivered at the session of the Directorate for the Development of Scholarship in January 1926, Hrushevsky made the following statement concerning the activities of the Ukrainian Academy of Sciences: 'And so, when it [Soviet power] began the energetic development of that supreme cultural centre dreamt of by generations of Ukrainian activists, in the eyes of Ukrainian society this became something of a symbol that Soviet power was taking these historic Ukrainian national tasks upon itself.'[117] Now it was time for the authorities to respond to this challenge.

Beginning in May 1926, when the communist leaders of Ukraine accelerated the linguistic and cultural Ukrainization of Ukraine's public sphere, following Stalin's recommendation to take over the cultural movement in Ukraine and free it from the influence of 'national deviationists,' the issue of who – communists or nationalists – were the true champions of Ukrainian nation- and state-building became an important topic in communist discourse. In June 1926, in his long speech at a session of the Central Committee of the Young Communist League of

Ukraine, Volodymyr Zatonsky handled this issue in the spirit of Soviet-style dialectics: 'If anyone should now attempt to present the matter in such a way as to suggest that the Bolsheviks, carrying on the social struggle, had no interest in the national question and stood aside from the building of Ukraine, while Vynnychenko, Hrushevsky, and others held the idea of national renewal in their hands, that is a lie. It is no less a revision than that of the social nature of the [Central] Rada. The dialectic of life consists in the fact that it was indeed those same Red Guards, who hated Petliura and everything Ukrainian along with him, the same ones who almost shot Skrypnyk and me in Muraviev's time – it was they, and not the Hrushevskys, who built Soviet Ukraine ... Objectively, was it not the Muravievists who almost shot me? Was it not in fact with their hands that possibilities for the development of Ukrainian culture were created?'[118] In 1918, when Kyiv was occupied by the Red Guards of Mikhail Muraviev, Zatonsky was almost shot dead by his comrades-in-arms merely for speaking Ukrainian on the street. By 1926, seeking to take over the Ukrainian revival so as to marginalize Hrushevsky and the Ukrainian national activists, Zatonsky was exploiting the fact of Hrushevsky's return to Ukraine as proof of the correctness of party policy.[119]

The celebrations of Hrushevsky's jubilee took place at the height of the Ukrainization campaign in Ukraine, pursuant to a resolution of the May 1926 Plenum of the Central Committee of the Communist Party of Ukraine. The jubilee marked the beginning of a period of some two years during which the authorities supported Hrushevsky in his scholarly undertakings, even though they did not allow him to take a more active part in the political and cultural life of Ukraine.[120] At his jubilee celebrations, which took place on 3 October 1926 in the conference hall of Kyiv University, Hrushevsky delivered a speech summarizing the major elements of his scholarly, cultural, and national agenda.[121] Hrushevsky clearly treated his jubilee as a manifestation of the triumph of the Ukrainian idea and insisted on the continuity of the Ukrainian scholarly tradition from the prerevolutionary era to Soviet times. He credited the authorities with creating conditions for the successful development of Ukrainian scholarship and culture but failed to repent his role as leader of the Ukrainian Central Rada and offered no assurances of his loyalty to the regime. Not surprisingly, his jubilee was treated by those present at the celebrations as the apotheosis of Ukrainian scholarship, not of the Communist Party or Soviet power.[122]

In his speech, Hrushevsky raised two important issues of clear political significance. The first was the formation of the Ukrainian proletariat, a previously missing component in the social structure of the Ukrainian nation, while the second was the problem of gathering all the Ukrainian lands within the borders of a Ukrainian state. Addressing the first issue, Hrushevsky declared his loyalty to the party's general line, which proclaimed that the proletariat defined the character of the current epoch. This formal acceptance of the party line allowed Hrushevsky to present his own cultural and national project in a manner congruent with official discourse. Dressing his national agenda in class trappings, Hrushevsky suggested that Ukraine would become a workers' state only when the nationally conscious masses of the peasantry joined the working class, providing a basis for its cultural Ukrainization. Accordingly, he called on the Ukrainian intelligentsia to continue its cultural work for the benefit of the Ukrainian peasantry. Seeking to justify his stand, Hrushevsky referred to the then popular communist slogan, 'Let's turn our face to the village' (*Lytsem do sela*). Hrushevsky was, in fact, advocating the continuing Ukrainization of the cities through the influx of peasants as a way of completing the formation of the Ukrainian nation.[123]

Hrushevsky's call for the unity of the Ukrainian lands was first presented in his main speech at the celebrations and repeated in his closing remarks. He reminded his audience about those parts of the Ukrainian nation that remained outside the 'workers' and peasants' Ukraine' and took no part in the national revival there. He specifically listed Ukrainian cities then under the rule of Poland (Kholm, Lviv, Ostrih, Lutsk), Czechoslovakia (Uzhhorod), and Romania (Chernivtsi, Khotyn, Akkerman). At first glance Hrushevsky's call for the unity of all Ukrainian lands within one 'Ukrainian state of workers and peasants' fully corresponded to the official party line, known as the Piedmont policy, which called for the accelerated development of Ukrainian national culture in the USSR so as to attract Ukrainians living in capitalist countries and destabilize the latter.[124] At the same time Hrushevsky departed somewhat from the official line. In quoting Ivan Franko's verses about the Ukrainian people as the future master of all its ethnic territory from the Carpathians in the west to the Caucasus in the east and the Black Sea in the south, he made a direct reference to Ukrainian ethnic territories within the boundaries of the Russian Federation. Hrushevsky's reading of Franko's verses was hailed with an ovation, and in the words of Hryhorii Kostiuk, a participant in the event, 'it can be said with certainty that at that moment, for all participants in the jubilee celebrations, with the exception of a few stooges who were undoubtedly in the audience, there was neither Soviet power nor the Communist Party nor its dictatorship. In their consciousness there was only the image of a great united Ukraine and its spiritual leader, Academician Mykhailo Hrushevsky.'[125]

The official line on Hrushevsky's jubilee was fully reflected in the speeches of the party and government officials present at the celebrations. Panas Liubchenko, who represented the Kyiv regional authorities, and Leonid Levytsky, who represented the government Directorate for the Development of Scholarship,[126] demanded a clear statement from Hrushevsky on his attitude to Soviet power. They claimed that unlike representatives of other scholarly disciplines, historians could not stay out of politics, and urged Hrushevsky to accept the proletarian revolution and Soviet power 'not only pro forma, but also in essence.' What the authorities really wanted was a formal declaration of Hrushevsky's loyalty to the Soviet regime; a statement supporting communist policy in Ukraine and presenting the new regime as a legitimate heir to the prerevolutionary Ukrainian national movement.

How far the authorities wanted Hrushevsky to go in demonstrating his political loyalty to the regime becomes apparent from the published materials of 1927 jubilee celebrations of another prominent historian, Dmytro Bahalii, who, it was claimed, wholeheartedly accepted the outcome of the Bolshevik Revolution. The historian Nataliia Polonska-Vasylenko, a supporter of Bahalii in the factional conflict within the Academy of Sciences, treated his jubilee as a reaction of the ruling group in the academy, led by academicians Iefremov and Krymsky, to the Hrushevsky jubilee, which received no more than formal approval from the academy.[127] As may be judged from the published texts of the speeches delivered at Bahalii's jubilee, its organizers made a great effort to outdo the Hrushevsky celebrations. Bahalii's jubilee, which attracted very little outside attention despite the full support of the Presidium of the Academy of Sciences and the political authorities, was presented as 'a Ukrainian national holiday, a demonstration of the strength of Ukrainian culture' – the very things with which the Politburo did not want the Hrushevsky jubilee to be associated.[128] Hryhorii Kostiuk, who was present at both ceremonies and heard the Russian-language speech delivered at Bahalii's celebrations by Pavel Postyshev, an influential member of the Ukrainian Politburo, considered the official praise for Bahalii a direct challenge to Hrushevsky and his interpretation of Ukrainian history.[129]

Bahalii's loyalty to the new regime, as well as his attempts to use Marxist methodology in his writings, created an ideal image of the Ukrainian historian and cultural activist to which the authorities wanted Hrushevsky to conform. The political dividends of such a metamorphosis on the part of Hrushevsky would be much greater than those derived from Bahalii. After all, in addition to significantly less impressive scholarly accomplishments, Bahalii was never regarded by the Ukrainian political and cultural activists as their leader, as was the case with Hrushevsky. How greatly Hrushevsky outranked Bahalii not only as a political figure but also as a scholar was demonstrated by the elections to the All-Union Academy of Sciences in 1928.[130] In June 1928 the People's Commissariat of Education of Ukraine suggested Bahalii (along with Hrushevsky) as a candidate for membership in the academy. Bahalii was the Ukrainian authorities' favourite candidate, but in Moscow only Hrushevsky's name appeared on the list of candidates supported by the Central Committee of the All-Union Communist Party. While the Ukrainian authorities admitted that Bahalii was a much less prominent scholar than Hrushevsky, he was politically far more desirable to them, and they believed that his failure to make the list would hurt their image, while building up Hrushevsky's reputation. The Kharkiv authorities tried once again to convince their superiors in Moscow to place Bahalii's name on the officially promoted list of candidates but failed to achieve any positive result.[131] The old-guard scholars in the Russian (now All-Union) Academy of Sciences did not consider Bahalii acceptable either in terms of his scholarly contribution or with regard to his political attitudes. Many of them, including Vladimir Vernadsky, could not reconcile themselves to Bahalii's excessively cosy relations with the authorities and the support he offered them in dismantling the traditional system of academic institutions in Ukraine.[132]

Hrushevsky, on the other hand, had impeccable academic credentials. At a meeting of the Humanities Division of the All-Union Academy on 12 December 1928, he received sixteen out of seventeen votes in favour of his election, and twenty-six out of thirty votes at a general meeting of the academy on 12 January 1929.[133] Among those who probably voted against Hrushevsky was the academic (permanent) secretary of the academy, Sergei Oldenburg. At a meeting of the nominating committee, he allegedly read a First World War–era letter written by Hrushevsky from exile to the president of the Russian Academy of Sciences, Konstantin Konstantinovich Romanov, in which Hrushevsky assured the latter of his loyalty to the regime. Oldenburg stated that there was no reservation about Hrushevsky's candidacy on academic grounds, but the letter to Romanov had to be taken into account as a negative factor. In the same presentation, Oldenburg mentioned that Hrushevsky's candidacy for election to the academy had first been considered in 1906, but Romanov had then suggested that the government would not approve his election. It is difficult to assess the influence of Oldenburg's revelation on the elections.[134] Most Russian academicians did not sympathize with the Bolshevik regime and probably did not consider the letter to Romanov a major factor in Hrushevsky's bid for membership in the academy. As for the authorities, they learned about the letter relatively late – in November 1928. The Ukrainian party and secret police officials, who wanted their republic to be well represented in the All-Union Academy, were quite sceptical about the whole affair. Not surprisingly under these conditions, Bahalii's great supporter, the Ukrainian Marxist historian and government official Matvii Iavorsky, recommended Hrushevsky for election to the All-Union Academy on behalf of the Ukrainian Marxist establishment.[135]

Hrushevsky's activities in the All-Union Academy give a unique insight into the ways in which his general views on Russian-Ukrainian relations turned into practical action within the context of academic politics. The All-Union Academy of Sciences was created by the authorities in Leningrad on the basis of the old Russian Academy of Sciences. Indeed, the Russian Academy took over the all-Union mandate, monopolizing access to central funding and marginalizing the republican scholarly institutions. The Russian scholarly establishment was becoming dominant over those of the other nations of the USSR – precisely the model of organization of academic work that Hrushevsky wanted to avoid at all costs. When Hrushevsky joined the All-Union Academy in 1929, he became part of an institution that he wanted to reconstruct according to his own model.

In 1925, when the Russian Academy was transformed into the All-Union Academy of Sciences, forty-two Ukrainian scholars signed a letter of protest. Hrushevsky took an active part in preparing the Ukrainian Academy's memorandum on the subject, which suggested that all-Union scholarly institutions could not be established merely by renaming Russian academic units. They could be formed only as associations of existing republican institutions, and only their organizational work, as well as the activities of units working on scholarly problems of common interest to members of the association, could be financed from the all-

Union budget. The memorandum referred to the Soviet constitution, which assigned issues of culture, education, and scholarship to the jurisdiction of the individual republics, and to the pertinent resolutions of the first all-Ukrainian congress for the study of Ukraine's productive forces. It also made use of a still vital Bolshevik dogma according to which the Soviet Union had been created to include all the communist nations of the world, which was at odds with the notion of allowing the Russian Academy of Sciences to monopolize all-Union scholarship.[136]

Hrushevsky's memorandum was supported by the Ukrainian Academic Assembly[137] and was fully consonant with the position formulated at that time by the Ukrainian Commissar of Education, Oleksander Shumsky. In a letter to the Russian Commissar of Education, Anatolii Lunacharsky, Shumsky wrote: 'The proclamation of the Russian Academy of Sciences as an all-Union institution is an attempt to subordinate the scholarly institutions of less developed national cultures to the scholarly institutions of Russia and to place the Russian Academy in a privileged position, in material terms as well ... Take the path of coordinating work, not guiding it,' Shumsky urged his Russian counterpart.[138] These protests from the Ukrainian party authorities and academic institutions had some resonance in Moscow. At a meeting of representatives of the republican directorates for the development of scholarship, the idea of an association of republican academies was considered but rejected on the grounds that most republics had only begun to develop their own scholarly programs and thus were not yet prepared to take part in an association. It was suggested instead that all academic institutions whose work had broader scholarly implications would be classified as all-Union institutions and financed from the all-Union budget. At the same time, they would remain under republican jurisdiction. In his speech at the session of the Ukrainian Directorate for the Development of Scholarship in January 1926, Hrushevsky welcomed the suggested compromise but requested that the Ukrainian Academy of Sciences as a whole be given all-Union status, making it equal to the Russian Academy of Sciences, and financed from the all-Union budget.[139]

In the long run, Hrushevsky's defence of the equal status of the Ukrainian Academy with the Russian proved unavailing, as the marginalization of non-Russian scholarly institutions proceeded apace.[140] In the first years after the Bolshevik takeover, the Russian Academy of Sciences, like its Ukrainian counterpart, took full advantage of the principle of academic autonomy in order to shield itself and its members from the dictate of the authorities. If in the Ukrainian case that attitude facilitated the promotion of Ukrainian scholarship within the academy, the Russian Academy preserved the prerevolutionary all-Russian mentality, which was particularly apparent in the structure of its humanities divisions. Under these circumstances, Hrushevsky was determined to do all he could to ensure that the new structure acquire as much of an all-Union character as possible and not remain the old Russian Academy under a new name.

In April 1929, at the first session of the All-Union Academy of Sciences following the election of its new members, Hrushevsky suggested a change in the name and structure of the division of Russian language and literature, which was responsible for research in all Slavic languages and literatures. He argued that leaving the old name unchanged would amount to the preservation of great-power imperialist traditions. The meeting of the new members of the division approved the change and endorsed Hrushevsky's proposal to establish separate institutes of the Ukrainian and Belarusian languages and literatures, as well as an institute for the study of the languages and literatures of the Western and Southern Slavs.[141] Hrushevsky was also a driving force behind the idea of the representation of non-Russian historiography in the All-Union Academy. He proposed the creation within the Humanities Section of separate institutes of Ukrainian and Belarusian history, as well as splitting the Caucasus institute of history and archaeology into a number of separate institutes dealing with the history of the Caucasian and Central Asian peoples. In May 1929 the Humanities Section approved Hrushevsky's proposal for the formation of an institute of Ukrainian history. Although that resolution was never carried out, the academy created a commission on Ukrainian history in the autumn of 1930.[142]

Hrushevsky, who genuinely regretted that the transformation of the Russian Academy into an all-Union one deprived the Russian scholars of their own academy, was working hard to give the All-Union Academy a pluralist character. As he had previously stated, he was so loyal to the USSR 'as to make the GPU gnash its teeth.' No doubt, the kind of USSR and all-Union institutions that he envisioned were meant to guarantee Ukraine and its culture equal status with Russia.

The Historian

According to Hrushevsky's own statements, he returned to Ukraine primarily to continue his scholarly work, although he was uncertain whether he would succeed in doing so. In a letter to Studynsky written in January 1924, several months before Hrushevsky left Vienna for Kyiv, he said: 'In my interview in *Nash prapor* (Our Banner) I deliberately outlined my scholarly plan in order to document why I made the journey and what I wanted. Perhaps it will prove impossible to realize any of it. I shall try.'[143] Indeed, Hrushevsky made his first attempts to carry out his scholarly agenda as soon as he settled in Kyiv. In July 1924, in an addendum to a letter addressed to his former party colleague Panas Butsenko, now secretary of the All-Ukrainian Central Executive Committee and an important figure in the Bolshevik administration of Ukraine, Hrushevsky sought to enlist his support. Among his major tasks, Hrushevsky listed the revival of the journal *Ukraïna*, publication of a bulletin of scholarly information for the outside world, and the continuation of his *History of Ukrainian Literature* and *History of Ukraine-Rus'*.[144]

How successful was Hrushevsky in attaining these goals? Did he accomplish what he had hoped for by returning to Ukraine, or were his expectations misplaced? Answering these questions is essential to determining the extent to which the Bolshevik regime allowed the realization of the scholarly agenda of the national project. I shall address them by taking a closer look at the aspect of Hrushevsky's scholarly activity that consumed most of his time and energy during the 1920s and early 1930s. This was the continuation of his 'big' *History of Ukraine-Rus'* and the archival research and archaeographic activities associated with that undertaking.

There is no question that the continuation of the *History of Ukraine Rus'* was one of the projects Hrushevsky wanted to advance by returning to Ukraine in the spring of 1924. His work on the *History* had been halted by the outbreak of the 1917 revolution. Hrushevsky completed part 3 of volume 8 of the *History* in early 1917, while in exile in Moscow. In the autumn of that year, he sent the corrected proofs of this part to his Moscow printer from Kyiv, where he was serving as head of the Ukrainian Central Rada. He reissued all three parts of volume 8 in the emigration in 1922.[145]

The uncertainties of émigré life, lack of archival materials, and growing difficulties in gaining access to library collections made it impossible for Hrushevsky to continue his 'big history' abroad. Instead, he focused his energies on organizing the Sociological Institute in Vienna, studied the history of primitive societies, which resulted in the publication of his *Origins of Society (A Genetical Sociology)* (1921), and began work on the multivolume *History of Ukrainian Literature*, which, unlike the *History of Ukraine-Rus'*, did not require archival research. As always,

Hrushevsky put long hours into his work on these projects. He wrote four volumes of the *History of Ukrainian Literature*, three of which were published while he was still in the emigration. He took the manuscript of the fourth volume to Ukraine, where it was issued in 1925. While abroad, Hrushevsky reprinted some of his earlier works, mainly to generate income but also in response to continuing demand for them. The new complete edition of volume 8 of the *History* was an especially important undertaking, given that part two of the volume had first appeared in an edition of a mere 500 copies, and the whole press run of part 3 had perished in Moscow in 1918. That part was reprinted from the only remaining copy, which Hrushevsky chanced to receive from the printer.[146]

In late 1923, when Hrushevsky and his family made their final decision to return to Ukraine, the historian turned to his old Lviv colleague and confidant Kyrylo Studynsky with a request to look for a number of books that he wanted to take with him to Ukraine. 'When I get to Kyiv,' wrote Hrushevsky, 'I want to set to work immediately on the continuation of the big *History*, 1650–1725.'[147] Two of the three works that Hrushevsky asked Studynsky to locate in his abandoned Lviv library were directly related to his planned continuation of the *History*. One of them was a collection of letters from papal nuncios pertaining to the Khmelnytsky Uprising and edited by Hrushevsky's former student Stepan Tomashivsky. Another was a multi-volume collection of studies by Ludwik Kubala, whom Hrushevsky later called 'the most ardent panegyrist' of Khmelnytsky.[148]

There is little doubt that in the last volumes of his *History*, Hrushevsky made a particular effort to shield his scholarship from the prevailing political biases of the period. In his foreword of 1921 to the second edition of part 3 of volume 8 of his *History*, Hrushevsky wrote that he had refrained from making 'any changes in it, so as to avoid introducing into the exposition any of the "politics" inspired by the events of the last few years. Let it stand as written at the time, when Ukrainians were not yet divided by contemporary politics.'[149] This desire to escape the influence of changing political circumstances was also expressed by Hrushevsky in his introduction to volume 9 of the *History*.[150] There is reason to believe that Hrushevsky's resistance to pressure from political supporters and opponents alike contributed to the way in which the Soviet-era volumes of the *History* were written. Both volumes (9 and 10) were extremely rich in source material and rather deficient in authorial interpretation of events. Hrushevsky's research, which was based predominantly on little-known or completely unknown sources from the Moscow archives, allowed him to make a tremendous contribution to his contemporaries' knowledge of that period and present many events and trends of the mid-seventeenth century in a new light. This is especially true of the diplomatic history of the period. The diplomatic relations of the Cossack state in the crucial years of 1654–8 (between the Pereiaslav and Hadiach agreements) with Muscovy, Poland, the Danube principalities, and Sweden were studied by Hrushevsky with a thoroughness as yet unsurpassed.

The continuation of Hrushevsky's magnum opus in Ukraine was no easy task, especially given its author's interest in archival materials. The regular cycle of work on the *History*, which involved Hrushevsky's students in archival research for future volumes of the *History* as their professor completed his current volume, was broken. Apart from that, Hrushevsky's own notes and copies of documentary sources on the Khmelnytsky era fell victim first to wartime hardships and police searches and then to the devastating fire at Hrushevsky's home caused by the Bolshevik bombardment of Kyiv.[151] Consequently, when Hrushevsky returned to Kyiv and presented his plans for the future in a letter to Butsenko, he did not mention the continuation of the *History* among his immediate priorities. Regarding the *History of Ukraine*, Hrushevsky wrote: 'I would also like to continue the big *History of Ukraine-Rus'*, which stopped with 1650 (volume 8). But as the prepared materials were burned in our house in 1917, one would need time to collect them again and resume work.'[152]

In October 1924 Hrushevsky left Kyiv for a short trip to Kharkiv, Moscow, and Leningrad. There he engaged in considerable lobbying on behalf of the academy's 'historical institutions' and familiarized himself with the new arrangement of the archival repositories with the intention of resuming his work on the 'big history.'[153] Hrushevsky was generally satisfied with the results of his trip. Writing to Studynsky from Leningrad (to which he referred by its pre–First World War name, St Petersburg), Hrushevsky noted: 'I was taking a look at conditions for scholarly work in connection with my plans to continue the big history. I see that in Kyiv we have no reason to complain too much about working conditions; we should just get down to work!'[154] That was exactly what Hrushevsky intended to do. In Kyiv he began his preparatory work on the *History* just as he had done in Lviv, by arranging an archaeographic expedition and recruiting young historians to participate in it. In his letter to Studynsky from Leningrad, Hrushevsky asked his old friend to look for a qualified person who could advance his projects in the archival repositories of Lviv and Cracow, promising to pay for the work.[155] In May 1925 he again asked Studynsky to find him a few qualified people in Lviv and Cracow to do archival research for the next volume of the *History* and wrote that he was under pressure on all sides to continue the work.[156] In June and July he appealed once more to Studynsky to help him find research assistants in Lviv and Cracow. He also mentioned that he was planning to complete the manuscript of the fifth volume of the *History of Ukrainian Literature* in September 1925; after that he wanted to begin preparing materials for the next volume of the *History of Ukraine-Rus'*.[157]

In 1925, on the basis of the 'historical institutions' of the Ukrainian Academy of Sciences, Hrushevsky organized an archaeographic expedition to the Moscow archives, which were particularly rich in materials on the Khmelnytsky era. The expedition began its work in 1926 and continued it on a regular basis until 1931. Participants included Volodymyr Ievfymovsky, Viktor Iurkevych, Dmytro Kravtsov, Sylvestr Hlushko, and Prokip Nechyporenko, with Mykola Petrovsky and Anatolii Iershov taking part on an occasional basis.[158] Members of the expedition studied an enormous number of Muscovite diplomatic sources pertaining to Ukrainian history for the years 1650–79 and sent copies of this material to Kyiv.[159] Thanks to the availability of additional government funding, Hrushevsky was able to pay salaries, award scholarships, and cover expenses not only of his graduate students who took part in the expedition to Moscow but also of those who, like the Nizhyn historians Mykola Petrovsky and Anatolii Iershov, participated in the expedition from time to time. Clerks were also hired in Moscow to speed up the copying of the documents. Moreover, Hrushevsky paid Vasyl Herasymchuk and Myron Korduba for their work in the Polish archives, as well as their copyists and other individuals working on the project.[160]

No doubt this diversion of funds to projects related to Hrushevsky's work on the *History* made many people unhappy in the cash-strapped academy.[161] Even Fedir Savchenko, who had once been close to Hrushevsky, complained in one of his letters to Studynsky that he could not get any travel money from the department, as all the funds were going to pay for trips taken by associates engaged in the archaeographic expedition to Moscow or to assist Hrushevsky's daughter, Kateryna, with her scholarly projects.[162] In the summer of 1930, when Hrushevsky found himself under direct attack by the authorities, the question of his alleged abuse of power was placed on the agenda of the academy's 'purge' commission. Oleksii Baranovych, Lev Okinshevych, and Mykola Tkachenko, all former graduate students of Hrushevsky's department[163] and members of the professional association committee at the time of the purge, asked one of the members of the archaeographic expedition, Volodymyr Ievfymovsky, what portion of his time in the archives he devoted to working on his own topic and how much of the materials collected he passed on to Hrushevsky. Ievfymovsky answered that approximately 10 per cent of the material was related to his own topic and the rest went to the Archaeographic Commission.[164]

Like all other members of the archaeographic expedition, Ievfymovsky, who was an official candidate for graduate studies (*kandydat v aspiranty*) in 1924–6 and became a graduate student at the Department of Ukrainian History in 1926–9, worked on his own thesis as well as on Hrushevsky's projects. The subject of his dissertation, 'Muscovite Voevodas in Ukraine in the Times of Bohdan Khmelnytsky,' was closely related to the materials that he was studying on behalf of Hrushevsky. He defended his thesis in 1930.[165] Also closely related to the themes being studied by Hrushevsky was the thesis topic of another active member of the archaeographic expedition, Dmytro Kravtsov. His subject was the impact of Stepan Razin's uprising on Ukraine.[166] Viktor Iurkevych was working on a thesis about Ukrainian resettlement to Muscovy in the Khmelnytsky era.[167] In Kyiv, as previously in Lviv, Hrushevsky sought to combine his own research interests with the topics studied by his graduate students. Conversely, there is little doubt that long stays in Moscow sometimes interfered with individual programs of graduate study at the academy. The correspondence between Hrushevsky and his students in Moscow often referred to their thesis work and progress in their examinations.[168]

Hrushevsky apparently had full control over the use of archival materials collected by the members of the archaeographic expedition. He approved the works of his graduate students for publication and was well acquainted with the research done by other members of the expedition, whose work in the Moscow archives he helped fund through the academy. Relations between Hrushevsky and his associates are well illustrated by letters to him from Anatolii Iershov, a Nizhyn historian, who worked as a temporary member of the expedition in 1927. In September of that year, he wrote to report on his findings in the archives and asked permission to use some of those materials to write an article on Ivan Vyhovsky's relations with the Ottomans. He was very careful and diplomatic in formulating his request: 'On the basis of these reports I would like to write a brief article on Vyhovsky's (Eastern) policy – only if this is appropriate in your opinion, of course. Otherwise, I shall make no use whatever of this material.'[169] Iershov was among the scholars whom Hrushevsky thanked for their assistance in the introduction to volume 9 of the *History*,[170] but we do not have his response to this particular request.

Hrushevsky stayed in close touch with his associates, following the progress of their work and often asking them to check and recheck documents that he needed at any given time.[171] He also did archival work himself while on short visits to Moscow and Leningrad. In order to save time, he would ask his associates to obtain advance permission for him to work in the archives, as well as to order the documents he was specifically interested in seeing.[172] Members of the archaeographic expedition conducted their search for archival documents in two ways. One would begin with Hrushevsky's specific request for a particular document cited in the works of Sergei Soloviev or Mykola Kostomarov.[173] The other method was a global search for documents in those archival collections where documents related to Ukrainian history were most likely to have been deposited. These included the collections of the Military Office (Razriadnyi prikaz), the Ambassadorial Office (Posol'skii prikaz, with its documents on Little Russian, Polish, Moldavian, Turkish, Crimean, Hungarian, and Swedish affairs), the Siberian Office, the Office of Secret Affairs (Prikaz tainykh del), and so on. The global search would be done on a year-by-year basis, but sometimes documents relevant to the period on which Hrushevsky was working would come from files pertaining to later periods. This was the case with the letters of Tymish Khmelnytsky's widow, Rozanda, to the Muscovite tsar, which were located by Viktor Iurkevych while studying documents of the 1660s. These letters were copied at Hrushevsky's request and cited at the end of the first part of volume 9.[174]

As a rule, members of the archaeographic expedition would read the documents, compare them with the published materials (mostly in the *Akty IuZR* [Documents on the History of Southwestern Russia]) and excerpts of documents quoted by Soloviev or Kostomarov, and then select excerpts for copying. The copyists hired by the archaeographic expedition would then transcribe individual documents, or parts of them. After that, a member of the expedition would check the copies against the originals and send them to Hrushevsky in Kyiv.[175] Sometimes the rolls (*stolbtsy*) were mixed up, and Hrushevsky's associates would have to do detective work to reestablish the original sequence of materials.[176] On occasion Hrushevsky would ask his associates to double-check the original or copy illegible words and passages on tracing paper. Ievfymovsky even suggested to Hrushevsky that typed copies of pages of the *History* containing excerpts from copied documents be sent to Moscow to be proofread there.[177] It is not clear whether Hrushevsky took this advice. Members of the archaeographic expedition worked closely with local archivists, including S.I. Porfiriev, who was thanked by Hrushevsky in the introduction to volume 9, and occasionally consulted scholars in Moscow, including Matvei Liubavsky and Vitalii Eingorn.[178]

The archival research conducted by members of the archaeographic expedition in Poland and Western Ukraine focused on the Lviv, Cracow, and Warsaw repositories. In Lviv, they worked in the Ossoliński Library, with its copy of the diaries of Albrycht Stanisław Radziwiłł, the compendium of Marcin Goliński, and the Stanisław Lukas files, as well as the Baworowski and Dzieduszycki collections.[179] In Cracow, they did research in the City Archives, with their Rusiecki and Pinocci collections; the Czartoryski Library, with its Naruszewicz files; and the Jagiellonian Library. In Warsaw repositories, special attention was paid to materials recently transferred there from Russia.[180] Both in Russia and in Poland, members of Hrushevsky's archaeographic expedition were able to collect an enormous amount of previously unknown material that presented many episodes of the Khmelnytsky Uprising in a new light. This explains, at least in part, Hrushevsky's decision to publish many of those documents in the text, notes, and appendixes of the Soviet-era volumes of his *History*.

Apart from work on Hrushevsky's assignments and their own scholarly projects, members of the archaeographic expedition were involved in preparing collections of documents. As head of the Archaeographic Commission of the Academy of Sciences, Hrushevsky had ambitious plans of continuing documentary publications initiated by previous generations of Ukrainian scholars but never brought to fruition.[181] These included the publication of a volume of documents on Cossack history covering the years 1628–38 compiled by Panteleimon Kulish and then taken over by the Archaeographic Commission of the Ukrainian Academy of Sciences in 1919. Hrushevsky considered the planned publication of Herasymchuk's collection of documents on the post-Khmelnytsky era a continuation of the documentary series started by the Archaeographic Commission of the Shevchenko Scientific Society in Lviv. He also planned the publication of a documentary series on the history of the Hetmanate, a project contemplated by the Archaeographic Commission of the Ukrainian Scientific Society in Kyiv prior to the First World War. In addition, there were plans to publish documents on the *haidamaka* movement, a project originated by Volodymyr Antonovych. Another project dealt with the publication of documents on Russian-Ukrainian relations: it was planned as a continuation of the *Akty IuZR* series, which had reached the year 1678 before it was terminated.[182] In terms of archaeographic work, Hrushevsky was often picking up where he himself or his colleagues and predecessors had stopped at the beginning of the First World War.

Hrushevsky's plans also included the publication of a new series of volumes of Ukrainian diplomatic documents (*Ukraïns'kyi dyplomatarii*). The first volume, comprising the proclamations of Bohdan Khmelnytsky, was planned for publication in 1932–3.[183] Needless to say, it never appeared. A variety of reasons delayed and then prevented the publication of Herasymchuk's collection of documents on the years 1657–65.[184] The published volumes of *Ukraïns'kyi arkhiv* (Ukrainian Archive, vols 1, 2, and 4) stand as a reminder of Hrushevsky's ambitious plans for the publication of Ukrainian source materials.[185] His major project in this sphere was never realized, initially for lack of funding and later because of the destruction of his 'historical institutions' at the academy. Yet there is little doubt that in Hrushevsky's mind, his most important task was not the publication of the materials collected by the archaeographic expedition but the continuation of his two multivolume histories of Ukraine and Ukrainian literature.

Hrushevsky was impatient to resume work on his magnum opus. In early 1926, without awaiting the results of the newly organized archaeographic expedition, he began writing the new (ninth) volume of the *History*. As Hrushevsky noted in his introduction to the volume, he initially wrote the parts covering the years 1650 and 1651, and later, in the course of 1926–8, when he gained access to more archival material, completed the narrative up to the death of Bohdan Khmelnytsky.[186] In April 1926 Hrushevsky wrote to Studynsky that he was working on the ninth volume of the *History*, most likely referring to this first draft of the volume.[187] By that time work on volume 9 had clearly become Hrushevsky's scholarly priority. Nevertheless, his administrative activities, academic politics, and lobbying in Kharkiv on behalf of the "historical institutions" were taking a great deal of his time and energy. In April 1928 Hrushevsky complained to Studynsky that he had had a very difficult year, and his work on the *History* was suffering as a result of constant commotion (*metushnia*).[188] The lack of progress on the *History* that so concerned Hrushevsky should, of course, be seen in relative terms. By early August 1928 the historian was already informing his Lviv colleague that he was completing the volume and planning to send its first chapters to the press later that month. Hrushevsky was tired and wanted to see the project completed. He complained about the lack of literature and difficulties in obtaining the books he needed but stressed that he wanted to get rid of the volume.[189] That was no easy task. The volume kept ballooning as a result of new archival material sent to Hrushevsky by his associates, and its final version consisted not of ten chapters, as originally planned, but thirteen.

Probably for the first time in his work on the *History*, Hrushevsky was approaching an era covered by an enormous amount of sources that were either unpublished or completely unknown to his predecessors. Hrushevsky could now not only offer his reader a new interpretation of known sources, as in the previous volumes of the *History*, but could also choose to allow the previously unknown sources to speak for themselves, thereby reducing to a minimum the role of the historian as interpreter of events. Hrushevsky expressed his fascination with the new sources in the introduction to volume 9: 'I have relegated the literary elaborations of the Khmelnytsky era to the background, giving preference to contemporary reports in documentary material collected in the publications of the last few decades, which I have supplemented with the help of my collaborators. This documentary material has been supplemented so considerably as to fill in some of the previous gaps and shed new light on events. This should be said particularly of the last years of the Khmelnytsky era, which have been very superficially treated in the scholarly literature to date. The factual content of the Khmelnytsky era has been considerably enriched, and its overall image appears much clearer, although the new material has rather complicated than simplified it. For my part, I have tried not to schematize this image or simplify it artificially, so as not to bend it to my subjective perceptions, even though I provide general comments in some places, especially at the end of the volume.'[190]

The first chapters of volume 9 were submitted for printing to the State Publishing House of Ukraine in September 1928.[191] The printing of book 1 of the volume was apparently completed by the end of April.[192] In his letter of 18 May 1929 to Studynsky, Hrushevsky wrote about sending him a copy of the book.[193] Hrushevsky sent the manuscript of the second part of volume 9 to the State Publishing House of Ukraine in September 1929,[194] but publication was long delayed, and the book did not come out until 1931. In his letter of 1934 to Viacheslav Molotov, Hrushevsky wrote that the volume was published before his arrest in the winter of 1930–1.[195] When exactly it was issued is hard to say. It is known that in December 1930 Hrushevsky was still busy proofreading the volume, making last-minute additions and corrections.[196] In February 1931 payment of the author's honorarium for the publication of the book was still being discussed by Hrushevsky's associates and the publisher.[197]

Meanwhile, Hrushevsky continued to work on new volumes of the *History*. On the agenda was the next (tenth) volume of his magnum opus. Some information about his work on this volume may be gleaned from an official report on the activities and plans of the Department of the Modern History of the Ukrainian People, one of the academic units chaired by Hrushevsky. It was reported there that in 1929–30, Hrushevsky was working on the history of the Vyhovsky era. It was also noted that in 1927–8 he had completed part 1 of volume 9 of the *History* (thirty-seven printed signatures), and in 1928–9 he had finished part 2 of the volume (close to fifty signatures). He was planning the completion of part 1 of volume 10 (about thirty signatures) in 1930–1 and part 2 of the volume (also close to thirty signatures) in 1931–2.[198]

Part of volume 10 of the *History* was issued posthumously by Kateryna Hrushevska in 1936. As published, it covers a two-year period (1657–8) and is limited to a discussion of the hetmancy of Khmelnytsky's immediate successor, Ivan Vyhovsky. There is no indication anywhere in the published text that what appeared in print was not a complete volume, although it is much smaller than the thirty signatures that Hrushevsky planned for part 1 of the volume in 1930. Most likely, volume 10 of the *History* as issued by Kateryna Hrushevska represents only the first chapters of the volume as originally planned. But did Hrushevsky's work end there? Was he able to extend his *History* beyond 1658? The question takes on particular significance in light of reports that the second part of volume 10 was seen in Kyiv repositories as late as the 1950s.[199] It is hard to say how well elaborated it really was.

Hrushevsky's plans to reissue the out-of-print volumes of the *History* in Ukraine remained unfulfilled. Soon after his return, he signed a contract with the State Publishing House of Ukraine to reprint those volumes. The publisher was also supposed to arrange the import of volumes 1–4 and 8 of the *History* from Lviv for sale in Soviet Ukraine.[200]

There were plans to reprint volume 5 of the *History* but, as Hrushevsky wrote in August 1926, the publisher failed to do so for lack of funds.[201] Moreover, in August 1925 the secret police issued a circular to its regional offices branding the *History* as a work hostile to the Soviet regime and recommending that GPU officials pay special attention to those interested in reading it.[202] The shortage of funds and the suspicious attitude of the authorities apparently prevented the republication of earlier volumes of the *History* in later years as well. Nevertheless, Hrushevsky and his associates continued their efforts in that regard. In January 1930 Fedir Savchenko informed Kyrylo Studynsky that the authorities had decided to reprint some of the volumes.[203] This decision, like all the previous ones, was never carried out.

Clearly, Soviet realities of the 1920s, particularly the reorientation of party policy in Ukraine of the early 1930s, prevented Hrushevsky from realizing many of his plans. This was an enormous disappointment, but it should be recognized that the achievements of Hrushevsky and his students were equally enormous. Even judged against Hrushevsky's most optimistic hopes at the time of his return to Kyiv, the results of his work in Soviet Ukraine surpassed all expectations. While in Ukraine, Hrushevsky was able to continue almost all the major projects initiated in Lviv prior to the First World War. He also trained a new group of scholars and managed to organize archival research on a scale previously unsurpassed. Was it indeed the case that Soviet power could take credit for an unprecedented flourishing of Ukrainian culture and scholarship, as was often declared in official pronouncements of the day? Not entirely. To begin with, Hrushevsky's achievements in Lviv, which were partly supported by funds provided to the Shevchenko Scientific Society by the Polish-controlled Galician Diet, were no less impressive than his accomplishments in Soviet Ukraine. Moreover, much of what Hrushevsky achieved at the Ukrainian Academy of Sciences came about not with the assistance of the authorities but against their will.

All this being said, it should be admitted that during the 1920s the Soviet authorities in Ukraine offered Hrushevsky and his coworkers better conditions to carry out their scholarly projects than they could have found anywhere else in contemporary Europe. Why did they do so? One reason was the official attempt to present Soviet Ukraine as a Piedmont for the Ukrainian intelligentsia and 'toiling masses' outside the USSR. Another was the policy of Ukrainization, especially the Bolshevik effort to find allies among the predominantly hostile Ukrainian intelligentsia. Under these circumstances, archival and scholarly projects like those undertaken by Hrushevsky were tolerated or even supported by the authorities to the extent that they did not directly contradict the party line and supported the official project of dismantling the ideological foundations of the old regime. That policy, which allowed Hrushevsky's archival projects to flourish, was implemented for most of the 1920s but came to an abrupt halt toward the end of the decade.

The 'Counterrevolutionary'

The year 1929 marked the beginning of officially sponsored attacks on Hrushevsky in Marxist publications. In January the Politburo of the Communist Party of Ukraine passed a resolution withdrawing its previous support for Hrushevsky's 'historical institutions' at the Ukrainian Academy of Sciences. That decision cleared the way for a well-orchestrated campaign of media attacks on Hrushevsky and his associates.[204]

The story of the Soviet authorities' persecution of Hrushevsky in the last five years of his life is well researched and familiar to scholars. The publication over the last decade of a number of monographs based on the archives of the party, the Academy of Sciences and, more importantly, the secret police has not only fully reconstructed the details of this campaign but has also added to our understanding of the inner workings of the Soviet regime in the non-Russian republics.[205] My account, then, will briefly summarize the official persecution of Hrushevsky as it emerges from formerly secret documents preserved in the Soviet archives. My main focus, however, will be on the nature of the argument used by the authorities to legitimize their actions. The questions I pose here deal mostly with the dominant Soviet discourse of the period and its transformation in the late 1920s and early 1930s. Hrushevsky found himself confronting an official effort to take full control of the main institutional symbol of knowledge and scholarship in the land – the Academy of Sciences and its publications. Arguably, never had the relations between power and knowledge been so starkly exposed as they were during the first decades of the Soviet regime. Hrushevsky's Soviet odyssey and the resulting human drama were thus characteristic of a profound change in the status of the Academy of Sciences, from relative autonomy in the former Russian Empire to political subservience in the USSR, as the coercive new regime sought to take over the country's academic and intellectual establishment.

Hrushevsky's fate was determined by the new Soviet policy of complete intolerance toward the 'old cadres' and the nationally conscious intelligentsia, who were banished from the public sphere, with little or no opportunity to respond in public to the accusations against them. This does not mean, however, that negotiations (in the postmodern sense of the term) between Hrushevsky and the authorities were completely abandoned. As has recently been argued with regard to the post–Second World War Soviet attack on Ukrainian historians, official accusations against actual and perceived enemies of the regime remained part of the negotiation process, even though the victims had very limited resources at their disposal to answer their accusers.[206] Thus, it is the shifting position of the dominant side in these 'negotiations' that is central to my discussion.

The change in the Kharkiv authorities' policy toward the academy, the termination of official cooperation with Hrushevsky, and the launch of an all-out attack on him and his associates should be viewed in the context of two interconnected processes that were under way in the USSR in the late 1920s. The first was the beginning of a new stage of the cultural revolution marked by an attack on the 'old cadres.' The second was the change in party policy toward the Ukrainian national revival. Both developments had a devastating effect on the Ukrainian Academy of Sciences.

In Russia the 1928 elections to the All-Union Academy of Sciences resulted in the virtual takeover of the academy by the authorities. They forced the academicians to vote for their candidates, such as Nikolai Bukharin and Mikhail Pokrovsky, and appointed party cadres to positions of power in the academy. That campaign was followed by the arrest of a number of scholars, including the prominent Russian historian Sergei Platonov. In Ukraine the GPU fabricated a case against the 'Union for the Liberation of Ukraine,' and scores of scholars from the Ukrainian Academy of Sciences, including Serhii Iefremov, were arrested and sentenced to imprisonment in the GULAG system.[207] The campaign against the Ukrainian intelligentsia went hand in hand with a propagandistic assault on 'Ukrainian nationalism,' a political offensive aimed at eliminating all manifestations of Ukrainian political assertiveness and opposition to Moscow's drive for the centralization of Soviet political, economic, and cultural life. Not surprisingly, the victims of the new policy included not only 'old cadres' but also highly placed party functionaries, such as the leading Marxist historian Matvii Iavorsky, who was severely criticized for alleged nationalism, forced to leave Ukraine, and later arrested.[208]

The party's assault on Hrushevsky came after the bogus trial of the 'Union for the Liberation of Ukraine' (March-April 1930), but the change in official policy toward him can be traced back to the end of 1927. The limits that Hrushevsky placed on his cooperation with the regime should be seen as an important reason for the party's reluctance to propose his candidacy for the office of president of the Academy of Sciences. The authorities' support for Hrushevsky all but evaporated by December 1927, once they realized that he and his allegedly irreconcilable foes, Iefremov and Krymsky, had reached agreement and formed a common front against the regime's policies within the academy. In the following year, the authorities removed Iefremov and his supporters from the leadership of the academy and resolved on its 'communization.' Once Iefremov was gone, the authorities lost interest in Hrushevsky as a natural counterweight to what they viewed as a 'constitutional-democratic' grouping in the academy. Official support was withdrawn, and funds earlier available to Hrushevsky were now allocated to establish an institute to be chaired by the new president of the academy, the biologist Danylo Zabolotny.[209]

By the summer of 1930 Hrushevsky found himself under continuous assault. At the academy, his 'historical institutions' were either taken away from him or their employees harassed by numerous commissions looking for signs of nationalism in Hrushevsky's scholarly work. Before his return to Ukraine in 1924, Hrushevsky had acquired two letters from the authorities guaranteeing his immunity from political persecution. The first was issued by the Ukrainian Central Executive Committee; the second was signed by the head of the government, Vlas Chubar, and the head of the GPU, Vsevolod Balytsky. Neither of these official guarantees was of any avail to Hrushevsky when on 22 March 1931 the Politburo of the Communist Party of Ukraine gave its approval for his arrest as leader of the fictitious 'Ukrainian National Centre.' The next day Hrushevsky was arrested in Moscow (where he had gone on a research trip), brought back to Ukraine, and interrogated by a number of GPU officers, including Balytsky himself. After that he was returned to Moscow, where he was unexpectedly released from custody and rescinded the self-incriminatory testimony that he had given under duress in Ukraine. Someone in the higher echelons of power had decided to spare the historian's life. Hrushevsky was allowed to continue his scholarly work in Moscow but remained under secret police surveillance until the end of his life and was never allowed to return to Ukraine.[210]

For a more detailed look at the political accusations levelled against Hrushevsky by Bolshevik propaganda, let us examine a government-sponsored pamphlet directly related to Hrushevsky's arrest. Its author was Andrii Khvylia, an official of the Ukrainian Central Executive Committee, and his pamphlet, 'The Bourgeois-Nationalist Tribune,' was published in *Bil'shovyk Ukraïny* (Bolshevik of Ukraine) soon after Hrushevsky's arrest.[211] This was the first political article specifically concerned with 'unmasking' Hrushevsky. In it, Khvylia revived many of the accusations made by Marxist reviewers of Hrushevsky's works prior to 1931 but also introduced some new elements into anti-Hrushevsky polemics.

The main purpose of Khvylia's article was to depict Hrushevsky as an ideologue of Ukrainian bourgeois nationalism and the journal *Ukraïna* as a mouthpiece of his ideas. Most of the charges levelled against Hrushevsky by the organizers of the new campaign did not pertain to his major work, the *History of Ukraine-Rus'*, but to his political writings of the revolutionary era, as well as his postrevolutionary publications in the journal *Ukraïna* on Ukrainian national historiography and the cultural revival of the nineteenth and early twentieth centuries. The articles published in that journal had been attacked by Marxist critics back in 1927 and 1929, and Mykola Skrypnyk himself went on record at least once with the claim that the journal was publishing articles of a political nature under the cover of scholarship. Hence it comes as little surprise that publications in *Ukraïna* served as the basis for Andrii Khvylia's attack on Hrushevsky.

Khvylia claimed that *Ukraïna* lacked articles dealing with topics important to Soviet society, such as class struggle and the history of the revolutionary movement. At the same time, he stated that *Ukraïna* had not become an 'archival journal' and was involving itself in politics. In his critique Khvylia suggested that as editor of *Ukraïna*, Hrushevsky was not only deliberately misrepresenting Ukrainian history and culture but also propagating bourgeois nationalism. Khvylia developed some of the charges that Oleksander Shumsky had brought against Hrushevsky in 1926 with regard to his article 'In Shameful Memory.' He also repeated arguments earlier voiced by Vlas Chubar and Volodymyr Zatonsky, who claimed that it was Hrushevsky who had joined the communists in the Ukrainian nation-building effort, not vice versa. There were also important new elements in Khvylia's attack on Hrushevsky. In order to discredit the journal and its editor even further in the eyes of the Soviet readership, Khvylia depicted *Ukraïna* as a tribune for the propaganda not only of nationalist and bourgeois ideas but also of religious ones.[212]

Hrushevsky emerged from the pages of Khvylia's article as a political enemy of the state who was summoning his supporters to an armed uprising. Clearly, the only proper place for such an individual was behind bars, and the main goal of Khvylia's article was to justify Hrushevsky's arrest. In making his case against Hrushevsky, Khvylia not only misinterpreted and decontextualized many of Hrushevsky's statements but also falsified some of them. In particular, he charged Hrushevsky with having stated that the national question could not be resolved within the framework of a proletarian state. He also insinuated that in writing about the 'emotional' as opposed to the 'rational' arguments of Ukrainian activists, Hrushevsky was in fact referring to armed struggle against the proletarian revolution. Khvylia concluded his attack on Hrushevsky and *Ukraïna* by noting the journal's failure to condemn the activities of the 'Union for the Liberation of Ukraine,' which had been fabricated by the secret police. According to Khvylia, the journal had kept silent on that matter because its editors did not approve the proletariat's verdict against the 'criminals.'

In the spring of 1931, during Hrushevsky's forced exile in Moscow, mock trials disguised as scholarly debates were staged by the authorities in Kyiv and Kharkiv for the purpose of discrediting Hrushevsky and his writings. Their other goal was the legitimization of the all-out attack on Hrushevsky's colleagues and students, as well as on the Ukrainian intelligentsia in general. Hrushevsky was probably the first Ukrainian scholar with an established prerevolutionary reputation whom the regime sought to destroy by means of public 'disputes.' Later the same year, new debates were held in order to 'unmask' the 'true' views of academicians Kostiantyn Vobly and Leonid Iasnopolsky, as well as to criticize the allegedly bourgeois scheme of Ukrainian history produced by Hrushevsky's antagonist at the time, Oleksander Ohloblyn.[213]

The three 'Hrushevsky debates' took place in Kyiv in May 1931. They were held in the building formerly occupied by the Central Rada, the conference auditorium of the Academy of Sciences, and the Kyiv Opera.[214] At these carefully orchestrated public discussions, party scholars would attack Hrushevsky for his non-Marxist and allegedly anti-Soviet views. The historian Nataliia Polonska-Vasylenko, who was present at the debates, later remarked that what she found most difficult to endure was listening to the speeches of 'repentance' given by former students and associates of Hrushevsky, who were forced to blame their leader for his alleged 'errors.' She also noted that there were individuals courageous enough to refuse to join the accusers.[215] The published text of one of the speeches delivered at the debates makes it apparent that some of those present at the debate of 5 May 1931 sent unsigned notes to the presidium reminding the audience that it was Hrushevsky who had led the Ukrainian people in their struggle for liberation.[216]

Texts of speeches delivered by some of the participants were later published in leading Ukrainian journals, giving us a better understanding of the discourse of denunciation employed by the regime to crush its real and imagined opponents. A reworked text of Andrii Richytsky's speech on Hrushevsky's sociological views appeared in the May 1931 issue of the Ukrainian party's main theoretical organ, *Bil'shovyk Ukraïny*, while an extensive tract on Hrushevsky's political views by Mykhailo Rubach (Rubanovych), based on his speech at one of the 'Hrushevsky disputes,' was published in *Chervonyi shliakh* (Red Pathway) in the latter half of 1932.[217]

Andrii Richytsky's presentation was devoted to 'unmasking' Hrushevsky's harmful views in the realm of sociology. As might be expected of a presentation at a politically charged 'dispute,' Richytsky not only attacked Hrushevsky's methodological 'errors' but also levelled a number of politically harmful charges against him. He claimed that Hrushevsky had never been a revolutionary populist himself and was responsible for Ivan Franko's decision to abandon the revolutionary populist platform and join the national-democratic camp. As an ideologue, Hrushevsky allegedly represented the views of the Ukrainian bourgeoisie of the 'Cadet' camp (that is, members of the Russian Constitutional Democratic Party). Richytsky characterized Hrushevsky's adherence to the UPSR not as the result of a genuine evolution of his views but as an opportunistic move intended to secure his influence over the masses. The fact that Hrushevsky's alleged former foe (and Constitutional Democrat) Mykhailo Mohyliansky[218] came to his defence during the 'dispute' was interpreted by Richytsky as evidence that various bourgeois groupings were prepared to create a united front against the dictatorship of the proletariat. Richytsky portrayed Mohyliansky as a representative of Russian Constitutional Democratic ideology, while Hrushevsky allegedly represented its Ukrainian equivalent. According to Richytsky, their ideological unity underlay the resistance of the bourgeois and capitalist elements to the advance of socialism, as well as kulak resistance to the collectivization of agriculture. Generally speaking, Richytsky made every effort to present Hrushevsky's case as an illustration of the party's then current slogan about the intensification of the class struggle as a result of the socialist offensive in the village. The final political blow came at the end of the article, where Richytsky stated that although Hrushevsky might not be a supporter of imperialist intervention against the USSR on the subjective level, objectively his scholarly activities represented nothing other than the intervention of bourgeois scholarship in the process of socialist cultural construction.

In his attack on Hrushevsky, Richytsky touched on a number of topics that were developed much more consistently by another inveterate critic of Hrushevsky, Mykhailo Rubach. For the Hrushevsky 'disputes,' Rubach prepared a paper devoted to a critique of the historian's socio-political views. It was first presented in April 1931 at a session of the Ukrainian Society of Marxist Historians and then delivered on 25 May at a joint session of the historical, philosophical, and sociological sections of the Ukrainian Academy of Sciences in Kyiv. A reworked and expanded version was published a year later, in the second half of 1932, in the journal *Chervonyi shliakh*. Rubach's career as a 'specialist' on Hrushevsky began in the mid-1920s in a seminar on Russian historiography conducted by Mikhail Pokrovsky. At that time Rubach prepared a long article on federalist theories in Russian historical thought that paid special attention to the works of Hrushevsky. In that article, which was published in 1930, Rubach developed Pokrovsky's view of Hrushevsky as a continuator of the federalist approach to Russian history first introduced into Russian historiography by Mykola Kostomarov.[219]

By contrast, Rubach's article of 1932 on Hrushevsky was less a scholarly discussion and more a direct political attack. The very title of the latter article, 'Bourgeois-Kulak Nationalist Ideology in the Guise of Democracy of the "Toiling People,"' indicated its main goal. Rubach proposed to unmask Hrushevsky as an ideologue not only of Ukrainian bourgeois nationalism in general but also of the Ukrainian kulaks (*kurkuli*) – well-to-do peasants who were then regarded as the party's main internal enemy. Taking Hrushevsky's autobiography and his political works as the basis of his 'class analysis,' Rubach presented the following picture of Hrushevsky's ideological and political evolution. In terms of social origin, Rubach described Hrushevsky as a descendant of a well-off clerical family, characterizing his father as a typical moderate liberal. All these markers of social and political identity, 'priest,' 'moderate,' and 'liberal,' were pejorative and dangerous words in the dominant Bolshevik discourse of the time. Rubach claimed that Hrushevsky had never been a socialist, and if he continued any tradition represented by Mykhailo Drahomanov, it was that of bourgeois liberalism, to which Drahomanov descended in the last years of his life, abandoning the platform of petty-bourgeois democratism. Although Hrushevsky had been persecuted by the tsarist authorities, Rubach maintained that he was no more radical than the Russian Cadets. According to Rubach, Hrushevsky had joined the UPSR during the revolution for the sole purpose of taking control of the masses and removing them from the influence of the proletariat.

Rubach presented Hrushevsky as the author of the theory of a 'single national front,' which had been conceived with that goal in mind. To make that theory work, Hrushevsky had allegedly advanced the supplementary thesis of the 'non-bourgeois' character of the Ukrainian nation, which Rubach characterized as a manifestation of nationalist, bourgeois-kulak ideology. That thesis made it possible for Hrushevsky to represent and defend the interests of Ukrainian landlords and bourgeois. According to Rubach, Hrushevsky did not regard the class struggle as the main agent of history – a Marxist view that became dogma under the Bolshevik regime – but as an anomaly of historical development. After Hrushevsky's return to Ukraine, continued Rubach, he had declared his support for the Soviet regime but remained opposed to the dictatorship of the proletariat and was hostile to industrialization. Instead, he had propagated a model of economic development that would benefit the kulaks, not the workers. Another of Hrushevsky's alleged transgressions was his call to unite the Ukrainian lands divided among the USSR, Poland, Czechoslovakia, and Romania. Rubach claimed that under cover of the national banner, Hrushevsky was attempting to downplay the opposition between the USSR and the capitalist world. In making his case against Hrushevsky, Rubach cited Lenin's maxim that within every nation there were two nations, one of the exploiters and the other of the exploited, just as there were two national cultures.

Rubach summarized and further developed many of the political accusations made against Hrushevsky by his predecessors during the 1920s and early 1930s, offering the most systematic account of the historian's 'subversive' ideas yet presented. Rubach had clearly read more of Hrushevsky's works than any other Marxist critic, which allowed him to present a biased but quite coherent critique (within the limits of party doctrine) of Hrushevsky's political views. The reason for the delay in the publication of Rubach's article, as compared with those of Khvylia and Richytsky, is not entirely clear. It appeared when the political campaign against Hrushevsky had long passed its peak of 1931, and the leaders of the party cell at the academy were even being reprimanded by their superiors for having treated the old cadres too harshly. The publication of the paper, which was later considered a classic example of the Soviet critique of Hrushevsky, in a predominantly literary journal rather than in *Bil'shovyk Ukraïny*, the party's main theoretical organ, also raises questions. The most plausible explanation of this anomaly is that by 1932 Rubach himself had fallen on hard times and found himself under criticism by the party. He was removed as director of the Kharkiv Institute of Party History, and his publications were attacked as national-democratic, rightist-opportunistic, and Trotskyite falsifications. Later he was accused of being a Iavorskyite and of treating the Ukrainian Revolution as a phenomenon separate from the Russian one.[220] The publication of the reworked version of Rubach's anti-Hrushevsky paper may be seen as a desperate attempt to demonstrate his continuing loyalty to the regime and eagerness to fight the enemies of the party on the historical front. Ironically, the article that Rubach apparently published to save his own skin during the 'intensification of the class struggle' later served as a basis for the formulation of the official view of Hrushevsky and his works for generations of Soviet historians.[221]

How different was the party-sponsored campaign of the early 1930s against Hrushevsky from the critical attacks of the 1920s? In 1931–4, as opposed to the officially sponsored attacks of previous years, Hrushevsky was presented by party ideologists not as an accomplice but as the main perpetrator. The objective of the new campaign was not to demonstrate the methodological shortcomings of Hrushevsky's writings, as was the case previously, but to 'unmask' him as a political enemy – a Ukrainian bourgeois nationalist and fascist allegedly working toward the separation of Ukraine from the USSR and its subjugation by the capitalist West.[222] The basis for bringing charges and fabricating evidence against Hrushevsky and other members of the Ukrainian intelligentsia was presented in January 1934 by the de facto ruler of Ukraine, Pavel Postyshev, in a speech to the Twelfth Congress of the Communist Party of Ukraine. Commenting on the 'findings' of the GPU, Postyshev claimed that the intensification of the class struggle within the country and the interventionist plans of foreign imperialists were leading to the activization of nationalist counterrevolutionary organizations.[223] The most serious political accusation against Hrushevsky was twofold, including elements of state treason (the violation of Soviet territorial integrity) and class-based subversion – the dismantling of the dictatorship of the proletariat and the restoration of the bourgeois order in Ukraine. These general themes of the officially sponsored attacks on Hrushevsky were worked out in detail in the list of 'crimes' imputed to him after his arrest. They included leadership of a clandestine organization that was allegedly preparing an armed uprising against the Soviet regime and the establishment and maintenance of conspiratorial ties with enemies of the USSR abroad. Hrushevsky's contacts with European and Western Ukrainian scholars were treated as incriminating evidence against him and his colleagues. In 1934, while in Moscow, Hrushevsky was investigated by the secret police as a member of the 'Russian National Party,' another clandestine organization fabricated by the GPU whose alleged members were accused of having contacts with fascist Germany and preparing to overthrow the Soviet regime.[224]

These and earlier charges brought against Hrushevsky by the GPU were a far cry from the official assessment of his political attitude in 1929. At that time, it was claimed that Hrushevsky belonged to a group of *smenovekhovtsy* who were pushing the authorities toward a more radical policy of Ukrainization but opposed foreign intervention or civil war in Ukraine, as they believed that under the circumstances only the Soviet regime could guarantee Ukraine's independence and cultural development. The GPU files on Hrushevsky show that within a relatively short period, between 1929 and 1931, the secret police made a drastic policy change: after having persecuted perceived enemies of the regime on the basis of charges that at least partly reflected their political views, they began laying completely trumped-up charges that reflected only the political goals of the regime, bearing no relation to the current or even former opinions of those accused.[225]

The key to understanding the nature of Soviet discourse of the 1920s and early 1930s lies in the party's complete control of the public sphere within which competing speakers were interacting. The print media were entirely subject to the Soviet regime, which consequently determined the scope and direction of public discourse. As demonstrated by the articles on Hrushevsky's jubilee of 1926 and the attacks on him in 1931, both positive and negative publications were given prior approval by the authorities. By establishing complete control over public space and determining not only what was said but also what was not said, the regime was able to turn press discussion into a forum in which the current party line was presented, its enemies crushed, and public hysteria and witch-hunting promoted.

When it came to official discussions of political and scholarly matters, only party members were allowed a voice, as was clearly indicated by Shumsky's response to Hrushevsky in the autumn of 1926. The regime also attempted to control all opposing discourse and later to eliminate it completely. Hrushevsky's experience and that of his colleagues in the Academy of Sciences affords numerous illustrations of this. In 1926 the authorities blacklisted Mykhailo Mohyliansky for publishing a short story in one of the Kyiv journals that was perceived as a nationalist attack on Hrushevsky. Since Hrushevsky was then considered loyal to the regime, the story was viewed as dangerous. In 1928 the authorities launched a campaign against Serhii Iefremov for publishing an article in the Lviv newspaper *Dilo*, which was out of reach of the Soviet regime. The campaign led eventually to Iefremov's arrest, which was followed by the fabrication of a criminal case against the so-called Union for the Liberation of Ukraine.[226]

Publications of the Academy of Sciences were initially exempt from Soviet censorship and consequently much freer than the rest of the Soviet press, but soon an unofficial censorship was established there as well. In his diaries, Iefremov noted a major difference between the old (tsarist) and the new (Soviet) censorship. If the old censorship confined itself to banning the publication of certain materials that it considered hostile to the regime, the new one went further, demanding the publication of materials favourable to the regime. This was exemplified by a Soviet censor's demand that Hrushevsky write and sign an article marking the anniversary of Lenin's birthday.[227] Under these new circumstances, the traditional significance of public statements by leading figures was subverted, and Hrushevsky's half-hearted declarations in support of the regime, as well as his condemnation of the Prague scholarly congress of 1926, acquired a new, negotiated meaning. As secret police reports make clear, the general public was convinced that Hrushevsky had been coerced into making his statement condemning the congress. A tacit code of public discourse gradually emerged in the USSR, with statements of exaggerated gratitude to the regime serving as warning signals to the public, which came to realize that such statements from the older generation of scholars, artists, and writers could not be taken at face value.[228] Within the framework of strictly controlled public discourse, a new meaning was assigned to silence. Iefremov's refusal to write for Soviet periodicals was viewed as a major insult to the authorities, who repeatedly attempted to force him to publish as an indication of loyalty. The fact that Hrushevsky did not publicly condemn the alleged members of the 'Union for the Liberation of Ukraine' was viewed by the authorities and the general public as a direct challenge to the regime.

After a series of public 'discussions' organized by the authorities to 'unmask' and 'ideologically disarm' Hrushevsky and his school, whatever was left of his 'historical institutions' in the Ukrainian Academy of Sciences was either completely dissolved or purged and taken over by his competitors. The campaign of criticism went on, and Hrushevsky was never allowed to return to Kyiv. The following years witnessed the man-made famine in Ukraine and an official attack on the proponents of national communism within the party ranks. Mykola Khvyliovy and Mykola Skrypnyk, the two members of the Communist Party of Ukraine whose names were most closely associated with the Ukrainization policy, committed suicide in order to avoid arrest. During that time, Hrushevsky's name was frequently mentioned in accusations against new victims of Stalin's terror. He was portrayed as one of the leaders of the Ukrainian fascists, and Mykola Skrypnyk himself was accused of sharing Hrushevsky's views on Ukrainian history.[229] The journal *Ukraïna*, which had been founded and edited by Hrushevsky, resumed publication in 1932 under new editorship. It was now full of brutal attacks on its former editor.

The political campaign against Hrushevsky was reactivated in early 1934 in connection with another purge of the Ukrainian Academy of Sciences. In January 1934 Hrushevsky was attacked by Volodymyr Zatonsky, the Ukrainian People's Commissar of Education, in his speech at a session of the Ukrainian Academy of Sciences.[230] In the same year the newly established Institute of Historical Archaeography issued the first volume of a serial, with two of its five articles devoted to 'uncovering' the 'fascist' and 'nationalist' character of Hrushevsky's conception of Ukrainian history.[231] Hrushevsky's anomalous position as the main enemy of the regime in Ukraine who remained at large in Moscow caused a number of problems for party officials in Ukraine, who demanded that Moscow clarify Hrushevsky's status. Suggestions (probably fabricated by the Ukrainian GPU) to the effect that Hrushevsky was contemplating defection to the West were forwarded to Moscow and served as a basis for putting him under close surveillance by the secret police. An undercover agent was sent to Kyiv to question Hrushevsky's relatives there, and Hrushevsky was followed by GPU agents while vacationing at the Academy of Sciences resort in Kislovodsk. It was there that he died under suspicious circumstances in November 1934.[232]

On 25 November 1934, the day after Hrushevsky's death in Kislovodsk, the Kyiv newspaper *Visti* (News) informed its readers of his passing and published the text of a Ukrainian government resolution announcing a state funeral for Hrushevsky and awarding his family a special government pension.[233] The enemy of the regime was buried with the honours reserved by that same regime for its major leaders. Hrushevsky's obituary was published by the Moscow *Pravda* and then reprinted in the Ukrainian media, appearing in some journals in the same issue as the bulletin about the assassination of Sergei Kirov on 1 December 1934.[234]

The authorities' unexpected 'change of heart' immediately following Hrushevsky's death and his officially sponsored funeral in Kyiv created an atmosphere that helped preserve some of his unpublished manuscripts. At its extraordinary meeting called to make preparations for Hrushevsky's funeral, the Presidium of the Ukrainian Academy of Sciences recommended to the Ukrainian People's Commissariat of Education that a special commission be established for the study of Hrushevsky's papers and suggested Hrushevsky's daughter, Kateryna, as a member. It was as part of her work on her father's manuscripts that Hrushevska managed to prepare for print and publish volume 10 of the *History* in 1936. Preparations for the publication of part 1 of volume 6 of the *History of Ukrainian Literature* also resumed. Moreover, a monument to Hrushevsky was erected on his grave.[235]

Part of the explanation of this change in official policy regarding Hrushevsky is related to the government's decision to reintroduce history courses in secondary schools and switch party support from Mikhail Pokrovsky's school of Marxist historians to the older generation of scholars trained before the revolution. The change of policy was felt by Hrushevsky before his death. In his letter to Molotov, Hrushevsky attempted to exploit the new policy line in order to improve his standing with the authorities. He wrote: 'Serious attention is now being paid to mastering the facts of history and literary history; sooner or later there will be an acute need for material prepared on a scholarly level. But it cannot be obtained immediately: it must be prepared well in advance, but work has now ceased.'[236] In the late 1930s, these changes in official policy modified attitudes toward the legacy of prerevolutionary scholars. It came to be believed that their works should not be rejected outright but could be used to educate younger generations, future builders of socialism. This period saw the reissue of works by Russian historians of the imperial period, including the writings of Pokrovsky's former professor and main ideological adversary, Vasilii Kliuchevsky. The rehabilitation process was mostly limited to works by Russian historians, but the publication of volume 10 of Hrushevsky's *History* attests that there was also some spillover of this policy in the realm of Ukrainian history.

There is sufficient evidence to assume that the new policy was extended to include Hrushevsky with the approval of none other than Joseph Stalin himself. In July 1939 Hrushevsky's widow, Mariia, wrote to Stalin requesting his intervention in the case of Kateryna, who had been arrested by the secret police in the previous year. In this letter, she wrote: 'You knew and valued the scholarly merits of my late husband, paid due respect to his memory, and acknowledged the value of his scholarly work in history. Your highly authoritative estimation of my late husband as a scholar whose works, according to your authoritative assessment, are a valuable contribution to Soviet scholarship, valuable as inexhaustible material for young Soviet historians, gives me grounds to appeal to you in connection with the misfortune that has befallen me.'[237] This statement on the importance of Hrushevsky's works for research conducted by young Soviet historians, which Mariia Hrushevska attributed to Stalin, was in complete accord with the new official line. That new policy even allowed some advocates of Hrushevsky's work to claim that his writings could be employed to counteract nationalist falsifications of Ukrainian history. It was on this basis that Oleksander Biletsky advocated the publication of the first part of volume 6 of Hrushevsky's *History of Ukrainian Literature*, claiming that his work was 'one of the monuments of the "cultural legacy" of the old world that we should study and critically assess. The content of this particular book, aside from its scholarly value, may also prove useful in our struggle against all sorts of nationalist falsifications of the historical development of literature.'[238] Unfortunately, the window of opportunity for the publication of Hrushevsky's works that opened briefly after 1934 closed too soon to allow his major unpublished works to reach their intended readers. In that context, Kateryna Hrushevska's publication of even an incomplete version of volume 10 of the *History* was nothing short of a miracle.

Was Hrushevsky right to return to Ukraine? He himself would probably have given different answers to this question depending on when it was asked. On a personal level, Hrushevsky and other members of the Ukrainian intelligentsia paid an enormous price for their bold attempt to exploit the Bolshevik regime in order to advance their national agenda. Nevertheless, during the first years after his return to Soviet Ukraine, Hrushevsky clearly did not regret his decision and even encouraged the son of his close friend Kyrylo Studynsky to follow his example.[239] But the excitement of the first years of Hrushevsky's work in Ukraine was short-lived. If GPU reports are to be trusted – and in Hrushevsky's case, at least until the late 1920s, they are quite reliable – by late 1927 or early 1928 he had become disillusioned about the prospects of work under the Soviet regime. By the early 1930s Hrushevsky and his family regarded the choice they had made in 1924 with a certain amount of fatalism. As Kateryna Hrushevska noted in a letter written prior to the family's exile to Moscow, there was no other Ukraine, and they had to serve the one that was there.[240]

Hrushevsky returned to Ukraine after admitting his political defeat. By 1924 he no longer expected the Bolshevik authorities either to turn over power to the Ukrainian national parties, as he had demanded in 1920, or to legalize those parties, as he called on them to do in 1921. Hrushevsky was coming back to Ukraine for the sole purpose of continuing his scholarly and cultural work. In his opinion, it was a unique opportunity to continue promoting the formation of Ukrainian national identity, which he and his colleagues had begun prior to the revolution. Indeed, Hrushevsky's activities in Ukraine during the 1920s contributed tremendously to the cause of Ukrainian nation-building. That contribution was manifested in his work at the Ukrainian Academy of Sciences, where he organized the 'historical institutions'; the publication of the journal *Ukraïna*, which was intended for a broader audience; and, last but not least, the continuation of the historical and literary national narratives – the multivolume histories of Ukraine and Ukrainian literature. Through his participation in public discourse, especially during the first four years of his residence in Ukraine, Hrushevsky promoted Ukrainian scholarship and culture, maintained and developed Soviet Ukraine's links with Galicia and Bukovyna, and defended the rights of Ukrainian culture and scholarship in the USSR.

There is little question that by returning to Ukraine, Hrushevsky was able to do much more to dismantle the ideological heritage of imperial Russia and promote the formation of Ukrainian national identity than he could have accomplished in the emigration. The Bolsheviks not only accepted the existence of the Ukrainian nation, culture, and history, but for most of the 1920s they also committed organizational support and resources to implementing their vision of a new interethnic order – one that at least in theory regarded Russia and Ukraine as equal partners in the Soviet Union. No doubt the Bolshevik regime was viewed as a natural ally by such left-leaning intellectuals as Hrushevsky and his socialist-revolutionary colleagues. What the Bolsheviks gained from this alliance was not just qualified cadres who returned to Ukraine and took part in the construction of socialism but also the partial legitimization of their regime in the eyes of its numerous foreign and domestic opponents. The fate of the returnees, including Hrushevsky and his colleagues, depended directly on shifts of Bolshevik policy in social and ethnic affairs, but it is clearly apparent from internal party and secret police documentation that they were never completely trusted by the regime.

Judging by Soviet publications of the time and secret police reports that are now available to scholars, Hrushevsky underwent an amazing political evolution during his decade of work in the USSR. On returning to Soviet Ukraine in 1924 as a former member of the UPSR, he denounced anti-Soviet political organizations in the emigration and for some time was even a leading official candidate for president of the Ukrainian Academy of Sciences. By the early 1930s, according to the secret police, he had allegedly joined his former party colleagues in creating a clandestine anti-Soviet organization, the 'Ukrainian National Centre,' which conspired to foment an armed uprising against the Bolshevik regime. On the basis of that charge, Hrushevsky was arrested, then released and exiled to Moscow. Judging by Soviet propaganda materials, Hrushevsky initially supported the Soviet regime because it tolerated Ukrainian statehood but then conspired to take Ukraine out of the Soviet Union in the interests of world imperialism and fascism. By the last year of his life, Hrushevsky had allegedly become involved in another anti-Soviet plot and was presumably planning to defect from the USSR.

If one attempts to trace the development of Hrushevsky's historical views as presented by his critics, the resulting picture is no less confusing than that of his alleged political evolution. According to the critics, Hrushevsky began as a populist and a follower of Kostomarov's federalist theory. From there he proceeded to economic materialism and eventually to Marxism, of which he adopted some important elements without ever grasping the historical importance of the class struggle. Although at different stages of his academic career Hrushevsky 'oriented' himself either on the toiling masses in general, the peasantry, or the intelligentsia, he also advanced a theory of the classlessness of the Ukrainian nation. He denied the existence of the Ukrainian bourgeoisie, and in so doing became its principal ideologue. In his historical writings, Hrushevsky allegedly resorted to documentalism, psychologism and, above all, nationalism, making him a quintessential eclectic. By the end of the 1920s Hrushevsky's main ideological platform became Ukrainian nationalism. From there, in the early 1930s, he descended to 'national democracy' (an opprobrious and dangerous epithet in the USSR at the time) and eventually to fascism. As a 'national democrat,' Hrushevsky abandoned his original populism and adhered to the statist school of Ukrainian historiography. As a fascist, he falsified the history of the Ukrainian peasant war of 1648–54.

Apparently, death itself could not stop the evolution of that great spirit. The obituary characterized Hrushevsky as one of the most prominent bourgeois historians of Ukraine who returned from the emigraiton in 1924, allegedly because of his realization that 'only Soviet power could ensure the social and national liberation of the Ukrainian people.' The death of the historian was the Bolshevik regime's last opportunity to derive political benefit from his return to Ukraine.[241] The calm tone of the obituary, which was in sharp contrast with the earlier attacks on Hrushevsky, clearly confused some party and Komsomol activists who for years had been exposed to articles and lectures accusing the historian of being the worst possible enemy of the Soviet state. When a disoriented young Marxist scholar asked the seasoned 'bourgeois specialist' Nataliia Polonska-Vasylenko how the government could give Hrushevsky such a funeral, she gave a sarcastic response: 'How can you fail to understand? This is the dialectic!'[242]

No less 'dialectical,' certainly, was the decision of the Kyiv city council in 1936 to carve Hrushevsky's tombstone out of a piece of granite that had served as a base for a monument to Emperor Nicholas I before 1919. The 'unmaking' of imperial Russia and the rise of a new Ukraine out of its ruins suddenly acquired an unexpected symbol in Hrushevsky's tombstone. It is unlikely that the council's decision-makers realized the significance of their action.

Chapter 5

Revisiting the Revolution

What impact did the revolutionary and Soviet experience have on Mykhailo Hrushevsky as a historian? The question is best addressed by looking at the new volumes of his magnum opus, written in the 1920s.

The Soviet-era volumes of the *History* continued Hrushevsky's discussion of the Khmelnytsky Uprising. Long before Hrushevsky, the Khmelnytsky era and its aftermath had been considered one of the most important periods in Ukrainian history. It was also endowed with particular significance for Hrushevsky. The Khmelnytsky Uprising featured prominently in all-Russian historiography, since it marked the point at which Ukrainian history reentered the imperial narrative, having virtually disappeared from it after the disintegration of the Kyivan state in the thirteenth century. With minor variations, the Russian imperial and national narratives both treated the uprising of 1648 as a revolt of the Russian Orthodox against Polish Catholic and Jewish subjugation in order to secure the reunification of the Rus' tsardom/nation. The uprising was also a crucial episode of the Little Russian historical narrative, which was conceived as an integral part of all-Russian history. Thus, claiming the Khmelnytsky era for the Ukrainian national narrative was a fundamental task of Ukrainian historiography. That process began with the publication of Mykola Kostomarov's three-volume study of Bohdan Khmelnytsky, the first scholarly monograph on the Ukrainian past, but Kostomarov still treated the uprising within the confines of all-Russian history, and it fell to his successors to separate the all-Russian and Ukrainian narratives at their most sensitive junction.

It was there that Ukrainian history acquired (more precisely, took over from the rival all-Russian narrative) its first real hero since the times of St Volodymyr – the Cossack hetman Bohdan Khmelnytsky. The period included two major events that in many ways defined Ukraine's subsequent relations with its two powerful neighbours, Russia and Poland. The first of these was the anti-Polish uprising of 1648, while the second was the Pereiaslav Agreement of 1654 between the Hetmanate and Muscovy, which made Cossack Ukraine a Muscovite protectorate. The interpretation of these two events could either promote the creation of a separate Ukrainian national identity, defined in opposition to its two major 'others,' the Poles and the Russians, or undermine that project. The Khmelnytsky era, as depicted in nineteenth-century historiography, linked two major myths of the Ukrainian national revival – the myth of Cossackdom and the myth of the people. Ukrainian activists also regarded that period as marking the emergence of a separate Ukrainian identity, while the new statist school in Ukrainian historiography considered it the cradle of early modern Ukrainian statehood.

The period from 1650 to 1657 encompassed an era that saw the transformation of Cossackdom from a rebellious stratum into a state-building force. After the bloody but victorious uprising against Polish domination in 1648 and the formation of a Cossack state – the Hetmanate – as a result of the Zboriv Agreement with the Polish king (1649), Cossackdom emerged as a significant political factor in Eastern Europe. It was a force to be reckoned with not only by the embattled Polish-Lithuanian Commonwealth but also by the neighbouring powers of Muscovy, the Ottoman Empire and its vassals, the Crimean Khanate, Moldavia, and Wallachia. Even after the Battle of Berestechko (1651), a disaster for the Cossack Host that entailed a drastic reduction of the territory subject to the Cossacks under the terms of the Peace of Bila Tserkva (1651), the Hetmanate managed to recover and defeat the Polish army at the Battle of Batih (1652). The leader of the Cossack state, Hetman Bohdan Khmelnytsky (1595–1657), even forced the hospodar of Moldavia, Vasile Lupu, to marry his daughter to Khmelnytsky's son Tymish, ensuring the rebel Cossack leader's entry into the exclusive club of East European rulers.

Further tests of strength with the Commonwealth, such as the indecisive Battle of Zhvanets (1653), obliged Khmelnytsky to seek protection from a stronger power. Although the Ottoman sultan first emerged as a possible protector of the Cossack polity, it was the tsar of Muscovy to whom the Cossack elite swore its allegiance at the Pereiaslav Council in January 1654. Not only was the tsar of the same Orthodox faith as the Cossacks, but he was also prepared (unlike the Muslim sultan) to commit his forces to war with the Commonwealth. The military success of the allied Muscovite-Cossack forces exceeded all expectations. They took away from the Commonwealth not only most of present-day Ukraine and Belarus but also the capital of the Grand Duchy of Lithuania, Vilnius, and a significant part of its territory. As Protestant Sweden and Transylvania entered the war, invading the Commonwealth from the north and south, and Lithuanian Protestant magnates joined their coreligionists, the once mighty Polish-Lithuanian state found itself on the brink of collapse – the ultimate goal of Cossack foreign policy of the time.

It was here that the interests of the Cossack hetman and the Muscovite tsar diverged. The former wanted the complete defeat of the old Cossack enemy, while the latter feared the unchecked strengthening of Swedish power in the region and signed an armistice with the Commonwealth in 1656 against the advice of his Cossack allies. Khmelnytsky sought an alliance with Sweden and Transylvania, undermining if not violating his agreement of 1654 with Moscow. His death in 1657 delayed the Cossack breach with the tsar, but it occurred in 1658 under his successor, Hetman Ivan Vyhovsky. The latter signed the Union of Hadiach with Poland, which positioned Cossack Ukraine as a third partner in the Commonwealth (along with Poland and Lithuania). The deal was rejected by most of the Cossack elite, which resented the very idea of returning to Polish control, while Muscovy opposed it with military force. Vyhovsky's brief hetmancy (1657–9) thus initiated a new round of Muscovite-Polish wars over Ukraine that saw the Cossacks themselves fighting one another under different banners, led by contending hetmans.[1]

What was Hrushevsky's interpretation of that crucial period of Ukrainian history, and how was it related to his general view of the Ukrainian and Russian past? I shall address these questions by considering the interrelation of the two most prominent discourses, populist and national, in Hrushevsky's writing. My discussion will begin with an analysis of the last ('Soviet') volumes of Hrushevsky's *History*, but the evolution of his views and interpretations over the years, especially as a result of the 1917 revolution, will also be taken into account. Hrushevsky was involved in research and writing on the Khmelnytsky era for most of his career, beginning with his essay of 1898 on Bohdan Khmelnytsky and his era and concluding with the publication of book 2 of volume 9 of the *History of Ukraine-Rus'* in 1931. One could hardly choose a topic that better demonstrates the evolution of his historical views and political sympathies over more than three decades of scholarly research. The subject also affords a unique opportunity to consider the interrelation between such elements of historical writing as evidence, research, and paradigm in the unmaking of imperial narratives and the construction of national ones.

The Revolution

In volume 9 of his *History*, Hrushevsky went so far as to state that the Khmelnytsky era was 'the most important epoch in the life of our people and the greatest revolution that it experienced.'[2] Was this his way of comparing the 'Ukrainian revolution' under Khmelnytsky with the one that he and all of Ukrainian society had just experienced? It is hard to tell, but there is reason to believe that the revolutionary epoch Hrushevsky was living through contributed significantly to his interpretation of the Khmelnytsky Uprising as a Ukrainian revolution. As an avowed positivist and historical sociologist, Hrushevsky believed in the evolutionary development of society from lower to higher forms of organization. For him, evolution was the way of social progress, but there was also a place for revolutions in this scheme. They could accelerate progress but not replace the evolutionary process.[3]

The application of the term 'revolution' to the Khmelnytsky Uprising was not Hrushevsky's invention, as it had figured in writings on the Khmelnytsky era at least since the early 1890s. In 1891 Hrushevsky's one-time fellow student Antin Syniavsky characterized the Khmelnytsky Uprising as 'a great popular revolution under the leadership of Bohdan that almost toppled Poland, but produced no actual results owing to lack of consciousness and political development.'[4] The term was also used in 1892 by the Polish scholar Tadeusz Korzon, who was very critical of the uprising,[5] as well by the dean of the Ukrainian populist school and Hrushevsky's professor, Volodymyr Antonovych, who took a positive view of it. In his lectures of 1895–6 on the history of the Ukrainian Cossacks, Antonovych compared the Khmelnytsky Uprising with 'revolutionary movements' in England and Naples. Taking issue with Polish historians who represented Khmelnytsky's personal grievances as the main cause of the uprising, Antonovych stated in his privately delivered lectures: 'A single individual cannot cause a revolution. The popular masses as a whole must be wronged for all of them to respond to one man's call for an uprising.'[6]

Apparently, Hrushevsky used the term 'revolution' for the first time in his essay of 1898 on Khmelnytsky and his era.[7] In the essay, Hrushevsky compared the significance of the Khmelnytsky Uprising to that of the French Revolution, asserting that the uprising had resulted in a 'radical social revolution' that took place independently of the wishes or even contrary to the intentions of the leaders of the uprising.[8] Hrushevsky made no specific comment on his understanding of the term 'revolution,' but it is clear from the context that, following in Antonovych's footsteps, he viewed it as a social upheaval and, more specifically, an uprising of the popular masses. In 1898 he termed it one of the most important outcomes of the Khmelnytsky era. For the next two decades, however, when returning to the subject in his writings, Hrushevsky not only did not develop his interpretation of the Khmelnytsky Uprising as a social revolution but virtually abandoned the term altogether. It recurred occasionally in volume 8 of the *History* (written between 1909 and 1917), but its use there lacked any system or consistency.[9]

During the decades in which Hrushevsky preferred to eschew the term 'revolution,' it was often employed by his future rival, but at that time his admirer and close associate Viacheslav Lypynsky. 'Revolution' even occurred in the title of one of the two major historical studies that Lypynsky published in 1912. Titled 'Two Moments in the History of Postrevolutionary Ukraine,' it appeared in a Polish-language collection of articles and source materials, *From the History of Ukraine*. There Lypynsky presented a number of views on the history of the Khmelnytsky Uprising that were later picked up and developed by members of the new statist trend in Ukrainian historiography. The author himself considered this study important enough to be translated from Polish into Ukrainian and published in revised form under the title *Ukraine at the Turning Point* (1920). In its new version, the work became a bible of the statist school.[10]

Like Hrushevsky, Lypynsky believed in the extraordinary importance of the Khmelnytsky Uprising. In his study of the Cossack colonel Mykhailo Krychevsky (Lypynsky's other major monograph, published as part of *From the History of Ukraine*), Lypynsky maintained that the Khmelnytsky Uprising was a revolution whose 'power and extent surpassed anything witnessed by contemporary Europe.'[11] Lypynsky clearly used the term 'revolution' to denote the 'uprising of the Ukrainian people' of 1648–9, which was in keeping with Hrushevsky's interpretation of revolution as a social upheaval. There were, nevertheless, important differences between Hrushevsky and Lypynsky in the interpretation of the 'Khmelnytsky revolution.' First of all, they differed on its chronology. If Hrushevsky saw it as an outcome of the Khmelnytsky era in general, Lypynsky limited it to the first two years of the uprising, treating it as a phenomenon that ended with the Treaty of Zboriv (1649). According to Lypynsky, after 1649 the 'revolutionary energy of the popular masses' was profoundly weakened as the Khmelnytsky revolt lost the characteristics of a social struggle.[12] Lypynsky viewed the revolution as 'a spontaneous upheaval (*przewrót*) carried out by the nation under the leadership of a titanic individual.'[13] Thus Lypynsky accorded Khmelnytsky a role of extraordinary importance in the whole revolutionary process. In his essay of 1898, Hrushevsky also used the term 'upheaval' (*perevorot*) to denote the Khmelnytsky Uprising but clearly limited its meaning to the political sphere, consequently excluding Khmelnytsky and his associates from the revolutionary process, which Hrushevsky defined predominantly in populist terms.

The Revolution of 1917 placed Hrushevsky and Lypynsky in opposite political camps and had an enduring impact on their historical writings. The most dramatic change occurred in Lypynsky's views and political beliefs. Emerging at the time of the Ukrainian Revolution as the most eloquent proponent of Ukrainian monarchism and a strong supporter of Hetman Pavlo Skoropadsky's political regime, which was established in 1918, Lypynsky felt a strong enmity toward the leaders and members of Ukrainian revolutionary parties, who worshipped the popular masses and revolution as an instrument of social liberation. The term 'revolution,' which Lypynsky had previously promoted, suddenly became a dirty word in his lexicon.

Lypynsky's new views were fully reflected in his postrevolutionary historical writings.[14] Telling in this regard is the change in the title of his historical study of 1912, 'Two Moments in the History of Postrevolutionary Ukraine': the Ukrainian-language version of 1912 was renamed *Ukraine at the Turning Point*. The term 'revolution' was thus eliminated from the title. Lypynsky still associated the Khmelnytsky Uprising with the 'great upheaval' (*velykyi perevorot*) of 1648–9 but generally referred to the events of those years as an 'uprising,' not a 'revolution.' The reference to the Khmelnytsky era as a revolution that surpassed anything witnessed by contemporary Europe was dropped from the text. Instead, the Khmelnytsky Uprising was characterized in more ambiguous terms, as a revolution 'started by a hundred fanatics at the moment of the seemingly complete downfall of the nation.' The reference in the 1912 edition to the declining 'revolutionary energy of the popular masses' was replaced in the new version with a comment on the declining 'participation of the Ukrainian peasantry in the uprising.' Thus the word 'revolution' was almost completely weeded out of the text, as were positive references to the participation of the masses in the revolt.[15]

The impact of the 1917 revolution on Hrushevsky's writings was quite different. In volume 9 of the *History*, especially its concluding chapter, Hrushevsky used the term 'revolution' more than in all his previous writings on this subject combined. The phenomenon referred to as the 'great uprising' or 'liberation struggle' in Hrushevsky's earlier studies was now termed a 'revolution.' The crucial role of the Zboriv Agreement in his account of the uprising now acquired a new justification as Hrushevsky observed that the 'arc of the revolution was broken at Zboriv.'[16] Hrushevsky also extended his comparison of the Khmelnytsky Uprising from the German Reformation and the French Revolution (parallels cited in his essay of 1898) to the Puritan Revolution of the mid-seventeenth century. He clearly welcomed the revolution as a liberation of the popular masses, despite all the tragedy and devastation that it entailed. Hrushevsky's fascination with the phenomenon of social revolution is clearly apparent in his interpretation of the diary of Paul of Aleppo, a Syrian Orthodox cleric who travelled in Ukraine in 1654 and 1656. Hrushevsky had already cited Paul of Aleppo's description of Ukraine in his essay of 1898 as evidence of the high level of education among the Ukrainian population at the time. In volume 9 of his academic *History*, Hrushevsky took another approach to the interpretation of the same source. He now followed Aleksandra Efimenko's reading of the diary as an eyewitness account of the gains achieved by the Ukrainian popular masses once they had freed themselves from the social and national oppression of the pre-Khmelnytsky era.[17]

Commenting on Paul of Aleppo's account of Ukrainian life in 1654 and 1656, Hrushevsky wrote: 'As a representative of a people oppressed for centuries, Paul had an extraordinarily intense feeling for the splendour of this heroic age in the life of the Ukrainian people: the pathos of revolution, the popular uprising, and the struggle for liberation, full of sacrifice, self-renunciation, and idealism. To the Poles and those looking through their prism, as well as to the Muslims and Muscovites (who nevertheless supported the Cossacks for political reasons), both the Cossacks and the Ukrainian masses in general were still nothing more than rebellious slaves, regardless of all their acts of heroism, military prowess, etc. But in the eyes of this uncultured Arab, they were bearers of the noblest human qualities, fighters for the dream of liberation, dearest to every individual. With delight he breathed this atmosphere of freedom, acutely aware of the tragic nature of this ephemeral balance between the enjoyment of liberty and the price of death to be paid for it, as well as the other horrors of war and captivity. His observations on the subject of the joy of liberation and the sacrifices with which it was purchased often show surprisingly keen awareness, so that the present-day reader is deeply moved. Such immediate enthusiasm is not to be found even in the Ukrainian literature. Paul's account in no way resembles the sour reflections of some Eyewitness or other, who peevishly tallies the number of windowpanes smashed in the course of this great conflagration.'[18]

For Hrushevsky, the term 'revolution' was associated first and foremost with the idea of liberation. Whether it took place in the seventeenth or the twentieth century, revolution was supposed to bring deliverance from social and national oppression. The social component in Hrushevsky's treatment of revolution, which comes across very clearly in his essay of 1898, also remained dominant in his Soviet-era writings. At the same time, Hrushevsky's treatment of revolution was much broader in 1920 than it had been in the 1890s. On the one hand, in Hrushevsky's opinion, the revolution was still the achievement of the 'Revolutionary Ukrainian People,' and the leadership of the uprising headed by Khmelnytsky was still viewed as having 'no desire for that revolution' and 'completely incapable of calculating its importance and consequences.'[19] On the other hand, the revolution was no longer completely divorced from Khmelnytsky and his associates. They were now represented as its leaders. Khmelnytsky was portrayed as the first leader to 'assemble the accumulated and as yet untouched resources of revolutionary energy.'[20] Unlike Lypynsky, Hrushevsky did not limit the revolution to the first two years of the uprising. To be sure, he maintained that the 'arc of the revolution was broken at Zboriv,' but that did not mark its end. He counted 1651 as the fourth year of the revolution[21] and used that term to define the whole epoch associated with Khmelnytsky. In Hrushevsky's eyes, Khmelnytsky was directly associated with the great victories of the '"springtime" of the Ukrainian revolution,'[22] and it was at the time of the hetman's death in 1657 that the 'terrible ruin and collapse of the Ukrainian revolution' became fully apparent.[23]

Another change in Hrushevsky's interpretation of revolution was his treatment of it as a creative factor. In the introduction to volume 9 of the *History*, Hrushevsky still used the term 'upheaval' (as in his essay of 1898) to define the change in the balance of international forces brought about by the Khmelnytsky Uprising,[24] but he also defined that change as an 'immense revolution that became the foundation of a New Ukraine and served to redraw the map of Eastern Europe.'[25] Commenting on Khmelnytsky's introduction of the subject of Ukrainian liberties in his negotiations with the Muscovite delegation at Pereiaslav in 1654, Hrushevsky wrote: 'In the given case it [the theme of the liberties] apparently signified the preservation of all the political and socio-economic gains of the Ukrainian revolution: Ukrainian statehood, citizenship, and economic privileges, the whole political and social system of Ukrainian life.'[26] For him it was as much a question of the creation of a new system as of the destruction of the old one.

There is little doubt that Hrushevsky's experience of the Ukrainian Revolution of 1917 affected his understanding of revolution in general and the Khmelnytsky-era revolution in particular. Hrushevsky's reference to the Khmelnytsky-era revolution as one that laid the groundwork for a New Ukraine was reminiscent of his pamphlet of 1918 that discussed the pressing problems and future of the contemporary Ukrainian Revolution and was titled *On the Threshold of a New Ukraine*.[27] Hrushevsky's treatment of the Khmelnytsky-era revolution became more inclusive and acquired clear national characteristics. As a rule, it emerges in volume 9 of the *History* not only as a 'great' revolution but also as a 'Ukrainian' one.[28]

Thus, following the events of 1917, Hrushevsky's use of the term 'revolution,' which was relatively rare in his pre-1917 writings, expanded immensely. Revolutionary discourse captivated the minds of Hrushevsky's contemporaries, and he himself, an outstanding leader of the Ukrainian Revolution, began to use the term more and more, not only in his political writings but also in his historical works. Hrushevsky's new interest in revolutions not only reflected his leftward drift during the Revolution of 1917 but also demonstrated the power of revolutionary discourse in the USSR. Hrushevsky's adherence to that discourse clearly helped bring about the separation of the Russian and Ukrainian narratives. Given Soviet conditions in the 1920s, endowing the Ukrainian historical narrative with a great revolution of its own was a significant way to legitimize it and establish Ukrainian history as a separate process that did not depend for its development on revolutionary impulses from Russia.

The Nation

In his writings on national issues, Hrushevsky generally avoided the term *natsiia*, preferring to speak of the *narod*. (Depending on context, the English 'nation' may be rendered by the Ukrainian *narod* or *natsiia*.)[29] In

Ukrainian political thought of the early twentieth century, there were two competing approaches to the use of the terms *natsiia* and *narod*. Writing in 1923, Stanislav Dnistriansky, Hrushevsky's former colleague at Lviv University, claimed that *natsiia* and *narod* denoted the same phenomenon and could be used interchangeably.[30] A different approach to the problem was taken by Dnistriansky's one-time subordinate Volodymyr Starosolsky. In his *Theory of the Nation* (1921), Starosolsky reserved the term *natsiia* for the modern national community, characterizing it as a product of the nineteenth century or, as he put it, 'the new era of history.'[31]

Hrushevsky presented his views on the issue in a series of pamphlets issued in 1917 to explain the history and goals of the Ukrainian movement to the general public. In the pamphlet *Who the Ukrainians Are and What They Want*, Hrushevsky developed a scheme according to which the Ukrainian nation had passed through a number of distinctive stages in its historical development. It began its history as an ethnos (*narodnist'*), then became a people (*narod*), and finally evolved into a nation (*natsiia*). Hrushevsky wrote in that regard: 'We have travelled our path of great struggle for freedom and equality, which other Rus' [East Slavic] ethnic groups have not known. Along that path, we were fully formed as the Ukrainian people, and current events are completing its transformation into the Ukrainian nation.'[32] In another pamphlet of 1917, *Where the Ukrainian Movement Came From and Where It Is Going*, Hrushevsky proposed a somewhat different hierarchy of these same terms and introduced a new one, *natsional'nist'* (nationality). He wrote that the era of Kyivan Rus' had laid the foundations for the unification of Ukrainian tribes into 'one people, one national body.' After the Khmelnytsky Uprising, the Ukrainian ethnos managed to distinguish itself completely from the Belarusian one. 'Then,' wrote Hrushevsky, 'the literary and political revival that began at the end of the eighteenth century led to the further development of the Ukrainian ethnos (*narodnist'*) into a true nationality (*natsional'nist'*) and has been completed by the contemporary political movement.'[33]

Whatever the inconsistencies in Hrushevsky's use of 'national' terminology, he believed in the historical continuity of the Ukrainian people. Regarding the Ukrainian national character as a phenomenon shaped by the Ukrainian historical experience, he was prepared to seek the origins of national identity as far back as the mid-seventeenth century. In his introduction to volume 9, Hrushevsky wrote that 'the new movement initiated by the sixteenth-century reawakening found its further development in that epoch. What in time was to become the *Ukrainian nation (natsiia)* was forged in that era.'[34] While avoiding the use of *natsiia* with reference to the early modern period of Ukrainian history, Hrushevsky discussed issues of national consciousness and identity at length, freely using the term 'national' (*natsional'nyi*).

As early as 1898, in his first essay on Khmelnytsky and his era, Hrushevsky discussed the role of the national factor in the Khmelnytsky Uprising. He believed that the development of the uprising had awakened the national consciousness of contemporary Ukrainians and that the whole movement, which he treated predominantly as a social and economic phenomenon, had acquired a substantial national colouring as it turned into a struggle of the oppressed Ruthenian strata against the Polish regime. It was also a time, according to Hrushevsky, in which the idea of a political entity encompassing the whole ethnic territory of Ukraine-Rus' came to the fore.[35] Hrushevsky was disappointed that instead of positing the achievement of social and national ideals as the goal of the uprising, its leaders gave the movement a religious (Orthodox) colouring.[36]

The notion that Ukrainian identity was awakened by the Khmelnytsky Uprising was not Hrushevsky's invention and can be encountered in the writings of leaders of the Ukrainian movement from the 1870s on. In his foreword to the first issue of the journal *Hromada* (Community, 1878), Mykhailo Drahomanov indicated the period of Cossackdom's greatest strength, between the Khmelnytsky Uprising of 1648 and the destruction of the Zaporozhian Sich after Mazepa's insurgency of 1709, as the time when 'awareness was growing among our people that they were a separate breed, whatever the state to which they were subject or even [differences] in faith itself.'[37] Ivan Franko, writing in 1895, suggested that Ukrainian 'national feeling' first became apparent at the end of the sixteenth century but noted that Ukrainian national consciousness (*ukraïns'ka svidomist' narodna*) manifested itself for the first time among the popular masses between 1648 and 1709.[38] The leaders of the Ukrainian cultural and political movement were convinced that it was Cossackdom that had given birth to modern Ukrainian national identity, but few professional historians were prepared to support that claim with scholarly arguments.

While Volodymyr Antonovych had presented the Ukrainian masses and the Cossacks, led by the officer stratum, as the main actors of the period, he had generally avoided any specific discussion of the national question in his lectures on the history of Cossackdom.[39] As was often the case, it fell to Hrushevsky to carry out that task. He gave a full account of his views on the role of the national factor in the Khmelnytsky Uprising in his discussion of its causes in volume 8 of his academic *History*. At the time of his work on the volume, Hrushevsky believed much more strongly in the importance of the national factor in Ukrainian history in general and in the Khmelnytsky Uprising in particular than at any previous point in his scholarly career. In his discussion of the causes of the uprising, Hrushevsky treated the national factor as a combination of political, economic, social, religious, and cultural elements. 'In pure, abstract form, this national element was scarcely apparent as a cause of the uprising and an agitational motif,' wrote Hrushevsky. 'However, it suffused all these instances of humiliation and injustice done to the Ukrainian element on various levels and from various viewpoints, sharpening their sting and painfulness and linking them into a single chain and a single image of the bitter enslavement of the Ukrainian people, an enslavement that was crying out for vengeance.'[40]

In discussing the role of the national factor in shaping the agenda of the uprising, Hrushevsky emphasized the ideas expressed by Khmelnytsky in his talks with the Polish commissioners in Pereiaslav in early 1649. On that occasion, Khmelnytsky spoke of his commitment to liberate the whole Rus' nation from the Polish yoke. This episode attracted Hrushevsky's special attention very early in his scholarly career, although there were profound differences in the way he treated Khmelnytsky's statements in 1898 and in 1909–17. In his first essay on the Khmelnytsky era, the young Hrushevsky interpreted Khmelnytsky's words as mere dreams, largely influenced by the religiously inspired thinking of the Cossack elites, which were unable to base the Cossack movement on a firm social and national foundation. In volume 8 of his academic *History*, Hrushevsky viewed the 1649 episode in a very different light. Now he treated Khmelnytsky's words as a manifestation of the future plans of the hetman and his entourage. In the second part of the volume (written between 1911 and 1915), Hrushevsky wrote: 'It is no wonder, then, that very quickly – just as soon as the war had unfolded on an appropriate scale, having drawn in great masses of the Ukrainian population and society, its ultimate goal emerged from behind particular reckonings and demands and was apprehended as a synthesis of these particular demands – the national liberation of Rus' ... Early in 1649 Khmelnytsky spoke quite unequivocally about the liberation of the "entire Ruthenian people" and of his "state," and this true nature of the Ukrainian-Polish struggle seemed entirely clear to its outside observers as well.'[41] Hrushevsky's interpretation of the Khmelnytsky era as a period of national and religious liberation shared important elements with the traditional interpretation of the epoch in Russian imperial historiography. Hrushevsky, though, treated the war as a struggle not for the liberation of the Rus'/Russian people from the Polish yoke but for the national and social liberation of the Ukrainian people. He now regarded the Orthodox element as a component not of Russian but of Ukrainian national consciousness and tradition, while the social aspect was closely linked to the predominantly peasant character of the Ukrainian nation at the time of the uprising.

Did Hrushevsky's views on the role of the national factor in the Khmelnytsky Uprising change as a result of the revolution? Was he still as enthusiastic about the role of the national factor in the uprising? There is no simple answer to these questions. On the one hand, in the Soviet-era volumes of the *History*, it is difficult to find examples of Hrushevsky's advocacy of the importance of the national factor in the uprising as passionate as those in volume 8. On the other hand, Hrushevsky's attention was now more than ever preoccupied with manifestations of national identity. In the introduction to volume 9, Hrushevsky wrote that he had paid special attention to all manifestations of Ukrainian national consciousness and was very glad that the new materials collected for the book included such examples.[42] In the last volumes of his magnum opus, Hrushevsky no longer had to prove the mere fact of the presence of a Ukrainian political and cultural agenda in the actions of the leaders of the uprising and its rank-and-file participants. Once the insurgency succeeded and the Ukrainian Cossacks created a polity of their own, the Hetmanate became the natural object of Hrushevsky's attention, bringing an end to his constant search for the ever-changing focal point of Ukrainian national history.

As in his pre-1917 writings, in the Soviet-era volumes of the *History* Hrushevsky narrated the history of the Ukrainian nation against the background of the histories of other nations of the region. In Hrushevsky's historical narrative, Ukraine's 'other' was represented by its immediate neighbours – the Russians, Poles, and Belarusians. The latter attracted Hrushevsky's particular sympathy as the ethnos that had shared the hardships of Polish and Muscovite rule with the Ukrainians. Hrushevsky admitted the existence of an undivided Ukrainian-Belarusian identity in the mid-seventeenth century but clearly treated the Belarusians as a separate entity and paid relatively little attention to

Cossack activities in Belarus. Although after 1654 the Cossacks showed much more interest in gaining control over some parts of Belarus than over Western Ukraine, Hrushevsky always treated Cossack involvement in Western Ukraine with more interest and animation than Cossack actions in and policy toward Belarus. As a national historian, primarily interested in Ukrainians and their ethnic territory, Hrushevsky paid special attention to historical efforts to bring all Ukrainian ethnic territories within the boundaries of a single state.[43]

Very different from Hrushevsky's attitude toward the Belarusians was his treatment of Ukraine's eastern neighbours, the Russians. Although Hrushevsky was critical of attempts to present Ukraine and Ukrainians as helpless victims of the 'evil' Muscovites, he found it difficult, especially in his popular and political writings, to avoid that tendency altogether. The interesting feature of Hrushevsky's writings on the subject is his application of the 'civilizational' argument against the 'colonizer.' Hrushevsky made use of the 'West-East' and 'Europe-Asia' dyads, in which the West and Europe served as indicators of positive values, while the East and Asia were associated with negative ones, to attack the imperial nation. In this system of coordinates, Ukrainians were presented as much closer to Western and European values than Russians.

This approach to the history of Russo-Ukrainian relations was expressed most clearly in Hrushevsky's essay 'Our Western Orientation' (1918). There he presented what actually amounted to a new scheme of Ukrainian history, placing special emphasis on the role played by the Varangians in the history of Kyivan Rus' and presenting Muscovy as the principal heir to the Byzantine tradition of Rus', while claiming that after the decline of the Kyivan state, Ukrainians developed mainly under the influence of practices and ideas coming from the West.[44] This essay was written after the Bolshevik invasion of Ukraine in January 1918 and the subsequent German takeover in the spring of the same year. Hrushevsky never developed this approach to the history of Ukraine in his later works, although his 'Western orientation' clearly manifested itself in the Soviet-era volumes of the *History*. There Hrushevsky not only referred to the Cossack officers as representatives of Western culture, while characterizing Muscovite officials as barbarians, but also indicated Ukraine's limited participation in the cultural life of the Catholic and Protestant worlds as one of the major shortcomings of its history.[45]

In volume 9 of the *History*, which covered the Khmelnytsky era from

1650 to 1657, Hrushevsky devoted special attention to the Council of Pereiaslav and the Cossack-Muscovite agreement of 1654 – a crucial juncture in Russo-Ukrainian relations at which the two historical narratives merged. There, Hrushevsky continued the line established in his political writings of 1917. As in his pamphlet of that year, *Where the Ukrainian Movement Came From and Where It Is Going*, Hrushevsky claimed that at the time of Pereiaslav Ukraine was in fact an independent state with a political structure of its own. He also wrote that the Muscovite government tolerated the de facto independence of the hetman's state, but only as a temporary phenomenon.[46] Surveying the works of his predecessors, Hrushevsky sided with Mykola Kostomarov against Gennadii Karpov in claiming that the Pereiaslav negotiations had in fact resulted in an agreement between the two parties, not merely in the subjection of the Cossack polity to the Muscovite tsar, as Karpov maintained.[47] The issue of whether there was a treaty or not had clear political ramifications, since a positive answer to this question allowed Ukrainian activists to advance their claim that the Muscovite authorities had violated the Pereiaslav Agreement, thereby releasing Ukraine from any obligation to Moscow.

The origins of the argument go back to the political demands put forward by the Cossack officers in the late seventeenth and, most particularly, the eighteenth century. In the early nineteenth century, the idea that Cossack rights had been guaranteed by the Russo-Ukrainian agreement of 1654 was popularized by the author of the *History of the Rus'*, but the first to introduce it into modern Ukrainian political discourse was Mykola Mikhnovsky in his *Independent Ukraine* (1900).[48] In it he argued that Russia had violated Ukraine's rights as granted to Khmelnytsky at Pereiaslav and called for the restoration of Ukrainian statehood. Mikhnovsky's legalistic and basically ahistorical approach initially did not impress either Ukrainian historians or the leaders of the Ukrainian political and cultural movement, who were also unmoved by his advocacy of Ukrainian independence. In 1917, though, the situation changed dramatically. Not only did the idea of independence find spokesmen and gain unprecedented popularity by the end of the year, but even the purism of professional historians gave way to the demands of the moment.[49] Under these circumstances, Hrushevsky's contemporaries looked to him to explain to the general public the significance of the Council of Pereiaslav for the history of Russian-Ukrainian relations in general and Ukrainian demands for autonomy in particular. To meet these demands, Hrushevsky published a brochure on the Pereiaslav

Agreement in 1917[50] and discussed the issue in his other contemporary writings on the history and political goals of the Ukrainian movement.[51]

Hrushevsky's view of the effect of the Pereiaslav Agreement on Ukraine's status evolved over time. If initially he considered Ukraine an autonomous entity that wanted to preserve its 'full autonomy' under the rule of the Muscovite tsars, later, during and after the revolution, he viewed it as a polity enjoying de facto independence. If at first Hrushevsky believed that the Muscovite authorities wanted to reduce Ukraine's legal status within the Muscovite tsardom to the level of an ordinary province, refusing to guarantee it even rights of 'provincial autonomy,' later he claimed that the tsarist authorities could not have had any such plans, given Ukraine's de facto independence prior to the agreement.[52] In the last volumes of the *History*, Hrushevsky also revised his earlier view of the legal nature of the Pereiaslav Agreement. If in his prerevolutionary writings he accepted the opinion of the Russian legal scholar Vasilii Sergeevich, who saw the Pereiaslav Agreement as an act establishing a personal union, now, after the revolution, he interpreted the agreement as one that established a Muscovite protectorate over Ukraine. Hrushevsky also referred to the Pereiaslav Agreement as a temporary military union, an arrangement that implied the equal status of both parties.[53]

Despite these and some other inconsistencies and contradictions in Hrushevsky's treatment of the Pereiaslav Agreement, which were all but inevitable in works written over a span of more than thirty years, it is quite clear that there was one guiding principle underlying all his writings on the issue. Consistent in treating the Pereiaslav arrangement as a diplomatic agreement, Hrushevsky objected to the teleological view of that agreement as a turning point in Ukrainian history. He rejected the approach to the agreement adopted by proponents of the idea of all-Russian unity. He also criticized Viacheslav Lypynsky's view of it as a turning point in Ukraine's struggle against Poland and an important step on its path toward independence. For Hrushevsky, the Pereiaslav Agreement suited the immediate needs of Khmelnytsky's administration in late 1653 and early 1654; at the time of its conclusion it did not differ very much from the formal acceptance of the Ottoman protectorate a few years earlier. Hrushevsky believed that the useful life of the Pereiaslav Agreement was about to expire at the time of Khmelnytsky's death and clearly ended under Vyhovsky as a result of the Union of Hadiach (1658) with the Polish-Lithuanian Commonwealth.[54]

Hrushevsky's treatment of the hetmancy of Ivan Vyhovsky in the last volume of his *History* gives a good idea of his changing interpretation of the role played in Ukrainian history by Ukraine's western neighbours, the Poles. Hrushevsky devoted many pages of his writings to challenging the historiographic tradition that treated Polish rule over Ukrainian territories in terms of a Polish 'civilizing mission.'[55] He not only welcomed the anti-Polish uprising of 1648 but also gave the most damning characterization of the Poles and their policies in Ukraine. Nevertheless, in the last volumes of the *History* one hardly feels the same anti-Polish animus as in its earlier volumes. From 1654 Cossack Ukraine had to fight on two fronts, against Poland and Muscovy, with the latter emerging as the main threat to Ukraine's interests. Hrushevsky therefore became reluctant to grant unconditional support to any anti-Polish initiative in the Cossack ranks. That was the case in his account of the decision of the Cossack officer council in the spring of 1655 to renew hostilities with the Polish-Lithuanian Commonwealth. Considering that shift in Khmelnytsky's policy to be the result of the victory of antinobiliary and anti-Polish circles in the Cossack administration, Hrushevsky did not welcome it. He considered the new course erroneous, believing that it would have been much more beneficial for Ukraine if the Hetmanate had continued its balancing act between Moscow and Warsaw.[56]

Also devoid of strong anti-Polish sentiment was Hrushevsky's interpretation of the Union of Hadiach, which was supposed to return Cossack Ukraine to Polish rule. Hrushevsky offered no serious criticism of the union's author, Ivan Vyhovsky, apparently because of the latter's attempt to break the Hetmanate's ties with Moscow. But even that rationale did not, in Hrushevsky's opinion, justify the renewed subordination of Ukraine to Poland, and while Vyhovsky himself was spared serious criticism, his brainchild, the Union of Hadiach, was not. Hrushevsky in fact parted ways with the long-established tradition, represented in both Polish and Ukrainian historiography, of praising if not the results of the Union of Hadiach, then the intentions of its instigators. In Ukrainian historiography, Hrushevsky saw manifestations of these tendencies in the writings of Mykola Kostomarov, as well as Volodymyr Antonovych and his students.[57] Rejecting this tradition, Hrushevsky sided instead with the views first expressed by Vasyl Vovk-Karachevsky, who blamed the authors of the agreement for neglecting the interests of the common people.

Hrushevsky's discussion of the Union of Hadiach comprised many elements of both populist and national discourse. In accordance with the principles of populist historiography, Hrushevsky interpreted the union as a response of the Cossack officers to the actions of the democratic elements of the Zaporozhian Host. He maintained that if the latter turned for support to Muscovy in their struggle with the officers, the Cossack officers made common cause with their erstwhile Polish enemies in an attempt to secure their social prerogatives within the social order of the Commonwealth.[58] Hrushevsky believed that the idea of basing the future Ukrainian state on the nobility resulted from the Cossack officers' attempts to take control of the Western Ukrainian territories, where Cossackdom as such had very little social support. To be sure, Hrushevsky welcomed the idea of uniting all Ukrainian ethnic territories within a single state, but considered it 'a great irony that it was precisely the western provinces that were torn out of the Grand Duchy of Rus' in the final version of the Treaty of Hadiach.'[59]

Thus Hrushevsky's critique of the Union of Hadiach was not limited to a condemnation of its antipopular character but proceeded to expose its shortcomings from the viewpoint of Ukrainian national interests. The critique of the Union of Hadiach for the failure of its instigators to take account of the interests of the peasantry and to include all of Ukraine's ethnic territories in the projected Grand Duchy of Rus' was initially voiced by Hrushevsky in his essay of 1898 on the Khmelnytsky era.[60] More than thirty years later, in the last volume of the *History*, Hrushevsky reinstated this interpretation of the Hadiach Agreement, thereby siding with Viacheslav Lypynsky, who in his study 'Two Moments in the History of Postrevolutionary Ukraine' (1912) declared the Union of Hadiach a setback for the territorial expansion of the Cossack state, its international relations, the authority of its leader, and the status of Cossackdom as a whole.[61] In Hrushevsky's interpretation, the Zaporozhian Host's opposition to the Union of Hadiach represented a case in which the interests of the popular masses coincided with those of the Ukrainian nation and state.

While treating the Russians and Poles as 'others' in opposition to whom Ukrainian national identity could be constructed, Hrushevsky was extremely critical, especially in the last volumes of the *History*, of any elements of Cossack politics that showed intolerance toward national and religious minorities in the Hetmanate. In his concluding remarks to volume 9 of the *History*, he severely criticized Khmelnytsky and his associates for their simplistic majoritarian approach to the restoration of Ukrainian national rights in the aftermath of their victories over the Commonwealth. He wrote in that regard: 'What a domi-

nant role is played here by purely mechanical methods: to destroy
Roman Catholic and Jewish shrines, expel not only clerics but even
adherents of other faiths, and not admit any priests, Catholic monks, or
Jews into Ukraine.'[62] This criticism of the Cossack administration may
have been provoked at least in part by Hrushevsky's own bitter experience of the first months of 1918, when he was unable to stop the
Ukrainian masses from engaging in anti-Polish and anti-Jewish attacks
and pogroms. But that could be only a partial explanation of his attitude. Even before the revolution, Hrushevsky had treated the plight of
the Jews in 1648 with great sympathy. In volume 8 of the *History*, he
critically analysed contemporary accounts of Jewish persecution of the
Ukrainian peasantry as a cause of the uprising, noting with regard to a
Polish account: 'The particular emphasis placed on the role of the Jews
among the various causes of the resentment of the Ukrainian people is
highly typical of the seventeenth-century anti-Semitism shared by Polish nobiliary and Ukrainian Cossack circles alike.'[63] Hrushevsky also
maintained that the Jewish writer Nathan Hanover, a contemporary of
the uprising, understood its social and national causes much better than
the Cossack author of the Eyewitness Chronicle.[64]

As in Hrushevsky's political activities, so in his historical writings the
Ukrainian national agenda was clearly incompatible with anti-Semitism
or the persecution of minorities, whether the initiators and perpetrators
were Polish, Russian, or Ukrainian. This attitude became even stronger
in Hrushevsky's writings after the Revolution of 1917.

The question that most attracted Hrushevsky's attention in the
Soviet-era volumes of the *History* was that of national unity or, more
specifically, the issue of the elites' responsibility for maintaining a united
front with the popular masses. His treatment of the question was most
probably informed by his experience as a leader of the Ukrainian Revolution. Hrushevsky formulated the set of problems that now preoccupied him as follows: 'As representatives of Cossackdom, how did
members of the ruling Cossack officer stratum understand their role?
To what degree did they govern themselves in their activities according
to their class interests and to what degree did they consciously establish
an aristocratic Ukrainian stratum? In so doing, did they take account,
and to what extent, of the interests of the whole people, the state, the
political independence and the national autonomy of the Ukrainian
people? Also, was the Khmelnytsky era at least to some degree a
national epos, as it appeared for centuries to the Ukrainian Cossack
officers, the Ukrainian intelligentsia, and even the popular masses?'[65]

These questions became especially important to Hrushevsky after the Revolution of 1917, but they were also present in his prerevolutionary writings. The following sections of this chapter trace the development of Hrushevsky's views on the main elements of his national equation: the role of the national leader, masses, elites, and the state.

The Hero

From the historiographic viewpoint, Hrushevsky's polemics with Lypynsky constitute the most interesting and intellectually provocative part of volume 9 – the longest volume of the *History of Ukraine-Rus'*. Hrushevsky organized the concluding chapter of that volume around his polemics with Lypynsky on the role of Bohdan Khmelnytsky in Ukrainian history.[66] He rejected Lypynsky's neoromantic view of Khmelnytsky as a titan, an all-powerful hero of the Ukrainian past. He did not cease to consider Khmelnytsky a hero but was more than eager to point out the negative aspects of Khmelnytsky's activities, insisting that the true hero of the Khmelnytsky era was not so much the hetman as the popular masses.

Hrushevsky's critique of Khmelnytsky's historical role recalled many elements present in his earlier writings on the subject and was generally characteristic of populist discourse of the late nineteenth and early twentieth centuries. At the same time, Hrushevsky's critique of Khmelnytsky in volume 9 of the *History* was much harsher than anything he had written previously. That harshness is to be explained, at least in part, by the heat of Hrushevsky's polemics with Lypynsky and by a strong desire to prove his political and academic opponent wrong. One might also assume that by attacking Lypynsky, Hrushevsky could count on scoring points with the Soviet authorities at a time when his own work was under attack in the USSR. Still, there was much more than pure politics in Hrushevsky's polemics with Lypynsky over Khmelnytsky's role in Ukrainian history. In many ways Hrushevsky's polemic contributed to the discussion of a much broader theme – the role of the hero in history. There were serious methodological differences between Hrushevsky and Lypynsky in dealing with this problem.[67]

Writing in the emigration in 1921 and explaining his scholarly method in *The Origins of Society (A Genetical Sociology)*, Hrushevsky sided with the founders of sociology, who made a clear break with the tradition that saw history as a manifestation of conscious will, either of gods or of heroes. Hrushevsky associated that historiographic tradition with the name of Thomas Carlyle, noting that most historians rejected approaches based on extreme individualism. He maintained that the social sciences were generally based on the concept of 'determinism,' which he took to mean the limitation of the human will and its dependence on the environment.[68] Hrushevsky considered the struggle between individualism and collectivism one of the major conflicts of post–First World War Europe. As he wrote in his introduction to *The Origins of Society*, the postwar era was characterized by a reaction against individualism and the class structure of the current 'mode of civilization,' which meant a return to collectivism and solidarity.[69]

Class-based thinking and individualism were the two major characteristics of Lypynsky's approach to Ukrainian politics as expressed in his collection of essays titled *Letters to Fellow Landowners*, written between 1919 and 1926.[70] Lypynsky and his followers on the one hand and the Bolsheviks on the other basically agreed on the class approach to politics and history, although they promoted it on behalf of different classes. When it came to the issue of individualism and collectivism, Hrushevsky was confronted only by Lypynsky, since the Bolsheviks were almost entirely on his side. With regard to the study of history, for Hrushevsky the conflict between individualism and collectivism came down to the question of who was the real hero of the Ukrainian past – the leader or the masses. Clearly, it was the revolution that reignited Hrushevsky's interest in the role of heroes in history, but his basic approach to the problem was rooted in his earlier writings on Ukrainian history. The idea of the limited power of the hero in history and the dependence of his/her actions on external social factors was inherited by Hrushevsky from Volodymyr Antonovych and reflected the dominant view of Ukrainian populists on the issue. It was also consonant with one of the basic dogmas of positivist scholarship and derived from the teachings of the very 'fathers of sociology' (Comte, Spencer, and others) whose writings Hrushevsky discussed in his *Origins of Society*.

Hrushevsky clearly took over from Antonovych his view of Khmelnytsky as a figure who represented the positive and negative characteristics of his milieu. Antonovych believed that Khmelnytsky's successes and failures were little more than a reflection of the positive and negative characteristics of the seventeenth-century Ukrainian nation. Both in his private lectures on Ukrainian Cossackdom delivered in the mid-1890s and in his public lecture of 1898 on Khmelnytsky, Antonovych explained the shortcomings of the hetman's rule by the generally low level of the Ukrainian people's political culture.[71] The major difference between Antonovych and Hrushevsky lay in their definitions of the hetman's milieu. For Antonovych it consisted of the people in general, while for the young Hrushevsky it was mostly limited to members of the Cossack order.[72] Hrushevsky's revision of Antonovych's approach contributed to the debunking of Khmelnytsky as a hero. In particular, it made him much more vulnerable to the populist critique, as it broke the link established by Antonovych between the hetman and the people. Any subsequent critique of Khmelnytsky reflected negatively not on the people, that sacred cow of populist ideology, but on the Cossack estate, which had already been condemned by Antonovych and his school for betraying the interests of the popular masses.

Hrushevsky's treatment of Khmelnytsky in his essay of 1898 presented some of his general views on the role of the hero in history as he understood it at the time. According to Hrushevsky, very few individuals acted on the basis of abstract motivations. He claimed that people were usually very subjective in their views and actions. While a higher level of culture allegedly entailed a greater degree of objectivity, even then human beings remained highly subjective in outlook. It was their personal experiences and ordeals that gave them a better understanding of the travails of the masses. Hrushevsky's ideal hero was supposed to identify his own misery and grievances with those of the people, and Khmelnytsky did not fit that category.[73] The historian was reluctant to include Khmelnytsky among the 'great souls' who cared about the 'whole world,' as he put it, since Khmelnytsky's grievances were those of the Cossack order alone, not of the popular masses. Hrushevsky sometimes presented Khmelnytsky as a member of the Ukrainian intelligentsia or of the Cossack officer stratum, but mostly as a representative of Cossackdom as a whole. It was in the interests of the Cossacks, claimed Hrushevsky, that Khmelnytsky pursued his policies, and it was their cause that he defended. The popular masses, who contributed most to the uprising, were allegedly used by Khmelnytsky as a mere instrument for achieving Cossack goals. According to Hrushevsky, Khmelnytsky was not a popular leader (narodnii vozhd'): he did not rise to the level of representing the interests of the whole people, and the result of his activity (a radical social revolution) was based on no clear plan of action or guiding principle. At the same time, Hrushevsky affirmed that the hetman was a person of outstanding ability and character and defended him against accusations of drunkenness. In the historian's opinion, Khmelnytsky was a highly gifted individual whose talents were particularly apparent if one compared him with his successors. He considered Khmelnytsky a gifted administrator and organizer, as well as a very successful diplomat, but a poor politician.[74]

Hrushevsky's low opinion of Khmelnytsky's political abilities tallied with Antonovych's appraisal of Khmelnytsky in his lectures on the history of Cossackdom,[75] but it was soon to change. The year 1904 saw the publication of two works in which Hrushevsky revisited the Khmelnytsky Uprising. The first was a short essay on the 250th anniversary of the Council of Pereiaslav (1654), while the second was Hrushevsky's *Survey History of the Ukrainian People*, his first synthesis of the subject. In the short essay Hrushevsky called Khmelnytsky a great politician – a major revision of his earlier assessment of the hetman's political skills – but in general the image of the hetman presented there was no more positive than that of 1898. The reason for this was the article's focus on the Pereiaslav Agreement, which Hrushevsky considered one of the low points of Khmelnytsky's career.[76] Discussing the Khmelnytsky Uprising in the *Survey History of the Ukrainian People*, Hrushevsky basically followed the narrative developed in his earlier writings on the period. Khmelnytsky emerged as a major historical actor but not a hero. The historian concentrated mainly on the hetman's actions, explaining his intentions and the consequences of his policies from time to time. For the most part, Hrushevsky skilfully avoided either a positive or a negative assessment of Khmelnytsky. He neither praised the hetman for the successes of the uprising nor blamed him for the failures of his policies. The image of Khmelnytsky in the *Survey* comes across as very faint and schematic: he is an ever-present but largely unheroic protagonist.[77]

Hrushevsky continued the revision of his original critical assesment of Khmelnytsky in his article of 1907 on the 250th anniversary of Khmelnytsky's death. The essay, titled 'Bohdan's Anniversary,' was written not only to commemorate Khmelnytsky's death but also to respond to celebrations held by the Polish community of Lviv in 1905 to mark the 250th anniversary of Khmelnytsky's unsuccessful siege of the city in 1655.[78] Those celebrations were accompanied by an attack on Khmelnytsky on the part of the Polish historian Franciszek Rawita-Gawroński in his pamphlet *The Bloody Visitor in Lviv*, which Hrushevsky considered an insult to the whole Ukrainian population of Galicia.[79] In 'Bohdan's Anniversary,' Hrushevsky made no secret of his desire to defend Khmelnytsky against the attacks of Polish nationalist historians. Another, no less important purpose of the essay was to claim the cult of

Khmelnytsky that already existed in the all-Russian historical narrative for the Ukrainian national movement. Hrushevsky wrote that false praise of Khmelnytsky rendered by defenders of the old regime and sophists of the imperial Russian ideology of 'Orthodoxy, autocracy, and nationality' had made the hetman *persona non grata* for adherents of the 'revived Ukrainian idea.' According to Hrushevsky, Khmelnytsky had been transformed into a hero of the established order, while opponents of that order turned away from him.[80] Hrushevsky called for the 'rehabilitation' of the hetman. 'The tragedy of Khmelnytsky,' he wrote, 'cursed in his lifetime by the popular masses that rose at his summons; crushed before his death by the unsuccessful results of political liberation; burned and scattered by an enemy hand after his death; apotheosized by the enemies of a free Ukraine and shrouded by the contempt of its new champions, endures to this day. But can time bring it to an end and, having condemned errors and shortcomings, acknowledge what was near and dear to us in him and his activity?'[81]

Hrushevsky was clearly claiming the famous hetman for the Ukrainian narrative and the Ukrainian cause. He introduced significant changes in the new editions of his *Survey History of the Ukrainian People* that appeared in 1906 and 1911. Hrushevsky decided to broaden his assessment of Khmelnytsky and present a psychological portrait of the hetman. He described Khmelnytsky as 'an experienced and skilful warrior and, in general, a highly talented individual, but impulsive, with no great stamina or persistence. A gifted chieftain and, one might say, an administrator of genius, a resourceful politician and diplomat, he was incapable of formulating and consistently carrying out plans reaching far into the future, especially as he did not rise above the level of the political and social opinions of the milieu that produced him.'[82] Hrushevsky also presented Khmelnytsky as a leader of the whole Ukrainian people. Commenting on Khmelnytsky's speeches at Pereiaslav in early 1649, Hrushevsky wrote in one of his additions to the original text of the *Survey*: 'It is hard to remain unmoved when following the growth of the political and social thought of this gifted man who embodied contemporary Ukrainian society and the whole Ukrainian people, which had unexpectedly freed itself of its age-old bonds of political, economic, and national subjection and was now contemplating, with rapture and confusion, the horizons opening before it and discovering in them the possibility of entirely new, previously inconceivable social and political relations.'[83]

The hetman who had earlier been castigated for neglecting and betraying the interests of the people was now portrayed as an authentic representative of the very same people. Was this change caused by Hrushevsky's experience at the time and after the Revolution of 1905? Was he abandoning his earlier views of Khmelnytsky as a representative of Cossackdom or the even more exclusive Cossack officer stratum and accepting the views of Volodymyr Antonovych? Or was it a more profound transformation that caused Hrushevsky to embrace a neoromantic view of the role of historical personalities? Whatever the case, there is little doubt that in the first decade of the twentieth century Hrushevsky's views on this matter had undergone a profound change, allowing certain elements of the romantic and old-fashioned populist approach to penetrate his original assessment of the Khmelnytsky Uprising.

The Ukrainian national revival, of which Hrushevsky had emerged as one of the most authoritative leaders in the course of the 1905 revolution, was engaged in a desperate search for its own historical legitimacy and its own heroes. The historical narrative that he offered the 'awakening' nation was very different from the one constructed in his populist writings of the 1890s. Now Ukrainian history emerged not as an account of the betrayal of the popular masses by their elites but as a story of the common struggle of masses and elites for national emancipation. Individuals such as Bohdan Khmelnytsky, whom Hrushevsky had treated in the 1890s as traitors to the masses, were now presented as national heroes. The populist historical narrative was quickly changing to meet the new demands of mass propaganda and mobilization, and in the process it was clearly acquiring the characteristics of a national epic. Hrushevsky could not afford to remain ambivalent with regard to Bohdan Khmelnytsky when both the Poles and the Russians were using the image of one of the most prominent figures of the Ukrainian past against the Ukrainian movement.

In elevating Khmelnytsky to the status of national hero, Hrushevsky was more and more adopting a language reminiscent of national discourse, deeply rooted in the romantic interpretation of history.[84] Hrushevsky's pen was guided by the conventions and requirements of that discourse when he delivered the following assessment of the Khmelnytsky era: 'A titan stirred – huge, dark, blind, fettered, beaten to the ground – as potent and dark as the black earth that he was to cultivate in chains. And ahead of him went his leader, no less titanic in strength and character, as a personification of that potent and blind popular strength, endowed with little more consciousness, but with the same titanic momentum of strength and energy. With his fearsome straining he shook the Ukrainian earth. As potent and elemental as nature, which in its elemental blindness cannot husband resources to attain its goal and sacrifices millions of specimens in mindless profligacy to preserve the species, the 'idea,' he expended the strength of the people, shed blood, and strewed his native land with corpses until the titan's elemental strength was exhausted by these incalculable and excessive losses, and his powerful hands were seized with impotent convulsions.'[85]

It is difficult to imagine a description of the Khmelnytsky era imbued with greater romanticism than the one presented in this case by the avowed positivist Mykhailo Hrushevsky. Next to the old populist hero, the collective 'people,' he placed a new protagonist, the Cossack hetman Bohdan Khmelnytsky, who emerged in Hrushevsky's essay as a romantic hero par excellence. In Hrushevsky's interpretation, Khmelnytsky's titanic power of leadership derived from the strength of the people, and it was the people who legitimized the new role carved out by Hrushevsky for the famous hetman. If in 1898 Hrushevsky was not entirely certain whether Khmelnytsky belonged to those 'great souls' who linked their own pain and suffering to those of the masses, by 1907 he seemed to have no doubt on that score. From a defender of Cossack interests, Hrushevsky transformed Khmelnytsky into a representative of the Ukrainian people, and in that incarnation he could not be wrong, any more than the people as a whole could be wrong. Hrushevsky maintained that seventeenth-century Ukraine, which lacked proper organization and culture because of its subjection to the Polish nobility, could not have expected a leader more able or talented than the one it obtained in Khmelnytsky.[86]

Hrushevsky took over from Antonovych the banner of Ukrainian national historiography, and in so doing he came to the defence of Ukraine's principal hero, using arguments similar to those of his former professor. Like Antonovych before him, Hrushevsky struggled to turn Khmelnytsky into a usable hero for the new generation of Ukrainian activists. Antonovych chose to do so by defending Khmelnytsky against attacks from young Ukrainian radicals who, in the tradition of Taras Shevchenko, could not forgive Khmelnytsky for the Pereiaslav Agreement and reproached him for not having created an independent Ukrainian state.[87] Hrushevsky, by contrast, saw it as his main task to wrest the image of Khmelnytsky from the embrace of proponents of Russia, 'one and indivisible.' That task, first formulated by Hrushevsky in his essay of 1907, was also addressed in his article of 1912, 'On Ukrainian Topics: "Mazepism" and "Bohdanism."' In it Hrushevsky protested attempts on the part of opponents of the Ukrainian movement to counterpose the image of Bohdan Khmelnytsky, allegedly a hetman loyal to Russia, to that of the disloyal Hetman Ivan Mazepa. Hrushevsky argued that this was a false dichotomy, as Khmelnytsky himself had been a 'conscious exponent of the ideology of Ukrainian statehood' and had sought a way of breaking with Muscovy. As Hrushevsky saw it, Mazepa's alliance with Sweden was little more than a continuation of the policy initiated by Khmelnytsky.[88]

In 1909 Hrushevsky published a brochure about Khmelnytsky written specifically for a mass audience. Titled *On the Cossack Father Bohdan Khmelnytsky*, it presented the image of a new hero of Ukrainian national history in a simple and understandable way. The brochure opened with a romantic description of the Khmelnytsky monument in Kyiv erected by the proponents of 'Russia, one and indivisible,' to praise Khmelnytsky for what he had done at Pereiaslav. Thus Hrushevsky was claiming for the Ukrainian movement not only the cult of the hetman, lavishly elaborated by its opponents, but also its main symbol, the Kyiv monument. Hrushevsky drew a very attractive picture of the famous hetman. All the events of the uprising were presented through the prism of Khmelnytsky's plans, ideas, and desires. In the brochure, Khmelnytsky exults and worries, happy and sad by turns; he is a wise leader but also a loving father. He is depicted as an archetypical romantic hero, an image created by Hrushevsky with the help of excerpts from the popular *dumy* (epic songs). Last but not least, in a brochure specifically written for the people, Khmelnytsky appears as their hero. In the last paragraph, Hrushevsky enhances that image as follows: 'The Ukrainian people did not fail to remember Bohdan for all the good that the famous hetman wanted for Ukraine. In songs and *dumy* it eulogized Bohdan's deeds as those of no other hetman. It handed down those songs and *dumy* to our own times as it handed down no memory of anyone or anything in all Ukrainian history.'[89] This positive image of Khmelnytsky also figured in Hrushevsky's *Illustrated History of Ukraine*, which was written in 1911, reworked in 1912, and subsequently issued in a host of new editions. This book was also addressed to a mass audience, but its account of Khmelnytsky was much more sophisticated than that of the folksy brochure of 1909.[90]

By 1912 Khmelnytsky's status as a hero of Ukrainian history was firmly established in the new Ukrainian historiography, not only by

Hrushevsky's own writings but also by the works of his students and followers. When Volodymyr Antonovych's lectures on the history of Cossackdom were reissued in Kolomyia in 1912, his critique of Khmelnytsky, very mild in comparison with Hrushevsky's early writings, was considered excessive by the editors. Hrushevsky's student Myron Korduba supplied the new edition of Antonovych's lectures with copious notes that often served as an antidote to Antonovych's critical remarks. Among other things, he called Antonovych's criticism of Khmelnytsky's retreat from Zamość at the end of 1648 'utterly mistaken' and offered a thoroughly positive assessment of the hetman's actions of the period, with references to the diplomatic correspondence.[91]

Another proponent of the heroic image of Khmelnytsky was Viacheslav Lypynsky. In his works on the Khmelnytsky era first published in 1912, Lypynsky gave a highly positive assessment of Khmelnytsky, calling him a 'great hetman' and 'liberator of Ukraine.' For Lypynsky one of Khmelnytsky's principal 'errors' was the Pereiaslav Agreement with Muscovy. Lypynsky explained those errors away by claiming that Khmelnytsky obviously did not foresee the consequences of his actions. In his attempt to rehabilitate the image of the famous hetman in the eyes of the younger generation of Ukrainian activists, Lypynsky quoted from Hrushevsky's essay of 1907, in which the latter had called upon his contemporaries to 'acknowledge what was near and dear to us in him and his activity.' He also found inspiration in the Polish historian Ludwik Kubala, whose extremely favourable evaluation of Khmelnytsky in the third volume of his *Sketches* (1910) clearly outdid the modest praise accorded the hetman in the works of Hrushevsky.[92] It is difficult to say whether in the years 1907–12 Hrushevsky led the way or followed the crowd in turning Khmelnytsky into a major hero of the Ukrainian national movement, but his work clearly reflected the advent of the romantically inspired hero in Ukrainian historical narrative.[93]

Did Hrushevsky the scholar differ from Hrushevsky the publicist in his assessment of Khmelnytsky? The question is best addressed by taking a closer look at Hrushevsky's magnum opus. Volume 7 of his academic *History*, which appeared in print in 1909, and the first part of volume 8, published in 1913, both discussed the pre-Khmelnytsky era, but the second part of volume 8, which was first published in 1916, dealt directly with the causes and the first stage of the Khmelnytsky Uprising. It was written before the outbreak of the First World War and contains an interesting assessment of Khmelnytsky, reflecting Hrushevsky's view of the hetman at a time of rapid development of the

Ukrainian national movement in Russian-ruled Ukraine. A reading of that part of the volume suggests that in the years preceding the world war, Khmelnytsky was as much a hero for Hrushevsky the academic historian as he was for Hrushevsky the political activist and essayist.

In volume 8 of the *History*, Hrushevsky called Khmelnytsky a 'great hetman' and rarely criticized him in any way. He gave the most positive evaluation he ever bestowed on Khmelnytsky, lauding him as a 'foremost hero of history.' In the second part of the volume, Khmelnytsky appears in the garb of a romantic hero, even more obviously than in Hrushevsky's essay of 1907. Hrushevsky's description of Khmelnytsky's revolt against the authorities and his decision to initiate the uprising is rendered in the most dramatic terms possible: 'This was a dreadful, critical moment in Khmelnytsky's life. A profound crisis occurred in his soul, in his whole being, all the more dreadful because of the restraint and moderation that had hitherto characterized this extraordinarily powerful and richly endowed nature. It may be said that Khmelnytsky before and after this moment was two different people.'[94] As was recently noted by Natalia Iakovenko, Hrushevsky's account of his hero's transformation as the dramatic culmination of his life represented one of the most popular topoi of romantic literature.[95] The romantic stirrings that awakened in Hrushevsky's mind around the time of the 1905 revolution and eventually overshadowed his earlier preoccupation with the plight and interests of the popular masses clearly continued to dominate his outlook at least until the outbreak of the First World War. At the same time, Hrushevsky the historian refused to sacrifice his scholarly principles and standards for the sake of his argument. He worked diligently to reconstruct every detail of Khmelnytsky's early biography and clear it of accumulated myths, including those potentially useful for reinforcing the image of the hetman as an infallible popular hero. For example, he rejected the well-established historiographic tradition according to which Khmelnytsky took an active part in earlier Cossack revolts and presented him as a loyal subject of the king prior to the outbreak of the 1648 uprising.[96]

As noted earlier, Hrushevsky began to write volume 8 of his academic *History* before the First World War. By the time his work on the volume was finished, he was no longer a resident of Lviv but an internee on the territory of the Russian Empire. His working conditions were different, as was the status of the Ukrainian movement, which the tsarist authorities now treated as a German and Austrian intrigue against the unity of the Russian nation. Did these new circumstances affect

Hrushevsky's treatment of Khmelnytsky? Was the image of the hetman in the third part of volume 8 (completed in early 1917) different from the one presented in its second part, written during the expansion of the Ukrainian movement? It is difficult to answer this question, as Hrushevsky avoided any further detailed discussion of Khmelnytsky's character, probably believing that the one he had given in the second part of the volume was sufficient. Generally speaking, there seems to have been no major change in Hrushevsky's view of Khmelnytsky's personality. On the one hand, he no longer emphasized Khmelnytsky's heroic characteristics, but on the other, he refrained from blaming the hetman directly for the grave consequences that the Zboriv Agreement of 1649 had for the masses. This time it was the leadership of the uprising in general, not Khmelnytsky as an individual, that took the blame.[97]

A real change in Hrushevsky's attitude toward Khmelnytsky becomes apparent only in volume 9 of the *History*, written after the revolution. In his conclusions to the volume, Hrushevsky presented his most detailed and critical, if not damning, evaluation of Khmelnytsky and his policies. As noted earlier, it was inspired by his polemics with the views expressed by Viacheslav Lypynsky in *Ukraine at the Turning Point* and demonstrated, probably better than any of Hrushevsky's writings of the period, the extent of change in his political and scholarly outlook between 1917 and the late 1920s. In regard to Khmelnytsky and his era, the change in Hrushevsky's interpretation was quite dramatic, but for the most part it did not represent the development of new views and ideas. Instead, Hrushevsky returned to many of his populist opinions of the turn of the century. The critical assessment of Khmelnytsky's activities that dominated Hrushevsky's essay of 1898 was now restated and further developed, while the much more positive evaluation of the hetman given in Hrushevsky's prerevolutionary writings, which had been influenced by concepts of national solidarity and neoromanticism, was modified or even openly rejected.

In volume 9 of the *History*, Hrushevsky reasserted his old idea of 1898 about the failure of the leaders of the uprising to develop an effective plan or a definite goal. That argument served as Hrushevsky's main instrument in his attempt to counter and discredit Lypynsky's portrait of Khmelnytsky (rendered in *Ukraine at the Turning Point*) as a great state-builder and an outstanding politician. Hrushevsky also revived another idea that he had never really abandoned even in his neoromantic period – the claim that Khmelnytsky was a poor leader of the popular masses. In that regard, he placed special emphasis on the policies of Khmelnytsky and his entourage that were harmful to the peasantry and the burghers. Khmelnytsky was also accused of relying too much on foreign alliances instead of securing the support of the masses, a policy that had begun, according to Hrushevsky, after the Zboriv Agreement of 1649. Last but not least, Hrushevsky returned to his earlier evaluation of Khmelnytsky as a poor negotiator in his dealings with Muscovy. According to Hrushevsky, at Pereiaslav Khmelnytsky had failed to secure Ukrainian statehood and thus betrayed the national cause.[98]

In the opening paragraph of his conclusions to volume 9, Hrushevsky wrote: 'Now, having made my way through it [the Khmelnytsky era] on the basis of the largest number of source materials ever assembled, I must clarify to what extent I stand by my earlier conclusions and to what extent I depart from them or make corrections of any kind, or at least present a newer version of my earlier theses.'[99] In fact, Hrushevsky's new interpretation of the era was influenced not only by the study of new sources but also by the change of his political orientation. His return to the ideas he had espoused at the turn of the century resulted in the outright rejection of many of the assessments he had made prior to the revolution. An example of such a drastic change is Hrushevsky's treatment of his old idea, first expressed in his essay of 1898, concerning the alleged lack of planning behind the Khmelnytsky Uprising. In his essay of 1907 on the 250th anniversary of Khmelnytsky's death, Hrushevsky had dismissed this argument, saying that those who witnessed the events of the 1905 revolution understood that one could not expect too much planning, given the low cultural level of the 'dark' masses.[100] In volume 9 of the *History*, he returned to his earlier view of the issue, accusing Khmelnytsky of failing to plan and organize the uprising properly. As Frank E. Sysyn has pointed out, 'In the late 1920s, he [Hrushevsky] did not find that the revolutionary events of 1917–1921 should make his contemporaries treat the hetman with greater understanding.'[101]

Another major change in Hrushevsky's interpretation of the Khmelnytsky era was his reevaluation of the significance of Khmelnytsky's leadership. If in 1907 Hrushevsky considered the hetman's death a turning point in the history of Cossack Ukraine, since Khmelnytsky's successors failed to match his level of leadership, he now claimed that there was no substantial difference between Khmelnytsky and his successors.[102] In his conclusions to volume 9, Hrushevsky criticized the view, 'harmful in its consequences for historical perspective,' that presented

Khmelnytsky as a 'titan among pygmies.' Ironically, it was Hrushevsky himself who in 1907 had called Khmelnytsky a 'titan,' while referring to his successors as 'tiny Lilliputians' who bound the Ukrainian people after Khmelnytsky's death.[103]

Apart from rehearsing his old grievances against Khmelnytsky, Hrushevsky presented a new list of the hetman's errors and shortcomings. Among them was his alleged inability or unwillingness to take full advantage of the rebels' military victories in the autumn of 1648, a 'failing' noted earlier by Antonovych. Hrushevsky was also unhappy with Khmelnytsky's failure to establish Cossack rule over Western Ukraine at the end of 1648. The hetman's other failings included waging war on his own territory, exploiting the masses as 'canon fodder,' involving the Cossacks in the conflict with Wallachia in 1653, neglecting to attack the Crimea in 1654, delaying the formation of a new league with Sweden and Transylvania in 1656, and unnecessarily (in Hrushevsky's opinion) worsening relations with Muscovy.[104] 'Thus,' wrote Hrushevsky, 'in the sphere of state policy, it is difficult to claim glory for the Khmelnytsky era, regardless of the fact that there was no shortage either of intelligent men or of brilliant ideas in its councils of state. I account for this, first of all, by the lack of a clear political plan, sovereign idea, and political leadership, i.e., the absence of a political master, so to speak.'[105]

In his conclusions to volume 9, Hrushevsky often repeated that he did not question Khmelnytsky's heroic status but was unhappy with the historiographic tradition that viewed the whole era through the prism of the hetman's life and actions.[106] He was also opposed to the 'unhealthy idealization of the age and individuality of Khmelnytsky that has frequently been asserting itself.'[107] Hrushevsky declined to view the events of the mid-seventeenth century through the actions and behaviour of a single individual, suggesting instead a more sophisticated approach in which the role of the leader was counterbalanced by other actors, including the ruling elite and the popular masses. The latter were Hrushevsky's traditional collective hero, while his interest in the role of the ruling elite or, in this instance, Khmelnytsky's circle of associates, was a relatively new element in his interpretation of the uprising. If for Antonovych Khmelnytsky was first and foremost the representative of the people and, for the young Hrushevsky, generally the representative of the Cossacks in general, for Hrushevsky of the 1920s Khmelnytsky was above all the representative of the Cossack officer elite. In the introduction to volume 9, Hrushevsky noted that further biographical study of the upper stratum of Cossack officers was one of the most important avenues for future research.[108] In his conclusions to the volume, he even recognized the primacy of the research conducted on that subject by his intellectual and political opponent Viacheslav Lypynsky.[109]

It would appear, nevertheless, that Hrushevsky and Lypynsky set themselves quite different goals in their studies of Khmelnytsky's associates. If Lypynsky was primarily concerned in his biographical study of Colonel Mykhailo Krychevsky with the role of the nobility in the Khmelnytsky Uprising and sought to present the noble stratum as a component of the Ukrainian nation, Hrushevsky was mainly concerned with the role of the Cossack officer elite in the leadership of the uprising. Hrushevsky claimed that Khmelnytsky had an entourage of talented associates, many of whom could have replaced him as leader, hence his primacy was largely a matter of luck.[110] By indicating the role of General Chancellor (and future hetman) Ivan Vyhovsky and others in the making of crucial decisions, Hrushevsky sought to put into perspective and, indeed, diminish the personal role of Khmelnytsky as a political leader. When he referred to the hetman and his associates as 'Khmelnytsky and Co.,' Hrushevsky was in fact shifting the focus of his narrative from the hero to his entourage, which, in Hrushevsky's opinion, often decided matters. Ironically, unlike Khmelnytsky and his administration, Vyhovsky and his hetmancy drew hardly any criticism from Hrushevsky, bolstering the historian's argument that the 'ruin of Ukrainian statehood' did not ensue after Khmelnytsky's death but began on his watch.[111]

Was Hrushevsky really protesting only the 'unhealthy idealization' of Khmelnytsky, as he claimed? In all probability, this was a candid statement. Hrushevsky's historiographic discussion in the concluding chapter of volume 9 evinces strong disapproval of attacks on Khmelnytsky by such historians as Panteleimon Kulish and Petr Butsinsky, as well as of the relentlessly negative assessment of the whole Cossack officer stratum given by Oleksander Lazarevsky.[112] The same concluding chapter of volume 9 features an extensive quotation, almost five pages in length, from the extremely positive assessment of Khmelnytsky by Ludwik Kubala.[113] Hrushevsky accompanied the quotation with the following statement: 'I have quoted this description at such length because I consider it highly penetrating. The author demonstrated not only a desire to be objective and to judge this enemy of Old Poland appropriately; in my estimation, he also correctly grasped much of Khmelnytsky's character: his unequaled temperament, extraordinary energy, adroitness, sensitivity, strongly developed imagination, effortless thought, and bent for hyperbole. Khmelnytsky had an extraordinary talent for psychological influence and suggestion, with a strong proclivity to histrionics. He was indiscriminate and ruthless in method and free of all moral constraints. He had an extraordinary and incredible attachment to power as a dogma of existence. In my opinion, all this is rendered very faithfully. Bohdan was indeed a born leader and ruler, politician and diplomat. He roused and moved the masses with ease and knew how to govern their moods, as much by bloody violence as by a gracious word or a humble gesture. There was something insuperably captivating in his nature that inclined people toward him. That is quite true. But was he also a politician in the higher sense – a builder of state and society, a civic and cultural organizer for the long term?'[114]

What these words in fact indicated was that Hrushevsky had little problem in accepting Khmelnytsky as a neoromantic hero – a talented rebel and an impulsive, charismatic leader – but declined to consider him a hero in the positivist sense. Khmelnytsky's actions allegedly were not constructive, a judgment that Hrushevsky repeated again and again in the conclusions to volume 9. For Hrushevsky, Khmelnytsky was a great leader of the Asian type (a 'Great Scythian') but not a state-builder of the European kind, while Ukraine, in his opinion, was part of Europe and deserved a leader with European qualities.[115] It was Lypynsky's depiction of Khmelnytsky as the hero of Ukrainian nation- and state-building (a 'builder of state and society, a civic and cultural organizer') that provoked Hrushevsky's criticism of the hetman. It can hardly be doubted that there was more than one image and cult of Khmelnytsky. As Sysyn has noted recently, 'the variety of cults of Khmel'nyts'kyi made him acceptable to very different constituencies in Ukraine.'[116] Hrushevsky apparently believed that the image of Khmelnytsky needed by the new democratic and revolutionary Ukraine was not that of a Cossack monarch but of a charismatic revolutionary leader of the popular masses. 'In the final reckoning,' wrote Hrushevsky in his conclusions to volume 9, 'from certain perspectives the tremendous agitation brought about by the Khmelnytsky era was beneficial to the people. It elevated the "simple folk" high above their slavery and humiliation. It allowed them to feel like human beings – not simple people but full equals. In their minds it revived their undying aspiration to regain their human status not just for a brief moment but "forever." As I have said repeatedly, Ukraine's new life began with the Khmelnytsky era. And as its principal agitator, Khmelnytsky will remain a hero of Ukrainian history.'[117]

What was behind Hrushevsky's refusal to recognize Khmelnytsky as a 'politician in the higher sense'? Why was he seemingly prepared to grant such recognition in 1907 but not in 1927? Was it Hrushevsky's renewed commitment to the interests of the popular masses, his return to the basic positivist denial of the importance of heroes, or the view of his own times as a confrontation between the principles of individualism and collectivism? Most likely, all these factors helped shape Hrushevsky's attitude of the late 1920s. One should also allow for the possible impact of pure politics. It is worth remembering that Hrushevsky the politician was deposed by a coup d'état carried out by Hetman Pavlo Skoropadsky, whose right to rule Ukraine was retrospectively legitimized by Lypynsky with references to the legacy of Bohdan Khmelnytsky. As early as 1917 Hrushevsky had opposed the idealization of the Cossack state, claiming that the Ukrainian movement did not aspire to a restoration of the Hetmanate but wanted to create a new order of state and society.[118] Following this line of argument, in volume 9 of his *History* Hrushevsky opposed the interpretation of the Khmelnytsky era as a paradise lost. Referring to the historical material presented in that volume, he wrote: '[The Khmelnytsky era] was neither idyll nor harmony. The Ukrainian people did not experience a paradise in Bohdan's time or in any other epoch of its past. Our social, political, and cultural ideals lie before us, not behind us.'[119]

This statement was reminiscent of the scepticism expressed by the Galician Ukrainophiles of the 1860s–80s with regard to Cossack history. It was also politically significant to Hrushevsky, as may be gathered from the fact that he chose to repeat it in his comments to a group of Kyivan workers in November 1929. A correspondent of the newspaper *Proletarskaia pravda* recorded Hrushevsky's words as follows: 'The [Khmelnytsky] era was only an episode in the life of the Ukrainian people. Our ideals lie before us, not behind us.' In the early 1930s, Hrushevsky's suggestion that Ukraine had yet to achieve its full social and national liberation were condemned by Soviet propagandists as an attempt to justify the restoration of the bourgeois order in Ukraine.[120] For Hrushevsky, meanwhile, as for his communist contemporary Mykola Khvyliovy, the national renaissance and, consequently, the 'golden age' of Ukraine lay not in the past but in the future.[121]

Masses and Elites

In his interpretation of the Khmelnytsky era in the Soviet-era volumes of the *History*, Hrushevsky remained a staunch populist in the sense that the good of the popular masses was his major criterion for assessing the uprising and its aftermath. Not surprisingly, it was to the 'creative sufferings' of the popular masses that Hrushevsky dedicated volume 9 of his *History*.[122] But who were the 'popular masses' for Hrushevsky? Judging by his writings, he used the term in the same sense as Volodymyr Antonovych and his circle of populists employed 'the people.'[123] For Hrushevsky, the 'popular masses' were first and foremost the peasantry but also often included the burghers and even rank-and-file Cossacks (the latter were sometimes considered part of Cossackdom in general). The elites consisted of the Cossack officer stratum, which included some elements of the Ukrainian nobility, while the intelligentsia included representatives of the nobility, Cossack officers, clergy, and even burghers, whom Hrushevsky otherwise considered part of the popular masses.

Hrushevsky saw relations between the masses and the Cossack elite as the crucial element of Ukrainian political and social life in the Khmelnytsky era. In his polemic with Lypynsky in the last chapter of volume 9, Hrushevsky argued that the contradictions in those relations were never resolved: 'The "fatal contradictions" between the social and economic strivings of the masses, set in motion by the leaders of the uprising and all of Cossackdom on the one hand and, on the other, by the landowning-officer tendencies of those leaders and the ruling Cossack order, were not levelled one bit.'[124] If Hrushevsky ultimately regarded the era as a failure, it was because of the hetman's perceived inability to resolve the contradiction between masses and elites.[125] In Hrushevsky's writings, the 'popular masses' almost always figured as a positive historical force, while the Cossack officer stratum, the powerful rival of the masses in Hrushevsky's historical scheme of the Khmelnytsky Uprising, was too often preoccupied with its own corporate interests, to the detriment of those of the masses and the nation as a whole. If Hrushevsky's view of the popular masses remained almost unchanged throughout his academic career, his attitude toward the Cossack officer stratum and the intelligentsia differed at various stages.

In his first essay on the Khmelnytsky era, published in 1898, he identified Cossackdom as a whole, not the Cossack officers, as the main rival of the peasantry. More than once he claimed that in the Khmelnytsky

Uprising the popular masses were an instrument in the hands of the Cossacks, who exploited the peasantry for their own ends as they gained autonomy for their corporate order.[126] In Hrushevsky's opinion, the main fault of Khmelnytsky and the Cossack officers was their inability to rise above the interests of the Cossack order and champion the cause of the popular masses.[127] Hrushevsky repeated this accusation in his essay of 1907 on the anniversary of Khmelnytsky's death, claiming that the hetman had started the uprising to promote the class interests of the Cossack order. Unable to appreciate the significance of the popular uprising, he limited his negotiations with the Polish king to the issue of Cossack privileges and was even prepared to end the revolt and abandon the popular masses in order to obtain those privileges.[128]

Hrushevsky showed much less antagonism toward elites in his later writings. That change of attitude first became apparent in his popular surveys of Ukrainian history. Very telling in that regard was Hrushevsky's approach in a brief survey of Ukrainian history that he prepared for a German publisher in the summer of 1905. He all but excluded the discussion of social conflicts in Ukrainian history from his short narrative, no longer blaming the Cossack elite for having betrayed the popular masses and led the Ukrainian people into Muscovite subjection. Instead, he portrayed Muscovy, specifically the Muscovite bureaucracy, as the main culprit of the troubles that befell the Ukrainian nation. In his *Illustrated History of Ukraine* (1912), also written for a popular audience, Hrushevsky assigned no specific blame for the tensions between the masses and the Cossack officers but treated them as an unfortunate reality that benefited the enemies of Ukraine.[129] In volume 8 of his academic *History*, Hrushevsky also spared the Cossack officer stratum direct criticism for its mistreatment of the popular masses. He wrote at length about popular opposition to the Zboriv Agreement and was clearly unhappy with the policies of Khmelnytsky and his associates at this stage of the uprising, but his criticism of the hetman and the officers for their alleged betrayal of the interests of the popular masses was much milder than his castigation of Cossackdom as a whole for the same alleged offence in his essay of 1898.[130]

The most controversial aspect of Khmelnytsky's policy at Zboriv, his implicit agreement to allow the Tatars to take captives among the Ukrainian population on their way back to the Crimea, was not only condemned but also explained by Hrushevsky: 'First of all, as we have seen, the hetman sought to maintain the integrity and validity of his alliance with the Horde, having stoically endured the khan's treachery at Zboriv and satisfied all his wishes, not even hesitating to bring down on himself the resentment and fury of the masses for his excessive acquiescence to the Tatars' will (in the matter of captives). By paying this high price, he indeed managed to preserve his close contacts and friendship with the khan's court and made a mockery of the boastings of the Polish government, which claimed by means of the concessions made at Zboriv to have severed the Cossack-Tatar alliance, so dangerous for Poland. That alliance remained intact and inviolate.'[131] Hrushevsky also provided an explanation for another policy of Khmelnytsky's that he had severely criticized – the hetman's agreement at Zboriv to allow the return of the Polish nobility to its estates outside Cossack territory and to compile a Cossack register, which effectively returned most of the Cossackized peasants to the authority of the Polish nobles.[132] Hrushevsky demonstrated that the hetman's administration did everything in its power to delay or sabotage the implementation of this provision of the treaty.

Writing before the revolution, Hrushevsky the national historian was much more willing to balance the interests of the popular masses and the elites than was the young Hrushevsky of the 1890s. The events of the 1917 revolution clearly put that attitude to the test. In some of his political writings of the period, Hrushevsky still praised Khmelnytsky for opposing the return of the nobility to Ukraine in 1649, but his motive for this was primarily to damage the political reputation of his opponents who signed the Treaty of Warsaw in 1920.[133] His new attitude toward the Cossack officer stratum is already apparent in some of his additions to parts 1 and 2 of volume 8 of the *History*, which he reprinted in 1922. To the concluding sentence of the second part of the volume, which read: 'The excessive agitation of the popular masses was a dangerous phenomenon for the Cossack leaders themselves,' Hrushevsky added a phrase taken almost verbatim from his essay of 1898 on Khmelnytsky, 'who still were by no means contemplating any kind of people's war against Poland, as we shall see in due course.'[134] In the introduction to volume 9 of the *History*, Hrushevsky reiterated his old belief in the existence of profound differences between the interests of the Cossack officers and those of the popular masses: 'The old historiography usually equated the class interests of this new social stratum with the spontaneous struggle of the masses and treated it as an expression of what was termed a "popular struggle," a "struggle for the liberation of Ukraine." Clearly, both the facts and socio-historical experience now require of us a careful differentiation of these two aspects of the process.'[135]

Hrushevsky indicated two sets of tensions in Ukrainian society during the Khmelnytsky era. The first was the contradiction between the interests of the Cossack officers and those of the peasantry, while the second arose from the Cossack officers' policy toward the Ukrainian burghers. Regarding policy toward the peasants, Hrushevsky believed that the Cossack elite's failure to guarantee freedom from feudal bondage to the serfs liberated by the uprising gave rise to peasant revolts against the hetman's regime and mass emigration to Muscovy. Commenting on Lypynsky's interpretation of Cossack officer-peasant relations, Hrushevsky wrote sarcastically: 'In his most recent work Lypynsky does indeed make out that the peasantry seemingly had nothing against "customary obedience," since it was supposed to submit to people on active service in the Zaporozhian Host. But such an idyllic picture is hardly convincing.'[136] Also unfortunate, if not malicious, in Hrushevsky's opinion, was Khmelnytsky's policy toward the burghers. He wrote in that regard: 'Cossackdom hurtled down upon urban life in such an unforgivable fashion. The Cossack officers showed such an undisguised desire to sweep up and retain in their own hands all that the elements liquidated by the rebellion – the office of castle chief, the hereditary landowners, and the Catholic Church – had managed to wrest from the burgher community.'[137]

Hrushevsky's overall conclusion was not favourable to the Cossack officer stratum. Returning to the tradition established by Antonovych and developed in his own populist writings of the turn of the century, Hrushevsky accused the Cossack elite of harbouring the desire to replace the Polish nobility and continue the traditional enserfment of the peasantry. An episode of 1654 involving the Cossack colonels Pavlo Teteria and Samiilo Zarudny, who managed to obtain land grants from the tsar along with permission to settle that land with peasants, was cited by Hrushevsky as proof of the Cossack officers' intentions to restore the traditional economic order and reintroduce serfdom in Cossack Ukraine.[138] In the conclusion to volume 9, Hrushevsky presented his final judgment on the issue: 'The masses expected that under the direction of the leaders of the revolution they would escape the Poles and serfdom. Meanwhile, these leaders were carving nobiliary latifundia for themselves out of this seemingly liberated land. That process began with the hetman himself, with his Hadiach estates, with Vyhovsky,

Zarudny, Teteria, and Zolotarenko, with their greater or lesser latifundia obtained by entreaties from the tsar in the course of bargaining for the sovereign rights of Ukraine.'[139]

Hrushevsky believed that by conducting a selfish social policy, the Cossack officer stratum had perpetrated wrongs not only against the masses but also against the political and national interests of Ukraine. In his opinion, there was no excuse for such a policy, and the arguments marshalled by Lypynsky, who himself had sided during the revolution with the landowning elite against the popular masses, could only make Hrushevsky's judgments harsher. Generally speaking, there can be little doubt that the revolutionary and Soviet experience made Hrushevsky a much stronger proponent of the interests of the masses and a more uncompromising critic of the elites than he had been before the 1917 revolution.

A social group that occupied a special place in Hrushevsky's analysis of relations between masses and elites in Ukraine was the intelligentsia. Like many of his contemporaries, Hrushevsky accepted Auguste Comte's view that the intelligentsia constituted the leadership of any society.[140] Hrushevsky defined it as including all educated groups in a given society and found its representatives among the Cossack officers and the popular masses alike. To define the latter group, Hrushevsky even introduced the term 'petty intelligentsia.'[141] The use of the term 'intelligentsia' to denote the educated classes of early modern Ukrainian society was not Hrushevsky's invention. Volodymyr Antonovych used it when writing about the burghers of the larger Ukrainian cities.[142] It was also generally used with reference to seventeenth-century classes by Ivan Franko and other Ukrainian authors of the late nineteenth century, including Trokhym Zinkivsky and Mykola Mikhnovsky.[143] What was interesting in Hrushevsky's writings on this problem was his varying assessment of the role of the educated classes in Ukrainian history – a process influenced by the changing political and cultural circumstances in which Hrushevsky found himself when he addressed the issue. From the end of the nineteenth century to the late 1920s, he often implicitly compared the role played by the intelligentsia of seventeenth-century Ukraine with the role of the intelligentsia in his own times.[144]

Hrushevsky introduced the term 'intelligentsia' into his discussion of the Khmelnytsky era in his essay of 1898. At that time his assessment of the role played by the intelligentsia in the Khmelnytsky Uprising was quite critical. He believed that the Cossack officer stratum and the entire Ukrainian intelligentsia had been raised on Polish social models. Hence Khmelnytsky, who, in Hrushevsky's opinion, did not differ in outlook from the rest of the Ukrainian intelligentsia, could not possibly understand the needs of the popular masses. Nor was he aware of the need to create a new political and social order based on the interests of the masses, not those of the Cossacks alone. In Hrushevsky's opinion, it was only his contemporaries, members of the new and 'progressive' Ukrainian intelligentsia of the late nineteenth century, who could fuse the Cossack ideals of equality and freedom with the aspirations of the popular masses, while freeing those ideals from Cossack-era social restrictions.[145]

In 1898 Hrushevsky was clearly in full agreement with Antonovych, who claimed that 'the intelligentsia usually attempts to assimilate with the ruling nation.'[146] A decade later, while writing volume 7 of the *History*, which covered the Cossack era to 1625, Hrushevsky presented a very different view of the intelligentsia. In his introduction to the volume, he identified the Cossack alliance with the Orthodox 'intelligentsia' as the factor that had elevated Cossackdom to a place of central importance in Ukrainian history.[147] Hrushevsky was no less enthusiastic about the positive influence of the intelligentsia on Cossackdom in volume 8 of the *History*. There he credited the Kyivan intelligentsia with bringing about a profound change in Khmelnytsky's ideology at the turn of 1649, when the Cossack hetman, in his conversations with the Polish commissioners, went far beyond the traditional Cossack demands and enunciated a plan for the liberation of all Orthodox Rus' from the Polish yoke.[148] In his essay of 1898, Hrushevsky was inclined to credit this change in Khmelnytsky's program to Patriarch Paisios of Jerusalem, with whom the hetman had held long conversations prior to the arrival of the commissioners. In volume 8 of the *History*, Hrushevsky clearly changed his mind, not only attributing the change of Khmelnytsky's policy to the influence of the Kyivan intelligentsia, which had not even been mentioned in the essay of 1898, but also questioning the role of Patriarch Paisios in changing Khmelnytsky's attitudes. Hrushevsky wrote: 'Whatever he may have brought with him from Jerusalem and Moldavia could hardly have sufficed for protracted heartfelt conversations or had any particular influence on the hetman.'[149] At most, Hrushevsky was prepared to consider the patriarch a spokesman for the Kyivan intelligentsia.

The ideas expressed by Khmelnytsky during his negotiations with the Polish commissioners in Pereiaslav in early 1649 were indeed much more reminiscent of the views developed by the Ukrainian Orthodox nobility and clergy throughout the first half of the seventeenth century than of any program that could possibly have been presented by the distinguished guest from Jerusalem. After all, it was on Khmelnytsky's initiative and direct order that Paisios was brought to Kyiv, there to await the hetman's triumphal entrance into the city. In all likelihood, it was the patriarch's sanction of Khmelnytsky's rule and not his ideas that interested the hetman at the time of his meetings with Paisios.[150] On the other hand, there is no evidence whatever of any significant contacts or discussions between Khmelnytsky and those whom Hrushevsky called the 'Kyivan intelligentsia' at the time of hetman's stay in the city in late 1648. Nevertheless, there is reason to believe that Khmelnytsky was acquainted with their ideas long before his solemn entrance into Kyiv. As Hrushevsky wrote, 'Among the Cossack officers who surrounded Khmelnytsky from the first stages of the people's war there was no lack of individuals who were more or less involved in the national movement of the Ukrainian intelligentsia.'[151]

As noted above, the revolutionary turmoil that took place between the writing of volumes 8 and 9 of the *History* changed many of Hrushevsky's prerevolutionary opinions and beliefs, including his view of the role of the intelligentsia in Ukrainian history. In volume 9 of the *History*, he generally avoided writing about the intelligentsia, using that term more often in relation to his contemporaries than to the educated circles of mid-seventeenth-century Ukraine. The Kyivan intelligentsia was mentioned only once and credited not with the 'formulation of the ideas and programs of statehood,' as in volume 8, but with promoting the liberation of the Ukrainian Orthodox Church. Hrushevsky wrote in volume 9: 'With the arrival of Khmelnytsky's circle in Kyiv at the end of 1648, it came under new influences: the Kyivan intelligentsia, the Ukrainian and Greek hierarchy, and the concept of the liberation of the Ukrainian church and Eastern Christianity – in short, the Ukrainian national problem in its ecclesiastical aspect.'[152]

What became of Hrushevsky's earlier worship of the intelligentsia and its role in the Khmelnytsky Uprising and Cossack history in general? It would probably be fair to conclude that the answer lies both in the main characteristics of the historical period studied by Hrushevsky at any given moment and in the more gradual changes in his political outlook. With regard to the first factor, it is worth noting Hrushevsky's differential treatment of the Ukrainian Orthodox clergy in the 1620s, when it supported Cossackdom, and in the latter half of the 1630s and most of the 1640s, when the clergy, led by Metropolitan Petro Mohyla, opposed the Cossacks. In the first case, the intelligentsia showed solidarity with the masses (as represented by the Cossacks), winning the highest praise from Hrushevsky. In the second case, it sided with the Polish regime against the masses (that is, the Cossacks) and, as a result, became the target of his greatest opprobrium.[153]

In discussing the change in Hrushevsky's political and cultural views and their impact on his treatment of the historical role of Ukrainian intelligentsia, it should be noted that the years of revolutionary turmoil, followed by émigré life in Central Europe, convinced Hrushevsky that the Ukrainian intelligentsia of the early twentieth century had not done its duty to the people. It neglected the interests of the masses, engaged in internal bickering, and, as a result, found itself on the losing side of the revolution. While in the emigration, Hrushevsky commented more than once on the shortcomings of the Ukrainian intelligentsia. In 1923 he noted in a letter to Kyrylo Studynsky: 'Just as you wrote that our people will now get what it deserves, and this is good, so now one must think that it will get very little, because its intelligentsia deserves very little, though the people deserves much more. But it is guilty of tolerating such a hypocritical, mendacious, vile, and egoistic intelligentsia!'[154]

Hrushevsky was not, of course, the only Ukrainian political activist to become disappointed with the Ukrainian intelligentsia during the revolution. His main political and scholarly opponent of the post-revolutionary era, Viacheslav Lypynsky, also experienced his share of disenchantment with the Ukrainian educated classes. True enough, in his studies of the Khmelnytsky era published in 1920, Lypynsky continued to view the intelligentsia as a contributor to the overall success of the uprising. Yet there were substantial differences in Lypynsky's treatment of the role of the intelligentsia as compared with his prerevolutionary writings. If in 1912 Lypynsky regarded the intelligentsia as a stratum composed of nobles and clergymen, in 1920 he presented the nobility as a group separate from the intelligentsia. The latter, unlike the nobility, had clearly lost the author's favour and was now lumped together with the Orthodox clergy. Both groupings were characterized as simple-minded and fanatical in their 'darkness.'[155] As was the case with Hrushevsky, Lypynsky's change of attitude toward the historical intelligentsia was directly linked to the change in his political views. In his *Letters to Fellow Landowners*, published in 1926, Lypynsky accused the intelligentsia, by which he meant primarily activists of the Ukrainian socialist parties, of dividing the nation and ruining Ukraine.[156]

In the aftermath of revolution, Hrushevsky and Lypynsky were both unhappy with the role played by the intelligentsia in the revolutionary events and, as a result, revised their views on its role in Ukrainian history generally. However, the nature of those revisions was quite different. If Lypynsky became even more convinced of the paramount role of the Ukrainian nobility in the Khmelnytsky Uprising, Hrushevsky returned to his populist-era fascination with the role of the popular masses, depicting them as the collective protagonist of Ukrainian history.

So far we have examined those elements of Hrushevsky's treatment of elite-mass relations in which his populist discourse not only did not contradict but actually reinforced the nationalist one. These were the cases in which the interests of the masses coincided, in Hrushevsky's opinion, with the interests of the Ukrainian nation as a whole. But the history of the Khmelnytsky Uprising was replete with instances in which the interests of the masses and those of the nation (even in Hrushevsky's opinion) were contradictory, making it necessary for the historian to choose between the two. Hrushevsky was becoming increasingly aware of such instances in the last, Soviet-era volumes of his *History*. As a result, when the populist elites that represented the interests of the masses at a given moment acted contrary to the national interests of Ukraine, Hrushevsky reluctantly sided with the ruling stratum and not with the popular masses. In such cases, Hrushevsky the national historian had to overcome Hrushevsky the populist.

Hrushevsky's desire to reconcile, if not harmonize, his populist and nationalist views was fully apparent in his treatment of mass Ukrainian emigration across the Muscovite border to Sloboda Ukraine after the Zboriv Agreement of 1649. From his early years as a scholar, Hrushevsky considered that phenomenon an important factor in the history of the Khmelnytsky era, and one of his best Soviet-era students, Viktor Iurkevych, even completed a dissertation devoted to the question. In his essay of 1898, Hrushevsky linked the beginning of the emigration with popular disappointment in the Cossack leadership in the aftermath of the Treaty of Zboriv. He blamed the negative consequences of the treaty partly on prevailing circumstances but also on the leadership of the uprising.[157] The accusatory tone was significantly modulated in Hrushevsky's later writings on the issue. In the *Illustrated History* (1912), Hrushevsky discussed the emigration of the peasant masses to Muscovy not so much in the context of Khmelnytsky's policy as in that of the unwillingness of the masses to sustain an uprising that had shattered their dreams.[158] In volume 8 of the *History*, he listed mass emigration to Muscovy among the factors that boded no good either for the hetman's government or for 'Ukrainian life' in general.[159]

Hrushevsky remained ambivalent on this issue in the Soviet-era volumes of the *History*.[160] On the one hand, he explicitly blamed Khmelnytsky for not caring enough about the interests of the masses and getting himself involved in Moldavian affairs instead of creating tolerable conditions for the peasantry.[161] On the other hand, Hrushevsky did not fully endorse the actions of the masses. Discussing Khmelnytsky's plans to take control of Western Ukrainian territories in 1656, Hrushevsky wrote: 'But as the wise heads of the Cossack leadership perspired over these combinations, the rank and file, weary of the endless war, campaigns, Polish and Tatar attacks, mobilization, and the interminable border postings with no opportunity for taking booty, were fleeing across the borders of the Cossack republic. And while political plans called for new operations in the west, Khmelnytsky was forced to contemplate punitive expeditions across the Muscovite border in order to eradicate and burn down the free villages there and return to their regiments Cossacks who had deserted there ... Therein lay the tragedy of those plans for statehood.'[162]

Hrushevsky did not condemn these punitive expeditions against Ukrainian settlers (he now called them the deserter element). Instead, he decried the establishment of a base for anti-Khmelnytsky activities across the Muscovite border and listed those settlements among the factors that contributed to the 'ruin of Ukrainian statehood' after Khmelnytsky's death.[163] Hrushevsky was prepared to let others judge whether the elites or the people were wrong in this situation: 'We leave it to the historian-publicists to determine who was more culpable here. Was it the Cossack masses, who, by deserting their political leaders and diplomats, were drifting farther away from campaigns, wars, and councils at such a critical moment in order to engage in homesteading as they pleased – establishing farmsteads, ponds, beehives, brewing mead and whisky, and relishing thoughts of an epochal struggle for liberation from a distance, in a shady spot? Or was it the upper stratum of Cossacks who, soaring intellectually among the various political constellations, were forgetting the national substratum that could not sustain such high politics beneath their feet?'[164] One of Hrushevsky's Marxist critics, Fedir Iastrebov, took his words about 'historian-publicists' as a derogatory reference to Marxist historians in general.[165] It is difficult to say whether that was indeed the case, although it is quite clear that Hrushevsky was truly disturbed by the question of whom to blame in this situation. While his sympathies were generally on the side of the masses, it was the elites that were building the Ukrainian state, planning to expand it with the Western Ukrainian territories, and defending its sovereignty against the encroachments of the Muscovite authorities. The masses, for their part, cared little about these issues, deserted the cause of Ukrainian statehood, and sided with the Muscovites in their attempts to destabilize the situation in Ukraine during the last years of Khmelnytsky's rule.[166]

Another case in which Hrushevsky did not side entirely with the masses was his treatment of the popular uprising against Ivan Vyhovsky led by Colonel Martyn Pushkar of Poltava and the Zaporozhian Cossacks (1658). There Hrushevsky followed in the footsteps of his former professor, Volodymyr Antonovych. The anti-Vyhovsky uprising, which met with some support and understanding in Moscow, had been treated by Antonovych with a measure of contempt. He believed that after the death of Khmelnytsky Ukrainian politics became a contest between two major forces: the Cossack officers who wanted to acquire nobiliary status, which required Polish support, and the popular masses, who opposed the return of serfdom. The plebeian leaders, however, relying on Muscovite support, knew no better than to introduce the Russian variant of the nobility and nobiliary-peasant relations into Ukraine. Antonovych was generally quite sympathetic to Vyhovsky and had no high opinion of his antagonists in the popular camp. He also believed that the plebeians' reliance on Moscow facilitated Muscovite attempts to curtail Ukrainian autonomy.[167]

In his essay of 1898 on Khmelnytsky, Hrushevsky further developed Antonovych's view, presenting the post-Khmelnytsky era as a period of conflict between the Cossack officers, with their autonomist aspirations, and the popular masses, who undermined those aspirations by siding with Muscovy. The reason for the conflict, in Hrushevsky's opinion, was the egoism of the Cossack officer stratum. Hrushevsky laid the blame at the feet of the Cossack officers, calling their social and economic agenda the 'internal gangrene that facilitated Muscovy's destructive work in Ukraine.' The Cossack officers traded away their political and national interests for economic gain, claimed Hrushevsky, while the popular masses, after having been exploited by Muscovy, were returned to the control of the Cossack officer stratum in order to be completely 'devoured' by it.[168] Five years later, in his *Survey History of the Ukrainian People* (1904), and subsequently in his *Illustrated History*, Hrushevsky did not put forward the 'masses vs Cossack officers' interpretation of Vyhovsky's hetmancy, focusing instead on the conflict between the hetman and his associates on the one hand and the Zaporozhians and Cossacks of the Poltava and Myrhorod regiments on the other.[169]

Uncharacteristically, given his other post-1917 writings, Hrushevsky actually remained loyal to this interpretation of events in volume 10 of his academic *History*. His critique of the Cossack officers' social and economic aspirations here was much less severe than in his essay of 1898. Writing about the atrocities committed by the rebellious masses against families of Cossack officer provenance, Hrushevsky noted that 'those who chose the class ways of the Polish lords and manifested their social and economic pretensions had to be prepared to face the repetition against them of the social revolution that they had so recently lived through.'[170] Thus, Hrushevsky was determined to hold the Cossack officers responsible for the popular revolt but made no attempt to put all the blame on the elites. The historian did not conceal his disgust with the atrocities perpetrated by Vyhovsky's foes, often referring to the rebels not as 'people,' 'masses,' or 'popular masses,' but as 'rabble.' Although Hrushevsky put the term in quotation marks, it is difficult to avoid the impression that he was far from supportive of that outburst of popular anger.

The reasons for Hrushevsky's negativism in treating this episode, which he might otherwise have regarded as a manifestation of the 'liberation struggle of the popular masses,' was spelled out in his comments on the rebels' plans for the reorganization of the Cossack order in Ukraine. Hrushevsky appraised them as follows: 'Ukrainian statehood was undermined. All the state-building accomplishments of the previous decade, of the times of Khmelnytsky, were [now] put into question.'[171] In making this assessment, Hrushevsky employed such derogatory terms as 'Host-rabble,' 'all the rabble of Zaporizhia and the settled area,' and so on. Hrushevsky was not opposed in principle to the rebels' desire to take power from the elite. What he could not accept was that in opposing the Cossack officers, the rebels were undermining the state and Ukrainian national interests. He gave the following evaluation of the actions of the 'rabble': 'It wants to wrest power from the hands of the ruling stratum that was turning this power into a tool of its social class strength, economic usurpation, and exploitation of toilers. But being unable to implement this in organized forms, this direct democracy plunges life into anarchic chaos on the one hand and, on the other, wants to paralyse the influence of its own bourgeoisie by means of the influence of the Muscovite bourgeoisie and bureaucracy, which is an even greater danger to its own strivings, for it is more strongly organized, utterly ruthless in its policies, and completely indifferent to the interests of Ukrainian life as such. Having made it the arbiter of its quarrels with the Cossack officers, direct democracy light-heartedly relinquishes to it the interests of Ukrainian life, its structure and leadership, instead of organizing those rank-and-file Cossacks in the settled area whose interests it was pleading and enabling them to build and control their own life.'[172]

Was this new approach to the post-Khmelnytsky era a result of the natural erosion of Hrushevsky's populist views by national ideas? Or was it a sign of Hrushevsky's rejection of Soviet-era fascination with the history of the class struggle? Probably, both factors influenced Hrushevsky's writing of the time. What strikes one, nevertheless, is that despite Hrushevsky's growing criticism of the masses, his language in volume 10 of the *History* seems much more influenced by official Soviet argot and class-based terminology than that of any previous volume. Hrushevsky used such terms as 'tool of class power' and 'exploitation of toilers'; he also accused 'direct democracy' of attempting to undermine 'the influence of its own bourgeoisie by means of the influence of the Muscovite bourgeoisie and bureaucracy.'[173] Hrushevsky had occasionally introduced class categories into his interpretation of Ukrainian history even in his prerevolutionary writings[174] and used terms such as 'exploitation,' 'toilers,' and 'bourgeoisie' in his political writings of the revolutionary period,[175] but generally he had avoided vocabulary of this sort in his academic *History*. What happened to Hrushevsky's use of terms in volume 10 of the *History*? Were these simple slips of the pen that allowed the dominant Soviet-era class-based discourse to take over Hrushevsky's narration? Or was he making a conscious attempt to rebuke the rebels for their excesses within the context of a generally mass-friendly, class-based discourse? Hrushevsky's text allows for more than one interpretation, but it is clear that in this case, as in many others, Hrushevsky the populist would not yield to Hrushevsky the nationalist and Hrushevsky the statist.

The State

Hrushevsky's treatment of the role of the state in the Khmelnytsky Uprising was closely linked to his evolving views on the role of the national factor in the Khmelnytsky era. Nevertheless, it requires separate treatment, partly because of the ongoing discussion in Ukrainian historiography on the question of whether Hrushevsky was a populist or a statist. That discussion originated with the publication of Dmytro Doroshenko's *Survey of Ukrainian Historiography* (1923), which characterized Hrushevsky as a 'representative of Ukrainian populism' and accused him of 'denying the significance of the Ukrainian state tradition.'[176] This argument was further developed in the article 'Ukrainian Historiography at the Turning Point' (1924) by Hrushevsky's student Ivan Krevetsky, who introduced a clear distinction between the 'populist' ideas of Hrushevsky and the 'national-statist' concepts of Viacheslav Lypynsky and Stepan Tomashivsky.[177] Viacheslav Zaikin, who reviewed Krevetsky's article, was apparently the first to speak of a 'national-statist' or simply statist school in Ukrainian historical discourse.[178]

The original discussion was provoked by Hrushevsky's political pamphlet *The Ukrainian Party of Socialist Revolutionaries and Its Tasks* (1920).[179] This was Hrushevsky's first major political statement to appear after the publication in 1918 of his collection *On the Threshold of a New Ukraine*. As noted in the previous chapter, the historian used this statement to present his views on the new political situation resulting from the defeat of the Ukrainian socialist parties in the wake of the Bolshevik takeover of Ukraine. Analysing the sympathies of the masses, Hrushevsky suggested that the Socialist Revolutionaries focus on meeting their social demands and expectations. In developing this thesis, he harked back to the political ideals of Ukrainian populism and presented himself as their devoted exponent: 'I was brought up in the strict tradition of Ukrainian radical populism, which originated with the Brotherhood of SS. Cyril and Methodius, and firmly believed that, in the conflict between the people and the government, blame attaches to the government, since the interests of the working people are the highest good, and if they are flouted, the people are free to change their social system.'[180]

In many ways Hrushevsky's statement not only reflected the atmosphere of Antonovych's school, in which he was moulded as a historian, but also manifested his revolutionary-era return to the ideological roots of Ukrainian populism. There is little doubt that Hrushevsky's remarks of 1920 on the role of the state in Ukrainian history were informed by the political struggle of the time. No less politically motivated were the accusations levelled against Hrushevsky by his opponents on the basis of this particular pamphlet. The attack, spearheaded by none other than Viacheslav Lypynsky in his *Letters to Fellow Landowners*, was quite brutal and often unjust.[181] Also far from objective was the criticism of Hrushevsky by his own students, such as Krevetsky, who indiscriminately claimed that he was 'hostile to the state.'[182] Even Doroshenko's moderate critique was wide of the mark. As noted in chapter 3, from the very beginning of his academic career, Hrushevsky did not shy away from discussing the role of the state in Ukrainian history. In his thinking, Antonovych's populism was counterbalanced by the task of creating a synthesis of Ukrainian history. While one could hardly expect a general history of Ukraine from the earliest times to the Khmelnytsky Uprising to employ statehood as its leitmotif, neither could such a comprehensive account be limited to the stateless periods of the Ukrainian past.

The fascination of Lypynsky and his followers with Ukrainian statehood was a novel phenomenon in their thinking that came to the fore only after 1917. By that time Hrushevsky had already published seven volumes of his *History*, which met with little if any criticism at the time on the part of the future statists. Writing in 1912, Lypynsky not only did not challenge any major points of Hrushevsky's interpretation of Ukrainian history but even sought help and advice from him. As his area of research, Lypynsky chose the history of the Ukrainian nobility, a topic that clearly distinguished him from Hrushevsky but hardly made him more of a statist than Hrushevsky himself. Lypynsky's fascination with Khmelnytsky's proclamation of 1657 to the Pinsk nobility, which he treated as an important indication that the hetman had acted as a head of state, was inspired by Hrushevsky's interpretation of the document. Even in 1920, when Lypynsky revised his earlier publications so as to put special emphasis on the role of the state in the Khmelnytsky era, his approach was hardly innovative, given the treatment of the issue in Hrushevsky's popular writings of 1917 and 1918. It is true, however, that unlike the statists, Hrushevsky did not view the state as an end in itself but treated it more as a means of achieving the political, social, and cultural objectives of the Ukrainian nation. It was in keeping with this objective that Hrushevsky consciously placed the goal of creating and preserving a Ukrainian nation-state at the top of his political agenda in 1917 and 1918.

After the revolution Lypynsky was the first scholar to place special emphasis on the history of Ukrainian statehood, which he consistently promoted in all his postrevolutionary (mainly political) writings. However, his single-minded insistence on the paramount importance of statehood for the development of the Ukrainian nation at a time when there was no hope of establishing such a state drew criticism even from the ranks of the statists themselves. In one of his private letters of July 1922, Stepan Tomashivsky went so far as to claim that statehood, in and of itself, could not be the goal of the national movement. He pointed out that state and nation were different categories, maintaining that Ukrainians would be better off if they stopped pursuing the ideal of statehood. Tomashivsky called on Ukrainian pedagogues to break down the premature fixation on statehood and focus instead on developing all the characteristics of a modern nation.[183]

There can be little doubt that framing the historiographic discussion of the 1920s as a confrontation between 'statists' and 'populists,' as was done by Hrushevsky's opponents in the 1920s, is misleading at best. At the core of the disagreement between Lypynsky, Tomashivsky, and other statists on the one hand and Hrushevsky on the other was not the issue of statehood per se but the question of what kind of state they wanted to build. In that regard, Hrushevsky indeed remained a populist who generally (if not invariably) put the interests of the popular masses at the top of his agenda. By contrast, Lypynsky, Tomashivsky, Doroshenko, Krevetsky, and others rejected the orientation on the masses: in their writings, they were much more inclined toward a positive assessment of the role played in Ukrainian history by the elites. If anything, they were 'elitist' in their interpretation of Ukrainian history. 'Elitism,' however, did not have as much appeal in postrevolutionary Ukrainian society as 'statism,' and, of course, it was much more effective to accuse one's opponent of being 'anti-statist' than egalitarian or anti-elitist.

For all its shortcomings and inaccuracies, the notion that Hrushevsky was an opponent of statehood in politics and historiography became an axiom in the writings of many proponents of the statist school. Only with the relative decline of the statist approach in Ukrainian historiography in the diaspora and the growth of a cult of Hrushevsky among Ukrainian historians in the West was that image of Hrushevsky challenged in the course of the 1960s and 1970s.[184] By the end of the twentieth century the statist/populist controversy all but died out in Ukrainian historical writing outside Ukraine. In Ukraine, on the other hand, the question of whether Hrushevsky was a 'statist' or a 'populist' historian is still being discussed and continues to engage some of Ukraine's most prominent historians.[185]

There is little doubt that Hrushevsky's early views on the role of the state in Ukrainian history were forged in the populist milieu of the friends and students of Professor Volodymyr Antonovych.[186] Hrushevsky himself presented the intellectual tradition of radical populism, in which he was brought up, as essentially antistatist. He did so not only in his politically inspired article of 1920 on the political tasks of the Ukrainian Party of Socialist Revolutionaries but also in his much more balanced article of 1928 on the scholarly legacy of Volodymyr Antonovych, in which he stated that Antonovych's 'democratism and populism acquired a clearly marked antistatist, anarchist character.'[187] Despite being influenced by the antistatist ideas of Ukrainian populism, Hrushevsky was also quite successful in shaking them off. Even in his early article 'The Communal Movement in Ukraine-Rus' in the Thirteenth Century' (1892), widely criticized for its populism and alleged antistatism, Hrushevsky did not question the positive role of the state in Ukrainian history per se. While praising one of the thirteenth-century communes for rebelling against the rule of its prince, Hrushevsky wrote: 'Although we do not depreciate the state as a form [for the development of] culture and progress, we can stand up for it only when it creates an opportunity for the spiritual, moral, economic, and political development of the community.'[188]

Generally speaking, Hrushevsky did not shy away from discussing the contributions of statesmen and government institutions to the development of Ukraine either in his academic *History* or in his numerous articles and popular writings. There is nothing to suggest that he harboured any nihilistic views concerning the role of the state in the Ukrainian past. The very fact that Hrushevsky devoted several volumes of his academic *History* to Kyivan Rus' and the Principality of Galicia-Volhynia after long decades of neglect of those states by populist historians was a clear indication of his new scholarly interests, which presaged the coming shift in the direction of Ukrainian historical research. Although Hrushevsky rarely used the term 'statehood' in his prerevolutionary works, it is quite apparent that from a very early point in his career he considered Kyivan Rus' not only part of Ukrainian history but also a Ukrainian state. Ten years after the publication of his article on the communal movement in medieval Ukraine, Hrushevsky addressed the issue once again in his famous article on the rational organization of East Slavic history (1904). There he did not deny the role played by state structures in the history of the Eastern Slavs. Instead, he acknowledged that the state had indeed been very important in the history of the Russian people but maintained that in the history of the Ukrainians, who had lived for centuries without a state of their own, it was of much lesser significance. He recognized the need to study the influence of foreign states on Ukrainian national life but argued that during the stateless periods of Ukrainian history the political element had been eclipsed by economic, cultural, and national factors.[189]

Let us now take a closer look at Hrushevsky's treatment of the statist idea in his discussion of Khmelnytsky Uprising. This seems especially appropriate, given the fact that all the leading members of the statist school, including Lypynsky, Tomashivsky, and Krypiakevych were not only specialists in the period but also developed and legitimized many of their ideas on the basis of their studies of the Khmelnytsky era. It should be noted at the outset that Hrushevsky, who did meticulous research on the political and diplomatic history of the Hetmanate, never discussed the issue of Cossack statehood as a theoretical problem. There is, nonetheless, enough occasional or incidental commentary in Hrushevsky's writings to make possible a reconstruction of his views on the issue.

Hrushevsky first applied the terms 'state' and 'statist' to the Cossack polity in his essay of 1898 on Khmelnytsky and his era. At that time, he believed that the idea of statehood was coming into focus only in the last year of Khmelnytsky's life. When discussing Khmelnytsky's circular to the Pinsk nobility (1657), Hrushevsky wrote that in this instance Khmelnytsky acted as a head of state and that the decree itself should be viewed as part of a plan to establish Ukrainian statehood.[190] What Hrushevsky meant by 'Ukrainian state' was the 'Rus' Principality,' a concept formally approved, in the historian's opinion, in Khmelnytsky's agreement of 1657 with Sweden and Transylvania on the partition of the Commonwealth. The principality was supposed to include the whole ethnic territory of Rus'-Ukraine, and its political structure was based on the idea that the entire principality would be represented by the 'Rus' hetman.' Hrushevsky believed that some elements of the 'Rus' Principality' project could be traced back to the Zboriv Agreement (1649), which defined Cossack territory and endowed its residents with specific rights. He also claimed that after the Pereiaslav Agreement, Ukraine found itself de facto a 'separate state,' linked to Muscovy on terms of personal union.[191]

In his article of 1904 on the anniversary of the Pereiaslav Agreement, Hrushevsky suggested that in Khmelnytsky's times Ukrainian-Muscovite relations were defined by the interaction of two factors – Ukrainian aspirations to statehood (*derzhavna okremishnist'*) and the Muscovite desire for centralism. In his article of 1912 on Mazepa and Khmelnytsky, Hrushevsky continued in this vein, presenting the latter as a 'fairly conscious representative of the idea of Ukrainian statehood (*derzhavna ukraïns'ka ideia*).'[192] Hrushevsky's growing interest in issues related to Cossack statehood can also be demonstrated by the extensive discussion that he added to the new edition of his *Survey History of the Ukrainian People* concerning the political and social order established in Ukraine as a result of the Khmelnytsky Uprising.[193] In the *Illustrated History*, a whole section ('The Hetmanate') was devoted to the organization of the Cossack polity in Khmelnytsky's times.[194] Hrushevsky's obvious interest in issues related to the history of Cossack statehood becomes particularly apparent in his political and popular historical writings of the revolutionary era. In the pamphlet *Where the Ukrainian Movement Came From and Where It Is Going* (1917), Hrushevsky listed the achievement of statehood among the goals of Ukrainian movement. Claiming historical legitimacy for those goals, Hrushevsky stated that Ukrainians were not inventing anything new but reminding others of the ideals for which their ancestors had fought and died. He maintained that Ukrainian statehood was a goal put forward by Khmelnytsky and his associates at the very beginning of the uprising.[195]

Hrushevsky's interest in the problem of Ukrainian statehood did not disappear in his post-revolutionary writings. Despite his much-criticized attempt to undermine the statist factor by emphasizing the social one in his pamphlet of 1920, *The Ukrainian Party of Socialist Revolutionaries and Its Tasks*, his treatment of the issue in the last volumes of the *History* is characterized by increased interest in the idea of statehood. As noted above, Hrushevsky's devotion to the interests of the masses revived in the 1920s. Nevertheless, this commitment ceased to be the only criterion by which the activities of individual actors and whole social groups were judged in Hrushevsky's writings. Reviewing Ukrainian historiography in the conclusions to volume 9 of the *History*, Hrushevsky noted the rise of the statist trend with obvious sympathy. He explicitly sided with the critics of Oleksander Lazarevsky, who rejected his class-based interpretation of the Cossack officer elite as a negative factor in Ukrainian history and stressed cultural, national, statist, and patriotic motives in the activities of Cossack officers. It is not clear whether Hrushevsky counted himself among those early critics of Lazarevsky and proponents of the statist approach in Ukrainian historiography, but it is quite apparent that the question of whether the Cossack officers not only represented the interests of their social stratum but also cared about the interests of the state and the nation as a whole was among those that most interested Hrushevsky in the Soviet-era volumes of his *History*.[196]

In those volumes, Khmelnytsky does not merely dream about the creation of a Ukrainian state but actually figures as the ruler of his own 'Cossack state' and the leader of a 'European state.'[197] While Hrushevsky clearly disagreed with Lypynsky's views on Khmelnytsky, he tried to discredit them not by attacking the latter's statist ideas but by showing that Khmelnytsky was a poor statesman who had failed to secure the interests of the Ukrainian state. Marshalling his arguments in his polemic with Lypynsky, Hrushevsky stressed that although he considered Khmelnytsky a great man, his greatness had little to do with statesmanship. According to Hrushevsky, Khmelnytsky's rule was completely bereft of an 'elementary state economy and the hand "of a political master of the Ukrainian land."'[198] The Cossack elites, for their part, failed to ensure the realization of the 'Ukrainian state idea' in relations with Muscovy and were 'completely indifferent to the statist aspirations of Cossackdom.'[199] Neither the very fact of the existence of a Ukrainian state under Khmelnytsky nor the paramount importance of its interests in the history of the Ukrainian nation were ever questioned by Hrushevsky in his polemics with Lypynsky. Their discussion did not centre on the idea of the state per se but on the question of what kind of state Ukraine needed, who had the right to rule it, and whose interests it was to serve. That was the true bone of contention between the 'statist' Lypynsky and the 'populist' Hrushevsky. If the former promoted the idea of a hierarchical, class-based monarchy, the latter had in mind the model of an egalitarian, classless state ruled by elites whose main purpose was to serve the interests of the popular masses.[200]

In the Soviet-era volumes of the *History*, the concept of statehood was closely associated with the idea of Ukrainian independence. It should be noted, nevertheless, that initially Hrushevsky was more than reluctant to accept the political independence of Ukraine as one of the goals of the Khmelnytsky Uprising. The major issue in his early interpretation of the Khmelnytsky era was that of Ukraine's autonomy, not of its independence. But even autonomy appeared in Hrushevsky's writing of the time as something quite marginal, if not completely alien, to the political thinking of the Cossack leadership. That was the context in which, in his essay of 1898 on Khmelnytsky, Hrushevsky criticized the Cossack officers' strategy at Pereiaslav, claiming that the idea of Ukrainian autonomy was absent from their demands, which focused only on the autonomy of Cossackdom as a social estate.[201] At that time, Hrushevsky apparently believed that the idea of territorial autonomy (*avtonomiia kraiu*) only began to be formulated in Khmelnytsky's day.[202] In this respect he was merely following Antonovych, who claimed in his survey of Cossack history that after the Pereiaslav Agreement Khmelnytsky became aware of his failure 'to guarantee the autonomous rights of Ukraine.'[203]

In a public lecture devoted to the 250th anniversary of the Khmelnytsky Uprising (1898), Antonovych generally praised Khmelnytsky but was very dismissive on the subject of Cossack statehood. Defending Khmelnytsky against accusations that he had failed to establish an independent Ukrainian state, Antonovych claimed that it was not the hetman but the Ukrainian (in his terminology, 'South Russian') people who were either uninterested in or incapable of creating one. According to Antonovych, the people strove for local autonomy instead.[204] Autonomy was the avowed goal of the late nineteenth-century Ukrainian movement, an objective that Antonovych, for whatever reason, read back into the times of Khmelnytsky. Did Antonovych believe what he was saying, or was he trying to provide historical legitimacy for the movement's moderate goal and implicitly threatening the authorities with the alternative of independence? The latter interpretation is not entirely untenable, although Hrushevsky himself later claimed that Antonovych's publicly expressed disbelief in the state-building potential of the Ukrainian people largely reflected his actual thinking on the issue.[205]

There can be little doubt that between the two revolutions, Hrushevsky's treatment of Cossack statehood was greatly influenced by the political goal of the Ukrainian movement – the achievement of territorial autonomy. In his essay of 1904 on the Khmelnytsky era, Hrushevsky identified the political autonomy of Ukraine as a goal of Cossack diplomacy at the time of Pereiaslav that was actually achieved by Khmelnytsky. If in his essay of 1898 he had accused the Cossacks of failing to put forward the idea of Ukrainian territorial autonomy, he now claimed that the Cossacks in fact desired 'complete autonomy,' while Muscovy refused to guarantee even 'provincial autonomy.' He also noted Moscow's policy of curtailing Ukrainian autonomy after Khmelnytsky's death.[206] In 'Bohdan's Anniversary' (1907), Hrushevsky traced the Ukrainian movement's goal of a 'free and autonomous Ukraine' back to Khmelnytsky's times and posed the following question to his reader: 'How close are we to the dreams of a Ukraine without serf or lord, free and autonomous, that entranced the old hetman and his collaborators and contemporaries?'[207] In his essay of 1912 on Mazepa and Khmelnytsky, Hrushevsky called the latter an 'outstanding autonomist.' Even Archbishop Lazar Baranovych of Chernihiv figured in that essay as a proponent of Ukrainian autonomy.[208]

In Ukrainian national discourse of the first months of the 1917 revolution, Cossack statehood was also intrinsically linked with the Ukrainian movement's efforts to secure broad territorial and national autonomy for Ukraine within a reformed federal Russian state. In his brochure of 1917, *What Kind of Autonomy and Federation We Want*, Hrushevsky defined autonomy as a broad concept that included various forms of government ranging from local self-rule to 'full statehood.' He illustrated this point by referring to the historiographic discussion on whether the autonomous Hetmanate had constituted a 'non-sovereign state' or an 'autonomous province' prior to its liquidation in the second half of the eighteenth century.[209] As the idea of Ukrainian national and territorial autonomy within the framework of a federalized Russia gained support within the Ukrainian movement, Khmelnytsky emerged in Hrushevsky's writings as an ever stronger supporter of Ukrainian autonomy. His subsequent transformation from autonomist into independentist corresponded in many ways to the evolution of Hrushevsky's own views.

Hrushevsky first employed the term 'independence' to characterize Khmelnytsky's views as early as 1904. In his essay on the 250th anniversary of the Pereiaslav Agreement, Hrushevsky wrote that as early as January and February 1649 the war for the interests of the Cossack order was transformed in Khmelnytsky's consciousness into a struggle for the interests of the whole people and the 'independence of Ukraine.'[210] In his *Illustrated History of Ukraine* (1912), Hrushevsky gave a similar interpretation of Khmelnytsky's statement to the Polish commissioners at Pereiaslav in early 1649. There, the historian claimed that Khmelnytsky had resolved to fight for 'the whole Ukrainian people, for all Ukraine, for its liberation, independence, and sovereignty.'[211] Hrushevsky, though, was far from consistent in his interpretation of Khmelnytsky's policy as one focused on Ukrainian independence. In the very same *Illustrated History of Ukraine*, he wrote about the autonomist aspirations of Khmelnytsky, the Cossack officers, and Ukrainian society as a whole.[212] In part 3 of volume 8 of his academic *History* (completed in early 1917), Hrushevsky approached the issue of Ukrainian independence in the same ambiguous fashion. On the one hand, he wrote that people were 'avid for a decisive struggle in the name of liberty and independence,'[213] but on the other, he failed to reassert his earlier claim about Khmelnytsky's orientation on independence as early as 1649. Hrushevsky confined himself to mentioning 'the idea of liberating Ukrainian Rus' from the rule of the Liakhs and securing its independence and statehood, in close alliance with its Orthodox neighbors,' as one of the topics discussed by Patriarch Paisios and Bohdan Khmelnytsky.[214]

Notwithstanding these inconsistencies, it would appear that the 1917 revolution turned Hrushevsky into a much stronger believer in Khmelnytsky's independentist aspirations. In his introduction to the second edition of volume 8, part 3, of the *History* (written in the emigration in December 1921), Hrushevsky noted that 'Khmelnytsky and his confederates' eventually arrived at the idea of a 'united, independent Ukraine.'[215] That statement was reinforced and further developed in volume 9 of the *History*. Writing about Khmelnytsky's aspirations in early 1649, Hrushevsky noted: 'He now posited the goal of Ukraine's complete political independence within its historical boundaries, and it was clearly in this sense that he referred to himself as "absolute Ruthenian ruler and autocrat" – not in the sense of a monarch with unlimited power, as Lypynsky interprets it, but as head of a sovereign state, in contrast to the royalism of yesteryear with its plans for an autonomous Cossack Ukraine under the direct rule of the king. Occasionally he would still go astray amid these royalist notes, but his policies were oriented quite clearly toward an independent Ukraine. I therefore resolutely reject the view that in 1649 Khmelnytsky and his supporters remained committed to the idea of Cossack autonomy within the framework of the Commonwealth, as they had been in 1648, and that the Zboriv Agreement supposedly gives us an expression of their political program.'[216]

Hrushevsky used the idea of Ukrainian independence as the basis for a rather detailed periodization of the Khmelnytsky era, which he presented in the concluding chapter of volume 9. Polemicizing with Lypynsky's interpretation of that crucial period, Hrushevsky presented his own version. In developing a statist concept of the Khmelnytsky Uprising, Lypynsky placed special emphasis on the legal treaties that defined the status of Cossack Ukraine at the time of the insurrection. He viewed the Zboriv Agreement of 1649 not only as an important treaty but also as an expression of Khmelnytsky's political aspirations at the time. Lypynsky also paid special attention to the Pereiaslav Agreement of 1654, as he believed that the treaty with the tsar effectively removed

Ukraine from Polish control and granted wider international recognition to the Cossack state.[217] Hrushevsky rejected this treaty-based periodization of the Khmelnytsky Uprising. As discussed earlier, he was more than critical of the merits of the Zboriv Agreement, nor did he praise the one reached at Pereiaslav.

In Hrushevsky's opinion, the first period of the uprising, which was characterized by mass participation and dominated by the political, social, and economic demands of the Cossack order, came to an end in December 1648. After his entrance into Kyiv, Khmelnytsky allegedly reformulated his program, striving for the liberation of the Ukrainian people and the political independence of Ukraine within its ethnic boundaries. From that perspective, the Zboriv Agreement was not an expression of the actual program of the Cossack elite but a compromise forced upon it by the Crimean khan. It was also a complete fiasco from the viewpoint of the interests of the Ukrainian masses and ended the growth phase of the uprising. Nor did the Pereiaslav Agreement promote the cause of the Ukrainian masses or Ukrainian independence. In Hrushevsky's opinion, the Cossack elite did not seize the opportunity to establish itself as the sole representative of Ukrainian society. Preoccupied instead with its own group interests, it opened the door to future intervention in Ukraine's internal affairs by the Muscovite authorities. According to Hrushevsky, the actual turning point of the Khmelnytsky era was the conclusion of the military alliance with Sweden in 1657. Even though the league never materialized, Hrushevsky considered it especially important, as it placed the political independence of Ukraine (within its ethnic boundaries) back on the agenda of Cossack politics.[218] Many elements of this scheme were already present in Hrushevsky's essay of 1898. This is true of his generally negative assessment of the Zboriv and Pereiaslav agreements and his positive attitude toward the Cossack alliance with Sweden and Transylvania. What was not always present in Hrushevsky's view of the great uprising was the idea of an independent Ukrainian state.

Hrushevsky's views on the history of Cossack statehood developed from initial scepticism with regard to Khmelnytsky's polity to full acceptance of the idea that Ukraine had been a state during his hetmancy; from a belief in the autonomous nature of that polity to enthusiastic endorsement of its complete independence. In many ways, this evolution of Hrushevsky's views paralleled his changing attitude toward the role of the national factor in the early modern history of Ukraine. Like his interpretation of the role of heroes, elites, and the popular masses, this evolution was of course influenced by the political and cultural environment in which Hrushevsky wrote his works. In an era marked by the disintegration of empires and the formation of nation-states, it was impossible to ignore the growing importance of issues of statehood and nationhood.

Since Hrushevsky's research on the Khmelnytsky Uprising was conducted over a long period, it was influenced by a number of political and historiographic trends and participated in several political and historiographic discourses. Clearly there was a relationship between changing political circumstances at the turn of the century, Hrushevsky's political and social views, and the type of history he was writing. But what kind of relationship was it? How did it influence another set of relationships – that between evidence, research, and paradigm in Hrushevsky's writings? Was Hrushevsky's paradigm formed by the historical evidence he uncovered during years of work in the libraries and archives of Eastern Europe, or was the selection and interpretation of evidence directed by his shifting historical paradigm?

When one analyses the reflection of Hrushevsky's evolving political, social, and cultural views in his historical writings, it appears at first glance that the succession of historical paradigms was determined by the prevailing characteristics of the historical period that Hrushevsky was studying rather than by the particular stage of his ideological transformation. The study of the religious movements of the sixteenth and seventeenth centuries presented an excellent opportunity to develop a concept of the national revival in early modern Ukraine, while the history of the Khmelnytsky Uprising was first-class material for researching the origins of early modern Ukrainian statehood. Nevertheless, a closer reading of Hrushevsky's works suggests that he managed his material in a way that corresponded to major shifts in the interests and goals of the Ukrainian national movement. For example, he treated the most divisive moment in early modern Ukrainian national history, the struggle centring on the ecclesiastical Union of Brest (1596), as a period of Ukrainian national revival – this at a time when Ukrainian leaders and organizations were concerned with the awakening and revival of their own nation. In the 1920s it was very difficult for Hrushevsky to abandon his research on the Khmelnytsky era, with its popular movements and state-building initiatives, and move on to later periods of Ukrainian history when Ukrainian political leaders were preoccupied with the painful question of why the Ukrainian Revolution and the Ukrainian national state had failed. As a result, Hrushevsky devoted two and a half books of his ten-volume, eleven-book *History* to an analysis of the Khmelnytsky Uprising.

The impact of changing political circumstances on Hrushevsky's selection of topics in Ukrainian history and their interpretation is difficult to deny. On the one hand, Hrushevsky's writings from the late 1890s to the early 1930s strike one as highly consistent in the range of ideas they project, since elements of populist, nationalist, and statist discourse are constantly present in them. On the other hand, depending on the period in question, one can discern clear differences among them as the populist, nationalist, and statist arguments are given varying degrees of prominence and move slowly from the periphery of Hrushevsky's thought to its centre, and vice versa. Hrushevsky, who began his scholarly career as a populist, evolved into a national historian deeply interested in the history of the Ukrainian state and its elites. Hrushevsky the historian apparently followed Hrushevsky the political thinker and cultural activist through the three major stages or periods of his intellectual transformation. He was an avowed populist in the 1890s; a national awakener who supported the idea of social solidarity on a national platform between 1905 and 1917; and a socialist who returned to his populist roots after 1917, having become a committed statist and even an independentist during the revolution.

Although the impact of the revolutionary era on his writings was significantly lesser, or at least less apparent, than in the writings of Hrushevsky's main intellectual opponent of this period, Viacheslav Lypynsky, whom he accused of reading the events of the revolution back into the Khmelnytsky era,[219] that impact was significant in Hrushevsky's reevaluation of Ukrainian history. One example is his different treatment of the outcome of the Khmelnytsky Revolution. Judging by the last volumes of the *History*, for Hrushevsky, the Khmelnytsky Uprising ultimately ended in defeat, as did the Ukrainian Revolution of 1917–20. Gone was the heyday of the 1917 revolution, when an optimistic Hrushevsky had declared the Khmelnytsky Uprising a victory. Writing in 1928 under the Soviet regime, he pronounced it a defeat, returning to the interpretation advanced in his 'populist' writings of the turn of the century. For Hrushevsky the politician, the main problem pertaining to the failure of the Ukrainian Revolution was that of responsibility for the division between the popular masses and the elites. The same question was at the centre of his attention in the last volumes of the *History*. It is hardly surprising that Hrushevsky the historian, like

Hrushevsky the politician, blamed the elites. The masses, on the other hand, returned to centre stage in Hrushevsky's *History* in a way reminiscent of his earlier writings. There were, nevertheless, important differences in Hrushevsky's treatment of the historical role of the masses before and after the Revolution of 1917.

The Ukrainian Revolution made Hrushevsky appreciate the importance of politics and diplomacy. In the last volume of the *History*, Hrushevsky occasionally even put reasons of state above the immediate interests of the masses. He sided with the elites that represented and defended the Hetmanate against the masses whose actions undermined it. There is also little doubt that Hrushevsky's view of the role of the state in the Khmelnytsky era, expressed in volume 9 of the *History*, differed significantly from his initial treatment of the issue. The 1917 revolution and Hrushevsky's own political experience, as well as the writings of Lypynsky and his followers, appear to have had a major impact on the evolution of Hrushevsky's historical views. In the final volumes of the *History*, Hrushevsky emerges as a historian who clearly appreciated the role of the state in Ukrainian affairs but was no less 'populist' in his views and judgments than in some of his earliest writings.

Thus the changing views and sympathies of the historian had a clear impact on his writings, affecting some important elements of his paradigm. Was there a reverse impact? Did new sources – and sources in general – influence his interpretation of events and alter his historiographic paradigm? Hrushevsky's writings on the Khmelnytsky era offer no simple answer to this question. By the time he began his research, the Khmelnytsky era was already one of the most closely studied periods in Ukrainian history, with dozens of interpretative volumes and collections of source materials published by Hrushevsky's predecessors available. Thus, from the very beginning Hrushevsky had a sufficient source base to formulate his views on the Khmelnytsky Uprising. Newly discovered archival materials added significantly to his interpretation of details but did not significantly change the general picture. This factor contributed to the impressive coherence of Hrushevsky's interpretation of the uprising throughout most of his academic career.[220]

Even so, there are indications that Hrushevsky's writings (if not his views) were influenced by new archival sources or by the lack of them. In the last volumes of the *History*, Hrushevsky was forever complaining that there were not enough sources for the history of the masses. New sources uncovered in the Moscow archives were primarily concerned with diplomatic history, turning Hrushevsky more into a historian of the state than of the masses. By contrast, new archival materials concerning the disastrous impact on the masses of Khmelnytsky's social policies and his alliance with the Tatars helped Hrushevsky make his populist case against the hetman and his entourage. In general, Hrushevsky's intimate knowledge of and attention to the sources and his refusal to bend the evidence to fit his own views contributed immensely to the quality of the last volumes of his *History*, which remain unsurpassed as a detailed and scrupulously balanced account of the era.

Hrushevsky's thorough study of the Khmelnytsky era, which resulted in two and a half books of his magnum opus, to say nothing of his numerous articles on the topic, decisively established the Khmelnytsky Uprising as an element of the Ukrainian national narrative, disengaging it from the history of Russia. In Hrushevsky's interpretation, the alliance with Muscovy became an alternative of the hetman's foreign policy, not a foregone conclusion, as it had been in the all-Russian narrative. The Khmelnytsky Uprising emerged in Hrushevsky's writings not as the culminating 'reunification' of the Rus' nation but as a turning point in the history of the Ukrainian nation, Ukrainian statehood, and the Ukrainian popular masses. As in the interpretation of many other episodes of Ukrainian history, Hrushevsky was not the first or the only historian to claim that era for the Ukrainian historical narrative, but his deep knowledge of the subject and the sheer volume of his writings on the period made him the historian who established his case better than any of his predecessors or contemporaries.

Hrushevsky was generally convinced of the objectivity of his scholarship.[221] In historical methodology, he was a thoroughgoing Rankean. As Hrushevsky saw it, historical writing was supposed to present a true picture of the past, not influenced by the historian's personal views or a priori concepts. This was the principle of 'objectivity' that Hrushevsky absorbed from his student reading of the 1880s and attempted to follow throughout his academic career. One way to achieve such objectivity, in Hrushevsky's opinion, was to carry out a thorough analysis of sources. In the last volumes of his *History*, Hrushevsky took that conviction so far as to prefer the publication of excerpts from historical documents to his own interpretation of events and the sources that described them. Early in his career, Hrushevsky was sometimes accused of being a poor theoretician and focusing mostly on the compilation of facts. He rejected such charges, claiming to avoid only premature and unsubstantiated generalizations: 'We cannot approach our material with an a priori program but are obliged to modify our questions in order to obtain reliable answers from the material.'[222]

In 1927, while working on volume 9 of the *History*, Hrushevsky published an article on the legacy of the populist historian Oleksander Lazarevsky, whom he criticized, among other things, for lack of interest in generalizations and conceptualization. In his critique of Lazarevsky, Hrushevsky nevertheless demonstrated some understanding of and sympathy for Lazarevsky's approach. He wrote: 'Profoundly sceptical by nature and, given the nature of all his life's work, constantly confronted with the verbal tangles of human guile, denunciation, bias, and tendentiousness, he did not want to take on the responsibility of interpreting, still less defending, one thesis or another; he did not want to stand between the reader and the bare, unadorned documentary fact, and he left it to the reader to draw conclusions and develop views at his own risk and responsibility. And as he was never a teacher – neither professor nor lecturer – he never even knew the responsibility of presenting ultimate conclusions, turning the material into a picture as full and finished as possible, bringing it to completeness, filling in lacunae and insufficiencies with the effort of one's own scholarly thinking and sharing its results with the public, and not leaving them only for oneself or an intimate circle of friends.'[223]

Hrushevsky himself was a university professor for most of his life, only too familiar with the pressure to draw conclusions and share his views on poorly researched aspects of the past. He did so at length in the earlier volumes of the *History*. Nevertheless, in the last, Soviet-era volumes of his magnum opus, Hrushevsky clearly surrendered to his natural inclination to prefer the analysis of sources to their synthesis. Unwilling to stand between the sources and the reader, he left it up to the latter to determine the true meaning of the documents liberally quoted in the volume. Did Hrushevsky adopt this approach because, like Lazarevsky before him, he had had to deal with too many 'verbal tangles of human guile?' Whatever the reason, his emphasis on historical sources and their publication created a standard of professionalism and a model of scholarship followed by those historians in the USSR who wanted to shield their research from official ideological interference.

Retreat to the sources and a 'scientistic' approach to historical scholarship was a development that helped save the historical profession under Soviet rule. As early as 1933 one of the most prominent American historians of the twentieth century, Charles A. Beard, recognized that potential of the 'scientific' method in historiography. In an address to the American Historical Association, Beard criticized those trends in historiography that had emerged under the influence of physics and biology, reassuring his listeners of the importance of the old-fashioned 'scientific' method. He asserted: 'It is the only method that can be employed in obtaining accurate knowledge of historical facts, personalities, situations, and movements. It alone can disclose conditions that made possible what happened. It has a value in itself – a value high in the hierarchy of values indispensable to the life of democracy. The inquiring spirit of science, using the scientific method, is the chief safeguard against the tyranny of authority, bureaucracy and brute power.'[224] The concluding volumes of Hrushevsky's *History* did indeed serve as a safeguard against the brute power of Bolshevik tyranny.

Chapter 6

Class versus Nation

For most of the 1920s, the Marxist historical narratives and the Ukrainian national narrative articulated by Mykhailo Hrushevsky existed side by side. Throughout the period, numerous conflicts and negotiations took place between these narratives. The rise of Marxist historical narratives in the USSR created a completely new situation with regard to competition between the Russian imperial, Russian national, and Ukrainian national narratives. Since the new Marxist historiography developed largely in conflict with the dominant Russian imperial narrative, it initially aligned itself with non-Russian historians in opposition to the old imperial school. From the very beginning, however, there were profound tensions between the Marxist and Ukrainian national narratives.

Very early on, Hrushevsky's paradigm of Ukrainian history became central to the historiographic debates of the time, and an examination of reactions to it affords a unique opportunity to elucidate relations between the Marxist and national narratives in the first decades of the USSR's existence. Such an examination demonstrates the extent of cooperation between Marxist and national historiography in the unmaking of the imperial Russian narrative and the construction of Ukrainian national history, while indicating the profound disagreements that arose between them over the primacy of class or nation in history. The Bolshevik regime was active in the construction of its own historical narrative, and an analysis of its role in that undertaking helps explain the relationship between power and knowledge in Soviet society, entailing the question of whether the outcome of negotiation between the competing historical narratives was predetermined by the position of the ruling party or whether that position was itself altered by the outcome of scholarly debate.

This chapter begins with the emergence of Russian and Ukrainian Marxist historical narratives of Ukraine and examines their relation to Hrushevsky's historical paradigm. It then details the conditions under which the Marxist and national narratives of Ukrainian history coexisted in the mid-1920s. This is followed by an account of the events leading to a split between Russian and Ukrainian Marxist historians, which made possible an all-out attack on Ukrainian national historiography by the Marxist historical establishment. The chapter ends with an analysis of the Marxist attacks on Hrushevsky in the late 1920s and early 1930s, considered as part of a larger effort of Bolshevik historiography to deconstruct and demolish the Ukrainian national narrative by means of a class-based analysis. Unlike the discussion in earlier chapters, my analysis here focuses less on Hrushevsky's writings than on the reaction to them on the part of other historians. Given Hrushevsky's reluctance to take part in historiographic discussions of the time or respond to his Marxist critics, this approach to the material seems most productive.

Marxist History and the National Narrative

If in the Russian Empire Hrushevsky's paradigm of Ukrainian history had to compete first and foremost with the Russian historical paradigm presented in the writings of Vasilii Kliuchevsky, in the USSR Hrushevsky's main counterpart on the Russian side was Mikhail Pokrovsky. A student of Kliuchevsky's, he was an early convert to Marxism and the only professional historian of stature among the old Bolshevik elite. Pokrovsky was instrumental in the formulation of party policy on the 'historical front.' Hence it was above all Pokrovsky's interpretation of history that Hrushevsky had to confront while continuing his work on Ukrainian history in Soviet Ukraine.[1]

Before the revolution, Pokrovsky, not unlike Hrushevsky himself, had been deeply involved in the delegitimization of the Russian imperial historical narrative. He led the charge of the Marxist historians, who undermined the old imperial narrative by means of materialist philosophy and the class-based method. Pokrovsky's interest in economic history, adherence to economic materialism, and strong emphasis on the history of classes and class struggle were at the core of the Marxist revolution in Russian imperial historiography. Pokrovsky's views on Russian history were fully presented in his five-volume *History of Russia from the Earliest Times*, the first edition of which appeared in print in 1910–13.[2] Judging by his introduction to the book, Pokrovsky saw his work as a contribution to the materialist interpretation of Russian history initiated by the publication of N.A. Rozhkov's *Survey of Russian History from a Sociological Viewpoint*.[3]

The *History of Russia* was written in Paris, where Pokrovsky settled after the defeat of the 1905 revolution. It was published in Moscow with the help of N.M. Nikolsky, who contributed a number of chapters to the book, and V.N. Storozhev, one of the few Russian scholars lauded by Hrushevsky in his article of 1904 on the traditional scheme of 'Russian' history.[4] Pokrovsky's *History of Russia* had enormous revolutionary potential when it came to restructuring the Russian historical narrative on the basis of the new materialist method.[5] It also broke with the old historiographic paradigm of the 'gathering of the Russian lands' by the grand princes of Moscow – an integral part of the traditional scheme of Russian history that was criticized by Hrushevsky. Pokrovsky rejected the notion of a centralized Kyivan Rus' state prior to the Mongol invasion, maintaining that the term 'Rus" had been applied mainly to the Kyivan Land and that pre-Mongol Russia consisted of a number of principalities. 'Since there was nothing to disintegrate, neither was there was anything to "gather"': such was Pokrovsky's summary dismissal of Karamzin's paradigm of the 'gathering of Russian lands.'[6]

Pokrovsky's rejection of this cornerstone of the Russian historical narrative can be traced back to the writings of Pavel Miliukov, who exposed the artificiality of Karamzin's scheme in his *Main Currents of Russian Historical Thought*. As discussed above, this work also influenced Hrushevsky's critique of the traditional scheme of 'Russian' history, but Pokrovsky and Hrushevsky took on the Russian grand narrative in very different ways. Unlike Hrushevsky, Pokrovsky rejected the concept of the 'gathering of Russian lands' not because he did not believe in the existence of one Russian people that was steadily reunited by the Moscow princes and tsars but because he did not believe in the existence of a united Kyivan Rus' state prior to the Mongol invasion. Pokrovsky's argument remained essentially statist. Thus, for all his criticism of Karamzin's scheme, Pokrovsky accepted the idea, legitimized by that scheme, of the shift of the centre of Russian life from south to north after the decline of Kyiv. He dated that process to the second half of the twelfth century and wrote that the decline of Kyiv 'conditioned the shift of the centre of the historical scene several degrees north and west, establishing for historical Russia the character of a northern country poorly endowed by nature that it did not yet possess in the mild climate and on the fertile soil of Ukraine.'[7]

With regard to the history of the non-Russian nationalities in general and the history of Ukraine in particular, Pokrovsky was following the traditional scheme of 'Russian' history in a version extremely close to the one described by Hrushevsky in his article of 1904. After covering the history of the Ukrainian lands up to the disintegration of Kyivan (in his terminology, 'ancient') Rus', Pokrovsky returned to the history of 'Western' and 'Southwestern Rus'' only in connection with the history of Russian foreign policy and the annexation of Ukraine in the second half of the seventeenth century. In this respect, Pokrovsky's historical narrative was not very different from that of Kliuchevsky. In fact, given the Marxist ambiguity in dealing with the national question at the time, Pokrovsky showed even less interest in the role of the national factor in history than did Kliuchevsky. Unlike his former professor, who revised and extended his discussion of nationality issues in the published version of his lecture course, Pokrovsky was utterly consumed with the idea of the materialist reinterpretation of Russian history and completely avoided the issue of the formation of separate East Slavic nationalities. His main concern was to establish the feudal character of 'ancient' Rus', whose population he called 'Russian.'[8]

Pokrovsky knew many of Hrushevsky's writings and made extensive use of them in his own work. Still, with regard to the interpretation of the major topics of 'Russian' history that were claimed for the Ukrainian national narrative, Pokrovsky's views often diverged from Hrushevsky's, mainly because of his different assessment of the importance of class and national factors in history. Characteristic of Pokrovsky's nihilism with regard to the role of the national factor in 'Russian' history was the fact that he took the whole discussion concerning the alleged depopulation of the Kyivan Land entirely out of its original context – the debate over the ethnicity of the Kyivan Rus' population. Judging by the text of Pokrovsky's *History*, the issue did not exist for him, as he made no mention of the problem of outmigration or resettlement of the area.

Pokrovsky was much more concerned with the role of the towns in 'ancient' Rus' history. In that regard, he gave special consideration to Hrushevsky's arguments concerning the Tatar attack on Kyiv. Commenting on the discussion of that issue in the historical literature, Pokrovsky concluded that the main effect of the debate had been to lead scholars to distinguish the fate of the city from that of the Kyivan Land. Pokrovsky believed that Kyiv had indeed been destroyed and took much longer to recover from the Tatar attack than the towns of the northeast. Pokrovsky saw proof of Kyiv's precipitous decline in Hrushevsky's assertion that the princes virtually abandoned Kyiv in the second half of the thirteenth century. He believed that such an exodus could occur only because the city was so devastated that it could no longer support the princes, not because the Kyivan community preferred self-rule to princely authority, as Hrushevsky claimed. 'To imagine, as our author is prepared to do,' wrote Pokrovsky with regard to Hrushevsky's hypothesis, 'that the Kyivans of that day were contented republicans is to transfer the concepts and relations of a much later time to the thirteenth century.'[9]

Despite the often sarcastic tone of Pokrovsky's commentary, he tacitly accepted Hrushevsky's main argument that the Kyivan Land (Ukraine) was not depopulated by the Tatar invasion. 'Thus, at no point in old Russian history was the territory of the old Russian principalities west of the Dnipro completely deserted,' wrote Pokrovsky.[10] His argument was informed by considerations of economic development and class structure. Pokrovsky wrote in that regard: 'They [the Tatars] could not allow the senseless extermination of the inhabitants, if only because they were preparing to exploit them and did indeed exploit, inter alia, the population of the Kyiv region.'[11]

Pokrovsky analysed the history of 'Western Rus'' under Lithuanian and Polish rule exclusively in social and economic terms, placing special emphasis on the development of feudalism in the Lithuanian and then in the Polish-Lithuanian state. He made a point of attacking the traditional Russian imperial presentation of the history of 'Western' and 'Southwestern' Rus' as an account of the survival of the 'Russian' nationality under foreign – Lithuanian and Polish – control. What Pokrovsky found questionable was not the traditional treatment of the inhabitants of the Ukrainian and Belarusian lands as 'Russians' but the assumption that relations between the 'Russian,' Lithuanian, and Polish nationalities were of any importance to the history of the region. 'Feudalism,' wrote Pokrovsky, 'is generally indifferent to national barriers: nationalism appears only at the subsequent stage of social development.'[12] Tensions and competition between the Ruthenian and Lithuanian elites in the Grand Duchy of Lithuania, which Russian imperial historians had traditionally interpreted as national in character, were seen by Pokrovsky as a contest between two religious traditions – Catholicism and Orthodoxy.

Having dismissed the national paradigm as the key to understanding the history of the Grand Duchy of Lithuania and its successor in the region, the Polish-Lithuanian Commonwealth, Pokrovsky focused primarily on the economic and social history of the region. In so doing, he based his discussion almost exclusively on Hrushevsky's treatment of the period, as well as on the documents published in the first volume of *Sources on the History of Ukraine-Rus'*, which was edited by Hrushevsky. As a result, Pokrovsky devoted particular attention to the history of economic and social relations in Galicia, a land all but ignored in his study of earlier periods of 'Western Rus'' history. Following Hrushevsky, Pokrovsky discussed the increasing demand for corvée labour, the reduction in the size of peasant plots, and the loss of land by the poor Galician peasantry. Unlike Hrushevsky, however, he explained these developments not by the disastrous impact of Polish rule on the Ukrainian economy but by the consequences of 'the emergence of early forms of a barter economy and, in that connection, the transformation of the feudal landholder into an agrarian entrepreneur.' He treated that process not as something unique to 'Western Rus'' or the lands of the Polish-Lithuanian Commonwealth but as a broader phenomenon, indicating parallels in the economic and social development of Muscovite Rus'.[13] In a way, Pokrovsky's fascination with social and economic factors and neglect of cultural and national ones was reminiscent of the political program of the Russian social democrats in general and the Bolsheviks in particular: the latter went into the revolutions of 1905 and (partially) 1917 without a clearly defined program on the nationality question. In that respect, the events of the latter revolution proved a great education for the Bolsheviks. The rise of the non-Russian national movements and the creation of independent national states on the territory of the former empire forced the Bolsheviks to learn as they went along and introduce changes to their nationalities policy, depending on particular circumstances of time and place.

In 1920 Pokrovsky published the first Marxist textbook of Russian history to appear in the postrevolutionary Russian Empire, titled *Russian History in Briefest Compass*.[14] Based on his lecture course delivered a year earlier at the Iakov Sverdlov Communist University in Moscow, it was reworked into a book in the course of Pokrovsky's brief leave from his duties as deputy People's Commissar of Education of the Russian Federation. The leave was granted for the specific purpose of enabling Pokrovsky to finish writing the book. Lenin himself welcomed its publication, suggesting that it be adapted as a textbook and translated into various European languages.[15] The book was indeed translated into numerous foreign languages, as well as the languages of the USSR, and reprinted more than ninety times, making it the most popular textbook of Russian history in the 1920s. It employed some of the basic ideas developed in Pokrovsky's five-volume *History of Russia*, with special emphasis on the history of the class struggle, the rise of the working class, and the role of commercial capitalism in early modern Russian history.

As the basis for his periodization of 'Russian' history, Pokrovsky used the Marxist idea of successive socio-economic formations. For Pokrovsky, 'Russian' history, as part of world history, began with the dominance in social relations of the clan system and went on to feudalism, then to merchant/commercial capitalism, and eventually to industrial capitalism. Seeking to present Russian history as a process subject to the same socio-economic laws as the history of Western Europe, Pokrovsky argued that feudalism in Russia was replaced by a capitalist economy in the sixteenth and seventeenth centuries. To prove the point, he developed a theory of 'commercial capitalism,' a socio-economic stage in Russian history in which commercial capital was used to acquire land. The advance of commercial capitalism resulted in the displacement of the old landowning class, the boyars, by a new one, the gentry (*dvorianstvo*). The new economy, based on corvée labour (*barshchina*) as opposed to the 'feudal' quit-rent (*obrok*), led to the enserfment of the Russian peasantry. According to Pokrovsky, the possessors of commercial capital and the gentry were also mainly responsible for creating the new Muscovite autocracy. The theory of commercial capitalism, whose principal agent was the burgher, was devised in order to guide Marxist historiography through the labyrinths of early modern Russian history. It remained almost unchallenged in Bolshevik historiography until the latter half of the 1920s.[16]

Pokrovsky's *Russian History in Briefest Compass* turned out to be a history of Russia proper to a degree not matched by any of the prerevolutionary histories of Russia. The compression of his narrative into one volume, as well as his new emphasis on the history of revolution and class struggle, significantly limited Pokrovsky's ability to deal with 'Russian' history before the seventeenth century. Among the main victims of that 'compression' was the history of 'Western' Rus'. Pokrovsky's brief discussion of its history in relation to the Khmelnytsky Uprising excluded the Grand Duchy of Lithuania altogether and was limited to a few pages – proportionally a tremendous decrease as compared with the treatment of the subject in his 'big' *History*.[17]

Pokrovsky's neglect of non-Russian history in his popular survey was also the logical culmination of the earlier tendency, associated with the names of Kliuchevsky and his students at Moscow University, to 'Russify' the Russian imperial grand narrative. But Pokrovsky, like the vast majority of his contemporaries in Russia, found it difficult to distinguish between Russia proper and the Russian Empire.

In the preface to the first edition of his book, Pokrovsky wrote: 'A conscious worker must know not only what communism is but also what Russia is. And so this book is dedicated to the history of the formation of contemporary Russia.'[18] It would appear that in that context, Pokrovsky used 'Russia' as a synonym for the Russian Empire, and it was the history of that country, not of the Russian nation, that Pokrovsky wanted to present to the 'conscious worker' along with the basics of communist doctrine. This particular interpretation of the terms 'Russia' and 'Russian' in the text of the book is confirmed by the author himself in the preface to its tenth edition (1931), where Pokrovsky characterized his survey as the most concise presentation of the subject 'that was known as "Russian history," that is, the history of *pre-revolutionary Russia*.'[19] Conversely, in a letter of 1932 to the director of the Crimean state publishing house, who planned the publication of Pokrovsky's survey in Tatar translation, Pokrovsky admitted that his work was a survey of the history of the Russian nation. As he put it: 'Its major flaw ... is that the book speaks only of one of the peoples of the USSR, and there is not a word about the other peoples.'[20] When Pokrovsky wrote his short survey of Russian history, he had no way of predicting the subsequent impact of his Russocentric narrative on the development of Marxist historiography in the non-Russian republics. But in the early 1930s, when there was a strong demand for a Marxist narrative of the history of the 'peoples of the USSR,' Pokrovsky regarded his exclusive focus on Russia as one of the shortcomings of his survey. There is no evidence that he thought in such terms in 1919–20.

The outbreak of the 1917 revolution, the disintegration of the empire, and the establishment on its ruins of new independent states, including the Russian Federation, removed the old constraints that hindered the 'purification' of the Russian imperial paradigm by the removal of non-Russian elements. After all, the lecture course that served as a basis for the new textbook of Russian history was delivered in Moscow, the new capital of the Russian Federation, by a deputy people's commissar of the Russian government at a time when the Moscow authorities had lost control over a significant part of the Russian Empire. Ukraine, in particular, was lost first to the forces of the Ukrainian People's Republic, led by Hrushevsky, and then to German troops, the Ukrainian Directory, and the White armies of General Anton Denikin. There existed (at least formally) a separate communist party of Ukraine and a separate Soviet Ukrainian government, while the formation of the USSR was at least two years away. Given these circumstances, Pokrovsky's focus on Russia proper was quite understandable. Because Pokrovsky's book painted the imperial past in dark colours and deprived Russian history of its traditional heroes, it was a poor instrument for nation-building.[21] Nevertheless, the new narrative managed to define the geographic and historical boundaries of the Russian national narrative to a degree unmatched by its predecessors. By focusing on Russia proper, it also left a vacuum to be filled with narratives produced locally by party historians in the non-Russian borderlands of the former empire.

In Ukraine there was a particularly strong demand for such a narrative, as evidenced by the hundreds of thousands of copies of brief textbooks and popular historical studies produced during the revolution that presented Ukrainian history from the Ukrainian national point of view. Hrushevsky's *Illustrated History of Ukraine* alone was reissued six times between 1917 and 1919.[22] For many Ukrainian cultural activists, the 'awakening' of their identity began with the reading of Hrushevsky's *Illustrated History*. A case in point was the prominent Ukrainian linguist and diaspora cultural activist George Y. Shevelov (Iurii Sheveliov), who read Hrushevsky's work in Kharkiv in 1923–4.[23] As becomes apparent from one of the recently discovered peasant chronicles written during the period of Ukrainization, Hrushevsky's *Illustrated History* served as a national narrative that allowed peasant historians of the 1920s to contextualize and nationalize their family histories. Before the revolution, these peasants had regarded themselves as *khokhly* with little if any national identity.[24] As noted above, the GPU, apparently realizing the danger posed by Hrushevsky's writings, instructed its local branches in Ukraine to collect information on those who showed an interest in Hrushevsky's *History of Ukraine-Rus'*.[25]

The task of constructing a Soviet Marxist narrative of Ukrainian history fell to one of the leading ideologues of the Soviet regime in Ukraine, Matvii Iavorsky. He was occasionally called the 'Ukrainian Pokrovsky,' but unlike his older colleague in Moscow, he was neither a professional historian nor an old Bolshevik. A lawyer by training, he formally joined the Communist Party only in 1920. Iavorsky was an ethnic Ukrainian who came to Eastern Ukraine from Galicia, where he graduated from Lviv University (having attended Hrushevsky's lectures on Ukrainian history) and, in addition to his law degree, completed a doctorate in political science (1912). During the First World War, Iavorsky served as an officer in the Austro-Hungarian army. In 1918 he was on the staff of an Austro-Hungarian military mission, first to the Central Rada and then to Hetman Pavlo Skoropadsky. Iavorsky's conversion to communism took place in 1919, when he prepared the defection of units of the Ukrainian Galician Army to the Bolsheviks. When the Galician sharpshooters abandoned the Bolsheviks in 1920, Iavorsky remained true to his communist convictions and stayed with his Bolshevik comrades.[26]

From the very beginning of his party career, Iavorsky was deployed on the 'educational front' because of his outstanding academic qualifications. In 1919 he was in charge of the 'Red officers' school' in Kyiv. In the following year he taught at a school of 'political literacy' in Kazan. Following relocation to Kharkiv in the autumn of the same year, Iavorsky began his teaching and administrative career there. He taught at the Institute of People's Education and at the Central Party School (from 1922, the Artem Communist University). With the establishment of the Ukrainian Institute of Marxism and Marxist Studies in Kharkiv in late 1922, Iavorsky joined its department of the history of culture. Between 1924 and 1929, he was also deputy head of the government directorate in charge of all scholarly activity in Ukraine. In that position, Iavorsky exercised enormous power over the development of the humanities and was one of the few top-level bureaucrats who oversaw the activities of the Ukrainian Academy of Sciences. As a pedagogue, he taught courses on political economy, historical materialism, the class struggle in Ukraine, the Communist Party of Ukraine, and the history of Ukraine. The latter became Iavorsky's field of specialization in both teaching and scholarship. During the 1920s, he not only wrote numerous articles on particular subjects in Ukrainian history (mostly of the nineteenth and early twentieth centuries) but also produced a number of textbooks on the subject for secondary schools and institutions of higher learning.[27]

Iavorsky's first surveys of Ukrainian history, which began to appear in print in 1923, were based on courses that he taught in Kharkiv's numerous educational institutions. All these works were published in Ukrainian, which undoubtedly reflected Iavorsky's personal preference and was also in line with the new party policy of Ukrainization, launched after the Twelfth Congress of the Russian Communist Party in April 1923.[28] If the choice of the language of the future Marxist narrative of

Ukrainian history came quite naturally, with no substantive discussion, the structure and content of that narrative were still to be decided. The first of Iavorsky's surveys, published in 1923, was a *Survey of Ukrainian-Russian History*.[29] It was a brief outline of the course that Iavorsky taught at the Artem Communist University. The title, which employed the word *rus'kyi* for 'Russian,' was reminiscent of the title of Hrushevsky's major work, with the important difference that in the latter case, *rus'kyi* was used in the meaning of 'Ruthenian.' Unlike Hrushevsky's *History*, Iavorsky's work was not concerned with linking Ukrainian history either with ancient Rus' or with Galicia but presented a comparative survey, juxtaposing chapters on particular periods of Russian and Ukrainian history. This approach was apparently influenced by prevailing circumstances, as most of Iavorsky's students at the Communist University knew very little about the history of Ukraine. Whatever Iavorsky's intentions, his attempt to present Russian and Ukrainian history within a single course drew strong criticism from the dean of Ukrainian historiography in Kharkiv, Dmytro Bahalii, who advised him to offer a separate course on Ukrainian history. Iavorsky followed Bahalii's injunction.[30]

The first year of the Ukrainization policy, 1923, proved highly productive for Iavorsky. Apart from publishing his outline course on 'Ukrainian-Russian' history, Iavorsky began issuing his *Survey of Ukrainian History*,[31] consisting of three parts, and published a history of the Ukrainian Revolution,[32] as well as a *Brief History of Ukraine* for secondary schools.[33] In the same year, Iavorsky delivered a paper on the tasks of Ukrainian historiography as a scholarly discipline that was discussed at a two-day debate with Kharkiv historians of the 'old' school. Taking as his point of departure Georgii Plekhanov's tenet that history was not the sum of known facts but a process subject to particular laws of development, Iavorsky asserted that instead of limiting itself to the mere presentation of facts, Ukrainian historiography should take on the task of revealing the 'causal regularity of social development as a dialectical process.' He argued that the main task of Ukrainian historiography should be the study of the 'processes of genesis, development, and change of relations within a given mode of production' and identified the periodization of those processes as the most important element in the philosophical explanation of history.[34] It is interesting to note that the existence of Ukrainian history as a particular scholarly discipline (*nauka*) was accepted by Iavorsky as a given, with no discussion whatsoever. For him the main issue was not the existence of the discipline per se but the elaboration of its philosophical foundations.

Iavorsky's unequivocal acceptance of Ukrainian history as a separate field of study can be explained by a number of factors. Of primary importance among them was the treatment of Ukrainian history as a separate discipline by the Ukrainian Academy of Sciences. In 1922 the academy's research department of Ukrainian history was established in Kharkiv. It was headed by Dmytro Bahalii, who had been teaching Ukrainian history as a distinct subject at Kharkiv University since 1917. Thus, when Iavorsky began his career as a historian, the formally unitary field of 'Russian' history had already been demarcated and divided by the academy. Under these circumstances, his task was not to change or abolish the established boundaries between scholarly disciplines but to take them over for Marxist scholarship. An even more important factor that could not but influence Iavorsky's outlook was the existence of a Ukrainian socialist state – at first formally independent and, after 1922, a republic of the USSR – with its own government and communist party. In 1922 an institute for Marxist studies was established in Kharkiv, the capital of the republic. Iavorsky taught at the institute's department of Ukrainian culture, which in itself made him little disposed to challenge the existence of Ukrainian history as a distinct field of study.

What really turned Iavorsky into a prolific writer on Ukrainian historical themes and made him a leading Marxist advocate of the independence of the 'Ukrainian historical process' was the policy of Ukrainization. The impact of Ukrainization on Bolshevik attitudes toward history becomes apparent in the foreword to Iavorsky's *Brief History of Ukraine* written by Khristian Rakovsky, who headed the Soviet Ukrainian government from 1919 to 1923.[35] Rakovsky's own path to Ukrainization was not a simple one and reflected some dramatic turns in the party elite's thinking on the nationality problem. Until 1921 Rakovsky, a Bulgarian who had been active in the Bulgarian and Romanian socialist movements prior to the 1917 revolution, refused to admit the existence of a separate Ukrainian nation. Subsequently he changed his position to one of strong support for Ukrainian autonomy vis-à-vis Russia. If in 1921 Rakovsky went on record as saying that victory for the Ukrainian language would mean rule by the Ukrainian petty-bourgeois intelligentsia and kulaks, in 1923 he demanded greater rights for the republics and was accused by Stalin of promoting confederation instead of a union of Soviet republics.[36] Rakovsky apparently subscribed to the 'internationalist' logic advanced by some influential members of the party, according to which the world revolution still lay ahead: if the world was destined to become a conglomerate of independent communist republics, why should Ukraine not be one of them? It would appear that by accepting this line of argument, Rakovsky was seeking to make his own position in Ukraine more secure and less dependent on the centre, as he became involved in the political struggle within the communist leadership on the side of Leon Trotsky.[37] Rakovsky's new pro-Ukrainian stand was fully reflected in his introduction to Iavorsky's book, where he wrote that his departure from Ukraine (not from the USSR, as one might expect him to have written under the circumstances) to take up a diplomatic post in England had not allowed him to produce a more substantial introduction.[38]

For Rakovsky the history of mankind was the history of class struggle, as he particularly stressed in the introduction. He stated that 'the whole history of humanity to the present day is precisely this preparation for the formation of two classes, the proletariat and the bourgeoisie, with which the whole history of classes will come to an end.'[39] The purpose of Iavorsky's book was thus to demonstrate that 'the history of Ukraine is not an exception to general historical laws, as nationalist historians think.' Rakovsky claimed that the nationalist view of Ukrainian history had been disproved by the events of the past several years and that the Ukrainian 'people' did not constitute a classless mass. 'In this apparently undifferentiated mass, the observant eye of the Marxist historian sees class differentiation and class struggle, which the superficial glance of the nationalist historian is incapable of discerning,' concluded Rakovsky.[40] If one accepted that the history of humanity was the history of classes, then it followed that the liquidation of the bourgeoisie would lead not only to the end of class-based history but also to the end of history in general, as the Bolsheviks understood its role and function.

Rakovsky's foreword effectively linked some basic elements of the Bolshevik Ukrainization project with the tasks of Marxist historiography. The main raison d'être of Ukrainization was to win over the peasantry to communism by conducting propaganda in the Ukrainian language and Ukrainizing the Russian-speaking city in linguistic and cultural terms, thereby making it possible for Ukrainian peasants to identify themselves with Soviet power, which was based mainly in the cities. In that context, the Ukrainian language of Iavorsky's book, which was addressed to young peasants, was in keeping with the latest version of the party line (Iavorsky devoted his work to the 'Communist Youth of Ukraine'). So were its contents. The book was supposed to tell the young peasant reader, whose ultimate destiny was to support and join the working class, 'how in the course of long centuries the peasantry had suffered unheard-of enslavement and exploitation merely because there was no revolutionary proletariat from which the peasantry could have drawn support.' The promotion of the Marxist view of history among the Ukrainian peasantry required a Marxist narrative of the Ukrainian past. Iavorsky's textbook was thus the result and continuation of the officially sponsored Ukrainization project.

What was the history of Ukraine for Iavorsky, not in methodological but in practical terms, and how different was his narrative of Ukrainian history from the one constructed by Hrushevsky? I shall try to answer this question on the basis of Iavorsky's two principal surveys – the *Short History of Ukraine* (1923), discussed earlier, and his *History of Ukraine in Brief Compass*, published in 1928 and addressed to students of 'professional schools' and workers' departments at institutions of higher learning. Iavorsky's *History of Ukraine* (1928) was based on his *Short History of Ukraine*, although the original text was significantly expanded and reworked. Some of the additions are of major importance for understanding the evolution of Iavorsky's views on Ukrainian history, while others are quite insignificant and at times inadvertently ridiculous, as they reveal Iavorsky's efforts to make his survey of 1928 more scholarly without devoting additional time to further research.[41] Still, most of Iavorsky's revisions reflected the change in his interpretations, while the text of his *History of Ukraine* (1928) generally attests to the greater professionalism of its author, as well as to the higher level of sophistication and complexity that the Marxist paradigm of Ukrainian history was acquiring in the course of the 1920s.

For Iavorsky the history of Ukraine was first and foremost the history of the Ukrainian nation (*narid*). If in 1923 he was anything but specific on where that nation lived, in 1928 he gave a detailed description of Ukrainian ethnic territory, both within the boundaries of the Ukrainian Socialist Soviet Republic and beyond, including southeastern Bessarabia, northern Bukovyna, eastern Galicia, western Volhynia, the Kholm region, and Polisia, which were 'under Romanian, Czech, and Polish occupation.'[42] Iavorsky explained the specific characteristics of nations on the basis of the territory and natural environment that shaped them. According to Iavorsky, a different habitat accounted for different cultural characteristics. Conversely, Iavorsky regarded communication and cultural encounters among nations, especially neighbouring ones, as important factors in the formation of common characteristics. 'Precisely because of these mutual relations [between neighbours], nowhere in history do we observe a people completely free and independent of foreign influences,' wrote Iavorsky.[43] This theoretical assumption acquired clear political ramifications as Iavorsky attacked representatives of Ukrainian 'bourgeois' historiography for their alleged attempts to build a 'Chinese wall' separating Ukrainian history from that of neighbouring nations, especially Russia. In the spirit of political correctness, which demanded a simultaneous struggle on two fronts – against the nationalism of formerly oppressed nations and the great-power chauvinism of formerly dominant ones – Iavorsky also attacked those Russian historians who were 'imbued with a great-power and imperial spirit' that made them deny the particularity of Ukrainian identity and history. Iavorsky stressed the factors that differentiated Ukraine from Russia but stopped short of asserting that their histories were completely separate and independent.[44]

Significantly, in the early and mid-1920s, Iavorsky's main adversaries were not Russian imperial historians but representatives of Ukrainian 'bourgeois' historiography, with whom he had to deal on a daily basis and compete for readership and influence within the Ukrainian Academy of Sciences. In Iavorsky's opinion, the major shortcoming of Ukrainian bourgeois historiography was its failure to recognize the existence of class divisions within the Ukrainian nation and demonstrate the 'class content of the Ukrainian historical process.' Iavorsky claimed that some bourgeois historians limited Ukrainian history to an account of princes and hetmans who ruled the state, while others, who admittedly studied the popular masses, viewed them only as a reservoir for the formation of the future nobility, completely ignoring the importance of the class struggle. When describing these two currents in Ukrainian bourgeois historiography, Iavorsky did not name names, but it may be assumed that among the 'statists' he counted not only Viacheslav Lypynsky and his followers but also anyone who did not belong to the populist school. The latter could include a long list of historians, starting with Bantysh-Kamensky and Markevych and ending with Mykola Arkas, the amateur author of a popular survey of Ukrainian history whose narrative was organized according to the statist principle, leading the reader from Kyivan Rus' to the era of Habsburg and Romanov rule over Ukraine.[45]

There is little doubt that among those Ukrainian 'bourgeois' historians who, according to Iavorsky, studied the popular masses but ignored the history of class struggle, Mykhailo Hrushevsky was first and foremost. Iavorsky gave the following evaluation of that group of Ukrainian 'bourgeois' historians: 'Others, although they did not remain silent about the life of the masses and the conditions of their existence, nevertheless forgot about the class struggle. Consequently, they have hitherto limited the history of Ukraine to the periods of its existence as a state, the periods of struggle for its political independence in the sixteenth and seventeenth centuries, and the periods of its enslavement in the seventeenth century. In the old scholarship neither the first nor the second took the history of Ukraine any farther, and it usually ended with the eighteenth century, when Ukrainian political independence was finally done away with. For that reason, whole volumes were written about Kyivan Rus', the Kingdom of Halych, the Lithuanian-Rus' State, the Cossacks (mainly about the Khmelnytsky era), and after that, interest in Ukrainian history fell off steadily. In the nineteenth century they did not even recognize it, or were content with mere observations about the national and cultural revival of the Ukrainian people.'[46] Iavorsky's attack on the account of Ukrainian history presented by historians of the second group clearly indicates the actual target of his critique – Hrushevsky's paradigm and periodization of Ukrainian history.

What alternative paradigm of Ukrainian history did Iavorsky offer his readers? He presented it as follows: 'True historical scholarship, based on historical materialism, does not regard the past and present of Ukraine in this manner. Princes and hetmans are of concern to it only insofar as they themselves are a consequence of the nature of social life in their times. Accordingly, for it the times of feudalism and serfdom are not the times of that selfsame independence to which one should aspire even today but constitute an era of historical preparation for capitalist bourgeois society. For the materialist school, the history of Ukraine should not terminate with the end of its existence as a state and political subjugation; on the contrary, it becomes more interesting insofar as preparations for the proletarian revolution appear more clearly in its historical preconditions.'[47] This scheme of Ukrainian historical development was very different from the one proposed by Hrushevsky; nevertheless, there were some striking similarities between them. Iavorsky's remarks about the degree to which the history of princes and hetmans should be of interest to Ukrainian historiography leave the impression that they were taken almost verbatim from Hrushevsky's inaugural lecture of 1894 at Lviv University, although it is doubtful that Iavorsky knew or remembered the content of a lecture delivered more than thirty years earlier.

The reason for the uncanny similarity between Hrushevsky's views of the 1890s and Iavorsky's beliefs of the 1920s was that in Ukraine both Marxist and national historiography grew out of the populist historical conceptions of the late nineteenth century and for a time employed the same arguments in fighting their common enemy, the Russian statist historiographic tradition. Another similarity between Hrushevsky's and Iavorsky's paradigms of Ukrainian history derives from their teleological approach to the past. One viewed Ukrainian history through the prism of the revival/liberation of a nation, while the other saw it as leading up to a victorious proletarian revolution. Both schemes concentrated on the changing fortunes of their respective historical agents – the nation for the national historians; class struggle and the proletariat for the Marxists.

The scheme of Ukrainian history suggested by Iavorsky in his survey of 1923 and further developed in his textbook of 1928 was a good illustration of the application of the Soviet Marxist paradigm to the subject.[48] By his own account, Iavorsky based his analysis of Ukrainian history on two main factors – economics and the class struggle. He divided it into four periods: the feudal era, dominated by the primitive economy; the period of landowners and serfs, characterized by the development of a money economy and the dominance of the latifundia; the bourgeois capitalist period, marked by the development of urban industrial production and capitalist enterprise in the village; and the era of socialist revolution, which began in 1917. In chronological terms, the first period lasted until the end of the fifteenth century and the second until the mid-nineteenth century, leaving the second half of that century and the early twentieth century for the third period.[49] Iavorsky acknowledged the national factor as a historical agent only in the last two periods of Ukrainian history. He defined the third period, inter alia, as a time of struggle of 'Ukrainian nationalism with Russian imperialism,' while the fourth period was dominated by 'the civil war of the proletariat with the Russian and Ukrainian bourgeoisie.'[50]

Iavorsky's periodization exemplifies what he meant by the concentration of 'true historical scholarship' on recent developments in Ukrainian history. His first period covered at least five centuries; the second, three and a half; the third, approximately seventy years; and the fourth, a mere decade. It was only in the Short History of Ukraine that Iavorsky devoted more or less equal attention to each of the four periods. In the 'big' History, he dealt with feudalism in twenty pages, covered the second period in 100 pages, allocated approximately 160 pages to the third period, and devoted thirty pages to the history of the

'Great Revolution.' With only two chapters ('The Era of Feudalism in Ukraine' and 'The Hetmanate') out of fourteen explicitly devoted to subjects other than class and social struggle, the 'big' *History* was above all a history of the 'liberation struggle' of the Ukrainian people against social oppression – a struggle that culminated in the Revolution of 1917. In terms of territorial coverage, both the 'short' and the 'long' *Histories* were accounts of 'Russian' Ukraine or, more precisely, the lands that constituted the territory of the Ukrainian Socialist Soviet Republic during the interwar period. Their history was discussed almost exclusively in the context of Russia and the Russian revolutionary movement. Galicia appeared in both works only in the early twentieth century, in relation to the history of the proletarian and socialist movement in that part of Ukraine.

For all Iavorsky's criticism of Hrushevsky, in many cases he accepted not only Hrushevsky's general postulate of the existence of Ukrainian history as a distinct field of study but also his treatment of many particular episodes and phenomena. In charting his course between Hrushevsky's paradigm of Ukrainian history and Pokrovsky's Russian Marxist narrative, Iavorsky quite often ended up closer to Hrushevsky than to Pokrovsky, especially when discussing pre-nineteenth-century history. He was guided by the set of ideas associated with the Ukrainization policy, as well as by his own vocation as a Ukrainian historian (in the scholarly literature he figures as a national communist par excellence).[51]

Iavorsky faithfully followed Hrushevsky's theory in his discussion of the genesis of the three East Slavic peoples – Russians, Ukrainians, and Belarusians – an issue completely ignored by Pokrovsky. Like Hrushevsky and a number of other national historians before and after him, Iavorsky listed the Polianians and Siverianians among the ancestors of contemporary Ukrainians.[52] In discussing the origins of the Russian ethnic group, Iavorsky initially linked it only with the Krivichians but added the Slovenes and Viatichians in his 'big' *History*. He wrote that by intermingling with the Finns, the northern East Slavic tribes gave rise to the Great Russian nation, while Ukrainians were descended from the southern tribes. Iavorsky believed that the disintegration of the original East Slavic language was complete by the end of the twelfth century.[53] With regard to the Normanist controversy, Iavorsky took an intermediate position between Hrushevsky and Pokrovsky. On the one hand, not unlike Pokrovsky, he believed that it was the Varangians who gave their Rus' name to the Kyivan state; on the other hand, like Hrushevsky before him, he did not consider the Kyivan princely dynasty to be of Varangian origin and regarded the famous Varangian military expeditions as joint ventures of the Norsemen and the Kyivan princes.[54] In both his short and long surveys of Ukrainian history, Iavorsky used the term 'Kyivan Rus',' as did Hrushevsky, not Pokrovsky's term 'Ancient Rus'.'[55] Also in line with Hrushevsky's presentation of Ukrainian national history, he paid special attention to the activities of Volodymyr the Great, one of the few Kyivan princes mentioned by name in Iavorsky's surveys. If Hrushevsky believed that Volodymyr's rule was followed by the decline of the Kyivan Rus' state, Iavorsky termed it the decline of the prince-and-retinue order.[56]

By far the most interesting example of the influence exercised by Hrushevsky's interpretation of Ukrainian history on Iavorsky's presentation of it is the latter's account of the Mongol (Tatar) invasion. As discussed earlier, throughout his career Hrushevsky paid special attention to the formation of communities not ruled by princes on territory conquered by the Tatars. He treated it as an indication of the democratic aspirations of the Ukrainian masses, to the great disdain not only of representatives of Russian imperial historiography but also of followers of the statist trend in Ukrainian historiography. Not surprisingly, in his treatment of the Tatar period, Iavorsky not only followed Hrushevsky but outdid him in his sympathy for the 'Tatar people.' He presented the same episode as the central phenomenon of the whole era, elevating it to the status of a 'great popular revolution' – an enormous distinction in the Marxist historical paradigm. He also attempted to undermine as class-based and elitist the image of the Tatar invasion cultivated for centuries in the Russian imperial narrative. 'The Tatar period,' wrote Iavorsky in his presentation of the era, 'is the name commonly given to the Tatar misfortune that befell Ukraine in the mid-thirteenth century, but, on giving proper consideration to the matter, we see that it was indeed a misfortune, only not for the working people but for the boyars.'[57] Iavorsky somewhat revised his presentation of this era in his 'big' History, where he replaced his term of 1923, 'Tatar revolution,' with the more neutral 'Tatar maelstrom,' but the remainder of the text was left almost without change.[58] There is no doubt that in this case, as in many others, Iavorsky, who conducted no independent research on pre-nineteenth-century Ukrainian history, simply followed Hrushevsky's discussion of events, occasionally taking some of the latter's conclusions and assertions out of context and blowing them out of proportion.[59]

If Iavorsky's presentation of Ukrainian history helped introduce some of Hrushevsky's populist assertions into the Marxist narrative of Ukrainian history, it also tended to ignore or reject those tenets that were based on the primacy of the national factor. The epoch presented in Hrushevsky's scheme as a 'transitional' stage between Kyivan Rus' and the Cossack era was similarly viewed by Iavorsky, but in his interpretation it was a transition from the feudal system to that of landowning and serfdom. That interpretative shift turned the question of the Kyivan inheritance, which was crucial to Hrushevsky's paradigm, into a secondary issue for Iavorsky's scheme. The incorporation of the Ukrainian lands first into the Lithuanian and then into the Polish-Lithuanian state, which was extremely important to Hrushevsky, was of far less consequence to Iavorsky, who saw it above all as part of the socio-economic history of the region. In this case, Iavorsky was siding with Pokrovsky, who rejected the interpretation of the Union of Lublin as a national issue – an approach that had dominated Russian imperial historiography for decades. There were, nevertheless, some important differences between Pokrovsky's and Iavorsky's treatment of the matter. If Pokrovsky looked to the social history of the region for an explanation of the union, Iavorsky found the reasons behind the incorporation of the Ukrainian lands into the Lithuanian and Polish-Lithuanian states in the realm of the economy, especially foreign trade.[60]

According to Iavorsky, the absorption of most of the Ukrainian lands into the Grand Duchy of Lithuania resulted from the Ukrainian boyars' desire to gain access to the Baltic Sea for trading purposes. But even the united Lithuanian and Ukrainian forces could not, in Iavorsky's opinion, defeat the knights who controlled access to the Baltic seaports. That, argued Iavorsky, was why the Lithuanian state entered into a union with Poland at Kreva in 1385. According to Iavorsky, the Union of Lublin (1569) was also a function of commercial interests. Poland, allegedly envious of the value of Ukrainian goods exported to the West across its territory, increased its duties on the transit of such goods, since Ukraine belonged to a foreign state. As the Polish elites were eager for rich Ukrainian soil, while the Ukrainian elites wanted access to Western markets, their interests coincided, leading to the incorporation of Ukraine into the Kingdom of Poland.[61] If, in Hrushevsky's scheme, every successive union of the Lithuanian Grand Duchy with Poland had negative consequences for Ukrainian political, cultural, and economic life, for Iavorsky, these same unions helped develop the Ukrainian economy, removing obstacles to foreign trade.

Iavorsky's interpretation of the annexation of the Ukrainian lands to the Grand Duchy of Lithuania and then to the Kingdom of Poland as a consequence of the shifting trade interests of Ukrainian elites and his view of the cultural conflict of the late sixteenth century as a manifestation of the struggle between the nobility and the burghers had little if any support either in the historical sources or in the historiographic tradition. Instead, these interpretations serve to exemplify the application of vulgar Marxist theories to the history of Ukraine. The only field in which Iavorsky felt completely at home was that of the 'revolutionary struggle' of the working class. That era was of particular importance not only to Marxist historians but also to national ones, who saw it as a time of glorious revival/liberation of their respective nations. Was the nineteenth-century liberation struggle against tsarism part of the onset of the proletarian revolution or of the national revival? Who, Marxists or nationalists, had the ultimate claim to the 'Great Revolution' of 1917? These were the questions at the centre of the Marxist historiography of Ukraine in the 1920s.

Marxist historical discourse of the 1920s leaves one with the strong impression that if it were up to the Marxist historians themselves, they would gladly have limited their research to the history of capitalist societies and the struggle for the liberation of the working class. They could not do so, as there was the nationalist challenge to be met, and the established discipline of history required the study of human development from the earliest times. As a result, the Marxist historians had little choice but to join battle with 'bourgeois' historical scholarship on its home ground, that of national history, which was deeply rooted in premodern times, and the study of which required a knowledge of languages, palaeography, archaeology, and so on – in short, qualifications that most Marxist historians clearly lacked. The only key to unlocking the 'ancient' past that Marxist historians were eager to use was the class method, frequently abused by Marxist neophytes in their fierce struggles with their professionally superior 'bourgeois' counterparts.

The Marxist narrative of the 1920s, constructed by authors who had scant historical training and could not meet minimum standards of scholarly rigour, was ultimately destined either to be discarded completely or drastically revised in order to produce an account more closely approximating professional criteria. For the time being, though, Iavorsky's narrative of Ukrainian history, whatever its shortcomings, acquired a life of its own, popularized in hundreds of thousands of copies of Iavorsky's own textbooks, pamphlets, and articles, as well as those written by his students and epigones. That narrative helped create a new Soviet Ukrainian identity firmly rooted in the idea of the existence of a separate Ukrainian people/nation. Like the historical narrative constructed and popularized by Iavorsky and his students, that identity was inspired and justified by the existence of a Soviet Ukrainian state. It regarded Soviet Ukraine as a Piedmont that would bring about the social and national liberation of other Ukrainian territories subject to the rule of foreign bourgeois states until the outbreak of the world revolution.[62]

Peaceful Coexistence

In May 1929 Mykhailo Rubach, a disciple of Mikhail Pokrovsky and one of the leading Ukrainian Marxist historians of the day, submitted a report to the Central Committee of the Communist Party of Ukraine on current discussions among Ukrainian Marxist historians. In his report Rubach divided the issues debated by party historians into two categories. The first concerned the question of the distinct (*samostoiatel'nyi*) character of Ukrainian history, while the second pertained to the content of the Ukrainian 'historical process.' 'Basically, the first problem of the distinct character of Ukrainian history, of its distinctness in relation to the history of Russia, Poland, and Belarus,' wrote Rubach, 'functionally depends on one or another resolution of the Ukrainian question in one historical period or another. Insofar as the Ukrainian people is a distinct people, its history is also completely distinct.' He concluded his argument as follows: 'The distinct character of Ukrainian history is acknowledged in a variety of ethnographic, territorial, and socioeconomic interpretations by M.S. Hrushevsky, and Dontsov, and Bahalii, and Hermaize and Iavorsky, and Rubach, Karpenko, and others.' At the core of the disagreement between Marxist and non-Marxist historiography, in Rubach's opinion, lay not the issue of the distinct character of Ukrainian history but that of its class content.[63]

Rubach's report was written at the height of Hrushevsky's career in Soviet Ukraine, just a few months before the start of a major attack on him, and in many ways reflected the extent of acceptance of Hrushevsky's main historical thesis in the USSR. The task of separating the Ukrainian historical narrative from the Russian one, placed on the scholarly agenda by Hrushevsky a quarter-century earlier, was all but accomplished. Under discussion was the issue of its content, with the Marxists insisting on the paramount importance of the class factor.

Hrushevsky and his followers, while not altogether denying the significance of class, were committed to defending the main elements of the national historical narrative. By all accounts, this state of affairs represented a major achievement for Hrushevsky, especially as compared with the treatment of his ideas in imperial Russia.

What made this achievement possible? An answer to this question requires a consideration of attitudes toward Hrushevsky and his work on the part of the Moscow-based Marxists (Pokrovsky and his students), and Marxist historians in Ukraine (represented by Matvii Iavorsky). I shall also discuss Hrushevsky's own attempts to adopt some elements of the dominant Bolshevik discourse of the time. My analysis here will cover most of the 1920s and end with the events of 1928 – the last year of 'peaceful coexistence' between Marxist and non-Marxist historians in the USSR.

One explanation of Rubach's position, as reflected in his statement of 1929, is to be sought in the generally tolerant attitude of Marxist historians of the 1920s toward Hrushevsky, whom they regarded as an accomplished scholar. As noted above, the dean of Russian Marxist historiography, Mikhail Pokrovsky, was positively disposed to Hrushevsky. In his lectures on Russian historiography delivered at the Grigorii Zinoviev Communist University in Petrograd in 1923, Pokrovsky stated that 'in his first volumes devoted to Kyivan Rus', Hrushevsky is the freshest and most European of researchers.'[64] Pokrovsky's overall assessment of Hrushevsky's work was also by no means antagonistic. He viewed Hrushevsky, along with Mykola Kostomarov, as one of the 'federalists of the petty-bourgeois branch' who could not produce a concept of the Russian historical process, 'because the whole essence of their activity consists in destroying the notion of a single Russian historical process.'[65] Pokrovsky offered a class-based explanation of Kostomarov's and Hrushevsky's position, asserting that the struggle of the petty bourgeoisie against the large, centrally based forces of capitalism often took the form of national self-defence. 'Consequently,' concluded Pokrovsky, 'nationalism is a particular form of petty-bourgeois defence against capitalism.'[66] That definition of nationalism as a form of anticapitalist struggle, coupled with Pokrovsky's positive assessment of Hrushevsky's contribution to the field of Russian history, reflected the atmosphere of general tolerance for non-Russian historiography prevailing in the early 1920s. Apparently, the Bolshevik historians of the period considered non-Russian populist historiography a natural ally in the Marxist offensive against the concepts of Russian imperial historiography.

Pokrovsky's views on Hrushevsky's historical method were further developed by his Ukrainian-born student Mykhailo Rubach, who prepared a lengthy study, 'Federalist Theories in the History of Russia,' that he submitted for publication in 1925.[67] In his essay, Rubach discussed federalist ideas reflected in the programmatic documents and activities of the Society of United Slavs and the SS. Cyril and Methodius Brotherhood, as well as in the works of three historians – Mykola Kostomarov, Afanasii Shchapov, and Mykhailo Hrushevsky. Rubach distinguished three types of federalism – feudal, petty-bourgeois, and national or statist – and identified Hrushevsky as a representative of the third category. According to Rubach, Hrushevsky's work represented not only the pinnacle of federalist theorizing in Russian historiography but also its terminus, since Hrushevsky ultimately rejected federalism as an option for future relations between Russia and Ukraine. In Rubach's opinion, Hrushevsky's idea of an independent 'Great Ukraine' spelled the end of the federalist orientation. He wrote in that regard: 'The counterposing of an independent Ukrainian people to the Great Russian; the rejection of elements of similarity between the two nationalities – not only those thought up by Muscovite historiography but also genuine historical and concrete elements – is organically a component of the process of transformation of federalist ideas into their national-statist forms, and then to the rejection of federalism itself.'[68]

Rubach held a generally high opinion of Hrushevsky as a historian. He credited him with completing the destruction of the scheme of 'all-Russian' history that his predecessors had begun. According to Rubach, Hrushevsky had also created an 'independent bourgeois-nationalist scheme of Ukrainian history.'[69] He welcomed both accomplishments, especially the first, and even believed that in his campaign against the concepts of the 'statist-juridical' school in Russian historiography, Hrushevsky had approached a Marxist understanding of history. This achievement was allegedly due to Hrushevsky's rejection of the primacy of the state in historical research; instead, he had based his idea of the continuity of Ukrainian history on a study of the territory, language, culture, and socio-economic development of the Ukrainian people. Hrushevsky's approach to Marxism was, in Rubach's opinion, only a temporary phenomenon. In the final analysis, Hrushevsky based his scheme of Ukrainian history on the selfsame statist idea, now given national colouration. Rubach concluded that for Hrushevsky the nation was not a historical but rather an eternal phenomenon whose history, along with that of the national movement, served as the 'criterion and highest goal' of his research.[70]

As noted above, Rubach welcomed Hrushevsky's successful deconstruction of the traditional scheme of 'Russian history,' meaning the scheme represented by the 'state-juridical' school. As for specific elements of Hrushevsky's project, Rubach particularly valued his attack on the Pogodin theory. Following Hrushevsky in his critique of Pogodin, Rubach also claimed that 'the history of the Kyivan state belongs *fundamentally*, in the first place, to the history of the Ukrainian people.' What Rubach refused to accept, however, was the thesis that 'the Great Russian people bears no direct relation to the history of the Kyivan period.'[71] Rubach believed that the origins of the history of the Russian people were also to be found in the history of the Kyivan state and claimed that 'his justified effort to prove the distinct character of the Ukrainian people ... led Hrushevsky to an unjustified rejection of elements of considerable kinship in the historical and prehistorical past of the two peoples.'[72] Although Rubach subscribed to Hrushevsky's thesis that Galicia-Volhynia, not Suzdal-Vladimir, was to be considered the principal successor to the Kyivan state, he also accused Hrushevsky of neglecting the historical links between the two parts of Rus'.[73] Rubach generally welcomed Hrushevsky's criticism not only of Russian but also of Ukrainian historical myths, among which he listed the theory of the Kyivan Rus' origins of Ukrainian Cossackdom.[74] He also welcomed Hrushevsky's conclusion that the failure of the Cossack revolution (that is, the Khmelnytsky Uprising) resulted from the Cossack officer stratum's betrayal of the national interests of Ukraine and the socio-economic interests of the popular masses.[75]

When it came to a critique of Hrushevsky's methodological paradigm, Rubach claimed that 'despite Hrushevsky's understanding of the role of the economic factor and class struggle, he basically remains an idealist.' He saw proof of this in Hrushevsky's rejection of historical materialism, as well as in his alleged 'eclecticism' and reliance on ethical criteria in the evaluation of historical developments. Rubach also questioned Hrushevsky's understanding of the role of class struggle in history, claiming that in his post-1917 works, Hrushevsky viewed the peasantry as an undifferentiated social group, neglecting class divisions within it. Nor did Rubach fail to point out Hrushevsky's critical attitude toward Marxism, which he saw as 'ruthless abstract oversimplification.'[76] Rubach's discernment of positive elements in the work of an author who treated Marxism with such scant respect was a reflection not only of his own views and attitudes but also of the relatively tolerant atmosphere of the mid-1920s.[77] If one treats Rubach's essay as a reflection of the broader consensus that emerged on the issue of the distinct character of Ukrainian history in the circle of young Marxist scholars working with Mikhail Pokrovsky, then Rubach's acceptance of the main elements of Hrushevsky's claim to Kyivan Rus' on behalf of the Ukrainian national narrative must be seen as a major gain for Hrushevsky's conception of Ukrainian history.

Even more impressive was the degree of acceptance of Hrushevsky's historical paradigm in Ukrainian Marxist historiography, thanks mainly to the 'Ukrainian Pokrovsky,' Matvii Iavorsky, whose dependence on Hrushevsky's interpretation of Ukrainian history has been discussed above. Iavorsky often charted his course between the ultrazealous Marxist critics of Hrushevsky and the latter's enthusiastic proponents in Ukraine. Iavorsky felt the strength of the Marxist purists as early as 1924, when he wrote a generally positive review of Hrushevsky's *Origins of Society (A Genetic Sociology)*. Iavorsky's review and Hrushevsky's book were soon severely criticized by Andrii Richytsky, who attacked Hrushevsky for disagreeing with Friedrich Engels's views on the history of primitive societies. Richytsky's negative review was aimed not only at Hrushevsky but also at the 'soft' communists within the ruling party. Richytsky attacked Iavorsky for being too 'tolerant' and issuing Hrushevsky and his work a passport to the world of materialist scholarship.[78]

Iavorsky's other opponent in the assessment of Hrushevsky's role in Ukrainian historiography was Hrushevsky's older colleague Dmytro Bahalii. When it comes to the attitude of the 'old guard' of Ukrainian historians toward Marxist historiography, Bahalii was clearly in a class by himself. Given prevailing circumstances and the almost complete control of public discourse by the communist authorities, the non-Marxists had only very limited opportunities to respond to their opponents. Many Ukrainian scholars avoided writing for state-controlled publications altogether. Others, including Hrushevsky, did not eschew the government-controlled media and publishing houses entirely but preferred not to respond to their Marxist critics in print. One of the few exceptions was Dmytro Bahalii. Quite early in his Soviet career, he became involved in open debate with his Marxist critic, Matvii Iavorsky. From the very beginning, Bahalii not only attempted to defend himself against groundless accusations but also tried to shape the parameters of the engagement.

The early polemic between Bahalii and Iavorsky, which spilled onto the pages of Kharkiv periodicals in 1923–4, not only gives us good idea of the nature of debates in Soviet Ukraine over the significance of Hrushevsky's paradigm but also illustrates the process of negotiation in which the Marxist and non-Marxist narratives of Ukrainian history were involved throughout the 1920s. The discussion was triggered by Bahalii's attempt to present in textbook format his views on Ukraine's revolutionary experience – the era considered by Marxist historians to be their exclusive turf. Bahalii wanted to present his overview of the period in a short essay on Ukraine's nineteenth- and early twentieth-century history to be appended to a Ukrainian translation of Aleksandra Efimenko's survey *History of the Ukrainian People*.[79] Bahalii's addendum was sent for review to Matvii Iavorsky, who not only accused Bahalii of 'objectivism' but also forbade the publication of the last part of his essay, which covered the events of 1918–22.[80] Bahalii was offended by the intrusion of the Bolshevik censor and submitted a written protest, charging Iavorsky with lack of scholarly expertise and indicating an apparent conflict of interest: even as he reviewed Bahalii's work, Iavorsky was preparing his own survey history of the revolutionary era in Ukraine for publication.[81]

Bahalii soon gained an opportunity to express his views on the historical qualifications of his opponent in public. In the Kharkiv journal *Knyha* (The Book) he published a review of Iavorsky's brochure-length *Survey of Ukrainian-Russian History*, which had recently appeared in print. In the same year (1923), he published a review of the first part of Iavorsky's *Survey of Ukrainian History*, which presented Iavorsky's views on the subject and his critique of non-Marxist historians of Ukraine.[82] Iavorsky, who readily admitted the shortcomings of the first publication, was clearly offended by Bahalii's second review, published in *Chervonyi shliakh*, and responded to it with a long article in the same journal.[83] Then it was Bahalii's turn to publish a rebuttal.[84] Apparently this heated polemic did not preclude a certain amount of cooperation between the two opponents, for in the same year the State Publishing House of Ukraine issued a brochure containing the text of Bahalii's paper on Hryhorii Skovoroda (delivered in December 1922 at the Artem Social Museum) and Iavorsky's short essay on the same subject.[85] It is quite obvious that both discussants were keeping their options open for the future.

In his evaluation of Iavorsky's works, Bahalii attempted to instruct his opponent and censor in some of the basics of historical research, as well as to teach him good manners in the conduct of scholarly polemics. Iavorsky, who attacked Bahalii in terms appropriate to a journalistic exchange, was mainly concerned to present his Marxist views on Ukrainian history and to give vent to his disappointment that Bahalii, having declared his interest in materialist methodology, had allegedly failed to understand the basics of the Marxist approach to the past. Among the major points of disagreement was Iavorsky's assessment of pre-revolutionary Ukrainian historiography. Bahalii protested Iavorsky's treatment of both Russian and Ukrainian historians as members of one bourgeois group, arguing that most Ukrainian historians should be considered populists. Iavorsky responded by accusing Bahalii and other Ukrainian scholars (above all Dmytro Iavornytsky) of continuing to indulge in romanticism and the heroic representation of the past, while neglecting class divisions within Ukrainian society. He insisted on his description of Ukrainian historians as bourgeois and once again attacked Bahalii for characterizing Ukrainian historiography as populist.

Iavorsky was nevertheless opposed to treating Hrushevsky as a member of the same group as Mykola Kostomarov, Volodymyr Antonovych, and Oleksander Lazarevsky. Hrushevsky alone, in Iavorsky's opinion, was a true populist, while the others merely used populist terminology to conceal their political goals. According to Iavorsky, Antonovych had become an opponent of populism under the influence of Drahomanov, while Kostomarov and Lazarevsky, whom Iavorsky called proponents of absolutism, allegedly promoted Cossack romanticism and ethnographism, writing about the Ukrainian popular masses only because they had no one else to counterpose to the Poles – the enemies of Ukrainian statehood. The fact that Iavorsky assigned Hrushevsky to a different group than the 'adherents of absolutism' Kostomarov and Lazarevsky did not save him from being classified as a representative of bourgeois historiography. Dividing all ideologies into bourgeois and proletarian, Iavorsky made the following reference to Hrushevsky: 'As for the fact that some Ukrainian historians deviated in the direction of petty-bourgeois ideology, even if it were the ideology of a Socialist Revolutionary, as in the case of Professor Hrushevsky, it is still bourgeois, whether great or petty-bourgeois.'[86]

Iavorsky also cited Hrushevsky to prove that even the 'true populists' sometimes followed sinister political agendas when they wrote about the people. 'Did not Professor Hrushevsky – he himself admits it now –

write his works about the Ukrainian people from the viewpoint of justifying efforts to attain Ukrainian independence, from the viewpoint of struggle for that independence, thereby obscuring the process of class struggle, the basic process in the history of the Ukrainian people?'[87] Hrushevsky's putative admission was a mere figment of Iavorsky's imagination, as he consciously misrepresented the former's words in the preface to part 3 of volume 8 of his *History*. There Hrushevsky wrote that Khmelnytsky and his associates had eventually arrived at the idea of establishing a united and independent Ukraine, noting that his book would be useful to readers with an interest in Ukraine's past, as well as to those interested in contemporary affairs.[88] In Iavorsky's opinion, Hrushevsky was much better than other pre-revolutionary historians of Ukraine but remained a bourgeois historian nonetheless.[89]

Quite different was Iavorsky's assessment of Bahalii. 'I know – not from an article,' wrote Iavorsky, 'that academician Bahalii, though at an advanced age, still wishes to go and is going in the direction of Marxism with his students, and is even teaching and urging others in that direction.'[90] Later, in his speech at the celebration of Bahalii's seventieth birthday in 1927, Iavorsky compared the contributions of Bahalii and Hrushevsky to Ukrainian scholarship. Unsurprisingly, the comparison did not favour Hrushevsky but revealed new elements in Iavorsky's assessment of prerevolutionary Ukrainian historiography. According to Iavorsky, both Bahalii and Hrushevsky, whom he called the patriarchs of Ukrainian historiography, were products of the historical school of Volodymyr Antonovych. In Iavorsky's opinion, that school was preoccupied with the study of historical sources, denied the importance of historical synthesis, neglected the role of politics in historical studies, and focused on the study of cultural manifestations of Ukrainian identity (*kul'turnytstvo*). Despite their common academic background, Hrushevsky and Bahalii had chosen to approach historical research from different directions. While Hrushevsky and his disciples devoted themselves to crafting an 'extraordinary beautiful nationalist necklace of scholarly historical synthesis,' Bahalii remained faithful to the tradition of the Antonovych school, avoided writing synthetic works, and took refuge behind the 'lifeless document.' The revolution, according to Iavorsky, changed the nature of Hrushevsky's and Bahalii's research. Hrushevsky and his school, incapable of producing a new historical synthesis, were obliged to revert to the old methods of Antonovych's 'documentary school.' Bahalii, on the contrary, took the opportunity to create a new historical synthesis, stringing his 'jewels' into a new 'necklace of red Ukrainian historiography.' Iavorsky wished Bahalii every success in that undertaking.[91] What Iavorsky failed to note in his analysis of Bahalii's evolution was that in assembling the new 'necklace of red Ukrainian historiography,' Bahalii availed himself of the design prepared by none other than Hrushevsky.

To Bahalii's credit, he fully recognized the priority of his younger colleague, producing the most detailed analysis of Hrushevsky's contribution to Ukrainian historiography ever published in Soviet Ukraine.[92] He first presented his views on the subject at Hrushevsky's jubilee celebrations in Kyiv (3 October 1926) and Kharkiv (10 October 1926). Later he published an extended version of his paper in *Chervonyi shliakh*.[93] Bahalii's essay showed few if any traces of bias and was entirely devoid of the deliberate misrepresentation of Hrushevsky's views that was common in Marxist critiques of him. In Bahalii's opinion, Hrushevsky was the first historian to separate the Ukrainian historical process from the Russian, to the benefit of both, and the author of the first scholarly history of the Ukrainian people, that is, a history of Ukraine based on the national paradigm. Bahalii stated that the publication of the *History of Ukraine-Rus'* made Hrushevsky supreme in the field of Ukrainian studies and secured for him the central place in Ukrainian historiography previously occupied by Volodymyr Antonovych.[94] Coming from Bahalii, himself a student of Antonovych and a distinguished historian in his own right, this was a flattering testimonial to Hrushevsky's accomplishments. It was also a slap in the face of the Soviet authorities, who had attempted to build up Bahalii's prestige at Hrushevsky's expense and sought to play off one historian against the other.[95]

Probably the most important point of Bahalii's essay was his statement that he agreed completely with the scheme of Ukrainian history employed by Hrushevsky. Bahalii acknowledged Hrushevsky's leading role in the development of the scheme and defended him against attacks from the 'traditionalists,' singling out the critique of Hrushevsky by another student of Antonovych (and Bahalii's one-time rival), Ivan Linnichenko.[96] Bahalii offered a twofold response to Linnichenko's attack, including old arguments based on the Ukrainian populist tradition and new ones reflecting the principal themes of Soviet discourse. Bahalii stated that he personally accepted Hrushevsky's scheme, as the Ukrainian people had indeed lived a 'historical life' for more than a thousand years: they had settled and developed their own territory; formed a nation with a distinct language and culture; obtained recognition from the other European nations; and, together with the Russians and Belarusians, founded the Soviet Union. In his critique of Linnichenko, Bahalii maintained that the Ukrainian people could not be denied a history of their own merely because they had long existed without a state. According to Bahalii, in exaggerating the historical role of the state, Linnichenko had neglected the importance of the socio-economic factor in history. He went on to charge Linnichenko with idealizing the role played in Ukrainian history by the Muscovite state, which had contributed to establishing an unjust socio-economic order in Ukraine and exploited the country's capital and human resources. Bahalii also strongly criticized Linnichenko's thesis that Ukraine had never had a culture of its own.

In the context of Soviet historiography of the mid-1920s, all these were serious deviations that contradicted the 'internationalist' reading of imperial Russian history promoted by the party authorities. Thus, Bahalii characterized Linnichenko's attack of 1917 on Hrushevsky as representative of the views of those all-Russian 'patriots' who had persisted in denying Ukraine autonomous status within the Russian state, even on the eve of the 1917 revolution. In pointing out that Ukraine had eventually become a union republic of the USSR, Bahalii was not only further discrediting the irredentist views of Linnichenko and the 'White Guard' circles but also endowing Hrushevsky's scheme of Ukrainian history with greater legitimacy in the context of the dominant Soviet discourse. According to that line of argument, every union republic had a self-evident right to a history of its own, and Hrushevsky's scheme made the writing of such a history possible.

Bahalii's 'complete agreement' with Hrushevsky's historical scheme was by no means unconditional.[97] His strictures concerning Linnichenko's neglect of the socio-economic factor in history also pertained to his interpretation of Hrushevsky's oeuvre. Bahalii defined Hrushevsky's main historiosophic approach as the study of national history in its three principal dimensions – territory, people, and state – with the main emphasis on the first two categories. On the one hand, Bahalii supported that approach because it undermined the traditional scheme of 'Russian' history, with its stress on the history of the state. On the other hand, he criticized it for its philosophical idealism, as opposed to materialism, and for subscribing to the wrong type of monism – that of nationality rather than the socio-economic factor. Bahalii was apparently the first student of Hrushevsky's writings to point out that the key element of his historiosophy was the Hegelian triad of thesis, antithesis, and synthesis. As applied by Hrushevsky to the history of Ukraine, this yielded a three-stage scheme of the development of the Ukrainian nation – its formation, decline, and revival. Bahalii asserted that Hrushevsky had studied the first two periods as a historian and contributed to the third as a political activist.[98]

Apart from philosophical and methodological principles, there were specific problems of Ukrainian history on which Bahalii did not agree with Hrushevsky. Some of them were of crucial importance for Hrushevsky's paradigm of the Ukrainian past. By far the most significant was the issue of the Kyivan heritage: Hrushevsky claimed that Kyivan Rus' was an exclusively Ukrainian formation, while Bahalii took a more cautious approach to the problem. He acknowledged that the history of Kyivan Rus' was mainly the product of the activities of Ukrainian tribes but maintained that it should be considered part of the Russian historical experience insofar as Russian tribes took part in it.[99] Another point of disagreement between Bahalii and Hrushevsky centred on the periodization of Ukrainian history. Arguing that Hrushevsky's periodization (Kyivan Rus', the Lithuanian-Polish and Cossack periods) was based mainly on a statist/political approach, Bahalii advocated a scheme based on the socio-economic factor.[100]

For all his criticism, Bahalii acknowledged Hrushevsky's *History* as the greatest achievement of pre-Marxist Ukrainian historiography, calling on older Ukrainian historians and the new generation of Marxist scholars to join forces in creating a Marxist synthesis of Ukrainian history.[101] It is difficult, if not impossible, to determine how much Bahalii believed in the importance of the materialist and socio-economic approach to history and to what extent he merely wanted to adjust to the new dominant discourse so as to legitimize the Ukrainian national narrative. After all, Bahalii's emphasis on the role of class struggle, his treatment of religion as a cover for socio-economic class interests, and his negative attitude toward the cult of personality in history reflected standard features of the Soviet Marxist historical paradigm of the mid-1920s. Bahalii's call for his colleagues old and new to 'provide new social content for the national idea and culture'[102] was basically an exhortation to reconcile the national and Marxist approaches to history.

It appears that even Hrushevsky himself did not exclude such a possibility, at least for the time being. As noted above, he had returned to Ukraine in 1924 as a committed socialist with a complete command of socialist terminology who observed politics through the prism of social and national revolution. By employing a vocabulary similar to that of the dominant discourse, Hrushevsky engaged in a process of negotiation with the Bolshevik regime, attempting both to further his political and cultural goals and to strengthen his position within the Ukrainian scholarly and cultural establishment. Hrushevsky's flexibility in selecting new strategies for the advancement of his national agenda clearly helped him achieve his political, scholarly, and cultural goals.

The concept of national revival – the cornerstone of Hrushevsky's paradigm – did not disappear from his political and intellectual horizon but was redefined within the framework of the new revolutionary discourse as the liberation movement of the Ukrainian people. In 1925, in the introduction to a special issue of *Ukraïna* devoted to the hundredth anniversary of the Decembrist Revolt (1825), Hrushevsky characterized the period between 1825 and 1925 as a 'campaign of Ukrainian economic and political emancipation, social and national liberation.' He also presented the following pro-Marxist interpretation of that period of Ukrainian history:

> In general terms, we understand how the growth of productive forces and resources led to a search for slogans of liberation and organizational forms now in the traditions of the old Ukrainian peasant-burgher and petty-bourgeois liberation struggle, now in models offered by the world revolution and particularly by French socialism, from Babeuf to Saint-Simon and Proudhon. We know the interest that the Decembrist uprising aroused in the Cyrillo-Methodian grouping and with what piety Shevchenko treated those martyrs for freedom in his works. We know that among Ukrainian activists of the 1870s and 1880s who considered themselves heirs of the Cyrillo-Methodians there was a parallel reflection, on the one hand, of the ideas of Fourier, Proudhon, and Marx, and, on the other, a search for the traditional thread that 'extends through our peasantry,' as Drahomanov put it, and should serve to intertwine the Ukrainian folk tradition with the new European liberation movement ... We know the unceasing search for a common line and a common front with the Great Russian liberation movement, and, at the same time, the effort somehow to part ways with tireless Russian centralism and make room for an independent place and independent movement for ourselves in the joint campaign for national and political liberation, to ensure the fulness of national life in an autonomous or independent Ukraine, a socialist federation, or a 'Free Union' – whichever of these was imagined by anyone at the time.[103]

On the one hand, there is good reason to believe that Hrushevsky's new reading of the era of Ukrainian national revival was more than a political pretence. It reflected many of the ideas that he developed during the 1917 revolution, when he emerged as one of the leading ideologues of the Ukrainian Party of Socialist Revolutionaries. On the other hand, there is little doubt that when it came to the presentation of his ideas, Hrushevsky was prepared to adjust some of his old formulas and even sacrifice secondary elements of his original paradigm in order to meet the requirements of the dominant Soviet discourse. The very fact that Hrushevsky was prepared to associate the beginning of the era of the social and national liberation of Ukraine with the Decembrist revolt of 1825, and not with the publication of Kotliarevsky's *Eneïda* in 1798, which he had earlier taken as the genesis of the Ukrainian national revival, gives a clear indication of his readiness to adjust his old interpretations of Ukraine's nineteenth- and twentieth-century history.

During the 1926 celebrations of his jubilee, Hrushevsky made good use of vocabulary either similar to or taken directly from the dominant Bolshevik discourse to present a class-based scheme of the development of Ukrainian historiography. He stated that early Ukrainian historical writing had developed on the basis of the feudal order, supported at first by the merchant and burgher strata and later by the agrarian boyars. In the fifteenth and sixteenth centuries, historical writing was oriented toward the needs of the burgher estate, which came into existence as a result of the new money economy. Then, according to Hrushevsky, the chroniclers began to orient themselves on the Cossack order, which combined elements of feudalism with the democratic tendencies of the masses. Nineteenth-century authors were preoccupied with the peasantry, while the new goal of the Ukrainian intelligentsia, declared Hrushevsky, was to complete the construction of the Ukrainian nation with the formation of a Ukrainian working class.[104] Hrushevsky's socialist terminology and class-based analysis thus helped endow the national paradigm of Ukrainian national historiography with new legitimacy.

The issue on which Hrushevsky would not compromise was that of the distinct character of Ukrainian history. He was determined to present Ukrainian history in general and the history of the Ukrainian social and national liberation movement in particular as processes separate from the historical development of Russia. Helping to enhance the idea of Ukraine's distinct path to liberation was a series of celebrations of the anniversaries of leading Ukrainian political figures and historians organized by Hrushevsky during the 1920s. These included Taras Shevchenko, Mykola Kostomarov, Panteleimon Kulish, Mykhailo Drahomanov, Ivan Franko, Volodymyr Antonovych, and Oleksander Lazarevsky. The commemorations resulted in the publication of numerous articles, as well as a special issue of the journal *Ukraïna* devoted to the history of the Ukrainian political and cultural movement.[105] The last article that Hrushevsky submitted to *Ukraïna* before his arrest in 1931 was devoted to the fiftieth anniversary of the assassination of Tsar Alexander II by members of the underground People's Will. There Hrushevsky discussed the fate of three members of the People's Will whom he considered to be Ukrainians or closely linked with Ukraine: Andrei Zheliabov, Nikolai Kibalchich, and Sofia Perovskaia. Although the article was never published because of the authorities' closing of the journal, it is of particular interest as one of Hrushevsky's last attempts not only to separate the history of the Ukrainian liberation movement from the Russian but also to claim for Ukrainian history an important part of the Russian revolutionary narrative.[106]

There can be little doubt that many of Hrushevsky's attempts to establish the distinct character of the Ukrainian liberation movement met with understanding among the Marxist historians of Ukraine. In his general courses on Ukrainian history and publications on the history of 'revolutionary struggle,' Matvii Iavorsky presented the Ukrainian 'revolutionary process' as a historical phenomenon distinct from its Russian counterpart. Portraits of Zheliabov and Perovskaia even made their way into Iavorsky's textbook of Ukrainian history for secondary schools.[107] Not surprisingly, for all his reservations about Hrushevsky's methodology, Iavorsky considered him, along with Ranke and Soloviev, one of the 'giants' of bourgeois historiography and regretted his absence at the International Congress of Historians in Oslo in 1926.[108]

Some Marxist historians were even willing to overlook Hrushevsky's 'idealism,' 'eclecticism,' and 'nationalism,' and worked hard to represent him as a scholar about to embrace the Marxist historiographical method. Such an interpretation of Hrushevsky's views was popularized by Osyp Hermaize, Hrushevsky's younger colleague in the historical institutions of the Academy of Sciences in Kyiv. In the autumn of 1926 Hermaize was entrusted by the party authorities with the task of writing an article for the journal *Zhyttia i revoliutsiia* commemorating Hrushevsky's birthday.[109] In discussing Hrushevsky's work, Hermaize stressed two principal achievements. The first was that of placing Ukrainian history on a national basis – a major accomplishment, given that before Hrushevsky, owing to the demands of Russian censorship, the Ukrainian element had been thoroughly concealed in the works of Ukrainian historians. Hrushevsky's second contribution was that of bringing together Ukrainian cultural forces from the Russian Empire and Austria-Hungary, a task postulated by Mykhailo Drahomanov.

Some of Hermaize's remarks about Hrushevsky and his accomplishments were taken directly from the introduction to the festschrift published by his students and colleagues in Lviv in 1906 on the occasion of Hrushevsky's fortieth birthday. Not unlike the editors of that festschrift, Hermaize wrote that Hrushevsky had placed the national idea at the foundation of his history of Ukraine and studied the continuity of the nation's life.[110] According to Hermaize, this approach to the history of Ukraine reflected Hrushevsky's own social and national aspirations without compromising the scholarly character of his work, which was based on thorough study of the sources. Indeed, Hermaize claimed that in quality of scholarly apparatus and analysis, Hrushevsky's works surpassed those of Sergei Soloviev and Vasilii Kliuchevsky. As proof of the high scholarly level of Hrushevsky's works, Hermaize cited the recognition of his contribution to the study of Ukrainian and East European history by the Russian scholar Dmitrii Korsakov and the acceptance of Hrushevsky's new scheme of Russian history by his colleague Aleksandr Presniakov, as well as by the leader of Soviet Marxist historiography, Mikhail Pokrovsky.[111]

One of the main tasks of Hermaize's article was to clear Hrushevsky of the charge of philosophical idealism pressed by many Marxist historians and even by some aspiring Marxists such as Bahalii. Hermaize claimed that it would be an error to consider Hrushevsky a complete idealist, as he had never considered 'spiritual activity' a factor in social development; did not believe in the spontaneous wisdom of the popular masses, as did Danylo Mordovtsev or Mykola Kostomarov before him; and had never idealized the past along the lines of Dmytro Iavornytsky. Hermaize saw Hrushevsky's interest in Ukrainian economic history as further proof of his lack of idealism. Nevertheless, what differentiated Hrushevsky from Marxist historians was, in Hermaize's opinion, his refusal to adopt a monistic approach to history. According to Hermaize, Hrushevsky was not an idealist but a pluralist who took account of all historical factors without reducing them to a common sociological denominator.

What Bahalii and some of the Marxist historians called 'eclecticism' was dubbed 'pluralism' by Hermaize. He also characterized Hrushevsky as a historian who could one day become a Marxist. Hermaize wrote that Hrushevsky was one of those scholars who were not afraid to reconsider their principles and adopt new methods of research. As an example of Hrushevsky's openness to new directions in scholarship, Hermaize indicated his work in sociology and specifically mentioned the similarity of Hrushevsky's views to those of Emile Durkheim's school, which, according to Hermaize, was reaching conclusions very close to those of Marx and Engels despite the bourgeois leanings of its members. Hermaize asserted that as a true scholar, Hrushevsky had no choice but to accept Marxism, for it was not only the most advanced but the only method of acquiring objective knowledge. He concluded with the wish that Hrushevsky's scholarship might continue to flourish in 'liberated socialist Ukraine.'[112]

Although Hermaize's depiction of Hrushevsky not as a philosophical idealist but as a would-be Marxist did not sit well with most Marxist historians and party apparatchiks,[113] the appearance of his article once again indicated the prospect of convergence of the Marxist and nationalist narratives in Soviet Ukraine. The rise of the Ukrainian national movement during the revolutionary era forced the Bolsheviks not only to recognize the existence of a distinct Ukrainian nation but also to make significant concessions to the Ukrainian national movement in the course of the 1920s. That policy could not but affect the balance of power between proponents and opponents of Ukrainian national historiography. Prior to the Revolution of 1917, Hrushevsky made use of the national paradigm to establish the distinct and separate character of Ukrainian people. Once the existence of the Ukrainian nation was accepted by the Bolsheviks, the whole historical scheme developed by Hrushevsky acquired legitimacy in their eyes. Hrushevsky's use of elements of the dominant class-based discourse clearly facilitated that process. Ironically, it also opened the door to a Marxist takeover of Hrushevsky's historical conception.

The Great Break

In his above-mentioned report of May 1929 to the Central Committee of the Communist Party of Ukraine, Mykhailo Rubach noted the relation between the notion of a distinct Ukrainian history and the particular 'solution' of the Ukrainian national question in the USSR. The problem with Rubach's view of the matter was that a different 'solution' could easily lead to the elimination of the distinct status of the Ukrainian historical narrative. After all, Rakovsky's foreword to Iavorsky's *Short History of Ukraine* implied that the question of right and wrong in historical debate was to be decided by political and military struggle.

The peaceful coexistence of Marxist and non-Russian national narratives, as well as their progressive convergence, came to an end in the course of 1929, dubbed by party officials the year of the 'great break' – a turning point in the politics of the period. In the USSR as a whole, it was marked by an all-out attack on the 'old cadres.' In Ukraine, the party signalled a reversal of official policy on the nationality question by sanctioning the first arrests among the intelligentsia in preparation for the show trial of the 'Union for the Liberation of Ukraine.' In the realm of historiography, the year began with a major disagreement between Marxist historians in Moscow and Kharkiv over the issue of establishing a distinct Marxist narrative of Ukrainian history. In the course of numerous discussions, Ukrainian Marxists were accused by their Moscow-based counterparts of following the nationalist views of Mykhailo Hrushevsky, and the outcome of this controversy had a profound impact on the development of the all-Russian, Great Russian, and Ukrainian historical narratives in the USSR.

The following discussion focuses on the conflict between Russian and Ukrainian Marxist historians, led respectively by Mikhail Pokrovsky and Matvii Iavorsky, in order to assess its significance for the national paradigm of Ukrainian history in the USSR. An important aspect of the controversy was Pokrovsky's use of class-based vocabulary to discredit and deconstruct the Ukrainian national narrative. This excursus into the historiographic debates of 1928–9 casts not only Iavorsky but also his main opponent, Pokrovsky, in a somewhat unaccustomed light. Rightly considered an enemy of the old Russian historical narrative and a committed internationalist in his writings and political activities in Moscow, Pokrovsky emerges in his relations with Ukrainian Marxist historians of the late 1920s not only as an opponent of the Ukrainian national narrative but also as a proponent of a Russocentric version of the new Soviet narrative.

The conflict between Russian and Ukrainian Marxists began as a bureaucratic dispute between Russian scholarly institutions taking on an all-Union role and Ukrainian institutions that were opposed to such expansion. Tension was already apparent at the First All-Union Conference of Marxist-Leninist Research Institutes, held in Leningrad in March

1928. There, Marxist scholars based in Moscow and Leningrad voiced their concern over the weakness of Marxist studies outside the two capitals. It was suggested that scholars from Moscow be dispatched to the provinces in order to raise the level of Marxist scholarship. The Russian Marxist establishment was then preparing for a takeover of the Russian Academy of Sciences but was also attempting to take control of Marxist scholarly centres in the Union republics, including Ukraine. Neither Iavorsky nor his superiors in Kharkiv, including Mykola Skrypnyk, could possibly have approved of that part of the plan. In his report to the conference, Iavorsky admitted the strength of bourgeois ideology in Ukraine but also noted the hold of Russian great-power chauvinism over the Marxist cadres,[114] thereby rejecting the offer of 'assistance' from Moscow.

The formation of the All-Union Society of Marxist Historians, initiated by Mikhail Pokrovsky, soon became a bone of contention between Kharkiv and Moscow. Iavorsky, apparently backed in this case by Skrypnyk, objected to the efforts of Pavel Gorin, one of Pokrovsky's closest associates and secretary of the society, to form a centralized all-Union organization, insisting instead on the formation of an all-Union association of republican societies of Marxist historians. To counter the Moscow plan, on 20 December 1928, immediately before the departure of the Ukrainian delegation for the First All-Union Conference of Marxist Historians in Moscow, Iavorsky and Skrypnyk formed the Ukrainian Society of Marxist Historians. Iavorsky announced this development from the podium of the all-Union conference and declared the society's intention to hold its own congress in May 1929 and begin the publication of its own journal under the same title as its Moscow prototype, *Istoryk-marksyst* (The Marxist Historian). Clearly, this was not what the Marxist scholars of Moscow had expected of their Ukrainian colleagues. In his organizational report to the all-Union conference, Gorin noted that sections of the All-Union Society of Marxist Historians had already been established in Belarus and the Trans-Caucasus, while in Ukraine this was taking longer to accomplish, although the need to bring together cadres of Marxist historians was more acute there than anywhere else.[115]

Iavorsky's main presentation at the conference was devoted to a critique of Ukrainian bourgeois historiography. This choice of topic was influenced by a number of factors, among them Iavorsky's attempt to clear the ground for the introduction of a new Marxist scheme of Ukrainian history that would treat it as a subject separate from Russian history not only in form but also in content. In order to accomplish this, Iavorsky had to demonstrate to his opponents that the old 'bourgeois' historiography was inadequate for the purpose. Opposing 'anti-Marxist' trends in Ukrainian historiography was also an opportune way to establish Iavorsky's Marxist credentials – a particularly important task, given the struggle between Moscow and Kharkiv for control of Marxist scholarly institutions in Ukraine. In his paper, Iavorsky apparently sought to anticipate possible attacks by his opponents based on the assumption that bourgeois influences in Ukraine were too strong to leave the local Marxist cadres to deal with them on their own. Iavorsky, for his part, maintained that despite the strength of bourgeois historiography in Ukraine, the Ukrainian Marxists had assessed the situation correctly, made serious progress in fighting the class enemy, and established their capacity to control the situation without help from Moscow. There was no better way to make these points than to criticize Hrushevsky and his followers among the 'pseudo-Marxist' historians.[116]

If that was indeed Iavorsky's plan, it clearly did not work. Comments made at the conference by some members of the Ukrainian delegation provoked a major controversy that set off a fierce attack on Ukrainian Marxist historiography and ultimately led not only to the end of Iavorsky's career but also to the dismantling of the Ukrainian Marxist grand narrative.

By no accident whatever, the debate that triggered the Russo-Ukrainian showdown at the Moscow conference was related to the Marxist historians' assessment of Hrushevsky's views. In his presentation, Matvii Iavorsky discussed and attacked the views not only of Viacheslav Lypynsky and various 'pseudo-Marxists,' including Oleksander Ohloblyn, Mykhailo Slabchenko, and Osyp Hermaize, but also of Hrushevsky. Iavorsky compared the political attitude adopted by Hrushevsky during and after the revolution to that of Otto von Bismarck, who was allegedly prepared for anything, even a revolution, to save Prussia.[117] What he apparently had in mind was Hrushevsky's readiness to accept the rules of official discourse without giving up his national convictions. In the discussion that followed Iavorsky's presentation, Hrushevsky was further criticized by Zynovii Hurevych and Mykhailo Rubach, members of the Ukrainian delegation at the conference.[118]

Hurevych even characterized Iavorsky's assessment of Hrushevsky's political attitude as too lenient. But in the process he also accused one of Pokrovsky's students, Militsa Nechkina, of Great Russian chauvinism in connection with her treatment of the Decembrist movement in

Ukraine. This accusation, which created a great uproar, was made in passing. Hurevych, whose main targets at that moment were Hrushevsky and Hermaize, struck out at Nechkina as part of the ritual, almost obligatory in Ukraine at the time, of fighting simultaneously on two fronts – against bourgeois nationalism and great-power chauvinism. In Moscow, the comment was viewed as an assault and served as a pretext for Pokrovsky and his group to launch a major attack on their Ukrainian colleagues. Pokrovsky himself rose in defence of Nechkina, while Gorin accused Iavorsky of harbouring non-Marxist views on the history of the revolutionary movement in Ukraine. At the end of the discussion, Hurevych felt obliged to withdraw his remarks about Nechkina. This was done under pressure from Pokrovsky, who accused Hurevych of being under Hrushevsky's de facto influence and of putting nationality ahead of class.[119]

Iavorsky, who clearly wanted to avoid an open conflict at the conference, tried to smooth things over after the confrontation. At the end of the conference, he unexpectedly rose to congratulate Pokrovsky on the thirty-fifth anniversary of his scholarly career. This obliged Pokrovsky to mute his attack on nationalist deviations in Marxist historiography (aimed first and foremost at Iavorsky) when he delivered his concluding remarks.[120] In the final analysis, though, Iavorsky's tactic failed. The conference adopted a resolution calling for the establishment of an all-Union organization of Marxist historians, not the decentralized association of republican organizations advocated by Iavorsky, and Pokrovsky welcomed that resolution in his closing statement. He said that before the conference he had been somewhat concerned about 'vestiges of nationalism' and supported the idea of a federal structure for the organization, but the unity shown by conference participants had convinced him that the organization should have a centralized, all-Union structure. He argued that the decision should not be viewed as an example of great-power chauvinism but as proof that conference participants were a 'true Marxist collective' capable of subordinating national interests to the common struggle on the class front. Pokrovsky had organized the First All-Union Conference of Marxist Historians as a reaction to the International Historical Congress held in Oslo in the summer of 1926, which he and Iavorsky had both attended, and expressed his pride in the Marxist historians' demonstration of unity at their conference, as opposed to the show of ethnic particularism among the bourgeois historians in Oslo.[121]

The image that Pokrovsky sought to project during the Russo-

Ukrainian debate was that of objective arbiter between the two groups of Marxist historians. Nevertheless, it was Pokrovsky himself who set the tone of intolerance at the conference and inspired the charges made against the Ukrainian historians. A report filed soon after the conclusion of the conference by an official of the Ukrainian commissariat of education named Semko indicates that it was Pokrovsky who influenced the conference vote on the issue of nationalist deviations in Marxist historiography. The conference condemned manifestations of bourgeois nationalism – a resolution that targeted the Ukrainian delegation – but failed to condemn manifestations of great-power chauvinism. Semko also protested Pokrovsky's attempt to lump Hrushevsky together with the Russian nationalist émigré Vasilii Shulgin and claimed that through Gorin Pokrovsky had influenced Moscow newspaper reports on the conference. Semko attached clippings of two articles from the newspapers *Vecherniaia Moskva* (Evening Moscow) and *Pravda* in which Gorin claimed that Ukrainian Marxist historians were under the influence of Hrushevsky, who, like Miliukov, was investing all his hopes in the outbreak of a peasant rebellion against Soviet power.[122]

The information supplied by Gorin to the Moscow newspapers was based on remarks made during the discussion of Iavorsky's paper by Pokrovsky himself. In his comments, Pokrovsky had effectively turned Hrushevsky and his historical paradigm into a weapon against the Ukrainian Marxist historians. He not only accused Hurevych of having fallen under the influence of Hrushevsky but also invoked Hrushevsky's name in order to argue for the creation of a 'united front' of Marxist historians of Russia and Ukraine. Pokrovsky claimed that Miliukov and Hrushevsky had a similar understanding of the 1917 revolution – the former viewed it as a peasant revolution, while the latter considered it a revolution of peasants and workers. According to Pokrovsky, Miliukov was hoping for a peasant uprising against Soviet power, as were all other political emigrants, whether they came from Russia or Ukraine. That line of argument led Pokrovsky to the conclusion that the counterrevolution had united its forces on the historical front and that the time had come to mobilize the forces of the Marxist historians as well. Pokrovsky formulated his view as follows: 'Comrades, this united front of historical counterrevolution shows that we must establish a firm and united front of Russian and Ukrainian historians, perhaps even forgetting for a time about Ukrainian, Belarusian, and Great Russian traditions, as they call them.'[123]

Pokrovsky's appeal for a united front of Marxist historians was little short of a call for a return to the prerevolutionary unity of 'Russian' historiography, presented by the leading Russian Marxist historian not in national but in class terms. Pokrovsky claimed repeatedly that the national factor was secondary to that of class. It was in this context that he referred to pan-Russian elements in the works of Russian Marxist historians not as manifestations of great-power chauvinism, as Hurevych described them, but as 'a certain disorderliness.' He asserted that Marxist historians should be interested in the social origins of the ideology of Decembrist organizations in Ukraine, not in the national origins of their individual members. Referring to national ideologies, he went on as follows: 'But, comrades, aside from these ideologies, there is yet another ideology that is known as Marxism and that made all these national ideologies obsolete long ago. Marxism knows only class ideology. True, in that class ideology one encounters a national refraction, but it is still based on class ... Thus, when Comrade Hurevych spoke so decisively about M.V. Nechkina's display of a great-power attitude, it was an incredible exaggeration, a tremendous exaggeration. And if such exaggerations are possible, that is the best explanation of Hrushevsky's influence to the present day.'[124]

Judging by Pokrovsky's statements at the conference, a true Marxist historian was not only supposed to subordinate nationality to class but was also free to neglect it completely. Disagreement with this view entailed an automatic accusation of solidarity with the camp of historiographic counterrevolution, represented by the names of Miliukov and Hrushevsky. That line of argument clearly helped Pokrovsky silence voices of opposition at the conference and later establish Moscow's organizational control over Marxist historiography in the national republics. It also had long-term consequences for the creation of a Russocentric paradigm of the 'history of the peoples of the USSR' and for the fate of the Marxist scheme of Ukrainian history that emerged in the late 1920s as the major obstacle to the restoration of the Russocentric outlook in Soviet Marxist historiography.

The issue of formulating a new Marxist scheme of the history of Ukraine distinct from that of Russia was privately discussed by conference participants and served as a background for the showdown between Russian and Ukrainian Marxist historians during the discussion of Iavorsky's paper. In his comments, another member of the Ukrainian delegation, Mykhailo Rubach, made a direct reference to those backroom discussions. 'I shall say openly,' stated Rubach, 'what is being said in the hallways: you [Ukrainian Marxists] are creating a scheme of your own. What kind of scheme is it? Are there really so many differences?'[125] The nature of Russian Marxist reservations concerning a distinct Marxist narrative of Ukrainian history was spelled out in Pavel Gorin's attack on Iavorsky at the conference. 'Of course, Ukraine has its own peculiarities of historical development, and no one is about to deny that,' argued Gorin. 'But I do not think that in their chase after a Marxist scheme of Ukrainian history the historians of Ukraine will give us, instead of Ukraine, a history similar to that of China, closed off with a "great wall of China" from historical developments in Russia. That would, of course, be a most ridiculous caricature, having nothing to do either with Marxism or even with "objective" bourgeois scholarship.'[126]

The creation of a Ukrainian Marxist historical narrative independent from that of Russia not only in form but also in content was something that Russian Marxist historians wanted to avoid at all costs. Iavorsky, on the other hand, apparently tried to use the forum of the all-Union conference to obtain approval for the creation of just such a narrative. He submitted a proposal for a paper titled 'A Scheme of Ukrainian History.' To Iavorsky's surprise, the paper was not included in the program: clearly, the organizers did not want to risk giving him an opportunity to achieve his goal. Nevertheless, once it became clear after the debate on Iavorsky's paper about 'anti-Marxist' historiography in Ukraine that most participants would not support him, Gorin suggested that Iavorsky be given an opportunity to read his second paper. Yet Pokrovsky did not support the idea, and the paper was not read at the conference.[127] A few months later it became a point of departure for a discussion among Marxist historians of Ukraine, who condemned Iavorsky's scheme as non-Marxist and nationalist, thereby burying the very notion of a distinctive Marxist narrative of Ukrainian history.

The attack on Ukrainian historians at the First All-Union Conference in Moscow by Pokrovsky and Gorin served as the basis for a political campaign against Iavorsky and some of his associates in Ukraine. Initially, the outcome of the Pokrovsky-Iavorsky confrontation was not clear. The Ukrainian authorities apparently continued to support Iavorsky. In February 1929 he was awarded a doctorate in the history of culture and in June of the same year elected a full member of the Ukrainian Academy of Sciences.[128] In the spring of 1929 he published a number of letters and comments in the Kharkiv journal *Prapor marksyzmu* (The Banner of Marxism) presenting his views on the conflict with Gorin and citing disagreements about the model of the future organization of Marxist historians as its main cause. In these publications,

Iavorsky not only rebuked Gorin but also attacked Pokrovsky on a number of theoretical issues, including the national question.[129] Pokrovsky's theory of commercial capitalism was under attack in Moscow at the time,[130] and Iavorsky apparently believed that he could prevail. He seems to have welcomed the initiative of the Ukrainian Institute of Marxism-Leninism in Kharkiv to arrange a presentation of his views on the new scheme of Ukrainian history.

The discussion took place at a meeting of the institute's department of history in May 1929 and lasted, with intervals, for five days. In his paper delivered at the beginning of the discussion, Iavorsky not only presented his own scheme of Ukrainian history but also attacked Pokrovsky's scheme of 'Russian' history. His position was supported by some of his students, including Volodymyr Sukhyno-Khomenko and Vasyl Desniak. Ultimately, however, Iavorsky lost the battle, and eventually the whole war. In the course of the discussion, Hurevych and Rubach, who had supported Iavorsky in Moscow, turned against him under the apparent influence of Pokrovsky and his group. Iavorsky was severely criticized for his alleged 'errors' along the lines laid out by Pokrovsky and Gorin at the conference.[131]

What were the main elements of the new Marxist narrative of Ukrainian history proposed by Iavorsky? Judging by the notes for his presentation (the proceedings of the first day of the discussion were not recorded),[132] he claimed that prerevolutionary Ukrainian historiography had not 'solved the problem' of establishing a scheme of Ukrainian history. The same was true, in his opinion, of Russian Marxist historiography, which had merely filled the old Russian imperial scheme with a new class content. Here, Iavorsky's main target was Pokrovsky and his narrative. Iavorsky claimed that because Russian Marxist historians were reluctant to accept the distinct character of the Ukrainian 'historical process,' pseudo-Marxist historians in Ukraine insisted on the absolute independence of that process from the Russian one.[133] Iavorsky had to be extremely careful in asserting the distinctness of the Ukrainian Marxist narrative so as to avoid being accused of nationalism. He presented his position as the only true Marxist approach to the problem, threading his way between the two 'mistaken' approaches – that of the Russian Marxists, who allegedly applied a 'formal Marxist' method to the study of history, and that of the pseudo-Marxist historians in Ukraine. One of those pseudo-Marxists, according to Iavorsky, was Hrushevsky's close collaborator Osyp Hermaize, who, as Iavorsky stated in his presentation in Moscow, 'most boldly applies the principle of ethnographic separation of the Ukrainian historical process from the Russian historical process in Ukraine.'[134] In Moscow, Iavorsky also decried the 'ethnographic' approach to the history of the revolutionary movement taken by Nechkina, who regarded the activities of the Decembrists in Ukraine as part of the Russian 'historical process.' Judging by his critique of Hermaize and Nechkina, Iavorsky was in fact arguing for the construction of a Marxist narrative of Ukrainian history on the territorial principle. 'When I speak of the Ukrainian revolutionary movement,' argued Iavorsky, 'I mean that it is not one national movement but that it is a revolutionary movement that took place on Ukrainian territory.'[135] At the same time, as his presentation at the Kharkiv discussion attests, he viewed that scheme as a national narrative. 'The history of Ukraine, like the history of any nation developing before the international proletarian revolution, is a national history.'[136]

The content of Ukrainian national history, according to Iavorsky, was supposed to be class-based. Iavorsky characterized Ukrainian history as a process leading to the socialist revolution. It had begun with feudalism and the autonomous existence of the Ukrainian lands between the tenth and fifteenth centuries, followed by the nobiliary and colonial dictatorship of the sixteenth and seventeenth centuries, going on to the period of primitive accumulation of capital and territorial self-determination of the seventeenth and eighteenth centuries, and culminating with the capitalist accumulation of the nineteenth century. The main agents of Ukrainian history, understood as the history of the movements of liberation and revolution, were the burghers and Cossacks who led the peasant masses in their struggle against feudalism, then the burghers and 'rural bourgeoisie' who headed the campaign against nobiliary serfdom, followed by the Ukrainian revolutionary proletariat, which allied itself with the Russian proletariat in competing with the Ukrainian petty bourgeoisie for leadership of the peasant revolution. In the culminating phase, the Ukrainian revolutionary proletariat, together with the Russian proletariat and the poor peasantry, led the struggle against the bourgeoisie for the social and national liberation of the masses in the socialist revolution, which figured in Iavorsky's scheme as part of the world revolution.[137] The particularity of the Ukrainian historical narrative in Iavorsky's account was ensured by the fact that all its principal actors were Ukrainian, while the introduction of the Russian proletariat as one of the major participants in the last two stages of prerevolutionary Ukrainian history was intended to show that that history was not separated from Russian developments by a 'great wall of China.'

Iavorsky's scheme was severely criticized by most participants in the discussion, but feasible alternatives to it were offered only by two historians, Shpunt and Rubach. Shpunt, who criticized Iavorsky for treating national and class factors as equally important, suggested as an alternative to Iavorsky's scheme his own view of Ukrainian history as part of 'East European history.' As the subsequent discussion showed, Shpunt's 'Eastern Europe' consisted mainly of the European USSR, with Poland and other countries of the region left out. That fact alone made Shpunt an easy target for accusations of attempting to revive the imperial scheme of Russian history and of indulging great-power chauvinism, and he eventually had to admit and repent his 'errors.' By the end of 1929 his theory of East European history had been officially condemned by the Ukrainian Central Committee as chauvinist, and Shpunt readily acknowledged the error of his ways in notes to the text of his presentation, which was published in the journal *Litopys revoliutsii* (Chronicle of the Revolution) in early 1930.[138] His repentance was taken into account, and there was no campaign against 'Shpuntism' paralleling the one against 'Iavorskyism' in the party press. The treatment of the Shpunt case was a clear indication that while the party was still proclaiming its readiness to fight on two fronts – against bourgeois nationalism and great-power chauvinism – it treated the first front much more seriously than the second. The fight against Ukrainian nationalism was clearly becoming the main task of party organs in Ukraine.

When Shpunt renounced his concept of 'East European history' in late 1929 and early 1930, the new concept to which he subscribed and declared his loyalty was that of the 'history of the peoples of the USSR,' advocated during the 'Iavorsky discussion' by Mykhailo Rubach. In his long presentation there, Rubach, following many other participants in the discussion, charged Iavorsky with exaggerating the role of the national question in history. Like Gorin before him, Rubach focused most of his critique on Iavorsky's treatment of the issue of the leading forces in the revolutions of 1905 and 1917, accusing him of inflating the role of the bourgeoisie in the revolutionary movement and minimizing that of the proletariat. He claimed that the main issue in establishing a scheme of Ukrainian history was not whether Russians or Ukrainians had the better claim to Kyivan Rus' but determining the social or class content of that scheme. According to Rubach, the separation of Ukrainian and Russian history had already been accomplished by the bourgeois historians, and Marxist scholars accepted the independence of the former. 'Hrushevsky and a whole series of historians before him,' argued Rubach, 'established the distinctness of the Ukrainian people. We part company with them here on the *method* of establishing the independence of Ukrainian history, in argumentation.'[139]

Rubach saw the solution to the problem of creating a Marxist scheme of Ukrainian history in the model of the 'history of the peoples of the USSR.' He strongly criticized Shpunt's notion of writing a history of 'Eastern Europe' and indicated the need to study the history of Asia. He also rejected Sukhyno-Khomenko's argument that writing a history of the territories constituting the USSR was all but impossible, given that significant parts of the national territories of the Belarusians, Ukrainians, Armenians, and other nations remained outside the Union. Rubach argued instead that the main obstacle was not the one noted by Sukhyno-Khomenko but the lack of specialists capable of writing a history of all the peoples of the Soviet Union. The solution proposed by Rubach was to begin by writing histories of individual peoples of the USSR, which in time would make it possible to write a history of all its peoples.[140] The whole project of writing a 'history of the peoples of the USSR' was little more than a temporary compromise between those Marxists who wanted to write their own national narratives and those who were bursting to produce a single historical narrative for the USSR, which was embarking on a project of administrative centralization, curtailment of non-Russian nationalism, and creation of a common identity. During the 'Iavorsky discussion,' Rubach emerged as the main promoter of the latter project in Ukraine.

Judging by the records of the discussion, Iavorsky devoted considerable attention to a critique of Pokrovsky's scheme of 'Russian' history, which was further developed by his supporters. Sukhyno-Khomenko claimed that Russian Marxist historiography had not abandoned the old imperial paradigm of the 'gathering of Russian lands' and asserted that the main problem with Pokrovsky was his continuing use of the old scheme of Russian history in an attempt to endow it with new class content.[141] Desniak based his critique of Pokrovsky not only on his five-volume *History*, written in the second decade of the twentieth century, but also on a Soviet-era survey of the history of Russian culture. He, too, maintained that Pokrovsky was completely dependent on the imperial scheme of Russian history.[142] But most Marxist historians spoke in defence of Pokrovsky. Hurevych, who changed his position completely after returning from Moscow, now argued that Pokrovsky's scheme needed some correction but could not be discarded entirely.[143] Another participant in the discussion, Karpenko, considered it inappropriate of Iavorsky to direct the brunt of his criticism against Russian Marxist historiography. He argued that it was incorrect to attack Pokrovsky on the basis of his pre-revolutionary works: while Pokrovsky could be accused of underestimating the importance of the national question, it was wrong to charge him with great-power chauvinism.[144] Another participant in the discussion, Shpunt, argued that Pokrovsky's errors (he allegedly accepted the thesis of Ukraine's separate historical development in the sixteenth and seventeenth centuries but denied it for the nineteenth century) should be placed in historical perspective, for at the time Pokrovsky was writing his 'big' History, the main task of Marxist historiography had been to combat the historiographic school of Soloviev, Chicherin, and Kliuchevsky.[145]

None of Pokrovsky's defenders was able to exonerate him completely, and all were obliged to admit his 'errors' in dealing with the national question in his historical works. The arguments set forth by Iavorsky, Sukhyno-Khomenko, and Desniak were clearly much more in keeping with official party discourse on matters of nationality policy than were the writings of Pokrovsky. The latter, while condemning Russian imperialism, still remained within the boundaries of the paradigm that Hrushevsky called the 'traditional scheme of "Russian" history' and either ignored the Ukrainian past or, as was the case with his prerevolutionary writings, presented it through the prism of the Russian historical narrative. Pokrovsky's defenders found the solution to their seemingly insoluble conundrum in his postulate about the secondary role of the national factor in history as compared with the class factor. That thesis was most eloquently formulated in the long paper delivered in the course of the Kharkiv discussion by Rubach, who stated that Pokrovsky's errors pertained to the national question rather than to the crucial realm of 'socio-economic' issues.[146] 'Errors' with regard to the 'national question' were indeed viewed by participants in the discussion as much more tolerable than 'errors' in matters of class. As Hurevych noted in the discussion, it was a good thing that Iavorsky had not delivered his paper on the new scheme of Ukrainian history in Moscow, for he would have been accused not only of nationalism but also of more serious failings.[147] Pokrovsky could be criticized in Moscow for his shortcomings in the treatment of various problems of Russian history but was next to invulnerable in what he had formulated as a struggle against nationalist deviations.[148]

How did the Pokrovsky-Iavorsky controversy affect Hrushevsky's standing with the Marxist establishment in Ukraine? Numerous references to Hrushevsky and his works in the Moscow and Kharkiv discussions, as well as a growing number of attacks on Hrushevsky and his associates in the academy, provide sufficient data for an answer to this question.

News of Pokrovsky's attack on Ukrainian historians at the Moscow conference reached Ukraine in January 1929, arousing a good deal of concern.[149] Hrushevsky was in a particularly bad mood and wrote to Studynsky that work on the proofs was distracting him from unpleasant thoughts, an apparent hint at the disturbing results of the First Congress of Marxist Historians.[150] The accusations directed against Hrushevsky at the Moscow conference and then in the course of the 'Iavorsky discussion' in Kharkiv were much harsher than anything he had experienced previously. The verbal attacks on Hrushevsky were soon followed by written ones. The first indication of the coming change was an article by the unwilling instigator of the Moscow showdown between Pokrovsky and Iavorsky, Zynovii Hurevych. Titled 'Pseudo-Marxism at the Service of Ukrainian Nationalism,' the article appeared in *Bil'shovyk Ukraïny* in May 1929. It was based on the text of a paper delivered by Hurevych on 25 March of the same year that attacked Hrushevsky's Marxist 'sponsor,' Osyp Hermaize. While Hrushevsky was not, for the time being, a primary target of the campaign, it is quite telling that Hermaize, who was later arrested and indicted at the show trial of the bogus 'Union for the Liberation of Ukraine,' was attacked first and foremost for his links with Hrushevsky. Hurevych denounced Hermaize for his attempts to present Hrushevsky as a Marxist while in fact sharing his nationalist convictions. He concluded with the statement, 'In the person of Osyp Hermaize we have an epigone of the historical school of Academician M.S. Hrushevsky.'[151]

A leitmotif of the new ideological campaign was that Hrushevsky, a bourgeois historian, could be expected to take this or that non-Marxist position, but that no Marxist historian could legitimately be an apologist for Hrushevsky or be influenced by him. Not only did that argument figure prominently in the 'Iavorsky discussion' of May 1929, but it also found its way into numerous articles and reviews that attacked Hermaize, Iavorsky, and other Marxist or near-Marxist historians, including Dmytro Bahalii.[152] A review of the first volume of Bahalii's *Survey of Ukrainian History on a Socio-Economic Basis* appeared in the autumn 1929 issue of *Prapor marksyzmu*.[153] It presents a good opportunity to examine how the 'great break' in party policy influenced Marxist perception not only of Hrushevsky but also of Bahalii – the regime's former favourite among prerevolutionary academics. The review was written by a young Marxist scholar, Fedir Iastrebov, who was filling a gap in the Marxist critique of non-Marxist publications indicated during the 'Iavorsky discussion.' (One of the participants had noted the failure of Marxist historians to comment either on the first volume of Bahalii's *Survey* or on the first book of volume 9 of Hrushevsky's *History*).[154]

In the new spirit of the times, Iastrebov accused Bahalii of being too lenient toward bourgeois historians and introduced an important maxim that signalled the arrival of a new era in party policy toward the intelligentsia: 'Either you are with proletariat or against it. There is no third way.'[155] Iastrebov dwelled particularly on Bahalii's attitude toward Hrushevsky's interpretation of Ukrainian history, attacking Bahalii for accepting it and failing to criticize it sufficiently in the historiographic section of his *Survey*. Iastrebov referred to Hrushevsky as the 'principal leader of the bourgeois-nationalist historical school in Ukraine'[156] and claimed that by accepting Hrushevsky's historical scheme, Bahalii was associating himself with subjective sociology and bourgeois nationalism. In his attack on Bahalii, Iastrebov consciously or unconsciously misinterpreted his views, as Bahalii accepted Hrushevsky's idea of the distinct character of Ukrainian history but not his paradigm of its development. The misrepresentation of an opponent's views was becoming more and more acceptable in theoretical discussions and ideological attacks of the time, and Iastrebov's review was no exception in that regard. The same method would often be applied by Marxist reviewers to the critique of Hrushevsky's works.

Unsurprisingly, the sharpest attack on Hrushevsky in 1929 came from a representative of Iavorsky's circle, whose members themselves were under suspicion and attack. In the eyes of many Marxist historians, attacking Hrushevsky was the best way to prove their own methodological purity. In December 1929 Mykhailo Svidzinsky, an associate of Iavorsky's who, along with Volodymyr Sukhyno-Khomenko, would soon be accused of Iavorskyism and national 'deviationism,' published a review of the 1927–9 issues of the journal *Ukraïna*, edited by Hrushevsky, in the Kharkiv-based *Prapor marksyzmu*.[157] Svidzinsky charged Hrushevsky with exaggerating the role of the intelligentsia, claiming that Hrushevsky and his journal were propagating the idea of the nonbourgeois character of the Ukrainian nation. Svidzinsky not only criticized Hrushevsky's methodological faults but also levelled a number of politically dangerous accusations against him. He claimed that Hrushevsky's positive assessment of the Act of Union of Eastern and Western Ukraine (1919) was proof of his hostility to the Ukrainian SSR and an endorsement of a united bourgeois Ukraine. Even more dangerous, given prevailing circumstances, was Svidzinsky's emphasis on the close relations between Hrushevsky and his 'first student,' Hermaize, whom Svidzinsky also characterized as a 'participant in the counter-revolutionary plot.' Svidzinsky concluded his review by invoking one of the leitmotifs of the cultural revolution in Ukraine. He asserted that socialist culture could be developed only by the worker and peasant intelligentsia, while the old cadres should be watched to prevent the emergence of new 'Unions for the Liberation of Ukraine.'[158]

In the course of the year 1929, Hrushevsky's name was generally used as a point of reference according to which the 'virtue' of Marxist historians was judged by their colleagues. If a Marxist historian wanted to establish his ideological probity, he would attack Hrushevsky; if he wanted to attack and discredit an opponent, he would accuse the latter of sharing or even defending Hrushevsky's views. This was the case during the debates at the First All-Union Conference of Marxist Historians and the Kharkiv discussion on Iavorsky's scheme of Ukrainian history. During the 'Iavorsky debate,' those who supported him indicated his achievements in replacing Hrushevsky's scheme of Ukrainian history with a Marxist one and in producing textbooks that superseded Hrushevsky's *Illustrated History of Ukraine*. Iavorsky himself was greatly agitated by well-founded accusations that his interpretation of the Mongol era in Ukrainian history was strongly influenced by Hrushevsky's: in the course of the discussion, he attempted to prove that there was no connection between them. Iavorsky claimed to approach the history of the Mongol invasion and rule over Ukraine from a class perspective; Hrushevsky, he maintained, had developed the whole concept of the classlessness of Ukrainian society on the basis of the Mongol period of Ukrainian history.[159]

Even though the officially sponsored ideological campaign was initially directed against the Marxist historians, Hermaize and then Iavorsky, it was potentially much more dangerous to Hrushevsky, whom the critics regarded as the main enemy. Marxist historians could err, but Hrushevsky and other bourgeois historians were beyond redemption. That understanding of the hierarchy of enemies was expressed in a comment made by one of the participants in the Kharkiv discussion,

Iavorsky's close associate Karetnikova. In the course of defending her superior against attacks by his opponents, Karetnikova remarked that if Iavorsky indeed belonged to the same ideological camp as Hrushevsky, as suggested by one of the discussants, then the accuser should go straight to the secret police and ask them to put Iavorsky under surveillance.[160] Karetnikova had no doubt that this had either already been done or was supposed to be done in Hrushevsky's case. In her opinion, and apparently in that of other Marxist historians, Hrushevsky was a subject for GPU surveillance, not for historiographic discussion.

The Suppression of the National Paradigm

Pokrovsky's attack on Iavorsky in Moscow and the latter's defeat in the Kharkiv discussion severely undermined the idea of a Ukrainian historical narrative independent from that of Russia. It came on the heels of the attack launched in 1927 on Moisei Ravych-Cherkasky's concept of the history of the Communist Party of Ukraine. That concept was based on the premise that the communist movement in Ukraine had different origins and, consequently, a different history from the Russian movement. Ravych-Cherkasky maintained that Ukrainian communism had two roots, Bolshevik and Borotbist.[161] The condemnation of his theory meant that the history of the Communist Party of Ukraine could no longer be treated in isolation from the grand narrative of Russian communism. The Moscow historians' accusations against Iavorsky and the subsequent official condemnation of 'Iavorskyism' put an end to the interpretation of the Ukrainian Revolution as separate from the Russian. With no distinct narrative of the history of the communist party and the revolutionary movement, the independence of the 'Ukrainian historical process' itself was in serious doubt.

These changes in the Marxist interpretation of Ukrainian history were accompanied by a major shift in the content of the officially sponsored campaign against Hrushevsky. Before 1929, while attacking Hrushevsky's non-Marxist methodology, the Marxist critics still treated his scholarly record with respect. Some of them, like Pokrovsky and Rubach, viewed him as a continuator of Mykola Kostomarov's federalist approach to Russian and Ukrainian history. Others, like Iavorsky, recognized in him a true populist with a genuine interest in the history of the popular masses. After 1929 Hrushevsky's critics placed ever greater emphasis on his refusal to accept the priority of the materialist approach and his failure to treat the class struggle as the main motive force of history. Hrushevsky was accused of regarding Ukrainian society as classless.

A new stage in the ideological campaign, this time with Hrushevsky as its sole target, began in early 1931. It was directly linked to Hrushevsky's arrest in March of that year and came in the wake of the prolonged harassment and destruction of Hrushevsky's historical institutions at the Ukrainian Academy of Sciences in the previous year. The anti-Hrushevsky campaign of 1931 gained impetus from an article by Trokhym Skubytsky, 'The Class Struggle in Ukrainian Historical Literature,' which appeared in the Moscow journal *Istorik-marksist* (Marxist Historian) in the autumn of 1930.[162] Skubytsky, a Dnipropetrovsk student who had moved to Moscow to continue his Marxist education, fiercely attacked Ukrainian historians in general (including Bahalii)[163] and Hrushevsky in particular for nationalism and subversive dissemination of bourgeois ideology. He asserted that both in his studies of the Khmelnytsky era and in his works on Ukrainian historians and cultural activists written in the years 1927–30, Hrushevsky had remained loyal to his populist and petty-bourgeois concept of Ukrainian history, which, in Skubytsky's opinion, reflected the views and served the political interests of former members of bourgeois and nationalist political parties.[164] Given that Skubytsky's article was published in Moscow, it signalled the centre's approval of further attacks on Ukrainian national historiography and Hrushevsky as its main symbol and exponent.

There was nothing new in the fact of a Marxist critique of his works and views per se. Indeed, Hrushevsky had become quite accustomed to critiques of his opinions in Marxist periodicals. His alleged failure to uncover the 'social causes' of the Cossack movements of the seventeenth century was condemned in the article 'Ukraine Old and New,' published in 1923 by Oleksander Shumsky, a former member of the Central Rada and at the time editor in chief of *Chervonyi shliakh*.[165] The articles on Hrushevsky and his works that appeared in Soviet publications upon his return to Ukraine already indicated some aspects of the subsequent Marxist critique of his views. These included reading Hrushevsky's political opinions of the revolutionary era into his historical writings and dispensing with a scholarly critique of his works in favour of a set of political accusations formulated according to the latest shifts in party policy. The early critique of Hrushevsky also exposed the main theme of later Marxist attacks on him – the alleged exaggeration of the national factor in history at the expense of class.

The attacks of the early 1930s were much harsher and more vulgar than those of the 1920s. One of the principles of the Soviet critique of the time was that the enemy had first to be 'unmasked' and 'disarmed' ideologically; in order to 'disarm' Hrushevsky, it was necessary to discredit and deconstruct the philosophical and historical foundations of the Ukrainian national narrative. That goal was most clearly articulated by Mykhailo Rubach in his article on Hrushevsky's political views (1932). Rubach identified Hrushevsky as the central figure of Ukrainian bourgeois historiography and called upon Ukrainian Marxist historians to demolish bourgeois ideology completely on the historical front, above all the complex of views represented by Mykhailo Hrushevsky.[166] The same task was put forward by the anonymous authors of the introduction to the first issue of the *Memoirs of the Institute of Historical Archaeography* (1934), in which two articles out of five were devoted to 'unmasking' the 'fascist' concepts of Hrushevsky and his school. They set forth their purpose as follows: 'To root out and demolish bourgeois nationalist and national-deviationist schemes and conceptions; to combat distortions and falsifications of history; to promote a correct Marxist-Leninist scheme of the history of Ukraine.'[167]

How did the official campaign against Hrushevsky in 1931–4 affect the fate of his national paradigm of Ukrainian history? It was Andrii Richytsky who best exemplified the new features of the anti-Hrushevsky campaign of the 1930s in his response to a statement made by Mykhailo Mohyliansky at one of the Hrushevsky 'disputes' of 1931. Mohyliansky distinguished Hrushevsky's political opinions from his historical views, suggesting that if the former should indeed be criticized, the latter called for no critique whatever. The task of Marxist historians in that sphere, argued Mohyliansky, was not to criticize Hrushevsky but to construct a new edifice of Ukrainian historiography alongside the one built by Hrushevsky.[168] In effect, Mohyliansky was suggesting that Hrushevsky's critics return to the pre-1929 status, with its relatively peaceful coexistence between the Marxist and national schools of Ukrainian historiography. What Mohyliansky did not yet realize, or perhaps did not want to admit, was that the era of peaceful coexistence was long gone. Responding to that suggestion of Mohyliansky's, Richytsky stated that Marxist historiography could not just exist alongside Hrushevsky's school. It could develop only in opposition to Hrushevsky's concepts, since the struggle against bourgeois scholarship was in fact only a reflection of the class struggle of the proletariat against the bourgeoisie.[169] Class struggle was thus promoted as the main task of Ukrainian historiography, with Hrushevsky and his paradigm of Ukrainian history designated as class enemies to be 'unmasked' and defeated. Unable to produce a substantial body of work on its own, Marxist historiography was commissioned by the party to begin destroying the 'edifice' of Ukrainian national historiography.

A good example of the application of Marxist principles to the deconstruction of Hrushevsky's national paradigm in his major historical work is offered by a number of reviews of volume 9 of Hrushevsky's *History* that appeared in Soviet periodicals between 1930 and 1934. Two such reviews, treating parts 1 and 2, respectively, of volume 9 of the *History* were written by Fedir Iastrebov, while a general survey of Hrushevsky's views on Ukrainian history, with particular emphasis on the last volumes of the *History*, was the work of Lev Okinshevych. What resources could the Ukrainian Marxist historians bring to bear against Hrushevsky's view of the Khmelnytsky era? When it came to actual historical research, they could offer very little. None of them was a specialist in pre-nineteenth-century history, and those like Iavorsky, Volodymyr Sukhyno-Khomenko, and Mykhailo Svidzinsky, who dealt with the history of the uprising in their general surveys of Ukrainian history, lacked a basic grounding in the premodern period. The forte of the young Marxist cadres was the construction and reconstruction of various schemes of Ukrainian historical development, all of which were based on class as the main agent of historical progress and class struggle as its 'motive force.' Marxist historians of the 1920s acted first and foremost as critics of the old bourgeois historiography. They were trained to uncover the 'true' ideological faces of their class enemies, deconstruct the latter's historical narratives by means of the class-based approach, and build their own historical schemes on the basis of factual material 'expropriated' from the bourgeois historians. In the course of the 1920s a whole generation of Ukrainian Marxist historians was instructed according to that model. As Hrushevsky wrote to Viacheslav Molotov in September 1934, defending his own work and the traditional values of the profession, 'one should have a critically assessed pool of facts in order to make it possible for party propagandists to produce books for mass consumption.'[170]

Fedir Iastrebov's review of book 1 of volume 9, which appeared in *Prapor marksyzmu* in early 1930, should be considered a direct echo of the discussion of 1929 concerning Iavorsky's scheme of Ukrainian history. Iastrebov, a beginning Marxist scholar and the author of a critical review of Bahalii's recent book, was in fact the first to offer a Marxist critique of Hrushevsky's *History of Ukraine-Rus'*. The charges made by

Iastrebov differed considerably from those presented in previous indictments of Hrushevsky. If earlier authors had criticized Hrushevsky for neglecting Marxist methods of historical analysis and ignoring the role of class divisions and class struggle in the Ukrainian history, he was now accused of being a nationalist historian and an ideologue of the Ukrainian bourgeoisie. 'This work is to the advantage of nationalism. And that is why we draw the conclusion that the first book of volume 9 is a book hostile to us,' concluded Iastrebov in his review. He argued that Hrushevsky regarded nationalism as the principal motive force of history and denounced him with all the naivety and aggressive fervour of a convert: 'It was proved almost a century ago that the main driving force of human history is class struggle, by means of which mankind proceeds first to the dictatorship of the proletariat and then to socialism.'[171] Developing his argument, Iastrebov linked Hrushevsky's nationalism with his alleged sympathies for social oppression and those responsible for it. He argued that Hrushevsky refused to admit the counterrevolutionary nature of some of the actions taken by Cossack officers in the course of the Khmelnytsky Uprising, thereby expressing solidarity with the oppressors. 'We say that it is the predicament of every nationalist to become an ideologue of the oppressors, not of the oppressed,' asserted Iastrebov.[172]

Iastrebov's review was written after the Kharkiv discussion of Iavorsky's historical scheme but before the publication of its proceedings. It is interesting in its own right as an attempt to develop, in the midst of the ongoing discussion, a coherent Marxist account capable of competing with Hrushevsky's interpretation of the Khmelnytsky era. What Iastrebov attempted was to bring together all the existing Marxist interpretations of the uprising, as long as they did not directly contradict one another. The starting point for the writings of all Ukrainian Marxist historians on the history of Ukraine was the corpus of Pokrovsky's writings. Not surprisingly, in his extensive review of Hrushevsky's *History*, Iastrebov wrote that Pokrovsky's brief chapter on the Khmelnytsky Uprising had done more to reveal its true significance than Hrushevsky's voluminous treatment. Accordingly, Iastrebov based his interpretation of the Khmelnytsky era on Pokrovsky's theory of 'commercial capitalism' and defined the Khmelnytsky Uprising as a commercial capitalist revolution. In examining its causes, he also drew on the views of Iavorsky and Sukhyno-Khomenko,[173] claiming that the revolution had been brought about by two factors: competition between large Polish and small Ukrainian landowners and the struggle of

Ukrainian commercial capitalists against Polish, Jewish, and other foreign competitors.

Iastrebov summarized the differences between Ukrainian Marxist historiography and Hrushevsky's work in the following statement: 'Thus, for Academician Hrushevsky the revolution of 1648–54 was a national revolution that led to the national liberation of Ukraine from Poland. He does not see the class-based, bourgeois nature of that revolution. For us this is one of the many revolutions brought about by commercial capital in many countries of the world. The revolution of 1648–54 destroyed the remnants of feudalism in Ukraine and cleared the way for the development of commercial capitalism, which was [earlier] severely obstructed by magnate landownership, Polish commercial capital, and the semi-feudal Polish state with its *szlachta* particularism.'[174]

Iastrebov also made an explicit attempt to link Hrushevsky's views on the Khmelnytsky Uprising with his alleged anti-Soviet political agenda. He cited an excerpt from one of Hrushevsky's newspaper interviews in which the historian stated that things only dreamt of in Khmelnytsky's day were beginning to be fulfilled in his own times. Politically speaking, Hrushevsky's statement was very carefully formulated and ambiguous enough to be treated as referring to the realization in Soviet Ukraine of either the social or the national ideals of those who took part in the Khmelnytsky Uprising. Iastrebov, however, in the best traditions of ideological witch-hunting, treated Hrushevsky's statement as an act of political dissent against the regime. He wrote: 'Is it possible that back then, bearers of revolutionary ideas (or, for that matter, "dreams") had any thought of socialism? Not at all ... According to Hrushevsky, this means that today we see the realization of something dreamt of by the former leaders of the "one (*iedynyi*) Ukrainian people," Khmelnytsky, Vyhovsky, and many others like them.'[175]

As noted earlier, Iastrebov's views on the Khmelnytsky Uprising lacked the originality shown by some of his Marxist predecessors. His only contributions to the Marxist interpretation of the era were the suggestion that the Orthodox struggle against church union was a struggle for a 'Ukrainian bourgeois state independent of Poland' and the assertion that while the Cossack officers sought to ally themselves with the Muscovite gentry, the Ukrainian bourgeoisie preferred an alliance with Sweden. Iastrebov's interpretation of the Khmelnytsky Uprising was far more anachronistic than those of his Marxist predecessors, and his text was loaded with terms borrowed from Bolshevik discourse, including such expressions as 'military specialists,' 'unprosperous peasants (*nezamozhnyky*),' 'the rightward wavering (*khytannia*) of the revolutionary forces,' and so on.

After Iastrebov, the next Marxist scholar to deconstruct Hrushevsky's views on the history of the Khmelnytsky Uprising was a research associate of the Ukrainian Academy of Sciences, Lev Okinshevych.[176] His article, 'The National-Democratic Concept of the History of the Law in Ukraine in the Works of Academician M. Hrushevsky,' was published in 1932 in the freshly 'purged' journal *Ukraïna*.[177] In the new spirit of the time, Okinshevych's essay contained not only a critical attack on Hrushevsky but also the author's self-criticism concerning his own errors and deviations. For example, Okinshevych claimed that he himself had been under the influence of Hrushevsky's ideas, had adopted the ideological orientation of the petty-bourgeois intelligentsia in his works, and had even wavered between an orientation toward 'bourgeois restoration' on the one hand and proletarian revolution and socialist construction on the other. In his earlier works, Okinshevych had allegedly followed a methodological approach promoting the idea of 'civil peace' and 'bourgeois falsification of the process of class struggle.' Okinshevych repented his errors, and the proof of his sincerity was apparently to be found in his critique of Hrushevsky.[178]

The thrust of Okinshevych's attack was that as a 'Ukrainian bourgeois nationalist,' Hrushevsky formulated and developed ideas that identified him with the camp of Ukrainian statist historiography. Given Okinshevych's own research on the history of the political institutions of the Hetmanate, it would be fair to ask to what degree he was reading his own views into Hrushevsky's work when he made this charge.

Okinshevych defined the Khmelnytsky Uprising as a 'peasant war,' a usage indicative of the change in Ukrainian Marxist historiography between 1930, when Iastrebov's review appeared, and 1932, which saw the publication of Okinshevych's article. The previously dominant view of the Khmelnytsky era as a revolution led by commercial capital was now rejected. This in turn led to a reinterpretation of the roles played by various social classes and groups in early modern Ukrainian history in general and the uprising in particular. If Iastrebov criticized Hrushevsky for neglecting the role of the burghers in Ukrainian history, Okinshevych attacked him for the exact opposite – exaggeration of their role. Okinshevych argued that as a bourgeois political activist, Hrushevsky was specifically interested in the history of his own class. Accordingly, when dealing with the history of Kyivan Rus', he attributed a hege-

monic role to the patriciate of Kyiv. He also distorted the social character of the 'peasant revolts' of the seventeenth century by presenting
them as influenced and led by the city patriciate. Thus, claimed
Okinshevych, Hrushevsky was reading back and attributing to feudalism the role played by towns in the formation of bourgeois states of the
capitalist era.[179]

Okinshevych further developed the Bolshevik critique of Hrushevsky
as an enemy of Russia by analysing his brochure on the Pereiaslav
Agreement (1654).[180] In that brochure, argued Okinshevych, Hrushevsky
set out to prove that after 1654 Ukraine possessed all the characteristics
of a state and that the gentry-based Muscovite government violated its
constitutional rights. In Okinshevych's opinion, the publication of
Hrushevsky's brochure served the purposes of the Ukrainian bourgeoisie – initially gaining autonomous status for Ukraine within bourgeois
Russia, and then going on to seek Ukraine's complete independence
from proletarian Russia.[181] In short, Okinshevych employed the prevailing class-based discourse to accuse Hrushevsky of providing historical justification for Ukraine's separation from Russia. According to
this line of argument, Marxists allegedly were not concerned about the
separation of one nation from another: what they could not tolerate was
any attempt to divide the working class or the toiling masses and to
sever Ukraine's alliance with the victorious Russian proletariat. The
party line was one of official impartiality in nationality policy: it was
fighting on two fronts against Russian great-power chauvinism and
Ukrainian bourgeois nationalism. This was reflected in Okinshevych's
critique of Russian populist historians (Venedikt Miakotin and Dmitrii
Odinets) who, in his opinion, had attempted to prove Russia's historical
claim to Ukraine. For Okinshevych, the issue of Hrushevsky's treatment of Russo-Ukrainian historical relations remained marginal, but
it would gain significantly in prominence as the officially sponsored
attacks on Hrushevsky continued.

For all its politically inspired accusations, Okinshevych's article was
by far the most intelligent and scholarly review of Hrushevsky's works
that Soviet Marxist historiography ever managed to produce. In style
and treatment of various issues of economic, legal, political, and church
history, it far outshone the vulgar Marxism displayed by Hrushevsky's
other critics. In the course of his critique, Okinshevych distinguished
some notable features of Hrushevsky's interpretation of the Khmelnytsky
era, pointing out his genuine interest in the history of the Ukrainian
state and its leaders. Nevertheless, declaring Hrushevsky a statist was

clearly an oversimplification of the issue. As a hostage of the regime's campaign against the Ukrainian intelligentsia, involved in a struggle for his own survival, Okinshevych was obliged not only to invent and exaggerate political motives for Hrushevsky's historical interpretations but also to link the main themes of the anti-Hrushevsky political campaign into a coherent whole. Okinshevych demonstrated sufficient flexibility and skill in repenting his own 'errors' and apparently had little difficulty in applying the same talents to his treatment of Hrushevsky.

At any given moment, the clichés obligatory for framing political denunciations were supplied by the communist propaganda apparatus: the 'repenting' scholars had only to insert their own names, or those of their professors and colleagues, into these prefabricated structures of political discourse. Okinshevych politically contextualized his attack on Hrushevsky by exposing the latter's 'statist' and 'national-democratic' views. He pressed his case by claiming that Hrushevsky's views served as the ideological basis for the creation of a Ukrainian bourgeois state during the revolution and for subsequent attempts at a bourgeois restoration. In the Soviet political jargon of the early 1930s, the term 'national democratic,' which Okinshevych used to characterize Hrushevsky's views, had extremely negative connotations, only slightly less opprobrious than 'fascist.' While avoiding the use of the latter term with reference to Hrushevsky (and thereby shielding himself against possible accusations of having shared Hrushevsky's 'fascist' views at some point), Okinshevych did not fail to point out that in the works of émigré authors Hrushevsky's national-democratic concepts had shown a tendency to develop into national-fascist ones. He named Lypynsky, Rostyslav Lashchenko, Serhii Shelukhyn, and Viacheslav Zaikin as émigré proponents of fascist ideology.[182]

The process of transforming Hrushevsky's ideas from 'national-democratic' into 'fascist' ones in Soviet Marxist literature on the Khmelnytsky Uprising was completed by none other than Fedir Iastrebov, who had reviewed the first book of volume 9 of Hrushevsky's *History* in 1930. In 1934 Iastrebov produced a long review of the second book of that volume. The review's title, 'The National-Fascist Conception of the Peasant War of 1648 in Ukraine,' was a clear indication not only of a new stage in the officially sponsored demonization of Hrushevsky but also of the unequivocal triumph of the 'peasant war' concept in Marxist historiography of the Khmelnytsky era.[183] In his new review, Iastrebov did not limit himself to criticizing Hrushevsky's ideas, as in

1930, but admitted and repented his own 'errors' in the interpretation of the Khmelnytsky Uprising. He wrote that he had shared some of the assessments of the uprising made by Mykola Skrypnyk and had viewed it as a 'great bourgeois revolution' along the lines suggested by Sukhyno-Khomenko. (By that time, both had been condemned by the authorities.)

With regard to the nature of the Khmelnytsky Uprising, Iastrebov wrote that since his first review of Hrushevsky's *History*, the issue had been 'finally settled.' 'It has been shown,' wrote Iastrebov, 'that this revolutionary movement was a peasant war and that along with the peasant masses, the oppressed tradesmen's element in the Ukrainian towns also participated in it.'[184] Iastrebov referred specifically to the resolutions of the Ukrainian Society of Marxist Historians, in which Iavorsky's interpretations of the uprising first as a gentry revolution and then as a revolution of commercial capital were condemned and rejected, and Sukhyno-Khomenko's interpretation of it as a bourgeois and national revolution was dismissed as erroneous. The 'final settlement' of the issue completely removed the Cossacks from the leadership of the uprising, in which they were now overshadowed by the peasantry. References to Cossackdom remained only in the official name given to the Cossack revolts of the late sixteenth and early seventeenth centuries, now designated as the 'era of peasant-Cossack wars of 1591–1638.'

Iastrebov's review of 1934 was one of the last examples of an exclusively class-based critique of Hrushevsky. The historian was not yet accused of being an enemy of the Russian people and of Russo-Ukrainian brotherhood and friendship – accusations that soon became obligatory in Soviet propaganda attacks on Hrushevsky. In his review, Iastrebov consistently presented Muscovite policy as a 'gradual takeover of Ukraine.'[185] 'For us,' wrote Iastrebov with reference to the Pereiaslav Agreement of 1654, 'this is a pact between two exploitative forces – Muscovite landowners and Ukrainian (to some extent also Polish) landowners.'[186] Iastrebov's treatment of the Pereiaslav Agreement as a 'lesser evil' casts light on the prevailing balance between class-based and nation-based elements in the Marxist interpretation of Ukrainian history. For him Pereiaslav was a lesser evil from the viewpoint of the Ukrainian Cossack officers, who had to choose between Moscovite suzerainty and the prospect of a popular uprising.[187]

The review, written at the height of the officially sponsored attack on

Hrushevsky, exemplified the worst features of Soviet 'criticism,' with its vulgar tone, unfounded political accusations, and falsification of the views of opponents. Iastrebov, for example, grossly misrepresented Hrushevsky's views on Khmelnytsky's role in Ukrainian history. He presented Hrushevsky, Kubala, and Lypynsky as authors who thought similarly on the issue and went on to claim that Hrushevsky had characterized Khmelnytsky as a superman. Iastrebov linked Hrushevsky's interpretation of Khmelnytsky's role in Ukrainian history with fascist ideology: 'And so, to the benefit of fascism,' he wrote, 'Khmelnytsky grows into a giant-sized figure not because he actually was such a figure but because Ukrainian fascism is seeking an individual along the lines of Khmelnytsky, Napoleon, Mussolini, Hitler, and other "fateful" figures with "characters of steel" and "superhuman energy" *for today.*'[188] Under the circumstances, one could hardly imagine a misrepresentation of Hrushevsky's views more ominous and politically damaging than this one.

Iastrebov's critique of Hrushevsky also represents one of the few instances in which a Marxist author unable to match Hrushevsky's level of professionalism sought to denigrate him not only as a politically harmful ideologue but also as a biased and unscrupulous researcher. Characteristic of Iastrebov's methods was his attack on Hrushevsky's treatment of the diary of Paul of Aleppo, an Arab cleric who visited Ukraine in the mid-1650s together with Patriarch Makarios of Antioch and left a diary in which he recorded his impressions. As noted earlier, Hrushevsky saw a reflection of the revolutionary spirit of the epoch in Paul's diary. For Iastrebov, by contrast, Paul's account was little more than an attempt to present an idyllic picture of class harmony in Khmelnytsky-era Ukraine – an image fully embraced by Hrushevsky, according to Iastrebov, for his own class-based purposes. 'Thus the bourgeois ideologue Hrushevsky juggles with the facts,' wrote Iastrebov, 'following Paul of Aleppo in making out Ukraine of the mid-seventeenth century, with its furious struggle of the masses for their liberation, as some kind of happy Arcadia.'[189] This passage echoed a point made by the People's Commissar of Education of Ukraine, Volodymyr Zatonsky, in a speech delivered in January 1934. Zatonsky quoted an excerpt from the diary in which the Arab author claimed that at the time almost all inhabitants of Ukraine were literate. He ridiculed this statement, along with a number of the diarist's other assertions, and commented as follows with regard to Hrushevsky's treatment of the historical source: '... instead of putting this source of Paul of Aleppo into question, the learned historian seeks a psychological justification for this all too obvious piece of nonsense.'[190]

Little did Zatonsky and Iastrebov realize that in ridiculing Paul of Aleppo's account they were in fact committing an act of communist sacrilege, as the same quotation from Paul's diary had been used by Lenin himself in a speech that he wrote in 1913 for Hryhorii Petrovsky (then a Bolshevik member of the Russian State Duma) to demonstrate the disastrous results of tsarist educational policy. According to Petrovsky's speech, official neglect of education over the centuries had dramatically reduced the number of literate people in Ukraine, which was known in the mid-seventeenth century for its high rate of literacy.[191] The fact that this unwitting insult to Lenin's memory went unnoticed by contemporaries does not mean that others who took it upon themselves to criticize Hrushevsky also escaped scot-free. In attacking Hrushevsky, his critics had to take a position that reflected the current party line. As the line changed, so did the interpretation of historical events, often exposing the critics themselves to very considerable danger.

As discussed earlier, in 1934 Iastrebov found it necessary to repudiate the 'erroneous' position he had taken in his first review of Hrushevsky's History, published four years earlier. This time he tried to be more careful in his assessments but again was in no position to predict future turns in the party line and its ramifications for historiography. Ironically, many of the historical issues that Iastrebov considered 'finally settled' in 1934 were soon reinterpreted by Soviet historiography, and Iastrebov had once again to adjust his views to the new doctrine. For example, in a Survey of Ukrainian History written in 1942 and edited by Iastrebov, Kost Huslysty, and Lazar Slavin, the Khmelnytsky Uprising was presented not as a 'peasant war' but as a 'national-liberation war of the Ukrainian people,' and Khmelnytsky was treated as a major hero. The incorporation of Ukraine into the Muscovite state after the Council of Pereiaslav was viewed as a 'lesser evil,' not as compared with the prospect of a popular uprising, as Iastrebov maintained in 1934, but in relation to the possible conquest of Ukraine by Poland or the Ottoman Empire.[192]

Hrushevsky never responded publicly to his critics. What he thought and felt about his attackers can be detected only from the unpublished review of volume 9 of the History of Ukraine-Rus' by his close associate Vasyl Herasymchuk. In his review of Hrushevsky's History, Herasymchuk commented on the 'abusive' reviews of Hrushevsky's work published in Soviet Ukraine. He stated that it was impossible to write the history of the seventeenth century without touching on the national issue, despite the contrary claims of Hrushevsky's critics, and maintained that 'nationalism' was the main historical factor of that era. He also claimed that under the cover of proletarian scholarship, the reviewers were propagating an imperialist brand of nationalism.[193]

What does the Marxist critique of Hrushevsky's views on the Khmelnytsky Uprising indicate about changes in the Marxist interpretation of Ukrainian history as a whole? One point that emerges quite clearly from a reading of the officially sponsored reviews of Hrushevsky's works is that after a relatively short period of unsupervised and chaotic efforts on the part of various groups of Marxist historians to apply the Marxist paradigm to Ukrainian history, the centre succeeded in imposing a uniform and obligatory interpretation of the Ukrainian past. That interpretation would change dramatically in the course of the 1930s, but open competition among various interpretations of history was effectively banned. The main victim of the new uniformity was the concept of nationhood and all historical symbols considered too closely related to the national paradigm of Ukrainian history. Cossackdom, for example, became a symbol of all that was wrong with the national paradigm in the eyes of Marxist historians: nationalism, statism, elitism, and lack of interest in problems of social differentiation and class struggle in Ukrainian society.

The rejection of Pokrovsky's theory of 'commercial capitalism' and the refusal to see the burghers as leaders of the Khmelnytsky Uprising (`bourgeois revolution') reflected a major shift in the official historiographic discourse on the bourgeoisie. The latter was no longer considered a progressive historical force, as Pokrovsky had earlier depicted it. The bourgeoisie was now regarded not only as the main enemy of the Soviet state but also as a major antagonist of the proletariat and the toiling masses in the past. The peasantry emerged as a major beneficiary of all these changes. On the one hand, the shift toward treating the peasantry as the protagonist of premodern history was influenced by the young Bolshevik cadres' growing acquaintance with the works of Marx and Engels, especially the latter's classic study of the peasant war in Germany. On the other hand, the further politicization of scholarship meant that the peasant issue, so crucial to the communist politics of the 1920s, was read back into the history of Ukraine. As a result, the new Marxist interpretation of the Khmelnytsky Uprising, as it emerged in the late 1920s and early 1930s, had much more in common with the interpretation of that event in the populist historiography of the late nineteenth and early twentieth centuries than it did with Marxism.

The Soviet critique of Mykhailo Hrushevsky and his political and historical views speaks volumes about the nature of the dominant discourse in the early years of the Soviet Union.

The regime's repressive policies eventually succeeded in turning Soviet political space into an area controlled by one hegemonic discourse. One of its main characteristics was an aggressive monism that represented every sphere of existence as defined exclusively by the class factor. In the sphere of ethnic relations, the party held that the national question was subordinate to that of class. Consequently, all national problems were supposed to be resolved by means of the class approach. In line with this approach, the Communist Party criticized and rejected both Dmytro Lebed's theory of the 'struggle of two cultures,' which advocated the continuing Russification of Ukraine, and Mykola Khvyliovy's idea of cutting ties with Moscow so as to orient Ukrainian culture toward the West. According to the party, both these approaches placed the national factor ahead of class. Criticizing Khvyliovy in 1926, Stalin changed the subject from nationality to class, claiming that in advocating a drive 'away from Moscow,' Khvyliovy was turning his back not on the capital of Russia but on the capital of the world proletarian movement, and consequently orienting himself on capitalist Europe. In 1930 Stalin rebuked Demian Bedny for his jokes about the negative features of the Russian national character by indicating the leading role of the Russian working class in the world proletarian movement.[194] Ukrainization itself was legitimized first and foremost within the context of class-based discourse and presented as an instrument for strengthening the unity of the Ukrainian-speaking peasantry with the Russian-speaking proletariat for the benefit of Soviet power in Ukraine. The policy was significantly scaled down in the course of collectivization and the famine of 1932–3 on the grounds that instead of making the peasantry more accommodating to the dictatorship of the proletariat, it had given nationalist ideological support to peasant resistance to collectivization.

Under these circumstances, anyone taking part in public discussion of issues of national culture and history had no choice but to adopt the terms of the dominant class discourse. It was within the bounds of that discourse that Hrushevsky sought to present his new vision of modern Ukrainian history in his articles and speeches of the mid-1920s. In his internal memoranda written at the Academy of Sciences before the complete destruction of his 'historical institutions,' Hrushevsky accepted the official Soviet periodization of Ukrainian history into periods of feudalism and merchant and industrial capitalism; he also protested the abolition of the academy's department for the study of commercial capitalism.[195] The application of the term 'commercial capitalism' to the sixteenth and seventeenth centuries was the only way to raise the status of that period in Soviet historical discourse, which was mostly concerned with the history of the working class and revolutionary struggle.

Not surprisingly, it was the class-based method of historical research that served as the basis for deconstructing the national paradigm of Ukrainian history. If Hrushevsky used the populist and nationalist approaches to dismantle the grand narrative of Russian history and clear the way for the construction of a national paradigm of Ukrainian history, his Marxist opponents used class-based analysis to deconstruct his own grand narrative.

How would the Ukrainian historical narrative have fared if Hrushevsky had deigned to correct his 'errors,' as did some of his colleagues? If the suggestions of his critics are a reliable guide, Hrushevsky's revised narrative would have been completely purged of historical heroes, including such 'semiheroic' figures as Khmelnytsky. The narrative would also have been stripped of one of its basic myths – that of Ukrainian Cossackdom. The statist idea and the paradigm of national revival would have been consigned to oblivion. The main 'other' of Hrushevsky's narrative would have acquired class characteristics instead of national ones and would have been embodied in the image of Ukraine's ruling classes throughout its history. The narrative would have presented the history of the popular masses – more specifically, of the peasantry – as one of continuous class struggle against their oppressors. In fact, Hrushevsky's revised narrative would have given an account of Ukrainian history remarkably similar to the one offered by Oleksander Lazarevsky – a populist whom Marxist critics of the 1920s and early 1930s characterized as the most reactionary Ukrainian historian of the nineteenth century.[196]

The historical narrative that Hrushevsky's critics wanted him to produce was very close to the one that he had inherited from the populist historiography of the 1880s. Having taken it over, Hrushevsky eventually turned that narrative into a national one, not only by separating it from the Russian grand narrative but also by enriching it with heroes, myths, elites, and the idea of statehood – all the elements that contributed to the nationalization of the Ukrainian past. The critics, for their part, demanded the exact opposite – the denationalization of the Ukrainian past. They did not openly question the distinct status of Ukrainian history but were intent on turning that status into a meaningless formality. The attack on Hrushevsky was thus also an attack on the national paradigm of Ukrainian history.

Conclusions

For more than a hundred years, from the last decades of the seventeenth century to the latter part of the eighteenth, the historical identity of educated Russian society took shape under the influence of the historical narrative composed by the monks of the Kyivan Cave Monastery and published for the first time in 1674 under the title *Synopsis*. By the 1830s the *Synopsis* had been reissued more than a dozen times, becoming the most popular historical work in the pre-nineteenth-century Russian Empire. The image of the past presented by the author(s) of the *Synopsis* was that of a common history of the two parts of Rus', Muscovite and Polish-Lithuanian. It was also the history of one *rossiiskii (slaveno-rossiiskii)* people that included the ancestors of today's Russians, Ukrainians, and Belarusians. The historical narrative introduced by the *Synopsis* stressed the role of Kyiv in all-Russian history, for its authors were determined to convince the tsarist government to maintain its control over the city despite the Muscovite-Polish Armistice of Andrusovo (1667), which assigned the ancient capital to the Polish side. For the author(s) of the *Synopsis*, the history of the Russian state and the Russian people was unimaginable without Kyiv. And so it continued for generations of readers of the *Synopsis* and for modern Russian historiography, which developed in that tradition.[1]

Some two-and-a-quarter centuries after the first appearance of the *Synopsis*, when Mykhailo Hrushevsky, another product of the Kyivan intellectual milieu, published his article on the traditional scheme of 'Russian' history (1904) and his *Survey History of the Ukrainian People* (1904) in St Petersburg, he forcefully rejected the notion of one Russian people and one Russian history, claiming Kyiv and its history for the Ukrainian nation. By nationalizing the Ukrainian past, Hrushevsky embarked on the project of unmaking Russian history as defined by generations of scholars and known to the educated public in the Russian Empire and abroad. In so doing, he undermined the founding myth of the Russian Empire and the imperial Russian nation, both of which looked to Kyiv for their historical roots. He also did away with a significant part of the Russian historical narrative that dealt with Ukrainian and Belarusian ethnic territory. Hrushevsky's deconstruction of the Russian imperial narrative – a project facilitated by the works of some Russian historians – proceeded simultaneously with (and in many ways was the result of) the construction of the Ukrainian historical narrative. Based on the primacy of the nation and the territory that it occupied, the new narrative grew out of the achievements of linguistics, anthropology (ethnology), and archaeology, which not only helped the national historians establish the continuity of their narrative but also made it easier to separate the past of their own nation from that of their dominant neighbours.

What were the main features that distinguished the Ukrainian historical narrative from the old Russian one? How did it differ from the Marxist narratives of Russian and Ukrainian history that appeared in the 1920s? Finally, how did it affect twentieth-century East European historiography?

To answer these questions, it is essential to define the main characteristics of the Ukrainian grand narrative as presented in Hrushevsky's writings. Hrushevsky contributed to the construction of the Ukrainian national narrative for most of his scholarly career. In the course of more than forty years, he underwent a remarkable intellectual evolution that could not but influence his philosophical views and the methods employed in his work on the *History of Ukraine-Rus'*. A number of discourses influenced his approach. Hrushevsky began his career as a committed populist, and his early writings on the Ukrainian past were dominated by a socially oriented, egalitarian, anti-elitist and often anti-statist populist discourse. Although that discourse had clear national overtones, it was poorly suited to the construction of a coherent and viable national historical narrative. It was utterly lacking in any notion of solidarity among diverse strata of society, recognizing only the solidarity of oppressed social groups.

As Hrushevsky's writings attest, the separation of the Ukrainian historical narrative from the all-Russian one required the transformation of populist discourse into a national one. The latter promoted as its paramount value the principle of national solidarity, suppressing anything in the populist discourse (from which it had developed) that might threaten that principle. The advance of the national discourse was promoted by the triumphs of neoromantic historiography in Eastern Europe in general and Ukraine in particular. It was also assisted by the rise of political conservatism and the growing interest in the history of social elites – a development fully exemplified in Ukrainian historiography by the writings of Viacheslav Lypynsky. The years of the revolution helped Hrushevsky restructure the Ukrainian historical narrative in a way that led to a synthesis of the views and historiographic approaches associated with the new ideological trends. The transformation of the populist discourse into a socialist one helped reemphasize the role of the popular masses in history, while the restructured national discourse helped promote the idea of the national state. For all the differences between these discourses and the historiographic approaches to which they gave rise, representatives of all Ukraine's historiographic camps accepted Hrushevsky's view of Ukrainian history as a narrative completely or largely separate from the Russian.

By deconstructing the Russian imperial narrative and separating Ukrainian history from that of Great Russia, Hrushevsky promoted the 'othering' of the Russian nation and history within the context of the Ukrainian national narrative. First the Russian authorities and then Russia in general took on the role of the 'other' in Hrushevsky's works. Hrushevsky accelerated that process in his political writings of 1918, when in reaction to the Bolshevik offensive against independent Ukraine he proclaimed 'the end of the Russian orientation' in Ukrainian politics. The 'othering' of Russia became an important turning point in Ukrainian historiography as it rejected the Little Russian identity, which was based on the exclusive 'othering' of the Poles and Tatars, precluding the rejection of the Russians. Hrushevsky was one of the first historians and political figures to begin the 'othering' of the Russians in Ukrainian political thought, which was fully accomplished by Dmytro Dontsov and Ievhen Malaniuk during the interwar period. Still, he was reluctant to employ the usual instrument of 'othering' – blaming the other national group for all the troubles that befell his own – against the Russians (a tactic he used much more willingly against the Poles). Instead, in analysing the course of Russo-Ukrainian relations, he turned the tables of colonial discourse on the Russians by characterizing Ukrainians as far more Westernized and culturally developed than their more powerful Russian masters.

How different was the new Ukrainian narrative from the Russian imperial one? This question may be approached by examining the following parameters of the two narratives: period of time covered and emphasized, territorial dimensions, main agency, teleology, and, finally, periodization of historical time. The Russian imperial narrative, as represented by the works of Russia's most influential historian at the turn of the twentieth century, Vasilii Kliuchevsky, covered a period that began with the first historical accounts of the settlement of the East European plain and continued to the mid-nineteenth century. It focused mainly on the territory settled by the Eastern Slavs before the thirteenth century and then switched to the history of the lands settled by the Great Russians, going on to discuss the territorial expansion of the empire. In this narrative, the Russian state and the Russian people figured as the main agents of Russian history, which was presented as an account of the formation, dispersion, and reunification of the Russian nation. Kliuchevsky's periodization of Russian history helped define the various stages of that complex process.

In defining the time frame of the Ukrainian historical narrative, Hrushevsky set out to present his nation as more ancient than the Russian, and thus deserving full support in its quest for sovereign cultural and political development, unhindered by interference from its younger sibling. In order to achieve that goal, he had to move the starting point of his narrative as far back as possible. Consequently, Hrushevsky not only established the Ukrainian claim to Kyivan Rus' in accordance with prevailing scholarly standards – an undertaking that put him on a collision course with traditional Russian historiography – but also presented the Ukrainians as direct descendants of the pre-Kyivan Antes. He also extended his narrative to his own day, not stopping in the mid-nineteenth century like Kliuchevsky but covering the events of the early twentieth century. For Hrushevsky, history did not end with the 'reunification' of the Russian people in the all-Russian Empire, as it did for Kliuchevsky, but with the 'national revival' and 'liberation' of Ukraine – a process that began to gain momentum in the latter half of the nineteenth century and reached the stage of mass mobilization at the beginning of the twentieth.

In terms of territorial scope, Hrushevsky was in a better position than Kliuchevsky, since his narrative did not require such dramatic geographical shifts (like the one from the Dnipro to the Volga basin) as did the traditional Russian narrative. Hrushevsky defined the territorial extent of his story by the limits of Ukrainian ethnic settlement and was not distracted in his narration by the ever-expanding boundaries of the

Russian Empire. In fact, he never limited his account to those boundaries but focused on tracing the history of the Ukrainian population and the territories that it settled, whether they belonged to the Lithuanian, Polish, Austro-Hungarian, or Russian states. The relative marginalization of the state in the Ukrainian past allowed Hrushevsky to present Ukrainian history as the product of a single agent – the people/nation. Kliuchevsky and Hrushevsky differed in their understanding of the nature of that agent, for Hrushevsky saw the 'Russian' (in his view, East European) ethnic conglomerate as divided into three culturally independent nations, not mere branches – a vision that he tried to substantiate and propagate through the writing of his *History of Ukraine-Rus'*. Still, not unlike Kliuchevsky's narrative, Hrushevsky's was teleological, although (as noted above) its objective was not the reunification of the Russian people but the deunification and emancipation of one of its parts from the oppression of another.

Hrushevsky's periodization of Ukrainian history was subordinated to that goal, following the development of the Ukrainian people/nation through a sequence of rises, declines, and revivals. This paradigm, based on an assumption of parallelism in the development of biological and social organisms and shared by many nation-builders of the nineteenth and twentieth centuries, postulated belief in the ultimate victory of the national cause despite all the setbacks of the past. The demands of scholarly criticism and Hrushevsky's own belief in the objectivity of historical scholarship helped him deconstruct many mythological features of the pre-national Ukrainian historical narrative. If he did not completely abandon other historical myths, he reevaluated and restructured them, as was the case with his treatment of Cossack mythology. Under the influence of neoromantic historiography, he interspersed his popular histories (and, to some degree, his academic *History of Ukraine-Rus'*) with heroic images of predecessors whom new generations of Ukrainians were meant to admire and emulate. For all the accusations of his Soviet critics, Hrushevsky never presented the history of Ukraine as that of a classless nation. On the contrary, he rejected the 'plebeian myth' of Ukraine as a peasant nation, with no elites or rulers of its own, that was promoted by populist historiography and picked up by Soviet historians of the 1920s and 1930s.

How was this narrative of Hrushevsky's related to the Marxist narrative of Ukrainian history? The latter was a product of class-based discourse that focused mainly on the theme of social antagonism. With regard to time frame, the new Marxist narrative placed its main emphasis on the revolutionary struggle of the nineteenth and early twentieth centuries – a development that brought it much closer to the Ukrainian national narrative than to the Russian imperial one. In terms of territory, Mikhail Pokrovsky's postrevolutionary coverage of events focused mainly on the Russian Federation, leaving the territory of Ukraine almost exclusively to the Ukrainian historical narrative. The new narrative viewed class as the main agent of history, as opposed to the state or the all-Russian nation, which had played that role in the old Russian historiography. Pokrovsky and his followers, including Matvii Iavorsky, presented East Slavic history as an account of the oppressed classes advancing toward the socialist revolution under the leadership of the proletariat, which was consonant with Hrushevsky's own revolutionary-era view of the Ukrainian people being liberated from social and national oppression by the great revolution. The Marxist narrative also accepted the Ukrainian view of the existence of three separate East Slavic nations, an approach that helped smooth out many contradictions between the Russian and Ukrainian historical narratives. It was this confluence of Marxist and populist/nationalist discourse that allowed the Ukrainian historical narrative to develop in the USSR for most of the 1920s.

The development of Ukrainian historiography in Soviet Ukraine benefited from the class-based deconstruction of the Russian imperial narrative and the separation of the Great Russian historical narrative from the all-Russian one undertaken by Mikhail Pokrovsky and his students, but by the end of the decade, Soviet Marxist historiography had launched a major attack on both the Russian imperial narrative and the Ukrainian national one. In Ukraine, the first victims of that offensive were the Ukrainian Marxists led by Iavorsky who strove to create a Marxist narrative of Ukrainian history separate from the Marxist narrative of Russian history. Next in line were the non-Marxist historians. The formulation of a historical paradigm acceptable to the political authorities and academic elites became increasingly subject to the dictate of the former. Academic historians, who became one of the main targets of the officially sponsored terror campaign, now hastily set about learning the basics of self-preservation and mastering the perverse rituals of criticism and self-criticism under the Soviet regime. During the 1920s, the intolerance cultivated within the party and the Marxist historical establishment was turned full force on the non-Marxist historians. The leaders of the national historiographic schools, such as Hrushevsky in Ukraine and Sergei Platonov in Russia, were accused of heading bogus anti-Soviet organizations, arrested, and exiled. On the historiographic level, Soviet Marxist discourse was restructured from a model founded on the coexistence of the class-based and national approaches to historical writing to one in which the class-based approach was turned against the national one.

During the 1930s the class-based discourse of Soviet Marxist historiography was adjusted to serve the purposes of the imperial project, which meant keeping the non-Russian nations of the USSR under Russian control. The Marxist attacks on the Russian imperial paradigm that were typical of Soviet historiographic discourse during the 1920s and even in the early 1930s proved short-lived and incapable of creating a coherent narrative to replace the Russian imperial account. Hence it was the gradual rehabilitation of the old imperial Russocentric paradigm that led the way to the creation of a new supranational Soviet narrative – the history of the peoples of the USSR.[2] The non-Russian historical narratives, including the Ukrainian one, were stripped of their national features and coordinated to fit the grand narrative of Soviet history. The 'denationalization' of the Ukrainian historical narrative in Soviet Ukraine was accompanied by official efforts to create a new supranational construct to be known as the 'Soviet people' – a term that entered political discourse in the 1930s.[3] The cultural basis for the creation of the Soviet people was necessarily Russian. As Oleksander Ohloblyn, a one-time opponent of Hrushevsky and later one of the creators of his cult in the Ukrainian diaspora, noted in his brief memoirs on the fate of Ukrainian historiography in the USSR, the concept of the Soviet quasi-nation was little more than the idea of the 'Russian nation' that the Constitutional Democrats had promoted before the revolution.[4]

Was the emergence of the Ukrainian national narrative in the late nineteenth century and the first three decades of the twentieth of any consequence for the construction of the official Soviet paradigm after 1934? I tend to give a positive answer to this question. It mattered largely because its emergence was an essential part of the larger revolution in the conceptualization of national relations in the former empire that occurred between 1917 and 1934. By the end of that period, the imperial Russian narrative with its concept of a tripartite Russian nation was largely gone. The new Soviet narrative was no longer concerned with supporting the concept of an all-Russian people, and the notion of the 'friendship of peoples' advanced by the regime and bolstered by official historiography after the Second World War was a pale shadow of its imperial predecessor. The Russian nationalism that re-

422 Unmaking Imperial Russia

turned to the political scene in the 1930s was not that of the old all-Russian tripartite nation but the Great Russian variety. The Russian narrative was now divested of its Ukrainian component (except for the history of Kyivan Rus' – the last refuge of the 'all-Russian' nationality), and a parallel Ukrainian narrative was permitted to exist within the bounds of the obligatory 'History of the (peoples of the) USSR.'[5]

To be sure, official Soviet historiography never stopped attacking the Ukrainian national narrative. Nevertheless, Hrushevsky's idea of Ukrainian history as a distinct scholarly discipline was never completely abandoned in the USSR. No matter how often it was rewritten according to the latest party directives, the history of Ukraine continued to be the subject of numerous historical surveys produced and published in the Ukrainian Soviet Socialist Republic. The very fact that there already existed a national narrative of Ukrainian history and that there were individuals and institutions abroad promoting the national paradigm of the Ukrainian past forced the Soviet authorities to begin publishing a separate Ukrainian historical journal in the 1960s and to maintain the Institute of History at the Ukrainian Academy of Sciences, which dealt almost exclusively with problems of Ukrainian history. It proved much easier for the Soviet regime to get rid of Mykhailo Hrushevsky than to discard his legacy and convince its own intellectuals that the historiographic revolution associated with his name had never taken place.

Appendix: Who Is Hiding the Last Volume of Hrushevsky's *History*?

One of the legends that still lives in the corridors of the humanities and social sciences institutes of the National Academy of Sciences of Ukraine is that there exists a manuscript, thickly covered with dust, of the eleventh volume of Hrushevsky's *History of Ukraine-Rus'*. It is lying somewhere waiting to be published, not unlike the first book of the sixth volume of his *History of Ukrainian Literature*, which was rediscovered and published in 1995. There has been talk of offering a reward to the finder of the volume in an amount irresistible to the former members of the secret police who allegedly are still in possession of it. Nevertheless, no award has been announced, nor is there any hard evidence that the volume ever existed. There are, however, people still living who claim to have seen the eleventh volume in the repositories of the Ukrainian Academy of Sciences Library back in the 1950s. Among them is the patriarch of Ukrainian archaeography, Ivan Butych. According to him, the volume was kept among Hrushevsky's materials in the library and covered Ukrainian history up to the hetmancy of Ivan Mazepa, or perhaps even Danylo Apostol.[1]

No one claims to have seen the volume since then. Did it indeed perish in the fire that decimated the library's collection in the early 1960s – a fire that alerted the Toronto businessman Petro Jacyk to the fate of Ukraine's vanishing cultural heritage and later influenced his decision to finance the translation of Hrushevsky's *History* into English?[2] Or was the manuscript destroyed in one of the numerous floods that have afflicted the library's outdated heating system (the last such flood took place only a few years ago)? Or was it perhaps exploited by one of the unscrupulous scholars who plagiarized parts of Hrushevsky's work for their doctoral dissertations? One such individual was recently exposed for publishing the work of a deceased historian of the inter-war period under his own name. We are unlikely ever to have a satisfactory answer to any of these questions. A question that we can explore, however, is whether the volume existed in the first place and, if so, what period of Ukrainian history it covered.

By far the best starting point for our investigation is volume 10, the last published volume of the *History*, which was issued posthumously by Kateryna Hrushevsky in 1936. It covered the period from 1657 to 1659, but was this indeed the period that Hrushevsky wanted to discuss in the volume? Apparently not. At the time of Hrushevsky's return to Ukraine in 1924, he planned to extend the *History* to 1725 – only two years short of the hetmancy of Danylo Apostol, mentioned by the 'eyewitness' of the eleventh volume Ivan Butych.[3] It would have been in line with this plan that one of Hrushevsky's students in Lviv, Ivan Dzhydzhora, worked before the war to collect materials on Cossack history of the first half of the eighteenth century.[4] A better understanding of the chronological limits of volume 10 can be obtained from the scope of the archival work carried out by Vasyl Herasymchuk, also a student of Hrushevsky's in Lviv, who continued collecting materials for his professor after 1924. Herasymchuk's period of study was 1657–67.[5] Another of Hrushevsky's students, Myron Korduba, who worked for his former professor in the Lviv archives, also treated his study of the period prior to 1667 as a separate stage of his archival research.[6] The decade from 1657 to 1667 also constituted a distinct period on which the work of Hrushevsky's archaeographic expedition focused in 1927–8. Before that, the members of the expedition worked on documents for the years 1650–7, the period covered in volume 9.[7]

It might be assumed from Hrushevsky's planning of his associates' work that he considered the period between 1657 (the death of Khmelnytsky) and 1667 (the Armistice of Andrusovo that divided Ukraine between Muscovy and the Commonwealth) an era of Ukrainian history that deserved a volume of its own, like the previous period of 1650–7. In the course of his work, however, Hrushevsky apparently decided to change the time frame of the volume. In late 1927 the journal *Ukraïna* reported that Herasymchuk was continuing his work on the collection of documents for the years 1657–65, not 1657–67.[8] In his letter of 1934 to Molotov, Hrushevsky wrote that the tenth volume of the *History* was to cover the period from 1657 to 1665. He characterized that period as the 'most interesting years' and the 'era of social differentiation' that had attracted the attention of Karl Marx, who took his information about it from Mykola Kostomarov's monograph on Stepan Razin.[9] Hrushevsky tried to convince Molotov of the importance of his work on the *History*, using language and arguments congruent with Bolshevik discourse of the time. Not all of Hrushevsky's statements in his letter to Molotov can be taken at face value, but if the time frame of volume 10 given there is correct, Hrushevsky intended to bring his account up to the beginning of Petro Doroshenko's hetmancy.

An examination of the manuscript of volume 9 shows that once Hrushevsky had written his text, he did very little subsequent editing. The text of volume 9 and the published portion of volume 10 also indicate that in the last volumes of his *History* Hrushevsky was primarily concerned with presenting source material, limiting his own commentary and discussion to a minimum. Considering that the preliminary work of copying sources was done by members of the archaeographic expedition in Moscow, Hrushevsky could indeed have made significant progress in his work on volume 10 and completed the preparation of its text by the middle of 1932, as originally planned. It did not turn out that way. The volume was not finished either in 1932 or in 1934.

In what state was the manuscript at the time of Hrushevsky's death? An answer to this question requires a closer look at the printed portion of the volume. That text, published by Kateryna Hrushevska as volume 10 of the *History*, is poorly edited, lacks transitions between some of its parts, and impresses the reader as an unfinished work, which in fact it is. In all likelihood, the rest of the volume was even less ready for print. Judging by Hrushevsky's requests to his associates in Moscow in 1930, at that time he was focusing most of his energy on preparing part 1 of volume 6 of his *History of Ukrainian Literature* for print.[10] A good deal of time was also consumed by Hrushevsky's efforts to protect his 'historical institutions' from increasing attack by the authorities. Clearly, the atmosphere of continuous persecution also prevented him from concentrating on the writing of the *History*. Under pressure from the authorities, even members of Hrushevsky's own staff began to criticize him for alleged methodological shortcomings in the *History*. Hrushevsky is said to have responded to one such attack with a jest: 'When you write such a work, Pylyp Vasyliovych,' he addressed one of his critics, 'you will do it according to your plan, and I shall do it according to mine.'[11] Such an atmosphere could only sap Hrushevsky's energy and enthusiasm. Apart from these troubles, Hrushevsky's eyesight was beginning to deteriorate. As early as 1930 Fedir Savchenko had written to Studynsky about Hrushevsky's eye problems, which grew even worse after his arrest and de facto exile to Moscow. Kateryna Hrushevska, who accompanied her father in exile, often had to read books and materials to him so that he could continue his work.[12] Hrushevsky also complained about his failing eyesight in his letter of September 1934 to Molotov.[13]

Most likely, Hrushevsky was unable to resume his work on the *History of Ukraine-Rus'* in Moscow or, if he did so, his progress was quite limited. In the same letter to Molotov, Hrushevsky referred to his work on volume 10 of the *History* as a project effectively interrupted by his arrest in 1931.[14] Kateryna remained her father's only assistant in Moscow, and when it came to work in the archives and reading handwritten Muscovite documents of the seventeenth century, she probably could offer him only limited assistance. Dmytro Kravtsov, the last member of the archaeographic expedition, ceased his work in the archives for lack of funds and left Moscow for Leningrad by the end of 1931.[15] Officially, according to the records of the Ukrainian Academy of Sciences, Hrushevsky was working in Moscow on the history of education and creative writing in the eighteenth and nineteenth centuries, a topic that suggests, if anything, the continuation of his work on the *History of Ukrainian Literature.*[16] Articles that Hrushevsky submitted for print in the journals of the All-Union Academy of Sciences indicate that he was working on topics related to Ukrainian chronicles of the first half of the eighteenth century,[17] a subject closely related to the history of Ukrainian literature.

There was also a problem of access to archival materials. Hrushevsky's failing eyesight apparently did not allow him to work in the archives, while copies of archival materials prepared by members of the archaeographic expedition remained in Kyiv. Obtaining copies from there was no easy task, as indicated by the scandal that arose in the academy when Kateryna Hrushevska asked that some of her folklore materials be sent to her in Moscow.[18] In Moscow Hrushevsky was also cut off from his Kyiv library.[19] His relatives in Kyiv knew that he was continuing to work as hard as ever in Moscow and were able to send him some of his books, but that led to unwanted complications with the authorities. Hrushevsky apparently had access to the library of his Moscow colleague Academician Mikhail Speransky, a specialist in the history of literature,[20] but in general, as he wrote to Molotov, conditions in Moscow did not allow him to 'conduct systematic scholarly work.'[21]

One might assume that, as in the case of Hrushevsky's period of emigration in the West, when he was cut off from library and archival materials, in Moscow he also chose to focus on the *History of Ukrainian Literature*, which did not depend on archival research. In a letter of November 1932 to Studynsky, Hrushevsky wrote mostly about his work on the literature project. He informed Studynsky that after completing volume 9 of the *History of Ukraine-Rus'*, he had returned to his work on the history of literature and had already sent the first part of the volume, covering the period 1600–32, to the press, but the printing was stopped in the spring of 1931. Concerning his work on the continuation of the *History of Ukrainian Literature*, he wrote: 'While living here, I have worked my way through the seventeenth and eighteenth centuries and even touched on the first third of the nineteenth century, but only in episodes, depending on the material that was available. There is very little Ukrainian and Polish literature here, and material is lacking for certain episodes: leaving them aside, my daughter and I are working on what we can cover. She is helping me and independently treating certain topics in cultural and literary history of the eighteenth and nineteenth centuries, without abandoning her work on the *dumy* and their exponents.'[22]

It is safe to assume that whatever work Hrushevsky did on volume 10 and any other volume of the *History* remained in Kateryna's hands after his death. After Hrushevsky's state-sponsored funeral, a special commission was struck by the Academy of Sciences to work on his papers. Kateryna Hrushevska was the only active member of the commission. She clearly worked on the manuscripts that were already in her possession but most probably also obtained access to the materials of the 'historical institutions' held in the academy. In June 1933 Hrushevsky's nephew Serhii Shamrai was able to remove some of Hrushevsky's archival materials from the academy to his apartment, but he himself was soon arrested, and the materials were returned to the academy.[23]

At the time of Kateryna Hrushevska's arrest in July 1938, the secret police confiscated all manuscripts remaining in the Hrushevsky family's apartment. Hrushevsky's widow, Mariia, wrote: 'Everything was turned upside down; everything jumbled together – manuscripts, notes, copies – so that the fruit of long and strenuous labour was lost. They threw some of those papers into a sack and took them away; others they took to my late husband's office, ordering me to open it, and sealed it afterwards.'[24] The arrest of Kateryna Hrushevska and the first search of the apartment took place on 10 July 1938. A subsequent search and confiscation of books and other materials followed on 23 August of the same year.[25] It appears that at least some of Mykhailo Hrushevsky's manuscripts were then in the apartment. In April 1939 Kateryna Hrushevska begged the members of the military tribunal that sentenced her to eight years of imprisonment to ensure the safety of Hrushevsky's materials confiscated at the time of her arrest. The tribunal agreed to send the materials to the Academy of Sciences for evaluation and possible use in scholarly work.[26]

It is not clear whether that decision was ever carried out. In June 1941 Kateryna wrote to her mother from imprisonment, asking about the fate of the books and manuscripts confiscated after her arrest. She was specifically concerned about the manuscript of volume 6 of the *History of Ukrainian Literature*, preserved at the time of her arrest in the Institute of Literature, where she had been employed as a research associate. Kateryna also asked her mother about the manuscripts that she had given to the academy,[27] which probably included the ones written by Hrushevsky in Moscow. The question that arises in this regard is whether the text that Kateryna enquired about was part 1 of volume 6 of the *History of Ukrainian Literature*, which Hrushevsky had sent to the printer in early 1931,[28] or volume 6 as a whole, which included the chapters written by Hrushevsky in Moscow. Most likely, Kateryna had both of these in mind. Oleksander Biletsky, who reviewed the manuscript of part 1 of the volume for publication after Hrushevsky's death, also recommended the publication of its second part, which, according to the review, covered the history of Ukrainian literature up to 'the last decades of the eighteenth century.'[29] Biletsky also referred to the second part of the volume in some of his later works, but no other proof of its existence has yet been discovered. This lack of reliable evidence caused the publishers of part 1 of the volume, which was finally issued in 1995, to question the existence of the second part of the volume altogether.[30]

The question that should be asked in connection with any future search for Hrushevsky's Moscow materials is in what language they were written. The first answer that comes to mind is that Hrushevsky wrote his works in Ukrainian. After all, in what other language could the Ukrainian-language *History of Ukrainian Literature* be continued? Nevertheless, the question is not so naive as it appears at first glance. There are indications that Hrushevsky may have written some of his last works in Russian. It is a well-known fact that Hrushevsky's articles of this period were written in Russian and published in Russian academic journals. According to a secret police report, that fact even drew criticism from the Kyiv intelligentsia, and members of the historian's family had to protect him from accusations of lacking Ukrainian patriotism. Responding to the question of why Hrushevsky, a Ukrainian academician, did not publish his works in Ukrainian but sent them instead to Leningrad to be published in Russian, Serhii Shamrai allegedly answered as follows: 'It would be strange if, after all they did to him in Ukraine, Mykhailo Serhiiovych had acted differently.'[31]

What Shamrai probably meant was that Hrushevsky did not want to send his materials to be published in the journals of the Ukrainian Academy of Sciences following its purge. The question, though, was not so much one of Hrushevsky's willingness to publish the results of his research in Ukraine but of the academy's refusal to accept his works for publication. After all, the publication of part 1 of volume 6 of Hrushevsky's *History of Ukrainian Literature* was halted after his arrest. The same fate befell Hrushevsky's articles and reviews prepared for publication in *Ukraïna* before his arrest.[32] While in Moscow, Hrushevsky repeatedly and fruitlessly applied for an invitation to attend a session of the Ukrainian Academy of Sciences. Without such an invitation, he could not leave Moscow for Kyiv.[33]

If Hrushevsky indeed wanted his new works to be published, he could count only on the central (Russian) publishers and would therefore have had to submit his manuscripts in Russian. An indication that this choice pertained to the publication of the *History of Ukrainian Literature* appears in Kateryna Hrushevska's letter of June 1941 to her mother: 'Do you know what happened to volume 6, which was in the institute, and to the other manuscripts that I submitted to the academy myself? And have you heard anything about the translation of volume 6?'[34] Did she mean the translation of the text from Russian? Or was she (more probably) referring to a translation from Ukrainian into Russian? One cannot exclude the possibility that Kateryna Hrushevska planned to publish her father's work, originally written in Ukrainian, in Russian translation.

If volume 6 of the *History of Ukrainian Literature* was not among the manuscripts confiscated at the time of Kateryna Hrushevska's arrest, which of Hrushevsky's works were? Could they have included new chapters of the *History of Ukraine-Rus'*? If so, did the military tribunal fulfil Kateryna's request and send those of Hrushevsky's materials confiscated during her arrest to the Academy of Sciences? If that was the case, then they may indeed have been delivered to the library of the Academy of Sciences and seen there by Ivan Butych, who assumed it to be eleventh volume of the *History*, since the tenth volume had already been published by Kateryna. This is definitely a possibility, but, unfortunately, no more than that. We have no answer to the question of what happened to the unpublished parts of Hrushevsky's *History*, either those that were just preparatory materials, an unpublished second part of volume 10, or an entirely new eleventh volume. Today, regrettably, all or almost all of the work done by Mykhailo and Kateryna Hrushevsky at the time of their exile in Moscow remains inaccessible to scholars. One can only hope that at least some of the Moscow manuscripts were not destroyed after Kateryna's arrest and will be made available in the future.

Notes

Introduction

1 *Encyclopaedia Britannica*, 11th ed. (New York, 1911), 15: 789.
2 *New Encyclopaedia Britannica*, 15th ed. (Chicago, 1993), 22: 487.
3 See *Encyclopaedia Britannica*, 11th ed., 15: 790; cf. *New Encyclopaedia Britannica*, 15th ed., 22: 487–9.
4 For the concept of the 'short twentieth century,' see Hobsbawm, *Age of Extremes*.
5 On the rise of the Ukrainian national movement in the nineteenth century and the policy of the Russian authorities toward it, see Hrytsak, *Narys istoriï Ukraïny*. 24–72; Savchenko, *Zaborona ukraïnstva*. Cf. Aleksei Miller, *'Ukrainskii vopros' v politike vlastei i russkom obshchestvennom mnenii*. For an English translation, see Miller, *The Ukrainian Question*. On the politics of Russification in the western provinces of the Russian Empire, see Weeks, *Nation and State in Late Imperial Russia*.
6 For a general account, see Kozik, *The Ukrainian National Movement in Galicia, 1815–1849*. On competing nation-building projects in pre–First World War Galicia, see Himka, 'The Construction of Nationality in Galician Rus'.'
7 For a standard account of Russian historiography, see Mazour, *Modern Russian Historiography*. On the relations between Russian and Ukrainian historiography in the nineteenth and twentieth centuries, see Velychenko, *National History as Cultural Process* and *Shaping Identity in Eastern Europe and Russia*; Prymak, *Mykola Kostomarov*; and articles by Zenon Kohut, Frank Sysyn, Bohdan Klid, and Thomas Prymak in *Historiography of Imperial Russia*.

On the interpretation of the non-Russian past in Soviet historiography, see Lowell Tillett, *The Great Friendship*. On Soviet Russian historiography, see Shteppa, *Russian Historians and the Soviet State*; Mazour, *The Writing of History in the Soviet Union*; Heer, *Politics and History in the Soviet Union*; Barber, *Soviet Historians in Crisis, 1928–1932*. For recent attempts at rethinking the Soviet historiographic legacy in Russia, see *Sovetskaia istoriografiia* and *Istoricheskaia nauka v Rossii v XX veke*.

8 For a political biography of Hrushevsky, see Prymak, *Mykhailo Hrushevsky*.

9 See Hroch, *Social Preconditions of National Revival in Europe*, 22–4.

10 See Hrushevs'kyi, *Istoriia Ukraïny–Rusy*. For a bibliography of Hrushevsky's works, see Vynar, *Mykhailo Hrushevs'kyi, 1866–1934: Bibliographic Sources*.

11 On the writing and publication of Hrushevsky's *Istoriia Ukraïny-Rusy*, see Sysyn, 'Introduction to the *History of Ukraine-Rus'*,' xxi–xlii.

12 The former approach has been applied successfully by the authors of *Historians as Nation-Builders* and, in the case of Hrushevsky, by the author of his political biography, Thomas Prymak (see his *Mykhailo Hrushevsky*).

13 On the role of history in the formation of national identities, see Chatterjee, *The Nation and its Fragments*; Hobsbawm and Ranger, *The Invention of Tradition*; Shaw and Chase, *The Imagined Past*; Deletant and Hanak, *Historians as Nation-Builders*; and Suny, 'History and the Making of Nations.'

14 See Anderson, *Imagined Communities*, 14–16.

15 See Szporluk, 'Ukraine: From an Imperial Periphery to a Sovereign State,' 367–8.

16 For a definition of 'othering,' see Ashcroft, Griffiths, and Tiffin, *Key Concepts in Post-Colonial Studies*, 169–73.

17 See Munslow, *Deconstructing History*, 186. On the role of historical narratives in the construction of national identity, see 'The Narration of the Nation' in Wodak et al., *The Discursive Construction of National Identity*, 23–7.

18 See Munslow, *Deconstructing History*, 181. For the application of discourse theory to the study of the formation of national identities, see chapter 2, 'The Discursive Construction of National Identities,' in Wodak et al., *The Discursive Construction of National Identity*, 7–49; for the interrelation between national and imperial discourses, see Wellings, 'Empire-Nation.' For an instance of discourse analysis applied to the study of the construction of Ukrainian national identity, see Kulyk, 'The Role of Discourse in the Construction of an Émigré Community.'

19 Like many other studies of discursive structures, my approach to the problem has been profoundly influenced by the writings of Michel Foucault. See especially his *The Order of Things*, *The Archeology of Knowledge*, and *Power/Knowledge*.

20 Kappeler, *The Russian Empire*, 8.

21 See Velychenko, *National History as Cultural Process, Shaping Identity in Eastern Europe and Russia*, and 'Rival Grand Narratives of National History'; Kohut, 'The Development of a Ukrainian National Historiography in Imperial Russia'; Brandenberger, *National Bolshevism*; Yekelchyk, 'The Grand Narrative and Its Discontents,' 'Stalinist Patriotism as Imperial Discourse,' and *Stalin's Empire of Memory*.

22 See Vynar, *Hrushevs'koznavstvo: geneza i istorychnyi rozvytok*; Prymak, *Mykhailo Hrushevsky*.

23 See Hrushevsky, *History of Ukraine-Rus'*, vols 1, 7, 8, ed. Sysyn et al., 1997–2002.

24 For a critique of that tradition, see Usenko, 'Mifolohiia na zavadi istoriï.'

25 For a discussion of the 'domestication' of Hrushevsky's image by Ukrainian political elites, see Hrytsak, 'Reabilitatsiia Hrushevs'koho i legitymatsiia nomenklatury.'

26 See Hrushevs'kyi, *Istoriia Ukraïny-Rusy*, 10 vols, 11 books (Kyiv, 1991–2000).

27 See Hrushevs'kyi, *Tvory u 50-ty tomakh*.

28 See Hrushevs'kyi, 'Spomyny,' *Shchodennyk*, and 'Shchodennyky M.S. Hrushevs'koho (1904–1910 rr.).'

29 For the latest publications on Hrushevsky, see Hranovs'kyi, *Mykhailo Hrushevs'kyi: pershyi prezydent Ukraïny, akademik: bibliohrafiia*.

30 See Pyrih, *Zhyttia Mykhaila Hrushevs'koho*.

31 See Sokhan', Ul'ianovs'kyi, and Kirzhaiev, *M.S. Hrushevs'kyi i Academia*; Iurkova, *Diial'nist' naukovo-doslidnoï kafedry istoriï Ukraïny M.S. Hrushevs'koho*.

32 See Prystaiko and Shapoval, *Mykhailo Hrushevs'kyi i HPU-NKVD* and *Mykhailo Hrushevs'kyi: Sprava 'UNTs' i ostanni roky*.

33 See Tel'vak, *Teoretyko-metodolohichni pidstavy istorychnykh pohliadiv Mykhaila Hrushevs'koho*; Masnenko, *Istorychni kontseptsiï M.S. Hrushevs'koho ta V.K. Lypyns'koho*, and *Istorychna dumka ta natsiotvorennia v Ukraïni*.

34 See Vashchenko, *Nevrasteniia*.

35 For debates on the issue dating from the first half of the century, see Meyerhoff's anthology *The Philosophy of History in Our Time*, 87–227.

36 For a discussion of postmodern methods of historical research, see Jenkins, *Re-thinking History* and his *The Postmodern History Reader*; Munslow, *Deconstructing History*; Berkhofer, Jr., *Beyond the Great Story*. For a critical analysis of postmodern approaches to history, see Windschuttle, *The Killing of History*.

37 'Forgetting, even getting history wrong, is an essential factor in the forma-

tion of a nation, which is why the progress of historical studies is often a danger to nationality.' Quoted in Hobsbawm, *On History*, 270. Cf. Renan, 'What Is a Nation?' 50.

38 On belief in the compatibility of 'scientificity' and political agendas in historical writing in nineteenth-century Western Europe, see Berger, Donovan, and Passmore, 'Apologias for the Nation-State in Western Europe since 1800,' 4–5.

39 See Anthony D. Smith, *National Identity*, 65–70, 128–9, 143–78.

40 The 'observations' of Stalin, Zhdanov, and Kirov on history textbooks were made public in January 1936. Earlier, in May 1934, the Soviet government issued a decree on the teaching of history in secondary schools. For a discussion of the changes in Soviet historiography initiated by the official intervention of 1934 in the writing and teaching of history, see the chapter 'The Turning Point on the Historical Front, 1934–1941' in Shteppa, *Russian Historians and the Soviet State*, 123–208; Brandenberger, *National Bolshevism*, 27–62.

Part 1

1 On Peter's acceptance of the title of emperor, see Pogosian, *Petr I – arkhitektor rossiiskoi istorii*, 183–243. On the importance of Peter's reforms for Russian nation-building, see Greenfeld, *Nationalism*, 192–9, and Tolz, *Russia*, 24–44.

2 On the Ukrainian role in the formation of the 'all-Russian' identity, see Keenan, 'Muscovite Perceptions of Other East Slavs before 1654: An Agenda for Historians,' 20–38, and 'On Certain Mythical Beliefs and Russian Behaviors,' 19–40; Plokhy, *The Cossacks and Religion in Early Modern Ukraine*, 274–333; Greenfeld, *Nationalism*, 195, 226, 236–9.

3 See Kappeler, *The Russian Empire*, 213–16, 220–30. Cf. his *'Mazepintsy, malorossy, khokhly:* Ukrainians in the Ethnic Hierarchy of the Russian Empire,' 162–81.

4 An interesting example of the hierarchy of these terms, in which 'Little Russia' already encompassed most of the Ukrainian territories, including Dnipro Ukraine, but had not yet been entirely replaced in the minds of the older generation of Ukrainian activists by the term 'Ukraine,' appears in a letter to Hrushevsky from Iakiv Shulhyn, a leader of the Ukrainophile Hromada in Kyiv. Writing to Hrushevsky in April 1899, Shulhyn informed him that he had moved from Ielysavethrad to Kyiv in order 'to elucidate the daily existence of the agriculturalist of Ukraine, Podilia, and Volhynia, and then of Little Russia as a whole.' See Shulhyn's letter of 13 April 1899

to Hrushevsky in TsDIAK, fond 1235, op. 1, no. 873, fols 270–3. For a brief biography of Shulhyn, see *Encyclopedia of Ukraine*, 4: 684.

5 The activists of the Ukrainian movement were recruited predominantly from the Kyiv, Poltava, and Chernihiv gubernias, the latter two of which were part of the Hetmanate in the seventeenth and eighteenth centuries. On the composition of the Ukrainian movement in the nineteenth and early twentieth centuries, see Kappeler, 'Die Formierung einer ukrainischen nationalen Elite im Russischen Reich, 1860–1914' in *Der schwierige Weg zur Nation*, 99–122.

6 On the early development of the Ukrainian national movement, see Subtelny, *Ukraine* (1988), 221–42; Magocsi, *A History of Ukraine*, 351–64.

7 For the application of Miroslav Hroch's scheme to the history of the Ukrainian national movement, see Kappeler, 'Die ukrainische Nationalbewegung im Russischen Reich und in Galizien: Ein Vergleich,' in *Der schwierige Weg zur Nation*, 70–87 and 'Die ukrainische und litauische Nationalbewegung im Vergleich,' ibid., 88–98; Szporluk, 'Ukraïns'ke natsional'ne vidrodzhennia v konteksti ievropeis'koï istoriï kintsia XVIII–pochatku XIX stolit',' 164. For Szporluk's periodization of the Ukrainian national movement, see his 'Ukraine: From an Imperial Periphery to a Sovereign State.'

For a general assessment of government policy toward Ukraine in the nineteenth century and the prohibitions on Ukrainian publications in 1863 (Valuev circular) and 1876 (Ems Ukase), apart from Miller's '*Ukrainskii vopros*,' see Saunders, 'Russia's Ukrainian Policy (1847–1905),' 'Russia, the Balkans and Ukraine in the 1870s,' 'Russia and Ukraine under Alexander II,' and 'Mikhail Katkov and Mykola Kostomarov.'

8 On the competition between the two projects, see Miller, '*Ukrainskii vopros*.'

9 On the role of the ethnic Ukrainian Mikhail Iuzefovich in the initiation of the Ems Ukase, see Miller, '*Ukrainskii vopros*,' 173–96.

10 See *Istoriia Rusov ili Maloi Rossii*.

Chapter 1: The Historian as Nation-Builder

1 Kohn, *The Idea of Nationalism*, 330.

2 Seton-Watson, Preface to *Historians and Nation-Builders*, 9. See also Georg Iggers's remark on Kohn's statement in his 'Changing Conceptions of National History since the French Revolution,' 132–4.

3 'Almost all of these constructed continuities,' write Stefan Berger, Mark Donovan, and Kevin Passmore with regard to British, French, German, and Italian national narratives, 'rooted in the past, created national theolo-

gies designed to legitimate the present and prevent future change. They read national histories backward to arrive at foundational dates of their respective histories ... Thus 1688 and/or 1832 for Britain, 1789 for France, 1861 for Italy and 1871 for Germany mark important foundational dates connected to the creation of foundation myths which were in themselves always contested by rival mythologies' ('Apologias for the Nation-State in Western Europe since 1800,' 11).

4 On Lelewel, see Skurnowicz, *Romantic Nationalism and Liberalism.*

5 On Kogălniceanu, see Jelavich, 'Mihail Kogălniceanu: Historian as Foreign Minister, 1876–8.' On Iorga, see Pearton, 'Nicolae Iorga as Historian and Politician.'

6 On Masaryk, see Szporluk, *The Political Thought of Thomas G. Masaryk.*

7 On Kostomarov, see Prymak, *Mykola Kostomarov: A Biography.*

8 On Antonovych, see Klid, 'Volodymyr Antonovych: Ukrainian Populist Historiography and the Cultural Politics of Nation Building.'

9 See the English translation of Doroshenko's *Survey of Ukrainian Historiography,* updated for the years 1917–56 by Olexander Ohloblyn; see also Doroshenko, *A Survey of Ukrainian History,* edited and updated by Oleh W. Gerus (Winnipeg, 1975).

10 On Lypynsky, see *The Political and Social Ideas of Vjačeslav Lypyns'kyj.*

11 Serhii Hrushevsky was apparently quite close to Lebedyntsev. The latter's wife was Mykhailo Hrushevsky's godmother.

12 See Vynar, *Molodist' Mykhaila Hrushevs'koho,* 6–7. On the government policy of Russifying the western regions of the empire, see Weeks, *Nation and State;* Miller, 'Ukrainskii vopros,' 138–52. One of the incentives used to attract teachers from other parts of the Russian Empire to the lands of the former Congress Kingdom was counting three years of service in the area as four years for pension purposes. See Weeks, *Nation and State,* 128.

13 An Orthodox Christian and a graduate of the Kyiv Theological Academy, Serhii Hrushevsky taught Russian at the Uniate (Greek Catholic) gymnasium in Kholm and later served as administrator of the teachers' seminary there. Appointments like his attest to government plans not only for the Russification but also the 'Orthodoxization' of the region. Arranging a rapprochement between the local Uniates and the Orthodox Church so as to bring about the eventual abolition of the church union was an important element of those plans. In Kholm, the Hrushevskys resided at the Greek Catholic seminary, where Mykhailo was born. See Hrushevs'kyi, 'Spomyny,' *Kyïv,* 1988, no. 9: 115–23. On the official 'Orthodoxization' of the Kholm region, see Himka, *Religion and Nationality in Western Ukraine,* 32–41, 57–63; Weeks, *Nation and State,* 172–92.

14 Hrushevs'kyi, 'Spomyny,' *Kyïv*, 1988, no. 9: 120. 'Under the influence of the stories told by my father, who remained warmly attached to everything Ukrainian – language, song, tradition,' wrote Hrushevsky in his autobiography, 'Ukrainian national feeling awakened within me and imposed itself on my consciousness at an early age, supported by reading and by those rare trips to Ukraine, which thus acquired the aura of a distant "homeland," in contrast to the "alien land," with its foreign tribes and languages' ('Avtobiohrafiia, 1906 r.,' 198). On the cult of the father in Hrushevsky's writings, see Vashchenko, *Nevrasteniia*, 124-82.

15 Hrushevs'kyi, 'Spomyny,' *Kyïv*, 1988, no. 9: 120, 123.

16 Ibid., 1988, no. 9: 148; no. 12: 116-17.

17 Ibid., 1988, no. 12: 119.

18 Hrushevs'kyi, 'Avtobiohrafiia, 1906 r.,' 198.

19 Hrushevs'kyi, 'Spomyny,' *Kyïv*, 1988, no. 12: 120.

20 See Rudnytsky, 'The Intellectual Origins of Modern Ukraine,' 133.

21 For a general discussion of Ukrainian populism, see Rudnytsky, 'Trends in Ukrainian Political Thought,' 96-8.

22 See Brock, 'Polish Nationalism,' 328-33; Walicki, *Poland between East and West*, 26-31.

    The neglect of activities intended to achieve political ends was also characteristic of Russian populism of the 1870s. See Walicki, 'Russian Social Thought,' 20-1.

23 Grushevskii, 'Dvizhenie politicheskoi i obshchestvennoi ukrainskoi mysli v XIX stoletii,' 52. The article was first published in *Ukrainskii vestnik*, no. 9 (16 July 1906).

24 Hrushevs'kyi, 'Spomyny,' *Kyïv*, 1988, no. 12: 121. In his memoirs, Hrushevsky also gave a positive assessment of the cultural and political program put forward by the journal at the time. He wrote: 'The culture of the Ukrainian word and of Ukrainian studies; the treatment of literary and scholarly interests not as political crimes or intellectual deviations but as normal and healthy manifestations of local life; a supportive attitude toward it instead of suppressing and trampling it under the boots of Russifying barbarians from the interior provinces – this was a minimal program capable of uniting a great many people and highly realistic at that point' (ibid., 120).

25 On the journal's importance for the development of the Ukrainian national movement, see Andreas Kappeler, 'Die Kosaken-Ära als zentraler Baustein der Konstruktion einer national-ukrainischen Geschichte: Das Beispiel der Zeitschrift *Kievskaia Starina*, 1882–1891' in *Der schwierige Weg zur Nation*, 123–35, and 'Nationale Kommunikation unter erschwerten Bedingungen:

Die Zeitschrift *Kievskaia starina* (1882–1891/1906) als Organ der ukrainischen Nationalbewegung im Zarenreich,' ibid., 136–50.

26 See Hrushevsky's diaries, edited by Leonid Zashkil'niak: 'Shchodennyky (1883–1893),' *Kyïvs'ka starovyna*, 1993, no. 3: 28–35; no. 4: 12–19; no. 5: 13–24.

27 Ibid., 1993, no. 4: 13. Hrushevsky used the terms 'Ukrainian,' 'Little Russian,' and 'Ruthenian' (*russ'kyi*) interchangeably to denote the Ukrainian language in which he wrote part of his diary.

28 Ibid., no. 3: 31.

29 In his diary entry for 14 November 1883, Hrushevsky wrote: 'It is a pity that some often forsake Ukrainian for Russian. Take even our great Hohol, for example: if he had written *po russki* [in Ukrainian], he could greatly have helped the Ukrainian people and their literature' (ibid., no. 5: 17).

30 Hrushevsky often complained in his diary that he had to spend his life far from Ukraine, surrounded by other nationalities. In his diary entry for 20 September 1883, Hrushevsky noted: 'You live and sometimes you do not hear your native language for a whole year – all around you Muscovites exalt themselves; Germans of all kinds; Armenians, Georgians, and other foreign-speaking people chatter. If only I could return to my native Ukraine as soon as possible: despite the woe, misfortune, and poverty among us in Ukraine, even that is better than [to be] here in a foreign land' (ibid., no. 3: 34).

31 Ibid., no. 5: 17 (15 November 1883).

32 Ibid., no. 3: 32 (18 September 1883). Apparently, what Hrushevsky meant by the desire to abandon one's own milieu was not aspiring to higher social status but abandoning Ukrainian culture for the dominant Russian one.

33 Ibid.

34 Ibid.

35 Ibid., no. 4: 13.

36 Ibid., no. 4: 17.

37 Ibid., no. 4: 18; no. 5: 18.

38 Petrov, 'Ocherki iz ukrainskoi literatury.'

39 Hrushevs'kyi, 'Shchodennyky (1883–1893),' *Kyïvs'ka starovyna*, 1993, no. 5: 17.

40 Hrushevs'kyi, 'Spomyny,' *Kyïv*, 1988, no. 12: 119.

41 On Pisarev and 'nihilism,' see Walicki, *A History of Russian Thought*, 209–15. Cf. his 'Russian Social Thought,' 22–3.

42 On Lavrov and his views, see Walicki, *A History of Russian Thought*, pp. 235–44. Cf. his, 'Russian Social Thought,' 26–8.

43 Hrushevs'kyi, 'Spomyny,' *Kyïv*, 1988, no. 12: 121.

44 Hrushevsky used his diary to monitor his spiritual condition, as he suspected that he had a psychological illness. As a result, the diary was very candid and sincere in portraying his moral and spiritual dilemmas. For the text of the diary, see Hrushevs'kyi, *Shchodennyk (1886–1894 rr.)*, ed. Leonid Zashkil'niak.

45 Hrushevs'kyi, 'Spomyny,' *Kyïv*, 1988, no. 12: 124.

46 On his uncle's request not to befriend students 'noticed' by the authorities, see *Shchodennyk*, 36 (23 January 1889).

47 Hrushevsky discussed the whole episode and its consequences in his article 'Iak ia buv kolys' beletrystom.' See p. 15.

48 Hrushevs'kyi, 'Spomyny,' *Kyïv*, 1988, no. 9: 120. For a postmodern analysis of Hrushevsky's psychological problems (addressed in his diaries as 'neurasthenia') as a cultural construct of the period, see Vashchenko, *Nevrasteniia*, 19–123.

49 Especially active in 'recruiting' Hrushevsky were his fellow students Luka Skachkovsky and Antin Syniavsky. In December 1888, Hrushevsky noted in his diary: 'On the evening of the eighth [of December], I went out with the boys. L[uka?] reproached me with hiding, saying that 'It cannot be done without sacrifices'; that he had heard about me from O[leksander] Ia[kovych Konysky]. I began to respond about psychological reasons, of course, but that went by without effect, but I was still stung by those reproaches' (*Shchodennyk*, 34 [10 December 1888]). The pressure on Hrushevsky continued, and in January 1889 he recorded in his diary: 'Syn[iavsky] seemed to know and picked up my track: about civic activity and duty' (ibid., 36 [21 January 1889]). Eventually Hrushevsky found that socializing with 'the boys' helped him deal with his mental problems. In September 1890, he wrote in his diary: 'I note that company dispels my melancholy; from that point of view it is a good thing for me, lest that melancholy drive me to distraction' (ibid., 58 [3 September 1890]).

On Hrushevsky's role in the activities of the 'seminarian community,' see Lotots'kyi, *Storinky mynuloho*, 1: 181, 225. On Syniavsky, see Zaruba, *Syniavs'kyi A.S. (Narys zhyttia i tvorchosti)*.

50 Hrushevs'kyi, *Shchodennyk*, 34 (12 December 1888). Still, Hrushevsky was an ambitious young scholar who wanted recognition, and the road to success led through the Russian language – a circumstance that caused him considerable agony. On 8 March 1891, Hrushevsky made the following observation in his diary: 'It is bad, as I note, that glory, simple glory attracts me very greatly; I desperately want to have many works that would be known to all, and therefore written in Russian,' ibid., 97 [8 March 1891]).

51 Zashkil'niak, 'M.S. Hrushevs'kyi u Kyïvs'komu universyteti (1886–1894 rr.),' 227–8.
52 Hrushevs'kyi [Khlopets'], 'Nova rozprava pro ukraïns'ku shliakhtu.' Cf. Zashkil'niak, 'M.S. Hrushevs'kyi u Kyïvs'komu universyteti,' 243–4. These ideas were further developed by Hrushevsky in his essay 'Khmel'nyts'kyi i Khmel'nychchyna. Istorychnyi eskiz.'
53 Hrushevs'kyi, *Shchodennyk*, 149 (18 January 1892).
54 Ibid., 159 (29 March 1892). Hrushevsky's Ukrainian patriotism apparently led to a disagreement with Nikolai Ogloblin. Hrushevsky seems to have been less open with other Russian historians concerning his Ukrainophile views. Ibid., 151 (10 February 1892) and 155 (25 February 1892).
   In his diary entry for 11 March 1892, Hrushevsky wrote about a lunch to which he invited ten Moscow historians: 'We drank to the Kyiv school in general and to Antonovych's school, and to me, who had produced a complete picture of the Kyivan Land for the first time' (ibid., 158).
55 For his final university exams, Hrushevsky read works by Nikolai Karamzin, Sergei Soloviev, Boris Chicherin, Ivan Zabelin, Nikolai Kareev, Vasilii Kliuchevsky, Dmitrii Ilovaisky, and Sergei Platonov. He was well acquainted with Polish historiography: aside from authors whose writings he knew because of his work on the history of Ukraine, he read general studies by Michał Bobrzyński, August Bielowski, and Oswald Balzer. Among Western historians, he read works by Alexis de Tocqueville, Thomas Carlyle, John Draper, and Ludwig Geisser. For references to the works of these and other authors in Hrushevsky's diary, see the index to Hrushevs'kyi, *Shchodennyk*.
56 Hrushevs'kyi, *Shchodennyk*, 88 (22 January 1891).
57 See Hrushevsky's note on a discussion of the role of the individual in history with Martyrii Halyn (ibid., 165 [30 April 1892]).
58 Ibid., 214 (27 June 1893).
59 Ibid., 50 (24 July 1889).
60 On Hrushevsky's reading, see ibid., pp. 76, 152, 175–7, 182, 184, 186, 187, 218. For the impact of European scholarship on Hrushevsky's interpretation of history, see Zashkil'niak, 'Istoriohrafichna tvorchist' Mykhaila Hrushevs'koho na tli ievropeis'koï istorychnoï dumky kintsia XIX – pochatku XX stolittia.'
61 Omeljan Pritsak made an attempt to reconstruct Hrushevsky's reading during his student years on the basis of the known reading lists of works by Russian historians of the period. He suggested that Hrushevsky was well read in contemporary European sociological literature, including works of Auguste Comte and Emile Durkheim, which later became a

major inspiration for his historical research and contributed to his self-designation as a 'historian-sociologist' (see Pritsak, 'Istoriosofiia Mykhaila Hrushevs'koho'). Hrushevsky's diary does not indicate an acquaintance with the works of those classics of positivist sociology during his years at Kyiv University, but his reading of Buckle, Malthus, and Tocqueville shows that he was indeed acquainted with positivist literature.

62 On Polish positivism, see Walicki, *Poland between East and West*, 28–35. Hrushevsky believed that Antonovych emulated the French positivists of the 1860s–1880s. See Hrushevs'kyi, 'Z sotsiial'no-natsional'nykh kontseptsii Antonovycha.'

63 For Hrushevsky's encounters with Luchytsky, a member of the Kyiv Hromada, see Hrushevs'kyi, *Shchodennyk*, 61, 63, 65, 90ff.

64 Hrushevsky and Kareev maintained friendly relations for a long time, exchanging letters and publications. Kareev also helped Hrushevsky secure the publication of his works in the Russian Empire. See Kareev's letters to Hrushevsky for the period 1900–12 in TsDIAK, fond 1235, op. 1, no. 518.

65 On Hrushevsky's encounters with Kareev and Kovalevsky during his stay in St Petersburg in the spring and summer of 1906, see his diaries, 'Shchodennyky M.S. Hrushevs'koho (1904–1910 rr.),' 16–17. On the positivism of Kareev and Kovalevsky, see Walicki, *History of Russian Thought*, 367–70. On the contributions of Luchytsky, Kareev, and Kovalevsky to historiography, see Sergei Pogodin, *'Russkaia shkola' istorikov.*

66 Pritsak, 'Istoriosofiia Mykhaila Hrushevs'koho,' xliv–lx; Vytanovych, 'Uvahy do metodolohiï i istoriosofiï M. Hrushevs'koho,' 48–51; Zashkil'niak, 'Istoriohrafichna tvorchist',' 40–2. Both Pritsak and Zashkilniak draw a strict distinction between positivism and Hrushevsky's sociological approach to history. On the development of social history in Ukraine, see Stel'makh, 'Sotsial'na istoriia v Ukraïni.' On Kovalevsky's historical views, see Natalia Shevchenko, 'Sotsial'no-ekonomichni aspekty anhliis'koï istoriï XVII st. u tvorchosti Maksyma Kovalevs'koho.'

67 On Hrushevsky's attempts to establish contacts with Ukrainian circles in Kyiv during his visit to the city in the summer of 1885, see his memoirs (Hrushevs'kyi, 'Spomyny,' *Kyïv*, 1988, no. 12: 134). On his impressions from reading Antonovych's articles in *Kievskaia starina*, see ibid., 120.

68 Grushevskii, 'Iuzhnorusskie gospodarskie zamki v polovine XVI veka. Istoriko-statisticheskii ocherk' and *Ocherk istorii Kievskoi zemli ot smerti Iaroslava do kontsa XIV stoletiia.*

Judging by Hrushevsky's autobiography ('Avtobiohrafiia, 1906 r.,' 199), he was dissatisfied with the level of education offered at Kyiv University and grew quite critical of his professors, including Volodymyr Antonovych. This assessment aroused protests from Hrushevsky's older colleague Dmytro Bahalii. Like Hrushevsky, Bahalii studied with Volodymyr Antonovych, and his opinion of the professors at the university and the courses they offered was much higher than Hrushevsky's. See Bahalii, 'Akad. M.S. Hrushevs'kyi i ioho mistse v ukraïns'kii istoriohrafiï (Istorychno-krytychnyi narys),' 165–7. One explanation for this difference of opinion is that Bahalii graduated from Kyiv University prior to the reform of higher education carried out in the Russian Empire in 1884. The reform curtailed university autonomy, modified curricula, and increased government control over the universities in general. Both Hrushevsky and Bahalii wrote about the negative impact of the reform in their autobiographies (Hrushevs'kyi, 'Avtobiohrafiia, 1906 r.,' 199; Bahalii, 'Avtobiohrafiia,' 103–23).

69 Grushevskii, *Barskoe starostvo; Akty Barskogo starostva XV–XVII vv.* (Kyiv, 1893) [=*AIuZR*, pt. 8, vol. 1]; *Akty Barskogo starostva XVII–XVIII vv.* (Kyiv, 1894) [=*AIuZR*, pt. 8, vol. 2]. Concerning Hrushevsky's work on his master's thesis, see Krykun, 'Magisters'ka dysertatsiia Mykhaila Hrushevs'koho.'

70 Filevich, 'Obzor glavneishikh sochinenii i statei po zapadnorusskoi istorii za 1891 god.' Hrushevsky was clearly pleased with Filevich's review: see his *Shchodennyk*, 167 (14 May 1892).

71 See Miliukov's unsigned review in *Russkaia mysl'*. Cf. Zashkil'niak, 'M.S. Hrushevs'kyi u Kyïvs'komu universyteti,' 237–8. Hrushevsky was upset by the review, whose authorship was no secret to him. He noted in his diary on 4 April 1893: 'Dobrovolsky brought Miliukov's review (no. 3 of *Russkaia mysl'*), which is very unpleasant; if it were at all just, that would be very distressing; I do not know' (Hrushevs'kyi, *Shchodennyk*, p. 204).

72 The irony – and potential danger to Hrushevsky's academic career – lay in the fact that the main proponent of the Pogodin theory at the time, the Russian philologist Timofei Florinsky, was also a professor at Kyiv University and dean of the faculty of history and philology when Hrushevsky graduated from the university and entered its master's program. As a dean and influential professor in the department, Florinsky was responsible for the scheduling of Hrushevsky's exams and was in a position to influence their outcome. See his postcard to Hrushevsky scheduling his master's exam for 19 May 1892 (TsDIAK, fond 1235, op. 1, no. 303, pp. 2–3). Hrushevsky mentioned the receipt of that card in his diary (*Shchodennyk*, 160). Hrushevsky was worried about possible negative actions on the part of Florinsky (ibid., 56, 68, 192).

73 Golubovskii, *Istoriia Severskoi zemli do poloviny XIV veka.*

74 Molchanovskii, *Ocherk izvestii o Podol'skoi zemle do 1434 g.*

75 Bagalei, *Istoriia Severskoi zemli do poloviny XIV st.* Commenting on Hrushevsky's monograph about the Kyivan Land, Bahalii later wrote that his younger colleague 'had been the ornament, in his day,' of the Antonovych school. See Bahalii, 'Akad. M.S. Hrushevs'kyi,' 167.

76 Zashkil'niak, 'M.S. Hrushevs'kyi u Kyïvs'komu universyteti,' 230–1.

77 Hrushevs'kyi, *Shchodennyk*, 94 (22 February 1891).

78 Ibid., 169 (22 May 1892).

79 Vozniak, 'Ol. Konys'kyi i pershi tomy "Zapysok" (z dodatkom ioho lystiv do Oleksandra Dukareva),' 375. Cf. Zashkil'niak, 'M.S. Hrushevs'kyi u Kyïvs'komu universyteti,' 251–2.

80 Hrushevs'kyi, 'Avtobiohrafiia, 1906 r.,' 200. The agreement between the Polish ruling circles of Galicia and the Ukrainian (Ruthenian) populists (*narodovtsi*) to which Hrushevsky referred in his autobiography inaugurated the 'new era' announced by a populist deputy of the Galician diet, Iuliian Romanchuk, in November 1890. The results of the 'new era' included the establishment of the chair of Ukrainian history at Lviv University, annual government grants to the Shevchenko Scientific Society, fellowships for Ukrainian scholars, the founding of a bilingual teachers' college in Sambir, the separation of the Ukrainian gymnasium in Peremyshl from the Polish one, and the opening of four-year schools with Ukrainian as the language of instruction in Lviv, Stanyslaviv, and Ternopil. See Chornovol, *Pol's'ko-ukraïns'ka uhoda 1890–1894 rr.*

81 On the Ukrainian chairs at Lviv University and competition between the dominant Polish academic community and the Ukrainian professors and students, see Grushevskii, 'Iz pol'sko-ukrainskikh otnoshenii Galitsii,' 212–30.

82 For sources on Hrushevsky's relations with Barvinsky, see Kupchyns'kyi, 'Do vzaiemyn Oleksandra Barvins'koho z Mykhailom Hrushevs'kym (dokumenty i materialy).'

83 See the text of von Gautsch's report of 22 March 1892 to the emperor in Vynar, 'Avstriis'ki uriadovi dokumenty,' 223–36, esp. 227–30. In his autobiography, Hrushevsky cited von Gautsch's alleged statement that 'ruthenische Geschichte ist keine konkrete Wissenschaft' (Hrushevs'kyi, 'Avtobiohrafiia, 1906 r.,' 201).

84 Chornovol, *Pol's'ko-ukraïns'ka uhoda*, 134–6; Zashkil'niak, 'Mykhailo Hrushevs'kyi i Halychyna,' 152; Batenko, 'Do pytannia pro zasnuvannia kafedry istoriï Skhidnoï Ievropy.'

85 Hrushevs'kyi, 'Avtobiohrafiia, 1906 r.,' 200, and *Shchodennyk*, 94 (24 Febru-

ary 1891). Once Hrushevsky decided to accept the Lviv position, he apparently began to work on improving his spoken Ukrainian, since lectures at Lviv University were to be delivered in Ukrainian, while in Kyiv the Ukrainian language was completely banned from the public sphere. There was a rumour among Hrushevsky's aquaintances that he would lock himself in a room for entire days and 'with the persistence of a Demosthenes, almost with a pebble in his mouth, he exercised his tongue in the Ukrainian language.' See Tsarinnyi (Andrei Storozhenko), *Ukrainskoe dvizhenie*, 173.

Hrushevsky was not the first Ukrainian activist from Dnipro Ukraine who was prompted to speak Ukrainian because of his contacts with Galician Ukrainians. In 1899 Iakiv Shulhyn, a leader of the Kyiv Hromada, wrote to Hrushevsky and apologized for his written Ukrainian: 'Since my early years, although I was born in Kyiv, I have not spoken Ukrainian. I acquired a consciousness of my homeland at Kyiv University and first began to speak Ukrainian in Vienna when I found myself in a group of Sich members there.' See Shulhyn's letter of 17 (24) January 1899 to Hrushevsky from Ielysavethrad in TsDIAK, fond 1235, op. 1, no. 873, fols 262–4.

86 Zashkil'niak, 'Mykhailo Hrushevs'kyi i Halychyna,' 153.
87 See the text of Hrushevsky's nomination to the position of full professor at Lviv University, approved by the emperor, in Vynar, 'Avstriis'ki uriadovi dokumenty,' 231–3. Oleksander Barvinsky presented his side of the story in his *Zasnovannie katedry istoriï Ukraïny v L'vivs'komu universyteti* (repr. in Kupchyns'kyi, 'Do vzaiemyn,' 157–73); Barvins'kyi, 'Zi "spomyniv moho zhyttia."'
88 Vynar, 'Avstriis'ki uriadovi dokumenty,' 231–3.
89 Before his appointment to the chair, on Barvinsky's insistence, Hrushevsky signed a letter stating that if there were no objection from the Russian government, he would become an Austrian citizen. See Hrushevsky's letter of 22 June 1898 to the Lviv newspaper *Dilo* in 'Iak mene sprovadzhdeno do L'vova,' repr. in Kupchyns'kyi, 'Do vzaiemyn,' 149–54, here 150.
90 See Hrushevs'kyi, 'Vstupnyi vyklad z davn'oï istoriï Rusy, vyholoshenyi v L'vivs'kim universyteti 30 veresnia 1894 r.' The text of the lecture was published by the Lviv newspaper *Dilo* a few days after Hrushevsky's inauguration. For a reprint of the lecture, see *Mykhailo Hrushevs'kyi i Zakhidna Ukraïna*, 5–14.
91 Compare Anthony D. Smith's remarks on the rediscovery of the ethnic past by national intelligentsias and their views of the role of the popular masses in history in his *National Identity*, 128–9.

92 Saunders, 'Mykola Kostomarov (1817–1885) and the Creation of a Ukrainian Ethnic Identity.'

93 Kyian, 'Kafedral'ne "viruiu" Volodymyra Antonovycha. Z neopublikovanoï spadshchyny.'

94 Prymak, *Mykhailo Hrushevsky*, 31.

95 For an example of Hrushevsky addressing his students as 'comrades,' see his letters to Ivan Krypiakevych in Roman Kryp'iakevych, 'Mykhailo Hrushevs'kyi ta Ivan Kryp'iakevych,' 333–72. On the impression that Hrushevsky made on the young Galician students, see Myron Korduba's memoir of his first meeting with Hrushevsky, 'Pryïzd prof. Hrushevs'koho do L'vova.' Oleksander Lototsky wrote in his memoirs that despite being older than other members of the Orthodox seminarian 'community' and superior to them in terms of talent, erudition, etc., Hrushevsky behaved as a 'sincere comrade' and equal (Lotots'kyi, *Storinky mynuloho*, 1: 181). Hrushevsky was also often addressed as 'comrade' in private letters dating from 1893. See TsDIAK, fond 1235, op. 1, no. 873, fols 107–18.

96 Hrushevs'kyi, *Shchodennyk*, 69 (11 October 1890).

97 See Hrushevs'kyi, 'Ukraïns'ka partiia sotsiialistiv-revoliutsioneriv ta ïï zavdannia. Zamitky z pryvodu debat na konferentsiiakh zakordonnykh chleniv partiï,' 12.

98 Rasevych, 'Evoliutsiia pohliadiv Mykhaila Hrushevs'koho,' 160.

99 Hrushevs'kyi, 'Avtobiohrafiia, 1906 r.,' 202.

100 Hrushevs'kyi, 'Iak mene sprovadzheno do L'vova,' repr. in Kupchyns'kyi, 'Do vzaiemyn,' 149–54.

101 Hrushevs'kyi, 'Era finansovo-ekonomichna,' 71–4.

102 'Having, perhaps, lost hope of completely denationalizing the Ruthenian population, the Polish ruling party (also supported, inter alia, in those efforts by Polish society) is seeking, by means of well-thought-out measures that constitute an integral system, to weaken the Ruthenian element numerically and qualitatively; to maintain it insofar as possible in the condition of an ethnographic mass; not to allow national life to develop,' wrote Hrushevsky in his essay of 1907 on Polish-Ukrainian relations in Galicia ('Iz pol'sko-ukrainskikh otnoshenii Galitsii,' 210).

103 Brock, 'Polish Nationalism,' 340–4.

104 Rasevych, 'Evoliutsiia pohliadiv Mykhaila Hrushevs'koho,' 158–9. Hrushevsky sought to attract Ivan Franko to the Shevchenko Society, which was headed by Barvinsky and did its best to keep such people out of its ranks. In February 1895 Hrushevsky warned Franko to be careful not to allow the Poles to exploit him against the conservative section of Ukrainian society. Under different circumstances in 1897, he welcomed

Franko's public attack on both the Ukrainian conservatives and the Polish political elite (see Hrushevsky's letter of 11 [23] February 1895 to Franko in *Lystuvannia Mykhaila Hrushevs'koho*, 77–8). In December 1898, Hrushevsky wrote to Franko that he had experienced considerable vexation in fighting the image of the Shevchenko Society as a 'new era' organization (see 'Lysty M. Hrushevs'koho do I. Franka,' 249).

105 On the revolt against 'organic work' in the Polish national movement, see Walicki, *Poland between East and West*, 43–4. On the founding of Ukrainian political parties in Galicia and Eastern Ukraine, see Rudnytsky, 'Trends in Ukrainian Political Thought,' 97–8, and 'Intellectual Origins of Modern Ukraine,' 134–5.

106 Hrushevs'kyi, 'Avtobiohrafiia, 1906 r.,' 202–3; Prymak, *Mykhailo Hrushevsky*, 54–8. For the formulation of the idea of Ukrainian independence by the Galician 'young radicals,' see Hrytsak, *Narys istoriï Ukraïny*, 94–5. For Franko's attitude to the slogan of an independent Ukraine, see his 'Ukraina irredenta.'

107 Hrushevs'kyi, 'Avtobiohrafiia, 1906 r.,' 207–13.

108 'Relations with Polish university colleagues, who wanted to have in me a submissive satellite of Polish domination, soon deteriorated completely and generated considerable unpleasantness. I did not lose courage or give up in the face of those difficulties,' wrote Hrushevsky ('Avtobiohrafiia, 1906 r.,' 202).

109 Hrushevs'kyi, 'Velyke dilo.'

110 Vynar, *Mykhailo Hrushevs'kyi i Naukove tovarystvo im. Tarasa Shevchenka, 1892–1930*, 56–8.

111 Hrushevs'kyi, 'Hromads'kyi rukh na Vkraïni-Rusy v XIII vitsi.'

112 Vynar, *Mykhailo Hrushevs'kyi i Naukove tovarystvo im. Tarasa Shevchenka*, 11–17, 29–33; Prymak, *Mykhailo Hrushevsky*, 41–43.

113 Hrushevs'kyi, 'Avtobiohrafiia, 1906 r.,' 202–4.

114 For a detailed discussion of the accomplishments of the Shevchenko Society, see Vynar, *Mykhailo Hrushevs'kyi i Naukove tovarystvo im. Tarasa Shevchenka*.

115 Grushevskii, 'Vopros ob ukrainskikh kafedrakh i nuzhdy ukrainskoi nauki,' 177, and 'Iz pol'sko-ukrainskikh otnoshenii Galitsii,' 222. Cf. Prymak, *Mykhailo Hrushevsky*, 59.

116 Rasevych, 'Evoliutsiia pohliadiv Mykhaila Hrushevs'koho,' 160–1.

117 Prymak, *Mykhailo Hrushevsky*, 59–60; Kachmar and Maryskevych, 'M. Hrushevs'kyi.'

118 For Hrushevsky's discussion of the issue of a Ukrainian university, see his 'Iz pol'sko-ukrainskikh otnoshenii Galitsii,' 224–30.

The crisis of 1901 brought no immediate results, and Ukrainian protests continued throughout the first decade of the twentieth century, until in 1910 one of the student meetings was attacked by the authorities. The attack led to the death of one Ukrainian student and the wounding of another. Subsequently, seventy Ukrainian students were arrested and tried for having participated in the altercation. The Ukrainians were outraged, their political lobby intensified its pressure on the authorities, and finally, in late 1912, after the obstruction of parliamentary proceedings by the Ukrainian deputies, the emperor was obliged to issue a decree announcing the opening of a Ukrainian university in Lviv on 1 September 1916. The outbreak of the First World War prevented the realization of that plan. See Kachmar and Maryskevych, 'M. Hrushevs'kyi'; Rudnytsky, 'Polish-Ukrainian Relations,' 64.

119 On Polish attempts to turn Galicia into a 'Polish Piedmont,' see Brock, 'Polish Nationalism,' 328–30.
120 Hrushevs'kyi, 'Avtobiohrafiia, 1906 r.,' 207.
121 Ibid. For Hrushevsky's description of the episode, see his 'Ukrainskii vopros,' 30. Cf. also his introduction to the published papers of the Galician would-be participants in the congress in ZNTSh 31–2 (1899).
122 Prymak, Mykhailo Hrushevsky, 25.
123 Commenting on the political atmosphere of the turn of the twentieth century, Hrushevsky wrote in his autobiography: 'At the same time, for their part, the local Russophile and Russian Slavophile "activists" à la Florinsky and Co. smeared me as the leader of Ukrainian separatism, indicating, for example, my signature under the manifesto of the re-formed populist movement, which put forward the political independence of Ukraine as the ultimate goal of its national program, and so on' ('Avtobiohrafiia, 1906 r.,' 203).
124 Kryp'iakevych, Mykhailo Hrushevs'kyi. Zhyttia i diial'nist', 467.
125 Vynar, Mykhailo Hrushevs'kyi i Naukove tovarystvo im. Tarasa Shevchenka, 35. Opposition to the participation of Galician scholars continued at subsequent archaeological congresses. As Hrushevsky's Russian colleague Vasilii Storozhev informed him in February 1906, the leaders of the organizing committee of the Fourteenth Congress (which took place in Chernihiv in 1908), Dmitrii Ilovaisky and Dmitrii Samokvasov, rejected a proposal of the Chernihiv delegates to schedule a special panel called 'Antiquities of Ukraine-Rus'.' They also turned down a proposal to open an office of the organizing committee in Lviv under the auspices of the Shevchenko Scientific Society. See Storozhev's letter of 10 February 1906 to Hrushevsky in TsDIAK, fond 1235, op. 1, no. 775, fols 6–7.

126 Prymak, *Mykhailo Hrushevsky*, 64–6. Hrushevsky learned about the cancellation of the congress from Franko in March 1904 during a prolonged bout of migraine and noted in his diary: 'Well, it's better that way, although I had already made various arrangements for this trip to St Petersburg.' See 'Shchodennyky M.S. Hrushevs'koho (1904–1910 rr.),' 13 (14 March 1904).

127 See Hrushevs'kyi, 'Zvychaina skhema "russkoï" istoriï i sprava ratsional'noho ukladu istoriï skhidnoho slov'ianstva.' The article, dated September 1903, was written after Hrushevsky completed work on the text of a Russian-language survey of Ukrainian history (Hrushevs'kyi, 'Avtobiohrafiia, 1906 r.,' 209).

Other Ukrainian-language papers that Hrushevsky submitted to the organizing committee of the Slavic congress included 'Spirni pytannia starorus'koï etnohrafiï' and 'Etnohrafichni katehoriï i kul'turnoarkheolohichni typy v suchasnykh studiiakh Skhidnoï Evropy.' Separate offprints of all three articles appeared in St Petersburg in the same year. For English translations of the latter works, see Chirovsky, *On the Historical Beginnings of Eastern Slavic Europe*, 13–38 and 39–52.

128 Much later, in 1928, Hrushevsky was one of those who sent congratulations to Polivka on his seventieth birthday on behalf of a number of institutions of the Ukrainian Academy of Sciences. For the text of Hrushevsky's address, see M. Zh., 'Iuvilei Iuryia Polivky.'

129 See Pypin's letter of 18 September 1904 to Hrushevsky in TsDIAK, fond 1235, op. 1, no. 270, fols 71–3.

130 Draft of Hrushevsky's letter of 30 October 1904 to Pypin in TsDIAK, fond 1235, op. 1, no. 275, fols 158–158v, 162–164v, here fol. 162.

131 For a brief biography of Pypin, see *Slavianovedenie v dorevoliutsionnoi Rossii*, 286–9.

132 Concerning Sviatopolk-Mirsky's views on the national question during his period of service as governor-general of Vilnius in 1902–4, see Weeks, *Nation and State*, 50–5.

133 See the draft of the letter in TsDIAK (Kyiv), fond 1235, op. 1, no. 275, fols 159–161v.

134 Hrushevs'kyi, 'Avtobiohrafiia, 1906 r.,' 211.

135 Ibid., 209.

136 Ibid.

137 See Grushevskii, *Ocherk istorii ukrainskogo naroda*. Cf. his *Iliustrovana istoriia Ukraïny, z dodatkom novoho periodu istoriï Ukraïny za roky vid 1914 do 1919*. This edition, which is cited throughout the present work, covered Ukrainian history up to 1907 and contained a special appendix written by

Hrushevsky, 'The New Period of the History of Ukraine,' dealing with events from 1914 to 1918.

138 See Hrushevsky's autobiographies in *Velykyi ukraïnets'*, 226, 235; Prymak, *Mykhailo Hrushevsky*, 70–9.

139 One reader, referring to Hrushevsky's article 'The Constitutional Question and the Ukrainian Movement in Russia' in *Literaturno-naukovyi visnyk* (1905), wrote: 'You do well, Esteemed Professor, to write ... and blame Ukrainians for keeping silent, but why do you yourself write so little and infrequently in Russian journals, although your articles, as those of a professor, would be published more readily than those of a Ukrainian writer?' (TsDIAK, fond 1235, op. 1, no. 874, fol. 20).

140 Hrushevs'kyi, 'Avtobiohrafiia, 1906 r.,' 203.

141 See Hrushevs'kyi, 'Frazy i fakty.' For a Russian translation, see 'Frazy i fakty,' *Kievskaia starina* (May 1905): 161–7. Hrushevsky exchanged letters with journalists working for the newspaper, who asked him to find them a correspondent in Lviv. See a letter dated 24 April 1905 from a staff member to Hrushevsky in TsDIAK, fond 1235, op. 1, no. 874, fols 10–13.

142 See the discussion of the issue in Hrushevs'kyi, 'Neveroiatno.'

143 See Hrushevs'kyi, 'Memorial Peterburs'koï Akademiï v spravi svobody ukraïns'koï movy v Rosiï.' Cf. his 'Na zlobu dnia' and 'Neveroiatno,' 108–9. For the text of the memorandum, see *Ob otmene stesnenii malorusskogo pechatnogo slova*. For a Ukrainian translation, see *Peterburs'ka Akademiia Nauk v spravi znesennia zaborony ukraïns'koho slova* (Lviv, 1905).

144 On the silent lifting of the ban, see Hrushevs'kyi, 'Hanebnii pamiaty.'

145 What awaited Hrushevsky in that regard was a severe disappointment. The prohibition on the import of Ukrainian books from Galicia was replaced by the imposition of a high tax on Russian publications imported from abroad. As Hrushevsky noted with irony in a note to the reprint of his article 'The Ukrainian Piedmont' in *Osvobozhdenie Rossii i ukrainskii vopros*, Ukrainian publications were not considered 'Russian' when the prohibition was in place, but once it was gone, they began to be treated as 'Russian' for customs purposes. See Grushevskii, 'Ukrainskii P'emont,' in *Osvobozhdenie Rossii i ukrainskii vopros*, 119–20.

146 Ibid., 116. Cf. Brock, 'Polish Nationalism,' 330.

147 Prymak, *Mykhailo Hrushevsky*, 76–7. On Ukrainian representation in the First Duma, see Andriewsky, 'The Politics of National Identity,' 163–99. On Hrushevsky's stay in St Petersburg, see his diaries, 'Shchodennyky M.S. Hrushevs'koho (1904–1910 rr.),' 16. While in St Petersburg, Hrushevsky met with the Ukrainian activists Oleksander Lototsky, Maksym Slavinsky, and Dmytro Doroshenko, his colleague Dmytro

Bahalii, and the Russian scholars Venedikt Miakotin, Aleksei Shakhmatov, Nikolai Kareev, and Ivan Grevs.

   Hrushevsky worked on his articles for *Ukrainskii vestnik* early in the morning. See, for example, his diary entry for 21 May 1906, where he recorded that he had written an article titled 'Question of the Day' and begun another article for the series 'Z bizhuchoï khvyli' (At the Present Moment. Cf. 'Shchodennyky [1904–1910],' p. 16). The first article was written for *Ukrainskii vestnik* in St Petersburg and the second for *Literaturno-naukovyi visnyk* in Lviv.

148 See Grushevskii, 'Ukrainskii P'emont.'
149 Grushevskii, 'Vstrevozhennyi muraveinik.'
150 See Grushevskii, 'Ukrainskii vopros' and 'Dvizhenie politicheskoi i obshchestvennoi ukrainskoi mysli v XIX stoletii.'
151 See Grushevskii, *Osvobozhdenie Rossii i ukrainskii vopros.*
152 Ibid., iii.
153 Mikhnovs'kyi, 'Samostiina Ukraïna.'
154 For Hrushevsky's reaction to Stolypin's circular of 1910, see his 'Na ukraïns'ki temy: Hymn vdiachnosty.' Cf. Prymak, *Mykhailo Hrushevsky*, 84–5.
155 On the policies of the Polish National Democrats in Russia, see Brock, 'Polish Nationalism,' 341–6; Zimand, *Narodowa Demokracja 1893–1939*.
156 See Grushevskii, 'Konets getto!' 146.
157 See ibid., 148. From a very early point in his political career, Hrushevsky was sympathetic to the plight of Ukrainian Jewry. Having been brought up as a devout Orthodox Christian in the atmosphere of official anti-Semitism that prevailed in the postreform Russian Empire, the young Hrushevsky had to rid himself of official attitudes toward Jews. That process was reflected in his student diary. Describing a visit to the home of a Ukrainian Jew on his way to the family estate in Sestrynivka, Hrushevsky wrote: 'I was also struck by the following thought: I heard a Jewess speaking with her daughter, and then I heard a child puffing and champing its little lips. That surprised me: it was as if I expected that a somnolent child, and so on, would behave somewhat differently from a Christian child, or something.' See Hrushevs'kyi, *Shchodennyk*, 74 (2 November 1890).
158 See Grushevskii, 'Vopros dnia (agrarnye perspektivy)' and 'Natsional'nye momenty v agrarnom voprose.'
159 On Hrushevsky's political activities in Galicia from 1905 to 1912, see Prymak, *Mykhailo Hrushevsky*, 91–103. In 1907 relations between Ukrainians and Poles deteriorated to such an extent that in the autumn of that

year Hrushevsky delivered some of his lectures with a gun in his pocket. See 'Shchodennyky M.S. Hrushevs'koho (1904–1910 rr.),' 21 (27 October 1907).

For Hrushevsky's attacks on the Russophiles, see his 'Het' z rutenstvom!' and 'Na ukraïns'ki temy: "Konets' rutenstva!"' For Hrushevsky's critique of Neoslavism, see his 'Na ukraïns'ki temy: Ukraïnstvo i vseslov'ianstvo' and 'Na ukraïns'ki temy: Na novyi rik.'

160 Kryp'iakevych, 'Spohady (Avtobiohrafiia),' 108.

161 In his autobiography, Hrushevsky explained the revolt against him in the Shevchenko Society as an intrigue masterminded by the National Democrats, who were seeking an alliance with the Poles. See Hrushevs'kyi, 'Avtobiohrafiia, 1914–1919,' 214; cf. his 'Avtobiohrafiia, 1926 r.,' 237. For a discussion of the conflict in the Shevchenko Society that cost Hrushevsky his position, see Vynar, *Mykhailo Hrushevs'kyi i Naukove tovarystvo im. Tarasa Shevchenka*, 59–69; Prymak, *Mykhailo Hrushevsky*, 104–6; Hrytsak, 'Konflikt 1913 roku v NTSh: prychyny i prychynky'; Horyn', 'Ostannii konflikt M. Hrushevs'koho v NTSh.'

162 See Hrushevs'kyi, 'Avtobiohrafiia, 1926 r.,' 235; Chykalenko, *Spohady (1861–1907)*, 481–2. On Hrushevsky's political activity at the time, see Prymak, *Mykhailo Hrushevsky*, 70–124.

163 'Shchodennyky M.S. Hrushevs'koho (1904–1910 rr.),' 22–4.

164 For the autobiography of V.I. Savva, see *Istoriko-filologicheskii fakul'tet Khar'kovskogo universiteta za pervye sto let ego sushchestvovaniia (1805–1905)*, 344–5.

165 Vasylenko's article was later included in a collection of articles, all of which, except Vasylenko's, attacked Hrushevsky in connection with his application for the position at Kyiv University. See *K voprosu o kandidature na kafedru russkoi istorii v universitete sv. Vladimira professora L'vovskogo universiteta Mikhaila Grushevskogo*. For Mykola Vasylenko's views on Hrushevsky and his scholarly achievements, see also Vasylenko's later article, 'Prof. M.S. Grushevskii kak istorik.'

166 On Hrushevsky's relations with Iefremov, which were long-lasting and became openly confrontational in the 1920s, see Hyrych, 'M. Hrushevs'kyi i S. Iefremov na tli suspil'no-politychnoho zhyttia kintsia XIX – 20-kh rokiv XX stolittia,' *Ukraïns'kyi istoryk* 33 (1996): 142–87.

167 For the struggle attendant on the transfer of Hrushevsky's activities from Lviv to Kyiv, see 'Shchodennyky M.S. Hrushevs'koho (1904–1910 rr.),' 17–21; Chykalenko, *Spohady*, 469–86; Prymak, *Mykhailo Hrushevsky*, 79–81. Characteristic of Dnipro Ukrainian attitudes to the Galician variant of Ukrainian was the stand taken by one of the most distinguished mem-

bers of the Kyiv Hromada, Iakiv Shulhyn. As he wrote to Hrushevsky in 1899, he first found himself obliged to speak Ukrainian among the Galicians in Vienna (cf. n. 86 above) but objected to Galician translations from the Russian because of their stylistic 'pecularities.' 'It would still be better,' wrote Shulhyn, 'for us to translate from the Russian than for your Galicians to do so, for their language often makes our eyes roll.' Shulhyn was prepared to make an exception only for the style of Ivan Franko. See Shulhyn's letter of 17 (24) January 1899 to Hrushevsky from Ielysaveth-rad in TsDIAK, fond 1235, op. 1, no. 873, fols 262–4.

168 Prymak, *Mykhailo Hrushevsky*, 87.
169 On Hrushevsky's cooperation with the Society of Ukrainian Progressives and the position he took during negotiations between the members of that organization and Pavel Miliukov in 1914, see Prymak, *Mykhailo Hrushevsky*, 107–14. In the spring of 1914, Hrushevsky expressed approval of Miliukov's extremely important speech on the Ukrainian question given in the Russian Duma on 19 February 1914. There the leader of the Russian Constitutional Democrats defended Hrushevsky and his colleagues against accusations of 'Mazepism' and attacked the Austro-philism of the Ukrainian radical Dmytro Dontsov, as well as the Russian nationalism of Anatolii Savenko and other Kyivan proponents of all-Russian unity. Welcoming the speech in a letter to Miliukov, Hrushevsky still maintained that the latter had unduly emphasized the position taken by Dontsov and his supporters, who advocated the separation of Ukraine from Russia and the establishment of Ukrainian autonomy in the Habsburg Monarchy. Hrushevsky also disagreed with Miliukov's position on federalism. See the draft of Hrushevsky's letter of 4 March 1914 to Miliukov in TsDIAK, fond 1235, op. 1, no. 270.
170 See Hrushevs'kyi, 'Na ukraïns'ki temy: Vidluchennia Kholmshchyny.' Cf. Prymak, *Mykhailo Hrushevsky*, 106. The Kholm province was established in September 1913. On the controversy attending this event, see Weeks, *Nation and State*, 173–92.
171 See Hrushevs'kyi, 'Na ukraïns'ki temy: Po koshmari.' Prymak, *Mykhailo Hrushevsky*, 91.
172 See Hrushevs'kyi, *Pro stari chasy na Ukraïni, Pro bat'ka kozats'koho Bohdana Khmel'nyts'koho*, and *Iliustrovana istoriia Ukraïny* (Kyiv, 1911, 1912, 1913, 1915).
173 See Saviovsky's letter of 15 May 1910 to Hrushevsky in TsDIAK, fond 1235, op. 1, no. 303, fols 155–7.
174 For a discussion of responses to Hrushevsky's historical writings from workers and members of the intelligentsia, see chapter 3 of the present work.

175 See Shelest's letter of 1909 to Hrushevsky in TsDIAK, fond 1235, op. 1, no. 303, fol. 128.

176 For a brief description of Hrushevsky's peregrinations during the First World War, see his autobiographies: 'Avtobiohrafiia, 1914–19 rr.', 214–16, and 'Avtobiohrafiia, 1926 r.,' 238.

177 Prymak, *Mykhailo Hrushevsky*, 117; Vynar, 'Chomu Mykhailo Hrushevs'kyi povernuvsia v Ukraïnu v 1914 rotsi.' A member of the Union for the Liberation of Ukraine, Volodymyr Doroshenko, later recalled: 'The Polish National Democrats hated Hrushevsky, considering him the main promoter of the Ukrainian national movement in Galicia. And given that the administration of Galicia was in Polish hands, any district head or chief of a local police station could destroy the "father of the haidamakas" under any pretext as a Russophile and enemy of Austria, using martial law as a cover' (Volodymyr Doroshenko, 'Pershyi prezydent vidnovlenoï ukraïns'koï derzhavy,' *Ovyd*, 1957, no. 2: 28).

178 The accusations were based at least partly on a denunciation made by Stepan Tomashivsky, one of Hrushevsky's former students and his adversary in the Shevchenko Society before the war. See Vynar, 'Chomu Mykhailo Hrushevs'kyi povernuvsia v Ukraïnu,' 191. On relations between Hrushevsky and Tomashivsky, see Bortniak, 'Stepan Tomashivs'kyi: do vidnosyn z Mykhailom Hrushevs'kym.'

The case was later dismissed by an Austrian military court, but the authorities did not warm to Hrushevsky and later suspected his influence behind the anti-Austrian campaign organized in the Ukrainian press in the United States. See the texts of documents of the Vienna Ministry of Internal Affairs dating from the first months of 1917 in Marko Antonovych, 'Sprava Hrushevs'koho.' Documents from that article are reprinted in *Velykyi ukraïnets'*, 367–79, here 376–8.

179 For excerpts from the police correspondence related to Hrushevsky's arrest and exile, see 'Sprava pro vysylku prof. M. Hrushevs'koho.'

180 Prymak, *Mykhailo Hrushevsky*, 117–20. See letters from Shakhmatov and Platonov to the president of the Russian Academy of Sciences, Grand Prince Konstantin Romanov (26 December 1914), in '"Ia nikogda ne vystupal protiv Rossii." M.S. Grushevskii i russkie uchenye, 1914–1916 gg.' See also Robinson, 'M.S. Hruševs'kyj, la "Questione ucraina" e l'élite accademica russa'; 'Ssylka M.S. Grushevskogo.'

181 See Shchegolev, *Ukrainskoe dvizhenie kak sovremennyi ètap iuzhno-russkogo separatizma*, 131.

182 Prior to the war, Hrushevsky had in fact protested against applying the term 'Mazepists' to the members of the Ukrainian movement. He claimed that the tsarist government had turned the Cossack hetman Ivan Mazepa

into a symbol of separatism when in fact his aspirations had not differed greatly from those of Bohdan Khmelnytsky, the major antipode of Mazepa in official Russian propaganda of the first decade of the twentieth century (see Hrushevs'kyi, 'Na ukraïns'ki temy. 'Mazepynstvo' i 'Bohdanivstvo'). In his *Iliustrovana istoriia Ukraïny* (1912, pp. 367–83), Hrushevsky eschewed any idealization of Mazepa and his motives in switching allegiance to Charles XII but treated the hetman with respect, noted his support of Ukrainian culture, and explained his revolt against the tsar as a consequence of increasing Russian interference in Ukrainian affairs and the demands of the Cossack elite.

183 See the text of the police report in Vynar, 'Chomu Mykhailo Hrushevs'kyi povernuvsia v Ukraïnu,' 191–3. On Russian policy in occupied Galicia, see Bakhturina, *Politika Rossiiskoi imperii v vostochnoi Galitsii v gody pervoi mirovoi voiny*. On the treatment of the Ukrainian question by the Special Political Department of the Russian Ministry of Foreign Affairs in 1916–17, see Miller, 'A Testament of the All-Russian Idea.'

184 Kulakovsky's article in fact echoed the accusations leveled against Hrushevsky by the Russian censor Shchegolev in his book *Ukrainskoe dvizhenie kak sovremennyi ètap iuzhno-russkogo separatisma*. The article was forwarded to Hrushevsky, who was then residing in Kazan, by Serhii Iefremov and his associates. Initially Hrushevsky was not sure whether a reply was warranted: as he noted to Iefremov, he usually did not respond to such 'voices in hiding' (*golosa iz ovraga*). Eventually he decided to write a response: see Hrushevsky's letters of 6 October (23 September) and 25 (12) October 1915 in *Lystuvannia Mykhaila Hrushevs'koho*, nos. 231, 232, pp. 172–4, here p. 174. As mentioned earlier, during his student years at Kyiv University Hrushevsky had turned down Kulakovsky's offer to specialize in ancient history under his supervision.

185 Hrushevsky's response to Kulakovsky, titled 'Vetkhii prakh,' appeared in *Ukrainskaia zhizn'* and in *Rech'*. It was interpreted by the Polish newspaper *Kurjer Lwowski* as anti-Austrian and provided the Lviv University authorities with an excuse to investigate not only the circumstances of Hrushevsky's departure but also his alleged anti-Austrian activities. A special commission was appointed by the academic council of the university to look into the matter. Having acquired a copy of Hrushevsky's article, it reached the conclusion that there were no grounds to accuse him of anti-Austrian activities. Hrushevsky was called upon to explain his reasons for leaving the university – easier said than done, given wartime conditions. For correspondence between the academic council of Lviv University and the Austrian authorities, see Marko Antonovych, 'Sprava Hrushevs'koho.'

186 See Shakhmatov's letter of 11 March 1915 to Hrushevsky in Simbirsk in TsDIAK, fond 1235, op. 1, no. 228, fols 34–34v.

187 See Hrushevsky's letter of 26 July [1915] in TsDIAK, fond 1235, op. 1, no. 275, fols 118–19v.

188 See Prymak, *Mykhailo Hrushevsky*, 120–1.

189 Ibid., 118.

190 Hrushevs'kyi, 'Avtobiohrafiia, 1914–19 rr.,' 215.

191 See the reference to Studynsky's testimony in the report of the Lviv University academic council (10 April 1916) to the chancellery of the Galician viceroy (*Velykyi ukraïnets'*, 367–70). Studynsky claimed that Hrushevsky left for Kyiv upon learning of a decree to the effect that Russian citizens would forfeit their property in the Russian Empire unless they returned there within six weeks of the publication of the decree.

192 Hrushevs'kyi, 'Avtobiohrafiia, 1914–19 rr.,' 215.

193 In Italy, on his way from Vienna to Kyiv, Hrushevsky met a correspondent of the Russian newspaper *Russkie vedomosti*, with whom he discussed the future federalization of Russia. See Prymak, *Mykhailo Hrushevsky*, 117.

194 See Smal'-Stots'kyi, 'Pochatok vidnovy Ukraïns'koï Derzhavnosty,' 93.

195 For the decrees (universals) of the Central Rada, see Hrushevs'kyi, *Na porozi novoï Ukraïny*, 197–214. For the minutes of Central Rada proceedings, see *Ukraïns'ka Tsentral'na Rada*. For a general survey of the 1917 revolution in Ukraine, see the chapter 'Revolutions in the Russian Empire' in Magosci, *A History of Ukraine*, 468–89, and the chapter 'War and Revolution, 1917–20' in Subtelny, *Ukraine: A History*, 339–54. For a history of the Central Rada, see Verstiuk, *Ukraïns'ka Tsentral'na Rada*.

196 Hrushevs'kyi, 'Promova na zasidanni Tsentral'noï Rady z 17 hrudnia 1917,' 151.

197 In his memoirs, Hrushevsky recalled the moment when he got news of the outbreak of the revolution: 'I was sitting in the Rumiantsev Library writing an article on Kostomarov's federative theory and collecting material about the discussion that it occasioned in the press of the day when the librarian shared with me the sensational news that they were just "taking the Kremlin"' (Hrushevs'kyi, 'Spomyny,' *Kyïv*, 1989, no. 8: 123).

198 Ibid., 124–5.

199 See 'Slovo Mykhaila Hrushevs'koho na ukraïns'kii manifestatsiï v Kyievi 19 bereznia (1 kvitnia 1917 r.).'

200 Hrushevs'kyi, 'Velyka khvylia.' Hrushevsky repeated the argumentation presented in this article in his speech at a meeting of the Society of

Ukrainian Progressives on 25–6 March 1917. See 'Spomyny,' *Kyïv*, 1989, no. 9: 113.

201 Hrushevs'kyi, 'Povorotu nema.'

202 Ibid., 146.

203 Hrushevs'kyi, 'Spomyny,' *Kyïv*, 1989, no. 9: 140. In his memoirs, defending himself against accusations that in his political program he was always a minimalist, Hrushevsky claimed that during the first stages of the revolution he had in fact been a maximalist, citing as proof his articles 'The Great Moment' and 'There Is No Turning Back.' He maintained that the latter article repeated the argument presented in the former (see Hrushevs'kyi, 'Spomyny,' *Kyïv*, 1989, no. 8: 144–5). In fact, in the first article, written after the demonstration of 19 March 1917, Hrushevsky only warned against minimalist Ukrainian demands but never stated what those demands should actually be. For a discussion of the autonomist and independentist elements in Hrushevsky's political outlook, see Verstiuk, *Ukraïns'ka Tsentral'na Rada*, 112–16.

204 Hrushevs'kyi, 'Narodnostiam Ukraïny,' 136.

205 Ibid., 136.

206 Hrushevs'kyi, 'Spomyny,' *Kyïv*, 1989, no. 9: 116.

207 Ibid., no. 10: 140. The Jewish deputies of the Central Rada supported the announcement of full Ukrainian autonomy in the third universal of the Central Rada (November 1917) but not the proclamation of Ukrainian independence in the fourth universal of January 1918. On Jewish attitudes toward the Central Rada and the participation of Jewish parties in its work, see Abramson, *A Prayer for the Government*, 34–66.

208 Hrushevsky's stand on the issue of Ukrainian-Jewish relations clearly helped curb anti-Semitism in Ukraine. As Henry Abramson notes, 'Taken together, the appointment of Hrushevsky to the presidency of the Central Rada, and the prominence of the USDLP [Ukrainian Social Democratic Labour Party] with the support of the popular UPSR [Ukrainian Party of Socialist Revolutionaries] effectively silenced any antisemitic voices in the early months of the Ukrainian Revolution' (*Prayer for the Government*, 36).

In 1918, after the first pogroms took place in Ukraine under wartime conditions exacerbated by the collapse of state authority, Hrushevsky called upon the Ukrainian community to do everything in its power to oppose anti-Semitism, which, in his opinion, was triggered by vulgar nationalism on the one hand and Jewish participation in Bolshevik atrocities on the other. Hrushevsky explained that the Jews who had joined the Bolsheviks had nothing to do with the Jewish national movement and expressed his conviction that Ukrainians and Jews would achieve a future understanding. See Hrushevs'kyi, 'Misto,' 45–6.

209 Hrushevs'kyi, 'Chy Ukraïna til'ky dlia ukraïntsiv?' 139. In 1918, after the proclamation of Ukrainian independence and the first military confrontations between the Bolsheviks and the Central Rada, Hrushevsky still warned against any drastic measures directed against Russians in Ukraine. He believed that part of the Russian population would indeed return to Russia, while those who were deeply rooted in Ukrainian life would stay and join the Ukrainian majority. 'One must await that moment patiently,' wrote Hrushevsky, 'without causing unnecessary irritation, without inflaming relations by means of impetuous Ukrainization, proceeding judiciously and as gently as possible in implementing the measures that are indeed required by the principle of Ukrainian statehood, the status of the Ukrainian language as the official language, and so on' (Hrushevs'kyi, 'Misto,' 43).

210 Hrushevs'kyi, 'Spomyny,' Kyïv, 1989, no. 8: 145.

211 Ibid., 141.

212 See Hrushevs'kyi, 'Misto,' 46–7.

213 See Hrushevsky's articles and statements on the issue of the Kholm region, 'Za Kholmshchynu' and 'Promova na ratyfikatsiï myrnoho dohovoru.'

214 Hrushevs'kyi, 'Promova na zasidanni Tsentral'noï Rady z 17 hrudnia 1917,' 153.

215 Hrushevs'kyi, 'Spomyny,' Kyïv, 1989, no. 8: 128–30. Hrushevsky was not happy about his treatment by the older generation of Ukrainian activists in Kyiv. He wrote in his memoirs: 'The Central Rada was relegated to the young people, and, as things turned out, the "elders" looked upon me as a "nanny" whose responsibility it was to keep them in check, but if, despite expectations, bread should come out of that flour, then I was to summon the "elders" to the table at the right moment' (ibid., 132).

216 See Ievhen Chykalenko, Uryvok z moïkh spohadiv za 1917 r., 24, cited in Prymak, Mykhailo Hrushevsky, 146.

217 On the role of the peasantry and military in forging the policies of the Central Rada, see Verstiuk, Ukraïns'ka Tsentral'na Rada, 73, 134–6, 183, 225–9; Hryhorii Savchenko, 'Ahrarni aspekty sotsial'nykh vymoh ukraïntsiv rosiis'koï armiï (berezen'-lystopad 1917 roku)'; von Hagen, 'The Russian Imperial Army and the Ukrainian National Movement in 1917.'

218 Hrushevs'kyi, Iliustrovana istoriia Ukraïny.

219 Hrushevs'kyi, Pro stari chasy na Ukraïni.

220 Hrushevs'kyi, Pereiaslavs'ka umova Ukraïny z Moskvoiu 1654 roku.

221 See Hrushevs'kyi, Z politychnoho zhyttia staroï Ukraïny. The book is listed under 1917 in Hrushevsky's bibliography, which was published in Kyiv in 1929 and was apparently approved by the historian himself. See the

reprint of that bibliography in Vynar, *Mykhailo Hrushevs'kyi, 1866–1934. Bibliographic Sources*, 29.

222 See Hrushevs'kyi, *Khto taki ukraïntsi i choho vony khochut'* and *Zvidky pishlo ukraïnstvo i do choho vono ide*.

223 See Hrushevs'kyi, *Iakoï my khochemo avtonomiï i federatsiï*.

224 See Hrushevs'kyi, *Pro ukraïns'ku movu i ukraïns'ku shkolu*.

225 See Hrushevs'kyi, *Vil'na Ukraïna*.

226 Vynnychenko, *Shchodennyk*, 1: 288.

227 Hrushevs'kyi, 'Spomyny,' *Kyïv*, 1989, no. 8: 145.

228 For the text of the Fourth Universal of the Central Rada and Hrushevsky's role in its drafting and adoption, see Hrushevs'kyi, *Na porozi novoï Ukraïny*, app. 6; Vynar, 'Chetvertyi universal UTsRady: vprovadzhennia,' 218–21. See also Hrushevsky's articles in which he promoted the idea of Ukrainian independence: 'Velyke Rizdvo,' 'Velykyi obov'iazok,' and 'Ukraïns'ka samostiinist' i ïï istorychna neobkhidnist'.'

229 Hrushevs'kyi, 'Velykyi obov'iazok,' 61.

230 Hrushevs'kyi, 'Ukraïns'ka samostiinist' i ïï istorychna neobkhidnist',' 64.

231 See Hrushevs'kyi, 'Ochyshchennia ohnem.'

232 Hrushevs'kyi, 'Povorotu ne bude,' 75.

233 Hrushevs'kyi, 'Ochyshchennia ohnem,' 67.

234 Hrushevs'kyi, 'V ohni i buri,' 71.

235 See Hrushevs'kyi, 'Ochyshchennia ohnem,' 68, and 'Kinets' moskovs'koï oriientatsiï,' 10.

236 Hrushevs'kyi, 'Ukraïns'ka samostiinist' i ïï istorychna neobkhidnist',' 64.

237 Hrushevs'kyi, 'Ochyshchennia ohnem,' 66.

238 Hrushevsky wrote: 'And it seems to me that what I am undergoing so acutely at this moment is also being undergone by all of Ukraine. That Ukraine has also buried what was old in this fire, as in a mother's grave ...' Hrushevs'kyi, 'Na perelomi,' 6.

239 Hrushevs'kyi, 'Kinets' moskovs'koï oriientatsiï,' 10.

240 Ibid., 11.

241 Hrushevs'kyi, 'Novi perspektyvy,' 21–2.

242 Ibid., 22.

243 See Hrushevs'kyi, 'Nasha zakhidnia oriientatsiia,' 'Oriientatsiia Chornomors'ka,' and 'Novi perspektyvy.'

244 See Hrushevs'kyi, 'Kul'tura krasy i kul'tura zhyttia.'

245 On Hrushevsky's political activities in 1918–19, see Prymak, *Mykhailo Hrushevsky*, 152–95.

246 Hrushevs'kyi, 'Spomyny,' *Kyïv*, 1989, no. 8: 111.

Chapter 2: The Delimitation of the Past

1 J.A. Helfert, *Über Nationalgeschichte und den gegenwärtigen Stand ihrer Pflege in Österreich* (Prague, 1853), 1–2, quoted in Walter Leitsch, 'East Europeans Studying History in Vienna (1855–1918),' 140.

2 As Stephen Velychenko has recently pointed out, in its focus on Russia proper the Russian imperial narrative resembled the British historical narrative of the nineteenth century, which focused on England proper and excluded from its scope not only the British overseas colonies but also Scotland. See Velychenko, 'Rival Grand Narratives of National History.'

3 For a general survey of the treatment of Ukrainian history in early modern Russian historiography, see Velychenko, *National History as Cultural Process*, 79–88. For a more detailed discussion of the Muscovite claim to the secular and ecclesiastical heritage of Kyivan Rus', see Pelenski's essays, collected in his *Contest for the Legacy of Kievan Rus'*, esp. 1–130. For the emergence of interest in Kyivan history in Muscovy during the late fifteenth and early sixteenth centuries and its relation to Muscovite historiography, see Ostrowski, *Muscovy and the Mongols*, 168–76.

4 For a reprint of *Synopsis*, see *Sinopsis. Kiev, 1681. Facsimile mit einer Einleitung*; on its popularity in Russia, see Samarin, *Rasprostranenie i chitatel' pervykh pechatnykh knig po istorii Rossii (konets XVII–XVIII v.)*, 20–76. On early modern Ukrainian views of Russia, see Kohut, 'Origins of the Unity Paradigm,' 'A Dynastic or Ethno-Dynastic Tsardom?' and 'The Question of Russo-Ukrainian Unity and Ukrainian Distinctiveness in Early Modern Ukrainian Thought and Culture'; Sysyn, 'The Image of Russia and Russian-Ukrainian Relations in Ukrainian Historiography of the Late Seventeenth and Early Eighteenth Centuries.'

5 On Karamzin, see Black, *Nicholas Karamzin and Russian Society in the Nineteenth Century*. On Karamzin's interpretation of Ukrainian history, see Velychenko, *National History as Cultural Process*, 90–1. For a survey of the interrelation of the Russian and Ukrainian historical narratives in modern times, see Velychenko, 'Rival Grand Narratives of National History.'

6 See Velychenko, *National History as Cultural Process*, xix–xx, and Kohut, 'The Development of a Ukrainian National Historiography in Imperial Russia.'

7 On the interrelation of monarchical and national principles in the Russian imperial narrative, see Wortman, 'National Narratives in the Representation of Nineteenth-Century Russian Monarchy.'

8 On the Pogodin controversy, see Pelenski, 'The Ukrainian-Russian Debate over the Legacy of Kievan Rus', 1840s–1860s'; Andriewsky, 'The Russian-

Ukrainian Discourse and the Failure of the 'Little Russian Solution,' 1782–1917.'

9 Here and below I use these designations for two groups of Ukrainian historians and intellectuals. The former thought of themselves as belonging to a distinct Ukrainian nation, while the latter regarded themselves as members of a branch of the all-Russian nation. Clearly, these contrasting self-images affected the history that they wrote. On 'Little Russianism' as a nineteenth- and twentieth-century phenomenon, see *Encyclopedia of Ukraine*, 3: 166.

10 See Hrushevs'kyi, 'Zvychaina skhema "russkoï" istoriï i sprava ratsional'noho ukladu istoriï skhidnoho slov'ianstva.' For an English translation, see Hrushevsky, *The Traditional Scheme of 'Russian' History and the Problem of a Rational Organization of the History of the East Slavs*, ed. Gregorovich. Gregorovich's translation was reprinted in Vynar (Wynar), *Mykhailo Hrushevsky: Ukrainian-Russian Confrontation in Historiography*, 35–42. Quotations are given below in my translation, with accompanying page references to Gregorovich's version.

11 Prymak, *Mykhailo Hrushevsky*, 65.

12 Hrushevs'kyi, 'Zvychaina skhema,' 167; cf. Hrushevsky, *Traditional Scheme*, 36.

13 Hrushevs'kyi, 'Zvychaina skhema,' 171; cf. Hrushevsky, *Traditional Scheme*, 40.

14 On Kliuchevsky, see M.V. Nechkina, *Vasilii Osipovich Kliuchevskii*; Byrnes, *V.O. Kliuchevsky*. Byrnes portrays Kliuchevsky as a Russian nationalist and pan-Slavist who had little interest in the history of the non-Russians. According to Byrnes, although Kliuchevsky was a close friend of Gennadii Karpov, an ardent opponent of Mykola Kostomarov, Karpov's views had little if any effect on Kliuchevsky's writings. See Byrnes, 'Kliuchevskii on the Multi-National Russian State.'

15 When writing his article on the traditional scheme of 'Russian' history, Hrushevsky apparently was not acquainted with the lithographic copies of Kliuchevsky's lectures. In the third edition of volume 1 of the *History* (1913), as well as in its Russian translation, *Kievskaia Rus'* (1911), Hrushevsky referred to the first volume of Kliuchevsky's *Course* as a recent work. See Hrushevsky, *History*, 1: 425; and *Kievskaia Rus'*, 471.

16 Kliuchevskii, *Kurs russkoi istorii*, 1: 272. Cf. Kliuchevsky, *A History of Russia*, 1: 182–3.

17 See *Kurs russkoi istorii*, 1: 32–3.

18 See editorial comments in the 1956 edition of the first part of the *Course* (Kliuchevskii, *Sochineniia*, 1: 377). Excerpts added by Klinchevsky for the 1924 edition of the *Course* are marked in the text of the 1956 edition.

19 Kliuchevskii, *Kurs russkoi istorii*, 1: 34.

20 Ibid., 1: 163.

21 Ibid., 1: 205.

22 Ibid., 1: 33.

23 Ibid., 1: 291.

24 Ibid., 1: 293.

25 Ibid., 1: 282–91.

26 Hrushevs'kyi, 'Zvychaina skhema,' 168; cf. Hrushevsky, *Traditional Scheme*, 36–7. For a detailed discussion of the Pogodin theory and Hrushevsky's contribution to the debate, see section 3 of this chapter.

27 Kliuchevskii, *Kurs russkoi istorii*, 1: 284–6. Cf. his 'Terminologiia russkoi istorii' in *Sochineniia*, 6: 135–6.

28 Hrushevs'kyi, 'Zvychaina skhema,' 167; cf. Hrushevsky, *Traditional Scheme*, 36.

29 See Kliuchevskii, *Kurs russkoi istorii*, 3: 92–120.

30 Ibid., 1: 336.

31 Ibid., 1: 292.

32 Ibid., 1: 351.

33 See Pipes, *Russia under the Old Regime*, 40.

34 In Velychenko's opinion, it was Linnichenko who complemented Ustrialov's scheme by augmenting it with the history of Galicia, which he treated as part of the Russian land. See Velychenko, *National History as Cultural Process*, xx–xxi. On Linnichenko, see Tolochko, 'Dvi ne zovsim akademichni dyskusiï'; Masnenko, *Istorychna dumka*, 217–22.

35 Linnichenko, *Malorusskii vopros*, repr. in *Ukrainskii separatizm v Rossii*, 253–4 (all references are to this edition).

36 See Pushkin, 'Klevetnikam Rossii.'

37 Linnichenko, *Malorusskii vopros*, 254.

38 On Efimenko, see Markov, *A.Ia. Efimenko – istorik Ukrainy* and a brief entry by Roman Senkus in *Encyclopedia of Ukraine*, 5: 765.

39 Efimenko, *Istoriia ukrainskogo naroda*, 1: 1.

40 Ibid.

41 Ibid., 1: 2.

42 Ibid. Cf. Grushevskii, *Ocherk istorii ukrainskogo naroda*.

43 Hrushevs'kyi, 'Zvychaina skhema,' 169; cf. Hrushevsky, *Traditional Scheme*, 38.

44 Liubavskii, *Ocherk istorii Litovsko-russkogo gosudarstva do Liublinskoi unii vkliuchitel'no*, 2.

45 Ibid., 1.

46 Ibid., 4.

47 Hrushevsky, *Traditional Scheme*, 41.

48 Ibid.
49 Hrushevs'kyi, 'Zvychaina skhema,' 169; cf. Hrushevsky, *Traditional Scheme*, 38.
50 Hrushevsky, *Traditional Scheme*, 35n. 2.
51 On Miliukov, see Riha, *A Russian European*; Stockdale, *Paul Miliukov and the Quest for a Liberal Russia, 1880–1918*. For the latest interpretations of Miliukov and his writings in Russian historiography, see a collection of articles, *P.N. Miliukov: istorik, politik, diplomat*.
52 See Miliukov, *Ocherki po istorii russkoi kultury* and *Glavnye techeniia russkoi istoricheskoi mysli*. See Hrushevsky's reviews of *Ocherki* and *Glavnye techeniia*.
53 *ZNTSh* 25 (1898): 31.
54 See *ZNTSh* 21 (1898): 15–16. In his review of Zagoskin's *History of the Law of the Russian People*, Hrushevsky confirmed his high opinion of Miliukov's writings. He criticized Zagoskin's historiographic introduction and noted that it could 'by no means be compared' to Miliukov's work. See Hrushevsky's review of Zagoskin, *Istoriia prava russkogo naroda*, 3.
55 On the young Miliukov's understanding of history, see his introduction to the first volume of *Ocherki* (1896), 1–20. Cf. the chapter on Miliukov's historical thought in Stockdale, *Paul Miliukov*, 53–80.
56 See Stockdale, *Paul Miliukov*, 313.
57 Quoted ibid., 312. Cf. Miliukov, *Ocherki*, 1: 114.
58 See Miakotin's review of the first volume of Miliukov's *Ocherki* in *Russkoe bogatstvo*.
59 See Hrushevsky's review in *ZNTSh* 21 (1898): 16.
60 Ibid., 25 (1898): 30.
61 See Miliukov, *Glavnye techeniia*, 1: 192–204.
62 Hrushevsky's review in *ZNTSh*, 25 (1898): 31. Hrushevsky also criticized Miliukov for commenting on the Kyivan *Synopsis* (1674) without embarking on a broader discussion of Ukrainian historiography of the sixteenth and seventeenth centuries.
63 Hrushevs'kyi, 'Zvychaina skhema,' 167; cf. Hrushevsky, *Traditional Scheme*, 36.
64 For Miliukov's views on the national question in Russia, see Stockdale, 'Miliukov, Nationality and National Identity,' in *P.N. Miliukov: istorik, politik, diplomat*, 275–87; Malinina, 'Dve kontseptsii "liberal'nogo natsionalizma." P.B. Struve i P.N. Miliukov.' As a leader of the Cadet (Constitutional Democratic) Party between the two revolutions, Miliukov often showed support for the cultural and political aspirations of the Ukrainian movement. In December 1909 he addressed the Russian Duma,

advocating the use of Ukrainian in the court system and attacking Russian nationalist deputies who opposed the adoption of the requisite law as follows: 'You say "Russia for Russians," but whom do you mean by "Russian"? You should say "Russia only for the Great Russians," because that which you do not give to Muslims and Jews you also do not give your own nearest kin – Ukraine' (quoted in Andriewsky, 'The Politics of National Identity,' 355). Of particular interest here is Miliukov's attack on Russian nationalists for confusing the terms 'Russian' and 'Great Russian.' Miliukov's stand was influenced by the 'revolt' of the Ukrainian members of the Cadet Party, who were dissatisfied with its ambiguous policies on the Ukrainian issue and demanded the party's support for the Duma bill on the use of the Ukrainian language in the courts (ibid., pp. 346–57).

65 See Miliukov, *Ocherki*, 1: 41–9.

66 Hrushevsky, *Traditional Scheme*, 36.

67 See Hrushevsky's review of Storozhev, *Russkaia istoriia s drevneishikh vremen do smutnogo vremeni.*

68 Hrushevs'kyi, 'Zvychaina skhema,' 168; cf. Hrushevsky, *Traditional Scheme*, 37.

69 See Korsakov, *Meria i Rostovskoe kniazhestvo.*

70 See Miliukov's unsigned review of Hrushevsky's *Ocherk istorii Kievskoi zemli.*

71 See Storozhev's letter of 18 April 1897 to Hrushevsky, in which he asked the latter's permission to reprint part of his book on the history of the Kyivan Land in a collection of articles on Russian history. Storozhev mentioned that neither he nor Hrushevsky's old acquaintance Nikolai Ogloblin were still working in the Archive of the Ministry of Justice, which they had had to leave because of Dmitrii Samokvasov (TsDIAK, fond 1235, op. 1, no. 775, fol. 1–1v).

72 Storozhev's letter of 7 January 1905 in TsDIAK, fond 1235, op. 1, no. 775, fol. 4v.

73 See Tel'vak, 'Naukova spadshchyna Mykhaila Hrushevs'koho v rosiis'kii istoriohrafii kintsia XIX – pershoi polovyny XX stolittia,' 69.

74 See Hrushevs'kyi, 'Odna z lehend Khmel'nychchyny.'

75 In his letter of thanks, Korsakov also expressed his pleasure at receiving Hrushevsky's greetings from '"Rus' abroad," constituting an ethnically and historically indivisible whole with Dnipro Rus'.' Indicative of Korsakov's views on the Ukrainian issue was the fact that he made no comparable statement concerning 'Great' and 'South' Russia. See Korsakov's letter of 10 December 1913 in TsDIAK, fond 1235, op. 1, no. 303, fols 340–1.

76 See Filevich, 'Obzor glavneishikh sochinenii i statei po zapadnorusskoi istorii za 1891 god.'

77 See Filevich, *Po povodu teorii dvukh russkikh narodnostei*, 17. Filevich, born into the family of a Ukrainian Greek Catholic priest in the Lublin area, was a strong proponent of all-Russian unity. Probably the only issue on which he agreed with Hrushevsky was the official plan to separate the Kholm region from the former Kingdom of Poland. For a brief biography of Filevich, see *Slavianovedenie v dorevoliutsionnoi Rossii*, 340–1.

78 Istrin, who became a corresponding member of the Russian Academy of Sciences in 1902 and a full member in 1907, replaced Shakhmatov as head of the academy's Department of Russian Language and Literature in 1920, a position that he held until the abolition of the department in 1930. See his brief biography in *Slavianovedenie v dorevoliutsionnoi Rossii*, 168–9.

79 Klymovych's second presentation was scheduled for 30 March. See his letter of 20 March 1905 to Hrushevsky in TsDIAK, fond 1235, op. 1, no. 874, fols 5–8. Klymovych, a personal acquaintance of Mykhailo Drahomanov, went on to serve as deputy minister of justice under the Central Rada and was killed by the Bolsheviks in 1920. For a brief biography, see *Encyclopedia of Ukraine*, 2: 567, as well as Serhii Bilokin's commentary in Syniavs'kyi, *Vybrani pratsi*, 377. Klymovych's alleged opponent, Boris Liapunov (a corresponding member of the Russian Academy of Sciences from 1907; full member from 1923), published an essay in 1919 titled 'Edinstvo russkogo iazyka v ego narechiiakh' in which he argued along Petr Struve's lines that the Russian literary and spoken languages were not Great Russian but constituted an all-Russian 'property' (*dostoianie*). The article appeared as part of volume 1 of *Sbornik statei po malorusskomu voprosu* (Odesa, 1919). It was reprinted in *Ukrainskii separatizm v Rossii*, 385–98.

80 Linnichenko, *Malorusskii vopros*, 253.

81 See Tsarinnyi, *Ukrainskoe dvizhenie*, in *Ukrainskii separatizm v Rossii*, 133–252. On the authorship of the work, see 404. On Andrei Storozhenko and his brother Mykola (Nikolai) Storozhenko (also a historian), see Masnenko, *Istorychna dumka*, 210–17. Both brothers belonged to the Little Russian current of the Ukrainian intelligentsia. After the revolution, they emigrated and apparently parted ways, as Andrei maintained his previous views, while Mykola became a Ukrainian patriot.

82 See Tsarinnyi, *Ukrainskoe dvizhenie*, 161. The confidential letters from Sergei Platonov and Aleksei Shakhmatov to the president of the Russian Academy of Sciences, Grand Prince Konstantin Konstantinovich Romanov,

concerning Hrushevsky's arrest and exile by the Russian authorities in 1914 reveal the attitudes that prevailed toward him in Russian academic circles. Shakhmatov, a strong supporter of Hrushevsky at the time of his forced exile, made every effort to counter accusations that Hrushevsky was engaging in anti-Russian activities and stressed his contribution to 'Russian' scholarship. He wrote that 'the critical apparatus of his eight-volume *History* may be termed classical and unique since Karamzin.' See Shakhmatov to Romanov (26 December 1914) in '"Ia nikogda ne vystupal protiv Rossii,"' 179. Platonov, on the other hand, was much more cautious in his assessment of Hrushevsky's political activities and advised Romanov against releasing Hrushevsky from exile in Simbirsk. But even he admitted that 'Hrushevsky possesses great scholarly talent and has done a great deal for scholarship, independently of his "theory"' (ibid., 178).

83 See *K voprosu o kandidature na kafedru russkoi istorii v universitete sv. Vladimira professora L'vovskogo universiteta Mikhaila Grushevskogo.*

84 Lotots'kyi, *Storinky mynuloho,* 3: 306. For an English translation of this extract, see Partykevich, *Between Kyiv and Constantinople,* 16–17.

85 Tsarinnyi, *Ukrainskoe dvizhenie,* 133.

86 See Volkonskii, *Istoricheskaia pravda i ukrainofil'skaia propaganda,* 25.

87 There were a very few cases in which Linnichenko either did not understand Hrushevsky or misrepresented him. He claimed, for example, that Hrushevsky was not sure of what to do with the history of 'Western Russia,' whether to treat it as a separate subject or attach it to Great Russian or South Russian history (see Linnichenko, *Malorusskii vopros,* 255). In fact, Hrushevsky advocated the creation of a separate field of Belarusian history. In another instance, Linnichenko revealed his poor knowledge of the history of the Polish-Lithuanian Commonwealth by questioning Hrushevsky's assertion that the Belarusian lands had been closely linked to the Grand Duchy of Lithuania and remained within it after the Union of Lublin (1569). Linnichenko wrote that he did not understand Hrushevsky's argument, as the Union of Lublin was followed by the incorporation not only of Little Russia but also of Belarus and Lithuania into Poland (ibid., 256). What Hrushevsky apparently meant was that unlike the Ukrainian lands, which were annexed to the Polish Crown after the Union of Lublin, the Belarusian lands remained within the Grand Duchy of Lithuania, which became part of the Polish-Lithuanian Commonwealth.

88 See Linnichenko, *Malorusskii vopros,* 257–8.

89 Ibid., 259. Cf. Hrushevs'kyi, 'Zvychaina skhema,' 171; Hrushevsky, *Traditional Scheme*, 40.

90 Commenting on the state of Ukrainian culture, Linnichenko wrote: 'One may, of course, regret such an absence of cultural independence; one may desire its establishment; but one cannot fail to acknowledge that absence as a fact of the past and present. For me as a Little Russian, that fact is perhaps no less burdensome than for Mr Hrushevsky, but I do not close my eyes to it; I strive to explain it; and I find a certain consolation and requital precisely in what Mr Hrushevsky finds so repulsive – *in the state'* (Linnichenko, *Malorusskii vopros*, 260).

In 1919 Linnichenko devoted an article to the subject of 'Little Russian' culture, developing many of the ideas first expressed in his 'open letter' of 1917 to Hrushevsky. See Linnichenko, 'Malorusskaia kul'tura.' It was issued as a separate brochure in the same year. See *Ukrainskii separatizm v Rossii*, 423.

91 See Linnichenko, *Malorusskii vopros*, 259. The reference was to Antonovych's public lecture of 1898 in which he sought to defend Bohdan Khmelnytsky against accusations of incapacity to establish a Ukrainian state by shifting responsibility for that failure to the people in general. See Volodymyr Antonovych, 'Kharakteristika deiatel'nosti Bogdana Khmel'nitskogo.'

92 Linnichenko, *Malorusskii vopros*, 260–1.

93 Ibid., 263.

94 Hrushevs'kyi, 'Avtobiohrafiia, 1906 r.,' 203.

95 See Bahalii, 'Akad. M.S. Hrushevs'kyi,' 174–5.

96 For a discussion of the role of founding myths in the formation of national histories, see Hosking and Schöpflin, *Myth and Nationhood*; Geary, *The Myth of Nations*.

97 See Hrushevsky, *History*, 1: 47.

98 Rostovtzeff, *Iranians and Greeks in South Russia*, 211.

99 Ibid., 238.

100 Hrushevs'kyi, 'Vstupnyi vyklad z davn'oï istoriï Rusy,' 141.

101 See Hrushevsky's review in *Ukraïna*, 1925, no. 4: 154–5. Writing a year later, Hrushevsky gave the following evaluation of Rostovtzeff's contribution to the field of Rus' history: 'Rostovtsev has reminded us in timely fashion of what was long considered self-evident but has not yet been duly researched and concretized – the prehistory of those great trading centres on which the Kyivan state was based in the ninth and tenth centuries' (Hrushevs'kyi, 'Poraionne istorychne doslidzhennia Ukraïny i obsliduvannia Kyïvs'koho uzla,' 16).

102 See Hrushevs'kyi, *Istoriia*, 1: 21.

103 See Hrushevsky, *History*, 1: 17–43, 62–121.

104 Ibid., 1: 233–5, 430–4. Hrushevsky's early caution with regard to the search for a Slavic anthropological type is to be explained at least in part by the lack of reliable data and research. As it turned out, this attitude was more than justified. In his review of Lubor Niederle's *Manuel de l'antiquité slave* (Paris, 1923), Hrushevsky wrote: 'The author acknowledges that his earlier efforts to establish the pre-Slavic archaeological type (dolichocephalic and fair-haired, as he argued) have yielded no positive result, and one is obliged, on the contrary, to consider the Slavic anthropological type primordially mixed. I adopted such a view in my *History of Ukraine-Rus'* quite some time ago, when Professor Niederle was still defending his Slavic type' (*Ukraïna*, 1924, nos. 1–2: 182).

105 Hrushevsky, *History*, 1: 1.

106 Ibid., 1: 54–60. Archaeological findings of the twentieth century generally confirm Hrushevsky's placement of the ancient Slavic homeland. See Baran, 'Velyke rozselennia slov'ian.' On theories of the location of the Slavic homeland, see Baran, *Davni slov'iany*, 6–10.

107 See Hrushevsky, *History*, 1: 55–6.

108 Hrushevs'kyi, *Istoriia ukraïnskoï literatury*, 1: 54.

109 On the Antes, see Sedov, 'Anten'; Zhukovsky, 'Antes' in *Encyclopedia of Ukraine*, 1: 76 (based largely on Mykhailo Braichevsky's entry in *Radians'ka entsyklopediia istoriï Ukraïny*, 4 vols. [Kyiv, 1969–72], 1: 58); Strumins'kyj, 'Were the Antes Eastern Slavs?'

110 See Poppe, Introduction to Volume 1 in Hrushevsky, *History*, 1: xlvii–liv, and his additions to Hrushevsky's notes, 420.

111 See Iordan, *O proiskhozhdenii i deianiiakh gotov: Getica*, 136.

112 See Zeuss, *Die Deutschen und die Nachbarstämme*, 604.

113 See Hrushevs'kyi, 'Anty. Uryvok z istoriï Ukraïny-Rusy,' 7. Cf. his *History*, 1: 131.

114 See Golubinskii, *Istoriia russkoi tserkvi*, 1: 15.

115 See Krek, *Einleitung in die slavische Literaturgeschichte*, 330.

116 Despite his belief in the Asian origin of the Antes, Kunik maintained that they ruled over a conglomerate of Slavic tribes. See Kunik, 'O vremeni, v kotorom zhil izrail'tianin Ibragim ibn-Iakub,' 1: 147.

117 See Hrushevs'kyi, 'Anty,' 7–10, and *History*, 1: 132–3, 418–20.

118 Hrushevsky, *History*, 1: 133.

119 Hrushevs'kyi, 'Anty,' 10.

120 Ibid. Cf. Hrushevsky, *History*, 1: 133.

121 See Hrushevsky, *History*, 1: 134.

122 Hrushevs'kyi, *Istoriia*, 1: 177. Cf. *History*, 1: 133–4.
123 See A.L. Pogodin, *Iz istorii slavianskikh peredvizhenii*. For a brief biography of Pogodin, see *Slavianovedenie v dorevoliutsionnoi Rossii*, 271–2. Later, Pogodin maintained good relations with Hrushevsky. See his letters to Hrushevsky in TsDIAK, fond 1235, op. 1, no. 700.

   Ironically, Hrushevsky's 'nationalization' of the Antes was completely overlooked by a reviewer of the German translation of the first volume of his *History* (1906), Aleksander Brückner, who was under the impression that Hrushevsky considered the Antes representatives of the Eastern Slavs in general. See Brückner, 'Dogmat normański,' 678.
124 Shakhmatov, *Vvedenie v kurs istorii russkogo iazyka*, 46.
125 See Shakhmatov, *Drevneishie sud'by russkogo plemeni*.
126 Hrushevsky, 'Poraionne istorychne doslidzhennia,' 19. Shakhmatov was often criticized for the superficiality of his theories by Russian and Ukrainian scholars alike. See, for example, Ahatanhel Krymsky's defence of Shakhmatov against Aleksei Sobolevsky's characterization of him as a 'linguistic dreamer' in Shakhmatov and Kryms'kyi, *Narysy z istoriï ukraïns'koï movy ta Khrestomatiia z pam'iatnykiv pys'mens'koï staro-ukraïnshchyny XI–XVIII vv.*, iv.
127 See Hrushevs'kyi, 'Poraionne istorychne doslidzhennia,' 18.
128 See Niederle, *Manuel*, 191–2.
129 Here Niederle referred to Shakmatov's studies on the history of the Little Russian language and nationality. Niederle was apparently prepared to accept the existence of the Little Russian branch of the 'Russian' people during medieval times, as long as that existence was postulated by Russian scholars.
130 See Niederle, *Slovanské starožitnosti*, 78.
131 See Hrushevsky, *History*, 1: 418–19. Niederle's scholarly disagreement with Hrushevsky did not stop him from recommending the latter for full membership in the Royal Czech Scholarly Society (see Niederle's post-card of 8 January 1914 informing Hrushevsky of his election to the society, TsDIAK, fond 1235, op. 1, no. 661, fol. 12). Some of Niederle's letters to Hrushevsky were written in Ukrainian (ibid., fol. 14).
132 See Hrushevs'kyi, 'Anty,' 16.
133 See Hrushevs'kyi, 'Poraionne istorychne doslidzhennia,' 19.
134 Hrushevs'kyi, *Istoriia*, 1: 177 and *History*, 1: 134. Cf. Grushevskii, *Kievskaia Rus'*, 1: 210. In the first volume of his *History of Ukrainian Literature* (1923), which was written in the emigration in the early 1920s, Hrushevsky referred to the Antes as 'East Slavic "Antean" tribes, ancestors of our people,' bringing together his belief in the Antes as ancestors of the

Ukrainians with the less controversial form of their identification as Eastern Slavs in general. See Hrushevs'kyi, *Istoriia ukraïns'koï literatury*, 1: 51.

135 See Hrushevsky's review of Niederle's *Manuel de l'antiquité slave*, 183. Cf. Niederle, *Manuel de l'antiquité slave*, 231, and the Russian translation of the Czech version of the *Manuel* (1953): *Slavianskie drevnosti*, 166. This argument was further developed in Niederle's *Původ a počátky Slovanů východních*, 211–13.

136 See E.K., 'M. Grushevskii protiv L. Niderle.'

137 See Hrushevsky's review of Niederle's *Slovanské starožitnosti* in *Ukraïna*, 135. Hrushevsky's critical notes appeared as an addition to the review of the volume by the linguist P. Buzuk (ibid., 130–4).

138 Hrushevsky's review in *Ukraïna*, 136. Significantly, Niederle's attacks on Hrushevsky were met with approval not only by Russian émigrés of the 1920s but also by Soviet historians of the 1950s. In the introduction to the Russian translation of Niederle's *Manuel de l'antiquité slave* (1956), Petr Tretiakov, a renowned Soviet archaeologist and director of the Institute of Slavic Studies of the USSR Academy of Sciences, praised Niederle for standing firm against nationalist concepts of the history of the Slavic peoples and rejecting the interpretation of the history of the 'East Slavic Antes' advanced by Mykhailo Hrushevsky. Tretiakov failed to mention that Niederle also disagreed with Aleksandr Pogodin and Aleksei Shakhmatov and relied heavily on Hrushevsky in his interpretation of many issues pertaining to the early history of the Eastern Slavs. (See Tretiakov, 'Liubor Niderle i ego 'Slavianskie drevnosti,' 6–7.)

139 Hrushevs'kyi, 'Poraionne istorychne doslidzhennia,' 19.

140 On the origins of the Normanist controversy, see Koialovich, *Istoriia russkogo samosoznaniia po istoricheskim pamiatnikam i nauchnym sochineniiam*, 109–13; Hrushevsky, *History*, 1: 472–4. For a discussion of the origins of the Normanist debate in relation to Russian nation-building, see Rogger, *National Consciousness in Eighteenth-Century Russia*, 202–20. For a general survey of the Normanist debate, see Moshin, 'Variago-russkii vopros'; Shaskol'skii, *Normanskaia teoriia v sovremennoi burzhuaznoi nauke*; Goehrke, *Frühzeit des Ostslaventums*; Khlevov, *Normanskaia problema v otechestvennoi istoricheskoi nauke*.

141 See Maksimovich, 'Otkuda idet russkaia zemlia' and 'O proiskhozhdenii Variago-Russov'; Venelin, *Skandinavomaniia i ee poklonniki ili stoletnie izyskaniia o variagakh*.

142 See Kostomarov, 'Nachalo Rusi.' Cf. Hrushevsky, *History*, 1: 475.

143 See Ilovaiskii, *Razyskaniia o nachale Rusi, Dopolnitel'naia polemika po*

voprosam variago-russkomu i bolgaro-gunnskomu, and *Vtoraia dopolnitel'naia polemika po voprosam variago-russkomu i bolgaro-gunnskomu.* On Ilovaisky's anti-Normanist stand, see Koialovich, *Istoriia russkogo samosoznaniia,* 502–5.

144 Hrushevsky, *History,* 1: 476. Sometime in 1895, after his move to Lviv, Hrushevsky sent Ilovaisky a copy of his book on the Kyivan Land. Ilovaisky responded with a letter thanking Hrushevsky and asking which of his publications the latter did not have. He also inquired where Hrushevsky was teaching and asked him for his mailing address. (See Ilovaisky's letter of 26 January 1896 to Hrushevsky in TsDIAK, fond 1235, op. 1, no. 303, fol. 323.)

145 Hrushevsky, *History,* 452, 476–7.

146 Ilovaisky's interpretation of the Russian past as the history of the Russian state and the tripartite Russian nation was often seen as the main rival of Hrushevsky's paradigm. Writing in the emigration in the 1920s, one of Hrushevsky's opponents, Andrei Storozhenko (A. Tsarinny), counterposed the two historians as follows: 'But then M.S. Hrushevsky comes onto the scene and with the freedom and ease of a jester, in his ponderous but scurrilous volumes, starts to assure the simple-minded "Ukrainians" in his Little Russian-Polish jargon that it is only the "Ilovaiskys" who could believe in the unity of the Russian people ...' (Tsarinnyi, *Ukrainskoe dvizhenie,* 180). For the impact of Ilovaisky's textbooks on historical consciousness in Ukraine, see Yekelchyk, 'The Grand Narrative and Its Discontents.'

147 Hrushevsky, *History,* 1: 482–91.

148 See Shakhmatov, *Razyskaniia o drevneishikh russkikh letopisnykh svodakh.* For Shakhmatov's views on the Normanist issue, see his *Skazanie o prizvanii variagov* and *Drevneishie sud'by russkogo plemeni.*

149 See Hrushevsky, *History,* 1: 450–69.

150 See Andrzej Poppe's editorial additions to Hrushevsky's excursus on the 'Earliest Kyivan Chronicle' in Hrushevsky, *History,* 1: 470–1. Cf. Łowmiański (Kh. Lovmianskii), *Rus' i normanny,* 72, 75 (Russian translation of idem, *Zagadnienie roli Normanów w genezie państw słowiańskich*); Zibrov, *O letopisi Nestora.*

151 Hrushevsky, *History,* 1: 465.

152 Ibid., 289–92.

153 See Poppe's additions to Hrushevsky's excursus, 'The Normanist Theory,' in Hrushevsky, *History,* 1: 491–2.

154 On the periodization of the Normanist debate, see Khlevov, *Normanskaia problema,* p. 43.

155 Hrushevsky, *History*, 1: 488.
156 See Brückner, 'Dogmat normański.'
157 Ibid., 669–70.
158 Hrushevsky, *History*, 1: 481.
159 Ilovaiskii, *Razyskaniia o nachale Rusi*, 229.
160 For a survey of the early stages of the discussion, see Pypin, *Istoriia russkoi ètnografii*, 3: 301–38; Pelenski, 'The Ukrainian-Russian Debate over the Legacy of Kievan Rus', 1840s–1860s.'
161 Maksymovych divided the Eastern ('Russian') Slavs into two categories: the northern Rus', consisting of Great Russians and Belarusians, and the southern or Ukrainian-Galician Rus'. He claimed to be following the example of Konstantin Kalaidovich. According to Maksymovych, the southern group of tribes consisted of the 'Polianians, Siverianians with Sulichians, Derevlianians, Tivertsians, and possibly the Croatians (Galicians)' (see Maksimovich, 'Otkuda idet Russkaia zemlia,' 8–9).
162 See Maksimovich, 'O mnimom zapustenii Ukrainy v nashestvie Batyevo i naselenii ee novoprishlym narodom (Pis'mo k M.P. Pogodinu),' 138.
163 See Andriewsky, 'The Russian-Ukrainian Discourse and the Failure of the "Little Russian Solution," 1782–1917,' 204–5.
164 See Sreznevskii, 'Mysli ob istorii russkogo iazyka' and 'O drevnem russkom iazyke'; Lavrovskii, *O iazyke severnykh russkikh letopisei*.
165 For the formulation of Mikhail Pogodin's hypothesis, see his 'Zapiska o drevnem russkom iazyke.'
166 Quoted in Andriewsky, 'Russian-Ukrainian Discourse,' 206n.63.
167 For Maksymovych's response, see Maksimovich, 'Filologicheskie pis'ma k M.P. Pogodinu,' 'Otvetnye pis'ma k M.P. Pogodinu,' 'O mnimom zapustenii Ukrainy,' and 'Novye pis'ma M.P. Pogodinu o starobytnosti malorossiiskogo narechiia.' From the Ukrainian side, the discussion was also joined by Oleksander Kotliarevsky. See his 'Byli-li malorussy iskonnymi obiteliami polianskoi zemli, ili prishli iz-za Karpat v XIV veke?'
168 See Mikhail Pogodin, 'Otvet na filologicheskie pis'ma M.A. Maksimovicha' and 'Otvet na dva poslednie pis'ma M.A. Maksimovicha.' Cf. his *Pis'ma M.P. Pogodina k M.A. Maksimovichu*.
169 See Sobolevskii, 'Kak govorili v Kieve v XIV i XV vv.?' (résumé of a paper delivered at a meeting of the Kyiv Historical Society of Nestor the Chronicler in 1882), his *Ocherki iz istorii russkogo iazyka*, and *Lektsii po istorii russkogo iazyka*. For the Ukrainian viewpoint, see Krymskii, 'Filologiia i Pogodinskaia gipoteza.'
170 See Vladimir Antonovich, 'Kiev, ego sud'ba i znachenie s XIV po XVI

stoletie (1362–1569)' and *Moia spovid'*, 577–92. Sobolevsky responded
to Antonovych's work with the article 'K voprosu ob istoricheskikh
sud'bakh Kieva (po povodu "monografii" V.B. Antonovicha).' Among the
linguists, Sobolevsky's most authoritative critic was Vatroslav Jagić. See
his critique of Sobolevsky's works in *Chetyre kritiko-paleograficheskie stat'i*
and *Kriticheskie zametki po istorii russkogo iazyka*.

171 See Hrushevsky's survey of the discussion in his *History*, 1: 423–7 (Note 6:
The Theory of the Early Settlement of Russians in the Dnipro Region).

172 See Grushevskii, *Ocherk istorii Kievskoi zemli ot smerti Iaroslava do kontsa
XIV stoletiia*.

173 Hrushevsky, *History*, 1: 151. Hrushevsky maintained this interpretation
of the Kyivan literary legacy throughout his career. See Hrushevsky,
'Poraionne istorychne doslidzhennia,' 22–3.

174 For a brief biography of Jagić, see *Slavianovedenie v dorevoliutsionnoi Rossii*,
377–80. Hrushevsky and Jagić corresponded in German. Jagić's letters to
Hrushevsky have been preserved in Hrushevsky's personal archive
(TsDIAK, fond 1235, op. 1, no. 870).

175 See Jagić, 'Einige Streitfragen,' *Archiv für slavische Philologie* 20 (1898):
30.

176 See Hrushevsky, *History*, 1: 425, and 'Chernihiv i Sivershchyna v
ukraïns'kii istoriï, 113. For Shakhmatov's change of mind, see his 'K
voprosu ob obrazovanii russkikh narechii' and 'K voprosu ob obrazovanii
russkikh narechii i russkikh narodnostei.'

177 See Hrushevsky, *History*, 1: 425. Cf. his review of Jagić, 'Einige Streitfragen.'

178 See Shakhmatov, 'K voprosu ob obrazovanii russkikh narechii i russkikh
narodnostei.'

179 See Hrushevs'kyi, *Spirni pytannia starorus'koï etnohrafiï*. Cf. his *History*, 1:
151, 425–6. This article of Hrushevsky's was published in the same collection as his more famous essay on the traditional scheme of 'Russian'
history. Petro Klymovych, who made a presentation in March 1905 at the
Odesa Historical and Philological Society on Hrushevsky's first, 'historiographic,' article and planned a talk about his 'ethnographic' article as
well, informed Hrushevsky that his opponent at the presentation, Boris
Liapunov, would 'maintain that the Siverianians were Old Russians (i.e.,
the selfsame Great Russians)' (TsDIAK, fond 1235, op. 1, no. 874, p. 8). It
would appear that Liapunov, who was a student of Jagić's at St Petersburg University, fully subscribed to the views of his former professor on
the Siverianian problem.

180 See Shakhmatov, 'Iuzhnye poseleniia viatichei.'

181 Shakhmatov, *Vvedenie v kurs istorii russkogo iazyka*, 100.
182 See Hrushevs'kyi, 'Chernihiv i Sivershchyna v ukraïns'kii istoriï,' 111–15.
183 Ibid., 115.
184 See Niderle, *Slavianskie drevnosti*, 165.
185 Among other things, Parkhomenko's theory was meant to solve the problem of why the Polianians, the ruling tribe of Kyivan Rus', were assigned such a minuscule territory (limited to Kyiv and its surroundings) in the Primary Chronicle, while the tribes controlled by the Polianians, such as the Derevlianians, Drehovichians, and others, inhabited much larger territories. The anomaly was supposed to be explained by the late arrival of the Polianians in the Dnipro region. The problem remains unsolved, for in archaeological terms the territory assigned to the Polianians in the chronicle is defined only by the special type of burial pertaining to the so-called retinue culture, which indicates an unusually high level of militarization but has no features distinguishing the local population from its neighbours in ethno-cultural terms. See Tolochko and Tolochko, *Kyïvs'ka Rus'*, 32–3.
186 See Parkhomenko, 'Novi istorychni problemy Kyïvs'koï Rusy.' On Parkhomenko, see Portnov, 'Do pytannia pro mistse V.O. Parkhomenka v ukraïns'komu ta svitovomu istoriohrafichnomu protsesi.'
187 For the text of Carpini's account, see Beazley, *The Texts and Versions of John de Plano Carpini*.
188 See Maksimovich, 'O mnimom zapustenii Ukrainy.'
189 See Vladimir Antonovich, 'Kiev, ego sud'ba i znachenie,' 534–9.
190 Grushevskii, *Ocherk istorii Kievskoi zemli*, 427–43.
191 For a brief biography of Sobolevsky, see *Slavianovedenie v dorevoliutsionnoi Rossii*, 311–13.
192 Grushevkii, *Ocherk istorii Kievskoi zemli*, 428–9.
193 Ibid., 436–40. 'If Professor Sobolevsky finds it possible to assert that Batu's horde "destroyed all the cities of the Kyivan Land, so that some of them, mainly in its southern portion, were not rebuilt at all or for a long time,"' wrote Hrushevsky, 'then that is his business, to be sure' (p. 436).
194 Hrushevs'kyi, *Istoriia*, 3: 144.
195 Ibid., 152.
196 'I cannot consider the Mongol invasion to have had a decisive, fatal significance for the condition of the land,' wrote Hrushevsky, concluding his remarks on the Pogodin theory. 'Conversely, as noted above, I attribute great significance to it in a different respect – that of the restructuring of political and social relations' (*Ocherk istorii Kievskoi zemli*, 443).
197 Ibid., 443–60.

198 See Hrushevs'kyi [Serhiienko], 'Hromads'kyi rukh na Vkraïni-Rusy v XIII vitsi.'

199 See Drahomanov's review of Hrushevs'kyi, 'Hromads'kyi rukh na Vkraïni-Rusy v XIII vitsi.'

200 See Hrushevs'kyi, *Istoriia*, 3: 83–7, 154–61, 535–6. This balanced treatment of the issue was also presented in Hrushevsky's popular *Illustrated History of Ukraine* (1912), where Danylo's struggle against the 'Tatar people' was explained by his concern that the communal movement would completely destroy 'Ukrainian political life' (see Hrushevs'kyi, *Iliustrovana istoriia*, 125).

201 See Hrushevs'kyi, 'Ukraïns'ka partiia sotsiialistiv-revoliutsioneriv ta ïï zavdannia.'

202 See Maksimovich, 'O mnimom zapustenii Ukrainy,' 1: 136.

203 Ibid., 137.

204 See Grushevskii, *Ocherk istorii Kievskoi zemli*, 440. Cf. his *History*, 1: 425; *Istoriia*, 3: 152.

205 See Hrushevs'kyi, *Istoriia*, 3: 151–2.

206 See Hrushevsky, *Traditional Scheme*, 37.

207 See Kliuchevskii, *Kurs russkoi istorii*, 1: 284–91.

208 See Hrushevs'kyi, *Istoriia*, 1: 555. Cf. *History*, 1: 425.

209 See Maksimovich (apparently influenced by Vasilii Tatishchev), 'Otkuda idet Russkaia zemlia,' 62.

210 Hrushevs'kyi, *Istoriia*, 3: 151.

211 See Hrushevsky, *History*, 1: 425. Cf. Spitsyn, 'Istoriko-arkheologicheskie razyskaniia.'

212 In his inaugural lecture, Hrushevsky presented the Kyivan state as a *sui generis* federation, 'in which the distinctiveness and autonomy of the lands was combined with the unity of the Rus' people, expressed in unity of language, culture, religion, and civic order' ('Vstupnyi vyklad,' 144).

213 See Klid, 'Dolia Kyieva ta Kyïvshchyny pislia monhol's'koï navaly 1240 r. v ukraïns'kii istoriohrafiï XIX stolittia i skhema M. Hrushevs'koho.'

214 See Kohut, 'The Development of a Ukrainian National Historiography in Imperial Russia,' 468.

215 For Bahalii's views on Hrushevsky, see chapter 6 of this book.

216 See Presniakov, *Obrazovanie Velikorusskogo gosudarstva*. For an English translation of the work, see *The Formation of the Great Russian State*.

217 See Tel'vak, 'Naukova spadshchyna,' 70.

218 Rostovtzeff, 'Les origines de la Russie Kiévienne,' 6.

219 Hrushevsky also suggested that Rostovtzeff's use of a single term – 'Russie' in his French-language writings and 'Russia' in his English

ones – to render both *Rus'* and *Rossiia* was confusing to the reader. See Hrushevsky's reviews of Rostovtzeff's *Ėllinstvo i iranstvo na Iuge Rossii, Iranians and Greeks in South Russia*, 'Les origines de la Russie Kiévienne,' and *Skifiia i Bospor*, 153.

220 See, for example, Vernadsky's discussion of early modern Ukrainian history in his *History of Russia*, vol. 4, *Russia at the Dawn of the Modern Age*, 220–92. George (Iurii) Vernadsky was the son of Vladimir (Volodymyr) Vernadsky, the first president of the Ukrainian Academy of Sciences and a rival of Hrushevsky's in academic politics in 1918–19. On the nature of their rivalry, see chapter 4.

221 See Vernadsky, Preface to Hrushevsky, *A History of Ukraine*, v.

222 Much more critical of that aspect of Hrushevsky's work was Michael Karpovich, who reviewed the English translation in *Yale Review* 31 (1942): 424–7. Cf. Budurovych, 'Mykhailo Hrushevs'kyi v otsintsi zakhidn'oevropeis'koï i amerykans'koï istoriohrafiï,' esp. 176–7.

223 For a discussion of the Eurasianists' interpretation of Ukrainian history, see Masnenko, *Istorychna dumka*, 194–200.

224 See Trubetzkoy, 'The Ukrainian Problem.' For a discussion of Struve's and Trubetskoi's interpretations of Ukrainian culture, see Ilnytzkyj, 'Modelling Culture in the Empire.' On Dmytro Doroshenko's polemics with Trubetskoi, see Masnenko, *Istorychna dumka*, 200–9.

225 Volkonskii, *Istoricheskaia pravda i ukrainofil'skaia propaganda*, 55.

Chapter 3: The Construction of a National Paradigm

1 See Velychenko, *National History as Cultural Process*, pp. 142–3; Doroshenko, *Survey of Ukrainian Historiography*, pp. 21–58. For the text of the chronicle, see *The Hypatian Codex, II: The Galician-Volhynian Chronicle*. On its composition, see Hens'ors'kyi, *Halyts'ko-Volyns'kyi litopys*. Hrushevsky studied the Galician-Volhynian Chronicle for his work on the *History of Ukraine-Rus'* and devoted an article to its chronology. See Hrushevs'kyi, 'Khronolohiia podii Halyts'ko-volyns'koï litopysy.'

2 On Sofonovych, see Mytsyk, *Ukrainskie letopisi XVII veka* and the introduction to Sofonovych, *Khronika z litopystsiv starodavnikh*. On the main themes of seventeenth-century Ukrainian historiography, see Sysyn, 'The Cossack Chronicles and the Development of Modern Ukrainian Culture and National Identity' and 'The Cultural, Social and Political Context of Ukrainian History-Writing: 1620–1690.'

3 Kohut, 'Development of a Ukrainian National Historiography,' 460.

4 On the relation of Ukrainian historiography to the Russian imperial narrative in the nineteenth century, aside from the above-mentioned article by Kohut, see Velychenko, 'Rival Grand Narratives of National History' and *National History as Cultural Process*, xxii–xxiii, 141–213. On the reception of the Russian imperial paradigm in Ukraine, see Yekelchyk, 'The Grand Narrative and Its Discontents.'

5 See *Perepyska Mykhaila Drahomanova z Melitonom Buchyns'kym, 1871–77*. Cf. 'Iuvilei akademika Dmytra Ivanovycha Bahaliia' in Bahalii, *Vybrani pratsi*, 1: 321.

6 On the views and activities of Antonovych, see Klid, 'Volodymyr Antonovych: Ukrainian Populist Historiography and the Cultural Politics of Nation Building.'

7 Drahomanov in fact shared the view of many national activists of nineteenth-century Europe, who believed that national histories (understood as histories of ethno-national groups) would eventually join together on an equal footing to create one European or universal history. Such a view, which can be traced back to the writings of Mazzini, was also adopted by Hrushevsky. For a discussion of the beliefs of romantic nationalists and their relation to history, see Pearton, 'Nicolae Iorga as Historian and Politician,' 162–4.

8 See Drahomanov, 'Chudats'ki dumky pro ukraïns'ku natsional'nu spravu' (1891), 490.

9 Syniavs'kyi [Katran], Review of Barvinsky's *Iliustrovana istoriia Rusy*. Reprinted in A.S. Syniavs'kyi, *Vybrani pratsi*, 34–41, here 34. On Syniavsky's views on Ukrainian history, see Zaruba, *Z viroiu v ukraïns'ku spravu: Antin Stepanovych Syniavs'kyi* and 'Skhema istoriï Ukraïny Antona Syniavs'koho.'

10 Hrinchenko, 'Lysty z Ukraïny naddniprians'koï' (1892–3), 37.

11 See Hrushevsky's autobiographies in *Velykyi ukraïnets': Materialy z zhyttia ta diial'nosti M.S. Hrushevs'koho*, 206, 229.

12 See Bahalii, 'Akad. M.S. Hrushevs'kyi,' 182–4.

13 Hrushevs'kyi, 'Avtobiohrafiia, 1906 r.,' 203, 210.

14 See Arkas, *Istoriia Ukraïny-Rusi*.

15 Grushevskii, *Ocherk* (1904), introduction.

16 Efimenko, *Istoriia ukrainskogo naroda*, 2.

17 See Bahalii, 'Avtobiohrafiia,' 75–7.

18 Ibid., 131–6. For a brief account of Bahalii's life and activities, see Kravchenko, 'D.I. Bahalii v svitli i tini svoieï "Avtobiohrafiï."'

19 These included courses such as 'History of Southwestern Rus' up to the Thirteenth Century,' 'The History of Southwestern Rus' from the Thir-

teenth to the Sixteenth Century,' and 'Historical Geography and Ethnography of Southern Rus" (see Markevych's obituary [1904] in Syniavs'kyi, *Vybrani pratsi*, 66–72; Masnenko, *Istorychna dumka*, 127).

20 The situation changed only during the Revolution of 1905, as the relaxation of government control allowed not only the publication of surveys of Ukrainian history but also the introduction of Ukrainian history courses at the university level. In 1906 Efimenko taught a course in Ukrainian history at the Higher Courses for Women in St Petersburg, while in 1907–8 Hrushevsky's younger brother, Oleksander, taught a course at Novorossiisk University in Odesa. See Masnenko, *Istorychna dumka*, p. 127.

21 See Bagalei, *Russkaia istoriia* and *Russkaia istoriia*, vol. 1, *Kniazheskaia Rus'*. Only the latter volume included a separate section on Ukrainian history.

22 On the persecution of Ukrainophile and liberal professors in Kharkiv University between 1884 and 1904, see Bahalii, 'Avtobiohrafiia,' 1: 103–23.

23 Ibid., 77.

24 See Efimenko, *Istoriia ukrainskogo naroda*, 1: 1–2, 211, 221, 242.

25 On the Ukrainian movement in Galicia, see Rudnytsky, 'The Ukrainians in Galicia under Austrian Rule,' 315–52; Kozik, *Ukrainian National Movement in Galicia: 1815–1849*; Hrytsak, *Narys istoriï Ukraïny*, 73–82; Himka, 'Construction of Nationality in Galician Rus',' *Galician Villagers and the Ukrainian National Movement in the Nineteenth Century, Religion and Nationality in Western Ukraine*, and *Socialism in Galicia*. On the Russophiles, see Magocsi, 'Old Ruthenianism and Russophilism'; Wendland, *Die Russophilen in Galizien*.

26 See Zubritskii, *Istoriia drevnego Galichsko-Russkogo kniazhestva*. On Zubritsky, see the entry by Roman Senkus in *Encyclopedia of Ukraine*, 5: 880.

27 Quoted in Turii, '"Rus'ka istoriia,"' 137.

28 See Sharanevych, *Istoriia Halytsko-Volodymyrskoi Rusy vid naidavnishykh vremen do roku 1453*.

29 See Deditskii, *Narodnaia istoriia Rusi*. The work first appeared as a series of articles in 1867–9. Apart from *Narodnaia istoriia Rusi*, Didytsky wrote *Russkaia letopis' (ot 862 do 1340)* and *Letopis' Rusi ot 1340 do 1887 goda*.

30 See Ripets'kyi, *Iliustrovannaia narodnaia istoriia Rusi*.

31 Velychenko, *National History as Cultural Process*, 172–6.

32 Turii, '"Rus'ka istoriia,"' 138. Taniachkevych's assertion partly resembled views expressed by Izydor Sharanevych, who stated in the preface to his *Istoriia Halytsko-Volodymyrskoi Rusy* that in publishing his history he did not want to 'multiply the number of dreamers' (quoted in Zayarnyuk, 'Obtaining History').

33 See Zayarnyuk, 'Obtaining History.'

34 Quoted in Hrushevs'kyi, 'Apostolovi pratsi,' 19.
35 See Turii, '"Rus'ka istoriia,"' 139–40. More than thirty years later, that idea was to bear fruit with the invitation of Mykhailo Hrushevsky to Lviv University.
36 See Stefan Kaczała, *Polityka Polaków względem Rusi.*
37 On Kachala's interpretation of Ukrainian history, see Velychenko, *National History as Cultural Process*, 173–4.
38 On Barvinsky, see the entry by Elie Borshchak in *Encyclopedia of Ukraine*, 1: 180–1.
39 Barvins'kyi, *Spomyny s moho zhyttia*, 225.
40 Ibid., 317–21.
41 See *Encyclopedia of Ukraine*, s.v. 'Rus'ka istorychna biblioteka'; Doroshenko, *A Survey of Ukrainian Historiography*, 260–1.
42 Linnichenko's study *Cherty iz istorii soslovii v Iugo-Zapadnoi (Galitskoi) Rusi XIV–XV v.* appeared in Ukrainian translation as volume 7 of *Rus'ka istorychna biblioteka* under the title *Suspil'ni verstvy Halyts'koï Rusy XIV–XV v.* It was published instead of Antonovych's prospective study on the history of Cossackdom, which was solicited by Barvinsky but apparently never written. See editorial preface to Linnichenko, *Suspil'ni verstvy*, iii–iv.
43 See Ilovais'kyi, *Kniazhyi period istoriï Ukraïny-Rusy.*
44 See Barvins'kyi, *Spomyny z moho zhyttia*, 332–3.
45 See Barvins'kyi, *Iliustrovana istoriia Rusy.*
46 On changes in the Russophile interpretation of the Ukrainian past, see Zayarnyuk, 'Obtaining History'; Hrytsak, '"Iakykh-to kniaziv buly stolytsi v Kyievi?": 85–6.
47 See Zayarnyuk, 'Obtaining History,' 4.
48 Syniavs'kyi, *Vybrani pratsi*, 40.
49 For the meaning and usage of the term 'Ukraine,' see the article by Ihor Stebelsky in *Encyclopedia of Ukraine*, 5: 343–4.
50 See *Istoriia Rusov ili Maloi Rossii*, iii–iv. Ironically, for all the 'anti-Ukrainian' animus of its introduction, the *History of the Rus'* became a bible of the nineteenth-century Ukrainian national movement, cited and cherished by Taras Shevchenko and his generation of national awakeners.
51 See Barvins'kyi, *Spomyny z moho zhyttia*, 322.
52 Hrushevsky, *History*, 1: 2.
53 A letter signed by five members of the reading hall in the village of Kupchyntsi (Barvins'kyi, *Spomyny z moho zhyttia*, 337–8).
54 Hrushevsky issued the first excerpt from the unpublished *Zherela* using the compound term 'Ukraine-Rus'' in 1894. See Vynar, *Mykhailo Hrushevs'kyi, 1866–1934: Bibliographic Sources*, 109.

55 See Kolankowski's review of Hrushevsky's *History*, 348.
56 See Frankiewicz's review of Hrushevsky's *Die ukrainische Frage in historischer Entwicklung*, 174.
57 See Rawita-Gawroński, *Kozaczyzna ukrainna w Rzeczypospolitej Polskiej do końca XVIII wieku*. This interpretative history of Ukrainian Cossackdom from its beginnings to the end of the eighteenth century appeared in print in the aftermath of the Polish-Ukrainian War of 1918–19 and was openly anti-Ukrainian in spirit and content.
58 See Kapystiański, 'Schemat historii Ruskiej w teoretycznym i praktycznym ujęciu prof. Michała Hruszewskiego.'
59 Storozhenko devoted an article, 'Malaia Rossiia ili Ukraina' (1919), to the usage of the term 'Ukraine.' He subsequently repeated his argument in the monograph *Ukrainskoe dvizhenie* (1925), published under pseudonym A. Tsarinnyi (cf. the reprint of both works in *Ukrainskii separatizm v Rossii*, 280–90, 133–252). For the treatment of the term 'Ukraine' as a product of Austro-German intrigue, see Volkonskii, *Istoricheskaia pravda i ukraino-fil'skaia propaganda*, 28–39.
60 Hrushevs'kyi, 'Vstupnyi vyklad,' 149.
61 For Hrushevsky's assessment of Kostomarov's contribution to Ukrainian history and ethnography, see his 'Etnohrafichne dilo Kostomarova.'
62 See Kyian, 'Kafedral'ne "viruiu" Volodymyra Antonovycha,' 68.
63 For a summary of Antonovych's views on Ukrainian history, see Klid, 'Volodymyr Antonovych,' 378–86; Ul'ianovs'kyi, 'Syn Ukraïny (Volodymyr Antonovych: hromadianyn, uchenyi, liudyna),' 60–5.
64 Hrushevs'kyi, 'Vstupnyi vyklad,' 145–9.
65 See Hrushevsky, *History*, 1: 12–13.
66 Ibid., 1: 13. For a more detailed discussion of the evolution of Hrushevsky's views on the role of people, nation, and state in early modern Ukrainian history, see chapter 5 of the present work.
67 Hrushevsky, 'Traditional Scheme,' 37.
68 Linnichenko, *Malorusskii vopros*, 262.
69 See Pelenski, 'Ukrainian-Russian Debate,' 219–21; Velychenko, *National History as Cultural Process*, 144–71; Kohut, 'Development of a Ukrainian National Historiography,' 460–7.
70 Oleksander Ohloblyn later considered Syniavsky a forerunner of Hrushevsky in the new conceptualization of Ukrainian history. In a letter to Syniavsky's daughter, Ohloblyn wrote regarding her father's review of Barvinsky's book: 'There A.S. [Antin Syniavsky] actually presented (for the first time!) a concept of the history of Ukraine that M.S. Hrushevsky only *later* repeated in his well-known works' (excerpt from a private letter

of 15 January 1976, quoted in Bilokin', 'Antin Syniavs'kyi i ioho doba,' 14. Ohloblyn was quite right to indicate parallels in Syniavsky's and Hrushevsky's approaches to Ukrainian history, although it should not be forgotten that both were products of the Kyiv milieu of Antonovych's students and collaborators; moreover, Syniavsky never developed his views in any detail. There were also important differences in their approaches, some of which will be discussed below.

71 See Hrushevsky, 'Traditional Scheme,' 37, and *Iliustrovana istoriia*, 5–6.

72 See Efimenko, *Istoriia ukrainskogo naroda*, 389.

73 See Maksimovich, 'O prichinakh vzaimnogo ozhestocheniia poliakov i malorossiian,' 250.

74 Cf. Syniavs'kyi, *Vybrani pratsi*, 34–5.

75 See Hrushevs'kyi, *Iliustrovana istoriia*, 5–6.

76 When it comes to 'friendly' criticism, Hrushevsky's periodization of Ukrainian history was criticized both for being excessively statist and for not being statist enough. Writing in 1926, Hrushevsky's colleague Dmytro Bahalii noted that although Hrushevsky regarded the national idea as the basis of his *History*, 'in dividing the Ukrainian historical process into eras, [Hrushevsky] lays the statist, political idea at its foundation, uniting it with the socio-economic and cultural element' (see Bahalii, 'Akad. M.S. Hrushevs'kyi,' 199).

Adrian Kapystiański, writing in 1935, suggested that Hrushevsky's 'Lithuanian-Polish' period be extended at least to the age of Bohdan Khmelnytsky and the 'origins of Ukrainian statehood.' Otherwise, in Kapystiański's opinion, Hrushevsky's periodization would create the mistaken impression that Polish control over Ukraine ended at the close of the sixteenth century. Kapystiański was implying that Hrushevsky should have been more thorough in following the statist principle employed in his periodization of early Ukrainian history. At the same time, he criticized Hrushevsky for inconsistency in his attempt to provide a periodization of Ukrainian history based on the national principle. Kapystiański believed that the Union of Lublin (1569), which separated the Ukrainian territories from the Belarusian ones, marked a crucial turning point in the formation of the 'Ukrainian-Ruthenian' nationality. He proposed to improve Hrushevsky's scheme by terminating the 'Lithuanian-Polish' era in 1569 and introducing a Polish period covering the years 1569–1648. In effect, he was suggesting a return to the periodization of early modern Ukrainian history advocated (among others) by Maksymovych, Efimenko, and Syniavsky (see Kapystiański, 'Schemat historii Ruskiej,' 74–5).

77 Concerning Drahomanov's views on nations and nationalism, see Kruhlashov, *Drama intelektuala*, 220–56.

78 Hrushevsky, *History*, 1: 4–5. For an interpretation of Hrushevsky's views on the formation of nations as modelled on the development of biological organisms, see Tel'vak, *Teoretyko-metodolohichni pidstavy*, 88–9. For a discussion of the evolution of Hrushevsky's views on the role of the national factor based on his interpretation of the Khmelnytsky era, see chapter 5 of the present work.

79 See Hrushevsky, *History*, 1: 14–16.

80 Ibid., 16.

81 See Prymak, *Mykola Kostomarov*, 45–50.

82 Concerning the influence on Hrushevsky of the ideas of social evolution developed by Herbert Spencer, see Tel'vak, *Teoretyko-metodolohichni pidstavy*, 88. For Hrushevsky's assessment of the impact of Spencer's views on the development of historical sociology, see his *Pochatky hromadianstva (genetychna sotsiologiia)*, 17–22.

83 For the application of this scheme, see Hrushevsky's *Iliustrovana istoriia*. For the use of the terms 'first' and 'second' revival, see volume 5 of Hrushevsky's *Istoriia ukraïns'koï literatury* (1960). The first edition of the volume, which appeared in Kyiv in 1926–7, bore the subtitle 'Cultural and Literary Currents in Ukraine in the Sixteenth and Seventeenth Centuries, and the First Revival (1580–1610).'

84 See Hrushevsky, *History*, 1: 15.

85 See *Sinopsis. Kiev, 1681. Facsimile mit einer Einleitung*.

86 See Grushevskii, *Ocherk* (1904), 67. Cf. Hrushevs'kyi, *Istoriia*, 2: 1.

87 See Hrushevs'kyi, *Istoriia*, 2: 1–2, and *Iliustrovana istoriia*, 11.

88 At that time, Hrushevsky believed not only that the people were the only hero of history but also that 'the state order in every age is of interest to us mainly insofar as it influenced the condition of the people, insofar as it was itself subject to the influence of the community, and insofar as it responded to the community's desires and strivings' (Hrushevs'kyi, 'Vstupnyi vyklad,' 149).

89 Hrushevs'kyi, 'Vstupnyi vyklad,' 149.

90 Hrushevs'kyi, *Iliustrovana istoriia*, 133. To be sure, in 1912 Hrushevsky still believed, as he had in 1894, that the popular masses suffered under the oppression of the elites. As a result, they did not share the political aspirations of the ruling class and were either indifferent or hostile to elite state-building projects. See Grushevskii, *Ocherk* (1911), 145–9; cf. his *Iliustrovana istoriia*, 132.

91 Ibid.

92 Hrushevsky the national historian, unlike Hrushevsky the populist activist, clearly distinguished between the Ukrainian and the 'foreign' state and was prepared to use all his resources as a historian to unmask and condemn the foreign oppressors of the Ukrainian people and their culture. In his *Illustrated History of Ukraine*, Hrushevsky presented the following picture of interrelations between the interests of the nation, state, elites, and popular masses: 'It is a terrible pity that the decline of sovereignty did not allow it [national and cultural life] to develop and cut it off at its very root. True, life was not sweet for ordinary people under their princes and boyars, and they gained little satisfaction from those cultural seedlings. But things became no easier for them when their own masters were replaced by foreign ones. Social and economic circumstances did not improve because of that, but worsened, as did the condition of the people. And national and cultural life was dealt a blow from which it could not recover, not even to the present day' (Hrushevs'kyi, *Iliustrovana istoriia*, 138).

93 See Hrushevsky, *History*, 1: 406; cf. his *Iliustrovana istoriia*, 72–82.

94 Hrushevs'kyi, *Iliustrovana istoriia*, 80–1.

95 Hrushevsky, who dismissed as fictitious the Primary Chronicle's story about the invitation to the Varangians, defended its account of the Christianization of Rus' (especially Volodymyr's 'trial of faiths') against Shakhmatov's deconstruction of that account. See Hrushevsky, *History*, 1: 444–8. Cf. Ševčenko, 'The Christianization of Kievan Rus''; Poppe, *The Rise of Christian Russia*.

96 On Hrushevsky's treatment of Volodymyr, Roman, and Danylo, see Iakovenko, 'Osoba, iak diiach istorychnoho protsesu v istoriohrafiï Mykhaila Hrushevs'koho,' 90–2.

97 See Hrushevs'kyi, *Iliustrovana istoriia*, 111. On the history of the Galician-Volhynian principality, see Kryp'iakevych, *Halyts'ko-Volyns'ke kniazivstvo*. For a brief account of its history and the current state of research, see Isaievych, 'Halyts'ko-Volyns'ke kniazivstvo doby Danyla Halyts'koho ta ioho nashchadkiv.'

98 Hrushevs'kyi, *Iliustrovana istoriia*, 81; Grushevskii, *Ocherk* (1911), 99–100.

99 Grushevskii, *Ocherk* (1911), 56–83.

100 Ibid., 100.

101 See Hrushevs'kyi, *Istoriia*, 4: 4.

102 See Hrushevsky, *History*, 1: 15.

103 *Istoriia Rusov*, iii–iv.

104 See Kostomarov's polemical works, 'Otvet na vykhodki gazety (Krakovskoi) *Czas* i zhurnala *Revue Contemporaine*,' 'Pravda poliakam o

Rusi,' 'Ukrainskii separatizm,' and 'Poliakam-mirotvortsam.' Kostomarov was especially critical of theories claiming that the Poles and Ukrainians were one people divided by the Norman intervention or that Ukrainians represented an ethnos whose language was little more than a dialect of Polish and that was destined to become part of the larger Polish nation. Kostomarov's attacks on the Poles were partly inspired by the theories of Franciszek Duchiński, who claimed that the Russians/Muscovites were not of Slavic stock. See Prymak, *Mykola Kostomarov*, 111–12. On Duchiński, see Rudnytsky, 'Franciszek Duchiński and His Impact on Ukrainian Political Thought.'

105 See Kostomarov, 'O kazachestve. Otvet *Vilenskomu vestniku*' and 'Otvet g. Padalitse.'

106 For Antonovych's critique of Polish historical myths pertaining to Ukraine, see his review of Henryk Sienkiewicz's classic novel *With Fire and Sword*, 'Pol'sko-russkie sootnosheniia XVII v. v sovremennoi pol'skoi prizme.' For Antonovych's response to Polish claims about the tolerant character of the Commonwealth's religious policies in Ukraine, see his 'Ocherk otnoshenii pol'skogo gosudarstva k pravoslaviiu i pravoslavnoi tserkvi.'

107 If Kostomarov's deconstruction of the Polish historical paradigm was mostly presented in the context of Russian-Polish debates concerning the Polish uprising of 1863 and was influenced by the political atmosphere of the moment, Maksymovych's main attack on the theory of Poland's civilizing mission in Ukraine took place before the uprising and was much more scholarly in character.

108 See Maksimovich, 'O prichinakh.' Maksymovych was responding to an article by Grabowski that appeared in Russian translation in the second of the two volumes of *Zapiski o Iuzhnoi Rusi* (St Petersburg, 1856–7), edited by Panteleimon Kulish.

109 It was in this context that Maksymovych went on to question the position taken by the translator and publisher of Grabowski's article, Panteleimon Kulish, who explained the Polish-Ukrainian conflict predominantly as a manifestation of social antagonism between the Ukrainian popular masses and the Polish landlords. In the long run, Maksymovych's critique of the views of Grabowski and Kulish on the role of the Ukrainian nobility in Polish-Ukrainian relations of the seventeenth century laid the foundations for subsequent research on the history of Ukrainian elites, as well as for Viacheslav Lypynsky's 'rehabilitation' of the nobility in Ukrainian historiography, which had been dominated for decades by representatives of the populist ideology.

110 Hrushevsky, *Istoriia*, 3: 146.

111 Ibid., 6: 412.

112 In volume 1 of the *History*, Hrushevsky devoted significant attention to the history of Ukrainian settlement on the ethnic Polish borderland (*History*, 1: 162–7). The question of who first settled the area, Poles or Ukrainians, had a clear political significance and remained a sensitive issue in relations between the two nations for most of the twentieth century. Accordingly, it comes as no surprise that Hrushevsky's argument in volume 1 of the *History* in favour of the original settlement of many border areas by Ukrainians met with criticism from a Polish reviewer of his work, Aleksander Brückner (cf. his 'Dogmat normański,' 676–7). For Hrushevsky's treatment of the issue of the 'Cherven towns' on the Polish-Ukrainian border, see his *History*, 1: 371–6, and *Istoriia*, 2: 577–9.

113 See Hrushevs'kyi, *Istoriia*, 6: 297.

114 Ibid.

115 Ibid., 4: 3–4.

116 See Hrushevs'kyi, *Istoriia*, 4: 63–99; cf. his *Iliustrovana istoriia*, 139–46.

117 See Hrushevs'kyi, *Istoriia*, 4: 180–4, 265–6, 338–423.

118 On the history of the Union of Lublin and its impact on Ukraine, see Pelenski, 'The Incorporation of the Ukrainian Lands of Kievan Rus' into Crown Poland (1569)'; Bardach, Leśnodorski, and Pietrzak, *Historia państwa i prawa polskiego*, 128–31, 191; Iakovenko, 'Zdobutky i vtraty Liublins'koï uniï'; Rusyna, *Ukraïna pid tataramy i Lytvoiu*, 196–204.

119 Hrushevs'kyi, *Iliustrovana istoriia*, 194.

120 Ibid., 194–7.

121 See Hrushevs'kyi, *Istoriia*, 5: 1–384; 6: 1–293.

122 Ibid., 5: 216–21; cf. his *History*, 7, and *Iliustrovana istoriia*, 197–201.

123 See Hrushevsky, *History*, 7: 201–2. The same view has been taken recently by Henryk Litwin in his monograph *Napływ szlachty polskiej na Ukrainę, 1569–1648* and in his article 'Katolizacja szlachty ruskiej, 1569–1647.' See also Iakovenko, *Ukraïns'ka shliakhta z kintsia XIV do seredyny XVII st.*

124 Volodymyr Vashchenko (*Nevrasteniia*, 224–6) has recently argued that Hrushevsky often subconsciously attributed features to Polish culture that he himself lacked and considered generally negative and decadent.

125 Quoted in Velychenko, *National History as Cultural Process*, 49. For a survey of Polish interpretations of Ukrainian history, see also 3–75. For Polish views on the history of Russia in the late nineteenth and early twentieth centuries, see Filipowicz, *Wobec Rosji*.

126 See Kolankowski's review in *Kwartalnik Historyczny* 27 (1913): 348–65.

127 Ibid., 356.

128 Hrushevs'kyi, *Istoriia*, 6: 299.

129 Hrushevsky, *History*, 7: 312.

130 See Hrushevs'kyi, 'Kul'turno-natsional'nyi rukh,' 143.

131 Hrushevsky, *History*, 7: lxiv.

132 According to Anthony D. Smith, 'the rediscovery of an ethnic past, and especially of a golden age that can act as an inspiration for contemporary problems and needs,' is an important factor in the 'cultural purification' of national movements. 'These pasts,' continues Smith, 'then [become] standards against which to measure the alleged failings of the present generation and contemporary community' ('Culture, Community and Territory,' 450).

133 See Armstrong, 'Myth and History in the Evolution of Ukrainian Consciousness.' On the role of myth in modern society, see Kolakowski, *The Presence of Myth.*

134 See Kohut, *Russian Centralism and Ukrainian Autonomy*, 59–63, 258–76.

135 On the development of early modern Ukrainian historiography, see Sysyn, 'The Cultural, Social and Political Context of Ukrainian History-Writing: 1620–1690' and 'The Cossack Chronicles and the Development of Modern Ukrainian Culture and National Identity.' On the cult of Bohdan Khmelnytsky in early modern Ukraine, see Plokhy, *Tsars and Cossacks*, 45–54.

136 For the history of the veneration of Cossackdom in Ukraine, see Sysyn, 'The Reemergence of the Ukrainian Nation and Cossack Mythology'; Plokhy, 'Historical Debates and Territorial Claims.'

137 For a general survey of literature on the history of the Cossacks published before 1965, see Vynar, 'Ohliad istorychnoï literatury pro pochatky ukraïns'koï kozachchyny.'

138 See Hrushevsky's autobiographies in *Velykyi ukraïnets'*, 198, 222.

139 See Rudnytsky, 'Intellectual Origins of Modern Ukraine,' 130.

140 Levitskii, *Ocherki vnutrennei istorii Malorossii*, 30–1.

141 Hrushevs'kyi, *Istoriia*, 9: 1482–3. Hrushevsky also noted Antonovych's lack of enthusiasm for Cossackdom in his article of 1928 on the legacy of his former professor. See Hrushevs'kyi, 'Z sotsiial'no-natsional'nykh kontseptsii Antonovycha,' 13–14.

142 See Hrushevs'kyi, 'Khmel'nyts'kyi.'

143 See Grushevskii, *Ocherk* (1904), 248–9.

144 See Hrushevsky's preface to volume 7 of the *History* (7: lxiv–lxvi) and my introduction to the English translation of the volume, 'Revisiting the Golden Age,' xxxvii, xl–xliv.

145 See Pritsak, 'Istoriosofiia Mykhaila Hrushevs'koho,' lxi. Compare

Hrushevsky's introduction with the third edition of the same volume (1913), where he added a comment on the leading role of the Cossack stratum in the popular movements of the period (Hrushevsky, *History*, 1: 15–16).

146 Hrushevsky, *History*, 7: lxiv.
147 Ibid.
148 See Hrushevs'kyi, 'Vstupnyi vyklad,' 149.
149 See Hrushevsky, *History*, 7: lxiii and lxiv–lxv.
150 Ibid., 54.
151 Volodymyr Antonovych's views on the origins of the Ukrainian Cossacks were developed in his 'Soderzhanie aktov o kazakakh' and *Besidy pro chasy kozats'ki na Ukraïni*. For a critique of Antonovych's 'princely' theory of the origins of the Cossacks, see Maksymovych, *Istoricheskie pis'ma o kazakakh pridneprovskikh k M.F. Iuzefovichu*.
152 See Hrushevsky, *History*, 7: 58, 102–8.
153 Ibid., 58.
154 Ibid., 236n.76.
155 Ibid., 109.
156 Ibid., 41.
157 Ibid., 101.
158 Ibid., 81–2, 100–1.
159 Ibid., 1: 9–12.
160 Ibid., 7: 209–10.
161 Ibid., 166–8, 185–91, 288–92, 366–7.
162 Ibid., 206–7.
163 Ibid., 39–41, 50–1.
164 Ibid., 120–1. Among those who disputed Hrushevsky's theory of the largely Ukrainian ethnicity of the Cossacks in the sixteenth century was a Polish historian, Władysław Tomkiewicz. He argued that Cossackdom was initially a multiethnic phenomenon, although eventually its non-Ukrainian elements were fully assimilated by the Ukrainian ethnic majority in the Cossack Host. Tomkiewicz clearly disagreed with Hrushevsky in his interpretation of Cossack social history, emphasizing the role of the Polish nobility in the formation of Cossackdom. See Tomkiewicz, *Kozaczyzna ukrainna* and 'O składzie społecznym i etnicznym Kozaczyzny ukrainnej na przełomie XVI i XVII wieku.' For the current state of research on the ethnic origin and national identity of the Ukrainian Cossacks, see Plokhy, *The Cossacks and Religion in Early Modern Ukraine*, 21–3, 145–75.

165 On the role of religion in Cossack ideology of the time, see Plokhy, *The Cossacks and Religion in Early Modern Ukraine.*
166 See Hrushevsky, *History,* 7: 303–5.
167 Ibid., 305n. 5.
168 Ibid., 305, 333–41.
169 Ibid., lxv.
170 Ibid.
171 Ibid., 401.
172 Ibid., 313.
173 Ibid., 304.
174 Ibid., 66–74, 449–52.
175 Ibid., 88.
176 See Hrushevs'kyi, 'Baida-Vyshnevets'kyi v poeziï i istoriï.' Owing to Vyshnevetsky's popularity in Ukrainian national historiography, Soviet historians viewed him as a symbol of Ukrainian nationalism and ardently rejected the assumption that Dmytro Vyshnevetsky and the Baida of the Ukrainian *duma* were the same person. The relatively moderate historian Volodymyr Holobutsky (1903–93), whose writings dominated Soviet historiography of the Cossacks from the 1950s to the 1980s, regarded attempts to identify Baida with Prince Vyshnevetsky as a direct challenge to the class-oriented approach to Ukrainian history. According to Holobutsky, the Zaporozhian Host had been created exclusively by the popular masses, not by magnates and nobles such as Vyshnevetsky. Even Vyshnevetsky's association with Tsar Ivan the Terrible did not save him from harsh criticism on the part of the Soviet historian. Holobutsky's views on the history of the Cossacks were formed back in the 1930s and differed from the prevailing historiographic trend of the 1980s, when the 'merits' of Ukrainian historical figures were determined not so much by their class origins as by their loyalty to Russia. See V. Golobutskii, *Zaporozhskoe kazachestvo,* 71–87, and *Istoriia Ukraïns'koï RSR,* vol. 1, bk. 2, ed. Holobuts'kyi, 124.
177 On relations between Hrushevsky and Jarosz, see Mytsyk, 'Z poshtovoï skryn'ky Mykhaila Hrushevs'koho.'
178 See Hrushevsky, *History,* 7: 118–24, 456–8.
179 See *Istoriia Rusov,* 34.
180 Hrushevsky, *History,* 7: 140.
181 Ibid., 164.
182 Ibid., 195–6, 197–8, 239. For a critique of this approach, see Korduba, 'Die Anfänge des ukrainischen Kozakentums.'

183 See Hrushevsky, *History*, 7: 210, 412.

184 Ibid., 140.

185 See Bahalii, 'Akad. M.S. Hrushevs'kyi,' 204–7.

186 For comparisons between Hrushevsky and Palacký, see Kryp'iakevych, *Mykhailo Hrushevs'kyi*, 480; Sysyn, 'Introduction to the *History of Ukraine-Rus'*,' xxii, xxv.

187 According to one of the letters to Hrushevsky, the information about the lifting of the ban was announced in a Russian newspaper, apparently in February 1905. (See a letter to Hrushevsky of 1 March 1905 from A. Denysenko, one of those interested in acquiring the *History*, in TsDIAK, fond 1235, op. 1, no. 303, fol. 308.) A Ukrainian activist in Odesa, Petro Klymovych, whose letter of 20 March 1905 was discussed in the previous chapter, also asked Hrushevsky about the *History* (see no. 874, fol. 5).

188 See TsDIAK, fond 1235, op. 1, no. 303, fols 301–6.

189 See, for example, letters to Hrushevsky from a political exile in Ust-Sysolsk, Hryhorii Porevych, and I.M. Bibikov, writing on behalf of a group of exiled Ukrainians in Turiansk (TsDIAK, fond 1235, op. 1, no. 303, fols 237–8, 240).

190 See Porevych's postcard of 29 March 1912 to Hrushevsky in TsDIAK, fond 1235, op. 1, no. 303, fol. 240.

191 TsDIAK, fond 1235, op. 1, no. 303, fols 301–2.

192 Iaronovetsky's letter of 25 February 1912 was forwarded to Hrushevsky by Iurkevych on 24 March 1912 with the following note: 'I received this letter from a Ukrainian worker who emigrated to Siberia and is working at a factory there. I had sent him some Ukrainian books – among others, your *Illustrated History*' (TsDIAK, fond 1235, op. 1, no. 303, 164–6).

193 Iaronovetsky then quoted a passage from the *Illustrated History* in which Hrushevsky noted problems arising from the exclusive nature of the Cossack officer councils that ruled Ukraine, which did not include representatives of other social strata.

194 Quoted in 'Ssylka M.S. Grushevskogo,' 209–10.

Chapter 4: Negotiating with the Bolsheviks

1 On Hrushevsky's return to Ukraine, see Pyrih, *Zhyttia Mykhaila Hrushevs'koho*, 16–17. Both Pyrih and Prymak (*Mykhailo Hrushevsky*, 205) give 7 March 1924 as the date of Hrushevsky's return to Kyiv. The secret police report about his return gives 8 March. For the text of the report, see Prystaiko and Shapoval, *Mykhailo Hrushevs'kyi i HPU-NKVD*, appendix 1, p. 130.

2 Mykyta Shapoval, 'Politychna smert' M. Hrushevs'koho.' Quoted in Prystaiko and Shapoval, *Mykhailo Hrushevs'kyi i HPU-NKVD*, 30.
3 See GPU report of 18 March 1924, ibid., appendix 2, p. 132.
4 See Shevchenko, 'Chomu Mykhailo Hrushevs'kyi povernuvsia na Radians'ku Ukraïnu?'
5 For Hrushevsky's brief references to his activities during the revolution, see his 'Avtobiohrafiia, 1926,' 239–40. For a discussion of his experiences under the Skoropadsky regime and his attitude toward it, see Prymak, *Mykhailo Hrushevsky*, 180–4.
6 See Prymak, *Mykhailo Hrushevsky*, 185–201.
7 The conference took place in Prague from 14 to 19 February 1920. For the text of its resolutions, see *Boritesia – poborete!* no. 1 (September 1920): 55–8.
8 For a summary of the Foreign Delegation's efforts to reach an understanding with the communist regime in Ukraine, see 'Vid Zakordonnoï delehatsiï Ukraïns'koï partiï sotsiialistiv-revoliutsioneriv do partiinykh orhanizatsii i tovaryshiv za kordonom,' 2. The statement was issued in Vienna on 3 August 1921.
9 The conference took place in Prague from 24 to 26 April 1920. For the text of its resolutions, see *Boritesia – poborete!* 1921, no. 9, 59–60.
10 The conference took place in Prague from 22 to 24 May 1920. For the text of the declaration, signed on behalf of the Foreign Delegation by Hrushevsky, Mykola Shrah, Mykola Chechel, and Oleksander Zhukovsky, see ibid., 61–4.
11 The letter was dated 19 July 1920 in Prague. For the text, see 'Lyst M.S. Hrushevs'koho do sekretaria TsK KP(b)U S.V. Kosiora' in *Velykyi ukraïnets'*, 268–74.
12 On changes in Bolshevik nationality policy in Ukraine, see Borys, *The Sovietization of Ukraine, 1917–1923*, 249–57; Martin, *The Affirmative Action Empire*, 78. The turning point in Bolshevik cultural policy in Ukraine is apparent in the 'Theses of the Central Committee RKP(b) Concerning Policy in the Ukraine' drafted by Vladimir Lenin. See Pipes and Brandenberger, *The Unknown Lenin*, 76–7. On Borotbism, see Maistrenko, *Borot'bism*.
13 Hrushevs'kyi, 'Mizh Moskvoiu i Varshavoiu,' 12–13. The resolution of the first conference of the UPSR abroad (Prague, 14–19 February 1920) explained the conflict between the two 'revolutionary governments,' Russian and Ukrainian, by indicating differences between the revolutions in the two countries. The authors of the resolution claimed that owing to insufficient industrial development and the lack of a sizable working class, as well as the predominance of colonial forms of exploitation, the revolution

490 Notes to pages 219–25

in Ukraine had taken on characteristics different from those developed by the Russian Revolution, turning into an agrarian-peasant and national-liberation movement. For the text of the resolution, see *Boritesia – poborete!* no. 1 (September 1920): 55.

14 Hrushevs'kyi, 'Mizh Moskvoiu i Varshavoiu,' 13.

15 Ibid., 4–13.

16 See Hrushevs'kyi, 'Ukraïns'ka partiia.'

17 See Hrushevs'kyi, 'Shevchenko iak providnyk sotsiial'noï revoliutsiï.'

18 See Hrushevs'kyi, 'Ukraïns'ka partiia,' 16–20.

19 See Hrushevs'kyi [M. Serhiienko], 'Hromads'kyi rukh na Vkraïni-Rusy v XIII vitsi.'

20 Hrushevs'kyi, 'Ukraïns'ka partiia,' 12.

21 Ibid., 11.

22 Ibid., 12.

23 Ibid., 16.

24 For Doroshenko's and Lypynsky's attacks on Hrushevsky based on statements made in that article, see chapter 5 of the present work.

25 Hrushevs'kyi, 'Ukraïns'ka partiia,' 50.

26 See Hrushevs'kyi, 'Lyst M.S. Hrushevs'koho do sekretaria TsK KP(b)U S.V. Kosiora,' 272.

27 See Pyrih, *Zhyttia Mykhaila Hrushevs'koho*, 25.

28 Hrushevs'kyi, 'Pam'iati Paryz'koï Komuny,' 7.

29 For an overview of UPSR contacts with the Bolshevik regime in Ukraine, see 'Vid Zakordonnoï delehatsiï Ukraïns'koï partiï sotsiialistiv-revoliutsioneriv.' For Hrushevsky's position on the issue, see Prymak, *Mykhailo Hrushevsky*, 197–200.

30 In the summer of 1921, the Foreign Delegation adopted a number of resolutions, first dissolving the party structures led by Shapoval, then prohibiting him from conducting any political activities on behalf of the party and, finally, expelling him from party ranks. Given that most party members supported Shapoval, not Hrushevsky, the impact of those resolutions appears to have been very limited. For the text of the resolutions, see 'Fakty i dokumenty.'

31 On Shumsky, see the article by Roman Senkus and Arkadii Zhukovsky in *Encyclopedia of Ukraine*, 4: 686–7; Maistrenko, *Borot'bism*; Mace, *Communism and the Dilemmas of National Liberation*, 86–119; Martin, *The Affirmative Action Empire*, 212–28.

32 See Chechel', 'Zvidomlennia z moieï komandirovky na Vkraïnu.' In a private letter of 3 June 1921 to imprisoned members of the Central Com-

mittee, Hrushevsky called on them to support Ukraine's cooperation with Soviet Russia, placing his hopes in the forthcoming negotiations with Oleksander Shumsky. See an extract from Hrushevsky's letter to the imprisoned members of the Central Committee in Vsevolod Balytsky's report of 8 February 1927 to Lazar Kaganovich and Volodymyr Zatonsky (Prystaiko and Shapoval, *Mykhailo Hrushevs'kyi i HPU-NKVD*, appendix 32, pp. 175–81, here 175).

33   For excerpts from the minutes of the Politburo meeting of 4 June 1921, see *Mykhailo Hrushevs'kyi: mizh istoriieiu ta politykoiu*, 18.

34   On the basis of Shumsky's information, Chechel later reported that the Politburo resolution considered desirable 'the return to Ukraine for participation in Soviet construction of individuals from the F[oreign] D[elegation], especially Comrade M.S. Hrushevsky. That return would be facilitated in every way and they would be given every opportunity at the disposition of the government of the Ukrainian SSR to conduct their work in Ukraine, but the precondition of that return would have to be the departure of those individuals from the UPSR' (Chechel', 'Zvidomlennia,' 9). Judging by Chechel's report, in May 1921 the Foreign Delegation received a telegram from the Soviet representative in Riga, who tried to arrange a meeting between Shumsky and Zhukovsky in order to convey the Politburo's message to the delegation. The meeting did not occur because of a change in Shumsky's travel plans.

35   See Chechel', 'Zvidomlennia,' 10–11.

36   Hrushevs'kyi, 'Vidkrytyi lyst,' 8.

37   See *Mykhailo Hrushevs'kyi: mizh istoriieiu i politykoiu*, 27. Cf. Pyrih, *Zhyttia Mykhaila Hrushevs'koho*, 30.

38   See Hrushevsky's letter of 17 November 1923 to Studynsky, *Lysty*, 133.

39   On Hrushevsky's criticism of Vynnychenko, see Prymak, *Mykhailo Hrushevsky*, 199.

40   *Lysty*, 12.

41   See Hrushevsky to Studynsky in *Lysty*, 43.

42   *Lysty*, 48.

43   See Prystaiko and Shapoval, *Mykhailo Hrushevs'kyi i HPU-NKVD*, 31.

44   See *Lysty* (17 November 1923), 133.

45   In a letter to his American correspondent Tymotei Pochynok mailed from Kyiv in September 1924, Hrushevsky wrote with regard to the status of his academic position: 'You remind me of my words that I was never an official and do not wish to be one – even a Soviet one, but I have not been false to them. I told them [so] when they proposed that I become an agent

for the publication of books abroad. Well, and if I have accepted election as a member of the academy, do you not understand that this is not a government post?' ('Lysty M. Hrushevs'koho do T. Pochynka,' 295).

46 See Pyrih, *Zhyttia Mykhaila Hrushevs'koho*, 34. That decision was also approved by the Politburo in Moscow. Quite telling with regard to Bolshevik interpretations of the status of Soviet Ukraine in the USSR were the terms used in Kharkiv and Moscow concerning Hrushevsky's return. If the Ukrainian Politburo voted in favour of allowing Hrushevsky to return 'to Ukraine,' the Politburo in Moscow voted on Hrushevsky's admission 'to Russia' and decided to allow him to return to 'the USSR.' See extracts from the minutes of the proceedings of the two politburos in *Mykhailo Hrushevs'kyi: mizh istoriieiu i politykoiu*, nos. 12, 13, p. 31.

47 See references to Hrushevsky's correspondence with the academy in his letters to Studynsky, *Lysty*, 69, 103, 106, 119, 129, 134, 137–8. For the text of one of those letters, see *Mykhailo Hrushevs'kyi: mizh istoriieiu i politykoiu*, no. 17, p. 33.

48 'Lyst M. Hrushevs'koho do T. Pochynka,' 294.

49 See Hrushevsky's letter of 1 October 1923 to Studynsky in *Lysty*, 125–6.

50 See Prymak, *Mykhailo Hrushevsky*, 202–3.

51 See Hrushevsky's letters of 1, 8, and 25 October 1923 to Studynsky in *Lysty*, 125–9.

52 See Prymak, *Mykhailo Hrushevsky*, 204.

53 *Lysty*, 134.

54 See Hrushevsky's letters to Studynsky in *Lysty*, 132, 136, 141.

55 In November 1921 Hrushevsky wrote to his American correspondent V. Kuziv with regard to his prospective return to Ukraine: 'I am making preparations with great anxiety. As far as getting there is concerned, I will probably manage, but getting back – who knows? And what awaits me there?' (quoted in Reshod'ko, 'Povernennia na Ukraïnu,' 386). In a letter to Pochynok, Hrushevsky stated that the authorities had promised him freedom to leave the USSR as he pleased. See *Mykhailo Hrushevs'kyi: mizh istoriieiu i politykoiu*, 33–4.

56 'Lyst M. Hrushevs'koho do T. Pochynka,' 294–5. There (295–6) and in a letter to Studynsky (*Lysty*, [19 January 1924], 139–41, here 141) Hrushevsky responded to those members of the Ukrainian political and cultural elite in Ukraine and abroad who condemned his decision to return.

57 'Lyst M. Hrushevs'koho do T. Pochynka,' 295.

58 See *Lysty*, 125.

59 *Lysty*, 133. The motif of the reunification of Ukrainian lands was also present in Hrushevsky's letter to Pochynok, where he wrote: 'Here,

regardless of all the defects, I feel that I am in the Ukrainian republic that
we began to build in 1917, and I hope that the defects will be smoothed
out in time, and that it will also unite the Ukrainian lands that are beyond
its borders today' ('Lyst M. Hrushevs'koho do T. Pochynka,' p. 296).

60 *Lysty*, 132.

61 For a recent discussion of some of these issues in relation to the communist takeover of the Russian/All-Union Academy of Sciences, see Tolz,
Russian Academicians and the Revolution.

62 On Hrushevsky's founding of the Ukrainian Sociological Institute and
his plans to transfer its activities to Ukraine, see Masnenko, *Istorychni
kontseptsiï*, 29–37, 39–41.

63 On Hrushevsky's view of the academy in 1918–19, see Prymak, *Mykhailo
Hrushevsky*, 182–3, 186; Polons'ka-Vasylenko, *Ukraïns'ka Akademiia Nauk*,
1: 17–18.

64 In 1922, when organizing relief for Ukrainian scholars through the network of the Ukrainian Scientific Society (by that time formally part of the
Academy of Sciences), Hrushevsky was in fact competing with the aid
effort arranged by the leadership of the academy. As it appears from
Hrushevsky's letters to Studynsky, his main concern and source of dissatisfaction with the academy was its non-Ukrainian character. See *Lysty*, 18,
21, 23, 103, 105, 106, 119, 120, 129, 134, 136, 137.

65 See the secret police report of 15 March 1924, addressed by the head of the
Kyiv gubernia branch of the GPU to the Kharkiv authorities, in Prystaiko
and Shapoval, *Mykhailo Hrushevs'kyi i HPU-NKVD*, appendix 1, pp. 130–2.
The GPU report of 20 March 1924 implies that Hrushevsky was prepared
for the reception he was given at the academy: 'Two hours after arriving in
Kyiv, he appeared at the All-Ukrainian Academy of Sciences for a meeting,
where, according to the expression of the secret operative, he issued a
challenge to the battle that will inevitably break out' (ibid., appendix 4, p.
133).

66 Judging by his diaries, Iefremov believed that Hrushevsky was concerned
primarily with his own projects and the promotion of his relatives in the
academy (see Iefremov, *Shchodennyky*, 85–6, 90). Hrushevsky, for his part,
believed that Iefremov belonged 'to the category of people who consider
themselves hard done by and undervalued under any circumstances'
(*Lysty*, 140).

67 Hrushevsky protested against entering Krymsky's statement, 'I am a
communist,' in the minutes of one of the academic meetings. See the GPU
report of 15 December 1925 in Prystaiko and Shapoval, *Mykhailo
Hrushevs'kyi i HPU-NKVD*, appendix 10, p. 139. According to the same

report, Krymsky and Iefremov were the ones who lobbied the authorities in 1923 to permit Hrushevsky's return to Ukraine (ibid., 138). On Krymsky's relations with Hrushevsky, see Pavlychko, *Natsionalizm, seksual'nist', oriientalizm*, 297–322.

68 According to GPU reports, Hrushevsky's opponents in the academy viewed him as an 'intriguer, a false and vengeful individual.' See the GPU report of 15 December 1925 in Prystaiko and Shapoval, *Mykhailo Hrushevs'kyi i HPU-NKVD*, appendix 10, p. 139. Cf. Iefremov, *Shchodennyky*, 172, 187, 206, 398–9.

69 For Hrushevsky's activities in the academy, see Sokhan' et al., *M.S. Hrushevs'kyi i Academia*; Iurkova, *Diial'nist' naukovo-doslidnoï kafedry istoriï Ukraïny M.S. Hrushevs'koho (1924–1930)*.

70 See Hrushevs'kyi, 'Lyst M. Hrushevs'koho do T. Pochynka' [16 September 1924], 294, 296. In a letter of 29 November 1924 to Studynsky, Hrushevsky wrote: 'The fact that I sometimes write about the difficulties here by no means signifies that I regret my return. On the contrary, we are all very glad to have returned, and, as you see, I am managing to get something done here after all' (*Lysty*, 165–6).

71 *Lysty*, 147–8.

72 Ibid., 155. On the Ukrainization policy, see Mace, *Communism and the Dilemmas of National Liberation*; Martin, *Affirmative Action Empire*, 75–124.

73 Before leaving for Kyiv, Hrushevsky expressed concern in a letter to Studynsky about the possible negative reaction of the Bolshevik authorities to the publication of the book, which was financed by Ukrainian Protestants in the United States. He completed the manuscript after his return to Kyiv and forwarded it to Studynsky from there. In a letter of 22 May 1924, he wrote conspiratorially: 'Do you already have my manuscript, which Havrysevych was to pass on through Iurii? (It begins: 'From the prehistoric depths'; there are 34 pages altogether.) I shall forward the conclusion soon via the mission. Kuziv is to send money for the publication' (*Lysty*, 152).

74 See extracts from the GPU report on Hrushevsky's stay in Kharkiv in April 1924 in Prystaiko and Shapoval, *Mykhailo Hrushevs'kyi i HPU-NKVD*, appendix 6, pp. 136–7. That information was later repeated by the head of Ukrainian GPU, Vsevolod Balytsky, in his report to the Ukrainian Politburo members Kaganovich and Zatonsky in February 1927. See ibid., appendix 32, p. 176. Judging by the original report, the GPU obtained its information either from Lyzanivsky's wife or from someone close to her.

75 Prystaiko and Shapoval, *Mykhailo Hrushevs'kyi i HPU-NKVD*, appendix 32,

p. 179. This statement has much in common with Hrushevsky's views expressed in his letters to Studynsky prior to his departure for Ukraine.
76 Ibid.
77 See Pyrih, *Zhyttia Mykhaila Hrushevs'koho*, 42.
78 See Prymak, *Mykhailo Hrushevsky*, 225. For an example of GPU documentation related to the secret police surveillance of Hrushevsky, see Prystaiko and Shapoval, *Mykhailo Hrushevs'kyi i HPU-NKVD*, appendix 27, p. 170.
79 See Prystaiko and Shapoval, *Mykhailo Hrushevs'kyi i HPU-NKVD*, appendix 3, p. 133. On Hrushevsky's loyalty to his old political convictions, see numerous secret police reports ibid., appendix 7 (6 March 1925), pp. 136–7, and appendix 10 (15 December 1925), pp. 138–9.
80 See an extract from Kaganovich's report, ibid., appendix 34, pp. 182–3. For protests against the application of this term to Hrushevsky and his comrades and associates, as well as the difference between *smenovekhovtsy* in Russia and Ukraine, see Maistrenko, *Istoriia moho pokolinnia*, 216–17.
81 See Prymak, *Mykhailo Hrushevsky*, 182–3.
82 See the reference to that faction in the GPU report of 15 March 1924 in Prystaiko and Shapoval, *Mykhailo Hrushevs'kyi i HPU-NKVD*, appendix 1, p. 130. In a letter to Studynsky from Vienna dated 23 September 1923, Hrushevsky mentioned his receipt of a letter from Ukraine informing him that discussions were going on in Kyiv about putting him in charge of the academy. Hrushevsky remarked that no one had invited him to head the academy; that he did not intend to purge it, as suggested in the letter from Kyiv; and that his only wish was to return to Ukraine in order to continue work on the histories of Ukraine and Ukrainian literature (see *Lysty*, 124).
83 See Pyrih, *Zhyttia Mykhaila Hrushevs'koho*, 51.
84 See the report of 15 March 1924 from the Kyiv GPU branch to GPU headquarters in Kharkiv in Prystaiko and Shapoval, *Mykhailo Hrushevs'kyi i HPU-NKVD*, appendix 1, p. 131.
85 See the response from Kharkiv headquarters to the request of the Kyiv GPU branch, dated 26 March 1924, ibid., appendix 5, pp. 134–5.
86 The latter apparently left the meeting without answering Kaganovich's question of whether he considered Soviet power best for Ukraine. A rumour to that effect was recorded in Iefremov's diaries (*Shchodennyky*, 249).
87 See *Mykhailo Hrushevs'kyi: mizh istoriieiu i politykoiu*, 64. Cf. Pyrih, *Zhyttia Mykhaila Hrushevs'koho*, 47.
88 See *Mykhailo Hrushevs'kyi: mizh istoriieiu i politykoiu*, 65. Cf. Pyrih, *Zhyttia Mykhaila Hrushevs'koho*, 48–50.
89 The demand for one continued for most of 1926. See, for example, the

statement made at the celebration of Hrushevsky's jubilee in October 1926 by the Kyiv official Panas Liubchenko (*Velykyi ukraïnets'*, 420–5). At some point Hrushevsky had promised to make a statement of loyalty to the regime in the form of an open letter to Vlas Chubar, the head of Ukrainian government, but apparently never signed the prepared text. For Ivan Lakyza's attempt to persuade Hrushevsky to sign the letter, see Prystaiko and Shapoval, *Mykhailo Hrushevs'kyi i HPU-NKVD*, 56–7. The text of Hrushevsky's statement, which apparently was submitted to the authorities but did not fully satisfy them, has never been found. See Pyrih, *Zhyttia Mykhaila Hrushevs'koho*, 50.

90 See an extract from the Politburo resolution of 14 April 1926 in *Mykhailo Hrushevs'kyi: mizh istoriieiu i politykoiu*, 65–6, and in Prystaiko and Shapoval, *Mykhailo Hrushevs'kyi i HPU-NKVD*, appendix 12, pp. 140–1.

91 See Pyrih, *Zhyttia Mykhaila Hrushevs'koho*, 50–1. In his speech, Hrushevsky stated: 'In the times of the Central Rada, the Hetmanate, and the Directory, measures were taken for that purpose [the development of the academy] but were interrupted by ever new explosions of civil war, and only Soviet power, once it had stabilized, gained the opportunity to put the matter on a firm footing.' Hrushevs'kyi, 'Perspektyvy i vymohy ukraïns'koï nauky,' 10.

92 See *Proletars'ka pravda*, 14 April 1926; cf. Pyrih, *Zhyttia Mykhaila Hrushevs'koho*, 52.

93 See *Lysty*, p. 186.

94 See an extract from an undated letter from Hrushevsky to Studynsky in the report of 25 May 1926 from the Kyiv GPU office to Vsevolod Balytsky in Prystaiko and Shapoval, *Mykhailo Hrushevs'kyi i HPU-NKVD*, appendix 13, p. 142.

95 On the reaction of the Ukrainian intelligentsia to Hrushevsky's statement, see ibid., 141–5.

96 That promise was allegedly made by Panas Butsenko, the secretary of the Executive Committee of the All-Ukrainian Supreme Soviet. See Vsevolod Balytsky's report on Hrushevsky, dated 8 February 1927, in Prystaiko and Shapoval, *Mykhailo Hrushevs'kyi i HPU-NKVD*, appendix 32, p. 181. The data used by Balytsky came from Fedir Savchenko, who was Hrushevsky's de facto personal secretary and close collaborator in the academy.

97 See Polons'ka-Vasylenko, *Ukraïns'ka Akademiia Nauk*, 1: 46.

98 See Hrushevs'kyi, 'Hanebnii pam'iati' (1926). Twenty years earlier, in 1906, Hrushevsky had published an article under the same title to mark the thirtieth anniversary of the Ems Ukase of 1876. See his 'Hanebnii pamiaty' (1906).

99 The metaphor was apparently based on Gerhart Hauptmann's play *The*

Sunken Bell, which was popular in Ukraine at the time. See Maistrenko, *Istoriia moho pokolinnia,* 192.

100 On the resonance of Hrushevsky's article among the Ukrainian cultural intelligentsia and Ukrainian students in Kyiv, see the memoirs of Kostiuk, *Zustrichi i proshchannia,* 188.

101 On the official discourse concerning the nationality policy of the time and its rationale, see Martin, *Affirmative Action Empire,* 2–9.

102 On Mykola Khvyliovy and his writings, see Shkandrij, introduction to Khvylovy, *The Cultural Renaissance in Ukraine.*

103 On Skrypnyk, see Koshelivets', *Mykola Skrypnyk* and *Mykola Skrypnyk: statti i promovy z natsional'noho pytannia;* Mace, *Communism and the Dilemmas of National Liberation.*

104 On the controversy surrounding the speeches of Larin and Enukidze, see Martin, *Affirmative Action Empire,* 36–9.

105 On Richytsky, see the article by Vsevolod Holubnychy and Arkadii Zhukovsky in *Encyclopedia of Ukraine,* 4: 367. For a contemporary reaction to Richytsky's article, 'Chy hude zatoplenyi dzvin?' (Is the Sunken Bell Tolling?), published in the Kharkiv newspaper *Komunist,* see Maistrenko, *Istoriia moho pokolinnia,* 191–3. Maistrenko, who, like Richytsky, belonged to the independent Ukrainian Communist Party until 1925, believed that Richytsky had not been coerced to write that particular article. According to Maistrenko, the authorities might indeed have asked Richytsky to write such an article, but he could easily have refused without negative consequences. In Maistrenko's opinion, Richytsky believed in the ultimate success of Ukrainization and considered it important to support the authorities, who were implementing that policy.

106 The text of the speech was published in early 1927, following Shumsky's removal from the post of People's Commissar for Education, and was accompanied by the critical remarks of Shumsky's successor, Mykola Skrypnyk. See Shums'kyi, 'Ideolohichna borot'ba.'

107 Shumsky accused Khvyliovy of adopting the theory of the 'struggle of two cultures.' That theory had been formulated by Dmytro Lebed, the secretary of the Central Committee of the Communist Party of Ukraine in the early 1920s, to justify the policy of Russification and had subsequently been condemned by the party authorities. According to Shumsky, Khvyliovy shared this mistaken interpretation of the nationalities question with Lebed, except that he advocated the rise to dominance of Ukrainian rather than Russian culture. On Lebed's theory of the 'struggle of two cultures,' see Mace, *Communism and the Dilemmas of National Liberation,* 88–9, and Martin, *Affirmative Action Empire,* 78–80.

108 Shums'kyi, 'Ideolohichna borot'ba,' 15–17.

109 See Skrypnyk's comments on Shumsky's speech in 'Khvyl'ovyzm chy Shums'kyzm.'

110 According to information obtained by the GPU from Fedir Savchenko, the historian believed that Shumsky held him personally responsible for his arrest during the rule of the Central Rada. See the Kyiv GPU report of 6 January 1927 to Vsevolod Balytsky and the latter's report of 8 February 1927 to Kaganovich and Zatonsky in Prystaiko and Shapoval, *Mykhailo Hrushevsky i HPU-NKVD*, appendixes 28 and 32, pp. 171, 175–81, here p. 180. In the first report, the information is attributed to an unnamed secret agent, while in the second it is attributed to Savchenko, which makes it apparent that Savchenko was recruited by the GPU prior to January 1927.

Hrushevsky's article may have been discussed by the special commission created by decision of the Kharkiv Politburo on 11 June 1926. The commission charged with the discussion of an unspecified article by Hrushevsky consisted of Dmytro Zatonsky (chair), Shumsky, Nikolai Popov, Andrii Khvylia, and Mykola Skrypnyk. See *Mykhailo Hrushevs'kyi: mizh istoriieiu i politykoiu*, 67.

111 For extracts from Stalin's letter, see 'Iz pis'ma tov. Kaganovichu i drugim chlenam TsK KP(b)U' in Stalin, *Marksizm i natsional'no-kolonial'nyi vopros*, 172–3. For extracts from the resolutions of the May 1926 session of the Central Committee of the Communist Party of Ukraine, see Skrypnyk's article 'Khvyl'ovyzm chy Shums'kyzm,' 32.

112 Shumsky also expressed the hope that Khvyliovy would admit his mistakes and reaffirm the party line. 'We are certain,' wrote Shumsky, 'that Comrade Khvyliovy, like any communist, will declare firmly and clearly to the Ukrainian nationalist camp: keep your dirty hands off' (Shums'kyi, 'Ideolohichna borot'ba,' 17).

113 In an article published in December 1926, Panas Liubchenko sent the same message to Hrushevsky, criticizing his focus on the peasantry as the main object of historical research (see Prymak, *Mykhailo Hrushevsky*, 222). Liubchenko, a former Borotbist like Shumsky, was apparently threatened by the development of the 'Shumsky affair' and may have sought to prove his loyalty to the party by attacking Hrushevsky.

Even Mykola Skrypnyk, whom Hrushevsky had sought to support in his article and who criticized Shumsky for devoting too much attention to a critique of Hrushevsky's views, failed to treat Hrushevsky's article as a legitimate voice in the discussion. See Skrypnyk, 'Khvyl'ovyzm chy Shums'kyzm,' 36. Skrypnyk's attack on that aspect of Shumsky's article might be interpreted as an attempt to shield Hrushevsky from public criticism at a time when the authorities considered it much more politically expedient to support his bid for the presidency of the academy.

114 For the minutes of the Politburo discussion on Hrushevsky's jubilee, see *Mykhailo Hrushevs'kyi: mizh istoriieiu i politykoiu*, 70–1, and Prystaiko and Shapoval, *Mykhailo Hrushevs'kyi i HPU-NKVD*, appendix 15, pp. 146–7.

115 For the GPU's concerns regarding the alleged efforts of former Socialist Revolutionaries to turn Hrushevsky's jubilee into a national celebration, see Vsevolod Balytsky's report to his Moscow superiors in Prystaiko and Shapoval, *Mykhailo Hrushevs'kyi i HPU-NKVD*, appendix 26, pp. 165–6.

116 The article on Hrushevsky as a political activist was written at the request of the Politburo by the Central Committee official Ivan Lakyza. See his 'Mykhailo Serhiiovych Hrushevs'kyi.'

117 Hrushevs'kyi, 'Perspektyvy i vymohy ukraïns'koï nauky,' 10.

118 Zatons'kyi, *Natsional'na problema na Ukraïni*, 80.

119 The same motif appeared in Vlas Chubar's speech to the Komsomol meeting of March 1926. See Prymak, *Mykhailo Hrushevsky*, 218.

120 There were rumours circulating to the effect that the party authorities and the GPU had funded the publication of Hrushevsky's autobiography in connection with his anniversary celebrations. See Iefremov, *Shchodennyky*, 413.

In early 1927, the GPU tried to play up to Hrushevsky and indirectly assisted him with the publication of collections prepared by his subordinates. See the GPU report of 6 January 1927 in Prystaiko and Shapoval, *Mykhailo Hrushevs'kyi i HPU-NKVD*, appendix 28, pp. 170–2. According to the report, the GPU helped secure funding for a collection of articles on Chernihiv and region (*Chernihiv i Pivnichne Livoberezhzhia* [Kyiv, 1927]) through its influence with the Kyiv regional committee of the Communist Party of Ukraine. The GPU claimed credit for finding the 3,000 rubles needed for publication. It appears that the secret GPU informer who persuaded his handlers to assist Hrushevsky with the publication was none other than Fedir Savchenko. Compare the statement of the anonymous 'secret associate' quoted in the Kyiv GPU report of 6 January 1927 with the one attributed to Fedir Savchenko in Vsevolod Balytsky's report of 8 February 1927 (ibid., 170–2, 180).'

In March of the same year, the Politburo confirmed its previous decision to support Hrushevsky's candidature for president of the Academy of Sciences. See the text of the Politburo resolution, ibid., appendix 33, p. 182; *Mykhailo Hrushevs'kyi: mizh istoriieiu i politykoiu*, 95.

121 The speech was published as part of the brochure about the celebration. See the reprint of excerpts from the brochure in *Velykyi ukraïnets'*, 393–440. For the texts of Hrushevsky's speech and his concluding remarks, see ibid., 414–20, 425–7.

122 See Kostiuk, *Zustrichi i proshchannia*, 186–96. Polonska-Vasylenko and
Oleksander Ohloblyn, who were associated with Dmytro Bahalii and did
not sympathize with Hrushevsky, were convinced that the jubilee had
ended in failure, as Hrushevsky's speech was disappointing to the
authorities (see Polons'ka-Vasylenko, *Ukraïns'ka Akademiia Nauk*, 1: 47–8,
and an extract from Ohloblyn's letter to his ally, the Odesa historian
Mykhailo Slabchenko, in Prystaiko and Shapoval, *Mykhailo Hrushevs'kyi i
HPU-NKVD*, appendix 24, pp. 162–3). On Slabchenko, see Vodotyka,
Akademik Mykhailo Ielyseiovych Slabchenko. Cf. his *Narysy istoriï istorychnoï
nauky URSR 1920–kh rokiv.*

Serhii Iefremov, a rival of Hrushevsky's at the academy, recorded in his
diary that the authorities were angry with Hrushevsky for introducing
last-minute changes into his autobiography, which was published on the
occasion of the anniversary. Hrushevsky apparently changed all references to himself in the appendix to the autobiography, which dealt with
the period after 1906, from personal pronouns to the abbreviation 'Hr.,'
thereby dissociating himself from the account of his life and work in
Soviet Ukraine (see Iefremov, *Shchodennyky*, 411–13). On Hrushevsky's
refusal to publish his autobiography, see the GPU report of 28 September
1926 in Prystaiko and Shapoval, *Mykhailo Hrushevs'kyi i HPU-NKVD*,
appendix 22, p. 154.

123 For a discussion of Hrushevsky's views on the role of the peasantry in
Ukrainian history and politics, see Masnenko, *Istorychna dumka*, 316–17.

124 As noted at the celebrations by the official party representative at the
event, Panas Liubchenko, there was no solution to the Ukrainian problem
outside the USSR. See *Velykyi ukraïnets'*, 424. On the Piedmont policy in
Soviet Ukraine, see Martin, *Affirmative Action Empire*, 8–9, 244–82. On the
role of the gathering of the Ukrainian lands in historiographic discourse
of the period, see Masnenko, *Istorychna dumka*, 286–300.

125 Kostiuk, *Zustrichi i proshchannia*, 193.

126 For the speeches of Levytsky and Liubchenko, see *Velykyi ukraïnets'*, 398–
400, 420–5. Lakyza's article was apparently written after the celebrations,
as it included a quotation from Liubchenko's speech.

127 See Polons'ka-Vasylenko, *Ukraïns'ka Akademiia Nauk*, 1: 47–8. Hrushevsky
himself was very suspicious of Bahalii's jubilee, regarding it as a possible
preparation of public opinion for the election of Bahalii as president of
the academy. See an excerpt from one of Hrushevsky's letters to Studynsky
that was intercepted by the secret police and quoted in Vsevolod Balytsky's
report of 8 February 1927 to Kaganovich and Zatonsky (Prystaiko and
Shapoval, *Mykhailo Hrushevs'kyi i HPU-NKVD*, appendix 32, pp. 175–81,

here p. 179). For a draft of Hrushevsky's greetings to Bahalii on the occasion of his jubilee, see TsDIAK, fond 1235, op. 1, no. 275, p. 112.

128 See 'Perednie slovo,' in *Iuvilei akademika Dmytra Ivanovycha Bahaliia (1857–1927)*, iii.

129 See Kostiuk, *Zustrichi i proshchannia*, 196–200.

130 On the elections to the All-Union Academy and its 'Sovietization,' see Tolz, *Russian Academicians and the Revolution*, 39–67.

131 See Pyrih, *Zhyttia Mykhaila Hrushevs'koho*, 86–7. Cf. the official correspondence concerning the elections to the All-Union Academy in *Mykhailo Hrushevs'kyi: mizh istoriieiu i politykoiu*, 109–15.

132 See Volodymyr Kravchenko, 'D.I. Bahalii v svitli i tini svoieï "Avtobiohrafiï,"' 44–5.

133 See Sokhan' et al., *M.S. Hrushevs'kyi i Academia*, 140.

134 See the GPU correspondence concerning Hrushevsky's letter to Romanov in Prystaiko and Shapoval, *Mykhailo Hrushevs'kyi i HPU-NKVD*, appendixes 70, 72, pp. 223–6.

135 See Sokhan' et al., *M.S. Hrushevs'kyi i Academia*, 140–1; Kravchenko, 'D.I. Bahalii v svitli i tini svoieï "Avtobiohrafiï,"' 44.

136 For the draft memorandum, see Sokhan' et al., *M.S. Hrushevs'kyi i Academia*, appendix 13, pp. 229–31.

137 Ibid., 136–7.

138 Quoted ibid., 136.

139 See excerpts from Hrushevsky's speech in his 'Perspektyvy i vymohy ukraïns'koï nauky,' 11–12.

140 The elections to the Russian (now All-Union) Academy that took place in late 1928 and early 1929 added a minuscule number of academics from the non-Russian republics to the Russian old guard.

141 See Hrushevs'kyi, 'U Vsesoiuznii Akademiï nauk. Zvidomlennia M. Hrushevs'koho.' Cf. Sokhan' et al., *M.S. Hrushevs'kyi i Academia*, 141–4.

142 Sokhan' et al., *M.S. Hrushevs'kyi i Academia*, p. 144. In October 1930 Academician Vladimir Peretts, who cooperated with Hrushevsky on the establishment of the Institute of Belarusian History, informed his colleagues in Kyiv that the All-Union Academy had approved a proposal to create a commission on the history of Ukraine. See Fedir Savchenko's letter of 19 October 1930 to Kyrylo Studynsky in TsDIAL, fond 362, op. 1, no. 379.

143 See *Lysty*, 140.

144 See the text of the letter in Sokhan' et al., *M.S. Hrushevs'kyi i Academia*, appendix 9, pp. 216–20. The letter was forwarded by Butsenko to Emmanuil Kviring, the supreme party official in Ukraine.

145 See Hrushevsky's introduction to volume 9 of his *Istoriia*, 5.
146 See Hrushevsky's preface to volume 8, part 3, of the *History*, 416–17. For a
     brief account of Hrushevsky's scholarly work in the emigration, see his
     autobiography of 1926 in *Velykyi ukraïnets'*, 240.
147 Hrushevsky's letter of 18 December 1923 to Studynsky from Baden in
     Lysty, 136.
148 Ibid. Hrushevsky also asked Studynsky to look for Józef Tretiak's book,
     Piotr Skarga w dziejach i literaturze unii Brzeskiej (Cracow, 1912), apparently
     needed for his work on the history of Ukrainian literature.
149 Hrushevsky, *History*, 8: 417.
150 Hrushevs'kyi, *Istoriia*, 9: 6.
151 'Burned were my manuscripts and materials, library and correspon-
     dence,' wrote Hrushevsky in his collection of pamphlets *At the Threshold
     of a New Ukraine* (1918). See Hrushevs'kyi, *Na porozi novoï Ukraïny*, 5.
152 See Sokhan' et al., *M.S. Hrushevs'kyi i Academia*, 219. Hrushevsky's house
     was actually bombarded on 24 January (6 February) 1918. See Prymak,
     Mykhailo Hrushevsky, 163.
153 In his official report on the activities of the 'historical institutions' for
     1927, Hrushevsky wrote that the purpose of his trip to Moscow and
     Leningrad had been 'to become acquainted with the current state of the
     archival repositories after the transfer of materials of Polish provenance
     to Poland, and with the new organization of archival work.' See 'Diial'nist'
     Istorychnoï sektsiï Ukraïns'koï Akademiï nauk v r. 1925,' xii. Nataliia
     Polonska-Vasylenko later wrote that Hrushevsky's visits to party officials
     in Moscow created a negative impression in Ukrainian academic circles
     (apparently she meant the leaders of the academy), as they demonstrated
     that Hrushevsky did not want to limit his activities to academic work but
     was also interested in taking part in politics. See Polons'ka-Vasylenko,
     Ukraïns'ka Akademiia Nauk, 1: 46.
154 The letter is dated St Petersburg, 11 October 1924. See *Lysty*, 161.
155 Ibid.
156 The letter is dated 17 May 1925. See ibid., 172.
157 See ibid., 172, 176.
158 On the work of the expedition, see Hrushevsky's introduction to volume
     9 of the *Istoriia*, 4, and Oksana Iurkova's exhaustive study of Hrushev-
     sky's Department of Ukrainian History at the Ukrainian Academy of
     Sciences, *Diial'nist'*, 178–90.
159 These materials are currently held in the Manuscript Institute of the
     Volodymyr Vernadsky National Library of Ukraine and in the archive of

the Institute of Ukrainian History, National Academy of Sciences of Ukraine. See Iurkova, *Diial'nist'*, 190.

160 For requests for payment from Hrushevsky's associates, see letters to Hrushevsky from Anatolii Iershov (20 August 1927, TsDIAK, fond 1235, op. 1, no. 468) and Vasyl Herasymchuk (27 November 1927, TsDIAK, fond 1235, op. 1, no. 411).

161 See Polons'ka-Vasylenko, *Ukraïns'ka Akademiia Nauk*, 1: 45.

162 See Savchenko's letter of 30 May 1930 to Studynsky in TsDIAL, fond 362, op. 1, no. 379.

163 On the promotion of Baranovych and Tkachenko from graduate students to research scholars in Hrushevsky's department, see 'Diial'nist' Istorychnoï sektsiï Vseukraïns'koï Akademiï Nauk ta zv'iazanykh z neiu istorychnykh ustanov v rotsi 1926,' xxxii.

164 See Savchenko's letter of 1 August 1930 to Studynsky in TsDIAL, fond 362, op. 1, no. 379.

165 See Iurkova, *Diial'nist'*, 189, 227.

166 Ibid., 188–9, 240.

167 Iurkevych's dissertation was later published under the title *Emihratsiia na Skhid i zaliudnennia Slobozhanshchyny za Bohdana Khmel'nyts'koho* (Kyiv, 1932). On Iurkevych and his publications, see Iurkova, *Diial'nist'*, 158–9, 347, 421–2.

168 Interesting in this regard is Viktor Iurkevych's letter of 18 October 1927 to Hrushevsky, in which Iurkevych asks his professor to allow him to postpone his exam on Marxism to Christmas 1927 (TsDIAK, fond 1235, op. 1, no. 855). Apparently the new Marxist requirements were no barrier to the observance of prerevolutionary calendar feasts in the Ukrainian Academy of Sciences. The graduate seminar on Marxism and Leninism was conducted by Hrushevsky's close associate Osyp Hermaize. See 'Diial'nist' Istorychnoï sektsiï Vseukraïns'koï Akademiï Nauk ta zv'iazanykh z neiu istorychnykh ustanov Akademiï v 1927 r.,' xxxiv.

169 See Iershov's letter of 14 September 1927 to Hrushevsky in TsDIAK, fond 1235, op. 1, no. 468.

170 See Hrushevs'kyi, *Istoriia*, 9: 5.

171 See, for example, Viktor Iurkevych's letter of 15 July 1927 to Hrushevsky and his apologies for errors/lacunae in the copied materials. See also his letter of 18 October 1927 concerning his work on the records of Boris Repnin's embassy of 1653 to the Commonwealth (TsDIAK, fond 1235, op. 1, no. 855).

172 See Hrushevsky's undated post card to Dmytro Kravtsov from Lenin-

grad, TsDIAK, fond 1235, op. 1, no. 855. Hrushevsky informed Iurkevych of his impending arrival in Moscow and asked him to order archival materials for 1650, including the account of the discussion on religious affairs at the Warsaw diet of 1650 that was later published as an appendix to vol. 9, pt. 2, of the *History* (*Istoriia*, 9: 1509–23).

173 See Viktor Iurkevych's letters of 15 July and 18 September 1927 to Hrushevsky, TsDIAK, fond 1235, op. 1, no. 855.

174 Hrushevs'kyi, *Istoriia*, 9: 600–1. Cf. Iurkevych's letters of 18 September and 5 and 18 October 1927 to Hrushevsky, TsDIAK, fond 1235, op. 1, no. 855.

175 Mariia and Elizaveta Shuiskaia, O. Balandina, and K. Grodskaia were employed as copyists (Iurkova, *Diial'nist'*, 185). See references to Elizaveta Nikolaevna Shuiskaia in Iurkevych's letter of 18 September 1927 to Hrushevsky (TsDIAK, fond 1235, op. 1, no. 855); also Ievfymovsky's letter to him dated 4 December 1927 (ibid., no. 470). Ievfymovsky also advised Hrushevsky to hire another copyist, Kateryna Ivanivna Mazurenko (letter of 13 December 1927). It is unknown whether the latter was ever hired.

176 See Viktor Iurkevych's post card of 30 October 1927 to Hrushevsky, in which he discusses confusion in the files pertaining to Boris Repnin's embassy of 1653 (TsDIAK, fond 1235, op. 1, no. 855).

177 See Ievfymovsky's letter of 26 September 1927 to Hrushevsky, TsDIAK, fond 1235, op. 1, no. 470. Ievfymovsky prepared detailed instructions for the members of the expedition on working with the documents (Iurkova, *Diial'nist'*, 185–6).

178 Èingorn recommended one of the copyists, an employee of the Rumiantsev (Lenin) Library in Moscow, to members of the expedition. See Viktor Iurkevych's letter of 18 October 1927 to Hrushevsky, TsDIAK, fond 1235, op. 1, no. 855; also Mykola Petrovsky's letter of 26 June 1927 to Hrushevsky, TsDIAK, fond 1235, op. 1, no. 692.

179 Myron Korduba was assisted in his work by the copyist Hrechukh. See Korduba's letters of 3, 7, and 30 August, 22 October, and 29 December 1927 to Hrushevsky, TsDIAK, fond 1235, op. 1, no. 552. Interesting are Korduba's opinions of Mykola Kostomarov and Ludwik Kubala, expressed in his letter of 30 August 1929 to Hrushevsky. There Korduba characterized both as historians for whom criticism of sources 'did not exist.'

180 See *Ukraïna*, 1927, no. 6, p. 194; 'Diial'nist' Istorychnoï sektsiï (1926),' xxxi. Cf. Vasyl Herasymchuk's letters to Hrushevsky from Warsaw (21 June and 27 November 1927), TsDIAK, fond 1235, op. 1, no. 411.

181 See Hrushevsky's introduction to *Ukraïns'kyi arkhiv*, 1: iii–iv. There Hrushevsky presented the Archaeographic Commission of the All-Ukrainian Academy of Sciences, which was formed in 1921 and which he chaired from 1924, as heir to the Kyiv Commission for the Study of Old Documents (1843), the Archaeographic Commission of the Ukrainian Scientific Society, formed in 1913, and the Archaeographic Commission of the Ukrainian Academy of Sciences, established in 1919. He also stated that the new (1921) commission had taken over projects from the Archaeographic Commission of the Shevchenko Scientific Society in Lviv. The release of volume 1 of *Ukraïns'kyi arkhiv*, initially prepared for publication by the Archaeographic Commission of the Ukrainian Scientific Society in 1914, gave Hrushevsky a good opportunity to present the genealogy of his archaeographic projects.

182 See 'Diial'nist' Istorychnoï sektsiï (1926),' xxviii–xxx. Cf. Hrushevsky's undated notes on the activities of the Archaeographic Commission and the Department of the Modern Ukrainian History of the Ukrainian People in the Vernadsky National Library of Ukraine, Manuscript Institute, fond X, no. 18622, p. 9, and fond X, no. 18652, pp. 1, 10.

183 See Iurkova, *Diial'nist'*, 187–8.

184 In his report on the activities of the 'historical institutions' for 1928–9, Hrushevsky wrote that the printing of Herasymchuk's collection was already under way, but in his report for 1930, he was obliged to note that publication of the collection had been delayed by Herasymchuk's departure from Kyiv for Galicia. See Vernadsky National Library of Ukraine, Manuscript Institute, fond X, no. 18622, p. 7; cf. Fedoruk, 'Vasyl' Harasymchuk ta ioho nevydani "Materialy do istoriï kozachchyny XVI viku,"' 23–6. Fedoruk concludes that the main reason for the delay was lack of coordination between Herasymchuk, who spent most of his time in Poland, and the academy's editors in Kyiv.

185 See *Ukraïns'kyi arkhiv*. Volume 2 was prepared for publication by Osyp Hermaize but issued after his arrest, hence without mention of his name. The third volume was never published.

186 Hrushevs'kyi, *Istoriia*, 9: 5.

187 In July of the same year he informed his friend in Lviv that he had completed some important organizational work. This would allow him to continue his 'big history,' a project he had not dared to take up ever since the loss of his manuscripts in the Kyiv fire. The archaeographic expedition was undoubtedly one of the organizational measures Hrushevsky had in mind. See *Lysty*, 187.

188 Ibid., 222.

189 Ibid., 229.
190 Hrushevs'kyi, *Istoriia*, 9: 5–6.
191 See Hrushevs'kyi, *Istoriia*, 9: 1539.
192 See Hrushevsky's report on the activities of the 'historical institutions' in 'Diial'nist' Istorychnoï sektsiï Vseukraïns'koï Akademiï Nauk ta zv'iazanykh z neiu istorychnykh ustanov Akademiï v 1928 r.,' ix. Cf. also Hrushevsky's report for 1930 in Sokhan' et al., *M.S. Hrushevs'kyi i Academia*, 279.
193 See *Lysty*, 236–7.
194 See Hrushevsky's report on the activities of the 'historical institutions' for 1930 in Sokhan' et al., *M.S. Hrushevs'kyi i Academia*, 279. In his report for 1929, Hrushevsky wrote that the second part of volume 9 was sent to the printer in April 1929 ('Diial'nist' Istorychnoï sektsiï [1928],' x). This report covered the activities of the 'historical institutions' until the summer recess of 1929 and was most probably written during the summer months of that year. Hrushevsky may have continued making corrections to the manuscript throughout the summer and submitted it to the press in September 1929, a development reflected in his report for the following year.
195 See Nikitin, 'Pis'mo istorika,' 95–7.
196 See Hrushevs'kyi, *Istoriia*, 9: 1539.
197 See Fedir Savchenko's letter of 13 February 1931 to Kyrylo Studynsky in TsDIAL, fond 362, op. 1, no. 379. Savchenko informed Studynsky about his meeting with the director of the State Publishing House, Mariia Abramivna Shmaionok, and wrote that after months of lobbying he had finally managed to convince her to raise the author's honorarium for the second part of the volume to 150 rubles (apparently per signature, i.e., 22–4 pages of typescript).
198 See Vernadsky National Library of Ukraine, Manuscript Institute, fond X, no. 18652 ('Kafedra novitn'oï istoriï ukraïns'koho narodu'), pp. 8, 10.
199 This information is based on my conversations with Iaroslav Dashkevych in Lviv on 7 and 8 June 2001. For a discussion of the possibility that part of the volume was never published, see Appendix.
200 In October 1924, Hrushevsky instructed Studynsky to leave between 50 and 150 copies of each volume of the *History* in Lviv. The remaining copies were to be shipped to Soviet Ukraine. See *Lysty*, 161–2.
201 See Hrushevsky's report on publication activities, dated 31 August 1926, in the Vernadsky National Library of Ukraine, Manuscript Institute, fond X, no. 15146.
202 See Verstiuk and Pyrih, *M.S. Hrushevs'kyi. Korotka khronika zhyttia ta diial'nosti*, 116.

203 See Savchenko's letter of 20 January 1930 to Studynsky, TsDIAL, fond 362, op. 1, no. 379.

204 Hrushevsky himself considered 1929 a turning point in government policy toward Ukraine and linked the change in official policy with the trial of those accused of membership in the 'Union for the Liberation of Ukraine.' See his letter of 4 September 1934 to Viacheslav Molotov in Nikitin, 'Pis'mo istorika M.S. Grushevskogo V.M. Molotovu,' 95–7.

205 In addition to the works discussed in the introduction on the last decade of Hrushevsky's life by Pyrih, Sokhan, Kirzhaev and Ulianovsky, Prystaiko and Shapoval, see also Shapoval, 'Mykhailo Hrushevsky in Moscow and His Death (1931–4)' and 'The Mechanisms of the Informational Activity of the GPU-NKVD.'

206 See Yekelchyk, 'How the "Iron Minister" Kaganovich Failed to Discipline Ukrainian Historians.'

207 On the communist takeover of the Russian/All-Union Academy of Sciences, see Tolz, *Russian Academicians and the Revolution*. On the Platonov case, see Brachev, *Russkii istorik S.F. Platonov, uchenyi, pedagog, chelovek*, 196–239; Paneiakh, 'The Political Police and the Study of History in the USSR,' 304–8, and *Akademicheskoe delo 1929–31 gg*. On the trial of the alleged members of the 'Union for the Liberation of Ukraine,' see Prystaiko and Shapoval, *Sprava 'Spilky vyzvolennia Ukraïny.'*

208 On Iavorsky, see Santsevych, *M.I. Iavors'kyi: Narys zhyttia i tvorchosti*.

209 On Communist Party and GPU politics in the academy, see Pyrih, *Zhyttia Mykhaila Hrushevs'koho*, 36–89; Prystaiko and Shapoval, *Mykhailo Hrushevs'kyi i HPU-NKVD*, 34–78.

210 On changes in the party's nationality policy and persecution of the Ukrainian intelligentsia and non-Russian party cadres, see Martin, *Affirmative Action Empire*, 236–60. Communist Party attacks on Hrushevsky and his 'historical institutions' are discussed in Pyrih, *Zhyttia Mykhaila Hrushevs'koho*, 90–123; Prystaiko and Shapoval, *Mykhailo Hrushevs'kyi i HPU-NKVD*, 79–104.

211 See Khvylia, 'Burzhuazno-natsionalistychna trybuna (Pro zhurnal 'Ukraïna').'

212 To prove his point, Khvylia quoted an excerpt from an *Ukraïna* article on the origins of the Cyrillic alphabet. Its author, M. Hrunsky, referred to a book on SS. Cyril and Methodius by the former minister of religion in the Petliura government, Professor Ivan Ohiienko (the future Metropolitan Ilarion of the Ukrainian Orthodox Church of Canada), and mentioned a breve of 1927 issued by Pope Pius XI on the life of St Cyril. Khvylia considered such references sufficient reason to claim that the editorial

board of *Ukraïna* was propagating religious 'obscurantism' and belief in miracles, as well as generally playing into the hands of the organizers of an anti-Soviet campaign launched in the West by Pius XI.

213 On the atmosphere of the 'disputes,' see Polons'ka-Vasylenko, *Ukraïns'ka Akademiia Nauk*, 2: 16–17; Mez'ko [Ohloblyn], *Iak bol'shevyky ruinuvaly*, 15–17.

214 See Polons'ka-Vasylenko, *Ukraïns'ka Akademiia Nauk*, 2: 16.

215 Ibid. Oleksander Ohloblyn, who later himself survived one such debate, claimed that lenient criticism intended to present the victims in a better light was potentially harmful to those who were criticized, as a new 'dispute' could be arranged to subject the victim to yet another round of criticism. See his pamphlet, published under the pseudonym Oles' Mez'ko, *Iak bil'shovyky ruinuvaly*, 16. For a detailed discussion of the Ohloblyn 'dispute' based on archival materials, see Verba, *Oleksandr Ohloblyn*, 221–5.

216 See Richyts'kyi, 'Proty interventsiï burzhuaznoï nauky,' 41.

217 See Rubach, 'Burzhuazno-kurkul's'ka natsionalistychna ideolohiia pid mashkaroiu demokratiï "trudovoho narodu."'

218 In 1926 Mykhailo Mohyliansky published a short story, 'The Murder,' describing the killing for treason of a national leader by his former followers. The authorities considered the story an attack on Hrushevsky and blacklisted Mohyliansky, prohibiting him from publishing in the republican press. See extracts from the party and GPU documents on the Mohyliansky case in *Mykhailo Hrushevs'kyi: mizh istoriieiu i politykoiu*, 66–7; Prystaiko and Shapoval, *Mykhailo Hrushevs'kyi i HPU-NKVD*, appendix 14, pp. 145–6.

219 See Rubach, 'Federalisticheskie teorii v istorii Rossii.'

220 See Pyrih, *Zhyttia Mykhaila Hrushevs'koho*, 130–1.

221 With the passage of time, Rubach's assessment of Hrushevsky as a political figure also came to be regarded as the standard Soviet Ukrainian view of Hrushevsky as a historian. The mere fact that Rubach was lucky enough to survive the 1930s and continued writing about Hrushevsky until the late 1970s contributed immensely to the popularity of his evaluation of Hrushevsky in Soviet publications from the 1950s to the 1980s. An important reason for the surprising longevity of Rubach's characterization of Hrushevsky, originally produced in the 1930s, is that unlike the 'vulgar Marxism' imputed to Mikhail Pokrovsky, the charge of 'Ukrainian bourgeois nationalism' against Hrushevsky was never reassessed during the existence of the USSR. As time passed, though, Rubach found himself obliged to add a few new 'errors' to his original list. The resur-

gence of the cult of heroism in Soviet historiography, the rise of the doctrine of the friendship of peoples, and, most particularly, the idea of Russian-Ukrainian brotherhood altered the basic premises of the Soviet critique of Hrushevsky. After the Second World War, Hrushevsky was accused not only of his old class-based transgressions but also of new, nationally based ones. It was noted that he did not treat Kyivan Rus' as the cradle of the three fraternal East Slavic peoples (Russians, Ukrainians, and Belarusians), ignored the close cultural bonds between the Ukrainian and Russian peoples, and, through his negative treatment of Bohdan Khmelnytsky and positive assessment of such anti-Russian hetmans as Ivan Vyhovsky and Ivan Mazepa, sought to detach Ukraine from Russia.

See Rubach's entry on Hrushevsky in *Radians'ka entsyklopediia istoriï Ukraïny*, 1: 483–4. For a biography of Mykhailo Abramovych Rubach, see ibid., 4: 32. There is also a brief biography of Rubach in *Vcheni Instytutu istoriï Ukraïny*, 273–4. For differing assessments of Rubach's career and personality, see Dashkevych, 'Borot'ba z Hrushevs'kym ta ioho shkoloiu u L'vivs'komu universyteti za radians'kykh chasiv,' 226–7, and Rybalka, *Taka nasha dolia* 18, 132.

222 Hrushevsky's name was probably first mentioned in connection with the term 'fascist' in the autumn of 1930. On 28 October, the Academy of Sciences announced that Volodymyr Iurynets would be working on a paper titled 'The Historiography of the Bourgeois Sociology of Iefremov, Hrushevsky, and the Ukrainian Fascists.' Hrushevsky, who was present at the meeting where the topic was announced, protested against being called a bourgeois sociologist and being associated with such company. See Fedir Savchenko's letter of 28 October 1930 to Studynsky in TsDIAL, fond 362, op. 1, no. 379.

223 See extracts from Postyshev's speech in Prystaiko and Shapoval, *Mykhailo Hrushevs'kyi: sprava 'UNTs,'* 237.

224 See the transcript of Hrushevsky's interrogations by secret police operatives and the official indictment of members of the 'Ukrainian National Centre,' allegedly headed by Hrushevsky, in Prystaiko and Shapoval, *Mykhailo Hrushevs'kyi i HPU-NKVD*, 249–50, 258–60, and *Mykhailo Hrushevs'kyi: sprava 'UNTs,'* 198–200.

225 On the change in the nature of GPU reporting over the years, see the section 'The Seksot [secret agent]' in Shteppa and Houtermans [F. Beck and W. Godin], *Russian Purge and the Extraction of Confession*, 171–81. The section was written by Shteppa, apparently on the basis of his own experience as a GPU informer. For his role in the 'unmasking' of Hrushevsky and his family, see Pyrih, *Zhyttia Mykhaila Hrushevs'koho*,

148–64; Prystaiko and Shapoval, *Mykhailo Hrushevs'kyi i HPU-NKVD*, 82, 301–2.

226 See Prystaiko and Shapoval, *Sprava 'Spilky vyzvolennia Ukraïny.'*

227 See Iefremov, *Shchodennyky*, 191.

228 This was the tactic used by Ahatanhel Krymsky on receiving an award from the Soviet government in 1941. Krymsky's speech included the following words: 'O Holy Party! Whose heart does not pound when thinking of you?' He later explained to Nataliia Polonska-Vasylenko: 'If I had said less, "our own people" would have believed in my sincerity, but in this way it is clear to all that it is not sincere, and "those people" will not believe it in the same way.' Quoted in Prymak, *Mykhailo Hrushevsky*, 272.

229 On the fate of Skrypnyk, see Mace, *Communism and the Dilemmas of National Liberation*, 296–301.

230 See Zatons'kyi, *Natsional'no-kul'turne budivnytstvo i borot'ba proty natsionalizmu*, 36–42. See excerpt in *Mykhailo Hrushevs'kyi: mizh istoriieiu i politykoiu*, 146–50.

231 See Ivan Kravchenko, 'Fashysts'ki kontseptsiï Hrushevs'koho i ioho shkoly v ukraïns'kii istoriohrafiï'; Iastrebov, 'Natsional-fashysts'ka kontseptsiia selians'koï viiny 1648 roku na Ukraïni.'

232 On Hrushevsky's arrest and last years in Moscow, see Prystaiko and Shapoval, *Mykhailo Hrushevs'kyi: Sprava 'UNTs'*; Shapoval, 'Mykhailo Hrushevsky in Moscow and His Death (1931–34).'

233 See Pyrih, *Zhyttia Mykhaila Hrushevs'koho*, 140–4. Time was required for the adoption of the government resolution and approval of the official obituary. The prompt publication of those documents in Kyiv on the second day after Hrushevsky's death continues to arouse suspicion that the authorities may have been making preparations for Hrushevsky's funeral before he actually died, and, by implication, that his death was in fact a murder arranged by secret police agents.

234 See 'Akad. M.S. Hrushevs'kyi,' *Chervonyi shliakh*, 1934, nos. 11–12: 171. For a report on the Kirov assassination, see ibid., iii. The Russian text of the obituary from *Pravda* for 27 November appears in Prystaiko and Shapoval, *Mykhailo Hrushevs'kyi i HPU-NKVD*, appendix 119, pp. 286–7.

235 For the minutes of the meeting of the Presidium of the Ukrainian Academy of Sciences concerning Hrushevsky's death, see TsDIAK, fond 1235, op. 1, no. 49. Work on the monument began in the spring of 1936 and was completed before Kateryna's arrest in July 1938. See Matiash, *Kateryna Hrushevs'ka*, 106–7.

236 Nikitin, 'Pis'mo istorika.'
237 Quoted in Pyrih, *Zhyttia Mykhaila Hrushevs'koho*, 119.
238 Bilets'kyi, review of Hrushevs'kyi, *Istoriia ukraïns'koï literatury*, 676.
239 That was in May 1926, when Hrushevsky nourished high hopes for the success of Ukrainization and his personal future at the Academy of Sciences. See Hrushevsky's letter of 25 May 1926 to Studynsky in *Lysty*, 187–9.
240 See Matiash, *Kateryna Hrushevs'ka*, 98.
241 *Pravda* obituary of 27 November 1934, in Prystaiko and Shapoval, *Mykhailo Hrushevs'kyi i HPU-NKVD*, appendix 119, pp. 286–7.
242 See Polons'ka-Vasylenko, *Ukraïns'ka Akademiia Nauk*, 2: 42–3.

Chapter 5: Revisiting the Revolution

1 For a discussion of the Khmelnytsky Uprising and the period that followed his hetmancy, see Sysyn, 'The Khmel'nyts'kyi Uprising: A Characterization of the Ukrainian Revolt.' Hrushevsky's *History* (vols 9 and 10) remains the most exhaustive and authoritative study of the period.
2 Hrushevs'kyi, *Istoriia*, 9: 1507.
3 See Pritsak, 'Istoriosofiia Mykhaila Hrushevs'koho,' il [*sic*]. On the impact of historical sociology on Hrushevsky, see also Zashkil'niak, 'Istoriohrafichna tvorchist' Mykhaila Hrushevs'koho,' 34–6, 41–3.
4 Syniavs'kyi, *Vybrani pratsi*, 39.
5 See Korzon, 'O Chmielnickim sądy PP. Kulisza i Karpowa,' 79. Cf. Sysyn, 'Chy bulo povstannia Khmel'nyts'koho revoliutsiieiu?' 571.
6 See Antonovych, *Korotka istoriia kozachchyny*, 90. The text of these lectures, so important for the present discussion, was prepared on the basis of notes taken by Antonovych's students Vasyl Domanytsky and Andrii Kuchynsky. It was later edited by Oleksander Konysky and appeared in Chernivtsi in 1898 under the title *Besidy pro chasy kozats'ki na Ukraïni* (see the preface to the second edition of the work, *Korotka istoriia kozachchyny*, xvi–xvii). Hrushevsky, who had certain reservations regarding the authenticity of the text, nevertheless used it in his analysis of the evolution of Antonovych's views. See his review of the book, 'Prymitky do istoriï kozachchyny,' and his 'Z sotsiial'no-natsional'nykh kontseptsii Antonovycha,' 14–15.
7 See Hrushevs'kyi, 'Khmel'nyts'kyi i Khmel'nychchyna. Istorychnyi eskiz.' Many of the ideas first expressed in this essay found their way into the last volumes of the *History*. This was also true of Hrushevsky's

overall assessment of the uprising. In the essay of 1898, it was defined as 'a movement that resulted in the complete transformation of the political system of Eastern Europe' (ibid., 1). The point was made in a very similar way in the introduction to volume 9, written almost thirty years later: 'At the focal point of the panorama is a great political transformation: Ukraine's passage from under the rule of the Polish Commonwealth "under the high hand" of the tsar of Muscovy' (Hrushevs'kyi, *Istoriia*, 9: 6).

8 Hrushevs'kyi, 'Khmel'nyts'kyi i Khmel'nychchyna,' 2, 22, 27.

9 See, for example, the use of the term 'revolution' in *History*, vol. 8, chapter 8, where Hrushevsky defined the period preceding the Khmelnytsky Uprising as a 'prerevolutionary era.'

10 See Lipiński, 'Dwie chwile z dziejów porewolucyjnej Ukrainy.' Cf. Lypyns'kyi, *Ukraïna na perelomi, 1657–1659*. On Lypynsky as a historian, see Bilas, 'Viacheslav Lypyns'kyi iak istoryk kryzovoï doby.' For a parallel presentation of Hrushevsky's and Lypynsky's views on the Khmelnytsky Uprising as a revolution, see Masnenko, *Istorychni kontseptsiï*, 176–89.

11 Lipiński, 'Stanisław Michał Krzyczewski,' 146.

12 Lipiński, 'Dwie chwile,' 520–2.

13 Lipiński, 'Stanisław Michał Krzyczewski,' 147.

14 For a discussion of Lypynsky's negative view of revolution and revolutionaries in Ukrainian history as expressed in his *Letters to Fellow Landowners*, see Masnenko, *Istorychni kontseptsiï*, 182–4.

15 Lypyns'kyi, *Ukraïna na perelomi*, 18–21; cf. his *Z dziejów*, 145, 520–2. See also Masnenko, *Istorychni kontseptsiï*, 184–5. In 1920 Lypynsky put much more emphasis on Ukrainian state-building and the role of the Cossacks, nobles, and wealthy burghers in the uprising, while downplaying the role of the Orthodox clergy, 'simplistic and fanatical' in its 'obscurantism,' and of the Orthodox intelligentsia, to which he attributed similar characteristics.

16 See Hrushevs'kyi, *Istoriia*, 9: 1494, 1496. Cf. his 'Khmel'nyts'kyi,' 12, and *Istoriia*, vol. 8, pt. 3, pp. 219–26.

17 Cf. Hrushevs'kyi, 'Khmel'nyts'kyi,' 12; Efimenko, *Istoriia ukrainskogo naroda*, 1: 243–5.

18 Hrushevs'kyi, *Istoriia*, 9: 969. The last sentence refers to the eighteenth-century Eyewitness Chronicle.

19 Ibid., 1486, 1501.

20 Ibid., 1486.

21 Ibid., 373.

22 Ibid., 1495.

23 Ibid., 1506.

24 Hrushevs'kyi, 'Khmel'nyts'kyi,' 1; cf. his *Istoriia*, 9: 6.

25 Hrushevs'kyi, *Istoriia*, 9: 1501.

26 Ibid., 757.

27 See Hrushevs'kyi, *Na porozi novoï Ukraïny*, 3–56.

28 Hrushevs'kyi, *Istoriia*, 9: 1486, 1494, 1495, 1507.

29 For a discussion of Hrushevsky's prerevolutionary views on the nation and its role in history, see chapter 3 of the present work.

30 For excerpts from Dnistriansky's *Zahal'na nauka prava i polityky* (1923), see *Politolohiia*, 689–702. In the Ukrainian translation of Volodymyr Antonovych's lecture on the Russian, Ukrainian, and Polish nations published by Oleksander Konysky in Lviv in 1888, the term *narod* (people) was all but avoided. Antonovych (or his editor) used *natsiia* (nation) and *natsional'nist'* (nationality) interchangeably. See Antonovych, 'Try natsional'ni typy narodni.'

31 See excerpts from Starosolsky's *Teoriia natsiï* in *Politolohiia*, 610–35, here p. 620. For a discussion of his views on nationhood, see Masnenko, *Istorychna dumka*, 27–30. In 1920, Starosolsky taught at the Ukrainian Free University in Prague, where Dnistriansky served variously as dean of the law school, president, and vice-president.

32 Hrushevs'kyi, 'Khto taki ukraïntsi i choho vony khochut" in *Politolohiia*, 181.

33 Hrushevs'kyi, 'Zvidky pishlo ukraïnstvo i do choho vono ide' in *Politolohiia*, 191.

34 Hrushevs'kyi, *Istoriia*, 9: 6–7.

35 See Hrushevs'kyi, 'Khmel'nyts'kyi,' 29.

36 Ibid., 7. In his later writings on the Khmelnytsky Uprising, Hrushevsky repeated some of these ideas. For example, in his essay of 1907 on Khmelnytsky's anniversary, Hrushevsky claimed that in their folklore the popular masses celebrated their Khmelnytsky-era victories over national oppression and ethnic and class privilege ('Bohdanovi rokovyny,' 211). In the *Illustrated History*, he wrote that for Khmelnytsky the national cause did not go beyond the religious one (*Iliustrovana istoriia*, 302).

37 Drahomanov, 'Perednie slovo (do *Hromady*),' in *Politolohiia*, 7.

38 See Franko, 'Ukraina irredenta,' 48–9.

39 See Antonovych, *Korotka istoriia kozachchyny*, 113–32.

40 Hrushevsky, *History*, 8: 356. For a similar treatment of the national factor as a combination of a number of different elements in Hrushevsky's pre-1917 writings, see chapter 3 of the present work. For a recent discussion of the impact of the Khmelnytsky Uprising on the formation of the Ukrainian nation, see Sysyn, 'The Khmelnytsky Uprising and Ukrainian Nation-Building.'

41 Hrushevsky, *History*, 8: 358. No less enthusiastic was Hrushevsky's assessment of Khmelnytsky's statements at Pereiaslav, recounted in the third
part of volume 8, which was written between 1915 and 1918. There
Hrushevsky placed special emphasis on Khmelnytsky's alleged ties with
representatives of educated Kyivan circles, whom he called the 'Kyivan
intelligentsia' and represented as the 'ecclesiastical and national center –
this hearth, now fanned into flame by the storm of the national uprising.'
These circles, in Hrushevsky's opinion, 'could not resist the mighty national force that found consonant tones in them; what is more, they themselves were part and parcel of that force' (ibid., 519–20).
42 Hrushevs'kyi, *Istoriia*, 9: 7.
43 In the last volumes of the *History*, Hrushevsky often evaluated the successes and failures of the Cossack administration on the basis of its policy
toward Western Ukraine, frequently reading modern Ukrainian identity
back into the minds of the leaders of the Hetmanate. See, for example, the
discussion of the successes and failures of Khmelnytsky's policy in the
conclusions to *Istoriia*, 9: 1491, 1504.
44 See Hrushevs'kyi, 'Nasha zakhidnia oriientatsiia.'
45 See Hrushevs'kyi, *Istoriia*, 9: 759, 1507.
46 Ibid., 857. Cf. his 'Zvidky pishlo ukraïnstvo,' in *Politolohiia*, 193.
47 See Hrushevs'kyi, *Istoriia*, 9: 751–60.
48 See Mikhnovs'kyi, 'Samostiina Ukraïna,' in *Politolohiia*, 126–35.
49 The simplistic Mikhnovsky-like interpretation of the Pereiaslav Agreement was rejected by Viacheslav Lypynsky, who in his *Ukraïna na perelomi*
(1920) criticized the view according to which Ukraine had joined Russia as
an equal partner, calling it a 'Pereiaslav legend.'
50 See Hrushevs'kyi, *Pereiaslavs'ka umova Ukraïny z Moskvoiu 1654 roku*. In the
second part of volume 9 of his academic *History*, Hrushevsky often quoted
Pereiaslavs'ka umova but gave few bibliographic references to it in the notes
(see, e.g., *Istoriia*, 9: 754, 756–7). On p. 754, for example, the number of the
note referring to *Pereiaslavs'ka umova* is given in the text, but the note itself
is missing. On pp. 756–7, there is a long quotation from the work with no
page reference. The tendency to avoid references to a particular work
struck me as quite suspicious, given that in the early 1930s, at the time of
the state-sponsored campaign against Hrushevsky, *Pereiaslavs'ka umova*
was among those of his writings that were criticized by Marxist historians.
A check of the manuscript of volume 9 (TsDIAK, fond 1235, op. 1, no. 145)
nevertheless established that this was a mere oversight on the part of one
of Hrushevsky's assistants. The historian himself did not copy quotations
from *Pereiaslavska umova* into his text, apparently leaving the task to one of

his graduate students, who inserted the quotations but in many cases neglected to give proper bibliographic references.

51 Apart from *Pereiaslavs'ka umova*, Hrushevsky discussed the Pereiaslav Agreement in 'Velyka, Mala i Bila Rus',' 'Spoluchennie Ukraïny z Moskovshchynoiu v novishii literaturi. Krytychni zamitky,' and *Khmel'nyts'kyi v Pereiaslavi*. He also reprinted his earlier essays on Khmelnytsky and his era in the collection *Z politychnoho zhyttia staroï Ukraïny*. They included 'Bohdanovi rokovyny,' 'Vyhovs'kyi i Mazepa,' '250 lit,' 'Na ukraïn'ski temy: "Mazepynstvo" i "Bohdanivstvo,"' and 'Khmel'nyts'kyi i Khmel'nychchyna.'

52 See Hrushevs'kyi, '250 lit,' 5. Cf. his *Iliustrovana istoriia*, 315; 'Zvidky pishlo ukraïnstvo,' in *Politolohiia*, 193; and *Istoriia*, 9: 757.

53 See Hrushevs'kyi, 'Khmel'nyts'kyi,' 23; '250 lit,' 5; *Istoriia*, 9: 757, 1494–5. The inconsistent treatment of the agreement in the last volumes of the *History* prompted criticism in one of the last Soviet-era reviews of Hrushevsky's writings. See Smolii and Sokhan', 'Vydatnyi istoryk Ukraïny,' xxxv.

54 See Hrushevs'kyi, *Istoriia*, 9: 1479–1508.

55 See, for example, Hrushevsky's sarcastic remark about the 'Polish civilizing mission' in his discussion of massacres of the Ukrainian population carried out by the Tatar allies of the Commonwealth in 1655 (*Istoriia*, 9: 1051).

56 Ibid., 9: 1218.

57 Ibid., 10: 354–6.

58 Ibid., 352.

59 Ibid., 353.

60 See Hrushevs'kyi, 'Khmel'nyts'kyi,' 10.

61 See Hrushevs'kyi, *Istoriia*, 10: 356–7.

62 Hrushevs'kyi, *Istoriia*, 9: 1504.

63 Hrushevsky, *History*, 8: 349.

64 Ibid., 348. On Hrushevsky's treatment of the Jewish factor in the Khmelnytsky Uprising, see Sysyn, 'Assessing the "Crucial Epoch": From the Cossack Revolts to the Khmelnytsky Uprising at Its Height,' introduction to Hrushevsky, *History*, 8: lxv–lxvi.

65 Hrushevs'kyi, *Istoriia*, 9: 1483.

66 In his magnum opus, Hrushevsky followed a policy of avoiding polemics with Marxist historians.

67 For a discussion of Hrushevsky's and Lypynsky's views on Khmelnytsky as a charismatic leader, see Masnenko, *Istorychni kontseptsiï*, 57–112. For Hrushevsky's interpretation of the role of the individual in Ukrainian

516 Notes to pages 300–4

history, see Iakovenko, 'Osoba, iak diiach istorychnoho protsesu v istoriohrafiï Mykhaila Hrushevs'koho,' and Tel'vak, *Teoretyko-metodolohichni pidstavy*, 112–20.

68 See Hrushevs'kyi, *Pochatky hromadianstva*, 36. For the young Hrushevsky's scepticism toward the views of Thomas Carlyle, see chapter 1 of the present work.

69 Ibid., 4.

70 See Lypyns'kyi, *Lysty do brativ-khliborobiv.*

71 See Antonovich, 'Kharakteristika deiatel'nosti Bogdana Khmel'nitskogo.' Cf. his *Korotka istoriia kozachchyny*, 110–11.

72 See Hrushevs'kyi, 'Khmel'nyts'kyi,' 27–8; cf. Antonovych, *Korotka istoriia kozachchyny*, 136–7.

73 Khmelnytsky also did not fit the image of the hero in the mind of the young Hrushevsky during his years at the Tbilisi gymnasium. In his memoirs, Hrushevsky described his ideal of the time as follows: 'My inner orientation was on a strong and independent individual with a firmly established goal who advances steadfastly, paying no heed either to the shallow temptations of life or to the world's opinion' (Hrushevs'kyi, 'Spomyny,' *Kyïv*, 1988, no. 12: 106).

74 See Hrushevs'kyi, 'Khmel'nyts'kyi,' 3, 17, 27–8.

75 See Antonovych, *Korotka istoriia kozachchyny*, 136–7.

76 See Hrushevs'kyi, '250 lit.' Back in his student days at the Tbilisi gymnasium, Hrushevsky, apparently under the influence of his reading of *Kievskaia starina* and Shevchenko's verses, regarded Khmelnytsky as a mainly positive figure of Ukrainian history, despite his hasty decision to unite with Russia. On 15 October 1883, Hrushevsky noted in his diary: 'That, in my opinion, is why we found ourselves enslaved to Muscovy, that having escaped Polish enslavement, we began to make approaches to Muscovy, but if Lord Zinovii (here he is not all that much to blame) had first settled everything nicely at home, putting Ukraine properly to rights, there would be none of this' ('Shchodennyky (1883–1893),' no. 4: 17).

77 See Grushevskii, *Ocherk* (1904), 226–49.

78 See Hrushevs'kyi, 'Bohdanovi rokovyny,' 208.

79 See Rawita-Gawroński, *Krwawy gość we Lwowie*. In the following year Rawita-Gawroński published a larger study, *Bohdan Khmelnytsky prior to the Election of Jan Kazimierz*, which was also very critical of the hetman. See Rawita-Gawroński, *Bohdan Chmielnicki do elekcji Jana-Kazimierza* (Lviv, 1906). Cf. Frank E. Sysyn, 'Grappling with the Hero,' 593–4.

80 In that regard, Hrushevsky specifically indicated the negative assessment of the hetman by Taras Shevchenko, whom the historian called 'the Prophet of the New Ukraine' (Hrushevs'kyi, 'Bohdanovi rokovyny,' 210).

81 Ibid., 210.
82 Grushevskii, *Ocherk* (1911), 239.
83 Ibid., 246.
84 For a discussion of neoromantic influences on Hrushevsky's writings, see Iakovenko, 'Osoba, iak diiach istorychnoho protsesu.' Cf. Zashkil'niak, 'Istoriohrafichna tvorchist' Mykhaila Hrushevs'koho,' 37–40.
85 Hrushevs'kyi, 'Bohdanovi rokovyny,' 210–11.
86 Ibid., 210. To be sure, Hrushevsky did not completely jettison his old grievances against the hetman. In his essay of 1907 he restated his positivist belief in the limited role of the historical actor/hero in history. He claimed that, like other historical figures, Khmelnytsky was important not per se but because of the significance of the events in which he took part. Hrushevsky also asserted that it was not Khmelnytsky who guided events but the events of the 'great popular struggle' that guided him. He reproved Khmelnytsky (as he routinely did) for defending the interests of the Cossack order instead of caring about the needs of the masses, as well as for yielding too much to Muscovy in 1654. These were the standard accusations levelled against the hetman in Hrushevsky's early writings, but now he put them into perspective and placed much stronger emphasis on the positive side of Khmelnytsky's activities than ever before.
87 See Antonovich, 'Kharakteristika deiatel'nosti Bogdana Khmel'nitskogo,' 190–3. In volume 9 of the *History*, Hrushevsky interpreted Antonovych's paper as a defence of Khmelnytsky against Kulish's attacks on the hetman. The paper itself indicates, nevertheless, that Antonovych was more concerned with attacks on Khmelnytsky's reputation by Ukrainian radicals. Hrushevsky's quotations from Antonovych's paper offer an interesting example of his efforts to bring Antonovych's ethnic vocabulary up to the standards of the 1920s. In translating the text from Russian into Ukrainian, Hrushevsky replaced Antonovych's identification of Khmelnytsky as a 'South Russian patriot' with the simple 'patriot' (*Istoriia*, 9: 1485).
88 See Hrushevs'kyi, 'Na ukraïns'ki temy: "Mazepynstvo" i "Bohdanivstvo,"' 98.
89 Hrushevs'kyi, *Pro bat'ka kozats'koho Bohdana Khmel'nyts'koho*, 74.
90 See Hrushevs'kyi, *Iliustrovana istoriia*, 296–320.
91 In seeking to prove Antonovych wrong, Korduba invoked the authority not only of his own professor, Mykhailo Hrushevsky, but also that of the Polish historian Ludwik Kubala, who could hardly be accused of nationalist excess. See Antonovych, *Korotka istoriia kozachchyny*, 111–15, 118, 122–4, 133, 135–7.
92 See Lipiński, 'Stanisław Michał Krzyczewski,' 148–51, 617. Cf. Kubala, *Wojna Moskiewska*, 7–18.

93 On the highly positive evaluation of Khmelnytsky rendered by Hrushevsky's students and followers of the period, see Sysyn, 'Grappling with the Hero,' 596–7.
94 Hrushevsky, *History*, 8: 385.
95 See Iakovenko, 'Osoba, iak diiach istorychnoho protsesu,' 96.
96 See Hrushevsky, *History*, 8: 376–87.
97 Ibid., 597–602; cf. his 'Khmel'nyts'kyi,' 11–12.
98 See Hrushevs'kyi, *Istoriia*, 9: 1491–1508.
99 Ibid., 1479.
100 See Hrushevs'kyi, '250 lit,' 210.
101 Sysyn, 'Grappling with the Hero,' 601.
102 See Hrushevs'kyi, *Istoriia*, 9: 1495–7, 1506–7. Cf. the discussion of changes in Hrushevsky's assessment of the importance of Khmelnytsky's death in Pritsak, 'Istoriosofiia Mykhaila Hrushevs'koho,' lxxi.
103 See Hrushevs'kyi, *Istoriia*, 9: 1496; cf. his 'Bohdanovi rokovyny,' 209, 211. 'Khmelnytsky burned as in a fire amid this struggle,' wrote Hrushevsky, 'which strained all his spiritual forces to the utmost, all his nervous energy, in unfathomable dread, in the consciousness of the terrible responsibility imposed on him by the task that had fallen to him and whose unfathomable dimensions were making themselves ever more apparent and clear to his consciousness. And he died in terrible travail, sensing that the strength of the people was becoming exhausted, that he was losing his moral sway over them, and that at the same time conditions were becoming ever more tangled and complex; that the people's problem was becoming ever more difficult. He died, and the blind titan was left without a leader. The tiny Lilliputians beset him and firmly bound him with a net of fine but strong fetters, chained him once again to the ground, and again drove him underground for long centuries' (ibid., 211).
104 See Hrushevs'kyi, *Istoriia*, 9: 1491, 1497–1501.
105 Ibid., 1500.
106 Ibid., 1485.
107 Ibid., 1507.
108 Ibid., 7.
109 Ibid., 1485.
110 Ibid., 1486.
111 Ibid., 1496–7.
112 Ibid., 1483–5.
113 Ibid., 1487–90.
114 Ibid., 1490–1.

115 Ibid., 1496–7. For attitudes toward Asia and Asians in Ukrainian and Russian academic circles, see Pavlychko, *Natsionalizm, seksual'nist', oriientalizm*, 157–80.
116 Sysyn, 'Grappling with the Hero,' 603.
117 See Hrushevs'kyi, *Istoriia*, 9: 1508.
118 See Hrushevs'kyi, 'Ukraïns'kyi herb.'
119 See Hrushevs'kyi, *Istoriia*, 9: 1508.
120 See Ivan Kravchenko, 'Fashysts'ki kontseptsiï Hrushevs'koho,' 27–8.
121 'The national revival is working miracles, and the nation is approaching its golden age at an accelerated tempo,' wrote Khvyliovy in his pamphlet 'Ukraïna chy Malorosiia' (1926). See *Politolohiia*, 648.
122 In the introduction to volume 9 of the *History*, Hrushevsky wrote: 'But we, more than anyone, must remember that the driving force of this great transformation [the Khmelnytsky era] was the struggle for the liberation of the Ukrainian masses, dictated by socio-economic conditions.' See Hrushevs'kyi, *Istoriia*, 9: 6.
123 See Rudnytsky, 'Intellectual Origins of Modern Ukraine,' 129–30.
124 Hrushevs'kyi, *Istoriia*, 9: 1505.
125 Ibid., 1492–6, 1507, 1508.
126 Hrushevs'kyi, 'Khmel'nyts'kyi,' 9, 18, 21, 23, 27.
127 Ibid., 18, 22, 27.
128 Hrushevs'kyi, 'Bohdanovi rokovyny,' 208–9.
129 See Hrushevs'kyi, *Iliustrovana istoriia*, 325.
130 See Hrushevsky, *History*, 8: 597–602; cf. his 'Khmel'nyts'kyi,' 9, 18, 21, 23, 27.
131 Hrushevsky, *History*, 8: 613.
132 Ibid., 599–602; cf. 638–9.
133 In his political essay 'Between Moscow and Warsaw,' written in May–June 1920 and directed against Symon Petliura's alliance with Poland, Hrushevsky praised Khmelnytsky for his policies after Zboriv. Comparing Khmelnytsky's and Petliura's policies toward Poland, Hrushevsky wrote that despite Khmelnytsky's decision to allow the Tatars to take captives in Ukraine after the Zboriv Agreement, the hetman had never allowed the return of the Polish nobility to Ukraine (implying that Petliura had relinquished Ukrainian territory to Poland). Hrushevsky wrote that Khmelnytsky had a good understanding of the people and knew that they would never compromise on that issue. He also expressed his conviction that the people would never tolerate Petliura's new 'manoeuvre' vis-à-vis Poland. See Hrushevs'kyi, 'Mizh Moskvoiu i Varshavoiu,' 3.

134 Hrushevsky, *History*, 8: 414. Hrushevsky made this addition, like many
others to the first two parts of the volume, in pencil. There were also
fourteen pages of more substantial additions in ink. The first two parts of
volume 8, with revisions by Hrushevsky for the 1922 edition of the
volume, are preserved in TsDIAK, fond 1235, op. 1, no. 142.

135 Hrushevs'kyi, *Istoriia*, 9: 6. It should be noted nevertheless that in the
introduction and conclusions to volume 9 Hrushevsky took a much more
ideological approach, presenting masses and elites as polar opposites,
than he did in the main text of the volume. Volume 9 differed from all
previous volumes of the *History* in that the historical account was clearly
separated from a more theoretically and ideologically informed discussion, which was limited to the introduction and conclusion of the
volume. In the text itself, when dealing with numerous Polish and
Muscovite sources that were generally either overtly hostile or unfavourable to the leaders of the uprising, Hrushevsky treated with
sympathy and understanding the attempts of Khmelnytsky and his
entourage to master the difficult situation in which the rebels found
themselves after the agreements concluded at Zboriv (1649) and especially at Bila Tserkva (1651). That sympathetic treatment was extended to
all aspects of Khmelnytsky's policy, including his attempts to calm the
popular masses. In the introduction and conclusions to the volume,
Hrushevsky's treatment of Khmelnytsky was much less friendly and
more ideologically oriented. The whole discussion was inflamed by
Hrushevsky's argument with Viacheslav Lypynsky, the proponent of the
idea of a Ukrainian toilers' monarchy, who claimed that just such a
monarchy, headed by the hetman, led by the Cossack elites, and supported by the masses, had begun to come into being in the times of
Bohdan Khmelnytsky.

136 Hrushevs'kyi, *Istoriia*, 9: 1501–2.

137 Ibid., 1502.

138 Ibid., 827–8. Cf. Hrushevsky's earlier treatment of the same episode in
'Khmel'nyts'kyi,' 22, and *Iliustrovana istoriia*, 325.

139 Hrushevs'kyi, *Istoriia*, 9: 1505.

140 See Pritsak, 'Istoriosofiia Mykhaila Hrushevs'koho,' xlviii–il.

141 See Hrushevs'kyi, *Istoriia*, 9: 1501. The term is reminiscent of 'petty
bourgeoisie,' often used in Soviet propaganda of the time, and may be
viewed as an example of the penetration of Soviet revolutionary-era
vocabulary into Hrushevsky's writings of the period.

142 See Antonovych, *Korotka istoriia kozachchyny*, 103.

143 See excerpts from their works in *Politolohiia*, 33–4, 48, 133.

144 See the section on 'The Cossack Mythology' in chapter 3 of the present work.

145 See Hrushevs'kyi, 'Khmel'nyts'kyi,' 5, 18, 28.

146 Like Hrushevsky after him, Antonovych was highly critical of the Cossack officers, whom he viewed as products of Polish culture. See Antonovych, *Korotka istoriia kozachchyny*, 103, 113.

147 Hrushevsky, *History*, 7: lxv.

148 Ibid., 8: 520.

149 Ibid.

150 For a discussion of Paisios's role in Khmelnytsky's political plans and Hrushevsky, *History*, 8: diplomacy, see my *Cossacks and Religion*, 308–9.

151 Hrushevsky, *History*, 8: 519; cf. his *Istoriia*, vol. 8, pt. 3, p. 127. To be sure, Hrushevsky understood that his interpretation of the role of the Kyivan intelligentsia in the dramatic shift of Khmelnytsky's political agenda was problematic. He admitted the lack of sources concerning Khmelnytsky's sojourn in Kyiv and the meetings that might have taken place there: 'Most regrettably, the contacts that Khmelnytsky and his officers made with the Ukrainian intelligentsia of Kyiv at the time – an immeasurably interesting moment from the standpoint of the development of political thought in Ukraine of that period, and so important for an understanding of further events – remain completely closed to us' (*History*, 8: 524). Despite this lack of sources, the historian strongly believed in his hypothesis that linked the Ukrainian intelligentsia of the period with Khmelnytsky's new plans to fight for the liberation of Rus' from Polish rule. 'I, for one,' wrote Hrushevsky in volume 8 of the *History*, 'have no doubt that it was first and foremost the circles of the Kyiv intelligentsia of the day, both secular and clerical, that constituted the laboratory for the formulation of the ideas and programs of sovereignty whose echoes later reach us from Cossack circles. It was to them that Khmelnytsky was indebted, both directly and indirectly, for the change in his disposition and plans that so greatly astonished his contemporaries' (ibid., 520).

152 Hrushevs'kyi, *Istoriia*, 9: 1492.

153 'Representatives of this new course,' wrote Hrushevsky about the members of Petro Mohyla's circle, 'were also distant and alien both to the social strivings of the people and to their national sentiments. In assessing everything from an exclusively ecclesiastical and confessional viewpoint, they became alienated from the people and from those strata that embodied national life, thereby preparing the way for the downfall of religious life itself' (Hrushevsky, *History*, 8: 332).

154 *Lysty*, 94.

155 See Lipiński, 'Dwie chwile,' 520–1; cf. his *Ukraïna na perelomi*, 19.
156 See Lypyns'kyi, *Lysty do brativ-khliborobiv*, vii–xlviii, 1–62.
157 Hrushevsky explained Khmelnytsky's attempts to delay the return of the
    Polish nobility to Ukraine (one of the conditions of the agreement) by the
    hetman's unwillingness to lose his 'right hand' – the support of the
    peasantry (Hrushev'skyi, 'Khmel'nyts'kyi,' 11–12).
158 See Hrushevs'kyi, *Iliustrovana istoriia*, 310.
159 See Hrushevsky, *History*, 8: 638.
160 This ambivalence has recently been noted by Masnenko in his *Istorychni
    kontseptsiï*, 149–50.
161 See Hrushevs'kyi, *Istoriia*, 9: 390–1, 428, 1496.
162 Ibid., 1167.
163 Ibid., 1227–8.
164 Ibid., 1231. In his conclusions to the volume, while attacking Khmelnyts-
    ky's policies in the course of his polemic with Lypynsky, Hrushevsky
    also raised the issue of mass emigration to Muscovy. 'The desertion of
    the Ukrainian masses across the Muscovite border during and after the
    Khmelnytsky era, leaving the Ukrainian ship of state stranded and
    undermining the struggle for independence, as well as for social and
    national self-determination, leaves one with a burdensome and oppres-
    sive feeling,' wrote Hrushevsky. 'Nevertheless, it is difficult to condemn
    the masses for such pusillanimity, short-sightedness, and irresolution
    when the leading officer circles displayed those very same flaws' (ibid.,
    1505).
165 See Iastrebov's attack on Hrushevsky in 'Natsional-fashysts'ka
    kontseptsiia selians'koï viiny 1648 roku na Ukraïni,' 95–96.
166 In the Soviet-era volumes of the *History*, Hrushevsky was gratified by all
    instances of close cooperation between the masses and the Cossack elites
    to promote the national interest. One such case was Khmelnytsky's
    effective mobilization of all available resources for the defence of Ukraine
    after the catastrophe at Berestechko in 1651. Hrushevsky, who otherwise
    was more critical than laudatory in assessing the policies of Khmelnytsky
    and his associates, now found that they had indeed demonstrated energy
    and talent in bringing the situation under control. In Hrushevsky's
    opinion, the actions of the elite helped the 'national organism' recover
    from the wounds it had suffered at Berestechko. 'The energy emanating
    from the centre of command,' wrote Hrushevsky, 'gave the people a sense
    of wholeness. No longer reckoning with defects in internal relations, it
    turned inward, marshalling all its forces for self-defence' (Hrushevs'kyi,
    Istoriia, 9: 318).

167 See Antonovych, *Korotka istoriia kozachchyny*, 139–42. Like Antonovych before him, Hrushevsky thought well of Vyhovsky. For all Hrushevsky's criticism of Vyhovsky's brainchild, the Union of Hadiach, the hetman himself received not even a scintilla of the criticism that Hrushevsky directed against Khmelnytsky. In volume 9 of the *History*, Hrushevsky effectively endorsed the high opinion of Vyhovsky held by his student Vasyl Herasymchuk and wrote that Vyhovsky was a European politician, while Khmelnytsky embodied the spontaneous force of Eurasian or Asian nature (see Hrushevs'kyi, *Istoriia*, 9: 1497). Coming from Hrushevsky, this was high praise for Vyhovsky's abilities and policies.

168 See Hrushevs'kyi, 'Khmel'nyts'kyi,' 24.

169 See Grushevskii, *Ocherk* (1904), 249–50, and *Iliustrovana istoriia*, 327–8.

170 Hrushevs'kyi, *Istoriia*, 10: 151.

171 Ibid., 117.

172 Ibid., 117–18.

173 Ibid., 118.

174 See, for example, Hrushevsky's reference to class conflict in his *Ocherk* (1911), 272. The reference does not appear in the first (1904) edition of the work.

175 See, for example, his political pamphlets 'Ukraïns'ka partiia sotsiialistiv-revoliutsioneriv ta ïï zavdannia' and 'Mizh Moskvoiu i Varshavoiu' (1920).

176 See Doroshenko, *Ohliad ukraïns'koï istoriohrafiï*. For an English translation, see Doroshenko, *Survey of Ukrainian Historiography*, 269–71.

177 See Krevets'kyi, 'Ukraïns'ka istoriohrafiia na perelomi.' Lypynsky was supposed to write a programmatic article for the same issue of *ZNTSh* under the title 'A Scheme of the Statist History of Ukraine' but failed to meet the deadline (see Masnenko, *Istorychni kontseptsiï*, 54–5). Hrushevsky's letters to Studynsky show that he viewed Krevetsky's article as a continuation of the conflict of 1913 in the Shevchenko Scientific Society. He believed that with its publication, 'the historians of the Shevchenko Society [were] breaking with me and other "older historians" in favour of Tomashivsky and Lypynsky!' See *Lysty*, 154.

178 See Zaikin's review of *ZNTSh*, vols 134–5. For the origins of the discussion, see Dashkevych, 'Mykhailo Hrushevs'kyi – istoryk narodnyts'koho chy derzhavnyts'koho napriamu?' 76–7; Hyrych, 'Derzhavnyts'kyi napriam i narodnyts'ka shkola v ukraïns'kii istoriohrafiï,' 61–3.

179 Hrushevs'kyi, 'Ukraïns'ka partiia.' For a discussion of Lypynsky's reaction to the publication of Hrushevsky's pamphlet, see Masnenko, *Istorychni kontseptsiï*, 37–9.

180 Hrushevs'kyi, 'Ukraïns'ka partiia,' 12. For an English translation of this
     extract, see Doroshenko, *Survey of Ukrainian Historiography*, 270. For a
     discussion of the political ideas expressed in the article, see chapter 4 of
     the present work. Antonovych's views on the role of the state in Ukrain-
     ian history are discussed in Klid, 'Volodymyr Antonovych,' 385–6.
181 On Lypynsky's attack on Hrushevsky, see Hyrych, 'Derzhavnyts'kyi
     napriam,' 62–4. For cases in which Hrushevsky was not mentioned by
     name but referred to as a 'university professor,' etc. (instances left out of
     Hyrych's analysis), see excerpts from Lypynsky's *Lysty* in *Politolohiia*,
     398–400.
182 Krevets'kyi, 'Ukraïns'ka istoriohrafiia,' 162–3; cf. Dashkevych, 'Mykhailo
     Hrushevs'kyi,' 76–7.
183 See an extract from Tomashivsky's letter of 29 July 1922 in *Politolohiia*,
     576–7.
184 Among the historians who maintained that Hrushevsky was far from
     hostile to the idea of a nation-state was Liubomyr Vynar. See his
     'Znachennia Mykhaila Hrushevs'koho v ukraïns'kii i svitovii istoriï.'
185 The most recent discussion of the issue took place between the dean of
     Ukrainian national historiography, Iaroslav Dashkevych, and his younger
     colleague Iaroslav Hrytsak. It ensued at a series of conferences held
     in Ukraine in 1994–6 to consider the legacy of Mykhailo Hrushevsky.
     Dashkevych and Hrytsak presented diametrically opposite views on
     the issue of whether Hrushevsky was a 'statist' or a 'populist.' Hrytsak
     argued that Hrushevsky began as a populist historian and basically
     remained one, although the majority of his Lviv students joined the
     'statist' camp. On that basis, he claimed that there are few grounds to
     speak of a Hrushevskian school in Ukrainian historiography. He consid-
     ered Hrushevsky a member of the populist school headed by Antono-
     vych and designated Hrushevsky's students of the prerevolutionary era
     as members of Viacheslav Lypynsky's 'statist' school. Dashkevych, for his
     part, argued that although Hrushevsky developed as a scholar under the
     influence of Antonovych and his circle, he was not actually a populist
     historian. Indeed, Dashkevych went on to claim that it was Hrushevsky
     himself who founded the national-statist school in Ukrainian historiogra-
     phy at the turn of the twentieth century. Dashkevych rightly dismissed
     the critique of Hrushevsky by members of the 'statist' school as politi-
     cally motivated. In the process, however, he all but hijacked the greatest
     Ukrainian historian for the statist school.
        For all the differences between Dashkevych and Hrytsak, both are im-
     plicitly agreed on two major issues: that there was a division in Ukrainian

historiography along 'populist'/'statist' lines and that Hrushevsky definitely belonged to one of these groupings. To strengthen their arguments, both Dashkevych and Hrytsak tend to present Hrushevsky's views as ideologically one-dimensional. Dashkevych minimizes the manifestations of Hrushevsky's populism in his pre-1898 writings, while Hrytsak claims that elements of the statist approach only became apparent in Hrushevsky's writings in the late 1920s. Our own reading suggests that Hrushevsky's views were much more complicated than this discussion makes them appear and thus do not easily fit the populist-statist paradigm of Ukrainian historiography.

See Dashkevych, 'Mykhailo Hrushevs'kyi – istoryk narodnyts'koho chy derzhavnyts'koho napriamu?' 65–85; Hrytsak, 'Chy bula shkola Hrushevs'koho?' For a more balanced approach to the problem, see Hyrych, 'Derzhavnyts'kyi napriam i narodnyts'ka shkola.'

186 For a discussion of the role of the state paradigm in Hrushevsky's interpretation of Ukrainian history, see chapter 3 of the present work.

187 Hrushevs'kyi, 'Z sotsiial'no-natsional'nykh kontseptsii Antonovycha,' 8.

188 Hrushevs'kyi, 'Hromads'kyi rukh na Vkraïni-Rusy v XIII vitsi,' quoted in Pritsak, 'Istoriosofiia Mykhaila Hrushevs'koho,' liii.

189 See the text of Hrushevsky's 'Zvychaina skhema "russkoï" istoriï i sprava ratsional'noho ukladu istoriï skhidnoho slov'ianstva,' in Politolohiia, 171.

190 See Hrushevs'kyi, 'Khmel'nyts'kyi,' 26.

191 Ibid., 21–4.

192 See Hrushevs'kyi, 'Na ukraïns'ki temy. "Mazepynstvo" i "Bohdanivstvo,"' 98.

193 See Grushevskii, Ocherk (1911), 260–9; cf. his Ocherk (1904), 246–7.

194 See Hrushevs'kyi, Iliustrovana istoriia, 320–5.

195 See Hrushevs'kyi, 'Zvidky pishlo ukraïnstvo,' in Politolohiia, 189, 193.

196 See Hrushevs'kyi, Istoriia, 9: 1483, 1485.

197 Ibid., 1497. Hrushevsky severely criticized Muscovite rulers for treating the Zaporozhian Host not as a state formation but as a rebel army (ibid., 1499).

198 Ibid., 1496.

199 Ibid., 1498.

200 For parallel presentations of Hrushevsky's and Lypynsky's views on Cossack statehood, see Masnenko, Istorychni kontseptsiï, 113–53, 176–89. In some of its elements, Hrushevsky's critique of Lypynsky followed the criticism expressed by Pylyp Klymenko in his review of Lypynsky's Ukraine at the Turning Point, published in 1922. Klymenko never challenged Lypynsky's views on the importance of the state but claimed that

he had exaggerated the role of the nobility in its creation and ignored the role of other social groups, especially Cossackdom, in the process of state-building. According to Klymenko, Lypynsky had also ignored the role of the masses, whose importance increased in revolutionary times, and failed to observe that the dominant 'spirit of the nation' at the time was democratic. See Klymenko's review in *Zapysky Istoryko-filolohichnoho viddilu*.
201 See Hrushevs'kyi, 'Khmel'nyts'kyi,' 21.
202 Ibid., 28–9.
203 Antonovych, *Korotka istoriia kozachchyny*, 135.
204 See Antonovich, 'Kharakteristika deiatel'nosti Bogdana Khmel'nitskogo,' 192.
205 See Hrushevs'kyi, 'Z sotsiial'no-natsional'nykh kontseptsii Antonovycha,' 14–15.
206 See Hrushevs'kyi, '250 lit,' 5–6.
207 Hrushevs'kyi, 'Bohdanovi rokovyny,' 212.
208 Hrushevs'kyi, 'Na ukraïns'ki temy: "Mazepynstvo" i "Bohdanivstvo,"' 97–8, 100.
209 See Hrushevs'kyi, 'Iakoï my khochemo avtonomiï i federatsiï,' in *Politolohiia*, 219.
210 See Hrushevs'kyi, '250 lit,' 1.
211 Hrushevs'kyi, *Iliustrovana istoriia*, 303.
212 See ibid., 322.
213 Hrushevsky, *History*, 8: 561.
214 Ibid., 519. For the use of the terms 'independent' and 'autonomous' as synonyms in Hrushevsky's political writings, see his 'Khto taki ukraïntsi i choho vony khochut',' in *Politolohiia*, 188, and 'Zvidky pishlo ukraïnstvo i do choho vono ide,' ibid., 194. For a clear distinction between the two terms, see his 'Iakoï my khochemo avtonomiï i federatsiï,' ibid., p. 218. Hrushevsky was only too well aware of the distinction between 'independence' and 'autonomy,' which raises the question of why he used the terms interchangeably in 1917. Was this an attempt to prepare the masses for a shift in the policy of the Ukrainian movement from autonomy to independence or an indication of the shift occurring at the time in Hrushevsky's own views? Perhaps it was a reflection of both processes taking place simultaneously.
215 See Hrushevsky, *History*, 8: 416.
216 Hrushevs'kyi, *Istoriia*, 9: 1493.
217 See Lypyns'kyi, *Ukraïna na perelomi*, 18–39.
218 See Hrushevs'kyi, *Istoriia*, 9: 1492–6.

219 See Hrushevsky's polemics with Lypynsky in *Istoriia*, 9: 1491. Hrushevsky was not the first historian to criticize Lypynsky for fighting too many political battles in his historical works. As noted above, Pylyp Klymenko claimed in 1922 that 'from the methodological viewpoint Lypynsky's work is not a pure scholarly [product].' Klymenko also believed that instead of engaging in the systematization and critique of his sources, Lypynsky simply used them to illustrate his historiographic scheme, developed under the influence of the Polish historians Ludwik Kubala and Wiktor Czermak. See Klymenko's review in *Zapysky Istoryko-filolohichnoho viddilu*, 246.

220 My research on Hrushevsky has convinced me of the general soundness of an observation made by Richard Pipes in his memoirs: 'In reality, "fresh sources" add less to knowledge than is generally believed. The art of the historian consists of selecting, according to his own criteria, some evidence from the boundless store of available facts and then weaving them in a convincing and, if possible, aesthetically satisfying narrative. Beyond this he seeks to arrive at some synthetic judgments about the story he tells' (Pipes, *Vixi*, 74). It would appear that the larger the scope of a given historian's narrative, the more this observation holds true.

221 For a discussion of Hrushevsky's views on the objectivity of historical research, see Tel'vak, *Teoretyko-metodolohichni pidstavy*, 125–33.

222 Quoted in Vytanovych, 'Uvahy do metodolohiï i istoriosofiï Mykhaila Hrushevs'koho,' 40–1. Among those who indicated Hrushevsky's tendency to analyse without synthesizing were Petro Holubovsky, Volodymyr Shcherbyna, and Ivan Franko. See Tel'vak, 'Naukova spadshchyna,' 66.

223 Mykhailo Hrushevs'kyi, 'V dvadtsiat' p'iati rokovyny smerty Ol. M. Lazarevs'koho,' 4.

224 Beard, 'Written History as an Act of Faith,' repr. in *The Philosophy of History in Our Time*, 149.

Chapter 6: Class versus Nation

1 On Pokrovsky, see Szporluk, Introduction to *Russia in World History*; Enteen, *The Soviet Scholar-Bureaucrat*.

2 See Pokrovskii with the assistance of Nikol'skii and Storozhev, *Russkaia istoriia s drevneishikh vremen*. See the reprint of the work in *Izbrannye proizvedeniia* (1965–6). The 1965–6 publication of Pokrovsky's *Russian History from the Earliest Times* was based on the seventh edition, which appeared in 1924–5.

3 See Rozhkov, *Obzor russkoi istorii s sotsiologicheskoi tochki zreniia*. Cf. Pokrovskii, *Izbrannye proizvedeniia*, 1: 75–6.
4 Storozhev helped Pokrovsky prepare the manuscript for print by selecting illustrations and compiling a bibliography and documentary addendum to the first edition of the book (see Pokrovskii, *Izbrannye proizvedeniia*, 1: 76). Thus it comes as no surprise that the title of Pokrovsky's multivolume *History* closely resembled that of a collection of articles, *The History of Russia from the Earliest Times to the Time of Troubles*, published by Storozhev in 1898. Pokrovsky contributed an article on the economic history of Kyivan Rus' to Storozhev's collection. As was noted in chapter 2 of the present work, in his review of the collection Hrushevsky welcomed Storozhev's suggestion that the history of Dnipro and Northeastern Rus' were products of the historical development of two different nationalities. He also singled out Pokrovsky's essay, which he praised, along with Storozhev's own article, as 'painstakingly and solidly' written. See Hrushevsky's review in *ZNTSh* 37.
5 The hostility to the government expressed in Pokrovsky's work led the Russian police to confiscate and destroy the print run of volume 5 of the *History* on the basis of a judicial finding that the book was an incitement to the terrorist overthrow of the empire's political system. See Szporluk, Introduction, 6.
6 See Pokrovskii, *Izbrannye proizvedeniia*, 1: 207.
7 Ibid., 208.
8 See ibid., 103–82, 450–517. Pokrovsky showed no interest in the ethnic origins of the population of 'ancient Rus'' and did not even mention the Antes.
9 Ibid., 455.
10 Ibid., 455–6.
11 Ibid., 455.
12 Ibid., 457.
13 Ibid., 461–7.
14 See Pokrovskii, *Russkaia istoriia v samom szhatom ocherke*. See the reprint of the 10th edition of the book (1931), *Izbrannye proizvedeniia*, vol. 3.
15 For the text of Lenin's letter to Pokrovsky welcoming the publication of *Russkaia istoriia v samom szhatom ocherke*, see Pokrovskii, *Izbrannye proizvedeniia*, 3: 3–4.
16 For a brief summary of Pokrovsky's views on 'Russian' history, see Szporluk, Introduction, 16–19; Barber, *Soviet Historians in Crisis*, 58–67.
17 The late sixteenth and early seventeenth centuries, presented in Hrushevsky's writings as a period of national revival, were treated by

Pokrovsky in his new book as the epoch of commercial capitalism. Comparing Russian and Ukrainian history of the period, Pokrovsky claimed that the major difference between the Russian and Ukrainian (Dnipro) Cossacks lay in the latter's ability to find allies in the local burghers. Organized in confraternities, the burghers fought against the church union – in Pokrovsky's interpretation, little more than a tool in the hands of the Polish government, which oppressed the petty Ukrainian burghers in the interests of the rich merchants. See Pokrovskii, *Izbrannye proizvedeniia*, 3: 80–1.

18 Ibid., 613.
19 Ibid., 616.
20 Ibid., 615.
21 For such an assessment of Pokrovsky's book, see Brandenberger, *National Bolshevism*, 18.
22 The fourth edition of the book appeared in 1917, while the fifth edition was published in 1918 and reprinted three times. The fifth issue of the fifth edition appeared in 1919. See Wynar, *Mykhailo Hrushevs'kyi, 1866–1934: Bibliographic Sources*, 29–35. For an impressive list of popular publications on Ukrainian history published between 1917 and 1919, see Masnenko, *Istorychna dumka*, 157–8.
23 See Shevelov's memoirs, *Ia – mene – meni ...* 1: 74–5.
24 See one such history, written by the peasant Vasyl Rubel, currently held in the Manuscript Collection of the Project for the Study of Southern Ukraine at Zaporizhia State University.
25 See the GPU circular of August 1925 in *Mykhailo Hrushevs'kyi: mizh istoriieiu ta politykoiu*, 64.
26 For a brief biography of Iavorsky, see Santsevych, *M.I. Iavors'kyi*, 5–27.
27 Ibid., 13–16, 37.
28 On the party policy of Ukrainization, see Mace, *Communism and the Dilemmas of National Liberation*; Martin, *Affirmative Action Empire*, 75–124, 211–72.
29 See Iavors'kyi, *Narys ukraïns'ko-rus'koï istoriï* (Kharkiv, 1923).
30 See Santsevych, *M.I. Iavors'kyi*, 29. For the text of Bahalii's review, see *Knyha*, 1923, no. 2: 48–50.
31 See Iavors'kyi, *Narys istoriï Ukraïny*.
32 See Iavors'kyi, *Revoliutsiia na Vkraïni v ïï holovnykh etapakh*.
33 See Iavors'kyi, *Korotka istoriia Ukraïny*. The book was reissued many times throughout the 1920s. All references in the present work are to the edition of 1927.
34 See the summary of Iavorsky's paper on the nature and tasks of Ukrainian

historiography in his 'De-shcho pro "krytychnu" krytyku, pro "ob'iektyvnu" istoriiu ta shche pro babusynu spidnytsiu,' here 168.

35 On Rakovsky, see Conte, *Christian Rakovski (1873–1941).*

36 See Martin, *Affirmative Action Empire*, 13, 78.

37 Rakovsky openly criticized Stalin's position on the national question at the Twelfth Party Congress in Moscow in April 1923. See John-Paul Himka's entry on Rakovsky in *Encyclopedia of Ukraine*, 4: 315; Mace, *Communism and the Dilemmas of National Liberation*, 72–3.

38 Rakovs'kyi, 'Do molodykh chytachiv.'

39 Ibid.

40 Ibid.

41 For example, a passage on Sarmatians and Scythians from Iavorsky's work of 1923, 'in the present-day Katerynoslav and Kherson regions various tribes migrating from Asia, such as the Sarmatians and Scythians, fought one another,' was revised in the survey of 1928 by adding the adverb 'apparently' before 'fought.'

42 See Iavors'kyi, *Istoriia Ukraïny v styslomu narysi*, 21.

43 Ibid., 10.

44 Ibid., 11–12. Iavorsky's position on the distinct character of Ukrainian history was a direct reflection of the ambiguous political status of the Ukrainian Socialist Soviet Republic in the USSR. While discussing the natural characteristics of Ukrainian territory, he compared it to those of Poland and 'our Muscovy.' Iavorsky used the term *rus'kyi* (Ruthenian) to denote the Russians and the term 'Muscovy' to denote Russia as a country and territory. This choice of terms reflected the linguistic practice of Soviet Ukrainian public discourse in the 1920s.

45 See Arkas, *Istoriia Ukraïny-Rusi.*

46 Iavors'kyi, *Istoriia Ukraïny*, 12.

47 Ibid., 13.

48 'The materialist method, which takes the economics of a society as its basis, is interested above all in class relations, relegating statist and political elements to the background; it spends less time describing antiquity and pays greater attention to stages closer to us, most particularly to the most recent stages of capitalist society,' wrote Iavorsky in his 'big' *History of Ukraine* (1928), 19.

49 See Iavors'kyi, *Korotka istoriia*, 13–15, and his *Istoriia Ukraïny*, 19–20.

50 Iavors'kyi, *Istoriia Ukraïny*, 20.

51 On the 'Iavorsky affair,' see Mace, *Communism and the Dilemmas of National Liberation*, 232–63.

52 See Iavors'kyi, *Korotka istoriia*, 18; cf. his *Istoriia Ukraïny*, 23.

53 See Iavors'kyi, *Korotka istoriia*, 28; cf. his *Istoriia Ukraïny*, 31.
54 See Iavors'kyi, *Korotka istoriia*, 22–3; cf. his *Istoriia Ukraïny*, 26–7. Pokrovsky
    was generally a strong supporter of the Norman theory. Basing his argu-
    ment on the work of Vilhelm Thomsen, *The Relations between Ancient
    Russia and Scandinavia* (Oxford and London, 1877), Pokrovsky sided with
    the Normanists in their claim that the Kyivan dynasty and the Rus' name
    itself were of Scandinavian origin.
        The editors of the 1960s edition of Pokrovsky's works were at pains to
    establish that he was not a Normanist. According to them, the 'Normanist
    theory' was a political tool used by bourgeois scholars to prove that 'the
    Slavs were incapable of independent political development.' By this logic,
    Pokrovsky was not a Normanist, as he did not consider the Normans to
    have been the founders of the Rus' state. For editorial comments, see
    Pokrovskii, *Izbrannye proizvedeniia*, 1: 97–8.
55 See Iavors'kyi, *Korotka istoriia*, 20; cf. his *Istoriia Ukraïny*, 25.
56 See Iavors'kyi, *Korotka istoriia*, 23–4; cf. his *Istoriia Ukraïny*, 27–8.
57 Iavors'kyi, *Korotka istoriia*, 29.
58 See Iavors'kyi, *Korotka istoriia*, 30–1; cf. his *Istoriia Ukraïny*, 32–3.
59 Natalia Iakovenko has recently explained Iavorsky's sympathetic treat-
    ment of the Tatar period by the success of Oriental studies in Ukraine. She
    treats Iavorsky's approach to the subject as evidence of the readiness of
    Soviet Ukrainian historiography of the period to admit the importance of
    foreign influences on Ukrainian history – a feature that all but disappeared
    in the post-1920s writings of Soviet historians. See Iakovenko, 'Ukraïna
    mizh Skhodom i Zakhodom: proektsiia odniieï ideï,' in *Paralel'nyi svit*,
    345–53.
60 Pokrovsky saw the treatment of the Union of Lublin in traditional Russian
    historiography as an instance of the erroneous application of the national
    paradigm to an event brought about, in his opinion, exclusively by social
    factors. 'The history of that union,' wrote Pokrovsky, 'presents an extra-
    ordinarily instructive example of the way in which an essentially social
    conflict is concealed by a national one' (Pokrovskii, *Izbrannye proizvedeniia*,
    1: 458). As the main object of his critique, Pokrovsky selected the interpre-
    tation of the union by Sergei Soloviev, who believed that the Lithuanian
    elites had initially opposed union with Poland but were obliged to curtail
    their opposition once they realized that the 'Russians' (against whom the
    Lithuanians often discriminated) did not support them. Pokrovsky dis-
    missed Soloviev's account, claiming that the privileges of the Lithuanian
    magnates were not significantly greater than those of their 'Russian'
    counterparts and that both groups had originally opposed the union.

Pokrovsky argued that the true proponent of the union in the Grand Duchy of Lithuania was the nobility as a class, irrespective of its members' ethnic affiliation. In his view, the Lithuanian and 'Russian' nobility wanted to take power from the magnates, as did the Polish nobility in the first half of the seventeenth century, and union with the Kingdom of Poland was the way to achieve that goal (ibid., 458–60).

61 See Iavors'kyi, *Korotka istoriia*, 32, 41; cf. his *Istoriia Ukraïny*, 34–5.
62 On the 'Piedmont' theory and rhetoric in Soviet Ukraine and the USSR, see Martin, *Affirmative Action Empire*, 8–9, 225–7, 274–82, 292–3, 312–19, 351–2.
63 See excerpts from Rubach's report in *Mykhailo Hrushevs'kyi: mizh istoriieiu i politykoiu*, 121–2.
64 Pokrovskii, 'Bor'ba klassov i russkaia istoricheskaia literatura,' 345.
65 Ibid., 344.
66 Ibid.
67 See Rubach, 'Federalisticheskie teorii.' According to Rubach, the original text of the work was longer than the published version. It contained sections on Mykhailo Drahomanov and on the attitude of the 'revolutionary Marxists' to federalism that were omitted in the published text for lack of space (ibid., 3). The work was not published until 1930. By that time, the authorities' 'soft' attitude toward Hrushevsky had been all but abandoned, and the officially sponsored attack on the historian, now branded a nationalist, national democrat, and even fascist, was gaining ever greater momentum.
68 Rubach, 'Federalisticheskie teorii,' 99.
69 Ibid., 107.
70 Ibid., 93.
71 Ibid., 87.
72 Ibid., 88.
73 Ibid., 89–90.
74 Ibid., 106.
75 Ibid., 92.
76 Ibid., 103–5.
77 The atmosphere of peaceful coexistence between Hrushevsky and the authorities on the political level, and between the Marxist and national paradigms of Ukrainian history on the theoretical level, was also reflected in reviews of publications edited by Hrushevsky. Quite characteristic in that regard was a review of the 1927 issues of the journal *Ukraïna* that appeared in the party's main theoretical and political journal, *Bil'shovyk Ukraïny*. The author of the review, one T. Stasiuk, generally attacked the journal for publishing articles dealing mostly with 'all sorts of antiquity'

when the popular masses were allegedly interested in the history of the revolution. In Stasiuk's eyes, *Ukraïna*'s editorial policy contradicted Hrushevsky's own statement that the Ukrainian Academy of Sciences was supposed to differ from bourgeois academies in not closing itself off from the masses with a Chinese wall but forging a link with them by means of scholarship and its achievements. Stasiuk was thereby indicating that Hrushevsky could still potentially improve the journal and change its direction. Quite telling in that regard was Stasiuk's positive evaluation of Hrushevsky's own article, published in *Ukraïna*, on the writings of Kulish. Stasiuk praised Hrushevsky for his attempt to go beyond Kulish's individual characteristics and analyse the historical, social, and economic causes of his conflicts with Ukrainian populists of the 1860s. He held up Hrushevsky as an example to other contributors to *Ukraïna*, who allegedly neglected social motifs in their explanations of historical events. See Stasiuk, review of *Ukraïna*, in *Bil'shovyk Ukraïny*, 1928.

78 See Richyts'kyi, 'Iak Hrushevs'kyi "vypravliaie" Engel'sa.' Richytsky criticized Hrushevsky for the alleged eclecticism (a mixture of materialism and idealism) of his outlook and attacked him for questioning the validity of Engels's views on the nature of primitive society. He also claimed that Hrushevsky failed to distinguish between the social organization of primitive and class-based societies, turning the state into a fetish. For Richytsky, who closely followed Engels in that respect, the state was a product of class society, hence there could be no state in pre-class society. In his critique of Hrushevsky, Richytsky also made a number of political accusations. He claimed that Hrushevsky fetishized the national (i.e., bourgeois) state, sharing the views of David Lloyd George – a politically dangerous association in the USSR.

79 See Iefymenko, *Istoriia ukraïns'koho narodu*. The publication of this book is an interesting example of the introduction into Soviet Ukrainian scholarly discourse of the populist paradigm of Ukrainian history, developed as part of the all-Russian historical narrative.

80 Iavorsky was also critical of Bahalii's treatment of the life and writings of Mykhailo Drahomanov. See Volodymyr Kravchenko, 'D.I. Bahalii v svitli i tini svoieï "Avtobiohrafiï,"' 35–6.

81 Ibid., 36.

82 See Bahalii, review of Iavors'kyi, *Narys ukraïns'ko-rus'koï istorii* and 'Persha sproba nacherku istoriï Ukraïny na tli istorychnoho materiializmu.' Cf. Iavors'kyi, *Narys istoriï Ukraïny*, vyp. 1, *Hospodarstvo natural'ne. Pervisne suspil'stvo. Kniazivs'ko-druzhynnyi vik. Feodalizatsiia Ukraïny. Feodalizm halyts'ko-volyns'kyi ta lytovs'koï doby.*

83 See Iavors'kyi, 'De-shcho pro "krytychnu" krytyku,' 167–82.
84 See Bahalii, 'Z pryvodu antykrytyky prof. M.I. Iavors'koho.'
85 See Bahalii and Iavors'kyi, *Ukraïns'kyi filosof H.S. Skovoroda.*
86 Iavors'kyi, 'De-shcho pro "krytychnu" krytyku,' 172–3.
87 Ibid., 174.
88 See Hrushevsky, *History*, 8: 416.
89 Iavorsky was especially critical of Efimenko, probably because her survey of Ukrainian history had recently appeared in print in Ukrainian translation.
90 Iavorsky lauded Bahalii for accepting the results of the proletarian revolution not only 'in word' but 'in deed.' He also praised Bahalii for his efforts to embrace Marxism and historical materialism and for treating the class struggle as the main motive force of history. Iavorsky presented Bahalii's academic career and intellectual and political biography against the background of the career and works of Hrushevsky. See Iavors'kyi, 'Deshcho pro "krytychnu" krytyku,' 178.
91 See Iavors'kyi, Address at the Bahalii celebrations in Bahalii, *Vybrani pratsi*, 1: 319–24.
92 For most of the 1920s, representatives of the old Russian historiography were also positive in their assessment of Hrushevsky's contribution to East Slavic history. The attitudes of the 'old guard' became fully apparent during the elections to the USSR Academy of Sciences in 1928. See chapter 4 of this book.
93 See Bahalii, 'Akad. M.S. Hrushevs'kyi.'
94 Ibid., 208–9.
95 During the presentation of his paper in Kharkiv, Bahalii kept repeating that he was going to speak about Hrushevsky exclusively as a scholar. According to a secret police report, these statements created the clear impression in the audience that Bahalii actually wanted to say something more (specifically about Hrushevsky's political activities) but was not permitted to do so by the authorities. See the GPU report on Hrushevsky's jubilee in Prystaiko and Shapoval, *Mykhailo Hrushevs'kyi i HPU-NKVD*, no. 26, pp. 164–69, esp. 169.
96 In discussing Hrushevsky's paradigm of Ukrainian history, Bahalii noted that Hrushevsky's scheme was not entirely of his own making, as it resembled the one developed in the 1890s by the editorial board of the Ukrainophile journal *Kievskaia starina* and followed by Aleksandra Efimenko in her *History of the Ukrainian People*. See Bahalii, 'Akad. M.S. Hrushevs'kyi,' 182–4. On the rivalry between Linnichenko and Bahalii, see Tolochko, 'Dvi ne zovsim akademichni dyskusiï.'

97 In paying due tribute to his colleague's accomplishments, Bahalii was nevertheless far from idealizing him. As he stated at the outset, it was not his intention to write a congratulatory speech but to discuss the scholarly significance of Hrushevsky's works and establish his place in Ukrainian historiography. See Bahalii, 'Akad. M.S. Hrushevs'kyi,' 182–4.

98 Ibid., 198–9, 209, 217.

99 Bahalii supported Hrushevsky in his attempt to claim for the Ukrainian historical narrative all territories eventually settled by the Ukrainian ethnos, including the history of the steppe nomads and the Greek colonies of the northern Black Sea region (ibid., 196–7).

100 Ibid., 206–7.

101 Ibid., 208, 217.

102 Ibid., 217.

103 Hrushevs'kyi, '1825–1925,' 4.

104 See the text of Hrushevsky's speech at his jubilee celebrations in *Velykyi ukraïnets'*, 417–18.

105 For a list of Hrushevsky's articles on Ukrainian cultural activists and historians published before 1929, see Wynar, *Mykhailo Hrushevs'kyi, 1866–1934: Bibliographic Sources*, 28–45. For Hrushevsky's publications in *Ukraïna* from 1924 to 1930, see *Naukovyi chasopys ukraïnoznavstva 'Ukraïna' (1907–1932)*, 46–7.

106 See Hrushevs'kyi, 'Vikopomna data,' Vernadsky National Library of Ukraine, Manuscript Institute, fond X, 17169, 34 pp. See also his short preface to the unpublished special issue of *Ukraïna* devoted to the seventieth anniversary of Taras Shevchenko's death (1861), 'V simydesiati rokovyny smerty Shevchenka. Na spomyn ioho i liudei iomu blyz'kykh,' ibid., fond X, 17166, 2 pp. There Hrushevsky called upon scholars to turn their attention to the study of Shevchenko's milieu.

In the late 1920s, the commission for the study of modern Ukrainian history, which was headed by Hrushevsky, worked on the history of 'revolutionary populism,' and its members published a number of articles on the history of Ukrainian populism. See Hrushevsky's report on the activities of the commission in 1929–30, ibid., fond X, 18626.

107 See Iavors'kyi, *Korotka istoriia*, 86, 87. For Iavorsky's presentation of the history of the revolutionary movement in Ukraine, which in his interpretation included such icons of the Ukrainian national revival as Shevchenko, Drahomanov, Franko, Lesia Ukrainka, and Mykhailo Kotsiubynsky, see ibid., 78–105, his *Istoriia Ukraïny*, 122–81, and *Narys istoriï revoliutsiinoï borot'by na Ukraïni*, vol. 1. In the latter survey, Iavorsky traced the history of the 'revolutionary struggle' from Kyivan Rus' all the way to the

'Cossack-peasant wars of the seventeenth century,' the *haidamaka* movement, the Decembrist revolt, the SS. Cyril and Methodius Brotherhood,
and the era of 'populist revolution.'

108 See Iavors'kyi, 'Providni dumky v rozvytkovi istorychnoï nauky,' 115,
and 'Shostyi mizhnarodnyi konhres istorychnyi,' 217–18, 220.

109 See Hermaize, 'Iuvilei ukraïns'koï nauky.' The article developed a
number of themes that were also enunciated in Hermaize's speech at
Hrushevsky's jubilee celebrations in October 1926; cf. the text of the
speech in *Velykyi ukraïnets'*, 406–14. A year earlier, Hermaize published a
positive review of Hrushevsky's *Z pochatkiv ukraïns'koho sotsiialistychnoho
rukhu: M. Drahomaniv i zhenevs'kyi sotsiialistychnyi hurtok* (Vienna, 1923).
See his 'Ukraïns'ki sotsiialisty ta osnovopolozhnyky naukovoho
sotsiializmu.'

110 The editors of the festschrift regarded Hrushevsky's *History* as a source
for the formation of Ukrainian national, political, and socio-cultural
consciousness and as a work that introduced Ukraine to the European
community of nations. See *Naukovyi zbirnyk, prysviachenyi profesorovi
Mykhailovi Hrushevs'komu*, vii.

In his speech at the jubilee celebrations (but not in the article),
Hermaize expressed agreement with Hrushevsky's statement that producing a complete history of Ukraine was a matter of national honour for
a whole generation of Ukrainian scholars (see *Velykyi ukraïnets'*, 410). In
the article, Hermaize also makes reference to this statement of Hrushevsky's without indicating his own attitude toward it (Hermaize, 'Iuvilei
ukraïns'koï nauky,' 96–7).

111 See Hermaize, 'Iuvilei ukraïns'koï nauky,' 96–7, 99.

112 Ibid., 98–9.

113 While Hrushevsky's socialist vocabulary undoubtedly helped Hermaize
present him as a historian ideologically close to the regime, if not an
outright Marxist, it did not deceive the authorities, who continued to
regard Ukrainian socialism as a major threat to their power. Among
those sceptics was Ivan Lakyza, head of the publications department of
the Central Committee of the Communist Party of Ukraine. As noted
above (chapter 4), at the request of the Politburo he wrote an article on
Hrushevsky's political views that was published in the same issue of
Zhyttia i revoliutsiia as the article by Hermaize. Lakyza restated the party's
long-held position that Hrushevsky's methodology was bourgeois and
went on to assert that Durkheim's school of sociology had generally
retained its bourgeois and idealistic outlook, although some of its research could indeed be of interest to Marxist scholarship. While Lakyza

did not mention Hermaize by name, his article represented the reaction of the party apparatus to Hermaize's effort to cast off Hrushevsky's image as a bourgeois scholar implicitly hostile to the regime. See Lakyza, 'Mykhailo Serhiiovych Hrushevs'kyi,' 101.

114 See 'Pervaia vsesoiuznaia konferentsiia marksistsko-leninskikh nauchno-issledovatel'skikh uchrezhdenii.' Cf. Enteen, *Soviet Scholar-Bureaucrat*, 80–2.

115 See the texts of Iavorsky's and Gorin's presentations on organizational matters in *Trudy*, 1: 16–27, 36–40, and a report on their presentations in *Istorik-marksist*, 1929, no. 11: 224–5.

116 See Iavorskii, 'Sovremennye antimarksistskie techeniia.'

117 See ibid., 435.

118 For the proceedings of the discussion, see *Trudy*, 1: 436–68; cf. a report on the conference in *Istorik-marksist*, 1929, no. 11: 229–42. For a summary of the discussion, see Prymak, *Mykhailo Hrushevsky*, 232–5.

119 For the text of Pokrovsky's comment, see *Trudy*, 1: 455–9; cf. a report on his presentation in *Istorik-marksist*, 1929, no. 11: 240–1.

120 See Artizov, 'M.N. Pokrovskii,' 1: 86. For the text of Iavorsky's greetings and Pokrovsky's reaction to them, see *Trudy*, 1: 75–82.

121 See Pokrovsky's concluding remarks at the conference in *Trudy*, 1: 75–9.

122 See extracts from Semko's report and from the Moscow newspapers in *Mykhailo Hrushevs'kyi: mizh istoriieiu ta politykoiu*, 116–20. Gorin's attacks on Iavorsky appeared in *Pravda* on 4 January and 10 February 1929.

123 See *Trudy*, 1: 456.

124 Ibid., 458.

125 Ibid., 455.

126 Ibid., 451–2.

127 Ibid., 467–8.

128 An indication of the strong support for Iavorsky's position among the Ukrainian leadership was the publication in the March 1929 issue of *Bil'shovyk Ukraïny* of a bulletin on the founding on 20 December 1928 of the Ukrainian Society of Marxist Historians and its forthcoming congress, scheduled for May 1929. This bulletin, issued on behalf of the society, was signed by Iavorsky as head and Karetnikova as secretary. For the text of the bulletin, see 'Do istorykiv-marksystiv Ukraïny.' Not until September 1929 was Iavorsky forced to 'admit' his alleged errors. See Rubliov and Cherchenko, *Stalinshchyna i dolia zakhidnoukraïns'koï intelihentsiï*, 88–93.

129 See Iavors'kyi, 'Don-kikhotstvo chy rusotiapstvo?' in *Prapor marksyzmu*, no. 2 (March–April 1929). See also Gorin's letter to the editor of *Prapor marksyzmu* and Iavorsky's comments on it in *Prapor marksyzmu*, no. 5 (October–November 1929): 227–9.

130 See Artizov, 'M.N. Pokrovskii,' 125.
131 For the proceedings of the discussion, see 'Dyskusiia z pryvodu skhemy istoriï Ukraïny M. Iavors'koho,' *Litopys revoliutsiï*, 1930, nos. 2, 3–4, 5.
132 See the text of Iavorsky's speaking notes in *Litopys revoliutsiï*, 1930, no. 2: 269–72.
133 This thesis is absent from Iavorsky's speaking notes but was apparently included in the full text of his presentation. See the objection to that assertion of Iavorsky's in the record of a presentation by Shpunt, a participant in the discussion (ibid., 274–6).
134 *Trudy*, 1: 434.
135 Ibid., 462.
136 See *Litopys revoliutsiï*, 1930, no. 2: 269–72.
137 Ibid.
138 Ibid., 279.
139 Ibid., 306. Rubach restated his position in that regard in his report to the Central Committee of the Communist Party of Ukraine on the results of the 'Iavorsky discussion.' Cf. excerpts from Rubach's report in *Mykhailo Hrushevs'kyi: mizh istoriieiu i politykoiu*, 121–2.
140 See *Litopys revoliutsiï*, 1930, no. 2: 315.
141 Ibid., 281–9.
142 Ibid., 297–302.
143 Ibid., 289–97.
144 Ibid., 272–4.
145 Ibid., 274–81.
146 Ibid., 302.
147 Ibid., 289.
148 Since the autumn of 1928, at the initiative of the head of the party propaganda apparatus in Moscow, A. Krinitsky, Pokrovsky had become active in the party campaign against 'right' deviations, a policy that resulted in fierce attacks on proponents of non-Russian nationalism in the republics. On Pokrovsky's standing in the party in 1928–9, see Artizov, 'M.N. Pokrovskii,' 84–5; Enteen, *Soviet Scholar-Bureaucrat*, 92–106.

David Brandenberger (*National Bolshevism*, 8, 20–4) traces the emergence of official support for the Russocentric interpretation of history to the war scare of 1929, when the Moscow Politburo began to doubt the potential of the internationalist ideology to mobilize the population for the defence of the regime.
149 On 16 January 1929, Serhii Iefremov noted in his diary: 'Through Iavorsky's lips they destroyed all previous Ukrainian historiography as bourgeois, and after that some Muscovite destroyed Iavorsky himself as

non-Marxist. And no righteous man was left to Ukraine ... People who make every effort to play up to Marxism, like Bahalii, for example, are extremely apprehensive. And rightly so: don't play up, don't stick your head where it doesn't belong' (Iefremov, *Shchodennyky*, 724–5).

150 See Hrushevsky's letters to Studynsky in *Lysty*, 234, 235–6, esp. 235. In the same month, much of the funding earlier allocated to Hrushevsky's projects by the Kharkiv authorities was withdrawn.

151 Hurevych, 'Psevdomarksyzm na sluzhbi ukraïns'koho natsionalizmu.'

152 Antin Kozachenko's review in *Prapor marksyzmu* of the second volume of *Studiï z istoriï Ukraïny*, published in 1929 by Hrushevsky's 'historical institutions,' should be seen as an exception to the common practice of using Hrushevsky's name to criticize Marxist historians in general and Osyp Hermaize in particular. Kozachenko specifically attacked Hermaize's article on recent Ukrainian historiography, maintaining that Hermaize treated all Ukrainian historians as a group and failed to discuss the social causes of recent developments in Ukrainian historiography. Attacking the 'bad' Hermaize, Kozachenko counterposed the 'good' Hrushevsky, who (in Kozachenko's account) accepted the interpretation of culture as one of the functions of society and urged historians to study that function. Kozachenko claimed that Hermaize was avoiding Hrushevsky's injunction. In a way, Kozachenko was continuing the pre-1929 tactic of shielding Hrushevsky from direct criticism. See Kozachenko's review of *Studiï z istoriï Ukraïny naukovo-doslidchoï kafedry istoriï Ukraïny v Kyievi*, vol. 2, esp. 214–15.

153 See Fedir Iastrebov's review of Bahalii, *Narys istorii Ukraïny*, 173.

154 See the proceedings of the 'Iavorsky discussion' in *Litopys revoliutsiï*, 1930, no. 5: 290. For a brief biography of Iastrebov, see *Vcheni Instytutu istoriï Ukraïny*, 380–1.

155 See Iastrebov's review, 169.

156 Ibid.

157 This was not Svidzinsky's first critical review of Hrushevsky's publications: in 1927 he had published a review of the collection *Za sto lit* (In One Hundred Years), edited by Hrushevsky, in which he criticized the latter for paying too much attention to the history of the Ukrainian peasantry while ignoring the existence of other social groups. See Svidzinsky's review in *Bil'shovyk Ukraïny*, 1927, no. 6: 139–45, esp. 139. Back in 1926, the first issues of Hrushevsky's *Ukraïna* were critically reviewed for *Bil'shovyk Ukraïny* by Volodymyr Iurynets. See Prystaiko and Shapoval, *Mykhailo Hrushevs'kyi i HPU-NKVD*, 36–7.

158 See Svidzinsky's review of *Ukraïna*, 240. Among other things, he attacked

Hrushevsky for failing to discuss social antagonisms in Ukrainian society in his article on Panteleimon Kulish. Ironically, only two years earlier the same essay had been praised in the party's main theoretical journal for its masterful application of sociological method in the analysis of Kulish's views. See Stasiuk's review of *Ukraïna*.

159 See the proceedings of the 'Iavorsky discussion' in *Litopys revoliutsiï*, 1930, nos. 3–4: 229.

160 Ibid., 224. The same understanding of the hierarchy of 'errors' was expressed in an attack on Hrushevsky's nephew Serhii Shamrai at the Academy of Sciences in February 1932. One of the participants in the 'discussion,' Denysenko, stated: 'But it cannot be said that Academician Hrushevsky's historical process can even be considered fundamentally erroneous. That process is not erroneous ... if an academic researcher upholds another methodology, another pathway to the benefit of the bourgeoisie, then we are dealing with a system, and not with errors, which, to repeat, may be found even among comrades who uphold the methodology of Marx and Lenin.' See the minutes of the discussion in the Vernadsky National Library of Ukraine, Manuscript Institute, fond X, 14627, p. 9.

161 See Ravich-Cherkasskii, *Istoriia Kommunisticheskoi partii (b-ov) Ukrainy*. On the official condemnation of the 'two roots' theory, see Mace, *Communism and the Dilemmas of National Liberation*, 102–3.

162 See Skubitskii, 'Klassovaia bor'ba.' In October 1930, Fedir Savchenko wrote to Kyrylo Studynsky that the issue of the journal containing Skubytsky's article had already arrived in Kyiv. Knowing that his letter might be read by the secret police, Savchenko limited his comments about the article to a minimum: 'There are three articles against bourgeois historians. The first is against Russian great-state chauvinism, the second against the Ukrainian bourgeois outlook, mainly Hrushevsky, but even Bahalii is sharply accosted, and the third against the Belarusian [bourgeois outlook].' See Savchenko to Studynsky (Kyiv, 12 October 1930) in TsDIAL, fond 362, op. 1, no. 379.

163 In his response to Skubytsky's critique, Bahalii sought to clear his name by saying that he acknowledged Hrushevsky's scheme of Ukrainian history only in that sense that it posited Kyivan Rus' as the starting point of Ukrainian history, while rejecting Hrushevsky's non-materialist interpretation. See Volodymyr Kravchenko, *D.I. Bagalei*, 148.

164 See Skubitskii, 'Klassovaia bor'ba,' 34. Like Svidzinsky before him, Skubytsky specifically attacked Hrushevsky for exaggerating the role of the intelligentsia in Ukrainian history, adducing a number of quotations

from Hrushevsky's *History*, including one in which the historian stated that the Kyivan intelligentsia, both secular and clerical, constituted a laboratory in which ideas and programs of state-building were formulated (ibid., 31; cf. Hrushevsky, *History*, 8: 520). In translating Hrushevsky's text into Russian, Skubytsky distorted the meaning of the quotation. While Hrushevsky wrote, 'It was to them [the Kyivan intelligentsia] that Khmelnytsky was indebted (*zavdiachuvav*), both directly and indirectly, for the change in his disposition and plans,' Skubytsky mistranslated *zavdiachuvav* as *blagodaril* (thanked). This made it appear that, according to Hrushevsky, Khmelnytsky had 'directly and indirectly thanked' the Kyivan intelligentsia.

In 1937 Skubytsky himself fell victim to the changing party line in history. He was arrested by the secret police for a number of ideological transgressions, including excessive criticism of Bohdan Khmelnytsky. See Yekelchyk, 'Stalinist Patriotism as Imperial Discourse.'

165 See Shums'kyi, 'Stara i nova Ukraïna,' 96.

166 This was the ideological goal established by Rubach at the beginning and end of his article. He began with the assertion that Hrushevsky was a historian and politician who had never concealed his political associations. His use of the past tense was very telling: a scholar who was still living and working had clearly been written off completely by the Ukrainian party establishment, as were hundreds of thousands of other victims of state-sponsored terror. Rubach claimed that at a time when the kulaks were being 'liquidated as a class' and the class struggle had entered an 'acute' phase, with capitalism itself in deep crisis, the bourgeois ideologues were using all sorts of ideological ruses to conceal their true intentions.

167 See [Kokoshko], 'Vid redaktsiï.' The editor in chief of the volume was S. Kokoshko, who probably was also the author of the introduction. Ivan Kravchenko, the author of the essay 'Fashysts'ki kontseptsiï Hrushevs'koho' in the same volume, saw the purpose of his article as 'uncovering the class content of the national-democratic and fascist conceptions in the historiography of Hrushevsky and his school' (ibid., 11).

168 As quoted in Richyts'kyi, 'Proty interventsiï,' 36. As noted above (chapter 4), Mohyliansky, who published a short story in 1926 characterizing Hrushevsky's return to Ukraine as an act of national treason, now tried to shield his former antagonist from an unfounded critique.

169 Ibid.

170 Nikitin, 'Pis'mo istorika,' 95–7.

171 See Iastrebov, 'Tomu dev'iatoho persha polovyna,' 147.
172 Ibid.
173 Sukhyno-Khomenko in fact became the main proponent of Pokrovsky's theory of 'commercial capitalism' and applied it to the history of the Khmelnytsky Uprising much more systematically than Iavorsky. See his *Odminy i bankrutstvo ukraïns'koho natsionalizmu*, 7–94, and his 'Dovidka tov. Sukhyno-Khomenka' in 'Dyskusiia z pryvodu skhemy istoriï Ukraïny M. Iavors'koho,' *Litopys revoliutsiï*, 1930, no. 5: 322–23.
     Later, when political circumstances required it, he employed his understanding of 'commercial capitalism' as a means of criticizing Iavorsky for alleged inconsistencies and deviations from the Marxist approach to Ukrainian history. Sukhyno-Khomenko was a 'soft' and unenthusiastic critic of Iavorsky: his critique was intended to help Iavorsky retain his position and authority in Marxist scholarship. Sukhyno-Khomenko even called upon his Marxist colleagues to fight 'Iavorskyism' together with Iavorsky. For his 'friendly critique,' see Sukhyno-Khomenko, 'Na marksysts'komu istorychnomu fronti,' *Bil'shovyk Ukraïny*, 1929, nos. 17–18: 47–52 and no. 19: 54.
174 Iastrebov, 'Tomu dev'iatoho persha polovyna,' 148.
175 Ibid., 147–8. The same words of Hrushevsky, published in late 1929 by the newspaper *Proletars'ka pravda*, were quoted by another of his critics, Skubytsky, who used them to indicate the role that Hrushevsky attributed to the Ukrainian intelligentsia. See Skubitskii, 'Klassovaia bor'ba v ukrainskoi istoricheskoi literature.'
176 On Okinshevych, see Padokh, 'Lev Okinshevych – vydatnyi istoryk derzhavnoho prava kozats'koï Ukraïny.'
177 See Okinshevych, 'Natsional'no-demokratychna kontseptsiia.' Okinshevych later recalled that he had to write a critique of Hrushevsky at the demand of the party secretary of the Academy of Sciences, F.A. Kozubovsky. He felt that he was in no position to ignore that demand. Ironically, when Okinshevych was later dismissed from the Nizhyn Pedagogical Institute at the behest of the secret police as a proponent of Ukrainian independence, one of the accusations against him was that in his article about Hrushevsky he did not so much criticize him as popularize his views. See Okinshevych, *Moia akademichna pratsia v Ukraïni*, 48, 58.
178 See Okinshevych, 'Natsional'no-demokratychna kontseptsiia.'
179 Ibid., 103–4.
180 See Hrushevs'kyi, *Pereiaslavs'ka umova Ukraïny z Moskvoiu 1654 roku. Statti i teksty*.
181 See Okinshevych, 'Natsional'no-demokratychna kontseptsiia,' 106.
182 The transformation of national-democratic ideology into fascism was a

major theme in the discussion of the historical views of Hrushevsky's nephew, Serhii Shamrai, which took place at the Ukrainian Academy of Sciences on 29 February 1932. Oleksander Ohloblyn, who chaired the meeting, and his student Ivan Kravchenko both indicated that such a transformation had taken place in the works of Hrushevsky and his school. Viktor Iurkevych, one of the members of that school and a close collaborator of Hrushevsky's, 'admitted' that this process was indeed taking place among Ukrainian historians abroad. According to him, the same tendency was apparent in the USSR, where the democratic element was disappearing from national-democratic ideology. Iurkevych indicated his own works and those of Shamrai as examples of that tendency. See the minutes of the discussion in the Vernadsky National Library of Ukraine, Manuscript Institute, fond X, 14627, pp. 19, 25, 38.

183 See Iastrebov, 'Natsional-fashysts'ka kontseptsiia,' 55–120.
184 Ibid., 60.
185 Ibid., 82.
186 Ibid., 73.
187 Ibid., 72.
188 Ibid., 112.
189 Ibid., 86.
190 See Zatonsky's speech in *Mykhailo Hrushevs'kyi: mizh istoriieiu ta politykoiu*, 149–50.
191 For the text of Petrovsky's speech, see *Stenograficheskie otchety Gosudarstvennoi dumy*, cols. 1778–92. On Lenin's authorship of the draft, see Lenin, *Polnoe sobranie sochinenii*, 23: 452.
192 See *Narys istoriï Ukraïny*, 67–72. The first edition was published in Ufa in 1942.
193 Herasymchuk's review was written in Western Ukraine, which was beyond Soviet control. For the text of the review, which remained in manuscript at the time, see Fedoruk, 'Vidhuk Vasylia Harasymchuka na IX tom "Istoriï Ukraïny-Rusy" M. Hrushevs'koho.'
194 On Stalin's critique of Bedny, see Martin, *Affirmative Action Empire*, 271–2.
195 See the text of Hrushevsky's internal memorandum of 30 August 1930 in Sokhan' et al., *M.S. Hrushevs'kyi i Academia*, 260–8.
196 See Iavors'kyi, 'De-shcho pro "krytychnu" krytyku,' 172; Kravchenko, 'Fashysts'ki kontseptsiï,' 21–2.

Conclusions

1 On the *Synopsis* and its readership, see Samarin, *Rasprostranenie i chitatel' pervykh pechatnykh knig po istorii Rossii*, 20–76.

2 On the 'rehabilitation' of the Russocentric paradigm in Soviet history, see Brandenberger, *National Bolshevism*, 43–62.
3 The 'denationalization' of the Ukrainian historical narrative was influenced by the major shift in Soviet nationality policy of the period. In many ways, the process of stripping national historiographies of their distinctive features and turning them back to the prenational stage paralleled the 'denationalization' of the Soviet republics. Stalin's shift to primordialism on the nationality question became fully apparent when the theme of building modern Soviet nations was abandoned in official discourse. The return to the populist paradigm in historiography coincided with the rise to prominence of folk culture as the main attribute of festivals of national culture in Moscow in the late 1930s. It also facilitated the centre's attempts to roll back the nationalization process in the Union republics and arrest the development of the respective 'nationalities' at the prenational level. For a discussion of the changing features of Soviet nationality policy in the 1930s, see the section titled 'Stalinist Primordialism' in Martin, *Affirmative Action Empire*, 442–51.
4 See Mez'ko, *Iak bil'shovyky ruinuvaly*, 47.
5 On the concept of the 'friendship of peoples' in Soviet historiography, see Tillett, *The Great Friendship*. For an in-depth analysis of the interrelation of the Russian and Ukrainian narratives in Soviet historiography from the late 1930s to the early 1950s, see Yekelchyk, *Stalin's Empire of History*.

Appendix

1 I am grateful to Iurii Mytsyk for interviewing Butych.
2 See Jacyk's statement in *The Hrushevsky Translation Project*, 29.
3 See Hrushevsky's letter of 18 December 1923 to Studynsky in *Lysty*, 136.
4 Hrushevsky searched for Dzhydzora's manuscripts after his return to Ukraine in 1924. In his letter of 8 September 1926 to Studynsky (*Lysty*, 193), he wrote that Dzhydzora's collection included documents covering more or less the first quarter of the eighteenth century, which was to be the terminus of Hrushevsky's multivolume *History*. In his introduction to the collection of Dzhydzhora's works published in Kyiv in 1930, Hrushevsky wrote that Dzhydzhora had collected materials for the first half of the eighteenth century (the period between the hetmancies of Ivan Mazepa and Kyrylo Rozumovsky). See 'Peredmova,' iv–v. On Dzhydzhora, see Pryshliak, 'Ivan Dzhydzhora.'
5 See Hrushevsky's letter of 8 September 1926 to Studynsky in *Lysty*, 193, and Fedoruk, 'Vasyl' Harasymchuk ta ioho nevydani "Materialy,"' 15–16.

6 See Korduba's postcard to Hrushevsky dated 29 December 1927, TsDIAK, fond 1235, op. 1, no. 552.
7 See 'Diial'nist' Istorychnoï sektsiï (1928),' x. Cf. Iurkova, *Diial'nist'*, 184.
8 See *Ukraïna*, 1927, no. 6: 194. Cf. Hrushevsky's reports on the activities of his 'historical institutions' in 'Diial'nist' Istorychnoï sektsiï (1926),' xxix; 'Diial'nist' Istorychnoï sektsiï (1927),' xxix; 'Diial'nist' Istorychnoï sektsiï (1928),' xxii; Hrushevsky's report for 1928–9 in the Vernadsky National Library of Ukraine, Manuscript Institute, fond X, no. 18622, p. 7.
9 See Nikitin, 'Pis'mo istorika.'
10 See Hrushevsky's letters of 15 February, 24 July, and 3 August 1930 to Dmytro Kravtsov in the Vernadsky National Library of Ukraine, Manuscript Institute, fond 262, nos 111, 112, 115.
11 Quoted in Polons'ka-Vasylenko, *Ukraïns'ka Akademiia Nauk*, 1: 15. The person in question was apparently Pylyp Vasyliovych Klymenko, whom Polonska-Vasylenko characterized as one of the oldest associates (he was born in 1880), but with very few publications (ibid., 15, 164). On Klymenko, see Iurkova, *Diial'nist'*, 78–9, 123–4, 151–2, 236–7, 291–3, 350–1.
12 See Fedir Savchenko's letter of 1 December 1930 to Kyrylo Studynsky in TsDIAL, fond 362, op. 1, no. 379. Savchenko complained that Hrushevsky showed no interest in the impending publication of his monograph on the prohibition of Ukrainian activities in 1876 and even refused to read the manuscript, citing the problem with his vision. Savchenko noted in his letter that the eye trouble was genuine. Cf. Kryp'iakevych, *Mykhailo Hrushevs'kyi*, 478.
13 See Nikitin, 'Pis'mo istorika.'
14 Ibid.
15 See Iurkova, *Diial'nist'*, 184.
16 Kateryna Hrushevska was assigned by the Ukrainian Academy to provide secretarial assistance to her father in carrying out this project. See Matiash, *Kateryna Hrushevs'ka*, 98.
17 Those articles include an abstract of a conference presentation, 'Ob ukrainskoi istoriografii XVIII veka. Neskol'ko soobrazhenii.'
18 See Matiash, *Kateryna Hrushevs'ka*, 100–3.
19 The third library collected during his lifetime, as Hrushevsky wrote in his letter to Molotov.
20 See a report by the secret police agent who met Hrushevsky's relatives in Kyiv in July 1934 (Prystaiko and Shapoval, *Mykhailo Hrushevs'kyi i HPU-NKVD*, 283–5). On Hrushevsky's relations with Speransky, see also Robinson, 'M.S. Hrušhevs'kyj.'
21 See Nikitin, 'Pis'mo istorika.'

22 *Lysty*, 250.
23 See Pyrih, *Zhyttia Mykhaila Hrushevs'koho*, 171–2; Matiash, *Kateryna Hrushevs'ka*, 100–2. Most of the returned materials have been preserved in the archive of the Institute of History of the National Academy of Sciences of Ukraine and the Vernadsky National Library of Ukraine. See Iurkova, *Diial'nist'*, 31.
24 Quoted in Pyrih, *Zhyttia*, 147.
25 Ibid.
26 See Matiash, *Kateryna Hrushevs'ka*, 114.
27 See Kateryna Hrushevska's letter to her mother in Matiash, *Kateryna Hrushevs'ka*, 207–8.
28 In his letter of 13 February 1931, Fedir Savchenko informed Kyrylo Studynsky that the 'next volume' of the *History of Ukrainian Literature* had been sent to the press, but the printer wanted the manuscript retyped, as Hrushevsky had made a large number of corrections and additions to it (TsDIAL, fond 362, op. 1, no. 379).
29 See Biletsky's review in Hrushevs'kyi, *Istoriia ukraïns'koï literatury*, 6: 677.
30 See Myshanych, 'Vid uporiadnyka,' 679. Myshanych questions the accuracy of Biletsky's information, noting his later claim that the first part of volume 6 had actually appeared in print after Hrushevsky's death, although there is no evidence of any such edition. Indeed, in June 1941, Kateryna Hryshevska still counted volume 6 among the manuscripts, and it is unlikely that the volume could have been published during or after the war (cf. Matiash, *Kateryna Hrushevs'ka*, 208).
       Even so, there is no reason to disregard all of Biletsky's evidence, as was done by Myshanych, who reasoned that if it took Hrushevsky three-and-a-half years to cover twenty-three years of Ukrainian literary history, it was unlikely that, given the conditions of the early 1930s, he could have written five to six thousand pages to cover more than 150 years of Ukrainian literature. The recent publication of Hrushevsky's letters to Kyrylo Studynsky shows that such a pace was not altogether impossible.
31 See the secret police report in Prystaiko and Shapoval, *Mykhailo Hrushevs'kyi i HPU-NKVD*, 284.
32 See Vernadsky National Library of Ukraine, Manuscript Institute, fond X, nos 2913, 15099, 15100, 17166, 17169, 17176, 17193, 17216, 17236.
33 See an excerpt from Hrushevsky's note appended to Kateryna Hrushevska's letter to relatives in Kyiv (Matiash, *Kateryna Hrushevs'ka*, 104).
34 Ibid., 208.

Bibliography

Abbreviations

AIuZR	*Arkhiv Iugo-Zapadnoi Rossii* (Kyiv)
Akty IuZR	*Akty, otnosiashchiesia k istorii Iuzhnoi i Zapadnoi Rossii* (St Petersburg)
ChIONL	*Chteniia v Istoricheskom obshchestve Nestora-letopistsa* (Kyiv)
ChOIDR	*Chteniia v Imperatorskom obshchestve istorii i drevnostei rossiiskikh pri Moskovskom universitete* (Moscow)
HUS	*Harvard Ukrainian Studies* (Cambridge, MA)
LNV	*Literaturno-naukovyi visnyk* (Lviv)
ZNTSh	*Zapysky Naukovoho tovarystra im. Shevchenka* (Lviv)
ZUNT	*Zapysky Ukraïns'koho naukovoho tovarystva v Kyievi* (Kyiv)

Archival Sources

Tsentral'nyi derzhavnyi istorychnyi arkhiv Ukraïny/Central State Historical Archive of Ukraine (Kyiv) [TsDIAK]
   Fond 1235, op. 1, nos. 49, 142–7, 151, 270, 275, 303, 393, 411, 468, 470, 518, 552, 661, 692, 700, 775, 828, 855, 870, 873, 874.
Tsentral'nyi derzhavnyi istorychnyi arkhiv Ukraïny/Central State Historical Archive of Ukraine (Lviv) [TsDIAL]
   Fond 362, op. 1, nos. 378, 379.
Natsional'na biblioteka Ukraïny im. Volodymyra Vernads'koho. Instytut rukopysu/Volodymyr Vernadsky National Library of Ukraine. Manuscript Institute (Kyiv)
   Fond 121, nos. 48–54.
   Fond 262, nos. 111, 112, 115.

Fond X, nos. 2913, 14627, 15099, 15100, 15146, 17166, 17169, 17176, 17193, 17216, 17236, 18622, 18623, 18626, 18652.
Zaporizhia State University. Archival Collection, Program for the Study of Southern Ukraine.
Vasyl' Rubel' manuscript.

Works of Mykhailo Hrushevsky

'250 lit.' *LNV* 7, no. 1 (1904): 1–6.
'1825–1925.' *Ukraïna*, 1925, no. 6: 3–4.
'Anty. Uryvok z istoriï Ukraïny-Rusy.' *ZNTSh* 21 (1898): 1–16.
'Apostolovi pratsi.' *Ukraïna*, 1926, no. 6: 3–20.
'Avtobiohrafiia' 1906, 1914–19, 1926 rr. In *Velykyi ukraïnets'*, 197–240.
'Baida-Vyshnevets'kyi v poeziï i istoriï.' *ZUNT*, 1909, no. 3: 108–39.
Barskoe starostvo. Istoricheskie ocherki (XV–XVIII v.). Kyiv, 1894. Repr.: *Bars'ke starostvo. Istorychni narysy*. Intro. Mykola Krykun. Lviv, 1996.
'Bekh-al'-dzhuhur.' *Dilo* (Lviv), nos. 66–68 (1885).
'Bezhluzda natsional'na polityka Rosiï.' *Dilo*, no. 100 (18 May 1905).
'Bidna divchyna.' *Step. Khersons'kyi beletrystychnyi zbirnyk*, 315–37. St Petersburg, 1886.
'Bohdanovi rokovyny.' *LNV* 10, nos. 8–9 (1907): 207–12.
'Chernihiv i Sivershchyna v ukraïns'kii istoriï. Kil'ka sposterezhen', zdohadiv i pobazhan'.' In *Chernihiv i Pivnichne Livoberezhzhia*, 101–17. Kyiv, 1928.
'Chy Ukraïna til'ky dlia ukraïntsiv?' In idem, *Na porozi novoï Ukraïny*, 138–40. First published in *Nova Rada* (Kyiv), no. 15 (1917).
'Dlia iuvileiu Ivana Kotliarevs'koho.' *ZNTSh* 2 (1893): 146–61.
'Do nashykh sprob spivrobitnytstva z USRR.' *Boritesia – poborete! Zakordonnyi organ Ukraïns'koï partiï sotsiialistiv-revoliutsioneriv* (Vienna), 1921, no. 9: 28–31.
'Dvizhenie politicheskoi i obshchestvennoi ukrainskoi mysli v XIX stoletii.' *Ukrainskii vestnik*, no. 9 (16 July 1906): 633–44. Repr. in idem, *Osvobozhdenie Rossii i ukrainskii vopros*, 42–54.
'Edinstvo ili raspadenie?' *Ukrainskii vestnik*, no. 3 (4 June 1906): 39–51. Repr. in idem, *Osvobozhdenie Rossii i ukrainskii vopros*, 55–67.
'Era finansovo-ekonomichna.' In idem, *Nasha polityka*, 71–88.
'Etnohrafichne dilo Kostomarova.' In [Mykola Kostomarov], *Etnohrafichni pysannia Kostomarova*, ix–xxiv. Kyiv, 1930.
Etnohrafichni katehoriï i kul'turno-arkheolohichni typy v suchasnykh studiiakh Skhidnoï Evropy. St Petersburg, 1904. English translation in Nicholas Chirovsky, ed. and trans., *On the Historical Beginnings of Eastern Slavic Europe*, 39–52. New York, 1976.

'Frazy i fakty.' *LNV* 8, no. 4 (1905): 132–7. Russian translation: idem, 'Frazy i fakty,' *Kievskaia starina* (May 1905): 161–7; *Syn otechestva*, no. 50 (14 April 1905). Repr. in idem, *Osvobozhdenie Rossii i ukrainskii vopros*, 94–100.

'Hanebnii pam'iati.' *Ukraïna*, 1926, no. 4: 46–51.

'Hanebnii pamiaty.' *LNV* 9, no. 6 (1906): 570–1. Russian translation: idem, 'Pozornoi pamiati ...,' *Ukrainskii vestnik*, no. 1 (21 May 1906): 39–41. Repr. in idem, *Osvobozhdenie Rossii i ukrainskii vopros*, 112–14.

'Het' z rutenstvom!' *Dilo*, no. 129 (22 June 1907): 1–2.

A History of Ukraine. New Haven, CT [1941].

History of Ukraine-Rus'. Ed. Frank E. Sysyn et al. Vols 1, 7, 8. Edmonton and Toronto, 1997–2002.

[M. Serhiienko, pseud.] 'Hromads'kyi rukh na Vkraïni-Rusy v XIII vitsi.' *ZNTSh* 1 (1892): 1–28.

'Iak ia buv kolys' beletrystom.' In idem, *Pid zoriamy. Opovidannia, nacherky, zamitky, istorychni obrazy*, 5–18. Kyiv, 1928.

'Iak mene sprovadzheno do L'vova.' *Dilo*, no. 137 (1898).

Iakoï my khochemo avtonomiï i federatsiï. Kyiv, 1917. Excerpts in *Politolohiia*, 217–30.

Iliustrovana istoriia Ukraïny. Kyiv, 1911, 1912, 1913, 1915, 1917. Repr. of 1913 edition: Kyiv, 1992.

Iliustrovana istoriia Ukraïny, z dodatkom novoho periodu istoriï Ukraïny za roky vid 1914 do 1919. Winnipeg, n.d. Repr. of Kyiv edition of 1918, with supplements.

Introduction to *Ukraïns'kyi arkhiv*. Vol. 1, *Heneral'ne slidstvo pro maietnosti Starodubs'koho polku*, pp. iii–iv. Kyiv, 1929.

Istoriia ukraïns'koï literatury. 5 vols. Kyiv and Lviv, 1923. Repr. New York, 1959–60. Vol. 6. Kyiv, 1995.

Istoriia Ukraïny–Rusy. 10 vols. 1st ed. Lviv and Kyiv, 1898–1937. Vols. 1–4. 2d ed. Lviv and Kyiv, 1904–7. Vol. 1. 3d ed. Kyiv, 1913. Repr. New York, 1954–8; Kyiv, 1991–2000.

'Iuzhnorusskie gospodarskie zamki v polovine XVI veka. Istoriko-statisticheskii ocherk.' *Universitetskie izvestiia* (Kyiv), no. 2 (February 1890): 1–33.

'Iz pol'sko-ukrainskikh otnoshenii Galitsii. Neskol'ko illiustratsii k voprosu: avtonomiia oblastnaia ili natsional'no-territorial'naia.' In idem, *Osvobozhdenie Rossii i ukrainskii vopros*, 195–264. Also separately: St Petersburg, 1907.

'Khmel'nyts'kyi i Khmel'nychchyna. Istorychnyi eskiz.' *ZNTSh* 23–4 (1898): 1–30.

Khmel'nyts'kyi v Pereiaslavi. Istorychni obrazy. Kyiv, 1917.

'Khronolohiia podii Halyts'ko-volyns'koï litopysy.' *ZNTSh* 41 (1901): 1–72.

Khto taki ukraïntsi i choho vony khochut'. Kyiv, 1917. Excerpts in *Politolohiia*, 178–89.

Kievskaia Rus'. St Petersburg, 1911.

'Kinets' moskovs'koï oriientatsiï.' In idem, *Na porozi novoï Ukraïny*, 10–13.

'Konets getto!' *Ukrainskii vestnik*, no. 7 (2 July 1906): 395–8. Repr. in idem, *Osvobozhdenie Rossii i ukrainskii vopros*, 146–8.

'Konstytutsiine pytannia i ukraïnstvo v Rosiï.' *LNV* 8, no. 6 (1905): 245–58. Also separately: Lviv, 1905. Abridged Russian translation: idem, *Osvobozhdenie Rossii i ukrainskii vopros*, 121–31.

'Krov.' *LNV* 11, nos. 4–6 (1908): 380–5.

'Kul'tura krasy i kul'tura zhyttia.' In idem, *Na porozi novoï Ukraïny*, 28–33.

'Kul'turno-natsional'nyi rukh.' In idem, *Dukhovna Ukraïna: zbirka tvoriv*, 136–255. Kyiv, 1994.

'Lyst M.S. Hrushevs'koho do sekretaria TsK KP(b)U S.V. Kosiora.' In *Velykyi ukraïnets'*, 268–74.

Lystuvannia Mykhaila Hrushevs'koho. Comp. Halyna Burlaka. Ed. Liubomyr Vynar. Kyiv, New York, Paris, Lviv, and Toronto, 1997.

'Lysty M. Hrushevs'koho do I. Franka.' In *Velykyi ukraïnets'*, 244–60.

'Lysty M. Hrushevs'koho do T. Pochynka.' Ed. M. Antonovych. *Ukraïns'kyi istoryk*, 1969, no. 4: 78–98; 1970, nos. 1–3: 168–83. Partial repr. in *Velykyi ukraïnets'*, 292–7.

Lysty Mykhaila Hrushevs'koho do Kyryla Studyns'koho (1894–1932 rr.). Comp. Halyna Svarnyk. Lviv and New York, 1998.

'Memorial Peterburs'koï Akademiï v spravi svobody ukraïns'koï movy v Rosiï.' *LNV* 8, no. 5 (1905): 160–3.

'Misto.' In idem, *Na porozi novoï Ukraïny*, 42–7.

'Mizh Moskvoiu i Varshavoiu.' *Boritesia – poborete!* no. 2 (October 1920): 1–18.

Mykhailo Hrushevs'kyi: iz literaturnoï spadshchyny. Comp. Halyna Burlaka and Al'bina Shats'ka. Ed. Liubomyr Vynar. New York and Kyiv, 2000.

Mykhailo S. Hrushevs'kyi: Vybrani pratsi. Vydano z nahody 25–richchia z dnia ioho smerty (1934–1959). Ed. Mykola Halii. New York, 1960.

'Na drugoi den'.' *Ukrainskii vestnik*, no. 11 (2 August 1906): 743–8. Repr. in idem, *Osvobozhdenie Rossii i ukrainskii vopros*, 6–11.

'Na perelomi.' In idem, *Na porozi novoï Ukraïny*, 5–9.

Na porozi novoï Ukraïny. Statti i dzherel'ni materiialy. Ed. Lubomyr R. Vynar. New York, Lviv, Kyiv, Toronto, and Munich, 1992.

'Na ukraïns'ki temy: Hymn vdiachnosty.' *LNV* 13, no. 5 (1910): 46–51.

'Na ukraïns'ki temy: "Konets' rutenstva!"' *LNV* 10, no. 10 (1907): 135–47.

'Na ukraïns'ki temy: "Mazepynstvo" i "Bohdanivstvo."' *LNV* 15, nos. 1–3 (1912): 94–102.

'Na ukraïns'ki temy: Na novyi rik.' *LNV* 12, no. 1 (1909): 115–26.

'Na ukraïns'ki temy: Po koshmari.' *LNV* 16, no. 11 (1913): 268–71.

'Na ukraïns'ki temy: Ukraïnstvo i vseslov'ianstvo.' *LNV* 11, no. 6 (1908): 540–7.

'Na ukraïns'ki temy: Vidluchennia Kholmshchyny.' *LNV* 15, nos. 7–8 (1912): 3–12.

'Na zlobu dnia.' *Syn otechestva*, no. 100 (August 1905). Repr. in idem, *Osvobozhdenie Rossii i ukrainskii vopros*, 104–6.

'Narodnostiam Ukraïny.' In idem, *Na porozi novoï Ukraïny*, 135–7. First published under the title 'Narodam Ukraïny' in *Nova Rada*, no. 6 (1917).

Nasha polityka. Lviv, 1911.

'Nasha zakhidnia oriientatsiia.' In idem, *Na porozi novoï Ukraïny*, 14–17.

'Nashi trebovaniia.' *Ukrainskii vestnik*, no. 5 (18 June 1906): 267–73. Repr. in idem, *Osvobozhdenie Rossii i ukrainskii vopros*, 86–92.

'Natsional'nye momenty v agrarnom voprose.' *Strana*, 1906, no. 154. Repr. in idem, *Osvobozhdenie Rossii i ukrainskii vopros*, 141–5.

'Natsional'nyi vopros i avtonomiia.' *Ukrainskii vestnik*, no. 1 (21 May 1906): 8–17. Repr. in idem, *Osvobozhdenie Rossii i ukrainskii vopros*, 68–80.

'Neveroiatno.' *Syn otechestva*, no. 187 (18 September 1905). Repr. in idem, *Osvobozhdenie Rossii i ukrainskii vopros*, 107–11. Abridged version: *Kievskie otkliki*, no. 261 (1905).

[Khlopets', pseud.] 'Nova rozprava pro ukraïns'ku shliakhtu.' *Pravda* 12, no. 35 (1892): 63–4; no. 36: 185–92.

'Novi perspektyvy.' In idem, *Na porozi novoï Ukraïny*, 21–7.

'O zrelosti i nezrelosti.' *Ukrainskii vestnik*, no. 4 (11 July 1906): 203–8. Repr. in idem, *Osvobozhdenie Rossii i ukrainskii vopros*, 81–5.

'Ob ukrainskoi istoriografii XVIII veka. Neskol'ko soobrazhenii.' In P. Sokhan' et al., *M.S. Hrushevs'kyi i Academia*, 316–17. Full text in *Bulletin de l'Académie des sciences de l'URSS. Classe des sciences sociales*, 215–33. Moscow, 1934. English translation: 'Some Reflections on Ukrainian Historiography of the XVIII Century.' Trans. Zenon E. Kohut. In *The Eyewitness Chronicle*. Harvard Series in Ukrainian Studies, vol. 7, pt. 10, 9–16. Munich, 1972.

Ocherk istorii Kievskoi zemli ot smerti Iaroslava do kontsa XIV stoletiia. Kyiv, 1891.

Ocherk istorii ukrainskogo naroda. St Petersburg, 1904. 2d ed. St Petersburg, 1906. 3d ed. St Petersburg, 1911.

'Ochyshchennia ohnem.' In idem, *Na porozi novoï Ukraïny*, 66–9.

'Odna z lehend Khmel'nychchyny: Khmel'nyts'kyi i lynchaïvtsi.' In *Sbornik statei v chest' Dmitriia Aleksandrovicha Korsakova*. Kazan, 1913, 510–13.

'Oriientatsiia Chornomors'ka.' In idem, *Na porozi novoï Ukraïny*, 18–20.

Osvobozhdenie Rossii i ukrainskii vopros. Stat'i i zametki. St Petersburg, 1907.

'Pam'iati Paryz'koï Komuny.' *Boritesia – poborete!* 1921, no. 9: 1–8.

'Peredmova.' In Ivan Dzhydzhora, *Ukraïna v pershii polovyni XVIII viku. Rozvidky i zamitky*, iii–xiii. Kyiv, 1930.

Pereiaslavs'ka umova Ukraïny z Moskvoiu 1654 roku. Statti i teksty. Kyiv, 1917. 2d ed. Kyiv, 1917. 3d ed. Kyiv, 1918.

'Perspektyvy i vymohy ukraïns'koï nauky (Kyïvs'ka sesiia UkrNauky).' *Ukraïna*, 1926, no. 1: 3–15.

Pochatky hromadianstva (genetychna sotsiol'ogiia). Vienna, 1921.

'Poraionne istorychne doslidzhennia Ukraïny i obsliduvannia Kyïvs'koho uzla.' In *Kyïv i ioho okolytsia v istoriï i pam'iatkakh*, ed. Mykhailo Hrushevs'kyi, 1–24. Kyiv, 1926.

'Povorotu ne bude.' In idem, *Na porozi novoï Ukraïny*, 74–5.

'Povorotu nema.' In idem, *Na porozi novoï Ukraïny*, 144–6. First published in *Nova Rada*, no. 4 (30 March 1917).

Pro bat'ka kozats'koho Bohdana Khmel'nyts'koho. Kyiv, 1909.

Pro stari chasy na Ukraïni. Korotka istoriia Ukraïny. St Petersburg, 1907; repr. St Petersburg, 1917.

Pro ukraïns'ku movu i ukraïns'ku shkolu. Kyiv, 1917.

'Promova na ratyfikatsiï myrnoho dohovoru.' In idem, *Na porozi novoï Ukraïny*, 110–15.

'Promova na zasidanni Tsentral'noï Rady z 17 hrudnia 1917.' In idem, *Na porozi novoï Ukraïny*, 150–4.

'Protiv techeniia.' In *Osvobozhdenie Rossii i ukrainskii vopros*, 1–5.

'Prymitky do istoriï kozachchyny z povodu knyzhky: "Besidy pro chasy kozats'ki na Ukraïni," Chernivtsi, 1898.' *ZNTSh* 22 (1898): 1–14.

'Ravnoiu meroiu.' *Syn otechestva*, no. 73 (12 May 1905). Repr. in idem, *Osvobozhdenie Rossii i ukrainskii vopros*, 101–3.

Shchodennyk (1886–1894 rr.). Ed. Leonid Zashkil'niak. Kyiv, 1997.

'Shchodennyky (1883–1893).' Ed. Leonid Zashkil'niak. *Kyïvs'ka starovyna*, 1993, no. 3: 28–35; no. 4: 12–19; no. 5: 13–24.

'Shchodennyky M.S. Hrushevs'koho (1904–1910 rr.).' Ed. Ihor Hyrych. *Kyïvs'ka starovyna*, 1995, no. 1: 10–30.

'Shevchenko iak providnyk sotsiial'noï revoliutsiï.' *Boritesia – poborete!* no. 1 (September 1920): 52–4.

'Slovo Mykhaila Hrushevs'koho na ukraïns'kii manifestatsiï v Kyievi 19 bereznia (1 kvitnia 1917 r.).' In idem, *Na porozi novoï Ukraïny*, 195–6.

Spirni pytannia starorus'koï etnohrafiï. St Petersburg, 1904. English translation in *On the Historical Beginnings of Eastern Slavic Europe*, ed. and trans. Nicholas Chirovsky, 13–38. New York, 1976.

'Spoluchennie Ukraïny z Moskovshchynoiu v novishii literaturi. Krytychni zamitky.' *Ukraïna*, 1917, nos. 3–4: 91–108.

'Spomyny.' Ed. Serhii Bilokin'. In *Kyïv*, 1988, no. 9: 115–49; no. 10: 131–8; no.

11: 120–37; no. 12: 116–39; 1989, no. 8: 103–55; no. 9: 108–49; no. 10: 122–58; no. 11: 113–55.

'Sprava ukraïns'kykh katedr i nashi naukovi potreby.' *LNV* 10, no. 1 (1907): 42–57; no. 2: 213–20; no. 3: 408–18. Also separately: Lviv, 1907. Russian translation: 'Vopros ob ukrainskikh kafedrakh i nuzhdy ukrainskoi nauki,' in idem, *Osvobozhdenie Rossii i ukrainskii vopros*, 149–94.

Tvory u 50-ty tomakh. Ed. Pavlo Sokhan' et al. Vol. 1, *Suspil'no-politychni tvory, 1894-1907*. Lviv, 2002.

'U Vsesoiuznii Akademiï nauk. Zvidomlennia M. Hrushevs'koho.' *Ukraïna*, no. 3 (May-June 1929): 167–72.

Die ukrainische Frage in historischer Entwicklung. Vienna, 1915.

'Ukraïns'ka partiia sotsiialistiv-revoliutsioneriv ta ïï zavdannia. Zamitky z pryvodu debat na konferentsiiakh zakordonnykh chleniv partiï.' *Boritesia – poborete!* no. 1 (September 1920): 1–53.

'Ukraïns'ka samostiinist' i ïï istorychna neobkhidnist'.' In idem, *Na porozi novoï Ukraïny*, 63–5.

'Ukraïns'ki zhydy.' *Pravda* (Lviv), 1889, no. 10: 27–40.

'Ukrainskii P'emont.' *Ukrainskii vestnik*, no. 2 (28 May 1906): 104–8. Repr. in idem, *Osvobozhdenie Rossii i ukrainskii vopros*, 115–20.

'Ukrainskii vopros.' In idem, *Osvobozhdenie Rossii i ukrainskii vopros*, 12–41.

'Ukraïns'ko-rus'ke literaturne vidrodzhennia v istorychnim rozvoiu ukraïns'ko-rus'koho narodu.' *LNV* 1, no. 4 (October 1898): 75–81.

'Ukraïns'kyi herb.' In idem, *Na porozi novoï Ukraïny*, 90–1.

'V dvadtsiat' p'iati rokovyny smerty Ol. M. Lazarevs'koho. Kil'ka sliv pro ioho naukovu spadshchynu ta ïï doslidzhennia.' *Ukraïna*, 1927, no. 4: 3–17.

'V ohni i buri.' In idem, *Na porozi novoï Ukraïny*, 70–1.

'Velyka khvylia.' In idem, *Na porozi novoï Ukraïny*, 141–3. First published in *Nova Rada*, 1917, no. 1.

'Velyka, Mala i Bila Rus'.' *Ukraïna*, 1917, nos. 1–2: 7–19.

'Velyke dilo.' *Ukraïna*, 1929, no. 1: 3–9.

'Velyke Rizdvo.' In idem, *Na porozi novoï Ukraïny*, 59–60.

'Velykyi obov'iazok.' In idem, *Na porozi novoï Ukraïny*, 61–2.

'Vetkhii prakh.' *Ukrainskaia zhizn'*, 1915, no. 10: 85–92; also in *Rech'*, no. 281 (1915).

'Vidkrytyi lyst Mykh. Hrushevs'koho, zakordonnoho delegata UPSR, Holovi Rady Narodnikh Komisariv Ukraïns'koï Sotsiialistychnoï Radians'koï Respubliky Kh. G. Rakovs'komu.' *Boritesia – poborete!* no. 19 (October–December 1921): 1–8.

Vil'na Ukraïna. Statti z ostannikh dniv (berezen'-kviten' 1917). Kyiv, 1917.

'Vopros dnia (agrarnye perspektivy).' *Ukrainskii vestnik*, no. 2 (28 May 1906): 75–82. Repr. in idem, *Osvobozhdenie Rossii i ukrainskii vopros*, 132–40.

'Vopros ob ukrainskikh kafedrakh i nuzhdy ukrainskoi nauki.' In idem, *Osvobozhdenie Rossii i ukrainskii vopros*, 149–94.

'Vstrevozhennyi muraveinik.' *Ukrainskii vestnik*, no. 6 (25 June 1906): 331–41. Repr. in idem, *Osvobozhdenie Rossii i ukrainskii vopros*, 265–77.

'Vstupnyi vyklad z davn'oï istoriï Rusy, vyholoshenyi v L'vivs'kim universyteti 30 veresnia 1894 roku.' *ZNTSh* 4 (1894): 140–50. Repr. in *Mykhailo Hrushevs'kyi i Zakhidna Ukraïna*.

'Vyhovs'kyi i Mazepa.' *LNV* 12, no. 6 (1909): 417–28.

Z pochatkiv ukraïns'koho sotsiialistychnoho rukhu: M. Drahomaniv i zhenevs'kyi sotsiialistychnyi hurtok. Vienna, 1923.

Z politychnoho zhyttia staroï Ukraïny. Rozvidky, statti, promovy. Kyiv, 1918.

'Z sotsiial'no-natsional'nykh kontseptsii Antonovycha.' *Ukraïna*, 1928, no. 5: 3–16.

'Za Kholmshchynu.' In idem, *Na porozi novoï Ukraïny*, 107–9.

'Za ukraïns'kyi maslak (v spravi Kholmshchyny).' *Rada*, 1907, nos. 2–4. Also separately: *Za ukraïns'kyi maslak (v spravi Kholmshchyny)*. Kyiv, 1907. Russian translation: 'Za ukrainskuiu kost' (vopros o Kholmshchine).' In *Osvobozhdenie Rossii i ukrainskii vopros*, 278–91.

Zvidky pishlo ukraïnstvo i do choho vono ide. Kyiv, 1917. Excerpts in *Politolohiia*, 189–202.

'Zvychaina skhema "russkoï" istoriï i sprava ratsional'noho ukladu istoriï skhidnoho slov'ianstva.' In *Stat'i po slavianovedeniiu. Sbornik Rossiiskoi imperatorskoi akademii nauk*, ed. V.I. Lamanskii, vyp. 1, 298–304. St Petersburg, 1904. Repr. in *Politolohiia*, 167–73. English translation: *The Traditional Scheme of 'Russian' History and the Problem of a Rational Organization of the History of the East Slavs*. Ed. Andrew Gregorovich. Winnipeg, 1965. Repr. in Lubomyr R. Wynar, *Mykhailo Hrushevsky: Ukrainian-Russian Confrontation in Historiography*, 35–42. Toronto, New York, and Munich, 1988.

Edited Works

Akty Barskogo starostva XV–XVII vv. (=AIuZR, pt. 8, vol. 1). Kyiv, 1893.
Akty Barskogo starostva XVII–XVIII vv. (=AIuZR, pt. 8, vols. 1–2). Kyiv, 1893–4.

Reviews by Mykhailo Hrushevsky

Jagić, Vatroslav. 'Einige Streitfragen.' In ZNTSh 26 (1898): 5–6.
Miliukov, Pavel. *Glavnye techeniia russkoi istoricheskoi mysli*. Vol. 1. Moscow, 1898. In *ZNTSh* 25 (1898): 30–2.

– *Ocherki po istorii russkoi kul'tury*. 2 vols. St Petersburg, 1896–7. Review of vol. 1 in *ZNTSh* 13 (1896): 2–5; of vol. 2, ibid., 21 (1898): 14–17.

Niederle, Lubor. *Manuel de l'antiquité slave*. Paris, 1923. In *Ukraïna*, 1924, nos. 1–2: 180–4.

– *Slovanské starožitnosti*. Prague, 1924. In *Ukraïna*, 1925, no. 6: 134–8.

Rostovtzeff, Michael. *Èllinstvo i iranstvo na Iuge Rossii*. Petrograd, 1918; *Iranians and Greeks in South Russia*. Oxford, 1922; 'Les origines de la Russie,' *Revue des études slaves* (1922): 5–18; and *Skifiia i Bospor. Kriticheskoe obozrenie pamiatnikov literaturnykh i arkheologicheskikh*. Leningrad, 1925. In *Ukraïna*, 1925, no. 4: 151–8.

Storozhev, V.N., ed. *Russkaia istoriia s drevneishikh vremen do smutnogo vremeni*. Vyp. 1. Moscow, 1898. In *ZNTSh* 37 (1900): 8–10.

Zagoskin, N.P. *Istoriia prava russkogo naroda. Lektsii i issledovaniia po istorii russkogo prava*. Vol. 1. Kazan, 1899. In *ZNTSh* 39 (1901): 2–5.

Secondary Sources and Literature

Abramson, Henry. *A Prayer for the Government: Ukrainians and Jews in Revolutionary Times, 1917–1920*. Cambridge, MA, 1999.

'Akad. M.S. Hrushevs'kyi.' *Chervonyi shliakh*, 1934, nos. 11–12: 171.

Akademicheskoe delo 1929–31 gg. Dokumenty i materialy sledstvennogo dela, sfabrikovannogo OGPU, 2 vols. St Petersburg, 1993–8.

Anderson, Benedict. *Imagined Communities: Reflections on the Origin and Spread of Nationalism*. London, 1983.

Andriewsky, Olga. 'The Politics of National Identity: The Ukrainian Question in Russia, 1904–12.' PhD thesis. Harvard University, 1991.

– 'The Russian-Ukrainian Discourse and the Failure of the "Little Russian Solution," 1782–1917.' In *Culture, Nation, and Identity: The Ukrainian-Russian Encounter (1600–1945)*, ed. Andreas Kappeler, Zenon Kohut, Frank Sysyn, and Mark von Hagen, 182–214. Edmonton and Toronto, 2003.

Antonovych, Marko. 'Sprava Hrushevs'koho.' *Ukraïns'kyi istoryk*, 1984, nos. 1–4: 262–77; 1985, nos. 1–4: 200–11. Partial repr. in *Velykyi ukraïnets'*, 367–79.

Antonovych, Volodymyr. *Besidy pro chasy kozats'ki na Ukraïni*. Chernivtsi, 1897.

– 'Kharakteristika deiatel'nosti Bogdana Khmel'nitskogo.' *ChOIDR*, 1899, no. 13: 100–4. Repr. in idem, *Moia spovid'*, 190–3.

– (Antonovich, Vladimir). 'Kiev, ego sud'ba i znachenie s XIV po XVI stoletie (1362– 1569).' *Kievskaia starina* 1882, no. 1: 1–48. Repr. in idem, *Monografii po istorii Zapadnoi i Iugo-Zapadnoi Rossii*, 1: 221–64 (Kyiv, 1885), and idem, *Moia spovid'*, 577–92.

– *Korotka istoriia kozachchyny*. Kolomyia, 1912.

– *Moia spovid'. Vybrani istorychni ta publitsystychni tvory.* Kyiv, 1995.
– 'Ocherk otnoshenii pol'skogo gosudarstva k pravoslaviiu i pravoslavnoi tserkvi.' In idem, *Moia spovid'*, 458–69.
– (Antonovich, Vladimir). 'Pol'sko-russkie sootnosheniia XVII v. v sovremennoi pol'skoi prizme.' In idem, *Moia spovid'*, 106–36.
– (Antonovich, Vladimir). 'Soderzhanie aktov o kazakakh. Issledovanie o kazachestve po aktam s 1500 po 1648 g.' *AIuZR*, pt. 3, vol. 1 (1863), 1–120.
– 'Try natsional'ni typy narodni.' In idem, *Moia spovid'*, 90–101.
Arkas, Mykola. *Istoriia Ukraïny-Rusi.* St Petersburg, 1908.
Arkusha, Olena, and Marian Mudryi. 'Suspil'no-politychna sytuatsiia v Halychyni naperedodni pryïzdu M. Hrushevs'koho do L'vova (kinets' 80-kh – pochatok 90-kh rokiv).' In *Mykhailo Hrushevs'kyi i Zakhidna Ukraïna*, 15–17.
Armstrong, John A. 'Myth and History in the Evolution of Ukrainian Consciousness.' In *Ukraine and Russia in Their Historical Encounter*, 125–39.
Artizov, A.N. 'M.N. Pokrovskii: final kar'ery – uspekh ili porazhenie?' *Otechestvennaia istoriia*, 1998, no. 1: 77–96; no. 2: 124–43.
Ashcroft, Bill, Gareth Griffiths, and Helen Tiffin. *Key Concepts in Post-Colonial Studies.* New York, 1998.
Bahalii, Dmytro. 'Akad. M.S. Hrushevs'kyi i ioho mistse v ukraïns'kii istoriohrafiï (Istorychno-krytychnyi narys).' *Chervonyi shliakh*, no. 1 (46) (January 1927): 160–217.
– 'Avtobiohrafiia.' In idem, *Vybrani pratsi u shesty tomakh*, 1: 5–211.
– (Bagalei, Dmitrii). *Istoriia Severskoi zemli do poloviny XIV st.* Kyiv, 1882.
– *Narys istoriï Ukraïny na sotsiial'no-ekonomichnomu grunti.* Vol. 1. Kharkiv, 1928.
– 'Persha sproba nacherku istoriï Ukraïny na tli istorychnoho materiializmu.' *Chervonyi shliakh*, 1923, no. 9: 145–61.
– (Bagalei, Dmitrii). *Russkaia istoriia.* Pt. 1, *Domongol'skii period.* Kharkiv, 1909. Pt. 2, vyp. 1, *Udel'nyi i moskovskii period.* Kharkiv, 1911.
– (Bagalei, Dmitrii). *Russkaia istoriia.* Vol. 1, *Kniazheskaia Rus'.* Moscow, 1914.
– *Vybrani pratsi u shesty tomakh.* Vol. 1. Kharkiv, 1999.
– 'Z pryvodu antykrytyky prof. M.I. Iavors'koho.' *Chervonyi shliakh*, 1924, no. 6: 149–60.
– Review of Matvii Iavors'kyi, *Narys ukraïns'ko-rus'koï istoriï.* Kharkiv, 1923. In *Knyha*, 1923, no. 2: 48–50.
Bahalii, Dmytro, and Matvii Iavors'kyi. *Ukraïns'kyi filosof H.S. Skovoroda.* Kharkiv, [1923].
Bakhturina, A. Iu. *Politika Rossiiskoi imperii v vostochnoi Galitsii v gody pervoi mirovoi voiny.* Moscow, 2000.
Baran, Volodymyr. *Davni slov'iany.* Ukraïna kriz' viky, vol. 3. Kyiv, 1998.

- 'Velyke rozselennia slov'ian.' In *Davnia istoriia Ukraïny v tr'okh tomakh,* vol. 3, *Slov'iano-rus'ka doba,* 83–90. Kyiv, 2000.
- 'The Veneti, Sclaveni and Antae in the Light of Archeology.' *Ukrainian Review* 45, no. 1 (spring 1998): 49–63.

Barber, John. *Soviet Historians in Crisis, 1928–1932.* New York, 1981.

Bardach, Juliusz, Bogusław Leśnodorski, and Michał Pietrzak. *Historia państwa i prawa polskiego.* Warsaw, 1979.

Barvins'kyi, Oleksander. *Iliustrovana istoriia Rusy vid naidavnishykh do nynishnikh chasiv pislia rus'kykh i chuzhykh istorykiv.* Lviv, 1890.
- *Istoriia Ukraïny-Rusy.* Lviv, 1904.
- *Spomyny s moho zhyttia. Druha chast'.* Lviv, 1913.
- *Zasnovannie katedry istoriï Ukraïny v L'vivs'komu universyteti.* Lviv, 1925. Offprint from *ZNTSh* 141–3 (1925): 1–18.
- 'Zi "spomyniv moho zhyttia." Sprava poklykannia prof. Volodymyra Antonovycha na katedru istoriï Ukraïny-Rusy na L'vivs'kim universyteti.' *Stara Ukraïna,* 1924, nos. 9–10: 137–9.

Batenko, Taras. 'Do pytannia pro zasnuvannia kafedry istoriï Skhidnoï Ievropy u L'vivs'komu universyteti.' In *Mykhailo Hrushevs'kyi i Zakhidna Ukraïna,* 23–4.

Beard, Charles A. 'Written History as an Act of Faith.' *American Historical Review* 39, no. 2 (January 1934): 219–29.

Beazley, C.R., ed. *The Texts and Versions of John de Plano Carpini.* London, 1903. Repr. Nendeln, 1967.

Berger, Stefan, Mark Donovan, and Kevin Passmore. 'Apologias for the Nation-State in Western Europe since 1800.' In *Writing National Histories: Western Europe since 1800,* 3–14. London and New York, 1999.

Berkhofer, Robert F., Jr. *Beyond the Great Story: History as Text and Discourse.* Cambridge, MA, 1997.

Bilas, Lev. 'Viacheslav Lypyns'kyi iak istoryk kryzovoï doby.' In Viacheslav Lypyns'kyi, *Tvory,* 3: xxiii–lxx. Philadelphia, 1991.

Bilets'kyi, Oleksandr. Review of Mykhailo Hrushevs'kyi, *Istoriia ukraïns'koï literatury,* vol. 6, 672–7.

Bilokin', Serhii. 'Antin Syniavs'kyi i ioho doba.' In A.S. Syniavs'kyi, *Vybrani pratsi,* 3–31.

Black, Joseph L. *Nicholas Karamzin and Russian Society in the Nineteenth Century: A Study in Russian Political and Historical Thought.* Toronto, 1975.

Bobrzyński (Bobrzhinskii), Michał. *Ocherk istorii Pol'shi.* Vol. 1. St Petersburg, 1888.

Bortniak, Nadiia. 'Stepan Tomashivs'kyi: do vidnosyn iz Mykhailom Hrushevs'kym.' *Ukraïns'kyi istoryk,* 1996, nos. 1–4: 291–6.

– 'Stepan Tomashivs'kyi: pochatky naukovoï ta hromads'koï pratsi do 1911 roku.' In *Ukraïna v mynulomu* (Kyiv and Lviv), vyp. 2 (1992): 93–115.

Borys, Jurij. *The Sovietization of Ukraine, 1917–1923: The Communist Doctrine and Practice of National Self-Determination*. Rev. ed. Edmonton, 1980.

Brachev, V.S. *Russkii istorik S.F. Platonov, uchenyi, pedagog, chelovek*. St Petersburg, 1997.

Braichevs'kyi, Mykhailo. *Pryiednannia chy vozz'iednannia?* Toronto, 1972. English translation: *Annexation or Reunification: Critical Notes on One Conception*. Trans. and ed. George P. Kulchycky. Munich, 1974.

Brandenberger, David L. *National Bolshevism: Stalinist Mass Culture and the Formation of Modern Russian National Identity, 1931–1956*. Cambridge, MA, 2002.

Brandenberger, David L., and A.M. Dubrovsky. '"The People Need a Tsar": The Emergence of National Bolshevism as Stalinist Ideology, 1931–1941.' *Europe-Asia Studies* 50, no. 5 (1998): 873–92.

Brock, Peter. 'Polish Nationalism.' In *Nationalism in Eastern Europe*, ed. Peter F. Sugar and Ivo J. Lederer, 310–72. Seattle and London, 1969.

Brückner, Aleksander. 'Dogmat normański.' *Kwartalnik Historyczny* 20 (1906): 664–79.

Budurovych, Bohdan, 'Mykhailo Hrushevs'kyi v otsintsi zakhidn'oevropeis'koï i amerykan'skoï istoriohrafiï,' *Vyzvol'nyi shliakh* 20, no. 1 (January 1967): 171–81.

Byrnes, Robert F. 'Kliuchevskii on the Multi-National Russian State.' *Russian History* 13, no. 4 (winter 1986): 313–30.

– *V.O. Kliuchevsky: Historian of Russia*. Bloomington, IL, 1995.

Chatterjee, Partha. *The Nation and Its Fragments: Colonial and Postcolonial Histories*. Princeton, NJ, 1993.

Chechel', Mykola. 'Zvidomlennia z moieï komandirovky na Vkraïnu.' *Boritesia – poborete!* 1921, no. 9: 7–16.

Chernov, E.A. 'Petrogradskie uchenye i ssylka M.S. Grushevskogo vo vremia pervoi mirovoi voiny.' In *Dnipropetrovs'kyi istoryko-arkheohrafichnyi zbirnyk*, ed. Oleh Zhurba, vyp. 2 (Dnipropetrovsk, 2001): 642–6.

Chornovol, Ihor. 'M. Hrushevs'kyi i problema "halyts'ko-rus'koho tertium."' In *Mykhailo Hrushevs'kyi i Zakhidna Ukraïna*, 20–3.

– *Pol's'ko-ukraïns'ka uhoda 1890–1894 rr*. Lviv, 2000.

Chykalenko, Ievhen. *Spohady (1861–1907)*. New York, 1955.

– *Uryvok z moïkh spohadiv za 1917 r*. Prague, 1932.

Chynczewska-Hennel, Teresa. 'The National Consciousness of Ukrainian Nobles and Cossacks from the End of the Sixteenth to the Mid-Seventeenth Century.' *HUS* 10, nos. 3–4 (December 1986): 377–92.

- '"Ruś zostawić w Rusi."' *Przegląd Historyczny* 78, no. 3 (1987): 533–46.
- *Świadomość narodowa szlachty ukraińskiej i kozaczyzny od schyłku XVI do połowy XVII w.* Warsaw, 1985.

Conte, F. *Christian Rakovski (1873–1941): A Political Biography.* Boulder, CO, 1989.

Dashkevych, Iaroslav. 'Borot'ba z Hrushevs'kym ta ioho shkoloiu u L'vivs'komu universyteti za radians'kykh chasiv.' In *Mykhailo Hrushevs'kyi i ukraïns'ka istorychna nauka*, 226–68. An earlier version of this article appeared in *Mykhailo Hrushevs'kyi i l'vivs'ka istorychna shkola*, 32–94.

'Mykhailo Hrushevs'kyi – istoryk narodnyts'koho chy derzhavnyts'koho napriamu?' In *Mykhailo Hrushevs'kyi i ukraïns'ka istorychna nauka*, 65–85.

Deditskii, Bogdan. *Letopis' Rusi ot 1340 do 1887 goda.* Lviv, 1887.
- *Narodnaia istoriia Rusi.* Lviv, 1871.
- *Russkaia letopis' (ot 862 do 1340).* Lviv, 1885.

Deletant, Dennis, and Harry Hanak, eds. *Historians as Nation-Builders: Central and South-East Europe.* Basingstoke, 1988.

'Diial'nist' Istorychnoï sektsiï Ukraïns'koï Akademiï nauk v r. 1925.' *Zapysky Istorychno-filolohichnoho viddilu* (Kyiv), 1927, no. 11: v–xiii.

'Diial'nist' Istorychnoï sektsiï Vseukraïns'koï Akademiï Nauk ta zv'iazanykh z neiu istorychnykh ustanov v rotsi 1926.' *Zapysky Istorychno-filolohichnoho viddilu*, 1928, no. 17: v–xxxv.

'Diial'nist' Istorychnoï sektsiï Vseukraïns'koï Akademiï Nauk ta zv'iazanykh z neiu istorychnykh ustanov Akademiï v 1927 r.' *Zapysky Istorychno-filolohichnoho viddilu*, 1928, no. 20: v–xliii.

'Diial'nist' Istorychnoï sektsiï Vseukraïns'koï Akademiï Nauk ta zv'iazanykh z neiu istorychnykh ustanov Akademiï v 1928 r.' *Zapysky Istorychno-filolohichnoho viddilu*, 1929, no. 24: v–xlii.

Dnistrians'kyi, Stanislav. *Zahal'na nauka prava i polityky.* Prague, 1923. Excerpts in *Politolohiia*, 689–702.

'Do istorykiv-marksystiv Ukraïny (pro vseukraïns'kyi z'ïzd istorykiv-marksystiv).' *Bil'shovyk Ukraïny*, no. 6 (31 March 1929): 122–3.

Dontsov, Dmytro. *Moderne moskvofil'stvo.* Lviv, 1917.

Doroshenko, Dmytro. *Moï spomyny pro davnie-mynule (1901–1914 roky).* Winnipeg, 1954.
- *Ohliad ukraïns'koï istoriohrafiï.* Prague, 1923.
- *A Survey of Ukrainian Historiography.* Updated for the years 1917–56 by Olexander Ohloblyn. New York, 1957.
- *A Survey of Ukrainian History.* Ed. and updated by Oleh W. Gerus. Winnipeg, 1975.

Doroshenko, Volodymyr. 'Pershyi prezydent vidnovlenoï ukraïns'koï derzhavy.' *Ovyd*, 1957, no. 1: 25–6; no. 2: 27–32.

Drahomanov, Mykhailo. 'Chudats'ki dumky pro ukraïns'ku natsional'nu spravu.' In idem, *Vybrane*. Kyiv, 1991.

– 'Perednie slovo (do *Hromady*).' Extracts in *Politolohiia*, 7.

– Review of Mykhailo Hrushevskyi [M. Serhiienko], 'Hromads'kyi rukh na Vkraïni-Rusy v XIII vitsi.' In *Narod* (Kolomyia) (1893): 77–8.

'Dyskusiia z pryvodu skhemy istoriï Ukraïny M. Iavors'koho.' *Litopys revoliutsiï*, 1930, nos. 2, 3–4, 5.

E. K. 'M. Grushevskii protiv L. Niderle.' *Vozrozhdenie* (Paris), 17 August 1925.

Efimenko, A. Ia. *Istoriia ukrainskogo naroda*. 2 pts. St Petersburg, 1906. Ukrainian translation: Iefymenko, Oleksandra. *Istoriia ukraïns'koho narodu*. 2 vols. Kharkiv, 1922.

Encyclopaedia Britannica. 11th ed. New York, 1911. S.v. 'Kiev.'

Encyclopedia of Ukraine. Ed. Volodymyr Kybijovyč and Danylo Husar Struk. 5 vols. Toronto, 1984–93.

Enteen, George M. *The Soviet Scholar-Bureaucrat: M.N. Pokrovskii and the Society of Marxist Historians*. University Park, PA, and London, 1978.

'Fakty i dokumenty. Vytiahy z protokoliv zasidan' Zakordonnoï delehatsiï UPSR.' *Boritesia – poborete!* 1921, no. 9: 17–25.

Fedoruk, Iaroslav. 'Vasyl' Harasymchuk ta ioho nevydani "Materialy do istoriï kozachchyny XVI viku."' In Vasyl' Herasymchuk, *Materialy do istoriï kozachchyny XVII viku*, 12–32.

– 'Vidhuk Vasylia Harasymchuka na IX tom "Istoriï Ukraïny-Rusy" M. Hrushevs'koho.' *Ukraïns'kyi arkheohrafichnyi shchorichnyk* (Kyiv), vyps. 3–4 (1999): 534–41.

Filevich, I. P. 'Obzor glavneishikh sochinenii i statei po zapadnorusskoi istorii za 1891 god.' In *Slavianskoe obozrenie* (St Petersburg), 1 (1892): 418–21.

– *Po povodu teorii dvukh russkikh narodnostei*. Lviv, 1902.

Filipowicz, Mirosław. *Wobec Rosji. Studia z dziejów historiografii polskiej od końca XIX wieku po II wojnę światową*. Monografie Instytutu Europy Środkowo-Wschodniej, vol. 2. Lublin, 2000.

Foucault, Michel. *The Archeology of Knowledge*. New York, 1982.

– *The Order of Things: An Archeology of the Human Sciences*. New York, 1973.

– *Power/Knowledge: Selected Interviews and Other Writings, 1972–1977*. Ed. Colin Gordon. New York, 1980.

Frankiewicz, Czesław. Review of Mykhailo Hrushevsky, *Die ukrainische Frage in historischer Entwicklung*. Vienna, 1915. In *Kwartalnik Historyczny* 31 (1917): 174–7.

Franko, Ivan. *Tvory v dvadtsiaty tomakh*. Vol. 20. Kyiv, 1956.

– 'Ukraina irredenta.' Repr. in *Politolohiia*, 48–61.

Gawlas, Sławomir, and Hieronim Grala. '"I na Rusi robić musi."' *Przegląd Historyczny* 78, no. 3 (1987): 547–56.

- '"Nie masz Rusi na Rusi." W sprawie ukraińskiej świadomości narodowej w XVII wieku.' *Przegląd Historyczny* 77, no. 2 (1986): 331–51.
Geary, Patrick J. *The Myth of Nations: The Medieval Origins of Europe.* Princeton, NJ, 2002.
Gellner, Ernest. *Encounters with Nationalism.* Oxford, 1994.
- *Nations and Nationalism.* Oxford, 1983.
Gerbel, N.V., ed. *Poeziia slavian: sbornik luchshikh poèticheskikh proizvedenii slavianskikh narodov v perevodakh russkikh pisatelei.* St Petersburg, 1871.
Goehrke, Carsten. *Frühzeit des Ostslaventums.* Darmstadt, 1992.
Golobutskii, V.A. (Holobuts'kyi, V.O.). *Zaporozhskoe kazachestvo.* Kyiv, 1957.
Golubinskii, E.E. *Istoriia russkoi tserkvi.* 2 vols. Moscow, 1901.
Golubovskii, Petr. *Istoriia Severskoi zemli do poloviny XIV veka.* Kyiv, 1881.
Gorin, Pavel. [Attacks on Iavorsky]. *Pravda,* 4 January and 10 February 1929.
- [Letter to the editor]. *Prapor marksyzmu,* no. 5 (October–November 1929): 227–9.
Greenfeld, Liah. *Nationalism: Five Roads to Modernity.* Cambridge, MA, and London, 1992.
Hall, J.R. 'Cultural Meaning and Cultural Structures in Historical Explanation.' *History and Theory* 39 (October 2000): 331–47.
Heer, Nancy Whittier. *Politics and History in the Soviet Union.* Cambridge, MA, and London, 1971.
Hens'ors'kyi, Antin. *Halyts'ko-Volyns'kyi litopys (Protses skladannia, redaktsiï i redaktory).* Kyiv, 1958.
Herasymchuk (Harasymchuk), Vasyl'. *Materialy do istoriï kozachchyny XVII v.* L'vivs'ki istorychni pratsi. Dzherela. Vyp. 1. Lviv, 1994.
Hermaize, Osyp. 'Iuvilei ukraïns'koï nauky. Sorok rokiv diial'nosty akad. M. S. Hrushevs'koho.' *Zhyttia i revoliutsiia,* 1926, no. 10: 93–9.
- 'Ukraïns'ki sotsiialisty ta osnovopolozhnyky naukovoho sotsiializmu.' *Zhyttia i revoliutsiia* 1925, nos. 1-2: 25-8.
Himka, John-Paul. 'The Construction of Nationality in Galician Rus': Icarian Flights in Almost All Directions.' In *Intellectuals and the Articulation of the Nation,* ed. Michael D. Kennedy and Ron Suny, 109–64. Ann Arbor, MI, 1999.
- *Galician Villagers and the Ukrainian National Movement in the Nineteenth Century.* Edmonton, 1988.
- *Religion and Nationality in Western Ukraine: The Greek Catholic Church and the Ruthenian National Movement in Galicia, 1867–1900.* Montreal, 1999.
- *Socialism in Galicia: The Emergence of Polish Social Democracy and Ukrainian Radicalism (1860–1890).* Cambridge, MA, 1983.
Hirsch, Francine. 'The Soviet Union as a Work-in-Progress: Ethnographers and the Category Nationality in the 1926, 1937, and 1939 Censuses.' *Slavic Review* 56, no. 2 (summer 1997): 251–78.

- 'Toward an Empire of Nations: Border-Making and the Formation of Soviet National Identities.' *Russian Review* 59, no. 2 (April 2000): 201–26.

Historiography of Imperial Russia: The Profession and Writing of History in a Multinational State. Ed. Thomas Sanders. Armonk, NY, and London, 1999.

Hobsbawm, Eric J. *Age of Extremes: The Short Twentieth Century, 1914–1991*. London, 1994.

- *Nations and Nationalism since 1780: Programme, Myth, Reality*. 2d ed. Cambridge, 1992.

- *On History*. New York, 1997.

Hobsbawm, Eric J., and Terence Ranger, eds. *The Invention of Tradition*. Cambridge, 1983.

Horyn', Vasyl'. 'Ostannii konflikt M. Hrushevs'koho v NTSh.' In *Mykhailo Hrushevs'kyi i Zakhidna Ukraïna*, 38–40.

Hosking, Geoffrey, and George Schöpflin, ed. *Myth and Nationhood*. London, 1997.

Hranovs'kyi, Borys. *Mykhailo Hrushevs'kyi: pershyi prezydent Ukraïny, akademik: bibliohrafiia (1885–2000)*. Kyiv, 2001.

Hrinchenko, Borys. 'Lysty z Ukraïny naddniprians'koï.' In Borys Hrinchenko and Mykhailo Drahomanov, *Dialohy pro ukraïns'ku natsional'nu spravu*, 35–148. Kyiv, 1994.

Hroch, Miroslav. *Social Preconditions of National Revival in Europe: A Comparative Analysis of the Social Composition of Patriotic Groups among the Smaller European Nations*. Cambridge, 1985.

The Hrushevsky Translation Project. Edmonton, n.d.

Hrytsak, Iaroslav. 'Chy bula shkola Hrushevs'koho?' In *Mykhailo Hrushevs'kyi i ukraïns'ka istorychna nauka*, 162–71.

- '"Iakykh-to kniaziv buly stolytsi v Kyievi?": do konstruiuvannia istorychnoï pam'iati halyts'kykh ukraïntsiv u 1830–1930-ti roky.' *Ukraïna moderna* (Lviv), no. 6 (2001): 77–98.

- 'Konflikt 1913 roku v NTSh: prychyny i prychynky.' *Ukraïns'kyi istoryk*, 1991–2, nos. 110–15: 319–32.

- '"Molodi" radykaly v suspil'no-politychnomu zhytti Halychyny.' *ZNTSh* 222 (1991): 71–100.

- *Narys istoriï Ukraïny. Formuvannia modernoï ukraïns'koï natsiï XIX–XX stolittia*. Lviv, 1996.

- 'Reabilitatsiia Hrushevs'koho i legitymatsiia nomenklatury.' *Den'* (Kyiv), 1996, no. 12.

Hurevych, Zynovii. 'Psevdomarksyzm na sluzhbi ukraïns'koho natsionalizmu (do ostannikh vystupiv O. Hermaize).' *Bil'shovyk Ukraïny*, no. 9 (15 May 1929): 55–69.

The Hypatian Codex, II: The Galician-Volhynian Chronicle. Trans. George Perfecky. Munich, 1973.

Hyrych, Ihor. 'Deiaki pytannia orhanizatsiï M.S. Hrushevs'kym arkheohrafichnoï roboty u l'vivs'kyi period zhyttia (1894–1914).' In *Materialy iuvileinoï konferentsiï, prysviachenoï 150–richchiu Kyïvs'koï arkheohrafichnoï komisiï (Kyïv, Sedniv, 18–21 zhovtnia 1993 r.),* 266–94. Kyiv, 1997.

– 'Derzhavnyts'kyi napriam i narodnyts'ka shkola v ukraïns'kii istoriohrafiï (na tli stosunkiv Mykhaila Hrushevs'koho i V'iacheslava Lypyns'koho).' In *Mykhailo Hrushevs'kyi i ukraïns'ka istorychna nauka,* 47–64.

– 'M. Hrushevs'kyi i S. Iefremov na tli suspil'no-politychnoho zhyttia kintsia XIX – 20-kh rokiv XX stolittia.' *Ukraïns'kyi istoryk* 33 (1996): 142–87.

– 'Orhanizatsiia M.S. Hrushevs'kym arkheohrafichnoï roboty u l'vivs'kyi period zhyttia i diial'nosti.' *Ukraïns'kyi istorychnyi zhurnal,* 1997, no. 1: 72–86.

'"Ia nikogda ne vystupal protiv Rossii." M.S. Grushevskii i russkie uchenye, 1914–1916 gg.' Ed. A.A. Varlygo. *Istoricheskii arkhiv,* 1997, no. 4: 175–99.

Iakovenko, Natalia. 'Osoba, iak diiach istorychnoho protsesu v istoriohrafiï Mykhaila Hrushevs'koho.' In *Mykhailo Hrushevs'kyi i ukraïns'ka istorychna nauka,* 86–97.

– *Paralel'nyi svit. Doslidzhennia z istoriï uiavlen' ta idei v Ukraïni XVI–XVII st.* Kyiv, 2002.

– *Ukraïns'ka shliakhta z kintsia XIV do seredyny XVII st. (Volyn' i Tsentral'na Ukraïna).* Kyiv, 1993.

– 'Zdobutky i vtraty Liublins'koï uniï.' *Kyïvs'ka starovyna,* 1993, no. 3: 77–85.

Iastrebov, Fedir. 'Natsional-fashysts'ka kontseptsiia selians'koï viiny 1648 roku na Ukraïni. (Z pryvodu 2–oï polovyny IX t. 'Istoriï Ukraïny-Rusy' akad. M. Hrushevs'koho).' In *Zapysky Istorychno-arkheohrafichnoho instytutu,* 1934, no. 1: 55–120.

– 'Tomu dev'iatoho persha polovyna.' *Prapor marksyzmu,* 1930, no. 1: 133–48.

– Review of Dmytro Bahalii, *Narys istoriï Ukraïny na sotsiial'no-ekonomichnomu grunti.* Vol. 1. Kharkiv, 1928. In *Prapor marksyzmu,* 1929, no. 5: 167–76.

Iavors'kyi, Matvii. [Address at Hrushevsky celebrations]. In Bahalii, *Vybrani pratsi,* 1: 319–24. Repr. from *Iuvilei akademika Dmytra Ivanovycha Bahaliia, 1857–1927,* comp. Mykola Levchenko, 73–80. Kyiv, 1929.

– [Comments on Pavel Gorin's letter to the editor of *Prapor marksyzmu*]. *Prapor marksyzmu,* no. 5 (October–November 1929): 227–9.

– 'De-shcho pro "krytychnu" krytyku, pro "ob'iektyvnu" istoriiu ta shche pro babusynu spidnytsiu.' *Chervonyi shliakh,* 1924, no. 3: 167–82.

– 'Don-kikhotstvo chy rusotiapstvo? (Z pryvodu odniieï retsenziï).' *Prapor marksyzmu,* no. 2 (March–April 1929): 207–13.

- *Istoriia Ukraïny v styslomu narysi.* Kharkiv, 1928.
- *Korotka istoriia Ukraïny.* Kharkiv, 1923.
- *Narys istoriï revoliutsiinoï borot'by na Ukraïni.* Vol. 1. Kharkiv, 1927.
- *Narys istoriï Ukraïny.* 3 vyps. Kyiv, Kharkiv, and Katerynoslav, 1923–5.
- *Narys ukraïns'ko-rus'koï istoriï.* Kharkiv, 1923.
- 'Providni dumky v rozvytkovi istorychnoï nauky.' *Prapor marksyzmu*, no. 1 (January–February 1929): 89–116.
- *Revoliutsiia na Vkraïni v ïï holovnykh etapakh.* [Kharkiv], 1923.
- 'Shostyi mizhnarodnyi konhres istorychnyi.' *Prapor marksyzmu*, 1928, no. 4 (5): 216–24.
- 'Sovremennye antimarksistskie techeniia v ukrainskoi istoricheskoi nauke.' In *Trudy*, 1: 426–35.

Iefremov, Serhii. *Shchodennyky, 1923–1929.* Kyiv, 1997.

Iggers, George. 'Changing Conceptions of National History since the French Revolution: A Critical Comparative Perspective.' In *Conceptions of National History: Proceedings of the Nobel Symposium 78*, ed. Erik Lönnroth, Karl Molin, and Ragnar Björk, 132–50. Berlin and New York, 1994.

Ilnytzkyj, Oleh S. 'Modeling Culture in the Empire: Ukrainian Modernism and the Death of the All-Russian Idea.' In *Culture, Nation, and Identity*, ed. Kappeler et al., 298–324.

Ilovaiskii, Dmitrii. *Dopolnitel'naia polemika po voprosam variago-russkomu i bolgaro-gunnskomu.* Moscow, 1886.
- (Ilovais'kyi, Dmytro). *Kniazhyi period istoriï Ukraïny-Rusy.* Rus'ka istorychna biblioteka, vol. 3. Ternopil, 1886.
- *Razyskaniia o nachale Rusi. Vmesto vvedeniia v russkuiu istoriiu.* Moscow, 1876.
- *Vtoraia dopolnitel'naia polemika po voprosam variago-russkomu i bolgaro-gunnskomu.* Moscow, 1902.

Iordan (Jordanes). *O proiskhozhdenii i deianiiakh gotov: Getica.* Moscow, 1960.

Isaievych, Iaroslav. 'Halyts'ko-Volyns'ke kniazivstvo doby Danyla Halyts'koho ta ioho nashchadkiv.' In *Halychyna ta Volyn' u dobu seredn'ovichchia. Do 800-richchia z dnia narodzhennia Danyla Halyts'koho*, 3–12. Lviv, 2001.

Istoricheskaia nauka v Rossii v XX veke. Ed. G.D. Alekseeva, A.N. Sakharov, and L.A. Sidorova. Moscow, 1997.

Istoriia Rusov ili Maloi Rossii. Sochinenie Georgiia Koniskogo, arkhiepiskopa belorusskogo. Moscow, 1846. Repr. Kyiv, 1991.

Istoriia Ukraïns'koï RSR. Ed. Iu.Iu. Kondufor et al. Vol. 1, bk. 2, ed. V.O. Holobuts'kyi. Kyiv, 1979.

Istoriko-filologicheskii fakul'tet Khar'kovskogo universiteta za pervye sto let ego sushchestvovaniia (1805–1905). Kharkiv, 1908.

Iurkevych, Viktor. *Emihratsiia na Skhid i zaliudnennia Slobozhanshchyny za Bohdana Khmel'nyts'koho.* Kyiv, 1932.

Iurkova, Oksana. *Diial'nist' naukovo-doslidnoï kafedry istoriï Ukraïny M.S. Hrushevs'koho (1924–1930).* Kyiv, 1999.

Iuvilei akademika Dmytra Ivanovycha Bahaliia, 1857–1927. Comp. Mykola Levchenko. Kyiv, 1929. Repr. in D.I. Bahalii, *Vybrani pratsi u shesty tomakh,* 1: 264–424.

Jagić, Vatroslav. *Chetyre kritiko-paleograficheskie stat'i.* St Petersburg, 1884.

– 'Einige Streitfragen.' *Archiv für slavische Philologie* (Berlin) 20 (1898): 1–53; 22 (1900): 11–45; 23 (1901): 113–29.

– *Kriticheskie zametki po istorii russkogo iazyka.* St Petersburg, 1889.

Jelavich, Barbara. 'Mihail Kogălniceanu: Historian as Foreign Minister, 1876–8.' In *Historians as Nation-Builders,* ed. Deletant and Hanak, 87–105.

Jenkins, Keith. *The Postmodern History Reader.* New York, 1997.

– *Re-thinking History.* New York, 1991.

K voprosu o kandidature na kafedru russkoi istorii v universitete sv. Vladimira professora L'vovskogo universiteta Mikhaila Grushevskogo. Kyiv, 1908.

Kachmar, Volodymyr, and Taras Maryskevych. 'M. Hrushevs'kyi i zmahannia za ukraïns'kyi universytet u L'vovi.' In *Mykhailo Hrushevs'kyi i Zakhidna Ukraïna,* 25–7.

Kaczała, Stefan. *Polityka Polaków względem Rusi.* Lviv, 1879.

Kappeler, Andreas. '*Mazepintsy, malorossy, khokhly*: Ukrainians in the Ethnic Hierarchy of the Russian Empire.' In *Culture, Nation, and Identity,* ed. Kappeler et al., 162–81.

– *The Russian Empire: A Multiethnic History.* Tr. Alfred Clayton. Harlow, UK, 2001.

– *Der schwierige Weg zur Nation: Beiträge zur neueren Geschichte der Ukraine.* Wiener Archiv für die Geschichte des Slawentums und Osteuropas, 20. Vienna, Cologne, and Weimar, 2003.

Kappeler, Andreas, Zenon Kohut, Frank Sysyn, and Mark von Hagen, eds. *Culture, Nation, and Identity: The Ukrainian-Russian Encounter (1600–1945).* Edmonton and Toronto, 2003.

Kapystiański, Adrian. 'Schemat historii Ruskiej w teoretycznym i praktycznym ujęciu prof. Michała Hruszewskiego.' *Ziemia Czerwieńska* (Lviv) 2 (1935): 66–75.

Karpovich, Michael. Review of Hrushevsky, *History of Ukraine* (New Haven, [1941]). In *Yale Review* 31 (1942): 424–7.

Keenan, Edward L. 'Muscovite Perceptions of Other East Slavs before 1654: An Agenda for Historians.' In *Ukraine and Russia in Their Historical Encounter,* 20–38.

– 'On Certain Mythical Beliefs and Russian Behaviors.' In *The Legacy of History in Russia and the New States of Eurasia*, ed. S. Frederick Starr, 19–40. Armonk, NY and London, 1994. Ukrainian translation: 'Rosiis'ki mify pro kyïvs'ku spadshchynu.' *Krytyka* (Kyiv) 3, nos. 1–2 (January/February 1999): 4–10.

Khlevov, A.A. *Normanskaia problema v otechestvennoi istoricheskoi nauke*. St Petersburg, 1997.

Khvylia, Andrii. 'Burzhuazno-natsionalistychna trybuna (Pro zhurnal 'Ukraïna').' *Bil'shovyk Ukraïny*, 1931, no. 6: 46–58.

Khvylovy, Mykola. *The Cultural Renaissance in Ukraine: Polemical Pamphlets, 1926–25*. Ed. Myroslav Shkandrij. Edmonton, 1986.

Khvyl'ovyi, Mykola. 'Ukraïna chy Malorosiia?' Excerpts in *Politolohiia*, 637–48.

Klid, Bohdan. 'Dolia Kyieva ta Kyïvshchyny pislia monhol's'koï navaly 1240 r. v ukraïns'kii istoriohrafiï XIX stolittia i skhema M. Hrushevs'koho.' In *Na sluzhbi Klio. Zbirnyk naukovykh prats' na poshanu Liubomyra Romana Vynara, z nahody 50-littia ioho naukovoï diial'nosty*, 196–204. Kyiv, New York, Toronto, Paris, and Lviv, 2000.

– 'Istoriia i polityka: borot'ba navkolo spadshchyny Mykhaila Hrushevs'koho.' *Ukraïns'kyi istoryk*, 1991–2, nos. 110–15: 186–99.

– 'Volodymyr Antonovych: Ukrainian Populist Historiography and the Cultural Politics of Nation Building.' In *Historiography of Imperial Russia*, 373–93.

Kliuchevskii (Kliuchevsky), V.O. *A History of Russia*. Trans. C.J. Hogarth. 5 vols. New York, 1960.

– *Kurs russkoi istorii*, pt. 1. In Kliuchevskii, *Sochineniia*, vol. 1. Moscow, 1956.

– *Terminologiia russkoi istorii*. In idem, *Sochineniia*, vol. 6: 129–275. Moscow, 1959.

Klymenko, Pylyp. Review of Viacheslav Lypyns'kyi, *Ukraïna na perelomi, 1657–1659*. Vienna, 1920. In *Zapysky Istoryko-filolohichnoho viddilu*, 1920–2, nos. 2–3: 239–46.

Knight, Amy. *Who Killed Kirov? The Kremlin's Greatest Mystery*. New York, 1999.

Kohn, Hans. *The Idea of Nationalism: A Study in Its Origins and Background*. New York, 1944.

Kohut, Zenon E. 'The Development of a Ukrainian National Historiography in Imperial Russia.' In *Historiography of Imperial Russia*, 453–78.

– 'A Dynastic or Ethno-Dynastic Tsardom? Two Early Modern Concepts of Russia.' In *Extending the Borders of Russian History: Essays in Honor of Alfred J. Rieber*, ed. Marsha Siefert, 17–30. Budapest and New York, 2003.

– 'Origins of the Unity Paradigm: Ukraine and the Construction of Russian

National History (1620–1860).' *Eighteenth-Century Studies* 35, no. 1 (2002): 70–6.

– 'The Question of Russo-Ukrainian Unity and Ukrainian Distinctiveness in Early Modern Ukrainian Thought and Culture.' In *Culture, Nation, and Identity*, ed. Kappeler et al., 57–86.

– *Russian Centralism and Ukrainian Autonomy: Imperial Absorption of the Hetmanate, 1760s–1830s*. Cambridge, MA, 1988.

Koialovich, M.O. *Istoriia russkogo samosoznaniia po istoricheskim pamiatnikam i nauchnym sochineniiam*. St Petersburg, 1884.

[Kokoshko, S.] 'Vid redaktsiï.' *Zapysky Istorychno-arkheohrafichnoho instytutu*, 1934, no. 1: 8.

Kolakowski, Leszek. *The Presence of Myth*. Chicago, 1989.

Kolankowski, Ludwik. Review of Hrushevs'kyi, *Istoriia Ukraïny-Rusy*. In *Kwartalnik Historyczny* 27 (1913): 348–65.

Kolesnyk, Iryna. *Ukraïns'ka istoriohrafiia (XVIII – pochatok XX st.)*. Kyiv, 2000.

Korduba, Myron. 'Die Anfänge des ukrainischen Kozakentums.' *Zeitschrift für osteuropäische Geschichte* 2 (1912): 367–81.

– 'Pryïzd prof. Hrushevs'koho do L'vova.' *Visnyk Soiuzu vyzvolennia Ukraïny*, no. 128 (10 December 1916): 795–6.

Korsakov, D.A. *Meria i Rostovskoe kniazhestvo. Ocherki iz istorii Rostovsko-Suzdal'skoi zemli*. Kazan, 1872.

Korzon, Tadeusz. 'O Chmielnickim sądy PP. Kulisza i Karpowa.' *Kwartalnik Historyczny*, 1892, no. 4: 34–79.

Koshelivets', Ivan. *Mykola Skrypnyk*. Munich, 1972.

Koshelivets', Ivan, comp. *Mykola Skrypnyk: statti i promovy z natsional'noho pytannia*. Munich, 1974.

Kostiuk, Hryhorii. *Zustrichi i proshchannia. Spohady. Knyha persha*. Edmonton, 1987.

Kostomarov, N.I. 'Nachalo Rusi.' *Sovremennik* 79 (1860): no. 1, otd. 1, 5–32.

– *Naukovo-publitsystychni i polemichni pysannia Kostomarova*. Ed. Mykhailo Hrushevs'kyi. Kyiv, 1928.

– 'O kazachestve. Otvet *Vilenskomu vestniku*.' In idem, *Naukovo-publitsystychni pysannia*, 57–68.

– 'Otvet g. Padalitse.' In idem, *Naukovo-publitsystychni pysannia*, 68–74.

– 'Otvet na vykhodki gazety (Krakovskoi) *Czas* i zhurnala *Revue Contemporaine*.' In idem, *Naukovo-publitsystychni pysannia*, 75–84.

– 'Poliakam-mirotvortsam.' In idem, *Naukovo-publitsystychni pysannia*, 252–9.

– 'Pravda poliakam o Rusi.' In idem, *Naukovo-publitsystychni pysannia*, 94–101.

– 'Ukrainskii separatizm.' In idem, *Naukovo-publitsystychni pysannia*, 193–6.

Kotliarevskii, Aleksandr (Kotliarevs'kyi, Oleksander). 'Byli-li malorussy iskonnymi obitateliami polianskoi zemli, ili prishli iz-za Karpat v XIV veke?' *Osnova*, 1862, no. 10: 1–12. Repr. in idem, *Sochineniia*, 1: 624–37. St Petersburg, 1889.

Kozachenko, Anton. Review of *Studiï z istoriï Ukraïny naukovo-doslidchoï kafedry istoriï Ukraïny v Kyievi*. Vol. 2. Kyiv, 1929. In *Prapor marksyzmu*, 1929, no. 2: 213–23.

Kozik, Jan. *The Ukrainian National Movement in Galicia, 1815–1849*. Ed. Lawrence D. Orton. Edmonton, 1986.

Kravchenko, Ivan. 'Fashysts'ki kontseptsiï Hrushevs'koho i ioho shkoly v ukraïns'kii istoriohrafiï (akademik Hrushevs'kyi i ioho shkola pislia povernennia z biloemihratsiï).' In *Zapysky Istorychno-arkheohrafichnoho instytutu*, 1934, no. 1: 9–54.

Kravchenko, Volodymyr. *D.I. Bagalei: nauchnaia i obshchestvenno-politicheskaia deiatel'nost'*. Kharkiv, 1990.

– 'D.I. Bahalii v svitli i tini svoieï "Avtobiohrafiï."' In Bahalii, *Vybrani pratsi*, 1: 9–56.

– *Narysy z ukraïns'koï istoriohrafiï epokhy natsional'noho vidrodzhennia (druha polovyna XVIII – seredyna XIX st.)*. Kharkiv, 1996.

– '"Rosiia," "Malorosiia," "Ukraïna" v rosiis'kii istoriohrafiï druhoï polovyny XVIII – 20kh rokiv XIX st.' *Zbirnyk Kharkivs'koho istoryko-filolohichnoho tovarystva*, n. s., 1995, no. 5: 3–16.

Krawchenko, Bohdan. *Social Change and National Consciousness in Twentieth-Century Ukraine*. Houndmills and London, 1985.

Krek, Gregor. *Einleitung in die slavische Literaturgeschichte*. Graz, 1887.

Krevets'kyi, Ivan. 'Ukraïns'ka istoriohrafiia na perelomi.' *ZNTSh* 134–5 (1924): 161–84.

Kruhlashov, Anatolii. *Drama intelektuala: politychni ideï Mykhaila Drahomanova*. Chernivtsi, 2000.

Krupnyts'kyi, Borys. 'M. Hrushevs'kyi i ioho istorychna pratsia.' In Hrushevs'kyi, *Istoriia Ukraïny-Rusy*, 1: i–xxx.

Krykun, Mykola. 'Magisters'ka dysertatsiia Mykhaila Hrushevs'koho.' In Hrushevs'kyi, *Bars'ke starostvo*, 577–622.

Krymskii, Agatangel (Ahatanhel Kryms'kyi). 'Filologiia i Pogodinskaia gipoteza.' *Kievskaia starina* 17, no. 6 (1898): 347–65; no. 9: 234–66; 18, no. 1 (1899): 9–29; no. 6: 307–16; no. 9: 277–311. Also separately: Kyiv, 1904.

Kryp'iakevych, Ivan. *Halyts'ko-Volyns'ke kniazivstvo*. Kyiv, 1984.

– *Mykhailo Hrushevs'kyi. Zhyttia i diial'nist'*. Lviv, 1935. Repr. in *Velykyi ukraïnets'*, 448–83.

– 'Spohady (Avtobiohrafiia).' *Ukraïna: kul'turna spadshchyna, natsional'na svidomist', derzhavnist'* 8 (2001): 75–140.

Kryp'iakevych, Roman. 'Mykhailo Hrushevs'kyi ta Ivan Kryp'iakevych (za materialamy neopublikovanoho lystuvannia ta memuariv).' *Ukraïna: kul'turna spadshchyna, natsional'na svidomist', derzhavnist'* 8 (2001): 333–72.

Kubala, Ludwik. *Wojna Moskiewska*. Szkice historyczne, 3d series. Warsaw, 1910.

Kuhn, Thomas. *The Structure of Scientific Revolutions*. 2d ed. Chicago, 1970.

Kul'chyts'kyi, Stanislav. *Komunizm v Ukraïni: pershe desiatyrichchia (1919–1928)*. Kyiv, 1996.

Kulish, Panteleimon, ed. *Zapiski o Iuzhnoi Rusi*. 2 vols. St Petersburg, 1856–7.

Kulyk, Volodymyr. 'The Role of Discourse in the Construction of an Émigré Community: Ukrainian Displaced Persons in Germany and Austria after World War II.' In *European Encounters: Migrants, Migration and European Societies since 1945*, ed. Rainer Ohliger, Karen Schönwälder, and Phil Triadafilopoulos, 211–35. Aldershot, UK, 2002.

Kunik, Arist. 'O vremeni, v kotorom zhil izrail'tianin Ibragim ibn-Iakub.' In *Izvestiia al-Bekri i drugikh avtorov o Rusi i slavianakh*. Vol. 1, ed. V.R. Rozen. St Petersburg, 1878.

Kupchyns'kyi, Oleh. 'Do vzaiemyn Oleksandra Barvins'koho z Mykhailom Hrushevs'kym (dokumenty i materialy).' In *Oleksandr Barvins'kyi, 1847–1927. Materialy konferentsiï*, ed. Mykhailo Hnatiuk et al., 142–78. Lviv, 2001.

Kyian, Oleksandr, ed. 'Kafedral'ne "viruiu" Volodymyra Antonovycha. Z neopublikovanoï spadshchyny.' *Kyïvs'ka starovyna*, 1992, no. 3: 63–9.

Lakyza, Ivan. 'Mykhailo Serhiiovych Hrushevs'kyi.' *Zhyttia i revoliutsiia*, 1926, no. 10: 99–105.

Lavrovskii, P.A. *O iazyke severnykh russkikh letopisei*. St Petersburg, 1852.

Leitsch, Walter. 'East Europeans Studying History in Vienna (1855–1918).' In *Historians as Nation-Builders*, 139–56.

Lenin, V.I. [Draft speech for Hryhorii Petrovsky]. *Polnoe sobranie sochinenii*, 23: 452. 5th ed. Moscow, 1967–70.

– [Letter to Mikhail Pokrovsky welcoming the publication of *Russkaia istoriia v samom szhatom ocherke*]. In Pokrovskii, *Izbrannye proizvedeniia*, 3: 3–4. Cf. Lenin, *Polnoe sobranie sochinenii*, 52: 24. 5th ed. Moscow, 1967–70.

– 'O natsional'noi gordosti velikorossov.' *Polnoe sobranie sochinenii* 26: 106–10. 5th ed. Moscow, 1967–70.

Levitskii, Orest. *Ocherki vnutrennei istorii Malorossii*. Vyp. 1. Kyiv, 1875.

Liber, George O. *Soviet Nationality Policy, Urban Growth, and Identity Change in the Ukrainian SSR, 1923–1934*. Cambridge, 1992.

Lieven, Dominic. 'The Russian Empire and the Soviet Union as Imperial Polities.' *Journal of Contemporary History* 30, no. 4 (October 1995): 607–35.

Linnichenko, Ivan. *Cherty iz istorii soslovii v Iugo-Zapadnoi (Galitskoi) Rusi XIV–XV v.* Moscow, 1894. Ukrainian translation: *Suspil'ni verstvy Halyts'koï Rusy XIV–XV v.* Rus'ka istorychna biblioteka, vol. 7. Lviv, 1899.

– 'Malorusskaia kul'tura.' In *Trudy podgotovitel'noi po natsional'nym delam komissii. Malorusskii otdel.* Vyp. 1, *Sbornik statei po malorusskomu voprosu.* Odesa, 1919. Also separately: Odesa, 1919. Repr. in *Ukrainskii separatizm v Rossii*, 315–29.

– *Malorusskii vopros i avtonomiia Malorossii. Otkrytoe pis'mo professoru M.S. Grushevskomu.* Petrograd and Odesa, 1917. Repr. in *Ukrainskii separatizm v Rossii*, 253–79.

Litwin, Henryk. 'Katolizacja szlachty ruskiej, 1569–1647: Stosunki wyznaniowe na Kijowszczyźnie i Bracławszczyźnie.' *Przegląd Powszechny*, 1985, no. 10: 58–70.

– *Napływ szlachty polskiej na Ukrainę, 1569–1648.* Warsaw, 2000.

Liubavskii, M.K. *Ocherk istorii Litovsko-russkogo gosudarstva do Liublinskoi unii vkliuchitel'no.* Moscow, 1910. Repr. The Hague, 1966.

Lohr, Eric. *Nationalizing the Russian Empire: The Campaign against Enemy Aliens during World War I.* Cambridge, MA, 2003.

Lotots'kyi, Oleksander. *Storinky mynuloho.* 4 vols. Warsaw, 1932–9. Repr. n. p.: Ukrainian Orthodox Church, 1966.

Łowmiański, Henryk. *Zagadnienie roli Normanów w genezie państw słowiańskich.* Warsaw, 1957. Russian translation: Kh. Lovmianskii, *Rus' i normanny.* Ed. V.T. Pashuto. Moscow, 1985.

Lypyns'kyi, Viacheslav (Lipiński, Wacław). 'Dwie chwile z dziejów porewolucyjnej Ukrainy.' In idem, ed., *Z dziejów Ukrainy*, 514–617. Kyiv and Cracow, 1912. Revised Ukrainian version: idem, *Ukraïna na perelomi, 1657–1659. Zamitky do istoriï ukraïns'koho derzhavnoho budivnytstva v XVII-im stolitti.* Vienna, 1920.

– *Lysty do brativ-khliborobiv. Pro ideiu i organizatsiiu ukraïns'koho monarkhizmu.* Vienna, 1926.

– (Lipiński, Wacław). 'Stanisław Michał Krzyczewski. Z dziejów walki szlachty ukraińskiej w szeregach powstańczych pod wodzą Bohdana Chmielnickiego (r. 1648–1649).' In idem, ed., *Z dziejów Ukrainy*, 145–513.

– (Lipiński, Wacław). *Z dziejów Ukrainy.* Kyiv and Cracow, 1912.

Mace, James E. *Communism and the Dilemmas of National Liberation: National Communism in Soviet Ukraine, 1918–1933.* Cambridge, MA, 1983.

Magocsi, Paul Robert. *A History of Ukraine.* Toronto, 1996.

– 'Old Ruthenianism and Russophilism: A New Conceptual Framework for

Analyzing National Ideologies in Late 19th Century Eastern Galicia.' In *American Contributions to the Ninth International Congress of Slavists*, ed. Paul Debreczeny, 2: 305-24. Columbus, OH, 1983.

Maistrenko, Ivan. *Borot'bism: A Chapter in the History of Ukrainian Communism.* New York, 1954.

– *Istoriia moho pokolinnia: spohady uchasnyka revoliutsiinykh podii v Ukraïni.* Edmonton, 1985.

Makovei, Osyp. 'Iuvilei 25–litn'oï literaturnoï diial'nosty Ivana Franka.' *LNV* 4, no. 2 (1898): 115–18.

Maksimovich, Mikhail (Mykhailo Maksymovych). 'Filologicheskie pis'ma k M.P. Pogodinu.' *Russkaia beseda*, 1856, no. 3: 78–139. Repr. in idem, *Sobranie sochinenii*, 3: 182–243.

– *Istoricheskie pis'ma o kazakakh pridneprovskikh k M.F. Iuzefovichu.* Kyiv, 1865.

– 'Novye pis'ma M.P. Pogodinu o starobytnosti malorossiiskogo narechiia.' *Den'*, 1863, nos. 8, 10, 15, 16. Repr. in idem, *Sobranie sochinenii*, 3: 273–311.

– 'O mnimom zapustenii Ukrainy v nashestvie Batyevo i naselenii ee novoprishlym narodom (Pis'mo k M.P. Pogodinu)' (1857). In idem, *Sobranie sochinenii*, 1: 131–45.

– 'O prichinakh vzaimnogo ozhestocheniia poliakov i malorossiian, byvshego v XVII veke (Pis'mo k M.A. Grabovskomu)' (1857). In idem, *Sobranie sochinenii*, 1: 248–76.

– 'O proiskhozhdenii Variago-Russov (Pis'mo M.P. Pogodinu).' *Sobranie sochinenii*, 1: 93–104.

– 'Otkuda idet russkaia zemlia, po skazaniiu Nestorovoi povesti i po drugim starinnym pisaniiam russkim.' In idem, *Sobranie sochinenii*, 1: 5–92.

– 'Otvetnye pis'ma k M.P. Pogodinu.' *Russkaia beseda*, 1857, no. 2: 80–104. Repr. in idem, *Sobranie sochinenii*, 3: 244–72.

– *Sobranie sochinenii*. 3 vols. Kyiv, 1876–80.

Malinina, O. Iu. 'Dve kontseptsii "liberal'nogo natsionalizma." P.B. Struve i P.N. Miliukov.' In *P.N. Miliukov: istorik, politik, diplomat*, 462–73.

Markov, P.G. *A. Ia. Efimenko – istorik Ukrainy.* Kyiv, 1966.

Martin, Terry. *The Affirmative Action Empire: Nations and Nationalism in the Soviet Union, 1923–1939.* Ithaca and London, 2001.

– 'Modernization or Neo-Traditionalism? Ascribed Nationality and Soviet Primordialism.' In *Stalinism: New Directions*, ed. Sheila Fitzpatrick, 348–67. New York, 2000.

Marwick, Roger. *Rewriting History in Soviet Russia: The Politics of Revisionist Historiography, 1956–1974.* New York, 2001.

Masnenko, Vitalii. *Istorychna dumka ta natsiotvorennia v Ukraïni (kinets' XIX – persha tretyna XX st.).* Kyiv and Cherkasy, 2001.

– *Istorychni kontseptsiï M.S. Hrushevs'koho ta V.K. Lypyns'koho. Metodolohichnyi i suspil'no-politychnyi vymiry ukraïns'koï istorychnoï dumky 1920-kh rokiv.* Kyiv and Cherkasy, 2000.

Matiash, Iryna. *Kateryna Hrushevs'ka. Zhyttiepys, bibliohrafiia, arkhivy.* Kyiv, 1997.

Mazour, Anatole G. *Modern Russian Historiography.* Westport, CT, 1975.

– *The Writing of History in the Soviet Union.* Stanford, 1971.

Meyerhoff, Hans. *The Philosophy of History in Our Time.* Garden City, NY, 1959.

Mez'ko, Oles' (Oleksander Ohloblyn). *Iak bil'shovyky ruinuvaly ukraïns'ku istorychnu nauku.* Prague, 1945.

Miakotin, V. Review of Pavel Miliukov, *Ocherki po istorii russkoi kul'tury.* Vol. 1. St Petersburg, 1896. In *Russkoe bogatstvo*, 1896, no. 11, section 2, 1–20.

Mikhnovs'kyi, Mykola. *Samostiina Ukraïna.* Lviv, 1900. Repr. in *Politolohiia*, pp. 126–35.

Miliukov, Pavel. *Glavnye techeniia russkoi istoricheskoi mysli.* Vol. 1. Moscow, 1898.

– *Ocherki po istorii russkoi kultury.* 2 vols. St Petersburg, 1896–7.

– Unsigned review article of Hrushevs'kyi, *Ocherk istorii Kievskoi zemli. Russkaia mysl'*, 1893, no. 3: 118–22.

Miller, Aleksei. 'A Testament of the All-Russian Idea: Foreign Ministry Memoranda to the Imperial, Provisional and Bolshevik Governments.' In *Extending the Borders of Russian History: Essays in Honor of Alfred J. Rieber*, ed. Marsha Siefert, 233–43. Budapest and New York, 2003.

– *The Ukrainian Question: The Russian Empire and Nationalism in the 19th Century.* Budapest and New York, 2003.

– *'Ukrainskii vopros' v politike vlastei i russkom obshchestvennom mnenii (vtoraia polovina XIX veka).* St Petersburg, 2000.

Mohylians'kyi, Mykhailo. 'Vbyvstvo.' *Chervonyi shliakh*, 1926, no. 1: 53–5.

Molchanovskii, Nikandr. *Ocherk izvestii o Podol'skoi zemle do 1434 g.* Kyiv, 1885.

Moshin, V.A. 'Variago-russkii vopros.' *Slavia* 10 (1931): 109–36, 343–79; 501–37.

Munslow, Alun. *Deconstructing History.* London and New York, 1997.

Mykhailo Hrushevs'kyi i l'vivs'ka istorychna shkola: materialy konferentsii, L'viv, 24–25 zhovtnia 1994 r. Ed. Iaroslav Hrytsak and Iaroslav Dashkevych. New York and Lviv, 1995.

Mykhailo Hrushevs'kyi i ukraïns'ka istorychna nauka: materialy naukovykh konferentsii, prysviachenykh Mykhailovi Hrushevs'komu, L'viv, 24–25 zhovtnia 1994 r., Kharkiv, 25 serpnia 1996 r., L'viv, 29 veresnia 1996 r. Ed. Iaroslav Hrytsak and Iaroslav Dashkevych. Lviv, 1999.

Mykhailo Hrushevs'kyi i Zakhidna Ukraïna: dopovidi i povidomlennia naukovoï konferentsiï (m. L'viv, 26–28 zhovtnia 1994 r.). Ed. Vasyl' Horyn' et al. Lviv, 1995.

Mykhailo Hrushevs'kyi: mizh istoriieiu i politykoiu (1920–1930–ti rr.). Zbirnyk dokumentiv i materialiv. Comp. R. Ia. Pyrih et al. Kyiv, 1997.

Myshanych, Oleksa. 'Vid uporiadnyka.' In Mykhailo Hrushevs'kyi, *Istoriia ukraïns'koï literatury,* 6: 678–81.

Mytsyk, Iurii. Introduction to Feodosii Sofonovych, *Khronika z litopystsiv starodavnikh,* ed. Iurii Mytsyk and Volodymyr Kravchenko, 5–53. Kyiv, 1992.

– *Ukrainskie letopisi XVII veka.* Dnipropetrovsk, 1978.

– 'Z poshtovoï skryn'ky Mykhaila Hrushevs'koho.' *Nashe slovo* (Warsaw), 6 July 1997, p. 9.

Narys istoriï Ukraïny. Ed. K. Huslystyi, L. Slavin, and F. Iastrebov. Ufa, 1942; Toronto, 1944.

Naukovyi chasopys ukraïnoznavstva 'Ukraïna' (1907–1932). Pokazhchyk zmistu. Comp. Raïsa Maiboroda and Volodymyr Vrublevs'kyi. Kyiv, 1993.

Naukovyi zbirnyk, prysviachenyi profesorovi Mykhailovi Hrushevs'komu uchenykamy i prykhyl'nykamy z nahody ioho desiatylitn'oï naukovoï pratsi v Halychyni (1894–1904). Lviv, 1906.

Nechkina, M.V. *Vasilii Osipovich Kliuchevskii. Istoriia zhizni i tvorchestva.* Moscow, 1974.

New Encyclopaedia Britannica. 15th ed. Chicago, 1993. S.v. 'Kiev.'

Niederle, Lubor. *Manuel de l'antiquité slave.* Paris, 1923. Russian translation of the Czech edition (1953): Niderle, L. *Slavianskie drevnosti.* Trans. T. Kovaleva and M. Khazanova. Ed. A.L. Mongait. Intro. P.N. Tretiakov. Moscow, 1956.

– *Slovanské starožitnosti.* Pt. 1, fascicle 4, *Původ a počátky Slovanů východních.* Prague, 1924.

Nikitin, E.N. 'Pis'mo istorika M.S. Grushevskogo V.M. Molotovu.' *Otechestvennye arkhivy,* 1998, no. 3: 94–98.

Ob otmene stesnenii malorusskogo pechatnogo slova. St Petersburg, 1905. Ukrainian translation: *Peterburs'ka Akademiia Nauk v spravi znesennia zaborony ukraïns'koho slova.* Lviv, 1905.

Ohloblyn, Oleksander. 'Mykhailo Hrushevs'kyi i ukraïns'ke natsional'ne vidrodzhennia.' *Ukraïns'kyi istoryk,* 1964, nos. 2–3: 1–6.

– 'Mykhailo Serhiievych Hrushevs'kyi (1866–1934).' *Ukraïns'kyi istoryk,* 1966, nos. 1–2: 6–14.

Okinshevych, Lev. *Moia akademichna pratsia na Ukraïni.* Lviv, 1995.

– 'Natsional'no-demokratychna kontseptsiia istoriï prava Ukraïny v pratsiakh akad. M. Hrushevs'koho.' *Ukraïna,* 1932, nos. 1–2: 93–109.

Ostrowski, Donald. *Muscovy and the Mongols: Cross-Cultural Influences on the Steppe Frontier, 1304-1589.* Cambridge, 1998.

P.N. Miliukov: istorik, politik, diplomat. Materialy mezhdunarodnoi nauchnoi konferentsii, Moskva, 26–27 maia 1999 g. Ed. V.V. Shelokhaev et al. Moscow, 2000.

Padokh, Iaroslav. 'Lev Okinshevych – vydatnyi istoryk derzhavnoho prava kozats'koï Ukraïny.' In Lev Okinshevych, *Moia akademichna pratsia v Ukraïni,* 8–24.

Paneiakh, Viktor M. 'The Political Police and the Study of History in the USSR.' In *Extending the Borders of Russian History: Essays in Honor of Alfred J. Rieber,* ed. Marsha Siefert, 301–14. Budapest and New York, 2003.

Parkhomenko, Volodymyr. 'Novi istorychni problemy Kyïvs'koï Rusy.' *Ukraïna,* 1928, no. 6: 3–5.

Partykevich, Andre. *Between Kyiv and Constantinople: Oleksander Lototsky and the Quest for Ukrainian Autocephaly.* Edmonton, 1998.

Pavlychko, Solomiia. *Natsionalizm, seksual'nist', oriientalizm. Skladnyi svit Ahatanhela Kryms'koho.* Kyiv, 2000.

Pavlyk, Mykhailo, comp. *Perepyska Mykhaila Drahomanova z Melitonom Buchyns'kym, 1871–77.* Lviv, 1910.

Pearton, Maurice. 'Nicolae Iorga as Historian and Politician.' In *Historians as Nation-Builders,* ed. Deletant and Hanak, 157–73.

Pelenski, Jaroslaw. 'The Incorporation of the Ukrainian Lands of Kievan Rus' into Crown Poland (1569): Socio-Material Interest and Ideology (A Re-examination).' In idem, *The Contest for the Legacy of Kievan Rus',* 151–88. Boulder, CO, 1998.

– 'The Ukrainian-Russian Debate over the Legacy of Kievan Rus', 1840s-1860s.' In idem, *The Contest for the Legacy of Kievan Rus',* 213–26. Boulder, CO, 1998.

'Perednie slovo.' In *Iuvilei akademika Dmytra Ivanovycha Bahaliia (1857–1927),* ed. Mykola Levchenko, iii–x. Kyiv, 1929.

Perepyska Mykhaila Drahomanova z Melitonom Buchyns'kym, 1871–77. Comp. Mykhailo Pavlyk. Lviv, 1910.

'Pervaia vsesoiuznaia konferentsiia marksistsko-leninskikh nauchno-issledovatel'skikh uchrezhdenii.' *Vestnik Kommunisticheskoi akademii* (Moscow) 26 (1928): 239–94.

Petrov, Nikolai (Petrov, Mykola). 'Ocherki iz ukrainskoi literatury. Psevdoklassitsizm v ukrainskoi literature nyneshnego veka i reaktsiia emu.' *Istoricheskii vestnik* 2, nos. 5–8 (1880): 577–614; 3, nos. 9–12: 25–57.

Pipes, Richard. *Russia under the Old Regime.* Harmondsworth, 1979.

– *Vixi. Memoirs of a Non-Belonger.* New Haven and London, 2003.

Pipes, Richard, ed., with the assistance of David Brandenberger. *The Unknown Lenin: From the Secret Archive.* Trans. Catherine A. Fitzpatrick. New Haven and London, 1996.

Plokhy, Serhii. *The Cossacks and Religion in Early Modern Ukraine*. Oxford, 2001.
– 'The Ghosts of Pereyaslav: Russo-Ukrainian Historical Debates in the Post-Soviet Era.' *Europe-Asia Studies* 53, no. 3 (May 2001): 489–505.
– 'Historical Debates and Territorial Claims: Cossack Mythology in the Russian-Ukrainian Border Dispute.' In *The Legacy of History in Russia and the New States of Eurasia*, ed. S. Frederick Starr, 147–70. Armonk, NY, and London, 1994.
– 'Revisiting the Golden Age: Mykhailo Hrushevsky and the Early History of the Ukrainian Cossacks.' Introduction to Mykhailo Hrushevsky, *History of Ukraine-Rus'*. Vol. 7. *The Cossack Age to 1625*, xxvii–lii. Edmonton and Toronto, 1999.
– 'The Symbol of Little Russia: The Pokrova Icon and Early Modern Ukrainian Political Ideology.' *Journal of Ukrainian Studies* 17, nos. 1–2 (summer-winter 1992): 171–88.
– *Tsars and Cossacks: A Study in Iconography*. Cambridge, MA, 2002.
Pogodin, A.L. *Iz istorii slavianskikh peredvizhenii*. St Petersburg, 1901.
Pogodin, Mikhail. 'Otvet na dva poslednie pis'ma M.A. Maksimovicha.' *Russkaia beseda*, 1857, no. 3: 97–107.
– 'Otvet na filologicheskie pis'ma M.A. Maksimovicha.' *Russkaia beseda*, 1856, no. 4: 124–41.
– *Pis'ma M.P. Pogodina k M.A. Maksimovichu*. St Petersburg, 1882.
– 'Zapiska o drevnem russkom iazyke.' *Izvestiia Imperatorskoi akademii nauk po Otdeleniiu russkogo iazyka i slovesnosti* (St Petersburg) 5 (1856): 70–92. Also published in *Moskvitianin* 1, no. 2 (1856): 113–39, and in idem, *Issledovaniia, zamechaniia i lektsii po russkoi istorii*, 7: 410–42. Moscow, 1856.
Pogodin, Sergei. *'Russkaia shkola' istorikov: N.I. Kareev, I.V. Luchitskii, M.M. Kovalevskii*. St Petersburg, 1997.
Pogosian, Elena. *Petr I – arkhitektor rossiiskoi istorii*. St Petersburg, 2001.
Pokrovskii, Mikhail. 'Bor'ba klassov i russkaia istoricheskaia literatura.' In idem, *Izbrannye proizvedeniia*, 4: 277–368. Moscow, 1967.
– *Izbrannye proizvedeniia*. 4 vols. Moscow, 1965–7.
– *Russkaia istoriia v samom szhatom ocherke*. Moscow, 1920. Repr. of 10th ed. (1931) in idem, *Izbrannye proizvedeniia*, vol. 3. Moscow, 1967.
Pokrovskii, Mikhail, with the assistance of N.M. Nikol'skii and V.N. Storozhev. *Russkaia istoriia s drevneishikh vremen*. 5 vols. Moscow, 1910–13. Repr. in idem, *Izbrannye proizvedeniia*, vols. 1–2. Moscow, 1965–6.
The Political and Social Ideas of Vjačeslav Lypyns'kyj. Special issue of *HUS* 9, nos. 3–4 (December 1985).
Politolohiia (kinets' XIX – persha polovyna XX st.). Khrestomatiia. Ed. O.I. Semkiv et al. Lviv, 1996.

Polons'ka-Vasylenko, Nataliia. *Ukraïns'ka Akademiia Nauk. Narys istoriï.* 2 vols. Munich, 1955–8. Repr. Kyiv, 1993.

Poppe, Andrzej. Introduction to Volume 1. In Mykhailo Hrushevsky, *History of Ukraine-Rus'*, 1: xliii–liv.

– *The Rise of Christian Russia.* London, 1982.

Portnov, Andrii. 'Do pytannia pro mistse V.O. Parkhomenka v ukraïns'komu ta svitovomu istoriohrafichnomu protsesi.' In *Osiahnennia istoriï: zbirnyk naukovykh prats' na poshanu prof. Mykoly Pavlovycha Koval's'koho z nahody 70-richchia*, ed. Liubomyr Vynar and Ihor Pasichnyk, 437–42. Ostrih and New York, 1999.

'Postanovy Tsentral'noho Komitetu UPSR dnia 5.VIII.1921.' *Boritesia – poborete!* 1921, no. 9: 25–6.

Presniakov, Aleksandr. *Obrazovanie Velikorusskogo gosudarstva.* St Petersburg, 1918. English translation: *The Formation of the Great Russian State.* Chicago, 1970.

Pritsak, Omelian (Omeljan). 'Harvards'kyi tsentr ukraïns'kykh studii i shkola Hrushevs'koho.' In idem, *Chomu katedry ukraïnoznavstva v Harvardi?*, 91–107. Cambridge, MA, and New York, 1973.

– 'Istoriosofiia Mykhaila Hrushevs'koho.' In Hrushevs'kyi, *Istoriia Ukraïny-Rusy*, 1: xl–lxxiii. Kyiv, 1991.

– 'U stolittia narodyn M. Hrushevs'koho.' In *Ideï i liudy vyzvol'nykh zmahan'*, ed. Bohdan Koval', 187–230. New York, 1966.

Prymak, Thomas M. 'The Hrushevsky Controversy at the End of the 1990s,' *Journal of Ukrainian Studies* 26, nos 1–2 (summer–winter 2001): 325–44.

– *Mykhailo Hrushevsky: The Politics of National Culture.* Toronto, Buffalo, and London, 1987.

– *Mykola Kostomarov: A Biography.* Toronto, 1996.

– 'Mykola Kostomarov as a Historian.' In *Historiography of Imperial Russia*, 332–43.

Pryshliak, Volodymyr. 'Ivan Dzhydzhora: zhyttievyi shliakh ta naukova spadshchyna.' In *Mykhailo Hrushevs'kyi i ukraïns'ka istorychna nauka*, 193–9.

Prystaiko, Volodymyr, and Iurii Shapoval. *Mykhailo Hrushevs'kyi i HPU-NKVD. Trahichne desiatylittia: 1924–1934.* Kyiv, 1996.

– *Mykhailo Hrushevs'kyi: Sprava 'UNTs' i ostanni roky (1931–1934).* Kyiv, 1999.

– *Sprava 'Spilky vyzvolennia Ukraïny': nevidomi dokumenty i fakty.* Kyiv, 1995.

Pushkin, Aleksandr. 'Klevetnikam Rossii.' In idem, *Sobranie sochinenii v desiati tomakh*, 2: 339–40. Moscow, 1959.

Pypin, Aleksandr. *Istoriia russkoi ètnografii.* Vol. 3. St Petersburg, 1891.

Pyrih, Ruslan. *Zhyttia Mykhaila Hrushevs'koho: ostannie desiatylittia (1924–1934).* Kyiv, 1993.

Radians'ka entsyklopediia istoriï Ukraïny. 4 vols. Kyiv, 1969–72.

Radziwiłł, Albrycht Stanisław. *Pamiętniki kś. Albrychta Stanisława Radziwiłła, kanclerza w. litewskiego, wydane z rękopisu.* Ed. Edward Raczyński. 2 vols. Poznań, 1839.

Rakovs'kyi, Khrystyian. 'Do molodykh chytachiv.' In Matvii Iavors'kyi, *Korotka istoriia Ukraïny,* 5–6.

Rasevych, Vasyl'. 'Evoliutsiia pohliadiv Mykhaila Hrushevs'koho v pershyi rik pislia prybuttia do L'vova.' In *Mykhailo Hrushevs'kyi i ukraïns'ka istorychna nauka,* 157–61.

Ravich-Cherkasskii, Moisei. *Istoriia Kommunisticheskoi partii (b-ov) Ukrainy.* Kharkiv, 1923.

Rawita-Gawroński, Franciszek. *Bohdan Chmielnicki do elekcji Jana-Kazimierza.* Lviv, 1906.

– *Kozaczyzna ukrainna w Rzeczypospolitej Polskiej do końca XVIII wieku. Zarys polityczno-historyczny.* Warsaw, 1922.

– *Krwawy gość we Lwowie.* Lviv, 1905.

Renan, Ernest. 'What Is a Nation?' In *Nationalism in Europe, 1815 to the Present. A Reader,* 48–60. London and New York, 1996.

[Report on the First All-Union Conference of Marxist Historians]. *Istorik-marksist,* 1929, no. 11: 229–42.

Reshod'ko, Leonid. 'Povernennia na Ukraïnu.' In *Velykyi ukraïnets',* 381–91.

'Rezoliutsiï Zakordonnoï delehatsiï UPSR 5.IX.1921.' *Boritesia – poborete!* 1921, no. 9: 26–7.

Richyts'kyi, Andrii. 'Iak Hrushevs'kyi "vypravliaie" Engel'sa.' *Chervonyi shliakh,* 1924, no. 3: 183–90.

– 'Proty interventsiï burzhuaznoï nauky.' *Bil'shovyk Ukraïny,* nos. 9–10 (May 1931): 34–47.

– *Taras Shevchenko v svitli epokhy (Publitsystychna rozvidka).* Kharkiv, Berlin, and New York, 1923.

Riha, Thomas. *A Russian European: Paul Miliukov in Russian Politics.* Notre Dame and London, 1969.

Ripets'kyi, Teodor. *Iliustrovannaia narodnaia istoriia Rusi.* Lviv, 1890.

Robinson, Mikhail A. 'M.S. Hruševs'kyj, la "Questione ucraina" e l'élite accademica russa.' *Slavica,* 2001, no. 4, *Pagine di ucrainistica europea,* ed. Giovanna Brogi Bercoff and Giovanna Siedina, 157–76.

Rogger, Hans. *National Consciousness in Eighteenth-Century Russia.* Cambridge, MA, 1960.

Rostovtzeff, Michael. *Iranians and Greeks in South Russia.* Oxford, 1922.

– 'Les origines de la Russie Kiévienne.' *Revue des études slaves,* tome II, fasc. 1–2 (1922): 5–18.

Rozhkov, N.A. *Obzor russkoi istorii s sotsiologicheskoi tochki zreniia*. 2 vyps. Moscow, 1905.

Rubach, Mykhailo. 'Burzhuazno-kurkul's'ka natsionalistychna ideolohiia pid mashkaroiu demokratiï "trudovoho narodu." (Sotsiial'no-politychni pohliady M.S. Hrushevs'koho).' *Chervonyi shliakh*, 1932, nos. 5–6: 115–35; nos. 7–8: 118–26; nos. 11–12: 127–36.

– 'Federalisticheskie teorii v istorii Rossii.' In *Russkaia istoricheskaia literatura v klassovom osveshchenii*, ed. M.N. Pokrovskii, 2: 3–120. Moscow, 1930.

Rubliov, O.S., and Iu. A. Cherchenko. *Stalinshchyna i dolia zakhidnoukraïns'koï intelihentsiï, 20–50–ti roky XX st*. Kyiv, 1994.

Rudnytsky, Ivan L. *Essays in Modern Ukrainian History*. Ed. Peter L. Rudnytsky. Edmonton, 1987.

– 'Franciszek Duchiński and His Impact on Ukrainian Political Thought.' In idem, *Essays in Modern Ukrainian History*, 187–201.

– 'The Intellectual Origins of Modern Ukraine.' In idem, *Essays in Modern Ukrainian History*, 123–42.

– 'Polish-Ukrainian Relations: The Burden of History.' In idem, *Essays in Modern Ukrainian History*, 49–76.

– 'Trends in Ukrainian Political Thought.' In idem, *Essays in Modern Ukrainian History*, 91–122.

– 'The Ukrainians in Galicia under Austrian Rule.' In idem, *Essays in Modern Ukrainian History*, 315–52.

Rusyna, Olena. *Ukraïna pid tataramy i Lytvoiu*. Ukraïna kriz' viky, vol. 6. Kyiv, 1998.

Rybalka, Ivan. *Taka nasha dolia. Storinky zhyttia moho pokolinnia*. Kharkiv, 1999.

Said, Edward. *Culture and Imperialism*. London, 1993.

– *Orientalism*. Harmondsworth, 1985.

Samarin, A. Iu. *Rasprostranenie i chitatel' pervykh pechatnykh knig po istorii Rossii (konets XVII–XVIII v.)*. Moscow, 1998.

Santsevych, Anatolii. *M.I. Iavors'kyi: narys zhyttia i tvorchosti*. Kyiv, 1995.

Sas, Petro. *Politychna kul'tura ukraïns'koho suspil'stva (kinets' XVI – persha polovyna XVII st.)*. Kyiv, 1998.

Saunders, David. 'Mikhail Katkov and Mykola Kostomarov: A Note on Petr A. Valuev's Anti-Ukrainian Edict of 1863.' *Harvard Ukrainian Studies* 17, nos. 3–4 (1993): 365–83.

– 'Mykola Kostomarov (1817–1885) and the Creation of a Ukrainian Ethnic Identity.' *Slavonica* 7, no. 1 (2001): 7–24. Ukrainian translation: 'Mykola Kostomarov i tvorennia ukraïns'koï etnichnoï identychnosti.' *Kyïvs'ka starovyna*, no. 5 (September–October 2001): 21–33.

– 'Russia and Ukraine under Alexander II: The Valuev Edict of 1863.' *International Historical Review* 17, no. 1 (1995): 23-50.

– 'Russia, the Balkans and Ukraine in the 1870s.' In *Russia and the Wider World in Historical Perspective: Essays for Paul Dukes*, ed. Cathryn Brennan and Murray Frame, 85–108. Basingstoke and London, 2000.

– 'Russia's Ukrainian Policy (1847–1905): A Demographic Approach.' *European History Quarterly* 25, no. 2 (1995): 181–208.

Savchenko, Fedir. *Zaborona ukraïnstva*. Kharkiv and Kyiv, 1930. Repr. Munich, 1970.

Savchenko, Hryhorii. 'Ahrarni aspekty sotsial'nykh vymoh ukraïntsiv rosiis'koï armiï (berezen'-lystopad 1917 roku).' *Istoriia ta istoriohrafiia v Ievropi*, 2003, nos. 1-2: 190–9.

Sedov, V. 'Anten.' In *Enzyklopädie zur Frühgeschichte Europas*, 28–32. Berlin, 1908.

Seton-Watson, Hugh. Preface to *Historians and Nation-Builders*, ed. Deletant and Hanak, 1–14.

Ševčenko, Ihor. 'The Christianization of Kievan Rus'.' In idem, *Ukraine between East and West: Essays on Cultural History to the Early Eighteenth Century*, 46–55. Edmonton and Toronto, 1996.

Shakhmatov, Aleksei. *Drevneishie sud'by russkogo plemeni*. Petrograd, 1919.

– 'Iuzhnye poseleniia viatichei.' *Bulletin de l'Académie impériale des sciences de St. Pétersbourg*, 6th series, 1, no. 16 (1907): 715–29.

– 'K voprosu ob obrazovanii russkikh narechii.' *Russkii filologicheskii vestnik* (Warsaw) 32 (1894): 1–12.

– 'K voprosu ob obrazovanii russkikh narechii i russkikh narodnostei.' *Zhurnal Ministerstva narodnogo prosveshcheniia* 322 (April 1899): 324–84.

– *Razyskaniia o drevneishikh russkikh letopisnykh svodakh*. St Petersburg, 1908.

– *Skazanie o prizvanii variagov*. St Petersburg, 1918.

– *Vvedenie v kurs istorii russkogo iazyka*. Pt. 1, *Istoricheskii protsess obrazovaniia russkikh plemen i narechii*. Petrograd, 1916.

Shakhmatov, Aleksei, and Ahatanhel Kryms'kyi. *Narysy z istoriï ukraïns'koï movy ta Khrestomatiia z pam'iatnykiv pys'mens'koï staro-ukraïnshchyny XI–XVIII vv.* Kyiv, 1924.

Shapoval, Yuri (Iurii). 'The Mechanisms of the Informational Activity of the GPU-NKVD: The Surveillance of Mykhailo Hrushevsky.' *Cahiers du monde russe* (Paris) 42, nos. 2–4 (April–December 2001): *La police politique en Union soviétique, 1918–53*, 206–30.

– 'Mykhailo Hrushevsky in Moscow and His Death (1931–34).' *Journal of Ukrainian Studies* 24, no. 2 (winter 1999): 79–100.

Sharanevych, Izydor. *Istoriia Halytsko-Volodymyrskoi Rusy vid naidavnishykh vremen do roku 1453*. Lviv, 1863.

Shaskol'skii, I.P. *Normanskaia teoriia v sovremennoi burzhuaznoi nauke*. Moscow and Leningrad, 1965.

Shaw, Christopher, and Malcolm Chase, eds. *The Imagined Past: History and Nostalgia*. Manchester, 1989.

Shchegolev, S.N. *Ukrainskoe dvizhenie kak sovremennyi ėtap iuzhno-russkogo separatizma*. Kyiv, 1912.

Shevchenko, Fedir. 'Chomu Mykhailo Hrushevs'kyi povernuvsia na Radians'ku Ukraïnu?' *Ukraïns'kyi istorychnyi zhurnal*, 1966, no. 2: 13–30.

Shevchenko, Natalia. 'Sotsial'no-ekonomichni aspekty anhliis'koï istoriï XVII st. u tvorchosti Maksyma Kovalevs'koho.' *Istoriia ta istoriohrafiia v Ievropi*, 2003, nos. 1–2: 94-101.

Shevel'ov, Iurii (George Y. Shevelov). *Ia – mene – meni ... (i dovkruhy). Spohady.* 2 vols. Kharkiv and New York, 2001.

Shkandrij, Myroslav. 'Mykola Khvylovy and the Literary Discussion.' In Khvylovy, *The Cultural Renaissance in Ukraine*, 2–42.

– *Russia and Ukraine: Literature and the Discourse of Empire from Napoleonic to Postcolonial Times*. Montreal and Kingston, 2001.

Shteppa, Konstantin (Kostiantyn Shtepa). *Russian Historians and the Soviet State*. New Brunswick, NJ, 1962.

Shteppa, Konstantin, and Friedrich Houtermans (published under the pseudonyms F. Beck and W. Godin). *Russian Purge and the Extraction of Confession*. London, 1951. Ukrainian translation: Shtepa, Kost', and Fridrikh Houtermans. *Chystka v Rosiï*. Kharkiv, 2000.

Shums'kyi, Oleksander. 'Ideolohichna borotba v ukraïns'komu kul'turnomu protsesi.' *Bil'shovyk Ukraïny*, 1927, no. 2: 11–25.

– 'Stara i nova Ukraïna.' *Chervonyi shliakh*, 1923, no. 2: 91–129.

Sinopsis. Kiev, 1681. Facsimile mit einer Einleitung. Bausteine zur Geschichte der Literatur bei den Slaven, vol. 17. Ed. Hans Rothe. Cologne, 1983.

Skrypnyk, Mykola. 'Khvyl'ovyzm chy Shums'kyzm.' *Bil'shovyk Ukraïny*, 1927, no. 2: 27–39.

Skubitskii, T. 'Klassovaia bor'ba v ukrainskoi istoricheskoi literature.' *Istorik-marksist* 17, no. 9 (1930): 27–40.

Skurnowicz, Joan S. *Romantic Nationalism and Liberalism: Joachim Lelewel and the Polish National Idea*. Boulder, CO, 1981.

Slavianovedenie v dorevoliutsionnoi Rossii. Biobibliograficheskii slovar'. Moscow, 1979.

Smal'-Stots'kyi, Roman. 'Pochatok vidnovy Ukraïns'koï Derzhavnosty.' In *Zoloti rokovyny: kalendar-al'manakh UNS*, ed. Antin Drahan, 88–106. New York, 1967.

Smith, Anthony D. 'Culture, Community and Territory: The Politics of Ethnicity and Nationalism.' *International Affairs* 72, no. 3 (July 1996): 445–58.

– *National Identity*. Reno, 1991. Ukrainian translation: *Natsional'na identychnist'*. Kyiv, 1994.

Smith, Jeremy. *The Bolsheviks and the National Question, 1917-23.* Basingstoke and London, 1999.

Smolii, Valerii, and Pavlo Sokhan'. 'Vydatnyi istoryk Ukraïny.' In Mykhailo Hrushevs'kyi, *Istoriia Ukraïny-Rusy,* 1: xiii–xxxix.

Snyder, Timothy. *The Reconstruction of Nations: Poland, Ukraine, Lithuania, Belarus, 1569-1999.* New Haven and London, 2003.

Sobolevskii, Aleksei. 'K voprosu ob istoricheskikh sud'bakh Kieva (po povodu "monografii" V.B. Antonovicha).' *Universitetskie izvestiia* (Kyiv) 25 (1885): 281–91.

– 'Kak govorili v Kieve v XIV i XV vv.?' *ChIONL* 2 (1888): otd. 1, 215–16.

– *Lektsii po istorii russkogo iazyka.* Kyiv, 1888.

– *Ocherki iz istorii russkogo iazyka.* Kyiv, 1884.

Sokhan', Pavlo, Vasyl' Ul'ianovs'kyi, and Serhii Kirzhaiev. *M.S. Hrushevs'kyi i Academia: Ideia, zmahannia, diial'nist'.* Kyiv, 1993.

Sovetskaia istoriografiia. Ed. Iu. N. Afanas'ev. Moscow, 1996.

Spitsyn, A.A. 'Istoriko-arkheologicheskie razyskaniia. I. Iskonnye obitateli Dona i Dontsa. II. Tmutarakan'. III. Teoriia massovogo pereseleniia pridneprovskoi Rusi na sever.' *Zhurnal Ministerstva narodnogo prosveshcheniia* 19 (1909): 67–98.

'Sprava pro vysylku prof. M. Hrushevs'koho.' In *Velykyi ukraïnets',* 365–66. First published in *Nova Rada,* no. 3 (23 March 1917).

Sreznevskii, I.I. 'Mysli ob istorii russkogo iazyka.' *Biblioteka dlia chteniia* 98 (1849): 1–55, 117–38.

– 'O drevnem russkom iazyke.' *Izvestiia Imperatorskoi akademii nauk po Otdeleniiu russkogo iazyka i slovesnosti* (St Petersburg), 5 (1856): 65–70.

'Ssylka M.S. Grushevskogo.' Ed. Pavel Eletskii. In *Minuvshee. Istoricheskii al'manakh,* no. 23, 207-62. St Petersburg, 1998.

Stalin, I.V. *Marksizm i natsional'no-kolonial'nyi vopros.* Moscow, 1934.

Starosol's'kyi, Volodymyr. *Teoriia natsiï.* Vienna, 1921. Repr. New York, 1966; New York and Kyiv, 1998. Excerpts in *Politolohiia,* 610–35.

Stasiuk, T. Review of *Ukraïna. Naukovyi dvomisiachnyk ukraïnoznavstva.* In *Bil'shovyk Ukraïny,* 1928, no. 2: 94–100.

Stel'makh, Serhii. *Istorychna dumka v Ukraïni XIX – pochatku XX stolittia.* Kyiv, 1997.

– 'Sotsial'na istoriia v Ukraïni: vytoky i tradytsiï svitohliadno-interpretatsiï̈noï paradyhmy (XIX – pochatok XX st.).' *Istoriia ta istoriohrafiia v Ievropi,* 2003, nos. 1–2: 81–93.

– 'Stanovlennia istorychnoï nauky v Ukraïni u pershii polovyni XIX stolittia.' In *Naukovi zapysky. Natsional'nyi universytet 'Kyievo-Mohylians'ka Akademiia.' Istorychni nauky* 19, ed. Iurii Mytsyk (2001): 53–8.

*Stenograficheskie otchety Gosudarstvennoi dumy, 4–i sozyv 1913 g. Sessiia 1–ia,
ch. 2.* St Petersburg, 1913.

Stockdale, Melissa Kitschke. 'Miliukov, Nationality and National Identity.' In
P.N. Miliukov: istorik, politik, diplomat, 275–87.

– *Paul Miliukov and the Quest for a Liberal Russia, 1880–1918.* Ithaca and London, 1996.

Storozhenko, Andrei. 'Malaia Rossiia ili Ukraina.' *Malaia Rus'*, 1918, no. 1.
Repr. in *Trudy podgotovitel'noi po natsional'nym delam komissii. Maloruskii
otdel.* Vyp. 1, *Sbornik statei po malorusskomu voprosu.* Odesa, 1919. Also
separately: Rostov-na-Donu, 1919. Repr. in *Ukrainskii separatizm v Rossii*,
280–90.

Storozhenko, Andrei. See also Tsarinnyi, A.

Strumins'kyj, Bohdan. 'Were the Antes Eastern Slavs?' *HUS* 3–4 (1979–80).
*Eucharisterion: Essays Presented to Omeljan Pritsak on His Sixtieth Birthday by
His Colleagues and Students.* Pt. 2, 786–96.

Subtelny, Orest. *Ukraine: A History.* Toronto, 1988. 2d ed., 1994. 3d ed., 2000.

Sukhyno-Khomenko, Volodymyr. 'Na marksysts'komu istorychnomu fronti.'
Bil'shovyk Ukraïny, nos. 17–18 (September 1929): 42–55; no. 19 (15 October
1929): 40–56.

– *Odminy i bankrutstvo ukraïns'koho natsionalizmu. Istoryko-publitsystychni
narysy.* Kharkiv, 1929.

Suny, Ronald Grigor. 'History and the Making of Nations.' In *Cultures and
Nations of Central and Eastern Europe: Essays in Honor of Roman Szporluk*, ed.
Zvi Gitelman et al., 569–88.

Svidzins'kyi, Mykhailo. Review of the the journal *Ukraïna*, 1927–29. In *Prapor
marksyzmu*, 1929, no. 6: 236–41.

Syniavs'kyi, A.S. *Vybrani pratsi.* Kyiv, 1993.

Sysyn, Frank E. 'Assessing the "Crucial Epoch": From the Cossack Revolts to
the Khmelnytsky Uprising at Its Height.' Introduction to Mykhailo
Hrushevsky, *History of Ukraine-Rus'*, 8: xxi–lxix.

– 'Chy bulo povstannia Khmel'nyts'koho revoliutsiieiu? Zauvahy do
typolohiï Khmel'nychchyny.' In *Prosphonema. Istorychni ta filolohichni
rozvidky, prysviacheni 60–richchiu akademika Iaroslava Isaievycha*, ed. Bohdan
Iakymovych et al., 571–78. Lviv, 1998.

– 'Concepts of Nationhood in Ukrainian History Writing, 1620–1690.' *HUS* 10,
nos. 3–4 (December 1986): 393–423.

– 'The Cossack Chronicles and the Development of Modern Ukrainian
Culture and National Identity.' *HUS* 14, nos. 3–4 (December 1990):
593–607.

– 'The Cultural, Social and Political Context of Ukrainian History-Writing:

1620–1690.' In *Dall'Opus Oratorium alla ricerca documentaria: La storiografia polacca, ucraina e russa fra il XVI e il XVIII secolo (=Europa Orientalis)* (Rome), ed. Giovanna Brogi Bercoff, 5 (1986): 285–310.

– 'Grappling with the Hero: Hrushevs'kyi Confronts Khmel'nyts'kyi.' *HUS* 22 (1998): 589–603.

– 'The Image of Russia and Russian-Ukrainian Relations in Ukrainian Historiography of the Late Seventeenth and Early Eighteenth Centuries.' In *Culture, Nation, and Identity*, ed. Kappeler et al., 108–43.

– Introduction to the *History of Ukraine-Rus'*. In Mykhailo Hrushevsky, *History of Ukraine-Rus'*. Vol. 1, *From Prehistory to the Eleventh Century*, xxi–xlii. Edmonton and Toronto, 1997. Repr. in *Historiography of Imperial Russia*, 344–72.

– 'The Khmel'nyts'kyi Uprising: A Characterization of the Ukrainian Revolt.' *Jewish History* 17, no. 2 (2003): 115–39.

– 'The Khmelnytsky Uprising and Ukrainian Nation-Building.' *Journal of Ukrainian Studies* 17, nos. 1–2 (summer–winter 1992): 141–70.

– 'The Reemergence of the Ukrainian Nation and Cossack Mythology.' *Social Research* 58, no. 4 (winter 1991): 845–64.

Szporluk, Roman. *Communism and Nationalism: Karl Marx versus Friedrich List*. New York, 1991.

– Introduction to *Russia in World History: Selected Essays by M.N. Pokrovskii*, ed. Roman Szporluk. Trans. Roman and Mary Ann Szporluk, 1–46. Ann Arbor, MI, 1970.

– *The Political Thought of Thomas G. Masaryk*. Boulder, CO, 1981.

– 'Ukraine: From an Imperial Periphery to a Sovereign State.' *Daedalus* 126, no. 3 (summer 1997): 85–199. Repr. in idem, *Russia, Ukraine and the Breakup of the Soviet Union*, 361–94. Stanford, 2000.

– 'Ukraïns'ke natsional'ne vidrodzhennia v konteksti ievropeis'koï istoriï kintsia XVIII–pochatku XIX stolit'.' *Ukraïna. Nauka i kul'tura* 25 (1991): 159–67.

Szujski, Józef. *O fałszywej historii jako mistrzyni fałszywej polityki. Rozprawy i artykuły*. Warsaw, 1991.

Tel'vak, Vitalii. 'Naukova spadshchyna Mykhaila Hrushevs'koho v rosiis'kii istoriohrafiï kintsia XIX – pershoï polovyny XX stolittia.' *Skhid-Zakhid. Istoryko-kul'turolohichnyi zbirnyk* 5 (2002): 64–77.

– 'Teoretychni problemy istoriï v tvorchii spadshchyni M.S. Hrushevs'koho-retsenzenta (1894–1914 rr.).' In *Dnipropetrovs'kyi istoryko-arkheohrafichnyi zbirnyk*, ed. Oleh Zhurba, vyp. 2: 209–24.

– *Teoretyko-metodolohichni pidstavy istorychnykh pohliadiv Mykhaila Hrushevs'koho (kinets' XIX – pochatok XX stolittia)*. Drohobych, 2000.

Thomsen, Vilhelm. *The Relations between Ancient Russia and Scandinavia and the Origin of the Russian State*. Oxford and London, 1877.

Tillett, Lowell. *The Great Friendship: Soviet Historians and the Non-Russian Nationalities*. Chapel Hill, NC, 1969.

Tolochko, Oleksii. 'Dvi ne zovsim akademichni dyskusiï (I.A. Linnychenko, D.I. Bahalii, M.S. Hrushevs'kyi).' In *Ukraïns'kyi arkheohrafichnyi shchorichnyk* (Kyiv), vyp. 2 (1993): 92–104.

Tolochko, Oleksii, and Petro Tolochko. *Kyïvs'ka Rus'*. Kyiv, 1998.

Tolz, Vera. *Russia*. London and New York, 2001.

– *Russian Academicians and the Revolution: Combining Professionalism and Politics*. New York, 1997.

Tomashivs'kyi, Stepan. Excerpts from correspondence in *Politolohiia*, 576–7.

Tomkiewicz, Władysław. *Kozaczyzna ukrainna*. Lviv, 1939.

– 'O składzie społecznym i etnicznym Kozaczyzny ukrainnej na przełomie XVI i XVII wieku.' *Przegląd Historyczny* 37 (1948): 248–60.

Tretiak, Józef. *Piotr Skarga w dziejach i literaturze unii Brzeskiej*. Cracow, 1912.

Tretiakov, P.N. 'Liubor Niderle i ego "Slavianskie drevnosti."' In Niderle, *Slavianskie drevnosti*, 5–12.

Trubetzkoy, Nikolai. 'The Ukrainian Problem.' In idem, *The Legacy of Genghis Khan and Other Essays on Russia's Identity*, 245–67. Ann Arbor, MI, 1991.

Trudy Pervoi Vsesoiuznoi konferentsii istorikov-marksistov, 28.XII.1928–4.I.1929. 2 vols. Moscow, 1930.

Tsarinnyi, A. (Storozhenko, Andrei). *Ukrainskoe dvizhenie. Kratkii istoricheskii ocherk preimushchestvenno po lichnym vospominaniiam*. Berlin, 1925. Repr. in *Ukrainskii separatizm v Rossii*, 133–252.

Turii, Oleh. '"Rus'ka istoriia" iak legitymizatsiia vyzvol'nykh zmahan' halyts'kykh ukraïntsiv.' In *Mykhailo Hrushevs'kyi i ukraïns'ka istorychna nauka*, 133–40.

Udod, Oleksandr. *Istoriia v dzerkali aksiolohiï. Rol' istorychnoï osvity u formuvanni dukhovnykh tsinnostei ukraïns'koho narodu v 1920–1930–kh rokakh*. Kyiv, 2000.

Ukraine and Russia in Their Historical Encounter. Ed. Peter J. Potichnyj, Marc Raeff, Jaroslaw Pelenski, and Gleb N. Žekulin. Edmonton, 1992.

Ukrainskii separatizm v Rossii. Ideologiia natsional'nogo raskola. Comp. M.B. Smolin. Moscow, 1998.

Ukraïns'ka Tsentral'na Rada. Dokumenty i materialy. Comp. Vladyslav Verstiuk et al. 2 vols. Kyiv, 1997.

Ukraïns'kyi arkhiv. Vydaie Arkheohrafichna komisiia Vseukraïns'koï Akademiï Nauk. Vol. 1, *Heneral'ne slidstvo pro maietnosti Starodubs'koho polku*. Ed. Kateryna Lazarevs'ka. Kyiv, 1929. Vol. 2, *Kodens'ka knyha sudovykh sprav*. Kyiv, 1931. Vol. 4, *Heneral'ne slidstvo pro maietnosti Lubens'koho polku*. Ed. Kateryna Lazarevs'ka. Kyiv, 1931.

Ulam, Adam. *The Kirov Affair*. San Diego, 1988.

Ul'ianovs'kyi, Vasyl'. 'Syn Ukraïny (Volodymyr Antonovych: hromadianyn, uchenyi, liudyna).' In Antonovych, *Moia spovid'*, 5–76.

Usenko, Pavlo. 'Mifolohiia na zavadi istoriï.' *Suchasnist'*, 2002, no. 6: 92–112.

Varlygo, A.A., ed. '"Ia nikogda ne vystupal protiv Rossii." M.S. Grushevskii i russkie uchenye, 1914–1916 gg.' *Istoricheskii arkhiv*, 1997, no. 4: 175–99.

Vashchenko, Volodymyr. *Lektsiï z istoriï ukraïns'koï istorychnoï nauky druhoï polovyny XIX – pochatku XX stolittia (M.I. Kostomarov, V.B. Antonovych, M.S. Hrushevs'kyi)*. Dnipropetrovsk, 1998.

– *Nevrasteniia: neprochytani istoriï (Dekonstruktsiia odnoho napysu – seans prochytannia avtomonohrafiï M. Hrushevs'koho)*. Dnipropetrovsk, 2002.

Vasylenko, Mykola. 'Prof. M.S. Grushevskii kak istorik.' *Ukrainskaia zhizn'*, 1916, no. 12: 30–45.

Vcheni Instytutu istoriï Ukraïny. Biobibliohrafichnyi dovidnyk. Ukraïns'ki istoryky, vyp. 1. Kyiv, 1998.

Velychenko, Stephen. *National History as Cultural Process: A Survey of the Interpretations of Ukraine's Past in Polish, Russian and Ukrainian Historical Writing from the Earliest Times to 1914*. Edmonton, 1992.

– 'Rival Grand Narratives of National History: Russian/Soviet, Polish and Ukrainian Accounts of Ukraine's Past (1772–1991).' *Österreichische Osthefte*, 2000, nos. 3–4: 139–60.

– *Shaping Identity in Eastern Europe and Russia: Soviet-Russian and Polish Accounts of Ukrainian History, 1914–1991*. New York, 1993.

Velykyi ukraïnets': Materialy z zhyttia ta diial'nosti M.S. Hrushevs'koho. Comp. A.P. Demydenko. Kyiv, 1992.

Venelin, Iu. *Skandinavomaniia i ee poklonniki ili stoletnie izyskaniia o variagakh*. Moscow, 1842.

Verba, Ihor. *Oleksandr Ohloblyn: Zhyttia i pratsia v Ukraïni*. Kyiv, 1999.

Vernadsky, George. *A History of Russia*. Vol. 4. *Russia at the Dawn of the Modern Age*. New Haven, CT, 1959.

– Preface to Michael Hrushevsky, *A History of Ukraine*, v–xiv. New Haven, CT [1941].

Verstiuk, Vladyslav. *Ukraïns'ka Tsentral'na Rada: navchal'nyi posibnyk*. Kyiv, 1997.

Verstiuk, Vladyslav, and Ruslan Pyrih. *M.S. Hrushevs'kyi. Korotka khronika zhyttia ta diial'nosti*. Kyiv, 1996.

'Vid Zakordonnoï delehatsiï Ukraïns'koï partiï sotsiialistiv-revoliutsioneriv do partiinykh orhanizatsii i tovaryshiv za kordonom.' *Boritesia – poborete!* 1921, no. 9: 1–7.

Visnyk Soiuzu vyzvolennia Ukraïny 3, no. 67 (3 December 1916).

Vodotyka, S.H. *Akademik Mykhailo Ielyseiovych Slabchenko. Narys zhyttia ta tvorchosti*. Kyiv and Kherson, 1998.

– *Narysy istoriï istorychnoï nauky URSR 1920-kh rokiv*. Kyiv and Kherson, 1998.
Volkonskii, A.M. *Istoricheskaia pravda i ukrainofil'skaia propaganda*. Turin, 1920. Repr. in *Ukrainskii separatizm v Rossii*, 25–123.
Von Hagen, Mark. 'The Russian Imperial Army and the Ukrainian National Movement in 1917.' *Ukrainian Quarterly* 54, nos. 3–4 (fall–winter 1998): 220–56.
Vozniak, Mykhailo. 'Ol. Konys'kyi i pershi tomy "Zapysok" (z dodatkom ioho lystiv do Oleksandra Dukareva).' *ZNTSh* 150 (1929): 339–90.
Vynar, Liubomyr (Lubomyr R. Wynar) 'Avstriis'ki uriadovi dokumenty pro pryznachennia Mykhaila Hrushevs'koho profesorom L'vivs'koho universytetu.' In idem, *Mykhailo Hrushevs'kyi: istoryk i budivnychyi natsiï*, 223–36.
– 'Chetvertyi universal UTsRady: vprovadzhennia.' In Mykhailo Hrushevs'kyi, *Na porozi novoï Ukraïny*, 218–21.
– 'Chomu Mykhailo Hrushevs'kyi povernuvsia v Ukraïnu v 1914 rotsi.' *Ukraïns'kyi istoryk*, 1967, no. 3–4: 103–8. Repr. in idem, *Mykhailo Hrushevs'kyi: istoryk i budivnychyi natsiï*, 188–93.
– *Hrushevs'koznavstvo: geneza i istorychnyi rozvytok*. Kyiv, Lviv, Paris, New York, and Toronto, 1998.
– *Molodist' Mykhaila Hrushevs'koho, 1866–1894*. Munich and New York, 1967.
– *Mykhailo Hrushevsky: Ukrainian-Russian Confrontation in Historiography*. Toronto, New York, Munich, 1988.
– *Mykhailo Hrushevs'kyi, 1866–1934: Bibliographic Sources*. New York, Munich, and Toronto, 1985.
– *Mykhailo Hrushevs'kyi i Naukove tovarystvo im. Tarasa Shevchenka, 1892–1930*. Munich, 1970.
– *Mykhailo Hrushevs'kyi: istoryk i budivnychyi natsiï. Statti i materialy*. Kyiv, New York, and Toronto, 1995.
– 'Ohliad istorychnoï literatury pro pochatky ukraïns'koï kozachchyny.' *Ukraïns'kyi istoryk*, 1965, nos. 5–6: 28–37; nos. 7–8: 17–38.
– 'Znachennia Mykhaila Hrushevs'koho v ukraïns'kii i svitovii istoriï (Z nahody 125–littia narodzhennia).' *Ukraïns'kyi istoryk*, 1991–2, nos. 110–15: 13–53.
Vynnychenko, Volodymyr. *Shchodennyk*. Vol. 1. Edmonton and New York, 1980.
Vytanovych, Illia. 'Uvahy do metodolohiï i istoriosofiï Mykhaila Hrushevs'koho.' *Ukraïns'kyi istoryk*, 1966, nos. 1–2: 32–51.
Walicki, Andrzej. *A History of Russian Thought from the Enlightenment to Marxism*. Trans. Hilda Andrews-Rusiecka. Stanford, 1979.
– *Poland between East and West: The Controversies over Self-Definition and*

Modernization in Partitioned Poland. Harvard Papers in Ukrainian Studies.
  Cambridge, MA, 1994.
– 'Russian Social Thought: An Introduction to the Intellectual History of
  Nineteenth-Century Russia.' *Russian Review* 36, no. 1 (January 1977): 1–45.
Weeks, Theodore E. *Nation and State in Late Imperial Russia: Nationalism and
  Russification on the Western Frontier, 1863–1914.* DeKalb, IL, 1996.
Weiner, Amir. 'Nature, Nurture, and Memory in a Socialist Utopia: Delineat-
  ing the Soviet Socio-Ethnic Body in the Age of Socialism.' *American Histori-
  cal Review* 104, no. 4 (October 1999): 1114–55.
Wellings, Ben. 'Empire-Nation: National and Imperial Discourses in England.'
  In *Nations and Nationalism* 8, no. 1 (2002): 95–109.
Wendland, Anna Veronica. *Die Russophilen in Galizien: ukrainische Konservative
  zwischen Österreich und Russland, 1848–1915.* Vienna, 2001.
Wilson, Andrew. *The Ukrainians: Unexpected Nation.* New Haven and London,
  2000.
Windschuttle, Keith. *The Killing of History: How Literary Critics and Social
  Theorists Are Murdering Our Past.* San Francisco, 1996.
Wodak, Ruth, Rudolf de Cilla, Martin Reisigl, and Karin Liebhart. *The Discur-
  sive Construction of National Identity.* Trans. Angelika Hirsch and Richard
  Mitten. Edinburgh, 1999.
Wortman, Richard S. 'National Narratives in the Representation of Nine-
  teenth-Century Russian Monarchy.' In *Extending the Borders of Russian
  History,* ed. Marsha Siefert, 52–64. Budapest and New York, 2003.
Yekelchyk, Serhy. 'The Grand Narrative and Its Discontents: Ukraine in
  Russian History Textbooks and Ukrainian Students' Minds, 1830s–1900.'
  In *Culture, Nation, and Identity,* ed. Kappeler et al., 229–55.
– 'How the "Iron Minister" Kaganovich Failed to Discipline Ukrainian
  Historians: A Stalinist Ideological Campaign Reconsidered.' *Nationalities
  Papers* 27, no. 4 (1999): 579–604.
– 'Stalinist Patriotism as Imperial Discourse: Reconciling the Ukrainian and
  Russian "Heroic Pasts," 1939–45.' *Kritika: Explorations in Russian and Eur-
  asian History* 3, no. 1 (winter 2002): 51–80.
– *Stalin's Empire of Memory: Russian-Ukrainian Relations in the Soviet Historical
  Imagination.* Toronto, 2004.
Zaïkin, Viacheslav. Review of *ZNTSh,* vols 134–5. In *LNV* 24, no. 5 (1925):
  85–95.
Zaruba, Viktor. 'Skhema istoriï Ukraïny Antona Syniavs'koho.' In *Dnipro-
  petrovs'kyi istoryko-arkheohrafichnyi zbirnyk,* ed. Oleh Zhurba, vyp. 2: 225–42.
– *Syniavs'kyi A.S. (Narys zhyttia i tvorchosti).* Dnipropetrovsk, 1998.
– *Z viroiu v ukraïns'ku spravu: Antin Stepanovych Syniavs'kyi.* Kyiv, 1993.

Zashkil'niak, Leonid. 'Istoriohrafichna tvorchist' Mykhaila Hrushevs'koho na
tli ievropeis'koï istorychnoï dumky kintsia XIX – pochatku XX stolittia.' In
Mykhailo Hrushevs'kyi i ukraïns'ka istorychna nauka, 31–46.
– 'M.S. Hrushevs'kyi u Kyïvs'komu universyteti (1886–1894 rr.).' In
Hrushevskyi, *Shchodennyk*, 222–54.
– 'Metodolohichni pohliady Mykhaila Hrushevs'koho.' *Ukraïna moderna*
(Lviv), 2–3 (1997–8): 233–53.
– 'Mykhailo Hrushevs'kyi i Halychyna (do pryïzdu do L'vova 1894 r.).'
In *Mykhailo Hrushevs'kyi i ukraïns'ka istorychna nauka*, 141–56.
Zatons'kyi, Volodymyr. *Natsional'na problema na Ukraïni*. Kharkiv, 1927.
– *Natsional'no-kul'turne budivnytstvo i borot'ba proty natsionalizmu*. Kharkiv,
1934. Excerpts in *Mykhailo Hrushevs'kyi: mizh istoriieiu i politykoiu*, no. 101,
pp. 146–50.
– 'Promova narkoma osvity USRR Akad V.P. Zatons'koho na pokhoronakh
Akad. M.S. Hrushevs'koho.' *Visti VUAN*, 1934, nos. 6–7: 36–9.
Zayarnyuk, Andrij. 'Obtaining History: The Case of Ukrainians in Habsburg
Galicia, 1848–1900.' Paper presented at a conference, 'Nationalist Myths and
Pluralist Realities in Central Europe.' University of Alberta, 27 October
2001.
Zelenov, M.V. *TsK RKP(b)-VKP(b): tsenzura i istoricheskaia nauka v 1920-e gody.*
Nizhnii Novgorod, 2000.
Zeuss, Kaspar. *Die Deutschen und die Nachbarstämme*. Munich, 1837.
Zh., M. 'Iuvilei Iuryia Polivky.' *Ukraïna* 1928, no. 3: 174–5.
Zherela do istoriï Ukraïny-Rusy. Vol. 8, *Materiialy do istoriï ukraïns'koï kozachchyny*.
[Vol. 1, *Dokumenty po rik 1631*]. Lviv, 1908. Vol. 12. Lviv, 1912. Vol. 16. Lviv,
1919.
Zibrov, V.K. *O letopisi Nestora*. St Petersburg, 1995.
Zimand, Roman. *Narodowa Demokracja 1893–1939. Ze studiów nad dziejami myśli
nacjonalistycznej*. Wrocław, Warsaw, Cracow, and Gdańsk, 1980.
Zin'kivs'kyi, Trokhym. 'Moloda Ukraïna: ïï stanovyshche i shliakh.' In idem,
Pysannia Trokhyma Zin'kivs'koho, ed. Vasyl Chaichenko [Borys Hrinchenko],
bk. 2: 81–119. Lviv, 1896. Repr. in *Politolohiia*, 33–46.
Zubritskii, Dionisii. *Istoriia drevnego Galichsko-Russkogo kniazhestva*. 3 vols.
Lviv, 1852–5.

Index

Academy of Sciences of the USSR, 249, 250, 252, 265, 426, 493n61, 501nn130, 131, 140, 142, 507n207. *See also* Russian Academy of Sciences

Advanced School of Social Sciences (Paris), 36, 53

Akkerman, 247

Aksakov, Ivan, 135

Akty IuZR, 258, 260

Aleksei Mikhailovich (tsar of Muscovy), 17, 55

Alexander II (emperor of Russia), 380

all-Russian narrative, 89, 94, 97, 101, 103, 149, 151, 159, 161, 281

all-Union (USSR) institutions, 235, 236, 240, 242, 249–52, 265, 383, 384, 386, 389, 397, 426, 493n61, 501nn130, 131, 140, 142, 507n207

America, North, 9, 228–30, 344, 345, 491n45, 492n55

American Historical Association, 345

Anderson, Benedict, 7

Andrusovo, Armistice of (1667), 415, 424

Annales Bertiniani, 130

Antes (Antae), 95, 120–7, 132, 134, 418, 467nn109, 116, 468nn123, 134, 469n138, 528n8

anti-Semitism, 66, 299, 456n208

Antonovych, Volodymyr, critique of Pogodin theory, 136, 140, 141, 143, 144, 146, 149, 472n170; and development of Ukrainian historical narrative, 155–75, 480n70; documentary school, 6, 20, 190, 373–5, 443n75, 524n186, 440n54, 441n67, 442n68; and Galicia, 37–41, 45, 478n42; as a historian, 36, 41, 62, 94, 103, 115, 118, 155, 260, 441n62, 524n181; at Kyiv University, 6, 35, 37, 44; participation in Ukrainian national movement, 20, 24, 27, 85, 88, 380; and Polish historiography, 183, 186, 190, 483n106; populist ideology, 220–2; research on history of the Cossacks, 195, 197, 198, 205, 485n141, 486n151, 511n6; study of Khmelnytsky Uprising, 284, 285, 291, 297, 301–8, 312, 316, 319, 321, 326, 329–32, 336, 466n91, 513n30, 517nn87, 91, 521n146, 523n167

Central Asia, 252. *See also* Asia
Central Rada, 9, 72, 73, 76, 78, 81,
    216, 217, 224, 253, 455n195,
    458n228, 496n91; and Bolsheviks,
    82, 83, 91, 236, 242, 246, 355, 399,
    457n209, 464n79, 498n110; and
    national minorities, 77, 78,
    456nn207, 208; and Ukrainian
    independence, 81, 82; and Ukrain-
    ian parties, 79, 86, 90, 457n215
Charles XII (king of Sweden), 18,
    454n182
Charles University (Prague), 24
Chechel, Mykola, 225–8, 489n10,
    491n34
Chernihiv (city, principality, region),
    138–41, 337, 435n5, 447n125,
    499n120
Chernivtsi, 247, 511n6
Chernivtsi University, 48
Chervonyi shliakh, 269, 270, 372, 375,
    399
Chicherin, Boris, 394, 440n55
Christianity, 3, 33, 99, 178–80, 192,
    196, 322, 450n157, 482n95
Chubar, Vlas, 236, 238, 266, 267,
    496n89, 499n119
Church Slavonic, 26, 87
Chyhyryn region, 26
Chykalenko, Ievhen, 65, 79
Cimmerians, 118
Circassians, 197
Colchis, 103
Commonwealth, Polish-Lithuanian,
    15, 93, 101, 105, 187, 189, 282, 283,
    296–8, 333, 338, 351, 424, 465n87,
    483n106, 503n171, 512n7, 515n55
Communist Party of Ukraine (Bol-
    shevik) [KP(b)U], Central Com-
    mittee, 218, 223, 236, 237, 244, 246,

367, 382, 392, 497n107, 498n111,
    499n116, 536n113, 538n139; Polit-
    buro, 225, 228, 236–8, 243, 244, 248,
    492n46, 494n74
Communist (Third) International,
    223, 225
Comte, Auguste, 301, 320, 440n61
Congress of Ukrainian Studies
    (Prague), 238, 239
Constantine Porphyrogennetos
    (Byzantine emperor), 130
Constitutional Democratic Party
    (Cadets), 59, 66, 73, 237, 266, 269,
    271, 421, 452n169, 462–3n64
Cossack chronicles, 154, 189, 204,
    207, 475n2
Cossack elites, 282, 283, 292, 316,
    317, 319, 335, 339, 454n182,
    520n135, 522n166. *See also* Cossack
    officers
Cossack Host, 184, 199, 202, 282,
    486n164. *See also* Zaporozhian
    Cossacks; Zaporozhian Host
Cossack mythology and history,
    193–207, 419
Cossack officers, 29, 195, 202–4, 222,
    295, 297–9, 302, 305, 312–13, 316–
    20, 322, 326–8, 334, 335, 337, 370,
    402–3, 407, 488n193, 521n146. *See
    also* Cossack elites
Cossack statehood, 178, 210, 255,
    282, 290, 333–9, 525n200. *See also*
    Hetmanate
Cossacks, Dnipro, 201, 207, 529n17;
    rank-and-file, 196, 203, 293, 316,
    328. *See also* Zaporozhian Cos-
    sacks
Cracow, 48, 256, 259; City Archives,
    259; Cracow historiographic
    school, 35

Lavrov, Petr, 32, 438n42
Lavrovsky, Petr, 135
Lazarevsky, Oleksander, 220, 222,
313, 334, 344, 373, 380, 412
Lebed, Dmytro, 411, 497n107
Lebedyntsev, Feofan, 25, 27, 436n11
Lelewel, Joachim, 24, 190, 436n4
Lenin, Vladimir, 82, 271, 274, 351,
409, 489n12, 540n160, 543n191
Leningrad, 250, 255, 258, 383, 384,
426, 429, 502n153, 503n172,
528n15. *See also* St Petersburg
Lermontov, Mikhail, 26
Lévy-Bruhl, Lucien, 36
Levytsky, Leonid, 248, 500n126
Levytsky, Mykhailo, 237
Levytsky, Orest, 195
Liakhs, 185, 338. *See also* Poles
Liapunov, Boris, 112, 150, 464n79,
472n179
Linnichenko, Ivan, 103–6, 112–15,
149, 151, 164, 173, 185, 186, 375,
376, 461n34, 465n87, 466n90,
478n42, 534n96
Literaturno-naukovyi visnyk, 47, 55,
65, 67, 68, 79, 450n147
Lithuania, Grand Duchy of, 101, 105,
107, 164, 186, 187, 283, 350, 352,
365, 465n67, 532n60
Lithuania, Lithuanian state, 18, 30,
37, 45, 53, 62, 93, 101, 104–8, 129,
146, 156, 161, 164, 165, 172–7, 182,
186–8, 200, 282, 283, 296, 297, 350–
2, 361, 365–7, 415, 419, 465n87,
480n76, 531–2n60. *See also* Commonwealth, Polish-Lithuanian
Lithuanian Rus', 104–6, 186
Lithuanian-Russian/Ruthenian
state, 105, 186, 361
Litopys revoliutsiï, 392

Little Russia (Ukraine), 4, 18–21, 28,
51, 52, 55, 58, 69, 80, 84, 87–90, 92–
4, 98–104, 109, 112–16, 124, 127,
135, 138, 139, 145, 149, 150–4, 158,
167–70, 174, 207, 211, 258, 281, 417
Little Russian identity, 84, 88, 89, 425
Litwin, Henryk, 484n123
Liubavsky, Matvei, 105, 106, 150,
151, 259
Liubchenko, Panas, 245, 248, 496n89,
498n113, 500nn124, 126
Lloyd George, David, 533n78
Lomonosov, Mikhail, 128, 132
London, University of, 24
Lototsky, Oleksander, 113, 216,
445n95, 449n147
Lublin, 161, 464n77
Lublin, Union of (1569), 101, 105,
175, 184, 186, 187–91, 365, 465n87,
480n76, 484n118, 531n60
Luchytsky, Ivan, 36, 441n63
Lukas Files, 259
Lupu, Vasile (hospodar of
Moldavia), 282
Lutsk, 18, 247
Lviv (Lwów, Lemberg, Lvov), 6, 28,
34, 40, 41, 44–6, 48, 49, 54, 65, 67,
68, 72
Lviv University, 6, 25, 37–40, 44–8,
68, 71, 72, 118, 148, 163, 166, 169,
171, 172, 179, 227, 290, 355, 361,
443nn80, 81, 444nn85, 87, 454n185,
455n191, 478n35
Lvov, Georgii, 74
Lybid (legendary figure), 131
Lypynsky, Viacheslav, 14, 24, 144,
222, 285–8, 296, 298–301, 308, 310,
313–16, 319–24, 329–35, 338, 341,
342, 360, 385, 406, 408, 425,
483n109, 512n15, 514n49, 520n135,